The Mooney Case

THE
MOONEY CASE

Richard H. Frost

Stanford University Press
Stanford, California
1968

Stanford University Press
Stanford, California
© 1968 by the Board of Trustees of the
Leland Stanford Junior University
Printed in the United States of America
L.C. 68-12332

To Robert N. Rodenmayer

Preface

THE San Francisco Preparedness Day bombing of July 22, 1916, interpreted at the time as the work of antimilitarist anarchists, was the origin of California's celebrated Mooney case. In an atmosphere of class tensions and hysteria abetted by irresponsible journalism, five local radicals were arrested and indicted for murder. Four were tried and two were convicted—Warren Billings and Tom Mooney. Billings was sentenced to life imprisonment, Mooney to death by hanging. During and after the trials, clear signs emerged of perjury, subornation of perjury, and the suppression of evidence by the prosecution. In 1917 Mooney became an international cause célèbre, a symbol of American capitalist oppression of militant labor. But Americans widely regarded him as a symbol of the radical threat to patriotism and to law and order during the First World War. In 1918 Mooney's sentence was commuted to life imprisonment, but the deeper issues of the case remained unresolved. For another two decades Mooney's name served as a rallying cry for radicals, organized labor, and defenders of civil liberties throughout the country, until Mooney and Billings were freed at last by Governor Culbert L. Olson in 1939.

Despite the considerable social and legal significance of the case, it has been slighted by historians. During its heyday it gave rise to several valuable works by publicists and legal scholars, notably *The Mooney-Billings Report* (1931), a legal study undertaken for the United States National Commission on Law Observance and Enforcement, and *What Happened in the Mooney Case* (1932), a reliable popular account by a former San Francisco newspaperman, Ernest J.

Hopkins. But scholarly historians, though long accustomed to remarking on the case in passing, have not treated it in depth. Perhaps this has been for want of the drama and tragedy that attend the execution of innocent men; perhaps it stems from a healthy regard for the subject's Byzantine complexity. Whatever the reasons, the case has deserved better.

There are many sources on the Mooney case, of all grades of reliability, all degrees of intimacy with moods and events. In preparing this book I consulted a number of unpublished collections, of which the richest and most important was the Mooney Papers in the Bancroft Library at the University of California, Berkeley. This collection of legal documents, correspondence, and other materials was in the process of being organized when I first began working on the case late in 1951 at the suggestion of John D. Hicks and with the encouragement and guidance of Robert E. Burke, at that time director of the manuscripts division of the Bancroft Library. In time I wrote both a master's thesis and a doctoral dissertation on the case; the dissertation is the basis of the present Chapters 1–15 and 17–19.

Among the many persons who have helped make this book possible, special thanks must go to the staff of the Bancroft Library for their unflagging assistance; to Walton Bean, who as director of my dissertation had both an abiding, constructive interest in the project and the restraint to let me fulfill my own conception of it; to Robert E. Burke, who gave of his time at the end as at the beginning, by reading proofs of the entire book and providing useful suggestions; to Muriel Bell, for editorial skill and assistance that has surely gone beyond the call of publishing duty; and to J. G. Bell, Editor of Stanford University Press, who, seeing in the original manuscript the promise of a better book, was instrumental in making its publication possible. I appreciate also the helpful advice of Stanford University's faculty publications committee.

I wish to acknowledge a generous predoctoral fellowship from the Haynes Foundation in Los Angeles, and research assistance on later occasions from the University of Winnipeg and from the Colgate University Research Council. Finally, to my wife, Barbara, I seal my gratitude here for her joy and her patience through preempted hours of uncounted days.

R. H. F.

July 22, 1968

Contents

Photographs follow pages 244 and 452

The Mooney Case

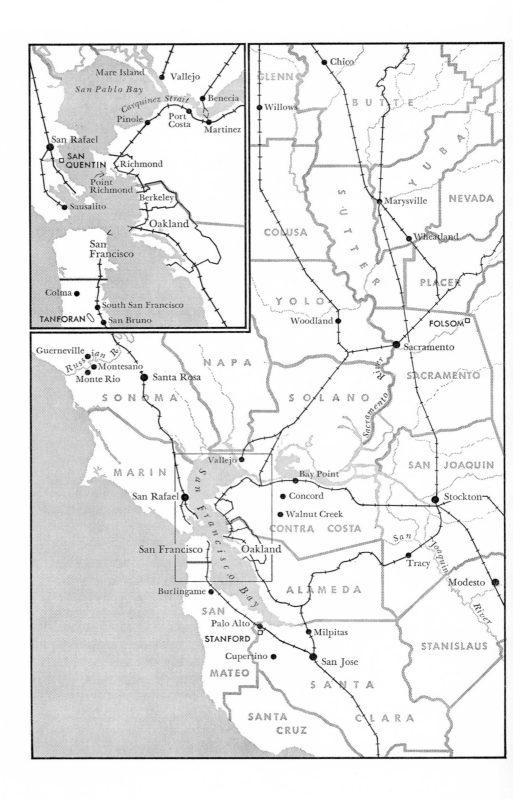

CHAPTER ONE

The Early Careers of Mooney and Fickert

What is life all about anyway Mrs. Jackson?
—Tom Mooney

UNTIL TOM MOONEY went to Europe in 1907, at the age of 24, his career was in no way remarkable. He was a laborer, a molder by trade and a union member, an energetic youth of strong build and average height, with thick dark hair, a full face, keen dark eyes, and an air of alertness. In later years he would be judged a dangerous and criminal radical, but his youthful deeds and appearance gave little hint of it.

His father, Bernard Mooney, was an Indiana coal miner, born of Irish parents in an Indiana railroad construction camp. His mother, Mary Heffernan Mooney,* had come to Massachusetts on a sailing ship from County Mayo after the American Civil War, and had settled in an Irish-Catholic neighborhood of Holyoke before marrying and moving west. Tom was born in Chicago on December 8, 1882, the first of five children, of whom three survived. Most of his childhood he lived around the coal mines of Washington, Indiana. When he was ten his father, age 36, died of tuberculosis. The family moved back to Holyoke. His mother found work sorting rags in a paper mill, 60 hours of labor a week for four dollars' wages, while he went to parochial school. Thrashed there one day by the priest for lying, young Tom rebelled and went off to public school with the Protestants. Long afterward he looked back on that incident as his first act of social rebellion.[1]

---

* Her maiden name was spelled variously. Bernard Mooney was also called Bryan Mooney. There were no family records, and his formal name is unknown. (Mooney to Tom Mooney Molders Defense Committee, October 27, 1932, Mooney Papers.)
  [1] Numbered notes will be found at the back of the book, pp. 501–48.

At the age of fourteen Mooney started to work in a local factory. A year later he was apprenticed as an iron molder, and four years after that he asked for a journeyman's wages. He joined an early union, which amalgamated with the International Molders Union in 1902. For the rest of his life he remained a member in good standing of the IMU, a fact that was a source of lasting pride for him.[2]

In his youth Mooney knew the hardships of unemployment in his trade. The need for work spurred his inclination to roam; one harvest season he spent in the Kansas wheat fields. Back in Buffalo he took a foundry job, and kept it long enough to save the money for a third-class passage to Europe. Sailing from Boston, *Baedeker* in hand, he journeyed through Ireland, and went on to the rest of the British Isles and to France, Belgium, and Holland. In a Rotterdam art museum Mooney fell to talking with a fellow American who wished to borrow his *Baedeker*. Nicholas Klein had just come from Stuttgart, where he had attended the International Socialist Congress. He was a well-informed and evidently persuasive Socialist, and the conversation, which began so casually, turned to Socialism and continued on that subject for two days. Mooney had heard Socialist arguments before, but they had never appealed to him. Now his interest was awakened. Resuming his travels, he began a crude, conscientious study of Socialism; he talked about it with people in Berlin, in Hungary, Switzerland, and Italy.[3]

Back in Massachusetts that winter he sought foundry work without success. In the short, acute depression that followed the panic of 1907, iron production dropped sharply and workers were out in the streets. To Mooney the new lessons of Socialism seemed forcefully borne out. He began to drift restlessly, finding occasional work as a day laborer but nothing in his own trade. West and south, to New Orleans, Vera Cruz, through Texas and on to California, he bummed his way. In March 1908 he reached Stockton, where he found work as an iron molder and stayed for six months.[4]

Mooney joined the Socialist Party in Stockton. He hawked Socialist literature in the evenings among the soapbox crowds and within a month was making speeches himself. In support of the 1908 Presidential campaign of Eugene Debs, he solicited funds through the city, raised $75, and was elected delegate to the California Socialist Convention in San Francisco. While he was at the convention, the spectacular "Red Special" came steaming north from Los Angeles on Debs's West Coast swing. Mooney met the train at San Jose, took the opportunity to sell Socialist literature in the crowds, and made such a success of it that he was asked to stay with the campaign party. The Red Special was almost stranded in Portland for lack of funds, but enough money was raised to head it back east and keep up its steam for the rest of the campaign. Mooney went along. Standing on the platform of the car and ballyhooing enthusiastically, he doubled the customary sales rate and brought in $1,000 for the Party's needy treasury.[5] Meanwhile, his Socialist convictions were strengthened by Debs. Debs appreciated the huckster's services: Mooney, he said, is "absolutely honest and trustworthy and is filled with energy and ambition to better the condition of his class."[6]

The campaign over and lost, Mooney wintered in Chicago, reading twelve hours a day in the reference library at Marshall Field's under the informal tutelage of the Socialist editor A. M. Simons, and meeting prominent Socialists at the national and state headquarters of the Party in Chicago. In the spring he left for the Northwest and found work in an Idaho iron foundry.[7]

Wilshire's Magazine, a national Socialist periodical, in 1909 offered a round-the-world trip to the person obtaining the largest number of subscriptions. Mooney hoboed 8,000 miles in his determination to win, smuggling himself into the Denver convention of the Western Federation of Miners and heading on to San Francisco. There, taking a foundry job, he bought an old motorcycle and visited local union meetings to solicit subscriptions. In the end he lost the contest, but he came in second with so fine a showing that the magazine gave him a special prize, a trip to Copenhagen for the International Socialist Congress to be held in 1910. He attended its two-week session, and for good measure stopped in England on the way back to San Francisco for the meetings of the British Labour Congress.[8]

II

The city to which Mooney returned for permanent residence was the Pacific Coast's leading center of commerce, finance, culture, and population, a proud city famous for its pride. Most recent among its splendid achievements was its recovery from the great earthquake and fire. With energetic self-confidence San Francisco was rapidly rebuilding. The scarred acres of burned city blocks were disappearing. Business was once again better than ever.

Slower to heal were the sores of municipal corruption that had developed during the rule of Boss Abe Ruef and his Union Labor Party, the first and last labor party to gain control of an American city government. The party had come to power in 1901. Ruef, Mayor Eugene E. Schmitz, and the "paint-eaters" of the Board of Supervisors were exposed after the earthquake by Fremont Older, Francis J. Heney, Rudolph Spreckels, and other reformers. Ruef was tried and convicted of bribery. The prosecution, under William Langdon, Heney, and Hiram Johnson, also sought to convict citizens who had bribed the administration for municipal franchise favors, notably Frank G. Drum of the Pacific Gas and Electric Company, the associates of William H. Crocker in the Parkside Realty Company, officers of the telephone companies, and Patrick Calhoun, Tirey L. Ford, and Thornwell Mullally of the United Railroads. The URR's bribe had been the most sensational of all: for overhead trolley privileges, Ford had paid Ruef $200,000 in the usual form of an attorney's retainer, $85,000 of which went to seventeen city supervisors. The trials of the URR officials were inconclusive, however, and as the case dragged on, the prosecution's public support faded. The conservative business community and fashionable society circles, which had followed the trials of the politicians with mixed feelings, began to protest that the prosecutors were eager for political power and were succeeding only in smearing San Francisco's good name. The taxpayers were constantly reminded by the defendants of the trials' mounting costs. These appeals gradually bore fruit.[9]

In 1907, at the end of the first year of the graft trials, the reformers won a decisive endorsement at the polls, when the voters defeated the Union Labor Party's candidate for Mayor, P. H. McCarthy, and its candidate for District Attorney by large majorities. The election was a mandate for continued action. But two years later, in 1909, the reformers again faced reelection, and the cases were still unsettled. Heney replaced the incumbent, Langdon, as the prosecution candidate for District Attorney. Despite the adverse climate, Heney's large, dedicated following gave him a fair chance of winning. During one of the graft trials he had been shot down in court; after months of convalescence he had recently returned to resume his crusade with renewed zeal. A man of probity as well as courage, he inspired strong loyalty among progressives of all parties in San Francisco. Against him there appeared in the summer of 1909 a youthful and politically unknown lawyer named Charles M. Fickert. Since Fickert was to play a crucial part in the Mooney case, his background is worth examining in some detail.[10]

Charles Marron Fickert was the son of a Tehachapi rancher. His father was a German-Polish immigrant from Königsberg, who reached California in 1847 or 1848, mined gold, and married an Irish girl; she bore him twelve children, half of whom died in childhood. Growing up on the cattle range, Charles became an excellent rider. He lived too far from Bakersfield to attend high school, but in 1893, at the age of twenty, having saved some money, he entered Stanford University as a special student.[11] "A big, boyish face, smooth-shaved, a ready smile, revealing fine, strong white teeth," a newspaper feature writer once wrote; "Fickert is like some big, handsome mastiff." The interviewer also described him as an amiable fellow with a dashing mental vagueness and blithely conflicting ideas.[12] He was an ambitious, callow, promising youth.

Fickert did not find the social adjustment from ranch to college easy. His more polished classmates treated him like a country hick. According to one of his later associates, he was "a great, big, awkward, pure-minded, honest farmer boy struggling to make his way through school, walking up and down the campus with tears in his eyes and sobbing at the indignities and insults and oppressions which he had to undergo."[13] He hated fraternities; he had little money, and had to "hash" to meet expenses. Majoring in history, he prepared for a law career, and graduated in five years.[14]

Compensations for his sensitivities were available. What Fickert originally lacked in social standing he gained in athletics. Strong, supple, of punishing stamina, he quickly excelled in field sports. In football he found his glory.[15]

Fickert had never seen a football game before he arrived at Stanford. After trying in vain for the varsity team his first year, he made it the year following, and for four seasons played varsity left guard in one of Stanford's most successful football eras. Fast, powerful, a hard-hitting, 60-minute player, standing 6'2" and weighing 205 pounds when in condition, he was Stanford's biggest lineman on the nation's heaviest team in 1897, and was considered one of the country's leading guards, "never . . . outclassed" on the gridiron. During his four years as "one of Stanford's great center trio," Stanford won every game against California, its first and—at the time—only intercollegiate football rival. In his junior year he was team captain. San Francisco sports writers idolized him. In the '96 game he "half picked up" fullback Stuart Cotton and "dragged him [a] full ten feet before the weight of a team stopped the procession"; Cotton gained ground "with Fickert in front pulling and almost the entire California team on his legs."

The *Chronicle* commented: "brawn, and not brain, is the fin-de-siècle fashion."[16] By his senior year he had won such renown that Harvard, having suffered from an ineffective line against Dartmouth and West Point, approached Fickert for an immediate transfer three weeks before the Yale game. (Mid-season raiding for players was not then illegal, but it was uncommon on a transcontinental basis.) Fickert turned Harvard down, and with his assistance California was trounced once again.[17]

Through football the Tehachapi farmer boy arrived socially. He was elected president of his junior class, and the following year was vice-president of the student body and president of the university's Philolexian Literary Society.[18] However unpolished his origins, his courage was proven, and his social contacts with Stanford men eventually bore fruit in San Francisco.

The Spanish-American War permitted Fickert, then a senior, a brief and obscure flirtation with military glamour. He organized a company of cavalry troops and stood at its head, Teddy-fashion, "ready and waiting for the President's call." As he told the story, the war came to an end and the company broke up without serving. Francis J. Heney told the story otherwise: Fickert tried to organize a company of Rough Riders but gave up the project when he was elected to a campus office paying $50 a month.[19] In either case, it was the end of Fickert's military career. Nineteen years later Theodore Roosevelt was to inspire him patriotically once again; the enemies then were not Spaniards, but radicals.

After graduation in 1898, Fickert stayed on at Stanford briefly to study law. The same year he entered the San Francisco law office of W. B. Kollmyer and Edward R. Taylor. Taylor was Dean of the University of California's Hastings College of Law in San Francisco, by marriage a close relative of Leland Stanford, a trustee of Stanford University, and a future Mayor of San Francisco.[20] The following year Fickert was admitted to the bar.[21] Although it was an auspicious beginning, the law failed to absorb his energy: he returned to Stanford in the fall of 1900 to serve as assistant varsity football coach under Fielding H. Yost. The following season he succeeded Yost as regular coach. Stanford, however, lost to California, and Fickert gave up coaching permanently.[22] But among Stanford students for years afterward, he was "still idolized as one of the most remarkable players that ever wore the cardinal."[23]

Three years later Presidents David Starr Jordan of Stanford and

Benjamin Ide Wheeler of the University of California were prevailed upon, perhaps by Dean Taylor, to recommend Fickert to the Department of Justice as a special Assistant United States District Attorney in San Francisco. Senator Thomas Robert Bard of California and United States District Attorney Marshall Woodworth concurred in the recommendation. These efforts on Fickert's behalf were not a reward for political labors; politically Fickert was inert, a nominal Republican. His appointment came in March 1904, subject to termination at the Attorney General's pleasure. He entered upon his duties at once.[24] But fifteen months later political complications disrupted his new career. His superior, Woodworth, had defied California's Republican machine to back Senator Bard for reelection; Bard lost, and was retired at the end of his term. Soon afterward Fickert was asked to resign.[25] He began working as a free-lance attorney, "a big, lumbering, good-natured sort of lawyer without much practice."[26] For the next four years he was out of the public eye. In 1905 he married Ethel Wallace, the daughter of a Southern Pacific official; they had Blue Book status in San Francisco society.[27]

Fickert admired the graft prosecutors until the summer of 1909, when he changed his mind. He had been suggested to the Union Labor Party as its candidate for District Attorney. James F. Brennan, a young lawyer and friend of Fickert's at the prestigious Olympic Club, was eager to obtain a position in the San Francisco District Attorney's office. He sensed that the surest way was to have a friend like Fickert elected District Attorney. Brennan exploited a connection with Tom Finn, chairman of the county committee of the Union Labor Party and for many years Sheriff of San Francisco. Fickert was introduced to Finn and other members of the committee. At that time Fickert was attorney for the boilermakers' union in the city. He appeared satisfactory to some of the committeemen.

Immediately Brennan started a "grass-roots" movement outside the party for Fickert's nomination. He rounded up a group of other young lawyers, mostly Stanford men, a few young University of California graduates, and a Stanford football coach. A committee of them called on P. H. McCarthy, the entrenched president of the powerful Building Trades Council, and on a group of other influential Union Labor Party leaders. Some of the labor men, including Andrew J. Gallagher, secretary of the San Francisco Labor Council, favored the graft prosecutions and wanted the party to support Heney, or at least to require a pledge from Fickert that he would give Heney a free hand with the prosecutions. But only a minority held this view. After three years of buffeting at the hands of reformers, the Union Labor Party was seeking to overthrow them and return to power. The party leaders backed Fickert and the county committee nominated him. Thus unexpectedly Fickert found himself the candidate of the Union Labor Party, running unopposed in the party primary with the support of men who had little more in common with him than a willingness to do business.[28]

Shortly thereafter the Supreme Court of California jeopardized Brennan's scheme by ruling that the 1909 direct-primary law prohibited a candidate's name from appearing on any party ballot except his own.[29] Fickert was officially a Republican. He had two possible maneuvers: the Union Labor Party nomination could be left blank and the party voters instructed to write in Fickert's name, or the Republicans could be persuaded to adopt Fickert as their own candidate. Both solutions were undertaken.

The Republican Party in San Francisco, like the Democratic Party, was divided over the graft prosecutions. The conservative business community condemned the reformers' "persecution" of Calhoun and his colleagues. Within the Republican Party conservative businessmen and fashionable society leaders were hoping to replace the Langdon-Heney fanatics with more understanding attorneys. The project was not simple, because Heney would be running in the Republican primary; in fact, his name could only be printed on the Republican primary ballots, in accordance with the Supreme Court's decision. At a mass meeting of bankers, investors, and merchants in the Chamber of Commerce, a committee of 25 was established under the chairmanship of I. W. Hellman, Jr., to draw up a conservative slate. Hellman, a leader of the anti-prosecution movement, was manager of the Union Trust Company, which had close financial connections with the Southern Pacific and United Railroads. Associated with him were several heavy investors in public-utility corporations that had bribed Ruef. And one of the committeemen was attorney Francis V. Keesling, who had been a Stanford classmate of Fickert's and was later to be partially responsible for the California fiasco in Charles Evans Hughes's 1916 Presidential race.[30]

The strategy of the Hellman committee was to accept the Union Labor Party's would-be candidate for District Attorney as its own. For Mayor the committee proposed William H. Crocker, son of the Southern Pacific magnate and a prominent banker, although he was president of the Parkside Realty Company, which had been involved in the bribery scandals. Crocker had personally made no bribes, in the judgment of the graft prosecutors, but he was known to oppose the trials. Whether or not Fickert actually promised the Hellman committee to drop the pending graft cases, it was clear what was expected of him, and the public understood him to be the anti-prosecution candidate.[31]

Thus Fickert found himself aligned with conservative business leaders and the earthy politicians of the labor movement. The progressive, middle-class reformers and the trade-union liberals were against him. This alignment was fixed in 1909 and continued for the rest of Fickert's political career.

Before the primaries, thousands of Union Labor Party voters and anti-prosecution Democrats switched their registration to the Republican Party, in order to swamp Heney's candidacy with votes for Fickert. Heney, if defeated on his own primary ticket, would be prohibited by law from running as a Democrat in the final election. To defeat these maneuvers, he withdrew from the Republican primary and ran only as a write-in candidate. Thus his name appeared on none of the three ballots, although he was the choice of the prosecution element in all three parties. Fickert won the Republican and Union Labor Party nominations comfortably, and almost defeated Heney for the Democratic as well.[32]

Fickert opened an impassioned campaign with a farrago of charges against Heney and remained on the offensive, never answering his opponent's rebuttals but constantly producing new sensations. Heney challenged Fickert to debate the issues, but Fickert refused. He had virtually no record of his own to defend. He did deny that he was the candidate of the millionaires; and when he was charged by a former president of the San Francisco Labor Council with scabbing during the teamsters' strike of 1901, he denied that also.[33] He accused Heney of obtaining the Democratic nomination by fraud, of opposing union labor, and of taking bribes from Spreckels to continue the graft prosecutions. He denounced the graft prosecutors as grafters themselves and betrayers of the public. He promised to prosecute the graft cases if he found sufficient evidence—which meant whatever he wanted it to mean. He labeled Heney "the biggest political faker and demagogue in existence," and declared that the prosecutors were afraid of being prosecuted themselves.[34] To all of this Hiram Johnson retorted: "Fickert has run riot with lies. I think he's gone stark, staring mad."[35]

Fickert made a direct appeal to the Stanford alumni for support.*

* San Francisco *Call*, July 23, September 16, 1909. (San Francisco newspapers are cited hereafter without city name.) Heney had attended the University of California. (Helene Maxwell Hooker, "Heney," *Dictionary of American Biography*, Supplement II.)

A group of them organized the Stanford Fickert Club, whose roster included Brennan, Keesling, and three younger Stanford graduates: Fred L. Berry, Aylett R. Cotton, Jr., and Edward A. Cunha, all subsequently Assistant District Attorneys under Fickert, and one of them, Cunha, Tom Mooney's prosecutor in 1917. Also included were Edward H. Hurlbut, a free-lance writer who managed Fickert's campaign publicity; Morris Oppenheim, later a police judge;* and W. F. Herrin, not a Stanford alumnus, but chief counsel for Southern Pacific.[36] Hailing Fickert, the club declared: "the same qualities of integrity, fearlessness and intelligence that marked his work upon the football field and made him a campus idol have been dominant characteristics of his professional life since leaving college."[37] Whatever the alumni may have thought of Fickert's candidacy, the Stanford faculty repudiated it: 120 of 152 faculty members in residence announced their preference for Heney.[38]

A few San Francisco labor leaders campaigned for Heney, notably Walter Macarthur and Paul Scharrenberg of the Pacific Coast Seamen's Union, and Andrew Furuseth, president of the International Seamen's Union. Furuseth was a gaunt, lonely seaman who had dedicated his life to ending the quasi-serfdom of American sailors; he hated corporations, capitalists, and chambers of commerce, and considered the San Francisco briberies one more capitalistic abomination. He called Fickert one of Calhoun's "latest maggots."[39]

By the end of the campaign, an exasperated Heney concluded that it was impossible to refute all Fickert's slanders. He concentrated on a few samples "to satisfy every voter that Mr. Fickert is utterly and shamelessly unreliable and untruthful."[40] But when the votes were counted, Fickert had won, 36,192 to 26,075. As the *Call* observed from its vantage point of editorial neutrality, the people of San Francisco had chosen not to press the graft prosecutions.[41]

Judge William Lawlor of the Superior Court did not concede, however, that the people of San Francisco had the right to nullify due process of law in California. Calhoun had been indicted, evidence had been gathered that might lead to his conviction, and the judge, whose sympathies had been with the prosecution, believed that the trial should proceed. Fickert, shortly after taking office, angrily asserted that Langdon, Heney, and Burns had removed graft prosecution records from the office. He took the matter before the San Francisco grand jury

* Oppenheim became involved in local bail-bond scandals in 1920. (*Call*, March 27, 1920.)

with a show of indignation that led to nothing. At the same time he announced that there was no evidence of wrongdoing by the URR. When a *Call* reporter suggested that his court motion for a dismissal might revive charges that he was Calhoun's flunky, Fickert retorted that he was considering asking the grand jury to investigate the *Call*.[42]

Lawlor had more than Fickert and Calhoun's attorneys to contend with: the major witness for the prosecution secretly left for an extended stay abroad on URR funds. As the months passed, the judge could only postpone the trial. After a year and a half, Calhoun's attorneys obtained an appellate court writ compelling Lawlor to dismiss the case. In the summer of 1911 the graft cases came to their tardy end.*

Such were the circumstances of Fickert's rise to power.

III

About the time Fickert took office, Tom Mooney returned to San Francisco and there continued his radical career. Like many native American radicals of his time, he was less concerned with dogma and organizational purity than with activity and propaganda. In the cause of preaching the revolutionary gospel, anyone going in the same general direction was good company. One of his first steps was to join the Industrial Workers of the World, America's home-made syndicalist, industrial-unionist organization, whose San Francisco local had perhaps three hundred members.[43]

The IWW in those years was repeatedly engaged in "free speech" crusades on the West Coast. Wherever local police interfered with IWW street-corner preaching, Wobblies from all over the West descended upon the offending town to exercise their constitutional right of free speech until thrown into jail. Singing, rioting prisoners filled the jails until local authorities, harassed by the overflow and the attendant embarrassing publicity, called a truce, expelled the prisoners from town, and left street speakers unmolested. As prisoners the Wobblies were roughly, sometimes brutally, handled. In a sense that was what they wanted, for it helped inspire fellow radicals to greater efforts

---

* California Supreme Court, "Habeas Corpus," XIX: 12,400; Walton Bean, *Boss Ruef's San Francisco* (1952), pp. 300–303; and *People v. Patrick Calhoun, Proceedings on Continuance* (1910–11). Years later, when Fickert was formally confronted with Franklin Hichborn's *"The System," as Uncovered by the San Francisco Graft Prosecution* (1915) and its charges against the dismissal of the graft prosecution cases, he dismissed the account as "very unreliable." "I know the man who wrote it," he said, "an associate of Lincoln Steffens." ("Habeas Corpus," XIX: 12,127–41.) Hichborn was an orthodox Progressive and not an associate of the famous radical journalist.

on their behalf and deprived the police of moderate community support. The issue, once joined, was substantially whether policemen or Wobblies were the more stubborn. In their zeal for freedom and punishment, the Wobblies usually won, at least until feelings died down. The bloodiest such contest in California was the San Diego free-speech fight of 1912. Other free-speech fights occurred in Aberdeen, Fresno, Los Angeles, Spokane, and, on a relatively minor scale, in San Francisco.[44]

Mooney joined the IWW in March 1910 to protest the persecution of its members in Spokane. His period of membership was brief. He did not participate in the Spokane fight, or do anything else memorable. After three months he let his membership lapse, having found the IWW too narrow and sectarian, its revolutionary vision too restricted. He criticized the IWW then and later for slighting the achievements of the American Federation of Labor and publicizing only its own part in the class struggle. He was nonetheless on friendly terms with national and local IWW leaders, including William D. Haywood, Vincent St. John, Elizabeth Gurley Flynn, C. L. Lambert, and George Speed.[45] (Lambert was secretary of the Sacramento local. Speed was founder and secretary of the San Francisco local; an austere old radical, he had been a division leader in Jacob Coxey's "army," and a friend and mentor of Jack London.)[46] Mooney thought of them as striving for the same revolution that he sought himself.

California's inhospitality to the IWW before the First World War issued partly from a hatred of radicalism and partly from a fear of rural arsonists and beggars. Seasonal agricultural employment in the fields and canneries meant unemployment each winter for the 30,000 homeless single men who comprised California's migrant labor force before the jalopy and the Dust Bowl changed the pattern. These men tended to winter in San Francisco or Los Angeles, where they were subjects for IWW recruitment. Others wandered in groups from town to town in the Central Valley; they were dispersed by the police, or fed and sheltered overnight and moved along the next day toward the next community. Some of these unemployed laborers, some of the time, were Wobblies. And some of them remained in the IWW during the work season. When field or cannery strikes occurred, or when fires unaccountably broke out in the packing sheds, the Wobblies were often blamed. Ordinary hoodlums, when arrested, frequently claimed that the IWW instigated their crimes, and newspapers reported these accusations.[47] The Wobblies were thus seen not only as street-corner agitators in the cities, but also as vagabonds, strike promoters, and agricultural incendiaries.*

While these circumstances did not personally involve Mooney, they bore on the Mooney case. His three months in the movement helped to determine his fate. His defenders in later years sometimes concealed or denied his membership, but his opponents capitalized on it.[48]

It was not in the IWW but rather in the Socialist Party that Mooney found his radical career between 1910 and 1913. The long-germinating, long-suffering Socialist Party of California reached a membership of 6,000 in 1910. Although a small number, it was 10 per cent of the Party's national membership, and represented a small fraction of the Socialist votes cast in California elections. This support came from the urban centers of Los Angeles, San Francisco, and Alameda County (Oakland and Berkeley). From Berkeley a popular Socialist minister, J. Stitt Wilson, ran for Governor against Hiram Johnson in 1910 and polled 13 per cent of the vote, the highest percentage ever polled by a Socialist gubernatorial candidate in California. A year later Wilson was elected the state's first Socialist mayor. In Los Angeles the Socialist Party allied in 1911 with the local trade-union movement in a violent struggle against Harrison Gray Otis, his Los Angeles *Times,* and an antagonistic business community. The Party made a strong bid under Job Harriman to capture the city government. He led in the primary but lost the final race, following the McNamaras' confession to the dynamiting of the *Times.* This setback did not prevent later growth. In 1912 the state gave Debs 79,000 Presidential votes, 11.7 per cent of its total, and Socialist candidates for Congress over 100,000 votes.[49]

However promising these developments, the Party was badly divided. The majority was dedicated to evolutionary Socialism, confident that rational appeals to all classes would convince enough citizens of the evils of capitalism to elect Socialist governments, which would then legislate the great change. A voluble minority of revolutionary Socialists, on the other hand, believed that the Socialist age would be inaugurated by the direct action of the proletariat. These militant Socialists envisaged not simply the public ownership of streetcars and waterworks, but the hegemony of the proletariat in every area

---

* Typical news reports included the following items: 150 IWW's headed for Marysville; a band of IWW's terrorizing Exeter and Lindsay; a cannery fire in Yuba City caused by the IWW; Fresno fruitpackers' strike taken over by the IWW, with rioting and the importing of 600 agitators. (See *Chronicle,* December 27, 1913, January 2 and 12, 1914, and August 26, 1916; *Examiner,* December 18, 1916; Sacramento *Bee,* August 24, 1915; and San Francisco *News Letter,* January 17, 1914.)

of society. The change would necessarily come about through social upheaval, since courts, ballots, newspapers, and employment offices were all in the hands of the enemy. "Revolution" and "direct action" in radical parlance did not mean communes and street barricades, but the irresistible economic power of a united and determined proletariat, organized in industry-wide, class-conscious labor unions which would transform society by collective action, particularly the General Strike. If their writings are indicative, the militant Socialists of the Bay Area said nothing about bombs or workers' militia. Ideally, violence was not supposed to be necessary, and advocating it was considered inimical to the revolutionary movement. For the most part, however, the matter was ignored.[50]

Mooney was attracted to the radical faction of the Socialist Party. Few of the Party's state officers were radicals. Job Harriman, J. Stitt Wilson, and most of the state Executive Committee opposed revolutionary Socialism. But the left wing was vigorous in San Francisco; although a minority there, it gained control of the local party organization, and in 1909 and 1911 nominated an advocate of industrial unionism, William McDevitt, for Mayor. McDevitt was the proprietor of a radical bookstore on Fillmore Street and a popular Socialist lecturer.[51] Another left-wing party leader in San Francisco was Austin Lewis. Born in England and educated in law at the University of London, Lewis came to California in the 1890's, was admitted before the bar, and practiced in Oakland and San Francisco. A well-known speaker and writer, he was the state's foremost left-wing Socialist intellectual, a Marxist and a student of European Socialist movements. With George Sterling and Jack London, Lewis was one of the founders of the California Writers' Club. In 1906 he had been the Socialist candidate for Governor of California.

Lewis was a far more articulate radical than Mooney. His writings presented the ideas that Mooney shared and continued to espouse after he had abandoned the Socialist Party. These ideas centered around industrial unionism, the class struggle, and the proletarian revolution. The Revolution would be achieved by the masses of unorganized labor, including the migratory workers but consisting primarily of the urban factory workers. No hope was placed in trade unions of the San Francisco variety, with their vested rights in particular trades, or in the capitalist-dominated "slum-proletariat," which could be found begging on the city's streets every winter.

Lewis despised white-collar Socialists, favored the IWW, and would probably have been a Wobbly himself had he not been—as he himself said in gleeful mimicry—a "cockroach lawyer," ineligible for membership. He defended industrial sabotage, but opposed attacks on individual lives as ineffective terrorism, and as a useless admission of the proletariat's political weakness. The "direct action" of the General Strike he approved, but only as a complement to political action. He judged the De Leonist Socialist Labor Party sounder in its revolutionary principles than the Socialist Party, which too often compromised with trade unions, intellectuals, and political expediency; but he joined the Socialist Party because its rival was trying to create revolutionary unionism by fiat and was numerically weak.[52]

By 1910 San Francisco's revolutionary Socialist leaders enjoyed the support of several loyal lieutenants, including David Milder, Selig Schulberg, and Tom Mooney. Milder was a tailor who had served nine years in the United States Navy, and now made sailors' suits on lower Grant Avenue. He helped with party chores, handled the funds of the Young People's Socialist League, and ran as the Party's candidate for city tax collector.[53] Schulberg was a waiter. An admirer of the IWW's Big Bill Haywood and formerly a member of the Socialist Labor Party, he was an acrid, facile party columnist and doctrinaire hack. He led the local branch of the Young People's Socialist League, and was a candidate of the Party for city supervisor.[54] With Milder and Schulberg, Mooney quickly found his place. He attended the 1911 state convention of the Socialist Party, where an able reporter, Ernest Jerome Hopkins of the San Francisco *Bulletin,* described him as a "lusty-voiced, aggressive, belligerent spokesman of the Socialist left-wing."[55]

Following the usual instincts of left-wing factions, the San Francisco revolutionaries founded their own weekly newspaper, the *Revolt,* "The Voice of the Militant Worker." McDevitt, Lewis, Milder, Schulberg, and others contributed. Mooney was circulation manager. The paper got off to a flying start in May 1911 with the blessings of Jack London, Eugene Debs, and other leading militant Socialists.[56] True to form, enthusiasm outran funds, and the paper was never long out of debt. Editor Cloudsley Johns, a professional newspaperman, reluctantly resigned after three months, at the insistence of the newspaper for which he regularly worked.[57] Thereafter the editorship was formally vacant. Mooney became the official "publisher." He did not edit the paper himself, for he lacked the ability; except for appeals for funds, he did not contribute a single article or editorial. His talent lay rather in soliciting subscriptions. With the aid of his new bride, Rena

Hermann, a San Francisco music teacher whom he had met three years earlier, he obtained about one-fourth of the paper's subscriptions and sold hundreds of copies on the streets. Primarily through his efforts the paper acquired a circulation of about 1,500 (of which not more than 600 were San Francisco subscriptions) and survived for thirteen months. Official journal for no organization, the *Revolt* lived and died of its own free enterprise.[58]

Preoccupation with factional squabbles within the Party weakened the *Revolt*'s appeal, but its message was consistent. The paper stressed industrial unionism, class consciousness, and international proletarian solidarity. It opposed the movement for public-school military training in California, and also the Boy Scouts, for scouts were future soldiers. The paper was friendly to the IWW. Anarchists it viewed with less enthusiasm, for they repudiated political action; yet it sought funds to help defend Arturo Giovannitti in New Jersey and Ricardo and Enrique Flores Magón in Los Angeles. Emma Goldman was respected but not admired. As Cloudsley Johns commented, anarchists pleaded for an ideal while Socialists worked for a revolution. Progressivism was ridiculed: Progressives were preoccupied with initiative, referendum, Sanskrit, and government ownership of the Express Company. As for the trade unions, they were as useless as conservative Socialists; one searches the paper in vain for favorable words about labor leaders.[59] In general, these views were undoubtedly shared by the paper's "publisher."

The *Revolt*'s militancy drew criticism from the majority wing of the Socialist Party, who called it sour and ill-tempered, a messenger of despair like "the radical publications of darkest Europe." The *Revolt* replied that it would not feed its readers taffy.[60] It spoke for revolution in the ideological sense of the American left wing. Its "extreme" views included no proposals that were not offered years before and after by Debs, Mother Jones, and other popular, fighting Socialists. Never did the *Revolt* advocate violence. Never was it sued or suppressed. In the hindsight of the First World War, the Mooney case, and the Red Scare of 1919–20, the long-defunct *Revolt* would be adjudged a vehicle of sedition—and thus proof of Mooney's wickedness and of his criminal intent to overthrow the government by violence. But there is no sign that the guardians of the state were mindful of such a view when the paper was in circulation.

In addition to working for the *Revolt*, Mooney was a Socialist Party candidate for Superior Court judge in 1910, and ran for Sheriff the following year. In both cases he was neither qualified nor hopeful of election; a Socialist political campaign was primarily an opportunity to spread the Party's message. The San Francisco left wing was so hardened about election prospects that the *Revolt* endorsed the Democratic candidate for Mayor, James Rolph, Jr., instead of William Mc-Devitt, in order to help prevent the reelection of the Union Labor Party's P. H. McCarthy. An honest enemy was better than a labor enemy, and the radicals were willing to lose votes to defeat McCarthy.[61] As the election turned out, Rolph won easily and needed no Socialist support. In the Superior Court contest, Mooney ran last in a field of twelve, with 5,890 votes. In the contest for Sheriff the next year his support sank to 2,764 votes, 3.5 per cent of the total. He was eliminated in the primary.[62]

IV

Mooney worked with the same fervor for his union as he had for his party. He believed that the International Molders Union was too conservative: "it is not advancing in the defense of Labor as is Capital in the exploitation of Labor."[63] The San Francisco IMU local, No. 164, was, like many of the city's other unions, a minor arena for conflicts between conservative and radical factions. The conservatives, loyal to the leaders and traditional policies of the American Federation of Labor, were in control, but the industrial unionists were strong enough to win an occasional fight.[64] Mooney was elected one of the local's delegates to the San Francisco Labor Council for one six-month term early in 1912. The published minutes of the Council show only that he was appointed to a committee with Schulberg to investigate Alameda County labor protests against police violations of free speech in Oakland.[65] But evidently he also made it a habit to introduce radical resolutions and to be a troublemaker in the Council. He was heartily disliked there for his conduct.[66]

That summer Mooney was not reelected to the Council, but he stood for election as his local's delegate to the International Molders Union convention. After repeated recounts of the ballots in an acrimonious, fist-swinging meeting, he won by a narrow margin. He was the only radical of the four delegates. At the convention, held in Milwaukee, he carried on a strenuous campaign to reform the IMU along industrial lines: he urged a general referendum of the international membership on changing the organization into an inclusive foundry union. Not more than one-fourth of the delegates, at most, were sympathetic.[67] He also took the floor to accuse employers of using increasingly brutal methods against labor: the injunction, the blacklist, and the kidnapping of labor officials, the last a reference to the seizure of Moyer, Haywood, and Pettibone for trial in Idaho and of the McNamaras in the Los Angeles *Times* case.[68]

To the IMU officers at the convention, Mooney was an irritant. They accused him of defaming their character. A fellow delegate, John I. Nolan, secretary of the San Francisco Labor Council and Progressive-Republican candidate for Congress, took him to task. In pique Mooney wired home that Nolan had made "personal attacks on my character as Union man by inference, insinuation, intimidation leaving impression I was a scab."[69] The local soothed him with a reendorsement and informed the convention that Mooney was "a thoroughly honest and true union man." More to the point was the comment of another San Francisco delegate, who told the convention that Mooney openly sympathized with the policies of the IWW.[70] At the convention Mooney ran as one of several left-wing candidates for national office; he placed well, but was not elected. At the end he showed no hard feelings. As he saw it, industrial unionism was the way to freedom, but "the Molders Union has made it possible for us to enjoy what little liberty we are enjoying."[71]

One project that he took back to San Francisco was the formation of an "International Foundry Workers Educational League," a propaganda organization that he undertook as a branch of William Z. Foster's Syndicalist League of North America. The Syndicalist League had been created earlier that year by radicals who disliked the IWW's principle of dual unionism—that is, existence apart from the established conservative unions. It was a minuscule and short-lived rival of the IWW. Like Foster, Mooney believed that the left-wing movement should develop within the established labor movement, with the aim of converting the conservative, skill-oriented unions of the AFL into class-conscious, industry-wide organizations. He was the Syndicalist League's organizer among the iron molders: in six months he chartered four locals with a membership of about fifty "Reds." But in the spring of 1913 other pastures lured him from his organizing work, and the foundry workers' league lapsed.[72] Mooney's new interest was San Francisco strike activity. In this field he first met Warren Billings.

CHAPTER TWO

Labor Strife, 1913-1914

Cain, the first of labor regulators, employed a club;
dynamite is now the favorite argument.
                    —H. H. Bancroft, 1915

WARREN KNOX BILLINGS was born of an old Massachusetts farming
family in 1893, at Middletown, New York, a small community near
the Catskill Mountains. His name commemorated two Boston heroes
of the Revolution; one of them, Joseph C. Knox, was his ancestor. His
father was a carpenter. His mother, a New Yorker, came from a German family that fled to America after the 1848 revolution. His father
died when Warren was two, leaving his mother a widow with nine
children. She did washing and scrubbing to support the family. When
Warren was seven his family moved to Brooklyn, and the boy worked
at his brother-in-law's dairy out on the edge of Jamaica Bay. Once he
ran away and lived in the meadows along the bay, raiding vegetable
patches and hunting muskrats until a policeman ended his adventures.
Finally, at the age of twelve, he refused to milk another cow. His
brother-in-law, no dairyman but a police officer, whipped him, but in
the end sold the dairy. The family moved into town and Warren
finished grammar school—and with it his formal education—at Brooklyn's P.S. 144.

Out of school, Billings drifted from job to job. Fights, hard luck,
irresponsibility, and a constant resentment of exploitation kept him
shifting. He learned to be a shoe lining cutter in a Brooklyn factory,
and moved on. At eighteen, swearing he was 21, he found work as a
streetcar conductor at 21 cents an hour on a Brooklyn Rapid Transit
line, but was shortly caught "nickeling," or pocketing fares, and was
fired. Once previously he had been arrested for possession of burglar's

tools; the charge was dismissed.[1] Turning to crap games, he lost what little he had saved, and settled into a life of odd jobs and vagrancy. For six months or so he drifted westward, riding the rods, sleeping in jails, washing dishes, dumping coal, picking apples, digging ditches. From Portland, Oregon, he set out for Mexico, to help Pancho Villa with his revolution.[2]

Billings got as far as San Francisco. He begged the five-cent fare for the ferry ride across the Bay from Oakland. It was a cold, foggy day in March 1913. After warming himself in a Howard Street poolhall, he hunted for a job, and soon learned of an opening for a shoe lining cutter. The workers at Frank & Hyman Shoe Company were striking to protest a wage cut; Billings could be useful to them by scabbing at the factory and getting inside information on customers and other strikebreakers. He learned of this job at the IWW's headquarters in Woodman's Hall. The strike had been called by the Boot and Shoe Workers Union, whose local membership was radical; some of the strike leaders were IWW's. Billings was not a Wobbly, but he knew of them; a strike in the Brooklyn shoe factory had taught him the advantages of industrial unionism over craft unionism. At the Frank & Hyman plant he was hired as a lining cutter. He was supposed to report secretly to the strikers at Socialist Party headquarters, but he feared that people there might take him for a genuine scab and beat him up, and so the meeting place was changed. He was directed to the house of Tom Mooney.[3]

This was Mooney's first strike. A pragmatic radical, he was dissatisfied with mere talk and organizing. He had been asked to help the shoe workers' union, which was small and without funds. That he was neither a shoe worker nor a Wobbly did not deter him; he lent a hand. The owner of the plant brought strikebreakers to and from the plant daily in an automobile; the strikers had no car in which to follow him, and so were unable to find out where the strikebreakers were living in order to persuade them to quit work. Mooney, with his motorcycle, trailed Hyman's auto for several weeks. He located the homes of the strikebreakers, who then were picketed. It was risky work for Mooney, since Hyman understood why he was being followed and several times tried to run Mooney down. He finally succeeded: when Mooney once made the mistake of passing the car, Hyman swerved into him and crushed his motorcycle. Mooney had Hyman arrested for assault, obtained legal help from Austin Lewis, and sued Hyman for $1,000. The matter was settled out of court for $150.[4]

Inside the factory Billings achieved his mission.* He also framed evidence on one of the key strikebreakers, so that the employers suspected the man of spying for the union and fired him. And one night Billings got the guard drunk in the course of a friendly crap game, after which someone broke into the factory and slashed hundreds of shoes. Billings then decided that the time had come to quit. When he went for his pay he got into a fight with one of the guards, who apparently suspected his complicity in the sabotage. During the scuffle Billings tried to get at his pistol, and so did the guard, assisted by a strikebreaker. The pistol went off in Billings's pocket, ripping through the end of his left thumb and hitting the strikebreaker in the foot. Billings was arrested, arraigned on charges of assault with a deadly weapon, and kept in jail two and a half months awaiting trial. Meanwhile the strike was settled.

Billings's arrest gave him an unhappy debut before the labor movement of the city: he was reported in the Labor Council's journal, the *Labor Clarion,* as a nonunion strikebreaker who went "wild with rage" and threatened to kill the guard for having had him discharged.[5] In time the case went before Judge Frank H. Dunne, a jurist then highly respected, like Judge Lawlor, for his courageous role in the graft cases. Billings's case was so clearly one of accidental shooting that when the jurors dallied for fifteen or twenty minutes in hopes of getting a free lunch before rendering their verdict, Dunne dismissed first the jury and then the case. Upon his release Billings went to the Mooneys' house to live. He was to appear before Dunne again three years later.[6]

II

In the summer of 1913 both Mooney and Billings were attracted by a far more serious strike. It involved the employees of the Pacific Gas and Electric Company (PG&E), northern California's largest light and power utility. In the International Brotherhood of Electrical Workers (IBEW), whose members comprised the largest single element of the PG&E labor force, a bitter factional war had been waged for five years. The radical, Reid-Murphy faction was condemned as the interloper and denied recognition by the AFL, but it was strong on the West Coast, especially in northern California, and was officially recognized

---

* As a *Bulletin* reporter recalled it, "Billings was a fink ... telling the goons outside who the strikebreakers were so they could take them up the back street and give 'em the moxie." (Author's interview, Edgar T. Gleeson, February 4, 1960.)

by the San Francisco Labor Council; P. H. McCarthy and the San Francisco Building Trades Council, however, recognized the smaller, conservative wing, the McNulty faction, as the legitimate one. The Reid-Murphy faction favored industrial unionism and, while not of course seeking its own premature demise, wished to join other trade unions in the electrical utilities industry to form a united bargaining front. In March 1913, the northern California locals belonging to this faction formed a Light and Power District Council with five other unions, the most important one being the machinists'. This council was a step in the direction of industrial unionism. It requested recognition from the utility companies as the sole bargaining representative of its six member unions, which had heretofore made separate wages and hours agreements with the utilities. To start matters off on the right foot, the Council also requested a wage increase of 50 cents a day across the board.[7]

PG&E, which had long employed union labor and considered its labor relations satisfactory, grudgingly recognized the Council but refused its demands for higher wages and exclusive bargaining rights. The Council therefore called a strike. On May 7 most of PG&E's union employees in northern California went out, thus commencing the company's first and only system-wide strike. The PG&E responded with a court injunction against picketing and boycotting, but the strike nevertheless became one of the most serious in the history of the American light and power industry. Communities from San Francisco to Sacramento and Chico to Fresno were threatened with the loss of light and power. Many places experienced dimouts and curtailed service. The company reported 1,625 employees out; union estimates were as high as 3,000. In San Francisco 800 struck, according to the *Labor Clarion*. Foremen and office employees who had been promoted from plant or line returned to maintenance tasks. To fill its depleted ranks PG&E turned to the electrical workers of the McNulty faction, who were willing to "scab" against a hated rival that the AFL had pronounced illegal. They had the support of McCarthy's Building Trades Council, but of virtually no other labor organization in the state: the strike was endorsed by every central labor council in northern California and by the California State Federation of Labor. In the San Francisco Labor Council—where prevailing opinion supported industrial unionism for the sake of collective bargaining, but decidedly not for the sake of a Socialist revolution—there was unusual unity between the regular leaders and the industrial-union radicals in strong support of the strike. (The strikers' keenest radical spokesman and fund raiser was Selig Schulberg, who in 1913 was not only a Labor Council delegate but also a trustee and executive committee member.)[8] PG&E's "stubborn directors," said the *Labor Clarion,* must be convinced that "this is an age of consolidation and solidarity in the labor movement."[9]

Throughout the summer of 1913 the strike was daily underlined with assaults and property damage. Between May and October, according to the vice-president and general manager of PG&E, John A. Britton, there were 770 depredations against the company, eighteen of them with dynamite. House transformers were blasted off street poles in Concord, Walnut Creek, and Berkeley; a PG&E substation in Placer County was wrecked by a heavy charge of dynamite; two PG&E steel towers south of San Francisco were dynamited, throwing local communities into darkness. Total property damage was estimated at $400,000. The extent of the strikers' responsibility for the damage was never determined; most of the crimes were never solved. A number of strikers or their abettors were arrested and held on charges ranging from short-circuiting high-tension lines to dynamiting and conspiring to dynamite power stations. Five men were sentenced to prison terms of one to five years on evidence presented by Pinkerton detectives. The Reid-Murphy faction of the IBEW charged "frame-up" and supported the prisoners' families.[10]

Tom Mooney was laid off his latest molder's job in August, and decided to join the Light and Power Council's picket lines. What else he may have done is a matter of conjecture: it is possible, though not demonstrable, that he was responsible for some of the dynamiting. Billings soon joined too. Neither had ever been employed by PG&E. For several weeks Billings worked for the striking electrical workers' union, Local 151, as an investigator. He tramped around the Bay Area along high-tension power-line routes to determine the number and distribution of company guards, so that expeditions could be made to short-circuit—and probably also to dynamite—these lines. Billings also stole dynamite from local quarries and construction-project shanties, using this time-honored technique to acquire explosives without sacrificing funds or anonymity.[11]

Edgar N. Hurley, an Oakland industrial unionist and officer of Local 151,[12] asked Billings one day in September to carry a suitcase of dynamite to Sacramento, for which he would be paid $25. Picking up the suitcase in Oakland, Billings caught a train to Sacramento and took a streetcar to the appointed rendezvous, a saloon. There he met no conspirator but two PG&E agents and two detectives. They arrested him. The electrical worker in Oakland who had made up the suitcase for Hurley, Billings learned later, had "sold out" to the Pinkerton Detective Agency and had given the agency advance warning of the trip. The fellow had said that Hurley would carry the suitcase himself, however, and the Sacramento detectives were disconcerted when Billings did not fit the description they had been given; but the suitcase was the same, and in it were 60 sticks of dynamite.*

In his possession Billings also had a number of percussion caps, a revolver and 50 extra cartridges, skeleton keys, a flashlight, and a jimmy. He had planned to burglarize powder shanties, although he did not tell that to the police. The detectives probed him for information that could be used in a conspiracy charge against Hurley, but Billings played dumb. Yet according to the Sacramento *Bee*, he confessed to being an IWW sympathizer and to believing that destruction of property was justified if it advanced the cause of labor.[13]

Billings was indicted for transporting explosives illegally on a public conveyance—namely, the Sacramento streetcar—and his trial was set for November. The Pinkerton detectives worked for weeks gathering evidence on the more serious charge that he had conspired with others to blow up a PG&E steam plant north of Sacramento. Although company agents and the District Attorney of Sacramento were convinced that this lay behind Billings's trip, they could find no evidence, and so he went to trial only on the lesser charge. The International Workers Defense League (IWDL) of San Francisco, a recently formed radical labor-defense organization to which both Billings and Mooney belonged, sent Austin Lewis, fresh from the Marysville IWW trials, to Sacramento to help. Billings, however, had obtained the services of a local lawyer, and Lewis's assistance was not needed. There was not much the defense could do, anyway, since the detectives had trailed Billings on the streetcar from the Southern Pacific station to the saloon, and had arrested him with the suitcase in his possession.[14]

As was usual in labor cases, union men and Socialists were rejected by the prosecution as unfit for jury duty. The prosecution was handled by a Deputy District Attorney with the assistance of an attorney from

---

* Billings contended that he did not know what the suitcase contained, but admitted later that he had "suspicions." (California Supreme Court, "In re Billings," II: 1410–11. See also Sacramento *Bee*, September 15, 1913, and University of California, Berkeley, Oral History Project, "Billings," pp. 91ff.)

PG&E, John J. Barrett.[15] It was neither illegal nor rare in such cases for corporation attorneys to sit beside the public prosecutor in the courtroom and help direct the prosecution, a circumstance that easily led to abuse and was repeatedly protested by trade unions and Progressives. In Billings's case the defendant was betrayed by a laborer through PG&E inducements, arrested by PG&E detectives, and prosecuted with the aid of a PG&E attorney. It was all quite legal. In any event Billings was obviously guilty.

During the trial the prosecution resorted to the hoary theatrical device, permitted by law, of bringing the suitcase full of the dynamite into the courtroom. The contents were noted by stipulation (i.e., by the agreement of attorneys for both sides), and the judge ordered it out of the building. Doubtless it had some effect on the jury. The effort to link Billings's crime with a general dynamiting conspiracy continued: Billings was asked whether Mooney was the leader of the gang. Mooney was believed to have been at the railroad station with Billings a few minutes before the arrest, and detectives had been looking for him since then. Billings, however, continued to deny knowledge of any associates. After a speedy trial he was convicted and sentenced to Folsom Penitentiary for two years. The judge regretted the brevity of the punishment: it was the most the law would permit.[16]

III

The detectives who arrested Billings were led by a San Francisco Pinkerton agent operating for PG&E, a blond, blue-eyed, 35-year-old Swede named Martin Swanson. According to Fickert, Swanson was a former Marine sergeant with an honorable discharge from the Navy. PG&E had hired him to head the investigations of strike activities and depredations against company property and personnel. The company officer with whom he worked most closely was the general property manager, Roy Cantrell, who was present at Billings's arrest.[17] Swanson was "not of the old type plug-ugly," but an inconspicuous man[18]—altogether too inconspicuous, unfortunately, for he was to be a key figure in the Mooney case. About his background little is known. He was not an undercover labor spy, but a detective known to union men, who despised his methods.

The defenders of Mooney and Billings have usually condemned PG&E's use of private detectives like Swanson, but company detectives were an inescapable necessity because in 1913 California neither had nor desired a state police force. The experience of striking workers in Europe and in Pennsylvania (which had the only state constabulary in the country) had convinced the labor movement that any state law-enforcement agency in America was far more likely to be used to protect property than to protect persons;[19] and businessmen and land-owners, for their part, took pride in their local resourcefulness, which included, in extreme cases, local vigilante traditions. In short, nothing could have been more alien to the concepts of freedom espoused by labor, business, and agriculture than a California state police force.* Rural crimes were the responsibility of elected county sheriffs and constables, whose skills were varied but generally elementary. When faced with unusual crimes, these officials sometimes turned to private detective agencies for the benefit of their experience and scope of operations.[20] Rural counties found it necessary to hire private detectives; and for similar reasons, so did corporations with extensive rural property, including PG&E.†

Detectives in California were not regulated by the state. In 1915 California did enact its first licensing measure, over the opposition of the detective agencies and the San Francisco Chamber of Commerce; but the act merely required from each private detective a small bond for good behavior, a small annual fee, and five letters of recommendation. Detectives "for whose good conduct in business, however, the employers shall be responsible" were exempt.[21] Thus the detective with a job like Martin Swanson's was not touched by even this bland measure. The corporations remained solely responsible for the character of their detectives, which was notably poor. Throughout the industrial West, false arrests and forced confessions taken by private detectives were common. In some cases evidence was framed. Labor and Progressive papers reported some of the more flagrant abuses, includ-

---

* As late as 1924 not a single state document or professional article favoring a state police had appeared in California. (Margaret Mary Corcoran, "State Police in the United States," *Journal of the American Institute of Criminal Law and Criminology*, February 1924, pp. 544–55.)

† In view of pro-Mooney propaganda after 1916, it is worth stating explicitly that PG&E was not antagonistic to organized labor. Prior to the 1913 strike, its labor relations were good. Nor was it generally hostile to the public interest. Its public relations among even the Progressives of northern California were quite good, despite its role in the San Francisco graft mess. John A. Britton, the general manager and vice-president of PG&E, was himself a right-wing Progressive. (*Call*, October 23, 1909; Bean, *Boss Ruef's San Francisco*, pp. 88–89; *Bulletin* editorials, July 1913–December 1916; Sacramento *Bee*, March 5, August 14, and November 29, 1913; Britton testimony, U.S. Commission on Industrial Relations, *Final Report*, VI: 5427, 5429; and Pauline Jacobson interview of Britton in *Call*, October 25, 1921.)

ing at least one murder; but even the most shocking reports aroused few Californians outside the trade unions and the Socialist Party, among whom there was a fruitless effort to legislate private detectives out of existence.[22] The lesser abuses, such as unrestricted jail access to grill suspects and their detention without charges, went on constantly. Sheriffs, police, and district attorneys gave their tacit consent; many of them did the same sort of thing. Lawless acts could be punished, but the prosecution of lawless detectives was unpopular. Against labor organizers, vagrants, burglars, and radicals, private detectives were generally protected as *ex parte* agents of the law.[23]

On occasion a district attorney and a powerful newspaper might combine to expose and punish a detective for some particularly outrageous offense. One such episode grew out of the Marysville IWW trial, following the Wheatland hopfield riot of August 1913. It happens also to have had some bearing on Mooney's destiny.

IV

The Wheatland riot originated in the filthy camp conditions, lack of water, and other abuses of the 2,800 migratory pickers on the hop ranch of Richard Durst, near Wheatland, south of Marysville, in Yuba County. During a protest mass-meeting at the ranch the sheriff tried to arrest "Blackie" Ford, an IWW orator who was haranguing the crowd. Angry workers attacked the sheriff, and an excited deputy on the fringe of the crowd fired in the air "to sober the mob." In the ensuing riot, a deputy sheriff, two laborers, and District Attorney E. T. Manwell were killed, and many others injured. The sheriff's posse withdrew. Governor Hiram Johnson sent several companies of the National Guard to Wheatland, but nearly all of the workers had fled during the night.[24]

Most of the hop pickers had come from outside the county. County officers accordingly called upon the Burns Agency for help. Burns detectives were sworn in as deputy sheriffs so that they could arrest suspects with blanket "John Doe" warrants. Operatives spread across the state and into Arizona, locating and arresting suspects, among them Blackie Ford and Herman Suhr, the two Wobblies who were later convicted.[25] Without interference from county sheriffs or other authorities in Yuba, Alameda, and Fresno counties, the Burns agents moved their suspects about from jail to jail, preventing attorneys from finding out where they were being held. From Suhr the detectives extracted a third-degree confession, which he repudiated on recovery; the prosecution quietly dropped it. One sixteen-year-old eyewitness of the riot was kidnapped from the Yuba City jail, where he had been placed following his arrest, and was taken into hiding so that neither relatives nor the court could locate him. Evidently he had information that would have been useful to the defense. His uncle, who happened to be the business agent of Molders Union Local 164 in San Francisco and a conservative colleague of Mooney's, pressed habeas corpus proceedings, but for the time being was unable to recover the boy.[26]

Meanwhile other prisoners were manhandled. One, a Danish alien, hanged himself in jail with a blanket rope; another went temporarily insane and was committed to the Stockton asylum after Burns detectives beat him and slit his ear. Henry C. Daken, Yuba County game warden, who was with District Attorney Manwell at the fatal riot and subsequently, as deputy sheriff, saw what was happening in the Marysville jail, was so incensed that he offered to be a witness for Herman Suhr "when his trial is over if he brings any action against the Burns men."[27] The Sacramento *Bee,* hearing rumors of the scandal, sent C. K. McClatchy, Jr., to Marysville to investigate, and published a series of muckraking articles and editorials based substantially on Daken's evidence. Other Progressive newspapers took up the cause. On top of these developments the Burns Agency and the William Mundell Detective Agency of San Francisco calmly presented the Yuba County supervisors a bill for $10,725 for their services in the case.* It was unquestionably the Burns Agency's conduct in 1913 that precipitated the regulatory legislation, such as it was, passed at the next legislature.[28]

Only one of the Burns Agency's abuses resulted in prosecution. An IWW suspect, Alfred Nelson, was arrested by Burns detectives in Guerneville in September 1913. They took him by a devious route to Martinez. There he was held in a room of the Martinez Hotel by Burns agent R. B. Cradlebaugh, who beat, kicked, and trampled on him to extract a hopfield riot confession. A hotel roomer, hearing the noises, climbed out on the fire escape to investigate. He saw the detective pistol-whipping the prostrate suspect. The affair became public knowledge in Martinez; but in Yuba County, District Attorney E. B. Stanwood proceeded to charge Nelson with the murder of District Attorney

---

* Burns Agency rates were $8 a day per detective, plus expenses—a rate that was at least twice the average daily wage of skilled labor in San Francisco. (Sacramento *Bee,* March 24, 1914.)

Manwell at Wheatland, and Nelson was formally indicted. The District Attorney of Contra Costa County, A. B. McKenzie, a man who despised private detective agencies, protested to Stanwood without success. McKenzie refused to let the matter drop. He had Cradlebaugh arrested and indicted for false arrest and assault. San Francisco private detective chief William Mundell berated McKenzie for meddling, and threatened to expose him for an alleged earlier dereliction in office if he did not drop the charges; but McKenzie was adamant. He prosecuted. Cradlebaugh was defended by the Burns Agency, assisted by Stanwood himself; the defense contended that Nelson had tried to escape! The jury convicted the detective without hesitation. He received a one-year sentence and was fined $1,000.[29] The San Francisco Labor Council commented that the IWW's were "guardian angels" compared to Burns men: "is it any wonder we have anarchists who are disgusted with our forms of government and who have no faith in our laws?"*

V

Mooney was evidently in Sacramento with his motorcycle the day of Billings's arrest, and chatted with Billings at the train station.† If he knew of Billings's mission, there is no evidence to connect him with it. Mooney learned a few days later, however, that Swanson and Cantrell were looking for him and concluded that they intended to frame him. He decided to go into hiding. He avoided his friends in San Francisco, grew a moustache, and for three and a half or four months lived "underground" in the Bay Area and central California, sleeping in rooming houses or out in the open, never staying long in one place. This furtive existence was suddenly cut short on December 27, 1913. He had planned—he said—to winter along the San Joaquin River on a "fishing expedition" with Ed (H. D.) Hanlon and Joe

---

* *Labor Clarion*, February 13, 1914. The case attracted national attention. In Washington William B. Wilson, the Secretary of Labor, declared that private detectives employed in labor disputes were an instrument of private warfare, and urged Congress to outlaw them in interstate commerce. (Martinez *Standard*, February 6, 1914.) District Attorney McKenzie later told the U.S. Commission on Industrial Relations that many public officials were cowed by private detective agencies because the officials were anxious to keep certain aspects of their own lives private; hence the agencies ran roughshod over them. "That has been the policy of those people in this State," he said. (*Final Report*, V: 4996.)

† [Anna] Marcet Haldeman-Julius, "The Amazing Frameup of Mooney and Billings" (1931), p. 65. Mooney later denied this but was apparently not always consistent about it. (California Supreme Court, "Habeas Corpus," XX: 13,074.)

Brown, fellow radicals and members of the striking electrical workers' union. At South Vallejo they purchased a battered old sailing skiff from a Greek fisherman and, loading in some supplies, set out into San Pablo Bay. Not knowing how to sail, they were unable to get the skiff through Carquinez Strait. They spent the night bailing out until they ran aground on the Richmond mud flats. In the morning, when the tide rose, they navigated to the nearest port, a dilapidated old wharf at Point Richmond, and went ashore to purchase requisite naval stores—oakum and putty. They slept all day in Richmond. Returning at twilight, they were confronted by a large posse with guns drawn. From the boat a Richmond police officer, tipped off by a telephone call from an undisclosed source, had extracted an impressive arsenal of weapons and dynamiting equipment.[30]

The three men were taken to the Richmond jail and held there without charges. Mooney gave his name as Charles King and demanded counsel. Hanlon was carrying an IWW card, the police said that Mooney was a Wobbly too, and it was agreed that all three were very dangerous radicals; but there was some uncertainty about just what they should be accused of doing. The Contra Costa and San Francisco newspapers reported that the skiff was loaded with enough explosives to blow up a city, that it was loaded with an infernal machine of nitroglycerine and guncotton wired to a wound clock scratched "I.W.W." on the back and set for 12:30, that the three had planned to blow up a Richmond industrial plant or rob a bank. "King" was considered the ringleader and by far the most dangerous of the trio. The Richmond police chief asserted that King was a professional dynamiter "connected with jobs in Indianapolis"—an allusion to the Structural Bridge and Iron Workers Union, whose officers, including two from San Francisco, were tried and convicted at Indianapolis on dynamite charges. But this hypothesis was dropped after the arrival of PG&E agents on the scene.[31]

The Richmond authorities did not at first connect the skiff with the PG&E strike, which was still officially on. Their oversight was remedied with the arrival of Martin Swanson and Roy Cantrell the day after the arrest. Swanson saw through King's moustache; possibly he already knew that Mooney had landed at Point Richmond. Assisted by Henry Balsz and W. E. Kramer, two Sacramento detectives who had helped to arrest and prosecute Billings, he "sweated" Mooney in the Richmond jail for several days and probed for information in a manner later described by police sergeant R. N. Ruiz as a modified third degree.* On December 30 the report went abroad that King was Mooney, and that he was implicated in a Sacramento PG&E substation bombing; subsequently it was announced that the trio had planned to blow up the PG&E tower on the north side of Carquinez Strait.[32]

Since PG&E high-voltage wires spanning Carquinez Strait carried electricity for the whole Bay Area (roughly, San Francisco and the eight neighboring counties), the last tower on either side was a natural objective for anyone planning to disrupt PG&E by dynamiting darkness upon San Francisco. No one thought of this in connection with Mooney, however, until Swanson arrived. Moreover, since there was no proof that this had been the trio's intention, the plan to charge them with conspiracy to dynamite the tower had to be dropped. Four days after their arrest they were formally charged with the lesser crime of illegal transportation of high explosives. But the newspapers, unrestrained by requirements of legal evidence, adhered to Swanson's hypothesis, and twenty years later it was still common and official opinion in California that Mooney had intended to dynamite the Carquinez tower.[33]

The defendants were transferred to the Contra Costa county seat at Martinez. Mooney, the supposed ringleader, was picked for the first trial. Austin Lewis attended the preliminary hearing to defend him, but dropped out before the trial. Mooney was represented by three attorneys: Henry B. Lister, defense counsel in the Marysville IWW trial; Maxwell McNutt, once a law partner of Supreme Court Justice Marcus C. Sloss, and from 1910 to the fall of 1913 an Assistant District Attorney of San Francisco under Fickert; and Thomas D. Johnston, a local attorney, a state Assemblyman, and later District Attorney of the county. Lister eventually withdrew, leaving the defense primarily to McNutt.[34]

The court proceedings were attended by San Francisco visitors, including novelist Inez Haynes Gilmore. The case stirred considerable interest: it was the first in the county to be prosecuted under the 1887 law restricting the possession of high explosives. Local newspapers an-

---

* Mooney was identified at the same time by Berkeley's police chief, August Vollmer. Vollmer or the PG&E detectives evidently told the Richmond police that Mooney was suspected of assisting in the bombing of a Berkeley PG&E substation by one C. W. McAlpine. Nothing ever came of the accusation, although McAlpine was tried and convicted. (*Chronicle*, December 30, 1913; Martinez *Contra Costa Gazette*, January 3, 1914; and California Supreme Court, "Habeas Corpus," XX: 13,088.) At the time of Billings's arrest in Sacramento, it was McAlpine, rather than Mooney, who was first reported as the accomplice on the motorcycle. (See Sacramento *Bee*, September 20, 1913.)

ticipated that the trial would be "one of the greatest legal battles ever fought in the county."[35]

District Attorney A. B. McKenzie was away during the first trial. Officially the prosecution was handled in his absence by Assistant District Attorney Ormsby. But as in the Billings case, PG&E's attorney John J. Barrett participated as "special prosecutor," and so did his PG&E colleague M. R. Jones, an able, conservative Contra Costa Assemblyman connected with the law department of Southern Pacific and president of the Contra Costa Chamber of Commerce. McKenzie had not refused to take part in the case, as Mooney later insisted, but he might as well have. Even the San Francisco *Chronicle* acknowledged that the prosecution was in the hands of Barrett and Jones; Ormsby was there only to officiate. At the request of the PG&E attorneys, Sheriff R. R. Veale of Martinez sat with them in the courtroom, advising them on the merits of prospective jurors—an extraordinary abuse of the Sheriff's office. Once again private detectives and PG&E were running the show. McNutt protested vigorously, and the Martinez *Standard,* which had recovered from its initial misrepresentation of the defendants to report the trials with restrained skepticism, agreed with him: "The Pinkerton sample of private detective is beginning to show at the trial of Thomas J. Mooney. They should keep away as the sheriff is capable of looking after things. The private gumshoe racket has a sinister aspect and it does not redound to the credit of a corporation displaying the need of them."[36]

In the San Francisco labor movement many insisted that Mooney was being framed; their feelings were shared by Progressives still indignant over the Cradlebaugh scandal. The San Francisco Labor Council protested that the defendants were held under excessive bail and were abused in jail. It cooperated with the International Workers Defense League in raising defense funds. At IWDL-sponsored mass meetings, militant San Francisco Progressives spoke from the platform with "revolutionaries" and an anarchist or two, on behalf of both the Marysville and the Martinez defendants. Mrs. Fremont Older, Inez Haynes Gilmore, the Socialists Austin Lewis and Selig Schulberg, and the anarchist Anton Johannsen all appealed for help against the persecution of left-wing workers in California's small-town courts.[37]

The first trial ended in a hung jury, split 6–6.[38] District Attorney McKenzie returned for the second trial, but again Barrett and Jones appear to have been in command. McKenzie disapproved of special prosecutors, but had once allowed a union to have a special prosecutor in a case involving a scab who had murdered a trade unionist. He therefore felt obliged to permit Barrett and Jones to participate in the prosecution of Mooney. McKenzie seems to have been surfeited with the case when the second jury split 7–5 for acquittal. Probably it was Barrett and Jones who insisted on the third trial.[39]

The main question before the jury was whether Mooney was responsible, along with Hanlon and Brown, for the weapons and dynamiting equipment found in the skiff, or whether someone—possibly an agent of Martin Swanson—had placed them there in their absence. No third alternative seemed feasible then, nor does one now. The prospects of a successful courtroom defense based on the frame-up thesis were poor, however, partly because there was no evidence that Swanson was in the vicinity until the day after the arrest. Therefore the defense built its case on the more technical and more manageable premise that there were no high explosives in the skiff.[40]

The articles found in the skiff by Officer Ruiz comprised an astonishing inventory: a 30–30 Winchester rifle with a Maxim silencer and a box of cartridges; a 38-caliber automatic Colt revolver and ammunition; a twelve-gauge double-barreled shotgun, its barrel painted aluminum, and a box of shells loaded with buckshot; thirteen dry-cell batteries connected in series and soldered to an alarm clock; a 500-foot spool of wire; fourteen electric exploders or caps, containing fulminate of mercury and attached at regular intervals to the wire; and gloves and tools. But there was no dynamite, no nitroglycerin, no guncotton. The ballyhooed mountain of explosives was reduced in fact to a molehill of caps. Were they a high explosive? The prosecution produced three expert witnesses—one of them John Bermingham, a former superintendent of the California Powder Works and currently M. R. Jones's secretary at the Chamber of Commerce—to testify that they were. The defense produced one expert witness, Ed Hurley of the striking electrical workers' union, who testified that the caps were no more harmful than pistol cartridges. Since the case rested on expertise and the experts disagreed, the jurors' indecision was understandable.

After the second trial Mooney's bail was reduced to a manageable $1,000, which was paid by the San Francisco Labor Council. But a new complaint was sworn out against him, this time by PG&E's Sacramento district manager, who alleged that Mooney had helped Billings carry the dynamite on the Sacramento streetcar. Mooney, protesting persecution, was taken in handcuffs to Sacramento for a preliminary hearing, and was then freed on bail to await the third trial. Detectives continued to harass him: one sought music lessons from his wife, and another the acquaintance of his sister.[41]

The third Martinez trial, pushed through in three days, was like the other two except in result. Barrett and Jones prosecuted with McKenzie; McNutt and Johnston defended again; this time the jury acquitted Mooney. McKenzie then moved for dismissal of the cases against the other two defendants, and Hanlon and Brown went free. Mooney, not yet a free man, was sent back to Sacramento, where Swanson, Balsz, and Kramer bore witness against him, but the evidence was so flimsy that the case was dismissed after the preliminary hearing.[42] Billings was brought from Folsom during the course of it to identify Mooney, but he refused to testify.*

Why was Mooney acquitted at Martinez? Labor radicals had been convicted on flimsier evidence. His jurors were not men of his class or political persuasion. They were farmers who might be expected to have little sympathy for Ed Hurley and his interpretation of fulminate of mercury. If the jurors distrusted Bermingham, they had only to accept the word of Colonel John W. Royce of the Benecia arsenal, or Leslie Oliver of the California Cap Works; Oliver told them that fulminate of mercury was the highest explosive made.[43]

There is one plausible explanation for the acquittal: in Martinez, it appears, nearly everybody read the *Standard*. (The *Standard*'s sole hometown competitor, the reactionary *Contra Costa Gazette*, was only a weekly.) The *Standard*'s folksy editor, Will R. Sharkey, was often inspired by McClatchy's *Bee* editorials, and occasionally also by those of Older's more radical *Bulletin*. Sharkey's first account of the arsenal in the skiff was as prejudiced as the *Gazette*'s, but when Swanson and PG&E arrived on the scene, Sharkey recalled Marysville and changed his mind. Private detectives, he said, were no more justifiable than a private judiciary.[44] Throughout the trials he published careful accounts of the proceedings, including Sergeant Ruiz's damaging testimony against Swanson.[45] Sharkey had no affection for radicalism or labor unions, but he plainly disapproved of Mooney's treatment. At

---

* The police judge presiding thereupon sentenced Billings to 100 days for contempt of court, but could not enforce the sentence because Billings was already a prisoner. Contempt-of-court sentences had to be served at once or they were not binding. (Oral History Project, "Billings," pp. 109–12.)

the third trial the prosecution asked prospective jurors whether they read the *Standard,* and in almost every case the answer was yes—the *Standard* or the Richmond *Daily News,* which was then an openly pro-labor paper. Some were dismissed after admitting that these papers had influenced their opinions about the "continuous prosecution" of Mooney. Others, whether or not so influenced, may have remembered that in the same jail with Mooney at Martinez was Cradlebaugh, put there by District Attorney McKenzie.[46]

Who put the arsenal in Mooney's sailboat? Two witnesses denied that the boxes alleged to have contained the equipment were in the boat when they saw it. Mooney claimed he never saw the articles until after his arrest. Why the trio might have wanted such an array of weapons is difficult to imagine. It was said that the shotgun barrel was painted aluminum for night shooting, and that the arsenal showed that the three men were desperadoes who would kill anyone interfering with their dynamiting. But such a collection of guns, two of which could not be concealed, would have jeopardized stealth, and to leave them in an open skiff in broad daylight was to invite discovery.[47]

As for the fulminate of mercury caps, the prosecution contended that they had been set along the wire in sufficient quantity and at the necessary intervals to explode dynamite charges at every leg of the Carquinez PG&E tower, and that Mooney, who had vacationed the preceding August at a shoreside resort not far from the tower, had already scouted the place. But the tower theory is unconvincing. Irrespective of the missing dynamite, its greatest flaw is that by December 1913 the PG&E strike was moribund. All the strikers who could return to work had long since done so. Negotiations were under way between the company and the IBEW, with the AFL mediating between the two wings of the IBEW; the final settlement was concluded January 7. There had been no depredations against PG&E property anywhere since October.[48]

What, then, might the wire and caps have been for? Billings's explanation that the skiff belonged to the Greek fisherman and that he had been dynamiting fish in the Bay is without merit. Police and newspapers supposed at the time of the arrest that the skiff was stolen, but at the trial the man testified that he had sold it to Mooney, and both sides accepted Mooney's ownership as a fact. Henry Lister suggested in the habeas corpus appeal before the first trial that the caps and wire might have been intended for dynamiting orchard land to plant fruit trees—a whimsical interpretation. Mooney himself had no explanation for the diabolical device, and seems to have discharged one attorney, either Lister or Lewis, for trying to explain it away. To rationalize, he insisted, was to compromise his innocence.[49]

Mooney's friends always believed that he was framed by Swanson; that Swanson, knowing Mooney to be a radical and a participant in the PG&E strike, was trying to get him at both Sacramento and Martinez.[50] But Swanson would hardly have bothered with all the weapons and the carefully prepared wire without including some sticks of dynamite. The guns and gear inflamed the imagination, but their possession was not illegal, and no charges involving them were formally made. Moreover, Swanson must have known that Contra Costa was the worst county in the state just then for a labor case arranged by a private detective. Even the IWDL was convinced that in Contra Costa County, Mooney would get an even break. Schulberg reassured Mooney before his first trial that many of the county officials were "directly connected with organized Labor."[51] If Mooney was framed, it was a careless piece of work.

In Martinez after the acquittal, John J. Barrett remarked to McNutt: "Well, Max, you got him off this time, but we have got a red shirt on the son-of-a-bitch now and we are going to put something good on him some day."[52] Mooney's friends would eventually look back upon the Martinez affair as a rehearsal for the final frame-up. There were, in fact, many ways in which the Martinez trials did prefigure the San Francisco Preparedness Parade bomb trials. Among the signs were the IWW label, the extra-judicial influences of the press and the public utilities, and the presence of Martin Swanson.

CHAPTER THREE

The Radicals

I am a Marxian.
—Tom Mooney, 1936

THE International Workers Defense League had been formed in San Francisco in 1912 to help radicals in the courts. It publicized their cases, raised funds, and provided legal counsel. These cases frequently developed during strikes and frequently turned into persecutions. Prosecutors, juries, and sometimes judges ignored or slighted the civil rights and courtroom testimony of radicals. The daily press usually prejudged the defendants. Against these elements the IWDL offered its support. The League was a practical expression of radical solidarity, perhaps the only effective American manifestation of thoroughly non-sectarian radicalism in its time. With the exception of the Socialist Labor Party, the IWDL included all radical elements: industrial unionists, trade-union radicals, militant socialists, Wobblies, anarchists, workingmen's fraternal organizations, and Socialist foreign-language federations.

There were a number of such leagues in industrial cities throughout the country. The first of them had been formed during the Moyer-Haywood-Pettibone trial, in Idaho in 1906. Local leagues were revived and reorganized on a more permanent basis as the IWDL during the trial of Joseph Ettor and Arturo Giovannitti, IWW-anarchist leaders in the textile workers' strike at Lawrence, Massachusetts, in 1912. By 1915 there were active defense leagues in New York, Chicago, Detroit, Pittsburgh, St. Louis, Kansas City, and Denver, as well as San Francisco. A Los Angeles branch was formed in 1916, to aid Ricardo and Enrique Flores Magón, the editors of a Mexican anarchist weekly.[1]

The IWDL of San Francisco represented over 50 local labor and radical organizations, about two-thirds of them Bay Area trade-union locals. The most active delegates were from San Francisco trade unions in which the left wing was dominant, or at least strong. The most powerful union in the group was the machinists' local (IAM 68), whose 1,500 members in 1915 constituted 90 per cent of the city's machinists. Many San Francisco unions refused to have anything to do with the IWDL, particularly the teamsters and most of the unions of P. H. McCarthy's Building Trades Council.* The San Francisco Labor Council was not directly represented, but even its conservative AFL leaders, on the whole, viewed the League's activities tolerantly. So did the California State Federation of Labor, the East Bay labor councils, and a few San Francisco building-trades unions with relatively strong radical elements.[2]

The IWDL was not primarily a propaganda organization, but the radicals could not have chosen a more effective means than labor cases to publicize their own causes. Its members believed in the proletarian revolution and in precipitating it through the industrial union, the boycott, and the general strike, and not through politics or arms. There is nothing to indicate that its members were engaged in criminal conspiracies or exhortations to violence, although their social philosophy was of course anathema to most San Franciscans. When San Francisco authorities seized the League's correspondence in 1916, considerable light was thrown on its views and activities; only to a prejudiced eye did these documents seem to show that the League germinated violence.[3]

Among the labor cases in which the San Francisco IWDL assisted between 1913 and 1916 were those of Mother Jones, Socialist folk heroine of the West Virginia and Colorado coal miners; the Colorado United Mine Workers, particularly Adolph Germer, one of their radical Socialist leaders; the IWW leaders arrested for murder during Michigan's Calumet mine strike; Max Sigman, Socialist officer of the International Ladies' Garment Workers Union of New York City; Joe Hill, IWW poet convicted of murder in Utah; and David Caplan and Matthew Schmidt, anarchists prosecuted in Los Angeles on conspiracy

---

* The Building Trades Council was deeply involved in cases concerning its own movement and leaders, especially the Los Angeles *Times* case and the Indianapolis trials of 1912. Its contributions to other labor defense cases were routine. (See *Bulletin,* December 15, 1913, January 24, May 1, 1914, and March 5, 1915.)

evidence arising out of the *Times* case.[4] The IWDL rarely concerned itself with any other type of cause.*

The San Francisco IWDL was run by half a dozen men. One of them was Tom Mooney, who became secretary after his release from Martinez. The others were all his friends. Schulberg and Milder he had known since *Revolt* days or before. Milder was his predecessor as secretary of the League. There was Anton Johannsen, the Chicago anarchist anonymously celebrated in Hutchins Hapgood's biographical sketch, *The Spirit of Labor*.† Johannsen had moved to San Francisco and was one of the labor leaders there who promoted the Los Angeles trade-union organizing campaign in 1910.[5]

There was Eric B. Morton, an anarchist and a member of the millmen's union, one of the few radicals on the San Francisco Building Trades Council, and also a Labor Council delegate until he was expelled for violating the taboo against employing Orientals. Morton was an associate of Johannsen, Caplan, and Olaf Tveitmoe in the Los Angeles organizing campaign, and was one of the group of organizers whom Louis Adamic chose to call "the San Francisco gorillas." He was suspected of complicity in the *Times* bombing, but was never arrested. A colleague of Alexander Berkman, the anarchist who had attempted to assassinate Henry Clay Frick during the Homestead strike in 1892, Morton had tunneled under the Pennsylvania State Penitentiary to rescue him and had almost completed the escape route before it was discovered. He was one of the few American radicals who had actually participated in a revolution, having gone to Russia with some crates of arms during the 1905 uprising. In San Francisco he was a chronic alcoholic.[6]

And there was the anarchist Edward D. Nolan, a machinist and local union organizer recently arrived from Los Angeles, where he had been a city labor council delegate in 1904 and in 1910–12. Nolan was a San Francisco machinists' union delegate to the Labor Council, 1913–14, and to the local Iron Trades Council in 1914. Berkman admired him as "one of the most intelligent and absolutely incorruptible Labor men."[7] It was Nolan who visited Billings in Sacramento on behalf of the IWDL, to arrange for Billings's defense. Nolan was fated

---

* An exceptional activity was the raising of funds for the unemployed in San Francisco. The IWDL was protesting the brutality meted out in Sacramento to Kelly's "army" of unemployed in March 1914. (*Bulletin,* March 16, 1914.)

† It is not clear whether Johannsen was a regular member of the IWDL or not, but he raised funds for it and participated in its crusades.

to be one of the defendants with Mooney in the Preparedness Day
bomb cases.*

In the Martinez trials the IWDL had assumed much of the financial
responsibility for Mooney's defense, and had obtained at least two of
the lawyers, Lister and Johnston. The first two trials alone cost $3,000,
part of which the IWDL raised. When Mooney was finally acquitted,
the League still owed his attorneys $1,075, which was particularly diffi-
cult to raise thereafter because the case was closed. Mooney made personal appeals at union meetings, and the IWDL sponsored picnics and
"Hobo Balls" to raise money for the Ford-Suhr and Mooney defense
funds; but by the end of 1915 only $700 or $800 had been raised against
the debt. The rest was never repaid.[8]

Mooney believed that he had been saved at Martinez by the IWDL.
In a letter to Mother Jones he described its activities, and confided
that had it not been for the IWDL, he would have been convicted:

> The California Light and Power Council called a strike against the Pa-
> cific Gas and Electric Co. one of the largest and most powerfull corpora-
> tions in this state. The Pinkerton Detective Agency was put on the Job by
> the Gas Co. at the time I was out of work and I at all times feel it my duty
> to do all in my power to aid and assist any or all aggragations of workers on
> Strike for better conditions. . . . Five of them were sent to the Penitentiary
> of this state for periods of from one to five years on evidence secured by
> Pinkertons. The Building Trades Council of Calif. Fought with the Gas
> Co. and aided in the Defeat of the strikers when the entire state Federation
> of Labor was supporting morally and financially the strike.
>
> There was several hundred thousand dollars worth of property of the
> Gas Co. destroyed by the strikers in various ways. I was in hiding for four
> months myself and finally arrested kept in Jail for five months going to
> the highest court of the state on habeas corpus, and then three Trials on
> the first Charge . . . and then the fourth trial at Sacramento, Cal. all finally
> resulting in my release. The Defense League carried on the defense in my
> behalf, and were it not for such a league I would be in San Quentin with
> the McNamara boys today and unable to write you as I am doing at this
> minute. . . .

---

* Oakland *World,* December 22, 1916; Oral History Project, "Billings," p. 104; and
Robert Minor to Frank P. Walsh, August 19, 1916 (Walsh Papers). Other active IWDL
men in the Bay Area were Jack Lofthouse, officer of local 42 of the millmen's union and
an industrial unionist; Henry Hagelstein, of the International Association of Machinists,
who appeared briefly for the Mooney defense on the witness stand in Martinez; Pete
Isaac, later president of IAM local 68; and Billings. (*Labor Clarion,* July 18, 1913; Oral
History Project, "Billings," pp. 105–6; and *Bulletin,* May 4, 1915.)

The defense League would like to have you come out here to help it pay off its debt that was incurred in my defense.[9]

San Francisco authorities, reading this letter two years later, interpreted it as a personal confession of guilt, and thereafter it was so regarded by his opponents.[10] But their conclusion was merely inferential. Since Mooney was asking Mother Jones to help the IWDL, he wrote in the manner that would appeal to her most. For Mother Jones, the significant fact was Mooney's struggle against Pinkertons and corporation lawyers, not his guilt or innocence according to law. He was on the fighting line in the class war. He might have dynamited corporation property, or he might not have. He was neither admitting nor denying it. Similarly, the mention of the McNamaras is inconclusive: both Mother Jones and Mooney probably believed (with many other radicals of the time) that the McNamaras had been successfully framed and had confessed only to save their lives.

Blackie Ford and Herman Suhr were under sentence of life imprisonment for the Wheatland riot killings when Mooney was acquitted at Martinez. Their case had been taken up vigorously by the IWW, the IWDL, and the San Francisco Labor Council. Pardon appeals were made to Governor Hiram Johnson. When Johnson chose to delay action until the State Supreme Court had reviewed the case, the state labor movement was irate and the radicals were outraged. The members of the IWDL decided to tell Johnson what they thought of him, but were divided over the message until Mooney, who had been campaigning among San Francisco unions for Ford and Suhr, and who knew Ford personally, drafted a threatening letter and persuaded his colleagues to accept it. He then wired it to the Governor, over his own signature, and sent copies to most of the papers in northern California. The message read in part:

The Governor's statement of his reasons for refusing to act at this time shows him up in his true colors, a cowardly cur, despicable beyond recognition, and resorting to the cunning, shrewdness, trickery and cowardice of the average district attorney in prosecuting a case.…

There are some workers at least, Governor Johnson, who will not accept as final your decision on the Ford and Suhr case, and from now on they will attempt to use the only kind of reasoning that will eventually reach you, and we hope it will be indulged in until Ford and Suhr are out of jail.

And so if violence is committed, Governor Johnson is responsible for it, as he has closed the last legal or governmental avenue of action.[11]

Mooney's was one of an "avalanche" of messages threatening Johnson with reprisals if Ford and Suhr were not reprieved.[12] Some of the messages were evidently IWW threats. Others were probably crank letters. This one, coming from the IWDL and bearing Mooney's name, was not dismissed as an emotional outburst. The inclusion of his signature surely discredits the view that he intended to attack the Governor physically, but it made the threat the more brazen.[13] The telegram was no common, anonymous threat such as Johnson was accustomed to receiving, and it left its mark. In the malevolence of Mooney's message Johnson formed his judgment of the man, and he never reopened his mind.*

Others besides the Governor were scandalized by the telegram. John A. O'Connell, secretary of the San Francisco Labor Council, condemned the "filthy document" and predicted that Mooney would soon be asking the Labor Council to dig him out of jail again.[14] The strongest word of all came from C. K. McClatchy: the *Bee* asserted that a lynching party was in order.† In the state labor movement, radicals and conservatives alike condemned Mooney's message. Paul Scharrenberg, chairing the annual convention of the California State Federation of Labor, declared that although Ford and Suhr had been unfairly tried, the Governor would not cringe before such contemptible pressure from the IWW arson brigade.[15] "It is such kind of stuff as this that is keeping Ford and Suhr in prison," he added, and obtained the cooperation of Hugo Ernst, San Francisco's best-known and most outspoken Socialist at that convention, in condemning Mooney's statement. (At the same time the convention unanimously recommended that Ford and Suhr be pardoned.) For Mooney himself, perhaps the hardest blow of all was that even Selig Schulberg disapproved.[16]

Undaunted, Mooney sent a similarly threatening appeal for clemency for Joe Hill, who was under sentence of death in Utah. On behalf of the IWDL, he wrote to Utah's Governor William Spry:

* In 1929 Walter W. Liggett wrote Roger Baldwin, "Hiram Johnson won't do a damn thing, altho he told me he knew Mooney was innocent and should have been freed long ago." (May 17, 1929, ACLU Papers, vol. 371. See also Older to Mooney, June 22, 1927, Mooney Papers, and Baldwin to Max Stern, January 13, 1932, ACLU Papers, vol. 561.) As George E. Mowry has written, "It is doubtful whether he [Johnson] ever really forgave what he considered a personal slight, whether real or fancied." (*California Progressives* [1951], p. 114.)

† Sacramento *Bee*, October 1, 1915. The *Bee* never named names when it called for the lynching of Wobblies, but since the same editorial that called for this lynching also condemned the letter "signed by Tom Mooney, Secretary-Treasurer of the I.W.W.," the newspaper's candidate was clear. (The supposition that the IWDL was an IWW organization was a common error.)

If you are not in favor of Justice, then you can only be expected to be treated as you would treat others. . . . We are not going to see any working man perish without being avenged, when we are satisfied he was not proven guilty of the crime charged in our estimation. Every principle of justice was denied this man. . . . If Utah takes this life it will pay dearly for so doing. Governor the Issue is up to you. Act, and Act Right, or other[s] will act right. Our demand is that Hillstrom be pardoned.[17]

In a last-ditch appeal Mooney appeared at the AFL national convention in San Francisco, and was permitted to address the gathering as secretary of the IWDL. He asked the convention to petition President Wilson for executive clemency. The request was received favorably; Gompers, who had already been concerned about the case, wired Wilson and Spry, protesting injustice, but Hill was executed forthwith. Meanwhile the Sacramento *Bee* condemned Mooney again as an "I.W.W. agitator" of the dynamiting sort, who had imposed upon the AFL by pretending to be a union man.[18]

What precisely Mooney thought his threatening messages might accomplish can only be surmised. He was not recognizably a vicious man, but he believed he was dealing with a vicious system. He was bumptious, foolhardy, and sometimes exasperating to his friends. It seems doubtful that he supposed he could intimidate either Johnson or Spry, but clearly he was willing to try. Many years later a close friend of Austin Lewis privately remarked that Mooney "always did just what he was told not to do, and was always making a fool of himself and getting into trouble."*

II

Though Mooney was never an anarchist, he made many anarchist friends through the IWDL and through his efforts on behalf of the Los Angeles anarchist defendants, Caplan and Schmidt. He worked earnestly for months in 1915, visiting Bay Area unions to raise IWDL funds in their behalf. He became a confidant of Alexander Berkman,

* Mary Hutchinson to Roger Baldwin, July 4, 1929, ACLU Papers, vol. 371. In this letter Miss Hutchinson also stated that Mooney "was operating in the terrorist movement" and that Lewis got him out of "more narrow scrape[s] than one," but she has since said that she does not know any details. (Author's interview, April 2, 1965.) Lewis's correspondence with Baldwin and others sheds no further light on Mooney's activities. On the contrary, in one letter he indicated that he knew little about them: "much of what is said is to [me] interestingly new." (Lewis to Henry T. Hunt, April 23, 1929, Lewis Papers.)

the fanatic who had attempted to assassinate Frick in America's first anarchist *attentat* 23 years earlier. Released from the Pennsylvania State Penitentiary in 1906, Berkman had resumed his leadership with Emma Goldman in the anarchist movement, though cured of the urge to awaken the masses by an *attentat*. He went to Los Angeles to see what he could do to save Caplan and Schmidt, and decided that an anarchist paper was the answer. A paper would publicize the defense and would report other news from "Labor's prisoners of war—on trial and in prison."[19] Berkman wanted a paper to stimulate radical solidarity, to encourage revolutionary activity, and "to keep the rebels throughout the world in closer touch with each other." He wanted particularly to encourage anarchist grammar schools founded on the principles of Francisco Ferrer, and to combat the growing spirit of militarism and armed preparedness in America. The West Coast was without an English-language anarchist paper to meet these needs. In order to avoid hindering rather than helping Caplan and Schmidt, Berkman took his project to San Francisco. There he was assisted by Morton, Ed Nolan, and Mooney.[20]

Mooney was enthusiastic. He shared Berkman's concern for the whole revolutionary cause and believed that any paper which embraced it in good faith was worth supporting. "I don't care what particular factional teaching any labor paper or radical paper has," he said; "if it supports the cause of the toilers in their struggle for freedom and emancipation, I am for that paper."[21] He disagreed with Berkman's political beliefs but wanted the paper to succeed, for it would be the only Bay Area working-class paper sufficiently radical to suit him. Mooney was involved at the time with a strike project and with his IWDL work, and had little time for the paper, but he encouraged friends to subscribe, sold subscriptions, and wrote one article.[22]

The paper was launched in January 1916 as the *Blast*. Under this redoubtable title issues appeared weekly, bearing articles by prominent philosophical, literary, and revolutionary anarchists and friends: in San Francisco, Sara Bard Field, Anton Johannsen; around the country, Charles Erskine Scott Wood, Emma Goldman, Mary Heaton Vorse, George Andreytchine; and from elsewhere in California, several little-known radical journalists, Luke North, Robert Minor, and Ed Gammons. Appropriate excerpts for anarchistic inspiration were reprinted from the writings of Shaw, Voltaire, Tolstoy, Nietzsche, Carlyle, and William Lloyd Garrison.

Berkman was editor. He was assisted by Morton and a red-headed young native-born admirer from Chicago, Mary Eleanor Fitzgerald. Cartoon covers were provided by Robert Minor, who in his time was one of America's most gifted political satirists with charcoal and paper. Lydia Gibson, who was later Minor's wife, supplied other art work. The editorials, articles, and cartoons together added up to an obscure, biting, but reasonably restrained sheet of anarchist social criticism, somewhat on the order of the more sophisticated and more culturally inclined *Masses* in New York, which Max Eastman was editing for the left-wing literati in the East. For a year and a half Berkman, more po-litical-minded and less witty than Eastman, turned out a competently edited paper, disseminating anti-militarism, anti-nationalism, labor de-fense, birth control, class war, and the Haymarket heritage. Comfort-able citizens of San Francisco might well have viewed the *Blast* with alarm had it come to their attention, but few were aware of its exis-tence.[23]

The paper was small but there were those who loved it. One was Ed Nolan. Like Mooney, he thought other labor papers anemic. He ap-plauded it vigorously and called for more vitriol:

I liked the first Blast [he wrote Morton], I like the second better, and god damn it[,] in the parlance of the miner if she don't start put in a bank shot and take down the whole mountain....

No gods to appease no leaders to bow to no dogmas to follow.

Shoot at the mark old boys and my fond hope is that we can furnish food for the seige.[24]

Within three months the paper was in trouble with the Post Office because of articles advocating birth control. Distribution by second-class mail was prohibited except after review of each issue by the Post-master General. Such harassment of a radical paper was common, and perhaps expected, for the Post Office had already denied mailing priv-ileges to the anarchist *Alarm* in Chicago and *Revolt* in New York. On the latter occasion Berkman had let loose the most caustic attack on the government the *Blast* ever made:

We are not going to say that it is an outrage. Why should the govern-ment not commit outrages? Invasion of personal liberty, suppression of free speech and free press, silencing non-conformists and protestants, shoot-ing down rebellious workers—all this is of the very essence of government.

We don't complain. We understand Wilson's position. He must do his master's bidding. This is the "sane policy." But we want to warn the weather cock in the White House that it may not prove *safe*. Suppression of the voice of discontent leads to assassination. *Vide* Russia.[25]

This editorial, signed and published, was cited a few months later as evidence that Berkman was a conspirator in the Preparedness Day bombing.[26] Meanwhile the *Blast* suffered added distribution costs. Berkman was irate: "We are tired of awaiting the pleasure of His Majesty, Postmaster General Burleson, and his Comstockian censorship. Who the hell is Burleson, anyhow, to presume to dictate what is or is not 'fit' to be read by the American public?"[27] With financial resources nearly exhausted, the "Blasters," as they called themselves, reduced publication to a monthly schedule. Subscriptions were sent unsolicited to San Franciscans whom Mooney thought might be interested enough to pay for them. This placed the *Blast* in the hands of some people who had never heard of it, and some may have been perturbed.[28]

Mooney's one article in the *Blast* was an attack on the Pacific Coast Defense League, a growing, San Francisco–centered civic organization spreading propaganda for military and naval preparedness. The San Francisco Board of Education had denied a request of the League for military training in the city's schools, and the labor movement approved the refusal. Mooney's protest was one among many: "I agree with the sentiments of a worker in this community when he said that if they [the League's officers] are not getting paid by labor's enemies they are scabbing on the job. This move of the League to trap the workers must be pushed back in the teeth of the labor crushers."[29] The article expressed a conviction shared by most Bay Area trade unionists, for they resented the established use of state and federal troops in breaking strikes. Mooney's words had nothing to do with the Preparedness Parade, which was not conceived for another month and a half, but his adversaries later quoted them widely against him.[30]

III

To be known as an anarchist, as all of the "Blasters" came to be, was to invite suspicion and trouble. The fear of anarchists was endemic in America during the first two decades of this century, from the assassination of McKinley to the Red Scare of 1919–20. San Francisco, with its cosmopolitan and relatively tolerant traditions, was less susceptible to hysteria than other communities. Nevertheless, the influence of narrow conservatism was also strong; anarchists were carelessly confused with the criminally insane; the will to resist anti-radical phobias was weakened by periodic bloodlettings in the Hearst papers; and with each new report of an anarchist assault on an American public official, priest, or policeman, public apprehension mounted. As a rule the radical orators of San Francisco's Jefferson Square were ignored by the police, but when the pressure was on, they were subjected to roundups, arrests, fines, imprisonment—and, occasionally, deportation proceedings.

The first severe anarchist scare in America since the assassination of McKinley developed in the spring of 1908. There occurred, in rapid succession, three crimes attributed to anarchists: an assassination of a Catholic priest in Denver, an attempted assassination of the police chief of Chicago, and a New York Union Square bombing that came within seconds of repeating the Haymarket carnage. During the outcry that followed, President Roosevelt requested Congress to pass more stringent laws against anarchism, and in particular to ban anarchist publications from the unsealed mails. He requested immigration officials throughout the country to cooperate with city police in rounding up and deporting anarchist aliens. In San Francisco the police and immigration officials complied. According to the city's police captain of detectives, some five hundred anarchists lived there at the time. The announced mission of the police was to bring all these men to police stations for identification and turn over those who were aliens to immigration officials for deportation.[31]

In 1914 and 1915 there were more anarchist scares, including three sensational ones in New York City. There was the Lexington Avenue bombing, an accidental explosion in an upstairs flat of a home-made bomb believed by some to be intended for John D. Rockefeller. That bomb killed four anarcho-syndicalist friends of Alexander Berkman. There was the bombing of the Bronx courthouse, on the twenty-seventh anniversary of the Haymarket executions. And there was the St. Patrick's Cathedral bomb plot, nipped in the fuse by New York police detectives, but subsequently revealed to be the work of two illiterate Italian anarchists inspired by a police *agent provocateur,* rather than the rumored inauguration of a city-wide reign of terror.[32] These events were reported in San Francisco newspapers, and readers were not left to draw their own conclusions. However, the local anarchists went right on meeting.

High-brow anarchists of San Francisco met with other malcontents —Socialists, Wobblies, Progressives, and eccentrics—in the International Radical Club, an informal organization of Bohemians, writers, professors, and other intellectuals who gathered monthly at the Fior d'Italia restaurant on Broadway and Kearny for conviviality, expostulation, lectures, and social criticism. The anarchists in attendance were "the most gentle of the lot," according to one Socialist member.[33] The club was founded in 1912. John D. Barry, a *Bulletin* staff editor and self-styled philosophical anarchist, was its first chairman, and Austin Lewis its first president; J. Edward Morgan was president in 1916. As for the anarchists of the streets, they met at Jefferson Square or in radical societies like the Gruppo Anarchico Volontà, with its library and reading room on Stockton Street, and the Union of Russian Workers, a foreign-language federation affiliated with the IWW. These circles had their favorite coffee shops, bookstores, and lecture halls, and the city officials usually left them alone.[34]

Emma Goldman, the famous dynamic anarchist, was a frequent visitor to San Francisco. On one occasion, in 1909, she was arrested and held on $4,000 bail for preaching doctrines inimical to government. Some of her followers who held a street meeting in protest were also arrested. Some of them were clubbed when police broke up the meeting. But the sequel is revealing: upon protest of the Socialist Party, through Selig Schulberg, the city police commission agreed to hold an inquiry on police department violations of free speech and free assembly in the city; and meanwhile Emma returned to the Dreamland Rink and expounded anarchism to a large crowd without police interference. So far, however, the anarchists had only threatened San Francisco with ideas.[35]

The spring of 1916 brought America a repetition of the 1908 fright. At Chicago's University Club an assembly of three hundred university and community leaders dining in honor of Archbishop George W. Mundelein were served chicken soup laden with arsenic. Fortunately the wretch who prepared the potion had dumped in far too much poison, so that the guests vomited, and none died. The deed was quickly traced to the cook's helper, Jean Crones, an immigrant from Cologne and allegedly a close friend of the widow of Gaetano Bresci, the Italian-born anarchist of Paterson, New Jersey, who had assassinated King Humbert of Italy in 1900. In Crones's room in Chicago were found anarchist literature, explosives, and vials of poison. The affair was emblazoned in the nation's press from the outset as an anarchist plot. Crones fled to New York, where he evaded police and amused himself writing letters to the New York *Times*.[36] Meanwhile Hearst's San Francisco *Examiner* reported the affair as "part of a world-wide plan of destruction by an anarchistic organization of tremendous power," whose program for Chicago included dynamiting buildings of the federal government, the Catholic Church, the Union League, and a public utility.[37]

Federal agents in Chicago entered the case and announced that they would seek to arrest every known anarchist in Chicago, New York, Pittsburgh, and San Francisco. The ringleader in San Francisco they reported as "the man who attempted to assassinate an Eastern financier several years ago,"[38] which may refer to Berkman and the Lexington Avenue bomb, in which Berkman's complicity had popularly been suspected. In San Francisco Berkman ridiculed the alleged plot, declaring that Crones was unknown to American anarchist leaders and that the story of an anarchist conspiracy behind the soup poisoning was "an old trick of the Chicago police."[39] A few days later the local newspapers signed off with the cryptic report from Newark, New Jersey, that a man fitting the description of Crones had shot himself.[40]

The Crones scare was prolonged for San Franciscans by the *Examiner,* which declared that private crime specialists were working in the city on "local strands in the gigantic web of anarchist plots to assassinate John Pierpont Morgan and other money and munitions barons of America." The heads of this plot were Germans, not Italians, "because the German anarchist has the shrewd, ever-anticipating brain, and is hard to catch." But many Italians were carrying messages and hiding away the "firing line workers" in the great plot.[41] Next it was discovered that the victims of "the projected death carnival" included Theodore Roosevelt. But the leaders of the plot, for all their "astute and trail-covering methods," had been traced to a large mid-western city, where detectives were ready to make the arrests at the moment of the assassination attempts. The possibilities of the situation were "keenly dramatic":

> The supreme delicacy of the task now in hand lies in giving these men [the anarchists] all the rope they can use—short of a successful assault. The threatened men must be protected, absolutely. But the assassins must be caught—at the very moment of their attempt. It is no child's play, nor do we play with children.[42]

The supreme delicacy of the task in hand had called for front-page publicity in the Hearst press, which served as a playbill for the conjured melodrama. Foiling villains offstage is no fun. Although the curtain never actually went up, Hearst had other shows for the romantic, the excitable, and the timid: German bomb plots, civilian preparedness drills, the Japanese yellow peril, and above all, war in Mexico.[43] And there were more anarchist events to come.

The *Chronicle* regretted, meanwhile, that public wrath against anarchy accumulated only after the deed, and was so short-lived. After considering alternative means for ridding the country of anarchists, the publisher, M. H. de Young, concluded that the only sensible plan was to buy a small island and deposit all the anarchists there.*

In late May a San Francisco police sergeant was slain by a suspected counterfeiter, also reported as a white-slaver, a Russian anarchist by the name of Vladimir Osokin, alias Philip Ward. According to the *Examiner*, Osokin had come of respectable family and university education in Russia, but from hatred of Tsarist authority had turned revolutionary; he had spent three years in a Moscow prison and five years in a Siberian coal mine, from which he escaped to China and thence to America. He had been in the United States several years, and in San Francisco only four weeks, during which time he gained the respect of local anarchists as an orator and a dedicated revolutionary. He was resisting arrest when he shot the officer. He thereupon barricaded himself in a bayshore boathouse and shot it out with more than a hundred San Francisco policemen until, repeatedly wounded, he expired, "proclaiming with his last breath his allegiance to the red banner of anarchy." According to the *Examiner*, an undertaker was engaged by Mary Eleanor Fitzgerald to prepare Osokin for burial, and the funeral was financed by members of the Union of Russian Workers and by "Russians of anarchistic tendencies who regularly gather at the office of 'The Blast.' "[44] Among the speakers at Osokin's memorial service were Selig Schulberg and Ed Nolan.†

The *Examiner* reminded its readers that there had been another like Osokin merely eight months before: one Gregory Chesalkin, alias George Nelson, from Los Angeles, a member of the Union of Russian Workers. An anarchist and a fluent speaker like Osokin, Chesalkin, too, had shot down the policeman who tried to arrest him. He, too, had barricaded himself and fought San Francisco police to his death. When would these acts of terrorism cease? Rumors circulated of an anarchist

---

* *Chronicle,* February 20, 1916. A feature writer for the *Call* (May 31, 1908) had concluded the same thing. These proposals were modeled on Devil's Island.

† *Examiner,* May 27 and 29, June 1 and 5, 1916. According to the *Chronicle* (May 27, 1916) he left a death note saying, "You dogs may say I am a bandit, though I am an anarchist-communist."

plot to slaughter the policemen of the Bay Area. In Oakland the District Attorney's office commenced a campaign to ferret out local anarchist colonies. In San Francisco, Police Chief D. A. White ordered his force out for target practice with its 1876 Springfields. He announced that an armored car, perhaps equipped with a machine gun, would be purchased for use against anarchist desperadoes.[45]

The armored car was not acquired. It would have been useless, anyway, in San Francisco's next anarchistic visitation, which came speedily. The Preparedness Parade was then but six weeks away.

CHAPTER FOUR

San Francisco Tensions, 1914-1916

Just arrived. San Francisco be damned!
—A '49er

I must not judge a State like California.
—Lincoln Steffens, *Autobiography*

THE BUSINESS community of San Francisco before the First World War was active and close-knit. Its most influential voice was the Chamber of Commerce. One of the oldest and most flamboyant in the country, the Chamber dated back to the days of the Gold Rush. It was reorganized in 1911 by amalgamation with three other civic-business organizations in the community. The Chamber's energies were largely absorbed in the details of trade and civic improvements that made possible the city's commercial growth and prosperity. It was also a community booster organization, seeking to attract new business and industry.

San Francisco was not highly industrialized. The Chamber of Commerce did not seek heavy industries, for the city could not and did not want to supply the large land sites and cheap labor such industries required. The Chamber sought smaller manufacturing plants and West Coast offices of national business concerns, for which skilled factory labor and office space would be needed. These would bring the city new commercial, banking, insurance, and advertising opportunities, as well as real estate development of the more desirable kind. Although San Francisco had always been the leading West Coast port, its future prosperity clearly required its continued expansion in the face of growing competition from Seattle, Portland, Sacramento, Stockton (which became a seaport in 1914), Oakland, and Los Angeles. Los Angeles in particular seemed a threat because of its new port, good climate, abundant cheap land, and expanding force of cheap labor.[1]

The attitude of San Francisco businessmen toward the local labor situation was mixed. Labor was more highly organized in San Francisco than in any other American city, and wage levels were the highest in the country. Whether the productivity level was commensurately high was keenly debated. Many of the employers feared that the unions were pricing San Francisco out of the race with Los Angeles, and this fear was combined with disgust at the arrogance with which unions sometimes inflicted their demands upon the city. These feelings were tempered, however, by the realization that it was often inexpedient to deny the unions recognition or refuse their demands; that where the unions had the upper hand, particularly in the building trades, the resulting handicaps were shared by competing employers in San Francisco; and that strikes supported by the powerful labor and building trades councils were apt to be long and costly. The power of the unions varied from trade to trade, and unskilled labor was little organized, but for most employers of skilled labor the unions were an inescapable reality. Some merchants, moreover, understood that a high-income labor population meant more retail trade. For these and other reasons the mediation of labor disputes and the tolerance of labor unions were widely accepted as practical necessities. But there was also a strong tendency to blame any economic recession, whether or not it was shared with the rest of the country, on the local unions.[2]

After its reorganization in 1911 the Chamber of Commerce was active on many fronts. It campaigned for Panama Canal toll exemptions for American coastal shipping, lower railroad freight rates, an improved California national guard and better coast defenses, and the Panama-Pacific International Exposition. (The Exposition was held in San Francisco in 1915.) The Chamber instituted lobbies and greatly expanded its publicity. In all of this there was at first no direct attack on trade-union power. But in 1913 and 1914 the pattern changed, as a moderate recession set in and the Los Angeles threat grew. At the 1913 Legislature the Chamber opposed the "ultra-radical" legislation backed by the State Federation of Labor, including regulation of private detectives, legal protection of pickets, and abolition of the state poll tax.[3] The Chamber began to challenge the trade-union movement openly:

At home and abroad the impression is general that our industrial conditions are not good and could be greatly bettered. There is strong conflict between labor and capital and many of our best men feel that we are not asking the most of our situation. . . .

Is union labor really holding back the growth of San Francisco? Is it a tyrannical power or is it a natural organization of working men and women under competent leadership combined to work for their own betterment? Have we a union labor oligarchy which has driven many industries from our city and is keeping many others from coming?[4]

In a comprehensive survey of 3,000 manufacturers in 1914, nearly one-third of the Chamber's respondents named labor as the most unfavorable local condition affecting their businesses.[5] Opposition to the unions mounted. "I have had it stated to me many times by many individuals," said the publisher of the *Call*, "that labor conditions in San Francisco were absolutely impossible; . . . that there must be violent conflict between capital and labor."[6]

Hostilities were postponed until after 1915 because the success of the Panama-Pacific International Exposition depended on cooperation from the unions. An accord was arranged with the Labor Council, providing that only union labor would be hired for the Exposition and that while it lasted no strikes would be called. With the fair's construction and provisioning contracts and the flood of tourists, as well as the wartime business orders that came to San Francisco in 1915, prosperity revived, and the call to arms of Chamber against Council temporarily subsided.[7]

II

The open-shop struggle that might have broken out in San Francisco in 1914 or 1915 was diverted to Stockton, sixty-five miles to the east. Stockton was a much smaller city, with a strongly organized labor movement, a militant Chamber of Commerce, and a newly organized Merchants and Manufacturers Association eager to pit its strength against the unions. It was an appropriate spot for a test of power that would affect the future of labor unions not only in Stockton but throughout the state. The Sperry Flour Company, an open-shop mill with one of the two largest payrolls in the city, was boycotted by the California State Federation of Labor in 1914 for rejecting a closed-shop contract. The Stockton M&M took this as justification for eliminating unions altogether, and in July its 403 members pledged themselves to employ nonunion labor. The Mayor secretly agreed to arrangements permitting the president of the M&M to name special policemen "to maintain order" during a strike.[8]

The ensuing conflict was one of the worst in the state's labor history. The M&M leaders planned to tear up all closed-shop contracts regardless of union records and possible injury to many individual businesses. The unions were aided by the San Francisco and state labor movements, which sent funds and organizers, including Anton Johannsen and Olaf Tveitmoe.[9]

Late in September the conductor of a Southern Pacific freight train passing through Tracy from Bay Point discovered and reported to Oakland headquarters that a seal had been broken on a car loaded with dynamite from the Hercules Powder Plant at Pinole. The railroad sent an agent to Martinez and Bay Point to investigate. On a lead from the Bay Point ticket agent, he interrogated a stranger in the station and discovered that his suitcase was filled with dynamite. The stranger, J. C. Emerson, turned out to have been employed since August on behalf of the Stockton M&M.[10] Emerson, held overnight in Martinez for questioning, asserted that the dynamite he was carrying was part of a "plant" he had discovered, claimed connections with prominent Stockton men, and threatened reprisals if he were detained. In the morning Sheriff R. R. Veale, having conferred with the Stockton police, released him and denied to newspapermen that any arrest had occurred.[11] At this point Tom Mooney entered the picture.

Mooney, by his own account, learned of Emerson's arrest and release through the *Chronicle*. Suspecting a plot, he at once brought the matter to the attention of the IWDL, which authorized him to go to Martinez with Ed Nolan to investigate. They did so the following day. Sheriff Veale again denied that anyone had been arrested, but at Port Costa they got the story from the constable who had arrested Emerson. Mooney and Nolan then demanded Emerson's rearrest and threatened to "expose" Veale for dereliction of duty. That afternoon Veale ordered Emerson's rearrest.[12] He was located in Oakland, brought back to Martinez, and charged with theft and illegal possession of dynamite. He made several conflicting confessions involving and exonerating Stockton M&M officials; one of his stories was that he was assisting in a plot to take dynamite to Stockton, where it was to be planted in the Sperry Flour Mill, the Stockton Iron Mill, the Stockton Hotel, and other key places, to be discovered in a way that would implicate union men. Emerson said he specifically had in mind Anton Johannsen, Olaf Tveitmoe, and Tom Mooney—although Mooney had not been participating in the Stockton fight before Emerson's arrest.*

* Sacramento *Bee*, October 2–3, 1914; Stockton *Record*, March 3, 1915; Mooney testimony, California Supreme Court, "Habeas Corpus," XX: 12,908–12. Emerson also admitted the participation of two other Stockton M&M agents in the transporting of stolen dynamite. These two men were subsequently arrested, and at their preliminary hearing it was shown that they had carted over 200 sticks of the dynamite around Stockton one

The outcome of the Emerson affair was as inconclusive as that of the Mooney affair at Martinez. Twice Emerson was tried in Martinez for illegal possession of dynamite, and once in Stockton on a parallel charge. The Stockton M&M provided his attorney but would not bail him out. He spent nearly six months in jail awaiting trials and was finally acquitted. On his release he was admonished by his trial judge, who apparently regretted the acquittal, for having impeded the settlement of the Stockton Labor War and "engender[ed] hatred and animosity that might have led to very serious consequences."*

In the end the Emerson affair succeeded only in strengthening the San Francisco labor movement's conviction that M&M associations were vicious, and Mooney's belief that the capitalists were out to get him. The case was far less clear-cut than the Cradlebaugh affair, but since Mooney and the unions were directly involved, it became, unlike the Cradlebaugh case, a permanent fixture in the radical version of the Mooney story. According to that version, capitalist attempts to frame Mooney were familiar by 1916: Swanson for PG&E and Emerson for the Stockton M&M had already made them.[13]

III

Behind the strikes and violence were more remote feelings of class allegiance, feelings woven into the social fabric of northern California. Perhaps San Francisco was no worse than other American cities, but relations between classes were tense. The hostility between banker and laborer, between Chamber and Council, involved wages and hours, power and prosperity, pride, and civic principles. The two groups clashed over labor legislation, the Los Angeles *Times* case, Oriental labor, civil liberties for radicals, municipal ownership of streetcars,

---

afternoon, awaiting orders for its disposal. The M&M ordered the dynamite sent back to Sheriff Veale in Martinez. (*Labor Clarion*, October 9, 1914; Stockton Police Court Judge Parker, quoted in *ibid.*, November 27, 1914.)

Meanwhile, in Stockton, a former gunman of the M&M, Hans Le Jeune, was caught attempting to plant dynamite in the room of Anton Johannsen. Le Jeune confessed that he had been paid $75 by F. J. Viebrock, a prominent Stockton merchant and a leader of the M&M, to beat up Johannsen. Viebrock admitted paying Le Jeune the money but said he did not know what it was for. Le Jeune also said he had heard that Johannsen and Mooney were selected by the unions to blow up the Sperry Flour Mill. (Haldeman-Julius, "Frameup," p. 68; *Labor Clarion*, October 9, 1914; Sacramento *Bee*, October 3 and 5, 1914.)

* Judge Plummer, quoted in the Stockton *Record*, April 3, 1915. Six years later Emerson was into mischief again. Employed during a strike as a guard for the Associated Oil Company, he was convicted of arson in the company's warehouse at Avon, and received a two-year-to-life sentence. (Contra Costa County *Labor Journal*, October 11, November 11 and 30, and December 7, 1921.)

cheap "jitney bus" transportation on Market Street, and community projects. Two minor episodes in San Francisco's civic affairs will suggest the tone of these frictions.

In the wake of the devastation wrought by earthquake and fire a new civic center was planned, which was to include an opera house. Years passed and no opera house was built. In 1915 a plan for its construction was laid before the city fathers by William H. Crocker, the leader of San Francisco's wealthy high society. Crocker proposed to raise $850,000 by private subscription from 850 San Franciscans. Much of this sum he had ready in pledges. The city was to put up only $1,000,000. In recognition of this private beneficence, the Board of Supervisors was to pass an ordinance creating a self-perpetuating board of managers for the new opera center. Ten members of the board would be from the subscribing families. All subscribers would have preferential rights to box seats in the opera house, rights that would descend to their heirs in perpetuity. The plan's supporters brought pressure on the city government, and the Supervisors accepted the plum; but Progressives descried the aristocratic principle of entail in the arrangement, and in response to their protests, Mayor Rolph vetoed the enabling ordinance. His veto was applauded by the Labor Council, whose leaders, whether or not they admired Madame Tetrazzini, recognized the high-handedness of Crocker's set. Of Crocker the Sacramento *Bee* commented, "The gall of some people seems to be limitless."*

The other incident also involved Crocker. The Labor Council accused him of profiting, through the Chamber of Commerce, from the city's Belgian War Relief program. With $125,000 that the Chamber had raised a few weeks after Belgium was overrun in August 1914, its committee on the purchase of relief supplies sought bids from West Coast mills on 1,500 tons of specified flour. After the bids were in, four-fifths of the contract was awarded to the Sperry Flour Company of Stockton, then deeply involved in the Stockton Labor War and boycotted by organized labor throughout the state. Sperry's largest stockholder, Crocker, was also chairman of the Chamber's committee on purchase of relief supplies, although it was said, lamely, that he did not

* *Bulletin,* November 21, 22, 24, 1913; *Labor Clarion,* November 28, 1913; and Sacramento *Bee,* November 24, 1913. The Crocker plan had provided for 400 general-admission seats in the family circle. Progressive attorney Matt I. Sullivan, later a State Supreme Court justice, remarked: "It is very kind of the Musical Association to recognize rights of the common people to this extent and give them, from that part of the theater next to 'nigger heaven,' the privilege of gazing down upon the domes of our leaders of society and the bejeweled backs of their ladies." (As quoted, *Labor Clarion,* November 28, 1913.)

attend the meetings at which contracts were decided upon. To make matters worse, the Sperry Flour Company's bid was not as low as one from a mill in Portland: after the bids were in, the committee had decided to consider only those which specified California flour. (The difference between the bids, allowing for transportation costs, amounted to $5,000, or more than 1,000 barrels of flour.) This scandal was brought to the attention of San Francisco labor leaders by one of the Labor Council's left-wing delegates, T. E. Zant, a carpenter and a member of the IWDL. The Labor Council verified the facts and held the Chamber up to ridicule, but was unable to find a legal remedy.[14]

IV

Following the Panama-Pacific International Exposition, the Chamber of Commerce faced the question of resuming an aggressive stand against unionism. Not all the Chamber's members favored an open-shop struggle. Business was flourishing; new firms were locating in San Francisco at a rate that was "nothing short of startling." To obtain authoritative information on labor costs in the city, the Chamber commissioned an industrial survey by Benjamin Rastall, a nationally recognized, independent industrial researcher trained at the University of Wisconsin. Apparently both friends and foes of unions in the Chamber believed that Rastall's findings would verify their own views.[15]

The president of the Chamber, Frederick J. Koster, had a foot in both camps on the union issue. Koster was a barrel manufacturer who employed union labor in a closed shop, paid his employees wages that exceeded the union scale, and maintained excellent employee relations. A director on the boards of four corporations and a prominent figure in the Panama-Pacific International Exposition, he was a civic leader, more flexible and more polished than the old moguls of California. He cut a figure quite different from that of Patrick Calhoun, Harrison Gray Otis, or Felix J. Zeehandelaar of the Los Angeles M&M. He had urged the hiring of Rastall; he insisted that the San Francisco Chamber of Commerce was not a militant organization like the recently formed San Francisco M&M (of which, nevertheless, he was an executive council member); and his published addresses to the business community were intelligent admonitions rather than the usual Better Business bromides. He cautioned Chamber members not to mouth "cheap, meaningless 'booster' trivialities."[16] Nonetheless, in the summer of 1916 Koster led the Chamber of Commerce in a bitter open-shop campaign.[17] It is hard to reconcile his attitude that summer with his own labor policy. Perhaps he was uneasy himself about the contrast.*

The Chamber's open-shop campaign was precipitated suddenly in June 1916 by the longshoremen's union. The longshoremen had demanded a pay increase in May; failing to receive it, they went out in a coast-wide strike on the first of June, breaking their contract with the San Francisco Waterfront Employers Union in the process. At the same time the members of the Bay and River Steamboatmen's Union, under the same pressure of rising living costs that other San Franciscans faced, went on strike and tied up boats operating between the Bay Area and Sacramento. Although neither the Sailors Union nor the Teamsters—the two remaining major waterfront unions—joined the strikes, the harbor's commerce was jeopardized and the prosperity of the city threatened. San Francisco faced its first major waterfront clash since 1901.[18]

Federal mediation efforts were of little help. Secretary of Labor William B. Wilson, a strong trade unionist himself, criticized the longshoremen for breaking their contract and asked them to return to work. They refused to do so at the existing wage rate. A truce arranged by the government temporarily sent the longshoremen back to their jobs, but no settlement was reached and tension continued high. Violence broke out on both sides of the Bay. According to the Chamber of Commerce, sixteen nonunion men, including a merchant and a police officer, were beaten up in San Francisco that month, and eighteen more in July. In the same two months, the Chamber acknowledged, six union men were assaulted.[19] Two union longshoremen were killed in June, one in Oakland and one in San Francisco. Officers of the International Longshoremen's Association demanded that armed strikebreakers and guards be withdrawn from the piers. The demand was rejected. The longshoremen thereupon broke the truce, and the strike was resumed on June 22. On the same day the directors of the Chamber of Commerce launched their open-shop campaign.[20]

The Chamber estimated that the waterfront strike held up exports worth $2,500,000 in June alone. Businessmen were angered not only by the commercial loss, but also by the violence and the strike leaders' effrontery in issuing permits for certain teamsters to pass through the picket lines. Since one of the drayage companies so favored was haul-

---

* Chester Rowell, a personal friend of Koster, considered Koster's open-shop campaign a "futile and dangerous policy." (Koster-Rowell correspondence, November–December 1917, in Rowell Papers; *California Outlook*, August 1916.)

ing for the Treasury Department, the Chamber leaders said that the strike leaders were dictating to the United States government. The bitterness of the struggle impressed all observers. The reporter for the uninvolved Socialist Labor Party described the fight as the most desperate struggle in the AFL's history. The San Francisco *Coast Review,* published for western insurance men, declared that "the notorious and anarchistic I.W.W." had instigated the strike; it protested that lawlessness, incendiarism, and "Mexican conditions" prevailed in the absence of firm civil authority.* Mayor Rolph in fact did refuse to provide extra police protection for the waterfront employers and their strikebreakers, fully realizing that it would contribute nothing to a just solution or to his own popularity. When a delegation of merchants called on him for special help, he turned them down. Himself an owner of coal schooners, Rolph had already granted the demands of the stevedores for his own ships.[21]

Koster, on behalf of the Chamber of Commerce, called together the merchants of San Francisco to consider the urgent need to maintain law and order. Two thousand businessmen attended the meeting, held on July 10 at the Merchants Exchange Building. There he denounced "the shameful, tyrannous, and uninterrupted rule of the waterfront" by the longshoremen's union, and demanded that law and order be restored. While insisting that the Chamber was not bent on destroying labor unions, Koster deplored the "class-ruled city" and defended the "right to work." "We insist upon the right to employ union labor or nonunion labor, in whole or in part."[22] In response to his appeal the meeting passed resolutions endorsing the open shop and authorizing him to form a five-man Law and Order Committee. Five minutes after its formation the Committee received voluntary subscriptions totaling $200,000 for its work, and within a week the sum came to $600,000.[23]

Following Koster several other prominent businessmen addressed the gathering. One was Captain Robert Dollar, a tart, wealthy, pious old Scot who owned the Dollar Steamship Lines and had fought La Follette's Seamen's Act. He was a past officer of the Chamber.[24] In words that became symbolic of the meeting, Dollar declared that waterfront peace had been established in a previous strike by sending ambulance-loads of pickets to the hospital. "Let's fight," he urged. "If a peaceful workingman is beaten up by strikers, then beat up two strikers

* According to one student of San Francisco maritime history, this strike aroused San Franciscans more thoroughly than any in the preceding half-century. (William Martin Camp, *San Francisco: Port of Gold* [1947], p. 415.)

in return."* Though none of the merchants followed his advice, they applauded him enthusiastically.

In naming the Law and Order Committee, the Chamber made a deliberate appeal to the city's Vigilante tradition, an appeal that reverberated in the conservative weekly press. "San Francisco needs a man of resolute, resourceful leadership like William T. Coleman of the Vigilance Committee," said the *News Letter*; Koster and a determined committee could save the day.[25] There were cries of "anarchy" and denunciations of the municipal authorities. To be sure, there was little danger that the Merchants Exchange Building would sprout gunnybags and gibbets, for the majesty of the law had accumulated considerable force in San Francisco since 1856. But the passions were there. Dollar recalled in his memoirs that he visited District Attorney Fickert with two other anti-strike leaders to tell him that if the waterfront violence did not stop, their vigilance committee would string him up to a telephone pole. He claimed that Fickert "at once promised to cooperate with us, and he did."[26]

The end of the longshoremen's strike later that month has no bearing on the Mooney case, but the formation of the Law and Order Committee was a critical event; some of its most important activities were to be connected with the case. The Committee was anathematized by organized labor and lauded by eastern business groups. Its creation aggravated local class tensions, for its primary purpose was to suppress the trade unions. As the Sacramento *Bee* concluded later that year, "Bitterness, civic warfare, and hate is all the Chamber of Commerce fight in San Francisco has succeeded in arousing."[27]

V

Apart from the clashes of the Chamber of Commerce with organized labor, there were other causes of civic tension in San Francisco in 1916. Foremost among them was the issue of national preparedness. By early 1916 the city's wealthy and well-situated citizens had devel-

---

* *Bulletin, Examiner,* July 11, 1916. According to another version he said, "When they compel us to send one ambulance to the receiving hospital, we send two of theirs." Dollar thought afterward that it was good advice. Twenty years later it was still part of the political lore of the city's waterfront. (New York *World,* May 16, 1923; *American Industries,* June 1923; Paul William Ryan [pseud. Mike Quin], *The Big Strike* [1949], p. 30.)

Paul Scharrenberg was present at the meeting. The trade unionists naturally resented the merchants' pose as champions of law and order. (*Coast Seamen's Journal,* August 2 and 23, 1916.)

oped a serious concern for national defense. Although war was raging in Europe, they were more worried about a possible war with Mexico or Japan, for in such a conflict California might be attacked. The state was unprepared. Her coastal defenses were unimpressive: artillery emplacements, such as those around San Francisco, were few and largely outmoded. Brigadier General E. M. Weaver, chief of the coast artillery, reported serious deficiencies in ammunition and manpower. The coast seemed vulnerable. Rear Admiral Cameron Winslow, commander of the Pacific Fleet, believed that one first-class enemy battleship could defeat the whole United States Pacific fleet.[28]

Apprehensions of unpreparedness were assiduously cultivated by the Hearst press, which made the most of every Mexican or Japanese move. When the Magdalena Bay incident occurred in 1911, when Japanese warships were sighted—or imagined—only 300 miles beyond the Farallones in March 1916, when Pancho Villa sacked Columbus, New Mexico, the same month, Hearst trumpeted patriotism, manliness, Anglo-Saxon superiority, preparedness, coastal defenses, border defenses, and reprisals, all in the name of peace. Others besides Hearst and the military commanders sought stronger defenses. Senator James D. Phelan's apprehension of the Japanese reflected a common attitude. And M. H. de Young's *Chronicle*, which daily mirrored the hopes and fears of the prosperous, had advocated improved defenses as early as the turn of the century.[29]

San Francisco's naval and military traditions were not grandiose, but they were the best on the West Coast, and the city's godfathers meant to keep them so. The military, as every member of the Chamber of Commerce knew, was good for business: naval construction and repair, provisionings, the splurging of sailors when the fleet, such as it was, came in—all contributed to San Francisco prosperity. Senator Phelan proposed that Congress allocate $10,000,000 for a national naval and aviation academy, to be located within 150 miles of San Francisco; more successful were efforts to have the government spend $500,000 in equipping Mare Island's navy yard.[30] Late in 1915 the directors of the Chamber urged the Secretary of the Navy to consider the Mare Island yard in awarding contracts for the construction of new battleships. As early as 1913 the Chamber had a standing committee on the California national guard and naval militia, and was pressing for army and navy establishments on the West Coast equal to those in the East.[31] The Chamber favored military training for civilians through the Boy Scouts and military summer schools, and publicized the coastal target practice of San Francisco's modest fortification, Fort Winfield Scott, as "an inspiring spectacle that no citizens should miss."[32] Inspiring perhaps, but the range of coastal artillery at San Francisco in 1916 was still short of the three-mile limit. There was room for improvement.[33]

The agitation for preparedness extended to high society. City branches of national women's organizations, the Daughters of this and that, held cocktail-hour preparedness *dansants* at the Palace Hotel and the Fairmont. "Society leaders, army and navy representatives, and women prominent in the executive circles of clubdom" organized the San Francisco chapter of the Women's Section of the Navy League early in 1916, and it soon became the most active of the women's preparedness social groups; one of its first acts was to form a committee on legislation to influence congressmen and arrange liaison with the Chamber of Commerce, men's clubs, and other women's leagues. The president of the League, Mrs. Frederick H. Colburn, was a banker's wife and had been the *Examiner*'s first newspaperwoman.[34]

The most dashing of all the preparedness advocates in San Francisco was Thornwell Mullally. Born and educated in the South, he came to San Francisco in the year of the earthquake as executive assistant to his uncle, Patrick Calhoun, president of the United Railroads. Like Calhoun he became involved in the graft prosecutions. Like Calhoun he lost little at the time save honor, and among his peers not even that. By 1912 he was one of the three URR directors who set up a blanket resolution under which Calhoun withdrew one million dollars of URR funds for speculation in Solano farmlands. Calhoun later went bankrupt and the stake was never returned. On the witness stand in 1914 before the State Railroad Commission to testify about this remarkable fraud, Mullally and the others disclaimed all responsibility for Calhoun's misdeeds, saying they had merely done what Calhoun asked of them! It was a shoddy performance. But San Francisco reserved ostracism for less elegant knaves than Thornwell Mullally. He was an executive director of the Panama-Pacific International Exposition, and a member in good standing of exalted social circles.[35]

As his first contribution to preparedness, Mullally in 1915 organized a volunteer cavalry troop of 35 businessmen and social blades, including most of the members of the polo team of Burlingame's exclusive country club. Once a week Mullally lunched with his troops at the Fairmont Hotel and led them to the Presidio or the beach for an afternoon drill. In May, assisted by a professional cavalry officer, he led them to the Burlingame woods, where they were attended by *Examiner* newsmen and country-club spectators in limousines. During the Mexican war scare Mullally accompanied Brigadier General John Pershing across the border, to Hearst's great delight.[36]

Reaction to Mullally was mixed. *Town Talk,* a sophisticated, reactionary weekly, was waggish but generally approving. Paul Scharrenberg in the *Coast Seamen's Journal* called him a "successful union-buster," which was factual enough. Fremont Older scorned him. The Oakland *Observer* regretted that no Ambrose Bierce lived to puncture Mullally's flatulence: "If he were here we might expect to see the Mullally hide neatly skinned and pegged out for desiccation."[37] It was Thornwell Mullally who was grand marshal of the San Francisco Preparedness Parade in July 1916.

Preparedness appeals were made to the general public constantly, through newspapers, pulpits, newsreels, and vaudeville shows. Many of the large numbers of nonunion clerks and white-collar workers in the Bay Area were favorably impressed. So, too, were some of the state's Progressive leaders, including McClatchy in Sacramento and Congressman William D. Stephens of Los Angeles, soon to become the Lieutenant Governor.[38] But the left-wing Progressives were opposed. They appealed to American anti-military traditions—isolation, anti-imperialism, Jeffersonian democracy, and the abhorrence of armed might in peacetime. Their leaders in San Francisco were Rudolph Spreckels and Fremont Older.

Spreckels was notoriously hostile to military expansion, which to him meant the creation of a military caste, the dissipation of national wealth, and the disruption of friendly relations with neighboring countries.* Older believed that militarism was a form of exploitation of the poor. Through his young editorial writer Robert L. Duffus, a Stanford graduate and a Wilsonian idealist, Older mocked the attraction of high society to the preparedness movement: "The rich, cultured and superior must first be aroused, and then the flame must pass gradually down the ranks of society . . . until the hungry, ragged, ignorant masses at the bottom throw up their tattered hats and march off to save their country." He feared the institution of compulsory military service: "The great defense societies—some of them reeking of

---

* He was also embroiled in a lawsuit with Mullally. *Town Talk* scornfully labeled Spreckels "Emperor Norton II," Norton I having been one of San Francisco's most colorful lunatics. (*Bulletin,* August 12, 1913; January 21, 1916; *Town Talk,* June 24, 1916.)

the munitions factories, some of them drunk with the crazy ambitions of half-baked aristocracies—are already singing the asinine praises of compulsion." The *Bulletin* urged that the government spend its money on conservation, education, and social welfare. It charged that the eager advocates of preparedness numbered among them "the despots of big business, the smug tyrants of 'company towns,' the cold-blooded financiers whose influence is always thrown against democracy." And since they included the Mullally crowd and "the [Harrison Gray] Otis school" of "drum and trumpet preparedness," they were not to be trusted.[39]

The preparedness movement was also opposed by organized labor in California. Although Samuel Gompers and the AFL in the East took an ambiguous stand, flirting with national defense while avoiding the more militaristic organizations and opposing the use of soldiers for strike duty, the AFL organizations in northern California refused to go along. Their resistance, being nearly unanimous, was formidable. It stemmed from their powerful Irish elements: preparedness was closely associated with sympathy for the English. It stemmed from the strong convictions of their Socialists, to whom wars were capitalistic struggles. (After the U.S. naval bombardment and capture of Vera Cruz in 1914, Hugo Ernst, a leader of the waiters' union in San Francisco, declared on standard international Socialist grounds that the working classes of the United States and Mexico had no quarrels and should unite against the capitalists of both countries. He protested that while the conflict with Mexico went on, working-class women and children were slain at Ludlow by hirelings of Colorado's big businessmen, without government interference.)[40] And it stemmed from the fear that military preparedness would simply mean more troops to suppress strikes. This belief ran deep among San Francisco trade unionists. To overcome it, the Chamber of Commerce and the Pacific Coast Defense League declared their opposition to using militia for strike duty and obtained the pledge of a number of Western governors, including Hiram Johnson, that they would not so use it; but organized labor remained unconvinced. It would wait to see new laws on the statute books. When officers of the California National Guard sought permission to address the San Francisco unions on preparedness, the secretary of the Labor Council told them not to waste their time; union men had not forgotten the role of the National Guardsmen in the Ludlow massacre, he said.[41]

Meanwhile the preparedness movement grew. The U.S. Army

sponsored summer training camps for civilians in 1915 and 1916 at Monterey, much like the renowned Plattsburg summer camp in upper New York. Hearst drummed enthusiastically for volunteers to attend, and the Chamber of Commerce requested its members to arrange vacations or leaves of absence for their employees. It was acknowledged on all sides, openly or tacitly, that this was a businessmen's program. Clerks might go, but no trade unionists showed up, nor were they invited.[42] The San Francisco unions continued to oppose preparedness almost to the entry of the United States into the First World War. They did not relax their opposition until the resumption of German submarine warfare on merchant shipping in February 1917.[43]

VI

Older's dedication to the anti-preparedness cause was intensified by his larger struggle with Hearst. The struggle has since been forgotten, partly because of the efforts of Fremont and Cora Older and of Older's biographer, Evelyn Wells, to play it down. Miss Wells has characterized the conflict as a cheerful, impersonal newspaper war, fought "furiously yet with respect."[44] That makes little sense, and does an injustice to Older's integrity. He and Hearst may have respected each other's success in journalism, but they despised each other's ideas and policies. The decade 1906–17 was a battle-scarred era of feuding between the two men. During the graft prosecutions Older was embittered by the apostasy of Hearst and the *Examiner* when the graft prosecution indictments shifted from the politicians to the bribers. Subsequently, Hearst's ample abuses of the public trust in his journalism scandalized Older, and editorial swipes at "Randolph the Fatuous" appeared constantly in the *Bulletin*. Hundreds of the *Bulletin*'s editorials analyzed, ridiculed, and excoriated Hearst. One of its most poignant indictments was a study of the Leo Frank murder case in Atlanta, Georgia, by a Kansas City *Star* reporter, who revealed that the anti-Semitism whipped up in Atlanta after Mary Phagan's murder was substantially the work of the Atlanta *Georgian,* a new Hearst paper. Three weeks after this story appeared in the *Bulletin,* Leo Frank was lynched.[45]

The clashes between Older and Hearst were not over principles alone. They were also over circulation. Beginning in 1913, when Hearst gained loose control of the *Call* and converted it into an afternoon journal,[46] the *Call* and the *Bulletin* competed for the afternoon trade. The *Bulletin* had a circulation lead of about 100,000 to 60,000, which the *Call* could not overcome. Consequently, F. W. Kellogg, the *Call*'s editor and nominal owner, made an arrangement with the joint circulation manager for the *Examiner* and the *Call* that required newsboys who sold Hearst's *Examiner* in the morning to take the *Call* and not the *Bulletin* in the afternoon. Since the *Examiner*'s circulation was very large, the threat to the *Bulletin*'s street sales was serious. Newsstand vendors were urged to pile *Calls* on top of *Bulletins* and were threatened with loss of the *Call-Examiner* franchise if they did not cooperate. Stubborn newsies were assaulted with bricks and fists in three years of intermittent fighting. The whole ugly affair reached its climax in 1916, when a *Bulletin* distributor, an ex-convict whom Older had helped to rehabilitate, was shot down by a *Call* distributor on the steps of the *Bulletin* building. In view of these circumstances and the content of *Bulletin* editorials, the claim that Older respected Hearst must be rejected.[47]

Older's staff was small but devoted. The paper's support of reform causes gradually built up its circulation, since every crusade brought it the loyal support of a minority group. The *Bulletin* circulated among union labor families and Progressives who liked Older's nerve. It is as difficult to imagine Robert L. Duffus, George P. West, John D. Barry, Maxwell Anderson, Carl Hoffman, Frederick Ely, or Pauline Jacobson writing for the *Examiner* as it is to imagine Edward H. Hurlbut of the *Call* or Edward H. Hamilton of the *Examiner* writing for Older.[48] Older's staff members were not embarrassed by their connections with society's outcasts and rebels; it was out of interest and sympathy—and a desire to sell the paper, as C. K. McClatchy kept insisting—that they befriended prostitutes, ex-convicts, derelicts, and radicals. Barry called himself a philosophical anarchist. Ely later went to the University of Southern California to teach sociology—a brash young discipline then. Maxwell Anderson turned to social criticism in the Broadway theater. Duffus eventually joined the editorial staff of the New York *Times*. In their *Bulletin* days these writers explored new ideas: Marxian economics, progressive education, Christian Science, reform penology. The *Bulletin* was not entirely above the sentimentalities and journalistic frauds of the times, to be sure; its standards for patent medicine advertising were remarkably low. But its newspapermen had the courage and skill to expose and ridicule the hypocrisies and follies of the age.[49] For some reformers they went too far. Chester Rowell, one of California's ablest Progressives, described the *Bulletin* as "radically,

wild-eyedly, crazily and fanatically on the progressive side of things."[50]
Certainly it had verve.

Older was a self-made editor, born in poverty, raised in typesetting,
a wanderer in his youth from Wisconsin to San Francisco, where he
arrived in 1873. He became editor of the conservative, failing *Bulletin*
in 1895. His education in local problems grew during Ruef's regime,
and the difficulty of coping with them was brought home to him in the
graft prosecutions. Spurred on by Clarence Darrow and Lincoln Steffens, he explored radical sociological ideas. Although a Progressive
reformer, he had little confidence that tinkering with political mechanisms could cure social ills. For Steffens the solution in later years
was Marxism. For Older no solution ever came; compassion was his
only way of coping with the insufferable while he struggled vainly for
an answer. He believed that he was as guilty as the rest: "It dawned
upon me . . . that I had been hurting others in order to make money
out of a successful newspaper; that I had been printing stories that
made others suffer that I might profit pandering to many low instincts
in man in order to sell newspapers; that I had told many half-truths,
and let many go undenied."[51] Older's repentance followed Ruef's departure to San Quentin Prison for a fourteen-year term. Other regrets were to come. He would always have to sell newspapers, and
would recurrently compromise his ideals under pressure from his publisher and evident business necessity.[52]

Older was loved and despised as a radical social critic and an in-
corrigible friend of social scum. Max Eastman called Older, Steffens,
Darrow, and Hutchins Hapgood "Sentimental Rebels":

> They had no historical tradition and they had no international con-
> nections. They were as purely American a phenomenon as the red Indians.
> They sometimes called themselves, or were called, "philosophical anar-
> chists," but that means little besides an irresponsible distaste for politics.
> Their defining trait was that they came into sympathy with the labor
> struggle, not by the road of theory or plan of action, but by the road of
> Christian sentiment bereft of Deity yet carried to a bellicose extreme. . . .
> They were all characterized by a distrust of intellect such as one finds
> among men of religious faith. And they were characterized by a Christlike
> fondness for the society of publicans and sinners. Indeed almost a cult arose
> among them of making friends with criminals.[53]

On the subject of criminology and penology Older was under
constant attack from civic leaders and from other northern California

newspapers, whose editors believed that any compromise in the traditional juridical principles of retribution and removal would let down
such bars as there were against crime, and the criminals would engulf
the state. For years the *Bulletin* crusaded for abolition of capital punishment, for a more humane treatment of prisoners, and for social rehabilitation of released convicts. The newspaper received thousands
of personal appeals for help, and Older did what he could.[54] Disclaiming sentimentality, he emphasized economic and moral determinism
in the making of criminals and derelicts: but as far as his critics were
concerned, that only made matters worse. They reminded him that
America was built on individual responsibility and self-reliance, and
that if moral determinism could be allowed criminals, it could not be
disallowed others.[55] Older was not actually a determinist; he stressed
determinism because he felt that no one else was giving it a hearing.
His philosophy of crime and punishment was best summarized in a
1914 editorial:

> The Bulletin has not taught ... that it is desirable to relieve men from
> personal responsibility for what they do. ... The truth which this paper
> seeks to bring home is not that there is no individual responsibility, but
> that our punishments and our judgments are not, and cannot be, based
> upon a just knowledge of the individual's responsibility.
>
> · · ·
>
> The Bulletin does not believe that Jesus thought that some men were
> scoundrels and some were not. It believes that there is evil in all men,
> preachers and prisoners and editors alike. It believes that the conquest of
> the evil comes about in two ways—by individual self-discipline and self-
> mastery, in which religious faith has a legitimate part; and by the substitu-
> tion, from without, of forces making for good for forces making for evil.
>
> Society has been too well satisfied with the first, which requires no
> sacrifice save on the part of the man to whom it is addressed.[56]

Older's ethics appealed to thoughtful members of the working class.
To the secretary of the Kern County Labor Council they represented
the "difference between clean sheets and dirty blankets."[57] Older's
was the one paper in San Francisco that did not lecture to the lower
classes but understood their needs and reflected their feelings, without necessarily representing their politics.

For the most part Older was accused not of doubting the freedom
of the will, but of harboring sheer sentimentality. How would for-
giveness and acceptance save California from rapists and anarchists,

labor thugs and dynamiters, footpads and yeggmen, from murder and from sudden death? Why did Older have to stir cesspools for feature stories? What was his sympathy for Ruef, if not quixotic? The *Bulletin,* "that champion of the slobbering classes," was a menace.[58] "The *Bulletin* is becoming not only an insult but a danger to the community."[59] Hearst agreed with de Young and other conservatives that Older's concept of crime was vicious. On one occasion, when a "notorious" San Francisco burglar got off with a four-year sentence, the *Examiner* commented:

> We ask, in all fairness, if this is not exactly the outcome to be expected of the slush and slobber and snivelling tears which it has become the habit of weak-brained sentimentalists to pour out on criminals?
> Isn't it about time to extend our sympathies, our aid and our consideration to honest men and women, struggling with poverty bravely, and cease, for a while, the unmanly and unreasonable and contemptibly silly adulation and commiseration of the base, mean, vile and dangerous criminals?

And the *Chronicle* explained: "There is no doubt that the rapid increase in crime in California, and especially in this city, is one of the consequences of the outpouring of sentimental mush with which this State has been deluged. It has lowered the virility of the whole community." Even McClatchy said that Older's sympathy for criminals was vicious.[60]

In sum, Older was an unusual editor, one who mixed rebellious, humanistic idealism with a tender hand, sold newspapers while doing it, and made enemies. Any journalist who propounded modern criminology and sociology in the early twentieth century invited severe criticism. But Older and his staff went on trying without success to figure out how society made such a mess of people, and how it could be changed. Older crusaded for the graft prosecutions and then for Ruef's freedom, he attacked local hypocrisy toward prostitution, he condemned militarism, he fought for the victims of capitalistic avarice. And he was soon to come to the defense of the two most "base, mean, vile and dangerous criminals" of them all, Warren Billings and Tom Mooney.[61]

CHAPTER FIVE

Mooney's Car Strike

If you were in San Francisco this afternoon, you'd have to walk.
— Jack London, *The Iron Heel*

BY 1916 the United Railroads was a partially reformed corporation. Patrick Calhoun, who had survived the graft prosecutions, had been removed as president in 1913 by the New York financiers who controlled the URR. His successor was Jesse W. Lilienthal, a Harvard Law School graduate and the son of a distinguished Cincinnati rabbi. Lilienthal was expected to cope with Calhoun's legacy of financial mismanagement, the popularity of San Francisco's new municipal streetcar line, and the political tide of Progressivism. He had practiced law in San Francisco for many years; he was twice president of the San Francisco Bar Association, active in many philanthropies, and moderately progressive in political views. Prior to his appointment he had had no connection with the URR. As president he set about to rebuild its finances and redirect its policy. In view of the overcapitalization and public ill will he inherited from Calhoun, his success was considerable. He withdrew the company from politics, promised to comply with the Public Utilities Act, and opened the company's books to the State Railroad Commission, thereby exposing Calhoun's knavery.[1]

Lilienthal did not share Calhoun's contemptuous indifference toward company employees. He supported the Progressives' Workmen's Compensation Act, instituted group life insurance for all employees, and established a revolving fund for short-term loans to employees, evidently to save them from the loan sharks. But the company drew the line at labor unions. With property valued at $25–30 million, a bonded debt of over $35,000,000, its common stock and some of its preferred stock worthless, and sweeping reorganization needed to squeeze out the water, the company sternly resisted union labor and union wages. The employees would have to continue paying for Calhoun's mismanagement. Burdened also with absentee ownership, worn-out equipment, and the competition of jitneys and the municipal streetcar system, the URR maintained its anti-union spying. No organizing of employees was tolerated.[2]

Against Lilienthal's determination to preserve the nonunion shop, the carmen of the URR—or those few among them who dared assert the right to organize—were stymied. Eight times after the major strike failure of 1907, and several times after Calhoun's departure, the Amalgamated Association of Street and Electric Railway Employees of America attempted without success to organize the company's carmen. On one occasion, in 1914, it had looked as if Lilienthal might accept the union, but when this hope was scotched, the officers of the national union wrote off the situation as hopeless.[3]

II

Tom Mooney dreamed of organizing the carmen. He believed that radicals could succeed where the regulars had failed. At the AFL national convention in San Francisco, late in 1915, he introduced himself to the union's international president, William D. Mahon, and presented his plan. Mahon referred him to the union's executive board, which turned him down. The carmen's union considered the timing poor (the last strike attempt had been the previous spring), and Mooney was not a member of the union anyhow. But Mooney was undeterred. Since no list of URR employees was available, he assembled one in his spare time from the city register, by indexing the names of 2,000 persons listed as streetcar employees and subtracting from it the names of those who worked for the municipal system. He got in touch with previous strike leaders, who had all been discharged from URR employment, and secured their support. They reckoned that Mooney would have the initial advantage of being unknown to the URR detectives.[4] When his job as a laborer for the Panama-Pacific International Exposition ended—foundry work being scarce in 1915—he took no other job, but devoted his full time to the preparations, moving into his wife's music studio to save rent.[5]

(His sister-in-law disapproved: "I always thought Tom was ... entirely too eager to mix into other strikes," she said later. "I felt that if he didn't have a wife that was making a living he would probably be at work himself.")[6]

Mooney planned to build a small organization of URR employees, call a wildcat strike, and stampede the rest of the carmen into the union. This technique was undependable, although it was often used against corporations whose labor-espionage systems prevented union organizers from approaching employees. Daniel Murphy, president of the Labor Council, believed that a successful strike against the URR required organizing at least 60 per cent of its carmen, but Mooney considered the requirement unreasonable and an excuse not to support his plan. For want of URR carmen who could be approached and trusted, he appealed to hundreds of his radical acquaintances in unions around the Bay Area, including Billings and Ed Hanlon and Joe Brown of Martinez days, to come to San Francisco and help spring the strike.[7]

Five months after commencing his secret work, Mooney still lacked Mahon's approval. Several carmen's union organizers who favored Mooney's scheme appealed to Mahon. They pointed out that although Mooney was a radical, he was an "absolutely honest and trustworthy" trade unionist, who had had some experience as a strike leader and was very enthusiastic, whereas the regular organizers were discouraged. In June 1916 Mahon finally agreed to contribute up to $60,000 to the strike fund, provided the Labor Council also gave its support. He disapproved of Mooney's radicalism but was anxious to see the URR organized. He sent Mooney $200 for living expenses. The Labor Council voted 80–4 against backing the strike, but Mooney went ahead anyway.[8]

The strike was originally scheduled for June 11. By that time Mooney's intentions and identity were known to the URR, and Thiel Detective Agency operatives were following him openly. He addressed circular letters to all the "Slaves of the U.R.R." urging them to organize.[9] In response the company posted notices in its carbarns stating that it was acquainted with the moves of one Thomas J. Mooney, an unemployed molder "who was arrested and confined in jail as a dynamiter," and that "any man found to be affiliated with Mooney or any union, will be promptly discharged."[10] Undismayed, Mooney proceeded with plans for a gathering of Muni streetcar men and other union supporters that evening at Woodman's Hall, popularly known as the IWW Hall, to prepare for the strike. Only two men at the meeting were URR employees, but URR detectives kept the building under surveillance.[11]

In the early hours of the morning on June 11 a high-voltage tower of the Sierra and San Francisco Power Company, which served the URR, was dynamited in the San Bruno hills south of San Francisco. With no incriminating evidence found at the scene, the URR shortly offered a reward of $5,000 for information leading to the arrest and conviction of the dynamiters.[12] The bombing was denounced as an incident in the "war of the direct actionists," whose dynamiting program had allegedly expanded since the Los Angeles *Times* case.[13] Mooney of course was suspected, as Lilienthal intimated in a statement to his employees. (Mooney asked Maxwell McNutt to help him sue the URR for injury to his reputation. McNutt refused, and Mooney dropped the idea.)*

The car strike did not come off as planned. Inadequate cooperation caused its postponement to July 14. Mooney appealed once again to organized labor, through handbills, to support the strike. Forewarned, the URR prudently assigned employees of uncertain loyalty to outlying routes for that day. Only one incident occurred. During the height of the evening rush hour, the conductor of a Muni system streetcar pulled his emergency brake at Lotta's Fountain on Market Street, stalling his car across the URR tracks and stopping scores of cars from the Ferry Building to Ninth Street. Groups of strike organizers, including Rena Mooney, "some of them believed to be I.W.W.," jumped onto the cars and urged the conductors and motormen to quit work. Only one did. The wildcat strike was a fiasco. After a while the trolleys that Billings and his friends had jerked off the wires were reset, service was restored, and nine agitators—including Rena

---

* *Examiner*, June 13 and July 13, 1916. Assertions by Mooney's defenders (e.g., Haldeman-Julius, "Frameup," p. 22) that the power companies damaged their own towers under Swanson's direction in order to throw suspicion on Mooney are supported by no evidence and seem improbable.

According to a contemporary statement to the police from Theodore Kytka, a criminology technician who soon afterward rendered services of crucial importance to the defense in the Mooney-Billings cases, McNutt retorted to Mooney that damages could not be recovered against the truth, and that Mooney and his friends would be caught sooner or later for the peninsula tower dynamiting. But McNutt himself, many years afterward and by then a judge of the San Mateo Superior Court, testified differently, saying that he asked Mooney why he didn't leave the platform men of the URR alone and warned him that he was likely to be victimized for his pains. (Theodore Kytka to Duncan Matheson, August 6, 1916, in California Supreme Court, "Habeas Corpus," XVI: 10,308–9; McNutt testimony, *ibid.*, III: 1761.)

Mooney but not, for some reason, her husband or Billings—were booked on charges of disturbing the peace. Mooney spent the next few days at the Hall of Justice arranging bail and counsel. On July 18 Rena was tried, given a suspended sentence, and released over the URR's protests. The daily press and the Labor Council treated Mooney to some contemptuous publicity, blaming him for IWW proclivities. Then, for the time being, the matter was dropped.[14]

III

Martin Swanson left the Pinkerton Agency in May 1914 to work for PG&E. In February or March 1916 he switched to a newly formed local detective agency, the Public Utilities Protective Bureau, which served PG&E and three other utility corporations, not including the URR but including its co-subsidiary, the Sierra and San Francisco Power Company, whose tower was dynamited June 11.* Swanson, among others, believed Mooney had set off that explosion.[15] Two days after the car strike he stopped a friend of Mooney's for a chat. The fellow was Israel Weinberg, a jitney bus driver who had known Mooney a few months and occasionally gave him free rides in his car. A naturalized Russian immigrant, Weinberg had come to San Francisco ten years earlier from Cleveland, where he had worked as a carpenter and a union organizer. He was an officer of the San Francisco jitney bus drivers' union, an organization quite low on the Labor Council totem pole. He owned his own jitney, enjoyed a working-class patronage of regular customers, and earned his living nickel by nickel. He had never been a radical. He was a modest, law-abiding family man and a property owner, and his son took music lessons from Rena Mooney. He had driven the Mooneys home from the car strikers' meeting of June 10, and also to an anarchist picnic at Colma Park, south of San Francisco, that Fourth of July.[16]

Swanson considered Weinberg suspect and perhaps usable. He warmed up the conversation. How was business? Fine now, responded

---

* The URR and the Sierra and San Francisco Power Company were both owned by the California Railway and Power Company, which in turn was owned by the United Railroads Investment Company of New Jersey, a holding company of Philadelphia and San Francisco utilities. (*Walker's Manual of California Securities ... 1916*, pp. 248–62.) The interests of the United Railroads and the electric utility were therefore intertwined. Swanson was never employed by the URR, but it does not follow, as he disingenuously suggested, that he was unconcerned about Mooney's car strike and that he would not have been trying to "get" Mooney on account of it.

Weinberg, but the prospects were gloomy. (The city supervisors, under pressure from the downtown merchants, the Chamber of Commerce, the URR, and people who could afford their own cars, had passed an ordinance prohibiting jitneys on Market Street during rush hours. It was a safety measure, but everyone knew it was also a measure to eliminate "unfair" jitney competition with the streetcars.) According to Weinberg, Swanson said with a snap of the fingers that Weinberg could earn the $5,000 reward offered by the URR in connection with the tower dynamiting. Would Weinberg tell him everything he knew about Mooney? Weinberg demurred. Swanson then threatened to have his jitney license taken away.[17] Weinberg responded:

> "I guess I can make a living without the jitney business," and he [Swanson] said, "Well, Weinberg, it is no use for you to talk like that; it is easier for you to make five thousand dollars, it would not take much to convict them,—just a little circumstantial evidence,—it would not be necessary for you to say that you remember all the details. . . ."[18]

Two days later Swanson jumped into Weinberg's machine again. He'd been talking the matter over with URR's chief attorney, he said, "and if you don't know enough to secure a conviction, I will pay you for what you know, and we will keep your name strictly confidential." Weinberg said he knew nothing. Swanson replied: " 'Is that the way you feel about it,' and I said, 'Yes,' and he shoved a nickel in my hand and got out and slammed the door and said 'I will get you yet.' "[19] That was Weinberg's later testimony. Swanson acknowledged that he had spoken to Weinberg, but denied he had shown him the reward notice or had tried to involve Mooney.[20]

Swanson also approached Billings. Billings had been paroled from Folsom at the first possible date, in December 1914—thanks to a $75 bribe which, he understood, was provided a member of the Parole Board by Ed Hurley. He returned to San Francisco, where, through the assistance of Fremont Older, he found a job with David Milder. Tailoring was respectable enough for the parole officers, but Billings did not know the trade and Milder could not pay him a normal wage. After a few months he left. Through Ed Nolan he found a job in the Ford assembly plant in San Francisco, and also worked nights as a poolhall poker shill. At the same time he served his old shoeworkers' local as their president; already blacklisted in the shoe manufacturing shops, he was immune to the treatment normally accorded union officers by the local manufacturers. He also represented the union on the Labor Council. After a few months, however, he resigned under pressure from the national president, who had heard false reports that Billings was a Wobbly. (Billings did occasionally associate with anarchists, including Berkman, and helped them raise funds.) Still as discontented as ever, he quit his Ford job over a wage dispute and went to Denver for six months, where he shifted from one job to another and was arrested and dismissed on a charge of theft and another of vagrancy. For a while he bummed his way among railroad towns between Cheyenne and Reno, then was arrested again in Sacramento, was released on a "six months' floater" out of town, and returned to San Francisco, where he barely escaped a waterfront shanghai. He worked seven weeks with the Cadillac garage, quit over a wage dispute, and amused himself with some other fellows from the Mission district by starting fights with scabs on the waterfront. When Swanson found him, on July 18, he was unemployed.[21]

Swanson was friendly. He showed no hard feelings over Billings's part in the 1913 strike. The next morning he offered to get Billings a job in the PG&E garage. While waiting to see the garage superintendent, Swanson (according to his own later testimony) handed Billings the URR handbill with the $5,000 reward notice,[22] and (according to Billings) asked for information connecting Mooney with the dynamiting. Billings had none, but drew the detective on, hoping to get some money out of him; Billings thought the URR might pay him a weekly salary while he pretended to try to get something on Mooney for Swanson. As soon as they separated, Billings sent word to Mooney through George Speed, the IWW secretary, to meet him at Berkman's office. Mooney disapproved of Billings's scheme, and so did Ed Nolan. Abandoning it, Billings returned and accused Swanson of trying to frame Mooney. The rapprochement dissolved in an angry exchange of words.*

* In Rena Mooney's trial Swanson denied that he had asked Billings for evidence connecting Mooney with the tower dynamiting. Years later he admitted only that he had been after "whatever information" Billings had on the tower bombing: "It was to find out about the explosion that I induced him to come to my office and it was to find out about the explosion that I was willing to give him a job." (Swanson testimony, San Francisco Police Commission, "In the Matter of Police Officer Draper H. Hand," April 13, 1921, in California Supreme Court, "Habeas Corpus," X: 5799–5800.) But Billings, Weinberg, and George Speed all testified that Swanson was after Mooney specifically, and was offering "incentives" to Billings and Weinberg for incriminating testimony. If he was circumspect enough not to display a bribe as a bribe, his intention was no less plain. (Swanson testimony, *People v. Rena Mooney*, IV: 1498–1506; Billings testimony, "Habeas Corpus," III: 1423–35, 1529–40; George Speed testimony, *People v. Mooney*, II: 1118–21. See also Henry T. Hunt, *Case of Thomas J. Mooney and Warren K. Billings* [1929], pp. 33–35.)

IV

Mooney's career prior to the Preparedness Day Parade of 1916 has been surveyed. It does not amount to very much. His type of radicalism defies classification; "radical trade-union Socialist" comes close. He was a left-wing activist with Marxist beliefs, industrial union aspirations, and anarcho-syndicalist sympathies. To call him a labor leader is to exaggerate considerably, for he had no following. He was "a particularly obstreperous agitator" who "never grew up," as George P. West commented. "He has a genius for antagonizing people." This opinion was shared by most liberals and labor leaders who knew him.[23] West also claimed that Mooney was malicious; bumptious and fractious are nearer the mark. In his dedication to radical causes Mooney was generous of time and energy. He was a pragmatic radical, committed to action rather than doctrine. Action meant organization, agitation, and propaganda. It may also have meant property destruction, but it cannot be shown that Mooney actually destroyed any property. And there is little if anything to suggest that action meant personal violence.* The sincerity of his radical dedication is probable enough. For all his "blustering conceit," he was distressed by the fate of the lower class, and in his tolerance of diverging radical beliefs there was an elevated hope for labor unity:

Many Reds all over the country [he wrote], get it into their heads that nothing can be done in the A.F. of L. This is bad. . . . We say the A.F.L. is separating Labor, there is no Solidarity, and in turn we propose to have solidarity by starting one more division of Labor, which is very pleasing to the Capitalist.

I have had considerable experience in the Radical Movements in the last five and one half years, and have come to the conclusion that we will never get our own by dividing ourselves up in many groups.[24]

Just look at the division of the Radicals. . . . [The] Socialist Party, and its factions, Radicals and reformers, the I.W.W. of Chicago, and the I.W.W. of Detroit, The Socialist Labor Party, the Syndicalist League of America, the anarchist, and numerous other groups of radicals all in different organizations working for the same end, . . . Their emancipation, from wage slavery. They preach solidarity, but they come a long way from practicing it.[25]

---

* Mooney did own a revolver in 1916. He was arrested in Oakland in 1913, during the PG&E strike, for carrying a concealed weapon; he pleaded guilty in a police court and was fined $5. Nothing was ever made of the incident. (California Supreme Court, "Habeas Corpus," XX: 12,817, I: 728.)

Himself a Socialist for the revolution, Mooney hoped to win other trade unionists to the industrial union movement directly, rather than through the Socialist Party. He had little to do with the Party after 1912. The IWDL was more productive. He was willing to support anyone, including anarchists, who championed labor's struggle with sufficient grit. Differences in radical persuasion did not disrupt his friendships; he remained on good terms with Berkman until Berkman's death, in 1936.[26]

Had there been no Preparedness Day bombing, Mooney in all probability would have remained a minor local figure or faded into obscurity. His mentality and character were not those of a leader. More characteristic than Debs or Berkman of the garden-variety radicals of their time, Mooney had none of Debs's magnetism, none of Berkman's commanding intellect. He was not a gifted strategist. His virtues were few, though enduring: concern for others of his class, tolerance of all radical sects, and enthusiasm.*

* Louis Adamic has represented Mooney as one of San Francisco's labor "gorillas" of 1910, with Tveitmoe and Johannsen, and Irving Stone more explicitly asserts that Mooney went to Los Angeles in 1910 to serve with the labor movement's General Staff in organizing the city. But there is no basis in fact for these claims. (Adamic, *Dynamite* [1935], pp. 206–7; Irving Stone, *Clarence Darrow for the Defense* [1941], p. 269.)

CHAPTER SIX

The Parade Is Bombed

The physical facts are the most important in any homicide case.
—Maxwell McNutt

PREPARATIONS for a monster demonstration in behalf of national preparedness started in San Francisco in May 1916, following the lead of New York City. The idea of holding a parade to demonstrate and strengthen public support for military armament was said to have first occurred to a New York businessman over a game of chess. The idea caught on swiftly. A hundred and fifty thousand New Yorkers, including 10,000 National Guardsmen, paraded on Fifth Avenue with bands, flags, armored cars, and field artillery in a twelve-hour demonstration reviewed by General Leonard Wood.[1] Other cities were inspired by this public display. Two days after the New York parade the Pacific Coast Defense League announced that San Francisco would have its own Preparedness Parade, to be headed by four western governors and ten adjutants-general of the western states.[2] Following the leadership of the League's chairman, Charles F. Hanlon—who was one day to contribute to the political repercussions of the Mooney case—San Francisco businessmen joined enthusiastically in laying plans. Mayor Rolph named Thornwell Mullally chairman of the parade committee. "We must make this a thorough, red-blooded American demonstration," said Mullally. "Every red-blooded American in San Francisco is aroused," said Hanlon.[3] An executive committee for the parade was formed; it included William H. Crocker, I. W. Hellman, Jr., John A. Britton, Herbert Fleishhacker, William Sproule (president of Southern Pacific), Jesse W. Lilienthal, William Randolph Hearst, M. H. de Young, William H. Metson (a law partner of Frank C. Drew, attorney for the Chamber of Commerce), and other prominent merchants, bankers, and businessmen. The committee sent to New York for plans and advice.[4]

As a gesture for labor support, Andrew J. Gallagher, a city supervisor and the sole labor member of the board of the Pacific Coast Defense League, and Sheriff Tom Finn were included among the parade organizers.[5] But the *Examiner* was playing Hearst's hoary game of manufacturing news when it announced that "labor, now lined up behind the preparedness programme, is expected to march shoulder to shoulder with militia companies."[6] Labor was not expecting to do anything of the kind. It was convinced, as William Jennings Bryan said of the New York parade, that preparedness parades were organized by interested financiers, munitions manufacturers, and controlled newspapers. The Labor Council denounced the report, denied the need for "artificial stimulation of patriotism within our city," and urged all workers not to join the parade.[7] The Building Trades Council was more severe: it issued a ukase prohibiting the participation of any affiliated member. It also promised to protect anyone who lost his job for refusing to march:*

Behind the military banners and martial glory they [the workers] see the grinning skulls of Homestead, Latimer, Coeur d'Alène and Ludlow— skulls of working men, women and children, shot, murdered and burned to death by militia men—soldiers.

And close in front appear the thousands of grave-yards in Europe—the international cemetery—and in liberty-loving America the ghastly, bleaching bone heaps, on the great desert, of the Mexican peons and poor people fighting unto death for the land and liberty.

Look, paraders and players for the bloody dripping dollars of the armament and munition trusts, the glorious human gore stream . . . is rushing to engulf the marchers. . . .[8]

The parade organizers had difficulty obtaining the promised governors and settling on a date for the city's grandest parade. The need to announce several changes of schedule must have caused some embarrassment. July 9, the eve of the departure of 3,000 businessmen for the Monterey training camp, appealed to some. Others favored Independence Day.[9] One committeeman, the Reverend Joseph McQuaide, advocated "a real 'insane' Fourth of July celebration." "Let

* *Organized Labor*, July 22, 1916. The Council's order was passed on May 18. The fear of dismissal from work for not marching was not groundless; one Bay Area Socialist said that his wife lost her job for refusing to march. (University of California, Berkeley, Oral History Project, "Herbert Coggins" [1956], p. 142.) In New York City the trade unions had similarly refused to join the city's preparedness parade there. (*New Republic*, May 20, 1916.)

us awaken the long sleeping spirit of patriotism by a burst of noise as in
the old days," he pleaded. "We are drifting backward and the real
American manhood has become lax."[10] But a delegation of San Jose
businessmen asked the San Francisco committee not to compete with
San Jose's frontier-day "round-up" celebration on the Fourth. The
date finally settled upon was July 22. Meanwhile President Wilson
had called for mobilization of California National Guard units on the
Mexican front. In California newspapers the Mexican crisis once
again crowded the European war from the headlines. Mexico was close
and real. San Francisco sons entrained for the border, some to die
there. Preparedness sentiment mounted. A hundred thousand marchers were predicted, an optimistic figure for a city of 460,000 people.[11]

Hearst's *Examiner* and *Call* did their best to ensure the parade's
success. So did the Chamber of Commerce. The *Chronicle,* chary of
preparedness coups for a Democratic administration and higher taxes
for armaments, was less enthusiastic. The liberal and pro-labor dailies,
the *Bulletin* and the *News,* offered no encouragement, nor did the
labor weeklies. Anti-preparedness sentiment in San Francisco was still
strong, Mexico or no. And alongside labor and liberals in opposition
to the parade were the radicals. The *Blast* protested as violently as
Organized Labor. Emma Goldman was scheduled to speak on July
20th against preparedness.[12]

Some of the opposition took an ugly, deranged aspect. Between
June 25 and July 22 some two hundred postcard threats were sent to
persons whose support of the parade had been announced. One received by the city treasurer was typical:

> Your extreme activity in promoting and glorifying militarism makes
> you the most vicious and dangerous jingo of all your brutal, greedy,
> thieving and war-making class, and the immediate extermination of you
> is going to be a sole and patriotic duty.
>
> EMPLOYES LIBERTY LEAGUE[13]

The treasurer thought this threat possibly a joke, but reported it to
the police and began carrying a revolver.[14] Subsequent warnings, apparently from the same source, were received by all the city newspapers on July 21. The one to Older declared:

> Our protests have been in vain in regards to this preparedness proppo-
> ganda, so we are going to use a little direct action on the 22nd which will
> echo around the earth and show that Frisco really knows how, and that

militarism cant be forced on us and our children without a violent protest. Things are going to happen to show that we will go to any extreme, the same as the controlling class, to preserve what little democracy we still have, Dont take this as a joke or you will be rudely awaken, *We have sworn to do our duty to the masses,* and only send this warning to those who are wise but are forced to march to hold their jobs, as we want to give only *the hypocritical patriots who shout for war but never go,* a real taste of w[ar.] Kindly ask the Chamber of Commerce to march [in] a solid body, *if they want to prove they [are] not cowards.* Our duty has been done so far, Thank Mr Older for his great work of the past in enlightening the masses and ho[pe] he will never allow himself to become the intellectual prostitute as the other dailys. . . .

TH[E] DETERMINED EXILES FROM MILITARISTIC GOVERNMENT

U.S.	Russia	
Holland	Italy	Russia
Italy	Germany	

The source of these warnings remained unknown.*

Two days before the parade, an anti-preparedness demonstration, strongly supported by the unions and publicized by the *Bulletin,* gathered in the Dreamland Rink, one of San Francisco's largest halls, on Steiner near Post Street. The sponsors of this meeting included many outspoken anti-militarist labor leaders and radicals. Among them were Paul Scharrenberg, Olaf Tveitmoe, Hugo Ernst, and William Spooner, the Socialist president of the Alameda County Central Labor Council. The IWDL was represented unofficially by Selig Schulberg, E. D. Nolan, E. B. Morton, David Milder, and Jack Lofthouse; several of these men were anarchists.† Theodora Pollack and Charlotte Anita Whitney, two social workers of impeccable family background and of growing left-wing persuasion (later to achieve unwanted and undeserved notoriety as criminal radicals), were sponsors. So were several writers and University of California professors. Mrs. David Starr Jordan, the wife of Stanford University's chancellor, brought the list a name nationally honored among pacifists. All told, four or five thousand persons, including many anti-preparedness businessmen and in-

---

* Original note (slightly mutilated), July 21, 1916, in Older Papers. For three or four years afterward attorney Maxwell McNutt, working with government postal inspectors, scrutinized handwriting samples and other threats mailed during the war, but to no avail. "I have been pretty well convinced that it was the work of an insane man," he concluded. (California Supreme Court, "In re Billings," II: 1267–69.)

† Mooney was not involved or present at the meeting, although he approved its purpose. (Mooney testimony, California Supreme Court, "Habeas Corpus," XX: 12,840.)

tellectuals, packed the auditorium to condemn munitions makers, hiss the name of Hearst, and applaud denunciations of armaments races.[15]

Rudolph Spreckels presided. Paul Scharrenberg, Mrs. Sara Bard Field (suffragist, poet, defender of labor causes), Rabbi Jacob Nieto, and William McDevitt were speakers. Spreckels reminded his audience that, though a banker, he was no representative of San Francisco's capitalists, some of whom he had fought in the days of Ruef:

Who is it that has organized this parade and will march in it on Saturday? Why, the public service corporations, who have grafted upon and debauched our community, and who now stand sponsor for and claim to represent patriotism. They ought to apologize for making such a claim. There are men who will wave the flag on our streets on Saturday who should hide themselves in shame because they have brought disgrace on our flag.[16]

There was not a single advocate of preparedness who also advocated government reform, declared Spreckels: all the promoters wanted was to get some of the money that would be spent on preparedness.[17] Scharrenberg denounced the same men in terms that reveal how inflamed class consciousness had become in the San Francisco fold of the AFL:

This great Republic may have foes abroad but some of its most deadly enemies are to be found right at home. They are the industrial vampires who undermine the Nation's vitality by cruel, merciless exploitation of labor. Special privilege, monopoly and greed are rampant. Starvation wages and long enervating hours of toil are imposed upon millions of American toilers, of whom one-third are poverty-stricken all the year around. Yet they have the nerve to ask Organized Labor to take part in military preparedness parades designed to intimidate some unknown foreign foe when the known foes of the Nation who live among us, are brazenly taking the lead in these demonstrations.[18]

McDevitt quoted G. B. Shaw's famous quip that soldiers should shoot their officers and come home:

If I thought the people in the Preparedness parade on Saturday afternoon were in a heroic humor and could take sound advice, I might be tempted to say to them:
"Shoot in the back of the neck, or somewhere else, in this parade, all of the corrupt corporation officials and minions, all of our bankers, all of the

representatives of those powers whose greed is lust for war, shoot them and call it a good day's work and come home."[19]

After the laughter and applause had subsided, McDevitt continued his address. The remark was well within the evening's rhetorical bounds; none of the next day's newspapers, not even the *Examiner,* quoted it or took McDevitt to task for it.[20] But it was soon to cause him acute embarrassment.

II

Thousands of American flags lined San Francisco's broad main thoroughfare for the Preparedness Parade. It was 1:30 P.M. Saturday, July 22, a hot, sultry afternoon. The traffic had been cleared from the street and police lined the curbs. The sidewalks and buildings along Market Street were crowded with spectators. There were few bands, no soldiers, no caissons, no artillery—just thousands of flags and thousands of citizens starting their march up Market Street. The police counted 22,400; the *Examiner* and *Chronicle* 51,000.[21] Corporation officials, bankers, and white-collar workers marched; if a labor unionist slipped into the ranks, it was not recorded. Cheers went up along the way as Grand Marshal Mullally and Mayor Rolph passed by (unaccompanied by Governor Johnson) at the head of the column.[22] Then the crowds lapsed into silence, watching the pageantry, neither applauding nor booing the marchers and the purpose to which patriotism that day was so brightly committed.

Early in the parade the last of the mysterious death threats was delivered. Mrs. William Hinkley Taylor, a prominent preparedness socialite, was waiting at the head of the women's division to lead her paraders into Market Street, when a note was thrust into her hand by a "rough-looking man" who disappeared in the crowds. The note warned that if she marched she would be bombed. She crumpled up the threat and proceeded into the line of march.[23]

Market Street parades usually formed along the Embarcadero, on both sides of the Ferry Building. Because of the large numbers in this parade, it had been necessary to assemble many of the marchers in side streets up from the waterfront and parallel to the Embarcadero. In Steuart Street, which lies a block from the Ferry Building and terminates at Market on the south side,* several parade units waited their

* See Map 2, p. 120.

turn to march. GAR veterans stood in line, followed by Sons of the American Revolution and a company of Spanish-American War veterans displaying a treasured battle flag of the First California Volunteers. Still other waiting divisions were behind them. Spectators lined the walks on both sides of the street. It was not altogether the best place from which to watch the parade, but some had come for a better look at the famous flag, and for East Bay residents the street was conveniently near the ferry.[24]

At four minutes past two the old GAR veterans in their faded blue uniforms began to move out into Market Street. The head of their column had about twenty feet to go before reaching the building line of Market, two minutes later, when off to the side, on the west sidewalk, a sudden explosion struck the crowd with shrapnel, concussion, and death.[25]

A heavy cloud of smoke obscured the scene, momentarily quiet. All around the sidewalk and the street lay the bodies of men and women in horrible, grotesque heaps. Blood flowed toward the gutter. The body of a young girl had crashed into a police officer; he got up and found one of her legs hanging by a shred. Another officer had been blown from his horse. Figures began to crawl on the pavement. Others moaned or lay silent. Some were partly stripped of their clothes. The back of a man's head had been blown off. Pieces of flesh lay about the sidewalk and street.[26]

There was no panic. The veterans regrouped and marched over the bloody pavement onto Market Street. The parade continued without interruption. As the uninjured began to realize what had occurred, some recoiled from the scene and fled. Others attended the wounded. More distant spectators pressed in to see what had happened. A garage man helped to cover bodies and became sick to his stomach. Many who heard the explosion from a distance mistook it for a signal bomb, announced in the papers, that was to be set off when Mullally passed the reviewing stand so that all the bands would play the "Star Spangled Banner" together.[27]

There happened to be one ambulance on Steuart Street when the explosion occurred. It was taking away a GAR veteran who had collapsed from the heat, and who died that night of shock. Other ambulances came, but not enough to remove all the wounded, and several delivery trucks were pressed into service. The Harbor Emergency Hospital, which was nearest, was quickly filled. Surgeons amputated mangled limbs and extracted such shrapnel as they could. Several more victims died in the next few days.[28] The final toll was ten dead and 40 wounded.*

The police took charge in a haphazard way—so haphazard that they later drew considerable criticism. No officer or any other authority roped off the area at the time, or supervised the gathering of evidence; evidence was picked up individually by police, spectators, and the detectives who arrived at the scene. Souvenir hunters had a field day. People found fragments as far away as the Embarcadero. One man picked up a hot and bloody ball bearing from the Steuart Street gutter. Others went up on the roofs, or dug metal out of a wooden fence or from their own clothing. The police department later had to publish a request that the articles found be turned in.[29]

The police officer supervising the parade in that section, Captain Duncan Matheson, was occupied with more pressing matters than the collecting of evidence. The parade had to be kept moving and the wounded rescued. Minutes after the explosion he left to supervise the arrival of a parade division from Oakland. Lt. Stephen Bunner, left without instructions, also departed to care for the wounded. When Bunner returned, at 3:30, he ordered the area flushed with a firehose "to get rid of a terribly nauseating sight." He did this without checking to see if the detectives had done their job. They had not, and the consequence of the cleanup was that powder burns and pieces of evidence were washed away along with the blood and flesh, and were irretrievably lost. This was to prove a critical error, for the nature of the explosion would never be fully determined.[30]

District Attorney Charles Fickert arrived an hour and a half after the explosion, accompanied by the secretary of the California Bankers Association, Frederick H. Colburn. Searching for bomb fragments, Colburn proceeded to enlarge with a hammer a small hole in the sidewalk where the pavement had been shattered. He also pushed through a brick or two in the adjacent wall, which the explosion had scarred but not penetrated. He produced a number of bullets and bomb fragments. But neither the sidewalk nor the wall had been measured or properly photographed before he began, and the pictures subsequently taken and widely circulated misrepresented the actual damage. One might have expected a more orderly approach to evidence from the District Attorney. It may be that Fickert's thoughts

---

* The death toll is often given as nine; the GAR veteran was not hit by the bomb, though it probably hastened his death.

were elsewhere: perhaps—as his chief clerk, Charles Brennan, told him while the *Examiner* photographers were taking pictures on the scene—perhaps the case would make him governor.[31]

Two and a half hours after the explosion Captain Matheson finally had the street roped off. A police detail was stationed around the area for several days to keep out sight-seers.[32]

III

Fear and rage invested San Francisco. The press spared few details of the bomb's horrors. The hideousness of the bomb's work was compounded by its defiance of patriotism and its defiance of understanding. The veterans were congratulated for averting panic and preventing the explosion from stopping the parade, but beneath these thoughts lay the uneasy knowledge that neither the time nor the place of the explosion could certify the anti-preparedness motive. Why Steuart Street? Why the sidewalk, the spectators, the hour, all so far removed from the parade's leading column? The casualness, the whimsy, the senselessness of it were terrifying. No evil mind or diabolical reasoning had selected its victims to maim and slay, or left the rest of the city unscathed on purpose; there on the spattered pavement, but for luck, lay each man and woman of San Francisco. And what was to prevent it from happening again? Raw nerves jangled at the suggestion. A newspaper editor, unaware that a photographer in the room was about to take a picture, jerked back in his chair with the flash and landed on the floor.[33] Ernest J. Hopkins, a *Bulletin* reporter, experienced a similar incident:

Some days after the bomb explosion I was going on an overnight visit, and I carried through San Francisco a suitcase containing harmless pajamas. People edged away from me on the streetcars; some spoke with nervous laughter. . . . I had to go into an office building, and I put down that suitcase in a well-filled elevator. Instantly there was a stampede; the elevator was emptied helter-skelter; someone shrieked: "For God's sake! Get that thing out of here!"[34]

In the two Sunday papers, the *Examiner* and the *Chronicle,* the atrocity was spread forth. The city was all wound: the parade and the bomb pushed every other news item from the first eleven pages of the *Examiner*; the *Chronicle*'s coverage was not far behind. The Battle of Jutland had been modestly reported by comparison.[35]

City leaders and editors lashed out, accusing preparedness opponents and anarchists and criticizing the police. For several days the lash of blame was laid on the leaders of the Dreamland Rink meeting. The speeches of Spreckels and McDevitt were dug up and scrutinized. Older, Spreckels, McDevitt, and Rabbi Nieto were castigated for inciting the crime. ("Nobody can quote Shaw," Older later said ruefully.) Whoever might have set the bomb, it was clear to the accusers that the anti-preparedness agitators had inflamed passions and caused the crime as surely as if they had made the bomb with their own hands. Free speech, free assembly, and free thought had run riot in San Francisco, unlicensed, irresponsible, anarchistic. Grand Marshal Mullally helped set the pace, singling out Spreckels for public condemnation. An army officer addressing the Commercial Club declared that the crime could be traced directly to the Dreamland Rink meeting. Ben Lamborn, brother of one of the bomb victims, demanded a coroner's investigation of McDevitt, Spreckels, Older, and Emma Goldman.[36]

These attacks were left far in the lee by Hearst. On the Monday after the bombing, the *Examiner* ran a scathing, full-page editorial assault upon Older and his colleagues—no names, but "you name them, because they are known to every one of us." Behind the wretch who bombed the parade, it said, were three "political and journalistic demagogues," men who befriended anarchists, petted and coddled infamous crooks, disseminated class hatred, crippled San Francisco's good name and prosperity, urged disloyalty to America, and "secretly rejoiced in their hearts over just such an infamous and wicked crime as this wholesale murder." These were men

who have incited riot, terrorized business and industry and defended and lauded dynamiters and murderers; who have seized control of and used to their own greedy ends labor organizations ... with the final result ... of the wicked and abominable crime which reddened our streets on Saturday's patriotic holiday with the innocent blood of the victims of this insidious and infamous propaganda.

The *Examiner* asked whether San Franciscans were going to be ruled and terrorized by these scoundrels, or whether they would "rid our city of these mean and loathsome vermin."*

* *Examiner,* July 24, 1916. Hopkins states that the editorial was written by a local Hearst subordinate. If so, the responsibility was nonetheless Hearst's. He had ample time between Saturday afternoon and Monday morning to set the editorial policy for his paper. Moreover, the *Call* ran the *Examiner*'s editorial the same day, which tends to show Hearst's hand. (Ernest J. Hopkins, *What Happened in the Mooney Case* (1932), p. 38n; *Call,* July 24, 1916.)

Older struck back. Hearst wanted more bloodshed: "He has seized upon dead and maimed bodies as a text for his cry of 'Exterminate!' 'Exterminate!' No soapbox agitator ever incited to violence more truly than Hearst. No madman, flinging the bomb of death, ever sought to take so many innocent lives."[37] Mullally also received his due. Where, demanded Spreckels, was Mullally's indignation in the days when James Gallagher's home was dynamited and Francis Heney was shot?[38] The old passions of the graft prosecutions reappeared also in the censure of Mullally by the Reverend Charles N. Lathrop, a Progressive social reformer, sometime adversary of Patrick Calhoun, and, by 1916, Dean of the Episcopal cathedral in Milwaukee:

> I have been profoundly astonished, upon my return to this city, to find a man like Thornwell Mullally at the head of a demonstration supposedly in behalf of the public welfare.
> I had never imagined that Mullally would have the cool effrontery to come out of his hole and take a stand in behalf of any movement that assumed to be for the general good.
> For Thornwell Mullally to point the finger of scorn at a man of the character of Rudolph Spreckels is to insult the feelings of every decency-loving person in the community.
>
> . . .
>
> On the question of preparedness, I do not agree with Mr. Spreckels, but the strongest argument I have met in his favor is to find this Thornwell Mullally leading the forces on one side and Mr. Spreckels on the other.[39]

The campaign against Older and Spreckels receded short of violence. Time sided with better judgment: Older was no more responsible for the Preparedness Day slaughter than Hearst had been for the assassination of McKinley. A preference for sanity was voiced from other communities in California. McClatchy defended the right of anti-preparedness citizens to express their convictions and protested the unfairness of holding them responsible. (He recommended that the real perpetrators be lynched.)[40] Irving Martin's Stockton *Record* similarly criticized the San Francisco newspapers for their "dunderheaded sensationalism": if the editors in San Francisco had dealt with the bombing more sensibly, "cheap attempts to make class or political capital out of it would never be spread in the papers before an excited public."[41] And the state's leading Progressive intellectual, Chester Rowell, editing the Fresno *Republican*, saw on both sides "a modicum of truth in these insincere distortions. Spreckels' pacifism and Bulletin parlor anarchy really are dangerous things, and dynamite outrages, by weak or crazed men, really are a byproduct of these forces. But when they are assailed in this spirit, from such sources, one instinctively runs to their defense."[42] If Chester Rowell ever ran to Fremont Older's defense, it was at a very cautious trot.[43] But he had a knack for asking the right questions. "Can't San Francisco find some better use of a historic crime than to wreak petty revenges or boost circulation?"[44]

The attack on the anti-preparedness leaders as dangerous molly-coddlers of the radicals and criminal stimulants to the weak-minded continued for some time in the *Chronicle* and the Hearst papers. F. W. Kellogg, editor of the *Call*, told the Law and Order Committee that Older had entertained Emma Goldman at his country home a few days before the bombing. He insinuated that the crime had been plotted there, and asked the Committee to retaliate by withdrawing advertisements from the *Bulletin*. (The Committee refused.) The offensive against the anti-preparedness leaders petered out in an unsuccessful attempt to remove McDevitt as the city's Socialist election commissioner in a hearing before Mayor Rolph. The Chamber of Commerce pressed the charges, but their own hands were as unclean as McDevitt's: Captain Dollar's incendiary words were flung back at their attorney, Frank C. Drew, by Paul Scharrenberg. In the last analysis Spreckels, Older, and McDevitt did not have the look of dynamiters, or instigators of dynamiters. Moreover, other scapegoats availed.[45]

IV

The scapegoats were the anarchists. The crime fit the popular stereotype of anarchists as furtive, inhuman dynamiters and terrorists. The outrage was compared to the Haymarket bombing, and anarchists were named as suspects from the outset along with Older and Spreckels.[46] The newspapers abounded with suspicions and opinions:

The particular local anarchists responsible—and they were probably local, since San Francisco was infested with them—had to be ferreted out and hanged. San Francisco had long been known as an anarchist center. There was the Gruppo Anarchico Volontà, for instance, on Stockton Street; it might have been involved. There was Alexander Berkman, who once tried to assassinate a man; he was in the city publishing a propaganda paper. Lucy Parsons, widow of one of the Haymarket anarchists, had visited the city in June. Alexander Horr was still loose, though he had once been arrested for deportation proceedings when he was running an anarchist bookstore with Mc-Devitt. And there was Emma Goldman. She was in town, and among her large following she doubtless had found some fanatics to fill with bombing schemes. They were all wicked, and if the San Francisco police had only been as vigilant as the Chicago police in suppressing them, there would have been no bombing. Chicago had more anarchists than San Francisco, but the preparedness parade in Chicago was not bombed. Maybe the plot was hatched there. Chicago was the city in which they had tried to poison the prelate. The headwaiter of the St. Francis Hotel in San Francisco had received an anonymous letter asking him to poison the hotel guests as an anti-preparedness demonstration. Emma Goldman had many friends in Chicago. She was said to have consulted friends of Jean Crones there, en route to San Francisco. Why had they let her speak, anyway, on Saturday night? She gave an anarchist talk to several hundred people just as though nothing had happened. The speech was even advertised on a Market Street billboard. It should not have been allowed. Chief White was an amateur who could not handle the anarchist menace. Something would have to be done about that. The anarchist mollycoddlers—Older and his kind—would also have to be dealt with.[47]

Emma Goldman was lunching with Berkman and Mary Eleanor ("Fitzie") Fitzgerald that Saturday when they learned of the bombing. Emma had come to San Francisco a few days before to give a series of lectures at Averill Hall, one of the radical culture centers, on anarchism, birth control, preparedness, German militarism, and atheism. She enjoyed San Francisco, where she had spoken many times before (this was her eleventh transcontinental lecture tour) and where she had attracted interested audiences and found many friends. Her lecture on preparedness had been announced for July 20, but she postponed it to the 22d when she found that it conflicted with the Dreamland Rink meeting. She felt keenly the good fortune of that postponement. The rescheduled lecture was not canceled after the bombing, nor were any of the fourteen others that she had arranged through August 6 for both sides of the Bay. But the strain was exquisite. At her preparedness lecture there were "more detectives than people," she reported. She evidently avoided discussing the parade, and if she said anything particularly inflammatory that evening it must have been

under her breath, for the newspapers did not pick it up.[48] The meeting
was chaired by Berkman. His words were preserved in the *Examiner*:

I understand that there was an explosion on Market Street, today. It is not
known who was responsible, and I hope that public judgment will be suspended. We do not know the possibilities underlying the tragedy, and I
will not discuss them. But I want to remind you all of the old saying that
he who lives by the sword, by the sword shall perish. Those who create
hatred in the minds of the people, those who favor training men to murder,
can expect that their teachings will bring thoughts of murder to others.
Those who are responsible for the preparedness movement are responsible
for violence.[49]

Although there were no arrests that evening, a group of veterans
gathered at the city hall to protest the anarchists' meeting. The campaign against the anarchists had already begun. "The fact is known
that wherever Emma Goldman goes, she is followed by a group of
anarchists, who are not insane, but have for their purpose the destruction of all forms of government," said private detective chief William
Mundell—he of the Cradlebaugh affair—who offered three dynamite
experts gratis to the police.[50] The de Young and Hearst papers maintained a flow of innuendo against Emma Goldman and her colleagues.
A cloth of red, erroneously assumed to be the badge of anarchism, was
rumored to have covered the suitcase that supposedly contained the
bomb. A minister who preached at the funeral of one of the bomb
victims blamed the outrage on "rank immigration laws" and the un-
inhibited dissemination of "publications in sympathy with crime,"
referring probably to both the *Blast* and the *Bulletin*. The United
States District Attorney, John W. Preston, blamed the anarchists; the
United States Immigration Commissioner, Edward White, said that
for the past four months immigration officials had been attending local
anarchist meetings, where anarchists made vague threats, "not specific
enough to be construed as treason." Preston and White both cautioned
that being an anarchist was not against the law, but in ignorance or
contempt of this fact the counsels of suppression mounted. Mayor
Rolph conferred with Fickert and Chief White to consider prohibiting anarchist meetings. Two city supervisors proposed instead that all
anarchists be driven from the city. While neither plan was adopted,
Rolph did promise to stamp out anarchy, and alluded to the Nelson
and Osokin cases:

We have had within a year two cases where anarchists have defied the law, murdered police officers and shot down citizens. And now comes this wholesale murder of men and women.

San Francisco will see that there are no further crimes of this kind. I have told Chief White to go the limit, and that means going to the root of the anarchistic canker in San Francisco and destroying it.[51]

Chief White likewise pledged himself to run the anarchist gangs out of business and put an end to their denunciations of law and patriotism. He reassured the public that every anarchist and Wobbly in the city would be shadowed, and swore in 85 special policemen, pledging them not to rest until the crime was solved.[52] Bitterly he protested that he had had too few detectives to keep track of anarchists in the past. "This is the most frightful thing that has happened in San Francisco since the fire."[53] The department had been unprepared for it.

With the heat turned on, some of the anarchists in the city wilted before they were touched. The Gruppo Anarchico Volontà denied anarchist responsibility for the bombing, but deserted its headquarters. Police found nothing there but radical literature. Before long Jefferson Square was closed once again to radical speakers.[54] On Dolores Street, however, the Blasters bided their time and continued publication.

The police appealed to police departments of eastern cities for cooperation in tracking the anarchists. Chicago's police chief ordered surveillance of everyone who attended anarchist meetings in his city, and word came back to San Francisco that there was "great rejoicing in the local anarchist colony over the San Francisco crime." It was said that the Chicago police had discovered indications that the bomb plot was hatched there. This lent weight to the view that the anonymous letter to the headwaiter at the St. Francis had emanated from Chicago.[55]

V

The immediate reaction to the bombing was manifested in two other ways: offers of rewards accumulated, and appeals went out for some up-to-date vigilante action. The first reward offer, $1,000, came from Ben Lamborn, brother of one of the bomb victims. A friend of another victim offered another $1,000. Mayor Rolph promised $5,000 from the city, but, discovering that the maximum reward allowed by the city charter was $1,000, he guaranteed $4,000 out of his own pocket while the Board of Supervisors looked for a way to get around the charter. The city had an emergency fund of $80,000. Supervisor Charles A. Nelson was in favor of spending it all, if necessary, to solve the crime; offering rewards was only one way to use it. A contribution from the state was also requested. Governor Johnson promised to ask the State Board of Control for a reward appropriation. The chairman of the Board, John Francis Neylan, said he would give the matter immediate attention; like many other people, he pointed out that in the McNamara case the state had paid the Burns Agency a reward of $10,000. The Chamber of Commerce pledged $5,000. By Thursday morning the total stood at $15,350. Before long it had reportedly reached $17,000.*

It was a large sum—a sweepstake for perjurers, as the New York *Times* pointed out. Such a large reward, the paper warned, was "an obnoxious remedy for desperate evils and one that always has, incidentally, deplorable effects." Even in the absence of perjury, justice might suffer: "More than once or twice the offer of these rewards has inspired a zeal of quite the wrong kind—a determination to catch and convict the real criminal if possible, but some one, anyhow."[56] Perspicacity of this caliber was not common among sideline observers of the case. In San Francisco the size of the reward caused no particular stir. It was quite modest, after all, in comparison to the $100,000 offered in the Los Angeles *Times* case.†

"The time has come for another Vigilance Committee in San Francisco. And I know a few people who should be the first to get attention from it." So spoke Colonel T. P. Robinson, an aide of Mullally's in the parade,[57] and many echoed the sentiment. "These outrages must be stopped with ropes."[58] It was up to the law-abiding citizens of San Francisco to "take matters in their own hands," to determine whether the city would continue to be advertised to the world as the home of anarchy.[59] Armed vigilantes might be a thing of the past, but a modern counterpart to the original Vigilance Committee

---

* *Examiner*, July 24 and 25, 1916; *Chronicle*, July 27, 1916; *Mooney-Billings Report*, p. 96. Most sources give the total as $17,000 or $17,500. But see Thomas P. Wickes's statement, in San Francisco Superior Court, "Argument on Audita Querela" (1921), p. 57, that the defense was unable to identify more than $15,350.

† Robert Glass Cleland, *California in Our Time (1900–1940)* (1947), p. 79. Even more modest was the fund started by Rolph for the families of the bomb victims, of whom only two had life insurance. A week after the bombing this fund reached $6,700. After the *Chronicle* stopped publishing the list of contributions, in mid-August, it may have reached $11,000. (San Francisco *Coast Review*, September 1916, p. 684; *Chronicle*, July 27 and 30, August 12 and 14, 1916.)

existed in the Law and Order Committee of the Chamber of Commerce. Some citizens wanted to use it.

Frederick J. Koster and Robert Newton Lynch, president and executive secretary of the Chamber, had definite ideas about the right action to take. They viewed the Preparedness Day bombing as a sequel to the waterfront violence of the preceding weeks. The bombing reinforced their judgment that San Francisco had suffered from too much labor lawlessness. Koster hurriedly called together the members of the Law and Order Committee, and announced that the Committee would sponsor a mass meeting in the Civic Auditorium July 26. "We want all decent-minded people to attend, . . . particularly the self-respecting trade-unionists," he said. "This outrage is another expression of that disease our law and order committee has started to combat, and which it is bound to stamp out." He added that the Committee had confidence in the great mass of union workers. "We feel that they look to us for conditions that will be safe."[60]

In a meeting on Monday, July 24, in the Merchants Exchange, Koster expanded the Law and Order Committee from five to 100 members. The new men were old hands: Crocker, Hellman, Dollar, Britton, Lilienthal, William Matson (of Matson steamship lines), Garret McEnerney, Herbert Fleishhacker, and William Sproule among them. Mullally was not included, but neither was Spreckels or any other anti-preparedness figure or labor leader. It was a certain kind of committee with a certain kind of law and order in mind. Funds for the Committee's campaign began to pour in, pledges of $25 to $25,000. On Tuesday the figure reached $600,000 and was climbing so fast that the Committee could not keep up with it.[61]

The excitement of a mass meeting staged by the Law and Order Committee was heightened by a report that the Committee had received an anonymous letter threatening to bomb the meeting if it assembled. The Civic Auditorium was thereupon carefully searched and guarded, and police were stationed to scan all entering persons. The threat did not deter some six thousand people from attending.[62]

The Committee obtained the cooperation of the city administration for the meeting. The Board of Supervisors provided the auditorium without charge,[63] and Mayor Rolph was one of the speakers. Koster spoke also. The occasion was solemn and the speakers were temperate. The pleas for restoration of order and respect for the law were earnest, dignified, and superficially unexceptionable. Koster alluded to "an earlier time in the city's history when she had to mend her ways,"[64] which was understood to mean the Vigilance Committee; but that was all. Rolph, in pledging the city to restoring peace, specified that law and order would be maintained by the "regularly constituted authorities."[65] No one spoke to the contrary from the platform, but the warning, if it was a warning, was timely. Sitting beside the Hearst reporters in the audience were the ghosts of Vigilantes:

They sat with us last night at the Auditorium, the brooding shades of the Vigilantes.

The high resolve that consecrated their work sixty years ago, recrudescent, spoke from the lips of the younger generation.

Grim, stern, patriotic, the sons of the sires of 1856 pledged themselves to carry on in sacred trust the fair name of a great city that these men of an elder time cleansed of stain and dishonor and passed along to us unsullied and glorious, a golden escutcheon without a blotch.

. . .

And the spirit of the mass meeting of last night can be interpreted in but one way—that if elected officials, truckling to vicious elements for votes to preserve their brief authorities, continue longer to permit conditions repugnant to every American spirit of liberty to exist in our midst, the unanimous spirit of the community will speedily find a means of solving the problem.

Times make the man. Leaders arise when the occasion is large. There was a Coleman in 1856; there is a Koster today.

But our vigilantes of 1916 . . . will not grip Winchesters. It is a spiritual host, it is a host that by sheer force of outraged public opinion will compel a correction of lawlessness and anarchy.[66]

The spirit of the occasion was as the Hearst press described it. The meeting may have been designed, as Koster said, "to crystallize sentiments"; but those sentiments were already crystal-clear to most San Franciscans, and the effect was to keep public emotions keyed up.

All week neither Koster nor Mullally nor de Young nor Hearst had found words to express confidence in the orderly processes of justice. There was an immense amount of irresponsible talk of "law and order" and ropes and the repression of anarchy and fanatics and radical mollycoddlers, all without reference to the established institutions of civil government. It was not really supposed that the Law and Order Committee was going to find and hang the villains itself. If it was to act, and act lawfully, it could act lawfully only by goading the lawful authorities. What Koster's committee was evoking was vigilante action in a modern style: early arrests, decisive action in the proper courts, and convictions, come hell or earthquake. Such pressure might secure justice if the right men were caught, but it might also destroy the safe-guards that made justice possible. The Law and Order Committee did not want the wrong men hanged, but its demands for action were preparing the way for the possibility of a frame-up.

VI

The day after the parade a Bomb Bureau, the first in the city's history, was set up by Chief White, to operate on a twenty-four-hour basis, as a division of the police detectives in the Hall of Justice. The Preparedness Day bombing was its sole responsibility. Placed in charge was Captain Matheson, a tall, scrawny, sandy-haired veteran officer of taciturn and systematic habits.[67] Lieutenant Bunner supervised the night shift. A dozen or more detectives and regular officers were as-signed to it, including a police detective veteran of the graft prosecu-tion, Sergeant Charles Goff, and a cynical rookie cop named Draper Hand. Their work was strenuous. Officers were often on the job six-teen or eighteen hours a day. Every police department in the Bay Area gave assistance, checking records and sharing hunches with Matheson.[68]

Pieces of the bomb, pieces of what might have been the bomb, were brought to the Bureau. The police tried to undo Bunner's fire-hose folly by cleaning out the drain traps in the sewers beneath Steuart Street. They did recover metal fragments which may have been from the bomb, but apparently these fragments were not critical and even-tually they proved inadmissible as legal evidence anyway.[69]

The Bureau was deluged with hunches and hysteria and with eye-witness accounts, genuine and imaginary. Tips came in of suspicious characters observed Saturday: descriptions conflicted, some indicating one or two swarthy men, probably foreigners, carrying a heavy suit-case. Known anarchists in the Mexican colony were shadowed. Several suspects were arrested, including a French-Indian Wobbly named Osmond Jacobs, found in Fresno with a powder burn on his cheek. Banner headlines proclaimed the news of an IWW arrest; the next day, his alibi accepted, Jacobs was released. A Finnish sailor, Frank Josefson, was arrested immediately after the explosion, when he was heard to say that it served them right; after a little while the police decided to hold him not for murder but for disturbing the peace. And there were other arrests and releases, false alarms attended by much publicity.[70]

Curiously, amidst all these reports of suspects and all the naming of anarchist names in the three or four days after the bombing, none of the newspapers mentioned Tom Mooney. Privately there were some persons who suspected him. One was Fremont Older, who knew personally most of the radicals in the city, including Mooney.[71] He decided that Mooney must have been responsible, on the grounds that Mooney was "the only one rash enough to do a thing like this."[72] He confided his suspicions to several people, including—according to Captain Matheson—Chief White. The idea that Mooney might be the man was also suggested to Matheson by Thornwell Mullally.[73] And, according to Theodore Kytka, the local criminologist, when Maxwell McNutt learned of the bombing, he turned to a friend standing beside him at the parade and said he would bet that Mooney had done it.[74]

These were only guesses, and more was made of them later than was warranted. It should not be supposed that because of the Martinez affair, the San Bruno tower bombing, and the recent car strike, Mooney was particularly in the thoughts of San Franciscans and the authorities after the Preparedness Day bombing. Older and McNutt, who knew Mooney personally, may have made their conjectures, but it did not occur to such an official as Assistant District Attorney James Brennan that Mooney might be responsible. Brennan knew of Mooney, but he and others like him did not connect Mooney with the case until Martin Swanson made the connection for them. Swanson was the only man whose inclination to associate Mooney with the crime was of transcending importance.[75]

VII

At 9 or 9:30 P.M. on July 22, Swanson called on District Attorney Fickert at the Palace Hotel to discuss the case and the likelihood that Mooney and Billings were guilty. There were no witnesses to the conversation. For nearly twenty years afterward it was only a matter of inference that Swanson even mentioned Mooney and Billings to Fickert that evening.[76] Fickert himself denied it.[77] Then, in 1935, the transcript of a police commission hearing of 1921 came to light,[78] in which Swanson stated that he had "quite a few men" on his mind that evening as possible suspects, including Mooney and Billings; Claude MacAlpine, the dynamiter of the Berkeley PG&E transformer in 1913; and "John Brown" (probably Joe Brown, Mooney's associate at Martinez). Swanson stated that he had discussed Mooney and Billings with Fickert. He also stated that the visit was made at Fickert's request, and that Fickert knew Swanson had had considerable experience with dynamite cases and wanted his assistance.[79]

Mooney's defenders claimed that PG&E and the URR were out to get Mooney, and that Swanson on their behalf went to Fickert that evening to frame him.[80] This claim is crude. It is implausible that such responsible, public-minded corporation officials as John Britton and Jesse Lilienthal would have encouraged Swanson to frame anyone, no matter how repugnant, for murder. Swanson may have seen in the bombing an opportunity to recoup his earlier failures to convict Mooney and Billings, and to enhance his own prestige by convicting men who were obnoxious to his employers. He may also have been under considerable non-directed pressure from his employers to justify himself and put an end to such unsolved property depredations as the San Bruno tower dynamiting.[81] But his immediate intention was probably not so much to focus exclusively on Mooney and Billings as to explore the possibilities and see what could be developed. The 1913 PG&E bombing suspects, or those among them whose presence in San Francisco on July 22 could be established, were good prospects. For instance, one of the dynamiters in the 1913 strike was one Lefler (or Leffler), convicted and imprisoned for a year for blowing up PG&E property. After the Preparedness Day bombing Lefler's name was mentioned in the papers as a suspect, but he was dropped after he convinced Fickert that he was employed out of town that day.[82] Mooney and Billings quickly proved the most promising of Swanson's candidates, whatever the number he may originally have had in mind. Whether it was Swanson or Fickert who initiated their first conference is of no moment. From July 22 on, they worked together.

Any well-informed detective might reasonably have considered Mooney and Billings in his initial investigations. Strange to say, the Bomb Bureau was not prepared to do so. The San Francisco police had their own dossier of known and suspected Bay Area dynamiters, with 98 entries, mostly safecrackers and a few IWWs, by July 1916. Neither Mooney nor Billings was included. This was not the fault of Swanson, but it does underline the responsibility he and Fickert took in centering the investigations on the pair.* What matters is not that Mooney and Billings were suspected, but that Fickert and the police quickly abandoned all their alternatives.

As of July 22, Swanson, according to his own testimony, was employed by the District Attorney. He resigned the same evening from the Public Utilities Protective Bureau and remained in Fickert's employ until after Mooney was brought to trial.[83] Fickert later insisted that he did not hire Swanson on July 22, but rather on August 1—that is, after the arrests.[84] August 1 may have been the day that the Board of Supervisors made a special appropriation of $2,500 to Fickert for expenses connected with the case; most of that money went for Swanson's salary.[85] But obviously Swanson did not just up and quit his job July 22. Fickert misrepresented Swanson's role in the Mooney case; indeed, in the later opinion of his own assistant, James Brennan, "he gave a more or less garbled account about everything he did at that time."[86]

Although Swanson was hired as an investigator for the bomb case, he was not attached to the Bomb Bureau. He worked with the police but was responsible only to Fickert. He was an anomalous figure in the investigation. The police did not know where he fitted in. Matheson stated that he did not even know who Swanson was until the day of Billings's arrest, July 26.[87] Even in the District Attorney's office Swanson was obscure: for a week or ten days Assistant District Attorney Brennan did not know what Swanson was doing there.[88] The police department and the District Attorney's office regarded each other with suspicion and distrust in those years. Goff, who had been a very close friend and bodyguard of Francis Heney, had fought Fickert

* On or after July 25, 1916, the following names, photographs, and descriptions were entered in the police dossier without date of entry showing: Billings, "carrying explosives," 1913 [no dates given with other entries]; Mooney, "explosives," "Martinez"; H. G. Hanlon, "explosives," "Martinez"; Ed Nolan, "Occupation, Anarchist"; Israel Weinberg, "Occupation, Anarchist"; Rena Mooney, "Occupation, Anarchist"; Emma Goldman, "Occupation, Anarchist"; Alexander Berkman, "Secretary to Emma Goldman." The dates of these entries were concealed and forgotten until the 1930's. Before then the volume was cited as evidence that the police knew what they were doing, were not dependent on Swanson for their leads, and had proceeded with an orderly investigation. (George T. Davis and Goff testimonies, examining the San Francisco Police "Safe-Cracker Book," in California Supeme Court, "Habeas Corpus," XII: 7357–82; San Francisco Police Commission, "In re Draper Hand," April 13, 1921, in *ibid.*, X: 5891. See also *Mooney-Billings Report,* pp. 72–73.)

On July 24, 1916, the Sacramento police advised the San Francisco police to investigate Billings. This might suggest that the police did investigate him in good faith, without Swanson's prompting. But in fact the suggestion at Sacramento was made by detectives Balsz and Kramer—which smacks of Swanson once again. See p. 30 above. (*Chronicle,* July 28, 1916; *Bulletin,* February 12, 1917.)

for years. Consequently the division of duties between Fickert's office and the police lacked coordination. Swanson's employment reflected this condition; as Brennan later commented, he should not have been around the office.[89] In later years the police as well as Fickert minimized Swanson's part, claiming that Mooney and Billings were arrested on the order of Chief White, in accordance with regular procedure and on the basis of eye-witness information.[90] But Swanson's participation in both the searches[91] and the gathering of evidence belies the claim of regularity. The District Attorney's office did not normally engage outside detectives for important cases.[92] Swanson was irregular, and he was making his own plans.

Swanson may have known where Mooney and Billings were the entire day of July 22. Until some undetermined hour during that day, three or more private detectives for the United Railroads were trailing them, in search of information connecting them with the June 11 dynamiting of the San Bruno tower, or with the subsequent attempted dynamiting of another tower in South San Francisco that supplied electricity to the URR.[93] These agents were Thiel Detective Agency operatives, not directly working with Swanson but cooperating with him in matters of mutual interest to the URR and the electric utilities for which Swanson worked.[94] They had trailed Mooney and Billings daily since July 19. It has never been shown that they abandoned their sleuthing or were shaken off before the early afternoon of July 22.* Yet neither can it be proven that they did know of Mooney's whereabouts throughout the afternoon. If they did, that tantalizing fact has been permanently withheld. Swanson claimed to know nothing of Mooney's and Billings's whereabouts during the parade, but to know a great deal about their previous dynamite activities.

Swanson's name did not appear in the early news reports on the bomb case. He operated quietly, participating in the searches and arrests but not in the publicity. By so doing he temporarily forestalled controversy over the District Attorney's employment of a private detective from the utilities.

---

* Maxwell McNutt, who had known Swanson for years, talked with him a few days after the explosion, and later related: "I said to Martin, 'You know perfectly well where the defendants were that day because Mooney had been to my office, complained to me just before the car strike that he could not move day or night but that he was followed by your men and by you.' And he told me that he had had Mooney under surveillance all the time and he said that for a few minutes that morning [July 22] Billings lost him." (California Supreme Court, "In re Billings," II: 1261–62.)

CHAPTER SEVEN

The Arrests

You do not go to a church to find dynamiters.
—James Brennan, testimony in
Billings rehearing, 1930

The evidence has nothing to do with it at all.
—Mooney, 1936

THE ARRESTS began on July 26, 1916. Lieutenant Bunner and Sergeant Goff, accompanied by Swanson, Fickert, and Chief White, picked up Billings at a medical clinic where he was being treated for psoriasis. They did not tell him why they were arresting him, but he went along quietly. The arrest was made without a warrant, and Billings was held without charge and without counsel. A few hours later Bunner and Swanson searched Billings's rooms (without a search warrant) at the boardinghouse of Mrs. Belle Lavin on Mission Street. They found a .22 rifle, a loaded .32 pistol, a can of .22 cartridges, two .38 cartridges, and some ball bearings. In Mrs. Lavin's room were some issues of the *Blast*. Mrs. Lavin was arrested. She had acquired notoriety as the woman who had boarded Matt Schmidt and J. B. McNamara before the Los Angeles *Times* bombing; this connection, emphasized by the newspapers, added to the sensation of the arrests. No warrant had been issued for her arrest, and probably none could have been obtained, since there was no evidence whatever linking her to the crime. She was released a few days later—after the grand jury indictments—without being charged with any offense.[1]

The same day Israel Weinberg was arrested in his jitney by Draper Hand. Like Billings, Weinberg was not told why he was being arrested. After two days and a sweating under a searchlight, he was told that he was charged with murder. The Mooneys' studio in the Eilers Building was broken into and searched by Bunner, Swanson, and three police detectives. They found some .32 and .38 lead and steel-jacketed bullets, a .38 pistol, copies of the *Revolt,* and various personal papers. (They had a search warrant this time, but neglected to file the legally required report of their findings with the magistrate who had issued the warrant.) Late in the evening of the same day, July 26, the fourth arrest was made when Ed Nolan was taken from his home. Nolan had been out of the city from June 10 to July 18, representing the local union at a convention of the International Association of Machinists in Baltimore.[2]

The attitude of the police and District Attorney toward the laws governing these arrests was casual. The officer who took custody of Weinberg, for instance, knew that no warrant had been issued for the arrest, but he did not take his prisoner to a magistrate, as the law required. He explained that he was acting under orders, and that obedience to his superior was sufficient justification for violating the law.[3] When Captain Matheson was asked why he ordered Weinberg's arrest without a warrant or an appearance before a magistrate, the head of the Bomb Bureau replied that he had acted "in the interest of justice."* Years later Fickert explained that there had been no abuse of Billings's rights because there was no "unnecessary delay" in his indictment and because Billings (he said) did not want counsel. Holding suspects without warrant or formal charge, he explained, "is the regular way it is done in all police departments, not only in this police department but all over."†

II

Mooney and his wife—according to their undisproved testimony— left San Francisco on Monday, July 24, for a week's vacation on the Russian River. They had planned to go earlier, but the car strike and arrests had necessitated a change of plans. Rena wrote a note to leave on the door of their studio in the Eilers Building, 975 Market Street, telling her music pupils that she had gone to Montesano. She inad-

---

* *People v. Mooney,* III: 1640. "That was quite typical of former days," commented Ernest J. Hopkins in 1931 on Matheson's remark. (Hopkins, *Our Lawless Police,* p. 161.)

† Fickert testimony, California Supreme Court, "Habeas Corpus," XV: 9711–12, 9732–33. Fickert also recollected, "Another thing we had to contend with was a threat of mob violence, and we had to protect them from the mob." What that may have had to do with the defendant's rights he did not explain. Whether in 1916 Fickert's understanding of the situation was woven around such fantasy as the fear of mob violence is a moot question, for he was not called upon at that time to justify himself. (*Ibid.,* 9712 and *passim.*)

vertently left it lying in the apartment. At the Ferry Building the Mooneys bought round-trip tickets to Montesano. They took a ferry across the Golden Gate to Marin County and caught an early train on the Northwestern Pacific line. (The Russian River was a natural destination, for it was a traditional summer playground for San Francisco's working classes.) At Montesano the Mooneys rented a tent and a rowboat. Rena, realizing she had failed to leave the note on the door, sent postcards to her pupils telling them where she was.

For three days the Mooneys enjoyed the river. On the fourth day they packed a lunch and rowed a few miles downstream to Monte Rio, where Tom bought some beer and the day's *Examiner,* just off the train. Rena wrapped the beer in a wet towel to keep it cold, while Tom, after a swim, brought the boat to a clump of willows for lunch. There Rena unfolded the paper and saw photographs of Billings and her husband, with frightening headlines:

DYNAMITING RECORDS
IN MRS. MOONEY'S STUDIO; MOONEY FUGITIVE

.   .   .

NATION-WIDE CALL SENT FOR ARREST OF MOONEY[4]

The paper detailed Mooney's radical career much as Swanson might have told it.

Mooney at once wired Chief White from Monte Rio:

Wife and I left San Francisco last Monday 8:45, for week's vacation at Montesano. See by Examiner I am wanted by San Francisco police. My movements are and have been an open book. Will return by next train to San Francisco. I consider this attempt to incriminate me in connection with the bomb outrage, one of the most dastardly pieces of work ever attempted.[5]

Mooney wired a copy of this to the *Bulletin.*[6]

Leaving the rowboat, they walked the railroad tracks back to Montesano and took the next train for San Francisco. They got only as far as Guerneville. There they were arrested by a San Francisco police officer, without a warrant, and were removed from the train.[7]

After several hours' delay an auto entourage of two cars and half a dozen policemen motored the Mooneys to Sausalito. They arrived there too late for the last ferry, and so the police chartered a launch. Shortly after midnight the Mooneys were delivered at the Hall of

Justice. Fickert, Swanson, and several police officers and assistant district attorneys awaited them. The grilling began at once, though without bright lights or physical abuse, and went on until 4 or 4:30 A.M.[8]

That night Mooney freely acknowledged his union activities against the URR, his opposition to preparedness, his radical sympathies, his current membership in the Socialist Party, his acquaintance with anarchists and activity in the IWDL, and his ownership of the firearms and other articles the police had found in Nolan's basement and considered incriminating. But he was not as cooperative as his interrogators wanted. He balked at discussing Billings or anyone else who had been mentioned in the newspapers as a suspect. He asked whether any formal charges had been placed against him, and learned that none had been and that no warrant had been sworn against him, but that he was being held for murder. He asked for counsel; the request was ignored. He insisted that he had a legal right to counsel. The District Attorney officials taunted him: What did he have to hide? Counsel could wait. Didn't he want to clear himself? If he was innocent he had no need for counsel. He was so disappointing, after having wired Chief White that he was coming in to clear himself.[9]

The police stenographer's record of the interrogation that night lay buried until 1935. When it came to light, extracted for the Mooney defense on the authority of the California Supreme Court,[10] it revealed a duel of wills:

Q. [BRENNAN] How long have you known Billings?
A. [MOONEY] *I insist that I have the right to counsel.* There is [no] fair minded, honest, liberty loving men that can deny me that right.
MR. FICKERT: We thought you wanted to make a statement.

· · ·

MR. BRENNAN: There are some circumstances can be cleared up. How long do you know Billings?
A. Listen Mr. Brennan,—Well, you don't intend to give us our rights?
Q. You sent a telegram for the purpose of making the people believe you are an innocent man.
A. To let you and Mr. Fickert and Chief of Police White know where I was.
Q. You knew we were right on your tail with five or six officers, right after you all the time. You knew you couldn't step ten feet without an officer being on top of you.
A. Why did you put in the paper a state wide search—a nation wide search—

Q. (Int'g) You knew they were after you. They were ready to grab you any time you made a move. If the telegrams you sent down here are not true, say so. If you are not an innocent man, say so.

. . .

Q. [BRENNAN] (Int'g) Let me tell you something. One of the most dastardly crimes that has been committed in this country has been committed in the last ten days.

A. *I know that. The most fiendish crime, the most heinous crime.*

Q. *Yes, and you are guilty of that crime.*

A. *Is that so!* [At this point Mooney rushed Brennan, calling him a "S.O.B." Police hauled him off and quieted him down.]*

. . .

A. . . . I am only a working man and there are many tricks in this game and I want my rights all safe guarded and I realize they cannot be safe guarded under these circumstances. I realize the seriousness of this charge that has been lodged against me. There is no provocation or justification for it, absolutely none, and you know it.

Q. Then if there is absolutely none your conscience is clear.

A. Absolutely.

Q. There is no reason why you should fear—have any fear of being contradicted.

A. I saw what was in the Examiner today.

Q. Then you are fore-warned of what might be asked of you?

A. I saw what was in the Examiner. I know why it was there and who put it there. *I am going to have counsel.*

MR. BRENNAN: Q. What was in the Examiner that came to your notice?

A. The whole paper.

Q. Give us just one idea of it, just one thing or suggestion.

A. All of it. All of my past. My trials at Martinez in connection with strikes and being tried for dynamite, which was not true, and all that stuff. It was to prejudice the minds of the people and inflame them, to make them believe I actually committed this dirty, dastardly crime. That is what it was done for.

. . .

Q. [BRENNAN] In this case, of course, nobody claims you, well known as you are, actually placed the bomb, . . . but if you are responsible for this crime at all it is because of the fact [that] you aided and abetted in its perpetration, and therefore, the only way to connect you up is to connect you with certain people who are claimed to be perpetrators . . . . As soon as we touch on any dangerous ground, that is, your connection with any of

---

* "They deleted that violent protest," Mooney wrote Jay Lovestone (May 19, 1936, Mooney Papers).

the parties who are responsible for this outrage, why, you immediately refuse to answer.*

During this detective-story interrogation Mooney controverted the prosecution with a consistent alibi which stood unchanged to the end of the case: that he and his wife were on the roof of their residence, 975 Market Street, more than a mile from Steuart Street, throughout the Preparedness Parade.

Forty-one times Mooney demanded counsel, and every time the request was sidestepped or ignored. He pointed firmly to two injustices that were to prove among the most serious in the history of the Mooney case: he was denied his legal rights, and he was prosecuted in the newspapers. When, in 1935, he saw in writing what he had said that night, he was proud.†

Rena Mooney, interrogated separately, did not know she was entitled to counsel and did not ask for it. On the whole she was decently treated that night. Then she was locked up in the jail toilet, where she slept on chairs for two nights.[11] The Mooneys and their fellow suspects were held on Fickert's unwritten *lettre de cachet* until the grand jury met. For six days Mooney was without counsel or communication with anyone outside the jail. The others were treated similarly. Reported the *Chronicle,* "All are now being held without any charge being placed against them, but some charge, probably murder, will be immediately lodged against any who attempt to invoke habeas corpus proceedings."[12] No charge was formally placed against Mooney until several days after he was taken, still protesting his right to counsel, before the grand jury.[13] Meanwhile the District Attorney and police were busy preparing their case and reporting progress to newspapermen.

III

The right of men to a fair trial often conflicts with the right of society to a free press. Justice requires that defendants be protected against inflamed public opinion, but society requires that it be in-

---

* Stenographer's transcript, in California Supreme Court, "Habeas Corpus," II: 661–731. (Excerpts from pp. 665–67, 670–71, and 705–6; italics are in source.) Mooney's statement that he was not tried for dynamite at Martinez is correct (see p. 33 above). The same issue of the *Examiner* (July 27, 1916) also revived the fiction that Mooney's boat was "loaded with explosives." Brennan's last words above suggest that Fickert had in mind at this early date prosecuting Mooney for conspiracy. The conspiracy charge later became part of the prosecution's strategy.

† California Supreme Court, "Habeas Corpus," II: 664–725, 731. Fickert later said that if Mooney had "named some counsel, we would have phoned him." (*Ibid.,* XV: 9736.)

formed about the administration of justice. The press serves a critical function as public watchdog, of seeing that the functions of the law are performed without fear or favor. At the same time, the press is also a courtesan of the public, offering its readers courtroom sensations as diversions in their daily lives. These two purposes conflict. For the opinions that a newspaper disseminates may reappear in the courtroom by prejudicing the participants, and by this means jeopardize the very justice which the newspaper presumes to guard. Because of this danger, a conscientious editor avoids exploiting criminal sensations between arrests and trials. Self-restraint is necessary, for no American court may prohibit news coverage of criminal cases.* To counter the harmful effects of newspaper prejudice, courts may resort to certain expedients, including delay of the trial, change of venue, isolation of the jury during adjournments, and the granting of a mistrial; but these measures often involve substantial inconveniences, and judges may be reluctant to invoke them. Whatever the reasons, courts have generally been insensitive to the possible effects of newspaper excesses.[14] The prejudicing of jurors is a serious matter; equally serious is the climate of prejudice that encourages unscrupulous acts on the part of the prosecution and its witnesses. Prompted and sustained by public indignation, their dishonesty may distort the procedures of criminal law and overwhelm its safeguards.

The judges who presided over the Preparedness Day bomb trials were men of unimpeachable integrity, and at least two of the three attempted to cope with the intrusion of newspaper prejudice. Many of the other participants, however, were swayed by the public reaction to the bombing and the arrests. This reaction was cultivated by the prosecution through the willing instrumentality of the press—Older's paper as well as Hearst's and de Young's, but particularly the last two. And the newspaper condemnation of Mooney and Billings operated as a feedback to the prosecution: Fickert was encouraged by his own publicity. Under the pressure of opinion in the days before the arrests,

---

* As the United States Supreme Court has commented in *Sheppard v. Maxwell* (384 U.S. 333 [1966], 350): "The press does not simply publish information about trials but guards against the miscarriage of justice by subjecting the police, prosecutors, and judicial processes to extensive public scrutiny and criticism. This Court has, therefore, been unwilling to place any direct limitations on the freedom traditionally exercised by the news media.... And where there was 'no threat or menace to the integrity of the trial,' we have consistently required that the press have a free hand, even though we sometimes deplored its sensationalism." For a critical commentary on the English practice of prohibiting newspaper discussion of impending trials, see John Hart Ely, "Trial by Newspaper and Its Cures," *Encounter*, March 1967, pp. 80–92.

he felt that his case was an important defense against radicalism, as well as a convenient way to bolster his own popularity. For his success the newspapers are partly responsible. Without them the community of hate could not have mustered sufficient strength to distort justice. To the early shaping of the Mooney case, de Young, Hearst, and Older each contributed his part.[15]

Newspaper misrepresentations of Mooney and Billings were rife in the four or five days between the arrests and the indictments, and spread in the following weeks. The *Chronicle,* a more responsible paper than the Hearst dailies (though with a smaller circulation than the *Examiner*), reported that the Mooneys "fled the city";[16] that Mooney's wire to Chief White was believed a ruse; that Mooney had not bought return-trip tickets when he left; that he burned his papers at Guerneville; that one of the suspects was willing to make a statement if granted immunity, but that the police had refused the offer; that Mooney's alibi did not stand up under police investigation; that Alexander Berkman and Alexander Horr were under police surveillance; that Ed Nolan was an IWW agitator; that letters of Mooney's had been found "which show in detail the ramifications of the dynamite gang";[17] that the police, aroused by this correspondence, had started a campaign to rid the city of anarchists; and that three men caught distributing anarchist literature had been turned over to immigration officials for deportation. About half of these statements were unsubstantiated or proven false. All were prejudicial.[18]

The Hearst papers published the same general lot of fictions as the *Chronicle,* a circumstance that points to a common origin for these reports. It is remarkable how easily a newspaper can prosecute and "convict" an unpopular criminal suspect. The little notations are often the most effective: "Billings was led back to his cell in the city prison, shielding his face with his hat as he left."[19] A familiar gesture, popularly associated with guilt.

The *Bulletin,* too, published some false reports, though far fewer than the *Chronicle* and *Examiner.* When Billings was arrested at the clinic, the *Bulletin* reported not that he was being treated for a skin disease, but that he was "suffering from injuries which apparently were caused by an explosion."[20] After hospital officials had been interviewed, this account was corrected. However, the same issue of the paper also reported that the Mooneys had left San Francisco at 4 P.M. on July 22; the implication was that they had run away after the crime.[21] The *Bulletin* did refrain from charging that Mooney and

Billings were anarchists, but this restraint was the consequence of Older's respect for anarchists rather than of any respect for Mooney and Billings. Since Older considered Mooney guilty, it is not surprising that he failed to criticize Fickert for the way he was handling the case. He accepted the prosecution's case for months, published many news releases from the District Attorney's office, and left Fickert alone.[22]

According to Ernest J. Hopkins, who covered the bombing and the first trial for the *Bulletin,* the reporters had no other source of information about the case before the trial than the daily interviews with officials at the Hall of Justice.[23] From the form the newspaper reports took, this statement appears to have been generally true; most of the newspapers' early reports emanated from the District Attorney's office or the police. That was a common procedure for reporting crimes, but it left the public dependent upon Fickert and the Bomb Bureau for information about the case.

Fickert made many accusations that were specifically credited to him. The bomb outrage, he announced, was the work of a nation-wide gang: "Nolan is one of the toughest of this gang; he is able to make the bombs himself." The Bomb Bureau's investigation, he said, showed that some of those under arrest were involved in the Los Angeles *Times* bombing and the Wheatland hop riots of 1913. "I believe Mooney had determined to bring about a reign of terror in San Francisco, and that he and Nolan had wild ideas about getting control of labor by what they call 'direct action,' which is another way of saying murder."[24] Fickert's propaganda was reinforced by the Bomb Bureau. Captain Matheson told reporters, "Any jury of American men cannot help but convict these murderers on the testimony which we now have."[25]

Accounts of several other unsolved dynamitings in the Bay Area began to center around Mooney and Billings. "It is the police theory that one gang is responsible for all the recent dynamite jobs in the vicinity of San Francisco."[26] A bomb explosion that wrecked a Southern Pacific overland passenger car in Oakland on June 30 had been assumed to be the work of Mexicans, but now Matheson and railroad detectives speculated that the bomb was being transported to San Francisco from the East for the use of the Preparedness crime gang and had exploded prematurely.[27] A rumored plot to dynamite a powerhouse of the Sierra and San Francisco Power Company was dramatized when two special policemen who had fired at a night prowler early in

July asserted positively that the prowler was Billings.[28] The "inside story" of the San Bruno tower dynamiting of June 11 was now "told . . . for the first time" by Assistant District Attorney Brennan, who declared that Mooney left the IWW hall at 8 P.M. the night of the 10th in order to blow up the towers in time to start the URR strike at midnight, and that Rena Mooney meanwhile kept the men locked in the hall. The plans went awry, he said, because Mooney did not give himself enough time to get to San Bruno.*

Yet another bomb, found unexploded in the countryside not far from San Bruno on June 23, was attributed to Mooney and Billings, with the explanation that they meant to blow up more towers. It was a time-clock suitcase bomb, similar to the one that was meant to kill Harrison Gray Otis at home in 1910, and to many others used in labor conflicts in the decade before 1916.[29] The bomb was found by one Mike McIntosh, a semi-literate horsetrader, who discovered it by the side of the road near the Tanforan racetrack. McIntosh showed it to an officer, who gave it to John Dowd, a URR detective. Later it was turned over to Fickert. Fickert publicized it as the type of bomb that Mooney and Billings favored. Since it was made with a cheap "Indian" brand alarm clock, a search was undertaken of shopkeepers who sold these clocks, and shortly afterward it was announced that an Oakland jeweler had identified Billings as a man to whom he had sold four of them. Fickert then introduced the suitcase—dynamite and all, but unaccompanied by the jeweler—to the San Francisco grand jury at the indictment hearings, on the theory that it resembled the obliterated Preparedness Day bomb.[30] The prosecution introduced no evidence connecting either Mooney or Billings with either the San Bruno bombing or the Tanforan suitcase. No one was ever indicted for either affair.†

Before Billings's trial, McIntosh was found in Fresno and brought to San Francisco. Dowd asked him to testify that he had seen Mooney and Billings with the suitcase. After Swanson showed him the two

---

* *Chronicle*, August 5, 1916. No evidence was ever adduced to substantiate these statements. (See [U.S. National Commission on Law Observance and Enforcement], *Mooney-Billings Report* [1932], p. 117.) The explosion occurred at 4 A.M.

† *Ibid.*, pp. 99n, 115, 117. The idea of linking Mooney and Billings to the San Bruno and Tanforan bombs, and of claiming that the Tanforan and Preparedness Day bombs were alike, was probably given to Fickert by Martin Swanson, whose employer owned the dynamited towers. In the judgment both of Henry T. Hunt and of the attorneys for the Wickersham Commission, Swanson brought the Tanforan suitcase to Fickert's attention and convinced him that the bomb at Steuart Street had been like it. (Hunt, *Case of Thomas J. Mooney and Warren K. Billings*, pp. 354–55; *Mooney-Billings Report*, p. 46.)

men, McIntosh said that he had never seen them before. Various inducements were dangled before him, according to his later testimony: Fickert promised him a ranch job, Dowd offered to set him up in an automobile business, and Swanson told him to name his own expense account. Could not McIntosh refresh his memory and recall Mooney and Billings? "They are dynamiters, and they are I.W.W.'s, and they are bad actors," Swanson told him. But the horsetrader would have none of it, and went back to Fresno.[31]

Several other radicals were arrested incidentally when the Mooneys, Billings, Weinberg, and Nolan were taken into custody. Mrs. Lavin was one. Another was an Italian anarchist and street agitator, Antone Fedoni. The police claimed he had inside knowledge of the bomb plot, but he was released shortly afterward without charge. An IWW speaker, Louis Frucht, was arrested, questioned about the bombing, and released. Perhaps these arrests were made in good faith, perhaps not. (They were made easily and had no repercussions, for the police had long been accustomed to arresting radicals—and derelicts—and holding them without charges.)[32] In addition, the office of the *Blast* was raided July 29 without a search warrant, although none of the "Blasters" there were arrested. All these actions contributed to the general impression that Mooney and Billings were members of a larger radical conspiracy.[33]

The police apparently intended also to arrest Alexander Horr, who was secretary of the jitney bus drivers' union as well as something of an anarchist, but the plan leaked. Horr learned of it through a reporter. He hired a lawyer and declared that he would prosecute anyone who arrested him without a warrant. He also enlisted the help of Supervisor Andrew J. Gallagher. Gallagher telephoned the police to ask what they had against Horr; nothing, they said, but Fickert was determined to have him arrested. Gallagher retorted that the police would hear from the Board of Supervisors if they reached into unions and arrested their secretaries without cause. After this conversation Fickert must have changed his mind, for Horr was not molested.[34]

The effect of the prosecution's propaganda on the public, including the citizens who became jurors, cannot be demonstrated, but it can be inferred. Fickert's usual critics were silent. Franklin Hichborn (to mention another besides Older) made no protest. Hichborn had campaigned against Fickert in 1909 and subsequently accused him of corruption, particularly in conniving with the politicians, police, and bail bond brokers who thrived on organized vice. But Hichborn accepted the reports concerning Mooney and Billings. He supposed that the suspects were probably guilty, and believed that Fickert's hand should be strengthened for the prosecution.[35]

IV

Once Mooney and Billings were arrested, every lead that did not indicate their guilt was abandoned. Eyewitnesses who told the police of suspicious persons were dismissed if the descriptions did not fit the two prime suspects. Several persons described two dark-skinned men, perhaps Mexicans, carrying a heavy suitcase near the bomb site. One of these witnesses, a retired seaman, was given a one-way passage to Stockton by the police and was never recalled. Another, an Oakland gardener named M. T. Pendergast, was more insistent; he was publicly denounced by Fickert as an IWW and a friend of Mooney and Billings. Pendergast, said Fickert, was trying to throw the investigators off the track: "The testimony Prendergast [sic] tried to give was a plain frame-up. We threw him out of the office."[36] Captain Matheson claimed that the police followed up hundreds of tips. Perhaps they did, but there were many important leads which they did not take seriously.[37]

Not a single witness prior to the arrests of Mooney and Billings offered the police information specifically incriminating them. Nor did the prosecution yet have any other evidence of their complicity in the Preparedness Day bombing.[38] The arrests were therefore false arrests. In the absence of evidence, no warrants for the arrests could have been obtained. The purpose of detaining the prisoners incommunicado was clear. As Ernest J. Hopkins explains, it was

to advertise the case, to give time for witnesses to come forward . . . and "identify," to enable a case against the suspects to be made. This backwards process—arrest first, get the evidence afterward—is the greatest curse of American police-work. Never was [there] a clearer example of the risks incurred by this hindside-before process, of the sound legal reasons for forbidding it as our Constitutions do, than the Mooney case.[39]

V

The grand jury met on August 1. The defendants were presented in a disreputable state. Mooney was unshaven, and his wife, having been roused from bed, appeared without her hair combed or her clothing properly arranged.[40] The Mooneys and Billings were then still without attorneys and without any contact with friends.* The defendants protested before the grand jury that counsel had been denied, but their protests were ignored. Mooney, Billings, and Nolan therefore refused to testify. Fickert acknowledged that refusing to testify was their legal right. (He may have expected the grand jury to regard their silence as evidence of guilty knowledge.) The defendants explained that they were protesting the denial of counsel. Said Fickert: "We can't arrange for lawyers and all that kind of stuff."†

The police had found in Nolan's basement an assortment of articles, which were described to the grand jury as "good for making bombs."[41] The articles included batteries, a sack of washers, slugs, some bullets, some plaster of paris, and other materials, including Epsom Salts, which were misrepresented as "a box containing saltpeter," and a bag that "looked like black powder."[42] According to Officer Burke, the metal articles were similar to those found in the vicinity of the explosion and in the bodies of the victims. Mooney's motorcycle was also in the basement, and Mooney reportedly had a key to the basement.[43] It was on the basis of the articles found in his basement, and in the complete absence of testimony about his activities or whereabouts on July 22, that Nolan was suspected and was indicted along with the others.

The grand jury returned eight indictments that night against each of the five defendants—Tom and Rena Mooney, Warren Billings, Israel Weinberg, and Ed Nolan—for the murder of the eight bomb victims who had died up to that time. (The last victim died on August 3.)[44]

VI

A week after the indictments Mooney saw Maxwell McNutt and once again obtained his legal help. The county jail authorities said that they had orders from Fickert not to let anyone see Mooney, but McNutt threatened habeas corpus proceedings, and was admitted.[45]

McNutt was chief attorney for Mooney and Billings for the next five months and labored in their behalf for years. The son of a wealthy

* Weinberg was allowed to see counsel July 31, after his attorney had initiated habeas corpus proceedings. Nolan was permitted to see an attorney for a few minutes on August 1. (*Mooney-Billings Report*, pp. 52, 63.)

† San Francisco Grand Jury, "Indictment of Billings *et al.*," p. 81. Under the law of California, the prisoners were entitled to the advice of legal counsel prior to but not during their grand jury appearance. (*Ibid.*, p. 115.)

surgeon, he was raised as a conservative: "a fastidious tory," George P. West called him.[46] He was a Native Son and a graduate of the University of California and Hastings College of Law. He had been an Assistant District Attorney of San Francisco from 1910 to 1913, and was "recognized by the San Francisco bar as one of the ablest prosecutors ever connected with the office of District Attorney."[47] Continual differences with Fickert had led to his resignation. He served as Mooney's attorney in 1914, and worked (unsuccessfully) on behalf of the State Federation of Labor for the pardon of Ford and Suhr. The price McNutt was to pay for defending the bomb suspects proved high: according to West, his practice was all but destroyed after he took the cases. His company disdained except by radicals, humanitarians, and laborites—persons with whom he shared little temperamentally— McNutt fought on, lonely and uncomplaining.[48]

For some reason McNutt did not force the issue of Mooney's right to counsel in the week after Mooney's arrest, though the illegality of the arrest was no secret. Perhaps Theodore Kytka was correct in stating that McNutt originally thought Mooney guilty. If so, he changed his mind after the indictments. He suspected a frame-up. One day not long after the arrests he met Martin Swanson, whom he had known for years. According to McNutt, the following conversation ensued:

Swanson asked me on the street—says, "What do you think now?" I said, "I think there is too much Swanson." He said, "What do you mean?" I said, "It is very evident to me that the arrest of these defendants was caused by yourself." I said, "You recollect that after the acquittal of Mooney in Martinez, Barrett, John J. Barrett, said to me in the presence of yourself and Cantrell, 'Well, Mac, you got Mooney out of this but we put a red shirt on him and we will get something on him some day' ", and he said, "Yes", and I said, "Martin, you are the man who caused the arrest of these defendants, and the identification is being sought afterwards", and he said it was so. He said, "Do you think if we keep private detectives in the background and make the public believe that the District Attorney and the police are prosecuting these cases that we will not get them?" I said, "Not if anybody is awake you won't." He said, "You won't take the case?" I said, "I am beginning to get interested." I said, "Are you going to hang anybody else along with them?" And he said, "Yes, Alexander Berkman." I said, "Who in the hell is Alexander Berkman?" I had never heard of him, strange as that may seem. And he pulled out of his pocket this pamphlet and handed it to me and he said he was an anarchist and he was going to hang him along with Mooney. On that pamphlet I wrote, "Handed me by

Martin Swanson opposite 110 Sutter Street in discussion of private detectives with the bomb cases", the day that he gave it to me. . . .*

McNutt had little financial support for legal assistance. He did have the help of John G. Lawlor, a local attorney and newspaperman who joined the Mooney defense eight days after the arrests. Lawlor came from the south side of Market Street (the wrong side); in his youth he made a hobo tour of the United States, and later, by reading law at night, gained admission by court order to the bar. He was no stranger to this sort of affair: as a Burns detective during the graft prosecutions he had been offered $200 by Luther Brown, the URR's chief detective, to filch documents from the Burns files. Lawlor was inclined to the defense of radicals. He was to help defend the IWW during the criminal syndicalism prosecutions of 1919.[49]

Assistant District Attorney James Brennan knew Lawlor slightly, and one day in August asked him to get Billings to turn state's evidence and share the reward. Lawlor asked if the prosecution had the evidence to convict. When Brennan replied affirmatively, Lawlor retorted: "What in hell do you want a confession for?"†

So the preparations for the legal ordeal began. There was not much time to get ready. When the defense attorneys took up the case, the first trial was but a month away.

* McNutt testimony in California Supreme Court, "In re Billings," quoted in *Mooney-Billings Report*, pp. 43–44. See also McNutt testimony, California Supreme Court, "Habeas Corpus," III: 1758–59. The Oakland *World*, December 8, 1916, stated that Swanson said, "Don't you think that if we can keep the names of private detectives out of it and make the public believe that the regular authorities worked up the case, we can hang Billings and then get Mooney, the man we want?"

† Lawlor testimony, California Supreme Court, "Habeas Corpus," X: 6347. Brennan substantially confirmed this conversation. He said he was joshing Lawlor. (Brennan testimony, *ibid.*, XVI: 10,348–49.)

CHAPTER EIGHT

The Prosecution Commences

Some of the facts seemed to be damaging.
— James Brennan, 1920

THE PREPAREDNESS DAY bomb cases were separately tried. The first trial was that of Warren Billings, in September 1916. He was convicted and sentenced to life imprisonment. Mooney was tried in January 1917. He was convicted and sentenced to hang. Rena Mooney was tried from May to July 1917. She was acquitted, but was kept in jail on the remaining indictments until March 1918, when she was released on bail. Israel Weinberg was tried in October and November 1917. He was acquitted, and was released on bail a few days before Rena Mooney. Ed Nolan was never brought to trial. He was released on bail two and a half months after Mooney's conviction.[1]

The prosecution's theory of the bombing can be simply outlined. Mooney and Billings were radical conspirators and experienced dynamiters who had been associated since 1913. Early in 1916 Mooney formed a conspiratorial anarchist society with Alexander Berkman. Their declared intention was to terrorize the preparedness movement. They made a time bomb out of an alarm clock and high explosives wired in a sealed pipe, and put it in a suitcase together with bullets and ball bearings. Billings carried the infernal machine to the roof of 721 Market Street, a two-story office building between Third and Fourth Streets, three-quarters of a mile from Steuart Street. He intended to throw it down on the parade. (The prosecution ignored the fact that throwing a time bomb would not have detonated it, and would probably have damaged the mechanism.) Finding the original plan unfeasible, Billings rejoined Mooney. They left the building, in front of which Weinberg's jitney was standing, and went to Steuart Street, arriving there shortly before 2 P.M. They placed the bomb on the sidewalk, where it exploded shortly afterward and killed certain persons nearby.

The prosecution held, further, that articles found in the residences of Billings, Mooney, and Nolan corroborated the other evidence of their conspiracy and identified them as the men who had made and set off the Preparedness Day bomb. The prosecution also held that actions of the defendants after their arrest indicated consciousness of guilt. Finally, both during and after the trials, it was the prosecution's contention that the defendants were the type of men who would have committed the crime.[2]

The response of the defense can also be simply outlined. The defense challenged the relevance of the "conspiracy" hypothesis and held that the prosecution had not established a convincing motive for the crime. It adduced testimony that the bomb was not a time bomb, but a percussion or fuse bomb. It produced evidence that the defendants were not at 721 Market Street or at Steuart Street before the explosion. From the very outset, and increasingly as time went on, the defense also challenged the good faith of the prosecution and impeached the character and credibility of the prosecution's major witnesses.[3]

As the prosecution elaborated its theory, beginning with the grand jury proceedings and progressing through four trials, there were a number of changes in its witnesses and their testimony. The nature of these changes, the question of whether or not they were made in good faith, and the character of the witnesses involved will be considered here and in later chapters.

Among the scores of witnesses in the cases, three were of primary importance for the prosecution: Estelle Smith, John McDonald, and Frank C. Oxman. Oxman, an Oregon cattleman, whose name in time became almost as widely known as Mooney's, did not enter the case until after the conviction of Billings. Estelle Smith and John McDonald appeared in Billings's trial, and prior to that at the grand jury hearings. Estelle Smith did not testify at Mooney's trial. The testimony of McDonald and Oxman incriminated both Mooney and Billings; Miss Smith's directly involved only Billings and Rena Mooney.

Miss Smith, with corroborating testimony from others, stated that Billings was at 721 Market Street with a heavy suitcase until about 1:30, or up to perhaps 1:50—her grand jury and trial testimonies

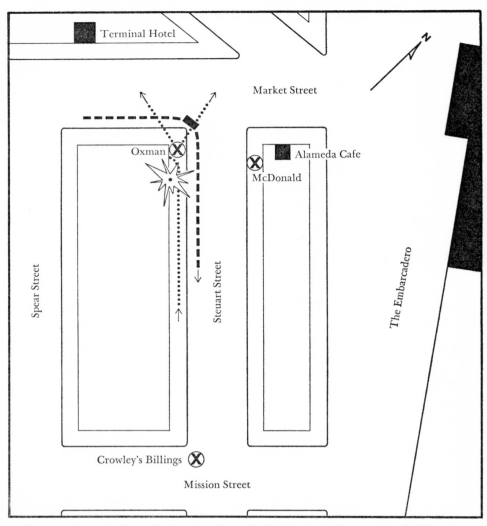

In the map above, the heavy dashes show the path of Weinberg's jitney as described by Oxman, which paused at the corner to discharge Mooney and Billings long enough for Billings to plant the suitcase (see pp. 179–80). The dotted line shows McDonald's Billings arriving on foot, depositing the suitcase, and entering the corner saloon, from which he and Mooney emerged and disappeared separately into the crowd. (All locations are approximate.) The map below shows the locations of the Eilers Building and 721 Market Street relative to the site of the explosion.

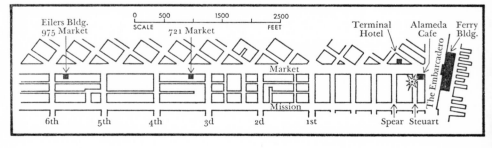

differed on this point and she claimed uncertainty of the time—on the afternoon of July 22. She said that she talked with Billings, and that Rena Mooney was also there briefly. John McDonald, without corroboration from any other witness until Oxman testified in Mooney's trial, stated that he saw Billings and Mooney with a suitcase at the scene of the crime, from about 1:52 P.M. until perhaps 2:00 or later (the explosion was at 2:06), but perhaps arriving about 1:45 and departing quickly. McDonald, like Miss Smith, changed his testimony concerning the time and claimed uncertainty about it. For the prosecution, a few minutes here or there were immaterial; witnesses could not be expected to have the exact time. But time was fundamental in the efforts of the defense to impeach the prosecution's witnesses and impugn the prosecution's good faith.

A second Steuart Street eyewitness, John Crowley, who did not appear before the grand jury, stated at Billings's trial that he saw Billings at Steuart and Mission Streets (that is, at the other end of the block) before and after the explosion. Crowley did not testify at Mooney's trial. He was replaced, as it were, by Oxman, whose testimony was of greater consequence than his.[4]

II

The manner in which the prosecution's witnesses identified the defendants was significant. The normal police procedure was for a witness to single out suspects from a lineup at the police station or jail. (A preliminary lineup might not have any likely suspects in it.) When properly administered, without coaching, this method was effective enough. In the Mooney-Billings case, however, it was not used: none of the witnesses identified the defendants in a lineup, and evidently there was no thought of having them do so. The major witnesses saw the defendants alone in jail. John McDonald saw their photographs in the Bomb Bureau's dossier of dynamiters and was taken to the cells where the defendants were confined. Estelle Smith saw Billings's picture in the *Examiner* the day after his arrest and went that day to the Bomb Bureau.[5] She was taken to see Billings in his cell.* During and after the later trials, the police represented some of the cell identifications as approximating lineups—Goff, for instance, said that McDon-

* At the grand jury hearing she said, "I know the man that you [C. M. Fickert] pointed out to me as Billings." ("Indictment of Billings *et al.*," p. 10, quoted in E. V. McKenzie, "In re Application of Warren K. Billings for a Pardon," p. 46.)

ald walked down the cell blocks until he found Mooney of his own accord—but this argument was countered with testimony of preliminary coaching. The police would have had little to lose by observing the formalities of the lineup, for by July 27 photographs of the defendants had appeared in the newspapers.[6]

Serious discrepancies existed between the original identification descriptions made by major witnesses and their subsequent testimony. John McDonald was the first major witness for the prosecution to appear before the police. With the possible exception of Estelle Smith, he was the only prosecution witness who attempted to identify the bombers before Mooney and Billings were arrested. (The Oakland gardener, M. T. Pendergast, and other persons offering eyewitness accounts of suspects to the police before July 27 were rejected by the prosecution.) In a statement McDonald made at the Bomb Bureau on July 24, two days before the first arrest, he described two men whom he said he watched placing a suitcase at the spot where the explosion occurred:

> Description of man who left the Suit case:
> 30 to 35 years of age, 5 ft. 7 or 8 in., 145 to 150 pounds, smooth shaven, rather dark complexion, brown hat, can not describe suit.
> Description of [man] with whom the man who had the suit case was talking:
> 25 to 30 years, 5 ft 8 in., 145 pounds, smooth shaven, medium complexion, dark blue serge suit, gray fedora hat.[7]

Billings was 5'4" tall and fair-complexioned, weighed 122 pounds, and was 22 years old but passed for a younger man: in Mooney's trial Oxman called him "the little auburn-haired boy."[8] Mooney was 5'10" and fair-complexioned, weighed 190 pounds, and had heavy black eyebrows. McDonald's descriptions therefore could not reasonably have been construed as descriptions of Billings and Mooney. But he changed his story after the arrests, and his original story was buried in the police archives, where it lay unknown to the defense until 1930.*

Estelle Smith's identifications were at least as doubtful. She stated

---

* *Mooney-Billings Report,* pp. 68, 71–72. Goff dismissed the discrepancies in 1930: "I have found very few men that will give an accurate description; the only one that is accurate in a description is one woman describing another woman's clothes." (California Supreme Court, "In re Billings," I: 333.) Billings's prosecutor, James Brennan, commented: "those statements . . . are filed away and nobody pays any attention to them." (*Ibid.,* II: 1073.)

before the grand jury on August 1 and at Billings's trial that Billings had a scar on his right thumb. The scar was rather on his left thumb, the one that was torn by a bullet during his scuffle at Frank & Hyman's shoe factory in 1913. Two San Francisco newspapers, the *Chronicle* and the *Call,* on July 27 made the same mistake; Miss Smith's error may have been a coincidence, but it seems more likely that she adopted it from the newspaper accounts. Also, she identified Rena Mooney on July 28 by her hat, "brown, low-crowned, of a peculiar coarse weave of straw, and shrouded in a lace veil"[9]—a description of the hat Rena Mooney was wearing when she was arrested. Miss Smith exclaimed that it was the one worn by the woman at 721 Market Street on July 22. But photographs later showed that Rena Mooney (at 975 Market Street) was wearing a black sailor hat at about 2 P.M. July 22.*

Estelle Smith made a favorable impression. She detailed her story with zest and assurance. When she first confronted Billings before the law agents and a battery of newsmen, she exclaimed, "Why, boy, I have a brother of my own, and I wouldn't say this about you if there were the slightest possibility of my being mistaken. But I am not mistaken, and you know that better than anyone else."[10] Her hearty bearing and her tale of wiping sweat from the dynamiter's brow added drama to the investigation. She helped the prosecution maintain public interest and a sympathetic press. At the grand jury hearing she and McDonald were the prosecution's major witnesses. Mayor Rolph personally congratulated her for her service to the city.[11]

Estelle Smith's mother, Mrs. Alice Kidwell, was another witness at the grand jury hearing. Mrs. Kidwell stated that she had seen the Mooneys standing on the sidewalk in front of 721 Market Street and waving to the man on the roof whom her daughter had identified as Billings.[12] Her testimony was significant not only because she corroborated her daughter's story, but also because she testified that Mooney was present at 721 Market Street, which her daughter never claimed. Mrs. Kidwell did not appear at Billings's trial, however, or at any subsequent trial. A week before Billings's trial opened, she wrote her husband, Daniel J. Kidwell, who was serving a two-year term at Folsom for forgery:

---

* *Mooney-Billings Report,* pp. 77–80; *Chronicle, Call, Examiner,* July 27, 1916; *Bulletin,* July 28, 1916; Hopkins, *What Happened in the Mooney Case,* p. 144; and *People v. Mooney,* III: 1359–60. That Rena Mooney might have changed hats for the pictures is untenable: the photographs were not taken by a friend and were made available to the defense only by court order.

San Francisco, September 2nd.

My dear Hubby:

I arrived here this P.M. The officers subpoenaed me for the trial and sent for me. I am very tired. Now, sweetheart, as soon as you receive this, just put your name up on the calendar, do it right away. The authorities are going to let you out and maby in a few days and maby by the 16th. Have got work for you in the Union Iron Works, anyway at 4 dollars a day, maby more. Captain Matterson [sic] and the District Attorney went to see two of the Board this A.M. and will see the others at Sac[ramento]. Now do as I tell you and you will be free in a few days. . . . I know I am needed for a witness and they are helping by getting you out. . . .

Your wife,
ALICE KIDWELL[13]

Kidwell mentioned the letter to a fellow convict named Hagen, who, unknown to him, had been a friend of Billings when Billings was in Folsom. Hagen sensed the letter's significance and, feigning innocence, obtained possession of it from Kidwell and smuggled it out to Maxwell McNutt.[14] McNutt checked the authenticity of the signature by having a registered package sent to Mrs. Kidwell. He took the signature on the receipt to Theodore Kytka, who compared the two and assured him that they were by the same person.[15] The defense was thus prepared for Mrs. Kidwell. But the prosecution apparently got wind of these developments, for it did not call her to the witness stand.* The defense could not put her on the stand to show up the prosecution, since the rules of evidence did not permit the impeachment of one's own witness.

After Billings was convicted, McNutt released Mrs. Kidwell's letter to the newspapers. Since it had not been introduced in court, the defense could not use it before the appellate courts as part of its case against the prosecution. But the letter was one item in the montage of evidence that the defense gradually assembled to show the prosecution's mode of operating. When the letter was published, Fickert commented: "Mrs. Kidwell and her daughter received a number of threatening letters when it became known that they were to testify. Mrs. Kidwell told me she feared for her life, and said she wished her husband was out of prison to protect her. Kidwell is eligible for

---

* According to Mooney, McNutt showed the letter to a personal friend on the *Examiner*, to provide him with a scoop on the understanding that it would not be published until the day Mrs. Kidwell took the stand, and word leaked out to Fickert through the *Examiner*'s managing editor. (Sara Eliaser to Humphrey Cobb, September 20, 1937, Mooney Papers.)

parole. . . . I saw nothing wrong in endeavoring to assist Mrs. Kidwell in the interest of justice."*

It is quite likely that Mrs. Kidwell did receive threats. According to Captain Matheson, over one hundred anonymous letters threatening death were received by prosecution witnesses and connected persons before and during Billings's trial. One letter to John McDonald's hotel proprietor, for instance, threatened to blow up his building with "fifty of the best gunmen here from Salt Lake" if he did not turn McDonald out.† It was sensible to take these threats circumspectly, and they undoubtedly added to the worries of the prosecution. Unfortunately they also provided Fickert with a convenient rationalization for some of his most questionable practices, among them his intercession for the parole of Mrs. Kidwell's husband. Before the trials were over, Fickert had claimed that threats were made against all his major witnesses—McDonald, Estelle Smith, and Oxman—and some of his less important ones. Perhaps the claims were truthful, but each time they were made in connection with the exposure of some unscrupulous method by the defense. Fickert's protests were readily accepted by the public, fitting as they did the public image of anarchists.[16]

"The type of mind possessed by Miss Estelle Smith," declared the *Examiner* on the morning of the grand jury hearing, "is the sort of mind which is of decided value to the world."[17] Before Billings's trial, however, the defense discovered that Estelle Smith had a police record. Along with her uncle, James L. Murphy, she had been indicted for the second-degree murder of a chorus girl at their boardinghouse in Los Angeles in 1913.[18] She was not prosecuted, but her uncle was convicted and sent to San Quentin. She may have been encouraged to believe that Fickert would intercede with the parole board to obtain his release. There is no proof of this, but it is noteworthy that Murphy, after serving only three and a half years of his twelve-year sentence, was freed by commutation on April 10, 1917, six months after Bil-

---

* As quoted, *Examiner*, September 25, 1916. Henry T. Hunt, in briefing the Mooney case for the National Mooney-Billings Committee of the American Civil Liberties Union, erroneously dated Mrs. Kidwell's letter February 2, 1917. This inadvertently concealed the significance of Mrs. Kidwell's absence from the witness stand in Billings's trial. (Hunt, *Case of Thomas J. Mooney and Warren K. Billings*, p. 327.) On January 5, 1917, two days after Mooney's trial opened, the *Chronicle* reported that D. J. Kidwell had been denied parole by the state board of prison directors. (*Mooney-Billings Report*, pp. 181–82.)

† *Bulletin*, September 26, 1916. Matheson had the good sense not to publish these letters before the end of Billings's trial.

lings's conviction.[19] Whatever Miss Smith's motive for testifying against Billings, the defense was inadequately aware of her record. Further knowledge of her past was to come to light after Billings's trial.

III

Billings's prosecutor was Assistant District Attorney James F. Brennan. A "big, virile young attorney," raised on an Iowa farm and trained in law at Stanford, Brennan was the man who had started Fickert toward his career as District Attorney. Like Fickert he was an ex–football star.[20] He was assisted in presenting the case against Billings by two other Assistant District Attorneys, Edward Cunha and Fred L. Berry, and by Fickert.

Brennan had misgivings about the reliability of his witnesses. He could not see any reason why Billings should have appeared at 721 Market Street, and he lacked confidence in both Estelle Smith and John McDonald. He had mentioned his doubts to Matheson, but Matheson in turn had begun to wonder about Brennan's loyalty to the prosecution, and had quietly instructed one of his police detectives, Draper Hand, to keep an eye on Brennan.[21] However, no disloyalty developed. Brennan shrugged off his doubts. It was no business of his, he thought, to determine whether his witnesses were reliable; his only duty was to present their testimony to the jury and let the jury decide. Certainly the long-standing conspiracy of the defendants was as convincing of their guilt as any man would want. Mooney, he thought, should be set with Alexander Berkman on one side and Emma Goldman on the other, "and you would have a trinity of anarchists the world could not equal."[22] To be sure, neither Berkman nor Miss Goldman had been indicted, but that was Fickert's responsibility. Fickert wanted to prosecute Billings himself. However, it was customary for an Assistant District Attorney to appear in court for the prosecution, and in all his years in office Fickert had not presented a case. Brennan was afraid that if the District Attorney undertook to prosecute Billings the case would be botched, and he succeeded in keeping Fickert's courtroom participation to a minimum. He had more faith in his own ability to get a conviction.[23] He also had his own career to consider.

The Hall of Justice, the only official building in the city that had survived the 1906 earthquake and fire, stood on Kearny Street a few blocks from Telegraph Hill, facing Portsmouth Square. There on September 11 Billings was brought to trial, in the court of Judge

Frank H. Dunne, for the death of Mrs. Kingsley Van Loo, one of the two women killed by the bomb and the mother of two children. The Mooneys, Weinberg, Nolan, and Tom Mooney's mother attended the opening sessions, along with Robert Minor and Selig Schulberg for the IWDL. The courtroom was packed, but standees were not permitted, and the spectators maintained good order throughout the trial. Billings was defended by McNutt.[24]

The jury box was quickly filled. The prosecution asked the veniremen, in addition to the usual questions, whether they had Socialist or anarchist affiliations and whether they subscribed to the *Blast*. McNutt asked them whether they had ever been connected with the United Railroads or PG&E. He knew some of them from previous cases; in fact, three had been on Billings's jury in the 1913 assault case before Judge Dunne. McNutt appeared to know which jurors he did not want, and did not find it necessary to use all of his peremptory challenges. The jurors were all men, for it was only some months later that women began to serve on California juries. It was an old jury; nine of the twelve jurors were retired.[25]

An odd incident occurred at this time. A subpoena was served in the courtroom on Robert Minor, IWDL secretary and reporter for the *Blast*, to appear as a witness for the prosecution. Minor was removed from the room along with the other witnesses. He protested that the prosecution had no intention of calling him to the stand, and that the subpoena had been served to prevent him from covering the case. McNutt protested the maneuver to Judge Dunne. Dunne consulted Prosecutor Brennan, who had meanwhile told reporters that the subpoena had been served because Minor had urged that Fickert be lynched. Since Brennan could not explain to Dunne's satisfaction why Minor should be a witness, he was permitted to return.[26]

In his opening statement to the jury Brennan dwelt on conspiracy. The grand jury indictments had not included conspiracy, but from an early date the prosecution had intended to present conspiracy evidence at the trials. Brennan had been to Martinez and Sacramento to discuss the earlier cases with local officials.[27] He told the jury of Billings's dynamite crime in Sacramento, of the San Bruno dynamiting, and of another bombing in Chicago in 1914 for which, he alleged, Billings had admitted being paid $250; he promised to show that on June 26, 1916, Billings took the Tanforan suitcase of dynamite down the peninsula by bus, and that on the evening of July 21 Billings delivered a borrowed "camera" to Mooney. The type of case Brennan sought to make was thus primarily a conspiracy case. It remained to be seen whether Judge Dunne would permit the trial to proceed on this basis. A conspiracy trial would open the doors of Billings's past and undoubtedly would facilitate a conviction. But the fact was that Brennan's claims, whether admissible or not, were inflated: there was little evidence, as we have seen, to sustain the San Bruno and Tanforan suitcase charges, and the alleged Chicago bombing was a complete myth. In the trial of Rena Mooney, when all the "conspiracy" testimony was admitted in evidence, the prosecution failed to prove any of the three charges.*

To begin the prosecution's conspiracy testimony, Fickert summoned William E. Kramer and Henry Balsz, the PG&E's Sacramento detectives.[28] When Kramer began his story the defense objected. Dunne then excused the jury and heard the attorneys' arguments. Brennan contended for the right to show a general conspiracy of Billings and Mooney against everyone who disagreed with their radical social theories. But Dunne was not disposed to allow so sweeping an interpretation of conspiracy evidence. He asked Brennan why the prosecution did not attempt to show a definite conspiracy against certain corporations; even that might not be acceptable testimony, he warned. "You do not seriously contend, Mr. Brennan," he said, "that there was a conspiracy in Sacramento three years ago extending to this present crime?"[29] And he cautioned him:

In order to prove a conspiracy it is necessary to show some definite purpose, and it is not permissible to prove a general conspiracy against the whole world. . . . If you do not take care, Mr. Brennan, you may find yourself proving that the defendant was guilty of transporting dynamite on a Sacramento street car, instead of proving him guilty of the murder of Mrs. Van Loo.[30]

Brennan responded that the State wanted to show that Billings was in the business of dynamiting people. He cited the trial in 1886 of

* *Bulletin*, September 12, 1916; *Chronicle*, September 13, 1916; *People v. Billings*, I: 2–10; and *People v. Rena Mooney*, III: 1257–81. In 1931 the U.S. National Commission on Law Observance and Enforcement, analyzing prosecution unfairness in American courts, stated: "The commonest sort of prejudicial evidence or reference improperly introduced is that which charges or insinuates that the prisoner has committed other offenses than the crime for which he is on trial. . . . when the attention of the jury is called to his other possible offenses there is danger that they may decide that he ought to be shut up as a bad man whether he actually committed the crime under investigation or not." (*Report on Lawlessness in Law Enforcement* [Report 11, 1931], p. 293.) The authors of this report were Walter H. Pollak, Zechariah Chafee, Jr., and Carl Stern, consultants of the Commission, who also prepared the *Mooney-Billings Report* for the Commission.

August Spies for the Chicago Haymarket riot, and other cases, to justify the introduction of evidence demonstrating a related conspiracy. But Dunne ruled the proposed conspiracy evidence irrelevant.[31]

The jurors were bored by their day-long exclusion from the proceedings. To pass the time they took a secret ballot and voted, 10–2, to hang, draw, and quarter the Prohibition movement. They also elected Charles Evans Hughes, 9–3, the next President of the United States.[32]

The closest the prosecution came to presenting conspiracy evidence in Billings's trial was the subpoenaed testimony of George Speed, the IWW secretary. Speed told of meeting Billings on Market Street three days before the bombing and of taking a note from Billings to Mooney, which Mooney answered with a message that he would meet Billings at the *Blast* office. This information was offered to prove that Mooney and Billings were in touch just before the parade. Speed also testified that Billings had told him of the approach of "the Pinkerton"—that is, Swanson—with an offer of $5,000 for information against Mooney.[33]

As for the Preparedness Day crime itself, the prosecution introduced scores of metal fragments and bullets that had been found on Steuart Street or in the bodies of the bomb victims. The missiles included .22 and .32 bullets and some ball bearings.[34] The prosecution intended to connect these with Billings by showing that there were .22 and .32 bullets and ball bearings in his room at the time of his arrest. McNutt argued that the connection was entirely inadequate. He pointed out that .22 and .32 caliber bullets were common possessions, and that the ball bearings in Billings's room differed in size from those found on Steuart Street.[35] The ball bearings found at the scene were nonetheless admitted in evidence by the court, and so were the ball bearings and cartridges found in Billings's room. McNutt subsequently represented these admissions to the appellate court as reversible errors.[36]

Seven witnesses for the prosecution testified that they saw Billings at 721 Market Street early in the afternoon of July 22. The first was a Honolulu school principal, Herbert A. Wade, who said that Billings, carrying a short, wide suitcase, pushed past him about 1 P.M. on the stairs going up to the dentists' office in the building.[37] The second was police officer Earl R. Moore, who was on duty in the street outside 721 Market Street during the parade. At 1:15, Moore said, he had questioned a man, whom he subsequently identified as Billings, about a Ford that was illegally parked at the curb.[38] The third witness, Peter Vidovich, a retired broker from Alaska, testified that as he left the dentists' office about 12:15, he passed Billings carrying a suitcase on the stairs. He agreed with Wade that the suitcase was of an unusual shape.[39] On cross-examination Wade described Billings as a man of 5'10", wearing a dark gray suit; Moore described him as 5'7" or 5'8", in a light brown suit; and Vidovich said the suit was of "light-dark color" with fine stripes. It was by no means clear that all three had seen Billings, or that any of them had.[40]

Wade, Moore, and Vidovich had all testified before the grand jury. But the fourth and fifth witnesses had not; they were surprises sprung by the prosecution. They were Mrs. Mellie Edeau, an Oakland dressmaker, and her daughter, Sadie Edeau. In time the pair became second only to Oxman in notoriety. Mrs. Edeau testified that on the afternoon of July 22, she and her daughter were on the sidewalk near the entrance of 721 Market, and that she saw Billings leaning over the roof with a suitcase in his hand and talking with a man on the sidewalk. She said that she saw Billings again on the sidewalk, about 1:30, talking at the curb with Officer Moore, and again, "talking with a woman and a man"; she overheard Billings say to the pair, "We have to make the ferry by 2 o'clock." Billings and the man and woman then left in the direction of the ferry (that is, toward Steuart Street). Mrs. Edeau thought Billings was wearing a brown suit; she was positive that he was Billings. Her daughter corroborated most of her testimony.[41]

Off the witness stand, Mrs. Edeau told reporters that she and her daughter had determined for weeks that they would not tell their story:

We were in deadly fear [she said] that if we did and were made witnesses in the trial we would be killed by anarchists. We have had anarchists among our neighbors and have had trouble with them.

We were torn between this fear and our desire to act the part of God-fearing Christian women and do our duty as citizens. We knew we were doing wrong by not telling, but we did not dare. But as days went by our guilty feeling preyed on our minds until we could not eat. We had to tell our friends to ask their advice. We were urged to go to the police, but we did not dare.

Our friends in the First Christian Church, of which we are members, begged us to give our information to the police. We were in such torment as the weeks went by that finally, after talking it over with church members, we decided to end it by doing our duty.

We went to San Francisco and told Captain Matheson all we had seen of Billings on the day of the parade.

Now that it is over we are happy. We are still afraid that our lives will be sought, and we intend to ask the Oakland police tomorrow to provide us with a guard. But we have a gun in the house and can defend ourselves if the need comes.[42]

Following the Edeaus, Estelle Smith took the stand to tell her story of how Billings, pale, nervous, and perspiring, had come with his suitcase to the dental offices where she worked, on the second floor of the building, and asked for permission to go on the roof, saying that he was a newspaper photographer. She told him, she said, to wait in the reception room until the doctor came back.

After a while he got up and walked up and down. He went out into the hall. I said to him, "What is the matter with you?" He said he was sick from the heat. I gave him a glass of water and wiped the perspiration off his face with a towel. . . . I suggested to Mr. Billings that he take a walk and get a little fresh air if he was affected with the heat. Well, when I stooped over to pick up his suitcase my back was to him and he said, "My God, girl, don't touch that." He said it so quick it made me jump. I said, "What is the matter with you?" He said, "I am afraid you will strain the lens in my camera." I said, "Oh, you frightened me you spoke so quick." . . . He was still wiping his face and was very nervous. I thought he was sick. I never dreamed it was anything serious. I just thought the man was sick from the heat.[43]

Then, said Miss Smith, she let Billings on the roof, and called a friend, Louis Rominger, to help him. She did not know when Billings came down, but thought it was about 1:40.* He said to her, " 'Good-bye, girl; I can't take advantage of your kindness. I have friends waiting for me downstairs.' " Miss Smith also told of seeing in the hall a rude stranger who looked like a Russian. When she asked him his business, he swore at her and left.†

* When she testified before the grand jury, Miss Smith said that Billings was still on the roof when Mayor Rolph passed and did not leave the building until five minutes later. It was later proven that the Mayor passed 721 Market at 1:51 P.M. (Edwin V. McKenzie, "In re Application of Billings for a Pardon" [1930], p. 55.)

† *People v. Billings*, I: 334–57. In her grand jury testimony Miss Smith said that he was "a very repulsive looking man, [with a] long moustache. I would say he was a Russian Jew or something that way." She said that while the man was there Mrs. Mooney ran up the stairs and called him away, and that five minutes later Billings left the building. (*Ibid.*, p. 365.) It may be that at the time of the grand jury hearing the prosecution had Alexander Berkman in mind. Whoever it was, in Billings's trial the prosecution did not pursue this line of testimony.

Louis Rominger testified that he helped Billings onto the roof with his heavy suitcase; that he saw him later on the sidewalk with the woman and two men, one with a black moustache; and that he saw Billings leave in the direction of the ferry.[44]

The prosecution had announced that Billings's reason for going to the roof of 721 Market Street was to throw the bomb down onto the parade. Brennan never developed this hypothesis during the trial. The defense therefore did not question the plausibility of a plan to throw a bomb that, according to the prosecution, was a time bomb rather than a fuse or percussion bomb. Brennan offered no other explanation of Billings's trip to the roof.[45]

John McDonald took the witness stand one week after the trial began. He was the prosecution's most important witness, for he— and, at this trial, he alone—claimed to have seen Mooney and Billings at the scene of the explosion. He said that he was standing on Steuart Street, across the street from the site of the explosion, at "eight or ten minutes to two," when he saw Billings on the other side approaching from Mission Street, carrying a suitcase, and looking from right to left as though his head were "on a pivot." Billings deposited the suitcase on the sidewalk "about two o'clock" and walked on a few steps to the entrance of the saloon on the corner. He went in and came out again with Mooney. They consulted their watches, and Billings went to the corner and disappeared in the crowd. Mooney looked at the Ferry Building clock after Billings left and then "took a hike out through the crowd." (All this was allegedly seen from across Steuart, which was lined with paraders and spectators.)* Then McDonald started for the Alameda Coffee House, about 125 feet away; when he got there, the explosion occurred.[46]

Another prosecution witness, John Crowley, then testified that he had seen Billings and another man, "either a Spaniard or a Mexican," standing at Steuart and Mission Streets at 1:55 and at the time of the explosion. He said that Billings was not carrying anything. Billings had attracted his attention by refusing to remove his hat when the band played "the colors."[47] This story conflicted with McDonald's testimony that Billings went off from the deposited suitcase in a direction away from Mission Street.

Finally, the prosecution offered testimony to show that there had

---

* On cross-examination McNutt brought out the fact that McDonald had told the grand jury that he saw Billings cross Market Street through the parade—an implausible claim, given the crowds and McDonald's location.

been a suitcase on the sidewalk at the point of the explosion. It had been noticed by at least one person.[48]

IV

Then came the turn of the defense. McNutt presented a witness who had been on the roof of 721 Market Street throughout the parade. This man, Al De Caccia, worked for a firm whose offices had been next door, and from the building next door he had reached the roof of 721 Market. De Caccia stated that Billings was not on the roof at any time during the parade, but that an unidentified photographer was there with a large camera case; that no one came up directly from 721 Market to the roof, which was accessible from the floor below only through the skylight; that he, De Caccia, was wearing a brown suit, and that he leaned over the coping and talked with his friends down on the street. His testimony was corroborated by three friends who had joined him on the roof during the parade. These witnesses surprised the prosecution. It was apparent that neither the District Attorney nor the police had interviewed anyone who had been on that roof.[49]

The defense also sought to impeach Officer Moore's testimony by putting on the stand a San Mateo resident, Thomas Dodge. Dodge swore that he had talked with Moore in front of the doorway of 721 Market Street about a parked automobile similar to the one Moore had described. (Moore, in rebuttal, denied having talked with Dodge. Whether Moore mistook Dodge for Billings was never settled. But it was shown from the San Francisco police archives twenty years later that Moore did not write out his description of the man he had talked to at 721 Market Street until after Billings's arrest. Even then he stated that the man had dark hair. Dodge had dark hair, but Billings's hair was red. It was also shown that Moore had gone to look at Billings in jail, after which he wrote out another report stating that Billings was the man.)*

Billings testified in his own defense. He denied that he was at either 721 Market Street or Steuart Street on July 22. Shortly after his arrest

* Dodge, Moore, testimonies, *People v. Billings*, II: 434–38, 647–48; police reports of Officer Earl R. Moore, July 31, 1916, in California Supreme Court, "Habeas Corpus," XVII: 11,284–85. Moore, confronted with this evidence in 1936, could not recall the incident, but still maintained that he had identified Billings correctly as the man at 721 Market Street. (*Ibid.*, XVII: 11,279, 11,286.)

he had worked out a description of his itinerary during the parade in careful detail for the police. He had named streets, parade formations, and incidental objects, such as a gray Hudson auto standing at Grant Avenue near Union Square. The police had not checked his statement; if they had, presumably they would have found, as Maxwell McNutt did, that there were in the city certain persons unknown to Billings who could verify parts of his story. On the stand he repeated the details—though with certain changes from his original story. Four corroborating witnesses were called. One of them, a physician who happened to be a personal friend of Judge Dunne, was the owner of the Hudson, and confirmed the fact that his car was at Grant Avenue at the time Billings had claimed it was. The testimony of the four witnesses indicated that Billings was in the vicinity of Union Square, nearly a mile from the scene of the explosion, at about 1:50 P.M., the time that McDonald said he was at Steuart Street.[50]

Unfortunately for Billings, there was one respect in which he showed badly. His explanation of his whereabouts July 22 to Police Sergeant Goff the afternoon of his arrest was not the same story he told Police Chief White July 29, nor the same as the one he told on the witness stand. He had told Goff nothing about being in the vicinity of Union Square July 22, but had said that he had gone from his residence to Ninth and Market Streets and had watched the parade in that area until about 2:45. The prosecution made much of the discrepancy, arguing with some plausibility that the change of story indicated a consciousness of guilt at the time of his arrest.[51]

At the time of his arrest Billings was, indeed, conscious of guilt—for an entirely different crime! He did not tell Goff the whole truth because he thought he was being picked up for defacing property. During the parade he had been spraying paint-remover on automobiles that had been painted by "scabs" during an automobile mechanics' strike. According to his own story, told long afterward, he had the license numbers of the autos written down on a cigarette paper in his possession at the time of his arrest, and sometime during the next day or so he took the piece of paper, rolled it into a cigarette, and smoked it, thereby destroying the evidence that could have convicted him of a misdemeanor—or possibly saved him from a murder conviction. After it was too late to retrieve the paper, he found out that he was accused of setting off the Preparedness Day bomb. Even then, he said, he was so sanguine about an acquittal, and so anxious not to admit the other crime, that he kept his story quiet: "I thought the mere fact alone that I was absolutely innocent of this crime would be sufficient enough for me to prove my innocence; consequently the other crime did not need to be brought forth."[52] He did not even tell his attorney. However, he did describe the cars to him, without saying anything about sabotage. McNutt was able to track down several of them, and was perplexed to discover that they were all similarly marred. Finally Ed Nolan explained to him in confidence what Billings had done. It was for Nolan's union that Billings had volunteered his acid-squirting services; besides Billings, only Nolan and Mooney knew the story. McNutt was anxious to use the information to strengthen Billings's defense, but Billings, Nolan, and Mooney, having conferred in jail, were against it, and Nolan refused to release McNutt from the confidence.[53] As Billings said later, "I did not think that it was necessary for me to prove anything against myself which would obviously be so prejudicial to a court as the commission of a crime of this nature."[54]

In his trial testimony Billings made numerous references to cars he had seen during the parade, without explaining why he remembered them. Fickert inferred that his alibi was phony. "You would think he was out buying a car that day, the way he looked at them," he told the jury.[55] For a year or so after his conviction Billings kept his story to himself. Without the full list of cars, it would have been of little value in establishing his innocence. Eventually he told Fremont Older and a few others privately, including Brennan in 1921 and Fickert in 1925 or 1926; but not until 1930 was the story brought out in the open, when his case was reviewed by the State Supreme Court.[56]

During the trial Mrs. Belle Lavin, Billings's landlady, testified about the articles the police had found in Billings's room. She, Billings, and a mutual friend had gone to the Russian River for a vacation early in July. The friend had taken along the .22 rifle and cartridges, which he left afterward at Billings's place. They had also taken along the .32 pistol, although its ownership and purpose were not explained by the defense.[57]

Because several of the prosecution witnesses had told of seeing Mooney as well as Billings on July 22, the defense undertook to establish an alibi for Mooney. On the witness stand the Mooneys, Rena Mooney's sister (Belle Hammerberg), and a cousin all stated that they were in the Mooneys' studio in the Eilers Building, 975 Market Street, until the head of the parade appeared down the street, and that they then went up on the roof and stayed there until the parade was over. Five other witnesses, three of them employees of the Eilers Music Company, swore that the Mooneys came on the roof before two o'clock, or five to ten minutes before the parade began to pass below.[58] The defense also introduced four photographs of the parade taken by an employee of the Eilers Music Company, Wade Hamilton. In these pictures the Mooneys—from the back, but without question the Mooneys—appeared as they leaned over the cornice. Hamilton's photographs became famous, but their full significance did not emerge until Mooney's trial.

The defense sought to undermine the prosecution's whole "suitcase" hypothesis of the bomb. McNutt and his witnesses showed that the nature of the bomb had never been clearly established by the authorities, and that, in fact, there was reason to doubt that the bomb's manufacture had involved either a suitcase or a clock mechanism. The prosecution had introduced three rings, which it claimed came from the clock; the defense showed that at best the three rings had come from two clocks,[59] and that perhaps the rings had not come from any clocks at all. Nothing else had been found of the putative clock. The prosecution also had introduced some bits of fiber, which probably had been part of a cheap leatherette suitcase, but it never proved that the explosion had come from within the suitcase; the bomb might have destroyed a suitcase incidentally. The prosecution, moreover, had never shown the type of explosive used, nor had it found any detonating wire or wood splinters, though time bombs required wiring and were normally constructed on wooden frames for safety.[60]

The defense did not deny that a suitcase had been involved in the explosion, and, in fact, produced M. T. Pendergast, the Oakland gardener whom Fickert had rejected, to testify that he had seen a suitcase, carried by a man who was neither Mooney nor Billings but a swarthy man, at the site of the explosion about three minutes before the bomb went off. And one of the GAR veterans who had marched in the parade, Major William J. Watson, stated for the defense that he saw a suitcase on the sidewalk at the same place "fully 20 minutes before the column moved out"—that is, fifteen minutes or more before Billings's arrival according to McDonald. Concerning the source of the explosion, Dr. J. Mora Moss, a San Francisco physician, testified that he saw, from a distance of sixty feet, a dark cylindrical object about fourteen inches long falling between the roof and the sidewalk an instant before the explosion. Like Pendergast, Dr. Moss was one of the witnesses whom Fickert had dismissed at the outset of the case.[61]

The defense elicited testimony to show that the prosecution's star witness, McDonald, was personally interested in the outcome of the case: he was expecting part of the reward. C. G. Requa, a Salvation Army captain, said that after McDonald's story had first appeared in the newspapers, he asked McDonald whether he realized that he might be eligible for a large part of the reward; and McDonald answered that Police Chief White had said he "would go back to Baltimore on the cushions with plenty of change in his pockets."* A restaurant worker testified that McDonald had told him the same thing; and a barber testified similarly, although less effectively. McNutt next offered to show that McDonald had been maintained in a hotel by the police with a $3 per diem allowance since August 16. Fickert conceded the fact, and said that the arrangement was necessary to protect the witness.[62]

Soon afterward the defense closed its case. In rebuttal the prosecution produced several witnesses to refute the contention that McDonald was after the reward.[63]

V

District Attorney Fickert opened the argument of counsel before the jury. Although court reporters usually do not include the attorneys' final arguments in trial transcripts, these arguments were fortunately taken down and incorporated in the Billings trial record. For the other Preparedness Day bomb cases, the newspaper accounts are the only records of the attorneys' final arguments.

Fickert's summary of the prosecution's case was fervent rather than closely reasoned. The anarchist menace, implicit throughout, was sometimes specifically involved. He discussed the purpose of time bombs: the Preparedness Day bomb was "fixed up with a clock, and timed, so that Mr. Mooney could have his picture taken on the Eiler[s] Building by the time it exploded." He said that Ortie McManigal's dynamiting of the Llewellyn Iron Works in Los Angeles showed how infernal-machine bombers could escape from the scene of their crime and establish an alibi. He said that a confederate of Billings had gone to Union Square while Billings was setting the bomb, and had made careful note of the scene so that Billings would have a convincing alibi. Billings "spent probably as much time working his alibi as he and his confederates did in constructing that bomb." He denounced several

---

* *People v. Billings*, II: 607. "On the cushions" was hobo slang meaning to ride as a regular passenger rather than "on the rods."

of the defense witnesses. Al De Caccia was Billings's "double," and the barber was a "wilful perjurer." Dr. Moss was mistaken about the falling cylinder: "what Dr. Moss saw was one of the legs or arms or heads or something else of one of these unfortunate victims." And, in spite of the court's ruling, Fickert referred to Billings's Sacramento record: "I trust, when your verdict is rendered, that you will have the same courage and stability that had the twelve men in Sacramento. He [Billings] never went back there. He comes here, and it is up to you, gentlemen of the jury, whether we shall tolerate this or not."[64]

Fickert opened and closed his appeal with particular stress on the hideousness of the crime and on Billings's cowardliness and lack of patriotism, and with incidental reference to his own courage as District Attorney:

Gentlemen, the case here is by far more serious than any other case that was ever submitted to any jury. It is not a question of this defendant against Mrs. Van Loo; that unhappy woman is at rest; those orphan children must go through life, thinking of the scenes that were enacted there. But here, gentlemen, was the offense: This American flag—this American flag was what they desired to offend. They offended that by killing the women and men that worshipped it. Here is another photograph of Mrs. Van Loo, dying on the streets of our city, and in a feeble hand she holds the American flag, and if that flag is to continue to wave, you men must put an end to such acts as these. So far as I am concerned, no personal consequences are going to swerve me one jot from my sworn duty. What are personal consequences, what are political consequences in a crisis like this? Gentlemen, the very life of the Nation is at stake. No foreign foes were on our land at this time, but some traitor, some murderous villain, who, with his associates, perpetrated this crime, and to disgrace the flag, they took the life of this unfortunate woman.

· · ·

Now, we have here, gentlemen, enough evidence at 721 Market Street— and God only knows, if it had not been for the action of Estelle Smith, and those who saw him there, God only knows, there may have been three or four hundred children of the working class of San Francisco blown into eternity.[65]

· · ·

He [Billings] probably delighted in hearing the cries of these women and children. My God! You have heard it described here, and I have seen it afterwards—women with babes in their arms, their legs shot away, crawling away from the wreck of the cruel shell, and if you could have heard the cries of some of those children, if you could have seen, like I have seen, my friend Lawlor there blown beyond recognition, you could not have thought lightly of it; if you could have heard little Baby Knapp crying for his mother—who was then about to expire—you would not take it as a joking matter, as this defendant has; you could not go upon the stand and grin, like the hyena grinned—I can find no comparison between this defendant and any other animal that breathes, except the hyena—and he is the cowardliest and most disliked of all the animal world.

MR. MCNUTT: I assign that as misconduct, deliberate and wilful, and ask the Court to note the same, and instruct the jury to disregard it.

MR. FICKERT: I have a right to make a comparison to the hyena as to courage. He is an animal of the desert and the night; he loiters around until the feeble victim is too far gone to resist; and then he satisfies his appetite on the dying victim, and of such character is the man that "pulled off" this bomb down here. He did not have the nerve to walk in front of that parade and place it; did not have the courage to walk and place it where the men that walked by had guns [sic], but went down where helpless men and women were, where the gray-haired old veterans were, because he wanted to make his insult to the flag as infamous as he could. It takes a black-minded, cold-blooded individual to do just such an act.*

. . .

Against the defendant I have no personal grievance [Fickert concluded], but as a man who had insulted the Flag, who is a man who has foully murdered men, women and children, it is my duty to see that he is placed where never again he can carry dynamite upon street cars or rob little children of their mothers, and I want you to consider that, gentlemen, consider it well, and place this fiend where never again he can repeat this act; and say to him, and to all of the anarchistic breed, "You cannot get by with that stuff. If you are not satisfied with these United States, go to Mexico, or some other place. We are going to have law and order here." And I want you to do your duty fearlessly, honestly, and conscientiously, [and so] when you leave this jury box and go home to your families, be in the position that you won't have to apologize to any man.†

McNutt objected twice during the course of the District Attorney's argument. Later, before the appellate court, he found many more

* *Ibid.,* Fickert argument, II: 12–13. Judge Dunne did not rule on McNutt's objection at the time. McNutt subsequently commented: "There is no evidence that the defendant at any time during the entire trial made any unseemly exhibit of himself or appeared to take the trial as a joking matter. The district attorney's insulting reference to the defendant was absolutely gratuitous and made for the mere purpose of discrediting and injuring him in the eyes of the jury." (*People v. Billings, Appellant's Brief,* p. 189.)

† *People v. Billings,* Fickert argument, II: 26. See comments of U.S. Supreme Court on malpractices of prosecuting attorneys in *Berger v. U.S.,* 295 U.S. 78 (1935): Justice Sutherland concludes, "improper suggestions, insinuations, and, especially, insertions of personal knowledge are apt to carry much weight against the accused when they should properly carry none."

faults with it, notably the inclusion of Fickert's own comments as an eyewitness.

McNutt's summary followed. He acknowledged that the trial, no thanks to the prosecution, had been "a fair and noble one."[66] He criticized the prosecution's injection of flag, government, Constitution, and patriotism into the case. But his argument was noteworthy primarily for his frank charge that a frame-up had been engineered by Martin Swanson. The history of Swanson's contacts with the defendants had scarcely been mentioned during the trial. It was no more admissible as evidence than the "conspiracy" evidence against Billings and Mooney. The defense did not even try to introduce it. But Swanson's participation in the arrests had been acknowledged by several prosecution witnesses, and also his reward offer to Billings. Said Mc-Nutt:

> This historic case was spawned in the brain of a private detective named Martin Swanson, and hatched in the super-heated per-fervid imaginations of the Smiths, the Kidwells, the Moores and the McDonalds, and fostered and brought into being and reared by the Fickerts, the Brennans, and the Traffic Squad—God save the mark!
> ... Every bit of evidence, with the exception of those four men that were on the roof of the Eiler's Building, every bit of evidence that has been produced before this jury, had been volunteered at some time or another to the Prosecution, and had been put in the ash-can. Why? Because it did not fit the "dream" of McDonald.[67]

McNutt ridiculed the interpretation that Mooney had had the Eilers Building pictures taken of him for his alibi:

> Now, where did we get the pictures of the Eiler[s] Building? Did we get them from the photographer who took them? No, he conceived it his Christian duty, and he lives at the Young Men's Christian Association—to refuse us even an interview, as to when, where or how he took these pictures, but the pictures, films and all were turned over to the Police Department, and not until the conclusion of the state's case did we have the permission so much as to look at them.[68]

He attacked the Bomb Bureau and the "more or less one thousand police officers that have been given free rein by the government"; they failed to find a single witness of their own searching, he pointed out, but they took witnesses who came to them and used or dismissed each one as he fitted their preconceived case. And he commented on Fickert's disclaimer of political considerations: "He starts out by saying that you are to try this case fairly, without fear and without favor . . . and without regard to political consequences to him. Who had mentioned any political consequences to him? . . . We know of no political consequences. We are not concerned with them."[69] So far McNutt had debated well. But thereafter, in his review and evaluation of the evidence, he rambled. His argument was neither precise nor moving.

The prosecution's rebuttal was made by Brennan. To the frame-up charge he replied, "That is always the policy of a man on trial, . . . to holler 'frame-up'; it is the old, old story; . . . it is the last card of a tripped man, and they always do it." Understandably, he made much of Billings's consciousness of guilt as shown by the changes in Billings's alibi. As for the Eilers Building photographs, Mooney had plenty of time to get back to 975 Market Street for his pictures; a jitney could easily go thirty miles an hour, and could get from 721 Market Street to Steuart Street in two minutes. (The refutation of this argument had to await Mooney's trial.) In response to the defense effort to impeach McDonald's testimony, Brennan minimized its importance: "An identification of Billings by McDonald, standing alone, I would not give a snap for it, not one snap of my finger for it, if it stood alone, but when you connect it up and weave it along with the others . . . then you get a substantial grip upon Billings."[70]

The issue of the case, as it closed, rested squarely upon conflicting testimonies. The *Bulletin* reporter commented that the case might go either way or end with a hung jury, depending on whose word the jurymen believed. Both the prosecution and the defense claimed confidence in the outcome.[71] But the prosecution was less confident of a conviction than it claimed. When Brennan closed his rebuttal, he unexpectedly intimated that in the event of a conviction the prosecution might not ask for the death sentence. Billings, he said, was in with the wrong gang and should be set right: "Gentlemen, this young man, I am sure, is a mere puppet; this young man is the one man who can clear up this story, . . . and I believe, you gentlemen . . . will render such a verdict as will enable us to see that this young man sees that the right thing is done, and enables us to do the right thing in this case."[72] He explained afterward that he believed Billings would turn State's evidence and tell what he knew if convicted. Observers commented that jurors who would vote for acquittal if Billings were likely to hang might now vote to convict him. The *Bulletin* speculated that Brennan had added materially to the chances of a conviction.[73]

According to the later testimony of Edgar T. Gleeson, Brennan told Gleeson in 1920 that during the trial he had had a violent row with Fickert over his refusal to ask the death penalty, and that at one point Fickert had threatened to throw him out of a fourth-story window in the Hall of Justice; but that Brennan saw discrepancies in the evidence, and felt enough doubt to have voted for an acquittal had he been on the jury.[74]

The jury withdrew, following a routine charge from Dunne. In the courtroom Brennan was sure that his final appeal had impressed the jury. He declared confidence in a conviction and a penalty of life imprisonment. But in the corridors of the Hall of Justice bets against a conviction went without a single taker, and "the wiseacres who claimed to have received an underground tip" declared that the jury was hopelessly hung.[75]

The jury took three ballots, found Billings guilty, and went to lunch. A restaurant workers' strike was on. Selig Schulberg handed the sheriff a list of "fair" restaurants, but the jurors were taken to a picketed cafeteria. An hour and three-quarters later they came back and agreed to fix Billings's punishment at life imprisonment. They returned to the courtroom, four hours after leaving, and announced their decision.

The courtroom was stunned. Dunne discharged the jury, set the date for sentencing, and left the room. No one else moved. The jurors sat in silence. After a while the police began to move the spectators toward the door. Then Billings was led back to jail.[76]

VI

It was said that all of the jurors were "thoroughly convinced" of Billings's guilt. If so, it is surprising that none of them insisted that he die. Billings had presumably committed one of the most heinous crimes in the memory of San Franciscans, and there was nothing in his record to recommend mercy. Yet the jurors did not even take a formal ballot on the sentence, but agreed orally on the lesser penalty.[77] Billings himself was quick to make this point:

> If I am guilty of the murder of ten innocent men and women [he said], the jury should have brought in no compromise verdict....
> It should have voted unanimously to impose the death penalty. The people are saying, "If Billings really placed that bomb, if the jury had no reasonable doubt as to his guilt, then hanging is too good for him." That's what I should say myself.[78]

Fickert showed no surprise at the verdict: "I can only say that many men do not believe in the death penalty. In such a case as this, I do believe in it. But the jurors, while believing Billings guilty, evidently did not believe in hanging. The McNamaras, you will remember, got a verdict of second-degree murder."[79] He doubted that he would try to induce Billings to confess and expose the higher-ups: "Billings is a smart fellow and I question whether an attempt to get a confession from him would be worth the effort. Besides that, our cases against the others are all complete and we don't need his testimony. We shall go ahead just as we have planned, regardless of what Billings may or may not do."[80] Thus did the District Attorney brush aside his assistant's final appeal to the jury.

An appeal to Judge Dunne for a retrial was made by McNutt and was turned down. On October 7, 1916, Warren Billings was sentenced to life imprisonment.

CHAPTER NINE

The Early Defense Movement

Just a few friends, that is all there are here.
—Ed McKenzie

Men who have friends get justice.
—Robert Minor

IN THE COURSE of its 23 years the Mooney case developed simultaneously along two fronts, law and publicity. Each affected the other. Without publicity there would have been neither funds nor political pressure; without legal defense there would have been nothing to publicize but the gallows and class strife. The relationship between law and publicity was not always close, and at times the two interests even seemed opposed. The publicists sometimes exasperated the defense attorneys by speaking up inopportunely. Yet the legal proceedings were but one-half—the more professional half—of the Mooney case. The other half was essential, too. The present chapter is concerned with the origins and development of the extra-legal defense from August 1916 to January 1917, the five months between the arrests and Mooney's trial.

Credit for establishing the Mooney defense movement has been claimed for various leaders of sympathetic groups. Anarchists and their admirers have assigned the credit to Alexander Berkman and Emma Goldman; Communists, to Robert Minor; some Irish-Americans, to Bourke Cockran; some liberals, to Fremont Older; some trade unionists and their supporters, to Samuel Gompers or to the Chicago Federation of Labor and its secretary, Edward Nockels.[1] The claims for all these persons have merit, with the reservation that Nockels, Older, and Gompers arrived later than Berkman, Emma Goldman, Minor, McNutt, and Cockran. Without the help of all of them and others as well, Mooney and Billings probably would have gone the way of Parsons and Spies, of Sacco and Vanzetti.

Beginning with the first news of the arrests, the question was argued whether the Preparedness Day bomb case was a labor case. The California labor movement itself was split in 1916 on this question; radicals took the affirmative and others the negative. The question was never entirely settled, but in time the labor movement generally accepted Mooney's cause as its own. In contrast, non-labor conservative opponents of Mooney rarely considered his case a labor case. Following Fickert's example, conservative and reactionary editors and pamphleteers for 23 years portrayed Mooney as a radical, often without even mentioning that he was also a labor unionist. In the labor movement some of Mooney's most sincere supporters, including Paul Scharrenberg of the California State Federation of Labor, conceded that his trade-union career was less significant than his friends claimed: Mooney was not a labor leader. But the trade unions made more of Mooney's radicalism before his trial than afterward, when the prosecution's malfeasance became public knowledge. The turning point was the exposé in April 1917 of the star witness in Mooney's trial, Frank C. Oxman. From that point on, the manifest injustice of Mooney's conviction overshadowed his radical record, in the judgment of organized labor.

II

When Mooney was arrested and indicted, the only people in San Francisco who stood up for him were the anarchists. Alexander Berkman, Emma Goldman, and a small group of their friends—loosely speaking, the "Blasters"—publicized the case from the outset. Other radicals either were too frightened to speak, or openly disavowed Mooney. George Speed told reporters that Mooney was not an IWW.[2] Staunch left-wing Progressives and labor reformers like Fremont Older and Andrew Furuseth knew from experience that the District Attorney was unscrupulous, but they had neither the evidence nor the faith in Mooney to declare that Fickert was framing him. The anarchists, for their part, required less evidence; their protests were based not so much on proof as on certitude. The indications of a rigged prosecution were still quite limited—the participation of Swanson, the lawless arrests, the smear campaign—but the proof of Mooney's innocence could wait. Succor could not. In spirit and action, Mooney had been with the anarchists for the revolution; they believed him incapable of such a pointless and abhorrent deed as the Preparedness Day bombing.

The "bosses of San Francisco," said the "Blasters," hated Mooney, and his persecution would follow the axioms of class warfare. If labor were not aroused to defend him, the Haymarket hangings would be repeated: "The enemy is athirst for blood: it is planning to transplant to San Francisco the gallows of 1887 when five of Labor's best and truest friends were strangled to death in Chicago. We feel that the workers of America will not permit a repetition of that five-fold judicial murder."[*]

Within a few days of the grand jury indictments, the "Blasters" sent a call for help to a fellow anarchist and friend of Berkman's then in Los Angeles, Robert Minor.[3] Minor was an accomplished cartoonist who had worked for several newspapers, including the St. Louis *Post-Dispatch* and the New York *Evening World*. He had joined the Socialist Party in 1907, taking his stand with the radical wing as an admirer of William D. Haywood; later, studying art in Paris, he "absorbed the anarcho-syndicalist philosophy that flourished in the studios and garrets of Montparnasse and Montmartre."[4] He drew cartoons for Max Eastman's iconoclastic *Masses,* and developed techniques of bold charcoal sketching that dramatized his radical messages. Minor had been to Europe as a war correspondent for the Scripps syndicate and the New York Socialist *Call,* and to the Mexican border to report the war skirmishes of the United States Army's expedition. When the border excitement dwindled he went to Los Angeles; he was there visiting Upton Sinclair when the call from the "Blasters" came. He left for San Francisco at once.[5]

On his arrival he went to the apartment of Mary Eleanor Fitzgerald, the red-headed associate editor of the *Blast,* whose place on Dolores Street in the Mission District served as the paper's headquarters. There he laid plans with the "Blasters" and Emma Goldman. Together with Schulberg, Milder, and other left-wing associates of Mooney's in earlier labor causes, the anarchists revived the IWDL, which had been inactive the previous year.[6] Minor became its secretary-treasurer.

The leadership in the radicals' publicity campaign for Mooney lay with Berkman and Minor, the former through his contacts with eastern radicals, and the latter through his organizing, pamphleteering, and local public speaking. In time, field representatives of the IWDL

[*] "Planning Another 11th of November," *Blast,* August 15, 1916. Of the Haymarket anarchists, four were hanged and one committed suicide; three others were pardoned in 1893 by the Governor of Illinois, John Peter Altgeld.

toured the country for the Mooney defense. The two major aims were propaganda and money—an aroused populace and a treasury supplied with the funds necessary for this work and for an effective legal defense. Berkman carried on his work until the spring of 1917, when American military conscription turned his criticism to another cause and the intervention of federal authorities landed him in the Atlanta Penitentiary. Minor carried on considerably longer, until early 1918, when he left the Mooney defense for an extended trip to Russia to observe the Bolshevik Revolution.[7]

Minor was without peer as publicist for the Mooney defense. He addressed mass meetings, attended the trials, and wrote regular news releases for the labor and radical weeklies of the nation. In speeches and writings his stand was aggressive and his plea for labor assistance urgent. Labor power, not legal argument, would free the defendants. At one of the first rallies he said: "Only great mobilized strength gets justice. If the sixty thousand union members of San Francisco had simply done the part of friends and gone down to visit the men on the morning after the arrest—a perfectly legal act—the men would have been freed in twenty minutes. Simply a peaceful visit. Men who have friends get justice."[8] For the IWDL and a parallel defense organization, the Tom Mooney Molders Defense Committee, he turned out pamphlets which they distributed by the hundreds of thousands. The first was published in December as "The Frame-up System." In it he reviewed the defendants' fights in labor's cause, condemned Swanson, and called the United Railroads "the cruelest beast in the jungle of unorganized labor."[9] He exposed as much about the prosecution's techniques as the defense then knew.[10] "The Frame-up System" was frequently revised during the following year to keep abreast of developments in the case. By the time the seventh edition appeared, in the fall of 1917, over 800,000 copies under various titles had been circulated.[11]

Like the San Francisco anarchists, the militant Socialists of Alameda County were stirred from the outset by the arrests. The radical weeklies in Oakland, the Socialist *World* and the Alameda County Labor Council's *Tri-City Labor Review,* took up the cause as quickly as the *Blast.* Even prior to the grand jury hearing, the *World* was blaming the Preparedness Day bombing on the munitions makers, militarists, exploiting merchants and manufacturers, corrupt politicians, land grabbers, Otis, and Hearst. The bomb, it asserted, had been set off by agents of capitalism paid to discredit the working people. When the indictments were returned, the *World* charged that the grand jury had acted on insufficient evidence at the District Attorney's request, and had indicted the accused because they were working people. The available evidence showed only that the public utilities wanted to get Mooney and Billings.[12]

Margaret Anderson, the publisher of an *avant-garde* literary monthly, the *Little Review,* happened to have brought her magazine to San Francisco shortly before Preparedness Day. She was a close friend of Emma Goldman's and put her columns at Minor's service that August. So Miss Anderson's subscribers (she had about 2,000, mainly in Chicago and New York), who generally picked up her magazine to read the poetry of Carl Sandburg, Edgar Lee Masters, and Ezra Pound, learned about the plight and class cause of the San Francisco defendants, whom "Dirty Hearst tried to lynch," long before eastern newspapers and national magazines carried reports on the case.[13]

Several weeks of strenuous effort were necessary to organize a defense movement among the radicals of the Bay Area. The "Blasters," assisted by foreign-language anarchist groups, distributed thousands of leaflets and beseeched friends for help.[14] The IWDL, once reorganized, grew rapidly. Only seven unions sent delegates to its first meeting in late August, but by December 1 the number rose to 38.[15] Funds were critically short. Few Bay Area unions considered the Mooney-Billings defense a deserving cause; only those with strong radical membership and IWDL connections lent support. Ed Nolan's local donated $1,000 to the IWDL in September, but no other union was so generous. Mooney's local sat tight.[16]

On the eve of Billings's trial, Minor arranged the city's first mass meeting to protest the frame-up of the Preparedness Day defendants. His advance publicity was spurned by the daily press; he lacked funds for advertising; prominent figures whom he asked to speak refused their support. Yet the meeting was held in one of the largest auditoriums in the city, the Dreamland Rink, and the house was three-quarters filled. The gathering was held under the auspices of the IWDL. Hugo Ernst, the Socialist president of the San Francisco waiters' union, presided. The speakers were William A. Spooner, secretary-treasurer of the Alameda County (Oakland) Central Labor Council, to which he was a delegate from the left-wing Cooks and Waiters Union (Local 31); Sara Bard Field, pacifist and suffragist, who had spoken at the Dreamland Rink meeting of July 20; and Robert Minor. All three assailed the authorities for the way they were handling the case. Spooner read from the grand jury transcript to show that Mooney had been denied counsel in jail.[17]

The audience was exhorted to contribute to the defense funds; $168 was collected. The modesty of this sum was pointed up by the contribution of $500 from a New York friend of Berkman's, Mrs. J. Sergeant Cram. Mrs. Cram was a social worker, a sympathizer of labor causes in the New York garment industry, and a friend of Pennsylvania's radical Progressive, Amos Pinchot. Her husband, a Tammany leader and former public service commissioner, was the wealthy scion of a long-established New York merchant family. She was the first of several women of wealth and secure social standing who were to contribute heavily to the Mooney defense.*

A telegram of support from Frank P. Walsh was read at the meeting. Walsh had been chairman of the Federal Commission on Industrial Relations, which he had guided through its two-year study of American labor conditions. He was a prominent lawyer, as well as a friend of radicals and an advocate of economic reforms more sweeping than most of his fellow Wilsonian Democrats would support.[18] Among radicals he was probably the most widely respected politician in the the country. Minor had sought his help as counsel in August. Because of the pressing need for competent legal assistance, McNutt had already been engaged, but the IWDL wanted Walsh. Like Clarence Darrow, he understood the social and economic aspects of labor cases. He had an enviable record as a defense attorney in murder cases, having saved at least eighteen men from the gallows.[19] He knew Mooney, admired Minor, and wanted to help, but after two years of absence from his legal practice in the service of the government, depleted finances and the press of neglected duties in Kansas City prevented him from taking the case. The IWDL, of course, could not have made him a remunerative offer, and did not attempt to. By then it had raised a total of perhaps $3,000, largely borrowed. Walsh promised a contribution of $250.[20] Years later, when Billings and Mooney were in prison, he was to become Mooney's chief counsel.

At the Dreamland Rink meeting, Minor excoriated Fickert and

* *Bulletin*, September 11, 1916; New York *Times*, July 24 and October 30, 1915, November 10, 1916, and January 19, 1936. Four other such women were Agnes Inglis of Detroit, Kate Crane Gartz of Pasadena, Alice Stone Blackwell of Boston, and Aline Barnsdall of Los Angeles.

accused him of planning judicial murder: "I want Mr. Fickert's servants here tonight to repeat this to him: a man can be murdered as easily and more safely with a legal rope than with a bomb. And, Mr. Fickert, whether it be dishonesty or whether it be stupidity, try to understand that these men are not to be and cannot be lynched."[21] Fickert had received the announcement of the Dreamland Rink meeting quietly: he did not intend to be carried away by side issues, he said, and if anyone had any evidence to show that the people under indictment were not guilty, the place to present it was in court.[22] Minor's speech, however, he interpreted as a personal threat, and he retaliated (as noted earlier) by trying to prevent the anarchist from covering Billings's trial.

Some time after the Dreamland Rink meeting, the District Attorney called on Sara Bard Field at her home. He came to ask why she was so sympathetic toward the defendants. She explained that she was concerned for their civil rights. He was not satisfied, and after he left he remained suspicious of her motives. She learned later from a friend who worked for the telephone company that her phone was being tapped by the prosecution.[23]

III

Compared to the anarchists and Socialists, other left-wing groups were slow to join the defense movement. The IWW did far less than the anarchists to publicize Mooney's plight, though Mooney's views were as close to theirs as to the anarchists'. To be sure, the IWW was preoccupied with defending its own members. About the time of the Preparedness Day bombing, several IWW's were arrested during an iron ore field strike in northern Minnesota on a false charge of murder; and in November nearly three hundred IWW's were arrested after a grim gunfight between a sheriff's posse and a boatload of Wobblies at Everett, Washington. One of them, Tom Tracy, was brought to trial for murder four months later.[24] Yet Mooney and Billings were not forgotten. George Speed condemned the prosecution in *Solidarity*; Elizabeth Gurley Flynn came to San Francisco after Mooney's conviction to observe and agitate; Ralph Chaplin denounced the San Francisco capitalists from Chicago IWW soapboxes.[25] One Wobbly wrote from San Francisco about Mooney and Billings: "While they are not members of our union, nevertheless they are fighters from the word go, and have always helped us in the past, and will certainly be needed in the future, in this greatest of all wars, the class war."[26]

The lack of American radical unity, which Mooney had deplored, was demonstrated in his own case by the attitude of the Socialist Labor Party. This "pure" Marxist splinter element of the revolutionary movement was oblivious to the Mooney case. The party was very small, though probably no smaller than the anarchist movement. Its weekly journal said nothing about Mooney for eight or nine months after the arrests. The party had a San Francisco local and a San Francisco correspondent, but the first news it published about the case was a reprint from the New York *Tribune*. To the anarchists and the IWDL, the apathy of the Socialist Labor Party in this "practical" labor cause was exasperating.[27]

IV

The mainstream of the San Francisco labor movement refused for months to help the Mooney defense. The conservative trade unionists held that Mooney was a radical, that he may well have been guilty, and that in any event it was not for them to accuse Fickert of planning to frame him. Their first concern was to dissociate the defendants from the labor movement. They did not want another black eye like the one the movement had suffered from the McNamara confessions after the Los Angeles *Times* bombing. A few days after the arrests three conservative labor leaders, Andrew J. Gallagher, Arthur Brouillet, and Michael Casey—all Union Labor Party politicians who had supported Fickert—called on the District Attorney and warned him that the Mooney case was not a labor issue. They did not want Fickert laying the case at the door of labor, they said. Fickert replied that he had no intention of doing so.[28] He kept his word: to him Mooney made sense only as an anarchist.

The attitude of the California State Federation of Labor toward the Mooney case was manifested at its annual convention at Eureka in early October. Paul Scharrenberg, the federation's secretary and the strongest leader in the state labor movement, ignored the case in his annual report. He might have listed the bomb prosecution along with the fight against the longshoremen's strike and the activities of the Law and Order Committee as aspects of the same campaign. But he did not believe that the Mooney case was germane to labor's cause. IWW's and anarchists were sincere, he said, but they did not care who they injured.[29] Left-wing delegates introduced the bomb cases. Two resolutions were submitted by a delegate from Ed Nolan's local. The first declared that the defendants were trade unionists who were being persecuted for their "constant activity in labor's cause." It condemned Martin Swanson, and called for an official fund-raising campaign. The second condemned San Francisco corporations for striving to convict Billings and "crush labor," and criticized the San Francisco jury system.[30] The proposals went to the resolutions committee, which was controlled by conservative Bay Area delegates. The committee affirmed the innocence of Mooney and Billings on the basis of the trial evidence, but denied that the labor movement was involved:

> As to the claims made that there exists a giant conspiracy against labor and that the men on trial are victims [it reported] . . . we submit that no one at this time is attempting to connect labor with the bomb outrage, and although statements were made in San Francisco immediately following the crime that the outrage "was the culmination of a series of crimes by organized labor," so well was our position defined and our policies defended and explained that attacks on us along that line have ceased.[31]

The committee substituted a resolution simply protesting the injustice of the verdict and the way juries were chosen.[32]

A spirited debate ensued. A representative from the IWDL, John H. Beckmeyer, who was also a union machinist from Ed Nolan's local, was permitted to address the convention on behalf of the stronger resolutions.[33] Hugo Ernst and a machinists' union delegate also defended them. On the other side Scharrenberg assailed the IWDL, blaming it for the continued imprisonment of Ford and Suhr. Michael Casey called the IWDL defense-fund solicitors "professional panhandlers."[34] The radicals were badly outnumbered and their resolutions were overwhelmingly defeated in a roll-call vote. The tiny minority consisted of Ernst, five machinists—two of them from Nolan's local— and three Oakland streetcar union delegates, who were probably resentful of the San Francisco movement's indifference toward organizing the URR. A lone delegate from Los Angeles voted with the minority. Only these ten men took an uncompromising stand on the Mooney case as a labor cause.[35] Not one was from Mooney's union.

The convention formally demanded fair trials but refused to endorse the IWDL: the state labor movement would try to assure justice, but insisted that it could "by no stretch of the imagination . . . be held in any way responsible for the conduct of the defendants."[36] The San Francisco Labor Council, whose unions dominated the state federation, took the same view. The *Labor Clarion* stated that Billings had "taken no active part in the bona fide labor movement," and that his conviction could not hurt the movement in the slightest degree. The journal also denounced the IWDL for its "campaign of lies."[37]

Confusion followed. Radicals, however disappointed, claimed that the state labor movement had joined the protest against the frame-up; conservatives claimed that it had rejected "the cause of our crew of dynamiters."[38] Frederick Ely tried to clarify the situation in a *Bulletin* article, but as long as Scharrenberg and the federation were defensive about the case, clarity was difficult. Eventually, when the California trade union leaders discovered they cared less about the past conduct of the defendants than the present conduct of the prosecution, a more vigorous stand resulted.[39]

V

Berkman, like Minor, had little faith that justice for labor could be won in the courts. He looked instead to agitation. As he had explained to Anton Johannsen in connection with the Caplan and Schmidt cases, all his experience had convinced him that in labor cases the chief objective should be to create favorable public sentiment.[40] Shortly after Billings's conviction he left San Francisco for New York on behalf of the IWDL.[41]

In the industrial cities of the East and Midwest, particularly in New York and Chicago, there were sizable left-wing labor groups that could be counted on to respond to a vigorous appeal for aid. The most important of these were the Socialist colonies of immigrant Jews from Germany and Russia, the garment workers who lived in the tenements of Manhattan and had linked their local unions in a city-wide federation, the United Hebrew Trades. It was to the UHT that Berkman turned for help. Founded in 1888 by Morris Hillquit and his Jewish colleagues in the Socialist Labor Party, the UHT had grown rapidly. It represented unions with a total membership of over 200,000. A few members were anarchists, but most were non-Zionist Socialists, who had helped send Meyer London to Washington in 1914 as the country's second Socialist Congressman. Until 1915 the UHT was affiliated with the AFL, but this connection was severed when the two organizations clashed over the recently formed, radically oriented Amalgamated Clothing Workers of America, an industrial union led by Sidney Hillman. To the AFL the new union was an interloper, a rival to the established and "legitimate" but weaker United Garment Workers of America. The garment-trades unions affiliated with the UHT had strong ties with the international Socialist and anti-war movements. It was in these unions that Berkman sought help for Mooney.[42]

Early in November Berkman arrived in New York. The radicals there knew little about the San Francisco situation. He addressed a UHT meeting on the open shop fight in San Francisco, the labor activities of the defendants, and the persecution of Mooney and Billings. The UHT delegates discussed his plea and voted to help. The officers then called a "national" conference of all Jewish labor and radical organizations to meet November 26 in the *Jewish Daily Forward* Hall on East Broadway. More than eighty unions and workers' societies, undoubtedly most of them in New York City, sent delegates.[43] A street demonstration was organized for the following weekend in Union Square, the city's major gathering place for radical demonstrations, not far from the garment district. The rally was held to protest the imprisonment of both the San Francisco defendants and the IWW defendants in Minnesota.[44]

By mid-November there had been organized, probably at Berkman's behest, a New York publicity committee of the San Francisco IWDL, which consisted mainly of friends of Emma Goldman and the left-wing intellectuals associated with Max Eastman's *Masses*.[45] This committee, in cooperation with the UHT, held a mass meeting at Carnegie Hall on December 2. Eastman presided. The speakers were Emma Goldman, who had returned two or three months earlier from San Francisco; Arturo Giovannitti, IWW leader of the 1912 strike in Lawrence, Massachusetts; Pat Quinlan, another IWW, just released from prison; Max Pine, secretary of the UHT; and Berkman.[46] At the box office equality bowed to the need for money: those who could pay, paid; those who could not sat in the balcony; boxes sold for $10. A thousand dollars, an exceptionally large amount for a labor defense collection, was raised that evening.[47]

Berkman's visit to New York had a second purpose. The IWDL, having failed again to obtain Frank Walsh, hoped to secure another prominent Irish attorney, Bourke Cockran, to defend Mooney. Cockran had already started publicity for Mooney in the New York *Irish World* before Billings's conviction. In October the IWDL appealed to Cockran for help. Berkman followed this up when he arrived. He did not visit Cockran personally, but appealed to him through local friends Mrs. J. Sergeant Cram and Mrs. John Sloan, the wife of a New York artist and an associate of Eastman's. Cockran read a copy of the Billings trial transcript and concluded from it that the State's evidence would not have justified a conviction even if it had remained wholly uncontradicted. He agreed to serve as Mooney's chief attorney without compensation. The IWDL would need funds to pay only his travel and living expenses.[48]

Cockran was an accomplished politician, a conservative, maverick Democrat. Born in County Sligo, educated in France, he came to New York in 1871, entered the law, and made a comfortable living. He often quarreled with Tammany's leaders and was critical of boss rule, but his popularity as an Irish orator and as a devout lay defender of Roman Catholicism helped maintain his political independence in the House of Representatives during the 1890's. He bolted for Mc-Kinley and the gold standard in 1896, but supported Bryan and anti-imperialism four years later. As Tammany's chief orator he campaigned against Hearst for New York's mayoralty in 1905, then about-faced with Tammany and supported Hearst for the governorship in 1906. He was reelected to Congress in this maneuver, although it was the last time for fourteen years that he took any active part in election campaigns for the Democratic Party. In 1912 he campaigned for Roosevelt and the Progressive Party. After Roosevelt's defeat he left politics, and for the rest of the decade was occupied largely with the law and non-political oratory.[49]

Cockran was not a veteran criminal lawyer. He had not the experience of Frank Walsh, nor the brilliance of Clarence Darrow or of Earl Rogers of Los Angeles. (Rogers had twice declined requests to take the Preparedness Day case.)[50] Yet Cockran was an unquestioned spellbinder. Some San Franciscans might look superciliously upon the importing of a fancy attorney from New York for Mooney's defense, but the defendants were overjoyed. Maxwell McNutt, too, was pleased; he had known Cockran for years.[51]

As Mooney's counsel Cockran was invited to speak at Carnegie Hall on December 2. As Mooney's counsel he declined. He countenanced the meeting as a necessary means of raising funds, but privately hoped that nothing would be said there that might be construed, even by the most prejudiced, as an attempt to influence the impending judicial proceeding in San Francisco.[52]

From the San Francisco county jail Ed Nolan warned Cockran that the prosecution would probably stress anarchism at Mooney's trial. He wrote that the defendants were to be tried "for ideas rather than acts, in short for heresy." He urged Cockran to deal with the social theories that the prosecution would raise to imply guilt: "Undoubtedly the air will be surcharged with such words as Anarchy, the Blast, Dynamiters, etc. and little else as regards real cohesive facts." He hoped that Cockran would not be discouraged by the coolness of the labor movement toward the cases: "It has been my experience that many union men and persons of little education . . . are more intolerant and dogmatic when they hear new ideas expounded than men who are well read and often on the other side."[53]

When Cockran took the Mooney case, the date for the trial had been set for late November. To accommodate him, and to avoid the possibility of having to lock up the jury over the Christmas holidays, Judge Franklin A. Griffin postponed the trial to January 3. Late in December Cockran was on his way to the West Coast.[54] The chief hopes of the defense movement went with him.

CHAPTER TEN

Jury Duty in San Francisco

Twelve men are drawn, usually from the more doltish element of the community....
—H. H. Bancroft, 1917

ONE OF the persistent problems in the bomb trials was the jury system. The caliber of the men who served as jurors and the mode of their selection raised recurrent doubts, particularly in the two months before Mooney's trial. Subsequently critics were preoccupied with more spectacular causes of injustice, but the administration of justice continued to be hampered by the jury system. It is appropriate to consider here, between accounts of the first two trials, the nature of these weaknesses.

The system of jury selection in San Francisco at the time of Billings's trial was not a satisfactory one. No method of choosing jurors is perfect, but some are worse than others. Statutory law in California allows the local courts considerable latitude in the selection process. The laws are few. A juror must be "in possession of his natural faculties and of ordinary intelligence and not decrepit."[1] Until 1915, no Californian was qualified to serve as a juror unless he had been assessed taxes, according to the last assessment roll of his county, on property belonging to him.[2] Until July 28, 1917, no woman in California could serve on a jury.[3] A 1905 law barred from jury duty everyone who had been discharged as a juror within a year.[4] Certain categories of citizens, including public officials, lawyers, ministers, teachers, doctors, sailors, telegraph operators, and railroad trainmen were exempted, although not excluded, from jury duty.[5]

There were no statutory requirements relating to class representation or cross sections of the local population. In recent years the

United States Supreme Court has emphasized the legal tradition that juries are representative cross sections of the community;[6] but in 1914 there was far less concern for this tradition than there has been in recent years. At best the principle is a difficult one to administer. In San Francisco, when Billings and Mooney were tried, it carried little weight.[7]

Apart from the statutory restrictions and certain procedural requirements, the local courts were generally left alone in the selection of jurors. The courts drew up the venire lists by whatever method the judges deemed suitable. The great register of voters was the most comprehensive source of names; at the other extreme—not in San Francisco, but in small counties—judges made lists of personal acquaintances. The use of assessment rolls was probably still common in 1916. The venire lists might and did diverge from approximate community representation, but attorneys could not challenge the panel on any grounds whatever. They could only challenge individual jurors.[8]

The Superior Courts of San Francisco, and particularly Judge Dunne's court, had for years filled jury lists with retired men who were willing to serve over and over again. They were known as "professional jurors." Retired shopkeepers and small businessmen, many of them seventy or eighty years old, these men had enough property to pay taxes and thereby (before 1915) to qualify for jury duty. For those who lacked sufficient property to make ends meet, jury duty was a way to eke out their income; jurors earned two dollars a day.[9] Whatever their financial circumstances, jury duty was work old men could do, after a fashion, and they relished it as a means of passing the time. They kept at it year after year—as long as the Superior Court judge was willing to keep their names on the venire list from which the court clerk selected potential jurors, and as long as practicing attorneys were willing to have them. They were a convenience for the court because they were willing to serve, and they were a convenience for the attorneys on both sides, who came to know them individually, because they reduced the need for preliminary courtroom examinations and the investigation of prospective jurors.[10] At Billings's trial observers noted that Maxwell McNutt appeared to know the veniremen. Since he knew three of them from one previous trial—that of Billings in 1913—and since he had been practicing in San Francisco for years, he probably knew most of the jurors well. The same may be said for the prosecution.

The professional jury system may have constituted a form of political-judicial patronage. Since the Superior Court judges were popularly elected, it was expedient for them to draw up their venire lists so as to provide jobs for voters who wanted to serve, and to keep off the juries voters who did not want to be inconvenienced. Judge Dunne by 1916 had been on the Superior Court bench eighteen years and had survived four elections. He probably made the most of his patronage opportunities.[11]

Some of the professional jurors served with remarkable frequency. After Billings's conviction the defense made a careful study and found that some of them had been serving regularly since 1906, which was as far back as the records went, and had earned as much as $600 or $700 in two years[12]—had served, that is, more than half the days courts were in session during that period. One juror in San Francisco had sat on 500 juries since the great earthquake.[13]

The legality of professional jury service was uncertain. According to the law of 1905 noted above, a person was not competent to serve on a jury if he had been discharged as a juror within a year, but qualifications in the wording of the law made it unclear whether such persons were barred if they did not claim exemption. Since professional jurors naturally did not claim exemption, they were perhaps not ineligible. By 1916 there was only one authoritative statement on the matter, in a State Supreme Court decision written by Justice Frederick W. Henshaw. This statement went against professional jurors, but it was an *obiter dictum,* not a ruling.[14] It went unheeded in Dunne's court.[15]

Certain practical defects inhered in the professional jury system. The professional jurors were not senile, but they were sometimes unable to keep up with the proceedings. One story was told of an old pioneer serving on an Oakland jury in 1914 who stepped out of the courtroom during a recess to refresh himself with a draught of beer. Returning by mistake to the wrong trial, he took his place in the wrong jury box, and no one was the wiser until the judge in the other room started an investigation for the missing juror.[16] In Mooney's trial a newspaper took one of the jurors to task for sleeping during the proceedings.[17] And in Rena Mooney's trial a 79-year-old juror had to be dismissed for incompetence.[18] There was some merit in the view that a man who was too old to manage his own business was too old for the responsibilities of jury duty.

Venality among professional jurors was common. Since the juries were dismissed as soon as they rendered their verdicts, the old men had a way of delaying their decision until after the noon hour so that they could have lunch at the state's expense. When they attempted this stratagem in 1913 at Billings's trial for assault, Judge Dunne, who knew what they were up to, countered by dismissing both the jurors and the case, the verdict by that time being obvious. But when they went to lunch at Billings's trial for murder, no such expedient was available.

More serious than the cadging of free lunches and the limitations of advanced age was the dependence of professional jurors on their income. Those who needed their jobs were sensitive to their records of convictions and acquittals. "Soft" jurors would be excluded by the District Attorney, either illegally, behind the scenes—tampering with jury lists was not unknown in San Francisco at the time[19]—or before the court by peremptory challenge. Of course, jurors who acquired the reputation of being "convicting" jurors were apt to be dismissed by defense attorneys, but it was better to err on the side of the District Attorney, especially in important cases, for the District Attorney was represented at every criminal trial.

It might reasonably be supposed that a jury of aged shopkeepers with a vested interest in their court positions would not be the citizens best equipped to pass judgment on the guilt or innocence of an alleged anarchist murderer against whom there was marked public prejudice. However, professional jurors were tolerated in San Francisco, partly because no one seems to have organized a determined protest until after Billings's conviction, but primarily because other citizens were not willing to serve. As Bourke Cockran wrote after Mooney's trial, "while competent men will sometimes serve as jurors through a sense of civic duty, no man who is fit to be a juror ever wanted to serve."[20] The problem is perennial. It contributed to the malfunctioning of the San Francisco courts in the 1850's, when conditions were so bad that the Vigilante Committee seemed the only way out.[21] Nearly a century later at the other end of the continent, Judge Harold Medina, presiding over the trial of eleven American Communist leaders in 1949, found that from a panel of about three hundred jurors, every single businessman and all other persons in positions of responsibility asked to be excused.[22] In recent years the courts of San Francisco have had to enroll eight to ten times as many veniremen as actually serve; the largest group seeking excuse from jury service, according to a 1952 survey, were the daily wage earners.[23] The easiest solution to this problem, and one that courts have to fall back on, is

the empanelling of persons who are willing to serve. If they fall back
a little farther, they empanel those who volunteer to serve. In the day
of the Mooney-Billings trials the volunteers were not housewives, as
they are now, but retired businessmen.

The method of selecting jurors in San Francisco [wrote Bourke Cock-
ran] is that each Superior Court Judge places in the box from which the
trial jurors are drawn the names of such persons as he may think proper.
In theory he is supposed to choose persons peculiarly well qualified to decide issues of fact. In actual practice he places in the box the names of men
who ask to be selected. . . .

The practical result is that a jury panel is a collection of the lame, the
halt, the blind, and the incapable, with a few exceptions, and these are well
known to the District Attorney who is thus enabled to pick a jury of his
own choice.[24]

The Ohio jurors who tried Eugene Debs in 1918 for obstructing
the war effort were, with one exception, retired merchants and retired
farmers; their average age was 72. A similar jury tried Victor Berger
for conspiracy under the Espionage Act the same year in Chicago.
Neither these jurors nor those who tried Billings were representative
of their communities. Nor is it likely that they were sufficiently fit for
jury duty, either in competence or in impartiality.[25]

Professional jurors continued to plague the defense after Billings's
conviction. The sixteen judges of the San Francisco Superior Court
discussed the professional jury system at their annual meeting in January, but turned down a resolution proposing to eliminate from the
1917 venires everyone who had served on more than one jury in 1916.[26]
Efforts in the succeeding bomb trials to avoid professional jurors were
only partially successful, for other citizens refused to serve. At Mooney's trial Judge Griffin called three special panels, from which but
eight jurors were obtained; hundreds of other veniremen found excuses. Some opposed the death sentence. Many said they were prejudiced against anarchists or against Mooney and Billings. (Mooney had
been up for public condemnation for so long that the veniremen with
no predispositions at all must have been philosophically well disci-
plined indeed, or deaf and blind.) Whether or not their prejudices
were strong enough to warrant dismissal by the court, many veniremen
so represented them.[27]

One consequence of Billings's conviction was a public outcry
against the professional jury system in San Francisco. The conviction

astonished many people. Even Robert Minor, who was not usually sanguine about the fairness of capitalistic courts, had believed halfway through the trial that there was "not one chance in a hundred of conviction."[28] Immediately after the verdict a protest against professional juries arose in the labor movement. The San Francisco Labor Council's weekly, disclaiming any interest in Billings personally, declared that the public, reading the daily press reports of his trial, believed he could not reasonably be convicted; the evidence offered at the trial did not justify the verdict. The fault, it said, lay with the professional jury system. The Socialists of the Bay Area also protested. A mass meeting to air these complaints was arranged for October 10 in the Dreamland Rink.[29]

The protests gained new impetus when Edwin V. McKenzie, an attorney and brother of an Assistant District Attorney, went to court before Judge Griffin early in November to defend one James Gaffene for murder. Griffin, having nearly exhausted his own jury panel, said he would have to draw on Judge Dunne's. McKenzie protested: Dunne's panel was one of professional jurors. The prosecution, he said, had boasted that it would hang his client with jurors from Dunne's panel.[30] He refused to proceed with the trial. Griffin sentenced him to five days in jail for contempt of court. The judge appointed two substitutes to defend Gaffene, but these attorneys in turn filed objections to professional jurors; one of them, Thomas O'Connor— later famous for his defense of Anita Whitney against the Criminal Syndicalist Law of 1919—quipped that the same men had probably been on murder case juries in Vigilante days.[31] The protest of these attorneys attracted popular notice. It was one thing if friends of a convicted anarchist complained, but for an attorney to go to jail for balking at the "nefarious institution" was another matter. The *Examiner* and *Town Talk* joined the critics: the professional jury system would have to go.[32] The Labor Council reiterated its criticism of the system. Supervisor Andrew J. Gallagher condemned it. Miss Anita Whitney, then known as a prominent social worker rather than a dangerous and criminal syndicalist, called it the greatest barrier to justice, a denial of democracy.[33]

Judge Dunne was apparently taken aback by all the criticism. He stated that he would compile his next roster from the Commonwealth Club, the Chamber of Commerce, and kindred organizations. To this Socialist journalist Ed Gammons retorted that labor wanted "neither professional jurors nor Koster jurors," but jurors drawn from the great register.[34]

Early in 1917 several unsuccessful attempts were made to eliminate the professional jury by legislation. Assemblyman Charles F. Goetting of San Francisco introduced a bill in the state legislature providing that a venireman might be challenged on the grounds that he had served on a jury in a criminal case within a year. (Thinly populated counties were exempted.) The bill was killed by the Assembly Judiciary Committee.[35] Several similar bills introduced at the same time in the State Senate by Senator Lester G. Burnett of San Francisco met the same fate. A more lenient bill by Senator J. M. Inman of Sacramento, providing for a 60-day limit per year (except to complete a trial), passed the Senate but died in the Assembly Judiciary Committee. Not until 1927 was an appropriate law passed: it prohibited a resident of a major county (defined as having a population of at least 300,000) from serving if he had served twenty days as a trial juror in the preceding two years.[36]

After McKenzie's protests the San Francisco courts made greater efforts to limit the use of professional jurors, but the system was hard to uproot. In Mooney's trial, as will be seen, the question also arose of whether the jury was entirely beyond the illicit reach of the prosecution. In San Francisco the caliber of jurymen, like the caliber of the prosecutors, fell far short of sound juridical standards.

CHAPTER ELEVEN

The Prosecution Shifts Witnesses

Few persons are ideal witnesses.
—James Brennan, 1920

BEFORE MOONEY came to trial the defense uncovered damaging information about John Crowley and Estelle Smith that impaired their usefulness to the prosecution as witnesses. In the same months of late 1916 Fickert found other witnesses and was quietly preparing to introduce the most important one of all, Frank C. Oxman.

Crowley, who had testified to seeing Billings at Steuart and Mission streets with a suitcase in hand before the explosion, was a witness of whom the defense had known nothing. He had not appeared before the grand jury. Within a few days of Billings's conviction it was discovered that Crowley had been arrested in 1911 for deserting his seventeen-year-old wife, whom he had infected with syphilis; he pleaded guilty to the desertion charge and was put on probation for two years. Subsequently he had been convicted of petty larceny for stealing a watch in a house where he was living with a group of female impersonators.

Fickert, who had signed the complaint against Crowley in 1911, contended long afterward that the man he put on the stand in Billings's trial was not the same John Crowley, but this assertion was refuted by Crowley's wife and brother. Crowley himself disappeared about 1918; according to reports, he was in military service and was killed when his ship was torpedoed off the coast of Ireland.[1]

Following up the information linking Estelle Smith to a Los Angeles murder charge, the defense discovered that she had been arrested in Los Angeles in 1914 for prostitution. She later quit her trade and was working respectably as a dental nurse in San Francisco. It is possible, however, that she was a drug addict at the time of Billings's trial: in 1929 she signed a statement, which she partially repudiated in 1930 ("after twelve or thirteen or fourteen years, I would believe almost anything"),[2] that in the summer of 1916 she was a morphine addict, that she was treated in San Rafael and at St. Mary's Hospital, San Francisco, where she was straitjacketed; and that during her day in court she had along her morphine tablets, which she took during recess.[3]

John McDonald had a hospital record, too. McDonald had been syphilitic for many years. The disease was arrested in 1914, but by that time it had attacked nerve and brain tissue. In 1914 he was diagnosed as having cerebral-spinal lues, a permanent syphilitic affliction, whose effects commonly include distortion of memory and hallucinations. As Billings's attorney pointed out in 1930, no physician would have accepted without reservation the word of a person so afflicted. By that time McDonald's mental condition had been amply demonstrated in his hopelessly self-contradictory course of statements about Mooney and Billings. At the time of their trials, however, his medical record was unknown.[4]

II

The prosecution was busy between the trials. Brennan went to Martinez after Billings's conviction and brought back most of Mooney's 1913 arsenal. Fickert told reporters that the weapons might be introduced at Mooney's trial.[5] However, he was less concerned with garnishing old tales than with finding new witnesses.

One of Fickert's new prospects was in Los Angeles: Charles Organ, a Negro convict departing for a three-year term at San Quentin for forgery, had asserted that in July 1915, Mooney offered him $500 and two bombs to blow up the Liberty Bell, which was passing through San Francisco on a national tour. He said that he took the offer but dumped the explosives off North Beach into the Bay. He also said that Mooney had vowed to blow up the militaristic "boobs" some day. Fickert announced that sea divers would be employed to search for the bombs, and that Organ would probably be called from prison to testify in Mooney's trial. However, he soon changed his mind and dropped the subject.*

* *Chronicle*, November 1, 4, and 7, 1916; *Bulletin*, November 1, 2, and 7, 1916; *Examiner*, November 3, 1916; and Minor, "Frame-up System," p. 12. Brennan later testified, evidently in this connection, "I remember in one case we had information that there was some very important witnesses in jail in Los Angeles that knew all about this bomb out-

III

The prosecution's most vital new preparation for Mooney's trial began with the discovery of Frank C. Oxman. Oxman was a genial, plain-spoken, suntanned cattleman of Durkee, Oregon, an unincorporated hamlet a few miles west of the Snake River. A man in his mid-sixties, he was born on a farm near Grayville, Illinois, had grown up there, and moved to Oregon some time between 1900 and 1904. Over the years he had been involved in several frauds. He deserted his first wife in Illinois, married another woman in Oregon, and lived with her for six years as a bigamist; he remarried her in 1911, after his first wife finally divorced him. In Princeton, Indiana, he was indicted in 1900 for obtaining property by false pretense, and through civil suit the property was recovered from him. (No criminal charge was pressed.) Among livestock men his word was as good as his money, but in Durkee some of his neighbors would not trust him under oath.[6]

The Oregon and Washington Railroad and Navigation Company, which Oxman regularly patronized in his cattle business, was sued in 1914 by one John Spain, a horse rancher and professional bucking-horse rider. Spain had been ejected from a train, in consequence of which, he alleged, the stump of his arm, which had been previously amputated, required a second operation. The railroad responded that the ejection was lawful because Spain was drunk and disorderly. Oxman came to the aid of the railroad. He told the company's claim agent, B. C. Wilson, that a friend, Edward Rigall, of Grayville, Illinois, had been on the train. Later he also told Wilson that he, too, had been on the train, and had witnessed Spain's removal; he said that his friend Rigall had purchased a bottle of liquor for Spain and had seen Spain drinking it on the train. Oxman said that Rigall was his employee and that they were returning together from Kansas City after delivering a shipment of cattle.

The railroad attorneys considered bringing Rigall to Oregon when Spain's suit came to trial, but decided against it because of the expense. Oxman they did put on the stand, although the conductor did not recall having seen him on the train. After the first trial, which the railroad lost, B. C. Wilson went to Durkee to learn more about Oxman's man Rigall, but discovered that no one there had ever heard of him.

---

rage, and Captain Goff . . . and I went down there, and we investigated the case. I talked to them about five minutes and found out that they were hoaxes." (California Supreme Court, "In re Billings," II: 1011.)

Although Wilson therefore doubted Oxman's veracity, Oxman testified for the railroad again at the second trial. Rigall was left in Illinois. Later Rigall denied that he had ever been in Oregon. It was a curious affair. More curiously, it exactly prefigured the course of Oxman's testimony two years later against Tom Mooney.[7]

On the morning of July 22, 1916, Frank Oxman was in Woodland, about twenty miles northwest of Sacramento. He had come to Sacramento from Portland on one of his many trips to buy or sell cattle, and stopped off at Woodland to see a friend of his, Earl K. Hatcher, a farmer and sheep-raiser. Hatcher, grandson of a forty-niner, was buying and shipping lambs in 1916 as Oxman's commission agent. He had great respect for Oxman's ability to judge livestock, and had wired Oxman in Portland asking him to come down to help him with the sale of ten or twelve thousand lambs to the Miller and Lux Company in South San Francisco. Oxman signed the register at the Byrns Hotel in Woodland, and the two men sat in the hotel lobby discussing cattle deals until late in the morning. According to Hatcher's later testimony, they went to Hatcher's house for lunch with his wife. Oxman was tired and took a nap. Then he and Hatcher walked to the Southern Pacific station, and Oxman caught the afternoon train for San Francisco, ninety miles away. If Hatcher was essentially truthful, then it was after 6 P.M. when Oxman got off the ferry at San Francisco and went to the Terminal Hotel on Market Street, near Steuart, to register.* He telephoned Hatcher to say he had made an appointment with a Miller and Lux representative, and asked if Hatcher had heard of the terrible explosion in San Francisco. Hatcher said he had. Oxman gave no details.[8]

Back in Durkee, Oxman confided to the railroad station agent, Frank Woods, on July 28—just after the arrests—that he had seen the Preparedness Day parade in San Francisco, and that he had been standing at the corner of Steuart and Market streets when a jitney bus drove up and certain persons whom he could identify left a suitcase on the sidewalk. He evidently asked Woods to keep mum about it, and said

---

* Hatcher recalled that the train left Woodland about 2:15. However, Southern Pacific Railroad records showed that the first train following the 9:13 A.M. train left Woodland at 2:55. See note, p. 353 below.

According to his own testimony in 1917, Oxman was at the Terminal Hotel twice before 2 P.M., but "the clerk told me he couldn't give me a room until night as he was crowded, and I disremember whether I put my name down then or whether I put it down later." (Hunt, *Case of Thomas J. Mooney and Warren K. Billings*, p. 115; California Supreme Court, "Habeas Corpus," VI: 3293. See also Oxman's affidavit of October 26, 1917, reproduced below in the Appendix.)

that he did not want to get mixed up in the case. But he changed his mind. Woods had noticed the offers of large rewards in the newspapers.[9] According to another account, it was common gossip in Durkee late that summer that Oxman offered Woods $1,000 to bring him to the attention of the San Francisco authorities.[10] Apparently the station agent was not keen on the idea at first, but later thought better of it and drafted a letter to the District Attorney of San Francisco. According to a local rancher who claimed to have overheard their conversation, Woods showed the letter to Oxman, and Oxman had him change the reference to himself from "a man" to "a reputable Oregon business man," and then approved the letter.[11] It was mailed to Fickert under the date September 21, 1916. After advising Fickert that the man had important eyewitness information, the letter concluded:

> Account neglecting his business by remaining in San Francisco to give evidence, this gentleman did not tell anyone what he knew of the case while there, and I don't believe he intends yet to offer his testimony. So if his testimony in this case will be of service to you I will put you in touch with the party for $2,500 payable upon conviction of the guilty parties.[12]

Fickert responded two days later. He was inquisitive but noncommittal. Woods then wrote a second letter, which within a year was lost or stolen from the District Attorney's files. On October 9 Fickert answered: "We have heard of a man from Oregon by the name of Oxman who has stated that he knows something about the explosion." He said that he had been unable to find him. Woods's information might prove useful.[13]

Whether Fickert had heard of Oxman before Woods wrote cannot be determined. Woods may have mentioned Oxman's name in the missing letter, in which case Fickert may have pretended previous knowledge of Oxman, to ward off the request for reward money. It is possible, however, that Fickert had heard of Oxman. From whom? Fremont Older, after his conversion to the Mooney defense, was informed by a detective who had been discharged by the San Francisco Chamber of Commerce that Fickert learned of Oxman through Frank Drew and Hugh M. Webster, the Chamber's attorney and the Law and Order Committee secretary; to these two officers of the Chamber Oxman was allegedly brought by a Western Meat Company representative, whose name, Older subsequently learned, was William Hough.[14] This account is plausible. While in San Francisco Oxman may have concocted his tale and confided it to Hough. Fickert himself in 1917 spoke of William Hough as a corroborating informant, without mentioning Drew or Webster. (In 1936 Fickert claimed that he had first heard of Oxman through an ex-District Attorney of Sacramento, Eugene S. Wachhorst, and that Wachhorst had received the information from Earl Hatcher of Woodland. The claim was false: Hatcher carefully concealed his information about Oxman until 1918, and anyway did not discover until 1917, according to his own testimony, that Oxman was involved in the case. As for Wachhorst, by 1936 he was in his grave and beyond questioning.)[15]

Back in Durkee, Frank Woods, in anticipation of his share of the reward and with Oxman's encouragement, purchased a store on credit. The previous owner, according to Woods's clerk, said he would get a thousand dollars of the payment when Mooney was hanged.[16]

Woods kept Fickert informed of Oxman's movements. He wrote him that on October 24 Oxman would be in the Kansas City stockyards with a shipment of cattle.[17] To find Oxman there and get a statement from him, Fickert engaged the Burns Detective Agency. The agency's San Francisco manager authorized the Kansas City office to "use as many men as necessary" to locate Oxman and coax him into making a notarized statement for Fickert. The manager warned that Oxman had to be approached cautiously, since the cattleman's time would be worth much more to him than the witness fees he would get if he could be persuaded to come to San Francisco.[18] With the assistance of Union Pacific freight agents from Idaho to Nebraska, the Burns Agency traced Oxman's journey eastward, and an operative found him in the Kansas City stockyard. Oxman told him about the jitney with "three men and a driver" and the suitcase that was set down before the explosion.[19] Oxman said he did not have time to go to San Francisco but was willing to make a notarized statement.

Numerous details in Oxman's affidavit of October 26 stand out because of their susceptibility to disproof or because of the discrepancies between them and his subsequent testimony at Mooney's trial. First, he averred that he arrived in San Francisco "about noon" from the town of Willows, California. Presumably this was to conceal his Woodland visit. Second, his description of San Francisco streets was incoherent. He did not name Steuart Street; the incident took place on the corner of "Washington Street" and a "side street leading out from Washington Street to the left," yet he also mentioned Market Street by name. (Washington does not intersect either Steuart or Market.) Third, he stated that while standing on the corner he saw a jitney with five persons in it; but according to the Burns Agency detective's report, Oxman at first said four persons. Fourth, in the affidavit Oxman said that two men got out of the back seat and that the second handed the first a suitcase; at Mooney's trial he testified that Mooney, sitting in the front seat, was holding the suitcase on the running board and that Billings jumped out and took it from him. Fifth, Oxman identified Mooney in the affidavit as the man who "remained in the car, sitting by the driver"; at the trial he said that Mooney got out and talked with Billings. Sixth, in the affidavit Oxman stated that the two who got out with the suitcase were "talking in a foreign language, and I could not understand what was said." This important point was later dropped; at Mooney's trial he related Mooney's alleged conversation with them in English. Seventh, Oxman described Mooney as weighing 155–60 pounds and having blue eyes; both facts, of course, were inaccurate. Finally, he stated in the affidavit that on the morning after the explosion he went by the bomb site and noticed lying there "some small pieces of grip," which he identified on the spot as parts of the grip he had seen the day before, and that he then realized the grip had contained the bomb. But no fragments offered at Mooney's trial were conclusively identifiable; and since souvenir hunters and Bunner's fire hose had already done their work by the morning after, it is unlikely that he saw any recognizable pieces of grip at all.[*]

Oxman's omissions of detail from his affidavit were almost as important as his assertions. He said nothing about the parade, although he mentioned the crowds. He said nothing about having copied down the jitney license number. And he said nothing about having seen an old acquaintance shortly before the explosion, a friend from Illinois by the name of Ed Rigall.

For a while the Kansas City affidavit lay around the District Attorney's office.[20] Then it disappeared permanently. The defense learned of its existence, but did not know and was unable to learn its contents during Mooney's trial, or at Oxman's trial, or at any time for the next seven years. The text first reached Mooney's hands in 1924, evidently having been transcribed from the Burns Agency files in Kansas City with the approval of Edward Cunha, who prosecuted Mooney. In 1926 the notary public who had certified the original was found in Chicago. He certified the copy.[21]

From Kansas City, Oxman went back to Durkee. There Fickert got in touch with him. The difficulties of arranging an interview with the

---

[*] The entire affidavit is set forth in the Appendix.

traveling cattleman were overcome, and in late November 1916, Fickert asked Assistant District Attorney James Brennan to go to Durkee. Brennan backed out of the assignment, and so Lieutenant Bunner went in his stead. Brennan privately distrusted the whole case by this time. He announced a few days later that he was going to resign to run for the office of city attorney, but he apparently changed his mind. He stayed with Fickert, without participating further in the bomb cases, until Mooney's conviction, and then left.[22]

Bunner found Oxman in Durkee. Oxman reaffirmed his story, but said that he did not want to go to San Francisco. His wife was ill; and testifying against those defendants, he said, was dangerous for any man.[23] Bunner pleaded with him: if Oxman's home and family were dynamited, would he not feel pretty hard if someone who knew about the crime refused to come forward and tell it? Oxman saw the point: "By God, I will go and tell them what I know."[24] And so the reluctant witness agreed to help Fickert. Woods, adding his bit to the deception, told Bunner that Oxman must not find out who informed Fickert: "If he finds out I tipped him off he has influence enough with the railroad to have me fired."[25]

Oxman arrived in San Francisco December 13 and registered again at the Terminal Hotel. In the lobby he met Fickert, and at the District Attorney's office he was introduced to Cunha. The three discussed the case. Either at this point or three weeks earlier, when Bunner visited Durkee, Oxman informed the prosecution that half an hour before the explosion he had met at Steuart Street an old acquaintance, his son's childhood friend from bygone years in Grayville, Illinois. He thought his name was Ed Rigall. Fickert and Cunha recognized the advantage there would be in having a witness to verify Oxman's presence at the scene of the explosion, and suggested to Oxman that he write his friend. Oxman did so.[26] The letter read:

Dear Ed.

Has been a long time since I hurd from you I have a chance for you to come to San Frico as an expurt wittness in a very important case. You will only haf to ansuer 3 & 4 questions and I will post you on them. You will get milegage and all that a witness can draw. Probly 100 in the clear so if you will come ans me quick in care of this hotel and I will manage the balance it is all ok but I need a witness. Let me no if you can come. Jan. 3 is the dait set for trile. Pleas keep this confidential. Ansuer hear.

Yours Truly
F. C. OXMAN[27]

Rigall wired back that he would come. On December 18 Oxman wrote again:

Dear Ed

Your telegram recived I will wire you Transportation in Plenty of time allso Expce money Will route you by Chicago, Omaho U.P. Ogden S.P. to San Frico. I thought you can make the trip and see California and save a little money as you will be allowed to collect 10¢ per mile from the Stake which will be about 200 besids I can get your Expenses and you will only haf to say you seen me on July 22 in San Frisco and that will be Easey dun. I will try and meet you on the way out and talk it ovr the State of California will Pay you but I will attend to the Expces. The case wont come up untill Jan 3 Or 4 1917 so start about 29 off this month. You know that the silent road is the one and say nuthing to any Body the fewer People no it the Better. When you arive Registure as Evansville Ind. little more milege.

Yours Truly
F. C. OXMAN

Will you want to Return by Los Angeles can route you that way.[28]

As an afterthought Oxman wrote Rigall's mother and invited her to come to San Francisco, too: "it might be that I can use you allso about the 10th. If so I can obtain you a ticket that you can see Californa if you would like the Trip adrees me care this Hotell tell F. E. to see [say?] nuthing untill he see me Can probly use a Extry witness. Been a long time I dont see you."[29] Mrs. Rigall did not accept the invitation. On December 27 Oxman wired Rigall that the money for his ticket and expenses was being wired him that day in care of the Illinois Central Railroad. As soon as he received it, Rigall left for San Francisco.[30]

CHAPTER TWELVE

Mooney's Trial

My name is Ed. Cunha, don't think I'm a luna-
Tic loosed from the Agnews confines;
I am from Milpitas 'mid mud and mosquitoes,
On politics I have designs.
                              —Stanford Quad '06

All loyal citizens appreciate Mr. Oxman's sacrifice
in coming here as a witness.
                              —Fickert, January 1917

JUDGE Franklin A. Griffin presided at Mooney's trial. Griffin's background was Progressive. As a young lawyer in Sacramento he had
worked with Hiram Johnson, had moved with him to San Francisco,
and campaigned for him in 1910. After Johnson's election he became
his executive secretary. A member of the Native Sons of the Golden
West, a society of native-born Californians, Griffin once tried to have
a Grand Parlor of that organization endorse the Johnson administration, but the proposal was howled down as an "unprecedented attempt
to foist politics on a nonpolitical and highly respected organization."*
In 1913 Johnson appointed him to the Superior Court of San Francisco. His reelection the following year was endorsed by Fremont
Older, and by Paul Scharrenberg and other labor leaders. He was
recognized in a *Chronicle* survey of the San Francisco bench and bar
at the time of Mooney's trial as "a most capable jurist, firm and trustworthy."[1] A conscientious judge, Griffin was to provide Mooney with
as fair a trial as lay within his power and knowledge.

The trial was prefaced by a raid on the *Blast* office December 31,

* Martinez *Contra Costa Gazette*, April 25, 1914. The Native Sons of the Golden West,
traditionally concerned about California pioneer history, was in fact influential in California politics by the 1910's as an organization anxious to keep the state a "White Man's
Paradise." (Carey McWilliams, *Prejudice: Japanese-Americans: Symbol of Racial Intolerance* [1944], pp. 22–24, 31. See also *Grizzly Bear*, the official magazine of the Native Sons
and Native Daughters of the Golden West, July, August, and November 1912, and March
1914, for anti-radical editorials.) Fickert, Cunha, and Judge Frank H. Dunne were members of the organization. (*Grizzly Bear*, September 1915, supplement; Lewis F. Byington
and Oscar Lewis, eds., *History of San Francisco* [1931], II: 479.)

the day after Bourke Cockran arrived in San Francisco. The prosecution had raided the *Blast* once before, but no papers were taken on that occasion, and Mary Eleanor Fitzgerald was courteously treated by Cunha and sympathetically described in the *Chronicle*.[2] The second raid was different. Swanson obtained a search warrant from Judge Griffin.[3] Then he, Cunha, and police detective Michael Burke went to the *Blast* office. "Fitzie" was there alone. They told her they had come for the papers, and began rummaging through the office. She tried to destroy some personal letters, which proved to be love letters from Berkman, but they were confiscated along with subscription lists, files of the *Blast*, cartoons, manuscripts, and some Mooney defense correspondence. Miss Fitzgerald was roughly handled. (The *Examiner* said that she "fought like a tigress.")[4]

Fickert explained the purpose of the raid. "The office of the *Blast* is the place where the bomb plot was hatched," he said. "They had some information there that we wanted, so we went and took it." He said that among the papers seized were letters showing that the radicals had anticipated just such an explosion as the Preparedness Day bombing. "These letters will be introduced at the trial, as they show that the explosion was not an accident, but was the result of carefully laid plans."[5] What specific information the letters contained he would not say, but he did announce from them that Cockran had been enlisted for the defense by Alexander Berkman.[6] The effect of the raid and Fickert's statements was to draw attention away from Cockran and remind the public of Mooney's anarchist associations.

The trial opened January 3. Cunha prosecuted and Fickert helped him. Cockran and McNutt for the defense were assisted by John G. Lawlor and by Frank G. Mulholland of Toledo, Ohio, the general counsel of the International Association of Machinists. Mulholland had attained national prominence a few years before as the defense attorney in the Danbury Hatters case.* He had come to San Francisco to help Ed Nolan.[7]

Two weeks were spent in selecting the jury. Many prospective jurors admitted prejudice against anarchists, and were dismissed. When the first panel was exhausted, Cockran exercised his right to request a special venire, which meant that the defense would have few

---

* In this case the United States Supreme Court found, in 1908, that a nation-wide union boycott of the products of a company constituted a conspiracy in restraint of trade, in violation of the Sherman Anti-Trust Act. The decision was a severe blow to the AFL. (Philip Taft, *The A.F. of L. in the Time of Gompers* [1957], pp. 266–67; Joseph G. Rayback, *A History of American Labor* [1966], pp. 223–25.)

professional jurors to contend with.[8] During the jury examinations
Fickert released to the press certain letters from the *Blast* papers. These
letters revealed some of Berkman's defense work; they revealed his
payment, allegedly to George P. West, of $300 for an eastern report
favorable to Mooney; they also revealed Berkman's affection for Miss
Fitzgerald.[9] There was nothing incriminating in them, but their publication harassed the defense. Cockran pointed out to Griffin that the
District Attorney had filed no return on the search warrant the judge
had issued, and added that the materials published were irrelevant
and prejudicial, that some had been altered, and that they were improperly being circulated in the community from which the jury was
being drawn.[10] Cunha responded that there had often been "slackness"
before in returning warrants to the court, and spoke slightingly of
Cockran: "we got along very nicely in San Francisco long before he
ever came here and our standing seems to be all right before the
people. . . . We don't want to go into his motives for coming out
here."[11] Griffin ordered the return made.[12]

Another flare-up occurred when a prospective juror drew a copy
of Minor's "Frame-up System" from his pocket and said that he had
received it in the mail that morning. Cunha suggested that Minor had
sent it. In reply, Cockran intimated that Fickert had sent the pamphlet
himself: "We know perfectly well how it was done, like every other
proposition in this frame-up."[13] He and Fickert then exchanged re-
criminations until Griffin restored order. The next day two more
jurors reported having received "The Frame-up System" in the mail,
and the accusations flew again.[14]

Fickert next published an IWDL form letter in which correspondents were asked for information on Mooney's prospective jurors, and
said that the form had been sent to a venireman. Minor denied that the
letter had been sent to any prospective jurors. He pointed out that the
one in question bore neither an IWDL signature nor an official IWDL
stamp; it was another prosecution fraud, he said.[15] In court Cockran
protested the District Attorney's publication of more prejudicial statements. Cunha replied that the prosecution officials had not objected
to Cockran's press publicity when he arrived in San Francisco, nor had
they asked the court "to stop a certain wagon which had been going
around this city with a big sign on it: 'District Attorney is Framing Up
this Case.' "[16]

Judge Griffin upheld the right of the defense to inquire into the
character of any juror, but deplored the newspaper accounts and

warned the eight jurors then sworn in not to read them. He admonished Cunha that such charges as the District Attorney had made should be threshed out in court and not taken first to the press: "I am going to try this case to the best of my ability, and I hope you will refrain from trying it in the newspapers."[17]

Mary Eleanor Fitzgerald then appeared in court displaying her bruised arm and accusing Officer Burke of manhandling her in the *Blast* raid. She requested the return of the *Blast* papers, saying that she needed them to publish the *Blast*. Cunha responded that he had personally supervised the removal of the papers and had taken only those which were relevant to the case. Cockran asked how letters concerning Miss Fitzgerald's affections were relevant. Cunha replied that they helped show the extent of the anarchist conspiracy, which included, he said, a plan by Berkman and Mooney to blow up public officials and assassinate the governor.[18] "GOVERNOR JOHNSON'S MURDER PLOTTED," announced the *Chronicle*; and even the New York *Times*, which was reporting little about the trial, repeated the accusation as it came off the press wires. In Sacramento Hiram Johnson, overlooking Mooney's threat of 1915, said that he had not heard of the matter before.[19] Griffin ruled that the prosecution did not have to return Miss Fitzgerald's papers, but that it did have to let the defense examine everything seized from her office.[20]

Cunha opened the case for the prosecution. Like Brennan at Billings's trial, he told the jury in his introductory remarks more about the alleged conspiracy than about the bombing on July 22. Mooney, he said, had conspired before 1916 with Berkman, M. E. Fitzgerald, E. B. Morton, Edward Nolan, and others, to bring about an uprising or revolution in California of propertyless workers, by confiscating property and destroying the government. These persons organized themselves as the "Blasters." In preparation for their revolution, they circulated papers in San Francisco to create prejudice against the government, law and order, the American Federation of Labor, and the army. They urged direct action. They urged violence. They urged the assassination of the President. They urged violent interference with the Preparedness Parade; and they achieved their effect through people who read and believed their ideas. Cunha promised to show the long association of Mooney and Billings, and their possession of materials from which the Preparedness Day bomb was made. He said the prosecution would expect a verdict of first-degree murder.[21] As for the events of July 22, his preliminary remarks were routine. He promised to prove that Mooney was at Steuart Street with Billings, but he gave only those details which McDonald had given at Billings's trial. There was no hint from Cunha of a new witness with new evidence. Frank Oxman was a well-guarded secret.[22]

The prosecution then began a prolonged presentation of the *corpus delicti* and circumstantial evidence. For the next week the trial was in substance a repetition of Billings's. Meanwhile, unforeseen events were taking place outside the courtroom.

II

While the jury was being selected, Oxman's old acquaintance, Ed Rigall, arrived in San Francisco. Since Rigall was soon to alter the course of the Mooney case, his background and character merit a brief examination.

Rigall was born and raised in Grayville, a town of 2,000 on the Wabash River in southeastern Illinois, 35 miles from Evansville, Indiana. He owned a poolhall and ran a poker table on the side. Summers he followed the county fairs with a teddy-bear wheel. (It was honest; somebody won a teddy bear every time.) Between gambling and pool he was putting $100 a week in the bank.[23]

Rigall had a police record of petty violations. He had been arrested and fined a number of times for breach of peace. He had been indicted and fined on five counts of illegally selling a beverage known as "jingo," a "temperance drink" with an alcoholic content of 2 per cent. He had also been in a scrape with a local girl by the name of Nora Biford, who accused him of abducting her for purposes of prostitution. He was brought to court, arraigned for a misdemeanor, and released on bail. The girl withdrew the charges, allegedly after Rigall had paid her grandmother $50, and the case was dismissed.[24]

That was about the extent of Rigall's known record. He was willing to make a fast dollar and perhaps to help a friend. From all outward appearances he did not amount to nearly so much as the prosperous cattleman who had appealed to him for assistance.

Rigall was pleased about going to San Francisco. On the other hand, he was not anxious to arrive there in time to help Oxman. The idea that he might have been in San Francisco on July 22 was ludicrous. He had never been in California in his life; on July 22 he had been on his way to Niagara Falls. He went to Chicago and wired Oxman that his arrival would be delayed until January 5. That, however, was all right with Oxman. At Salt Lake City, Rigall stopped off, got drunk, and wired Oxman again, advising that the trial go ahead without him:

"Got left. Cockeyed. Let 'er buck." Rigall apparently thought that by showing up three days late he would be too late to testify, but he knew nothing about the time consumed in jury selection. When he arrived, testimony had not begun.[25]

Rigall went to the Terminal Hotel and registered as L. O. Charles from Evansville, Indiana. At the hotel he met Oxman, whom he had not seen for eight or ten years. Oxman did not recognize him. Rigall was surprised, too: he had thought it was for Oxman's son, whose name was also F. C. Oxman, that he had come. Oxman told him about the bomb outrage. He had never heard of it before. In the absence of earlier information from Oxman, he might have expected anything; but testifying in this case was more than he had anticipated. According to his own account, which Oxman denied ("There never was no testimony went over," Oxman said), Rigall raised some objection but was easily coaxed out of it: Oxman told him that no one was going to investigate him, and that in any event the state would take care of its own witnesses. Oxman took him to Steuart Street and 721 Market Street and showed him around. A day or so after his arrival Oxman introduced him to Lieutenant Bunner and Captain Matheson, and to the staff at the District Attorney's office. Rigall told Fickert that he had seen Oxman at Steuart Street on July 22. Four or five days after his arrival Rigall re-registered at the Terminal Hotel under his own name. He decided to say that he had arrived on the morning of July 22 by Western Pacific from Salt Lake City. He and Oxman went to the downtown Western Pacific office to check the train schedules. They also went out to the police station to examine Weinberg's jitney bus.[26]

According to Rigall, Oxman expanded his initial request that Rigall merely identify him: he wanted Rigall to say that they had met on Steuart Street, that Oxman had stepped over to a fruit stand and bought some fruit, and that they had walked across the street and were standing there when a Ford drove up with five people, one of whom was sitting in the front seat holding a suitcase on the running board. Rigall balked: Oxman wanted too much. Oxman, according to Rigall, promised to give him a personal check for $250 if he would go through with it. It was understood between them that Rigall's share of the reward money would be considerably more. He and Oxman discussed the reward on several occasions with Bunner and Fickert, according to Rigall (Oxman and Fickert, the latter by implication, both denied it in 1917), and Rigall understood from Oxman that his share of the reward would amount to $2,000 or $3,000.[27]

Rigall and Oxman were entertained by the police and members of the District Attorney's staff during their stay in San Francisco. They were taken for a harbor ride in a police launch; they were motored to San Jose; they dined at the Cliff House one evening with Fickert and Cunha.[28] Fickert gave Rigall a pass as his guest at the Olympic Club. Detective Draper Hand was informally assigned to look after the needs of Oxman and Rigall. He wined and dined them at police department expense.[29] One evening, it seemed, Oxman accidentally admitted to him that he intended to commit perjury. The three men were watching wrestling matches, when Oxman said, "Draper, don't you think they will know we are lying?" Hand responded that they could *think* whatever they liked; and Oxman was silent.[30] Hand thought that the slip was as good as a confession, but he never mentioned it to other officers.[31] He had a cynical notion of what was expected of him as a "good detective," and acted accordingly. When Rigall's spirits flagged, Hand (as he later recalled) "went over the old regular routine, telling him the patriotism and the duty they owed to the country by sending these people to jail, and that they were guilty of it, and the country might deify them in later times—you know, that old bolster-up stuff. You never was a detective?"[32]

The night before Rigall was to take the stand against Mooney, he called on Cunha in the Hall of Justice to go over his testimony. By his own account, he was not very cooperative: when Cunha asked him where he had spent the night of July 22, he replied that he had stayed all night with a young woman in her hotel room. "Well," said Cunha, "that shows you too much of a rounder."[33] So Rigall told him that he had been lying, that in fact he had not been in San Francisco at all and that he didn't know a damn thing about the case. Cunha said that if that was so, the prosecution would not put him on the stand. Rigall then asked to be reimbursed for his expenses. Cunha offered $150, but held him off for a day or two, since he did not want Rigall to leave town until after Oxman had testified.[34]

III

Toward the end of the prosecution's case Oxman took the stand. He stated that business with the Western Meat Company and with Miller and Lux had brought him to San Francisco on July 22, and that he arrived between twelve and one P.M. He said that he was standing on the southwest corner of Steuart and Market streets* at 1:40 or 1:45

* See Map 2, p. 120.

("I ain't going to testify to minutes")[35] when he saw an old Ford, headed toward the Ferry Building, approach along Market and stop at the corner. A man whom he identified as the defendant was in the front seat with his hands outside holding a suitcase on the running board. The "little auburn-haired boy" jumped out of the back seat and took the suitcase from Mooney. A second man got out of the back seat. He was not Nolan, but a working man with a stubby moustache; he came and stood on the corner near Oxman. Billings was very excited. He rudely pushed Oxman out of the way. ("I said, 'You are a pretty smart boy that will push a big fat man.' ")[36] Billings and the other man—who was perhaps intended to be Berkman—walked down Steuart, the latter carrying the suitcase. Billings took the suitcase from him and set it on the sidewalk. Meanwhile Mooney stepped out of the automobile. The other two men came back to him. Mooney said to Billings, " 'Give it to him and let him go; we must get away from here; the bulls will be after us.' " The other man left. Mooney looked at his watch and at the Ferry Building clock, and the two returned to the automobile. The automobile turned into Steuart and went up the street. The driver was Weinberg; Mrs. Mooney was a passenger.[37]

On cross-examination Oxman said that he did not know how the prosecution had learned of him, but that he had mentioned in a local restaurant on July 23 that he had nearly been blown up, and that a representative of the District Attorney had approached him in Kansas City. He also told of Bunner's visit to Durkee. Oxman said that his identifications were absolutely certain. He could not, however, describe the clothing the defendants had been wearing. Cockran pressed him: he could identify four people after only one sight of them, but could not describe their clothes? "If the Court please," answered Oxman, "I would like to answer that in my plain way of speaking":

I thought these people were a set of thieves. . . . I thought they had stolen this suitcase and were caching it out. . . . My idea was that that grip—probably they had taken the valuables out of it, and were probably leaving the grip there. . . . When people steal things, they naturally would remove the valuables from the suitcase and deposit that where it could be concealed. . . . They were kind of putting it behind those steel doors [that is, beside an open pair of sidewalk elevator doors].[38]

He did not look for a policeman, however. He did not know that when Mooney said "the bulls" would be after them, he meant cops. ("I never heard a policeman called a 'bull.' I am a cattleman. We call a male cow a bull.")[39] Nor did he want to report anything to the police after the explosion occurred: "I didn't want to tell anybody; I didn't want to get mixed up and I had about five thousand cattle on my ranches in Oregon and Idaho that needed my presence there, and I couldn't afford to, because I didn't want to get mixed up in that connection with anybody that throwed a bomb. I didn't want to come and testify."[40] But as the auto drove away down Steuart Street, he said, he wrote down its license number. Thereupon Oxman drew out of his pocket a yellow envelope on which he had written a number. It was the number of Weinberg's jitney license.[41]

Throughout his courtroom appearance Oxman seemed to be an honest, simple cattleman. He did not know what a jail "tier" was ("—you accused me this morning of being a country gentleman, Professor, which I am proud to say is true"), but he would try to answer Cockran's questions if Cockran would ask them "in common language." At the end, in response to Griffin's request that he return if needed, he said, "I have a wife that is sick, and I may be telegraphed at any minute, and there ain't enough courts in California to hold me."[42] A loyal husband.

The prosecution had kept Oxman a complete surprise for the trial, and Oxman had kept his jitney-license notation a complete surprise for the cross-examination. The strategy succeeded. Cockran was unable to shake his testimony. He might have asked for a court recess in order to see what could be learned about Oxman, but that was not his manner, and he probably could not have impeached Oxman anyway; the defense had never heard of Ed Rigall or Earl Hatcher. Cockran asked Colonel C. E. S. Wood, an attorney and poet of Portland and San Francisco and the husband of Sara Bard Field, to check Oxman's background at Durkee. Wood wrote confidentially to the two best-posted men he knew in Oxman's county, who replied that Oxman's general reputation was good. That Cockran did not send an investigator in person to Durkee undoubtedly discomforted the defense attorneys later, but they could not have done everything; many other problems besides Oxman's background claimed their limited time and resources.[43]

Oxman declared that he was trailed in San Francisco after he testified. He told the police that he grabbed one sleuth in front of the Terminal Hotel, shook him up a bit, and told him to run along.[44] If the defense did set anyone on Oxman's trail in San Francisco, the results were disappointing.

Oxman's testimony raised serious questions. McDonald had testified before Oxman, and also at Billings's trial, that the defendants had come and gone on foot. Only Oxman saw the jitney. Why? Why would Mooney have been holding the suitcase in public view on the running board? And how could the jitney possibly have driven three-fourths of a mile along Market Street, from 721 Market to Steuart, against the flow of the parade, without being stopped by a policeman? The police had general orders to turn off Market Street any automobile without a special pass. According to Captain Matheson and Sergeant Goff, there were automobiles on Market Street, and at least one or two of them were authorized; one that reached Steuart Street was a press car, carrying Andrew Gallagher and two reporters. Goff, who was stationed at Third Street, said that he did not allow any unauthorized vehicles past him. (Matheson was at the Embarcadero at 1:40 and therefore would not have seen the jitney reach Steuart Street.)[45]

The whole matter of the jitney journey was not carefully examined at Mooney's trial. The best men to question were the eighteen policemen stationed along the ten blocks of Market Street from Third to Steuart, the hypothetical path of the jitney.* The prosecution did not put any of these officers on the stand, although had any of them seen the jitney pass by, their testimony would have strengthened the case against Mooney. The defense attorneys did not put them on the stand, either; they did not know who the officers were. They repeatedly asked Captain Matheson for their names, but Matheson, who sat with Fickert throughout the trial, said he could not find the list. Cockran refrained from compelling Matheson to produce it by court order, for he did not want to put adversary witnesses on the stand. After Oxman's exposure the hostility of the police department grew decidedly relaxed, and in Rena Mooney's and Weinberg's trials all eighteen officers testified for the defense to the effect that the jitney had not passed.[46]

Ed Rigall returned to Fickert's office the afternoon Oxman testified. Fickert gave him the expense money. According to Rigall, Fickert

---

* According to McNutt, the prosecution's case was untenable unless the prosecution had the jitney run down Market. With the Hamilton photographs in the defense's possession, he contended, time did not permit any other hypothesis. (McNutt testimony, California Supreme Court, "Habeas Corpus," III: 1769.) This is probably true. But even if the jitney had turned off Market and had run along Mission, which parallels Market, it would have had to return to Market before reaching Steuart, to fit Oxman's description; and it would have had to pass at least two officers. Moreover, the point was brought out in Weinberg's trial that the traffic on Mission Street was very heavy at that hour. (See testimonies of five jitney bus drivers, *People v. Weinberg*, II: 1162–75.)

started to write a check, but Cunha stopped him; Fickert then bor-rowed some gold pieces from other men in the room and handed Rigall $150 in cash. The same day Rigall left San Francisco.[47] The prosecu-tion had not heard the last of him.

Rigall's visit to San Francisco seems to have inspired a prosecution fantasy. The day after he left, Cunha announced that a Chicago cattle-man, whose identity was being kept secret, would corroborate Oxman's testimony at the next trial session. The man would testify, said Cunha, that Billings bumped him with the suitcase and that he remarked to Oxman, " 'Gee, that thing must be full of bricks!' "[48] The anonymous cattleman never materialized. Fickert explained that he was satisfied with Oxman alone, for Oxman, "disinterested and straightforward," could not possibly have been moved to interrupt his ranching for any other purpose than to see justice done.[49]

IV

Mellie and Sadie Edeau followed Oxman to the stand. Once again their testimony concerned supposed events at 721 Market Street. Sadie, who at the former trial had merely supplemented her mother's testi-mony, now took the important part. In her earlier account she had mentioned a "man and a woman" on the sidewalk. She now identified them as the Mooneys. When McNutt asked her why she had not done so formerly, she replied that she had not been asked. She again de-scribed Billings and the man and woman as walking off in the direction of the Ferry Building; but this time the automobile at the curb was Weinberg's, and a few minutes later Weinberg cranked it, got in, and drove off toward the Ferry Building, too. And Weinberg was not alone: in his back seat was a laboring man with a stubby moustache.[50] These were new revelations. She had not even mentioned them to the prose-cution before Billings's trial, she said. McNutt was exasperated. Per-haps Miss Edeau, too, had written down the jitney license number? She had not.[51]

Mrs. Edeau corroborated her daughter's testimony. Cockran asked her if she had seen anything about a reward in the paper. She replied that she had not; such a thing would never appeal to her. "I would like to swear that I am not after the reward."[52] (Later she changed her mind. In 1919 the Edeaus filed a claim with Mayor Rolph for payment of their share of his $4,000 contribution to the reward.)[53]

V

The prosecution closed its case with some technical testimony on explosives, and the defense began. Mooney's alibi was, as before, that he and his wife were on the Eilers Building throughout the parade. Twelve other persons, including Belle Hammerberg and Rena's cousin Martha Timberlake, gave corroborating eyewitness testimony, unshaken by the prosecution.[54] In presenting the alibi the defense had one source of evidence whose full significance was not clear at Billings's trial. The Wade Hamilton photographs of the parade, taken from the Eilers Building, had been in the District Attorney's possession during that trial. McNutt had asked for them repeatedly. The prosecution refused to give contact prints or let him use the negatives, but did furnish inferior enlargements, which the defense used during Billings's trial.* They served to show that the Mooneys were on the Eilers Building sometime early in the parade. They also showed a blurred jeweler's clock standing on the sidewalk across Market Street. The hands of the clock were indistinguishable. After Billings's conviction the defense secured the use of the negatives by court order and made its own prints. Under a microscope the hands on the jeweler's clock could be read: the pictures had been taken at 1:58, 2:01, and 2:04. The defense then hired Theodore Kytka, the handwriting expert, to enlarge the clock 25,000 diameters in his laboratory. These enlargements, made in the presence of two police detectives, were introduced at Mooney's trial.[55]

The Hamilton photographs did not prove that Mooney was never at Steuart Street during the parade. They did prove that he was on the Eilers Building, 975 Market, which was 1.15 miles from the corner of Steuart and Market, at 2:01 and 2:04, that his wife was with him, and that she was on the Eilers Building at 1:58 as well as 2:01 and 2:04. Beyond that, one had to reason how quickly he could have moved during the parade from 721 Market Street to Steuart Street before the explosion (2:06), and then back to the roof of 975 Market Street. None of the prosecution witnesses left him much time. Oxman's testimony allowed perhaps fifteen minutes for him to reach the Eilers Building from Steuart Street. McDonald had to change his testimony to give Mooney any time at all. At Billings's trial he had testified that he saw

---

* Maxwell McNutt, *Before the Special Commission Appointed by the President of the United States* (1917), pp. 33–35. In 1936 Fickert denied that any request was made of him during Billings's trial or before Mooney's trial for the negatives. (Fickert testimony, California Supreme Court, "Habeas Corpus," XV: 9980–81.)

Billings about eight or ten minutes of two; that Billings placed the suitcase about two o'clock; that Billings had then joined Mooney, and that after Mooney had left, "I started down Market Street and got as far as the Alameda Coffee House on Market Street when the explosion occurred."[56] The distance to the cafe was ninety feet—half a minute's walk for McDonald, according to his own demonstration in the courtroom at Mooney's trial. All of his statements at Billings's trial about the time were rendered obsolete by the Kytka enlargements. At Mooney's trial he said that Billings had arrived about a quarter of two, and he refused to confirm the rest of his earlier testimony concerning the time.[57]

The refusal of the prosecution to allow the defense to use the Hamilton negatives until the court ordered it to do so was one reason why McNutt did not have the clock evidence at Billings's trial. By the time the defense developed that evidence, it was too late to refute McDonald's testimony against Billings. At Mooney's trial Cunha pointed out that the District Attorney was not bound voluntarily to let the defense see the pictures; McNutt could have obtained them by court order at any time, he said.[58] Strictly speaking, that was true, and McNutt was at fault; Cunha's attitude was unexceptionable according to the conception of the District Attorney's office that admitted solely the duty to prosecute. "You know," Cunha once said, "the prosecution in a criminal case is not a wet nurse for the defense."[59] However, it has long been recognized that a District Attorney is a quasi-judicial officer as well as a prosecutor. In the words of a California Supreme Court decision of 1884: "Equally with the court, the district attorney, as the representative of law and justice, should be fair and impartial. He should remember that it is not his sole duty to convict. . . ."[60] From this point of view it was Fickert's duty to share the photographs with McNutt before he was commanded to do so.*

It is by no means clear that Fickert willfully suppressed the clock evidence at Billings's trial. Had he known that the clock hands could be read and found out what they said, he would surely have persuaded McDonald before Billings's trial that McDonald was recalling the time inaccurately. At the same time Fickert undoubtedly realized that the Hamilton photographs would corroborate Mooney's alibi in a general way, and so he kept them from McNutt as long as he could, parry-

---

* As the *Mooney-Billings Report* declared in 1931 (p. 189): "The function of a prosecuting attorney is not to harass the defense, but to aid in the development of the truth at the trial, whether that may tend to establish or defeat his own case. The conduct of the prosecution with regard to these photographs does not satisfy an exacting standard of fairness."

ing McNutt's informal requests and furnishing only low-grade enlargements.[61]

At Mooney's trial the defense offered new evidence that the bomb had been hurled. In addition to the account of Dr. J. Mora Moss, who testified as at Billings's trial, three Oakland residents stated that they had seen a dark object flashing downward before the explosion.[62] Another witness, Mrs. Jane Compton, from Chicago, testified that she had seen a man walk across the roof and lean over the cornice above the site of the explosion a second before the bombing occurred. (From her position she could not see whether he had dropped anything.)[63]

Several days before Mrs. Compton took the stand, a man had called on her in the lobby of the Kensington Hotel. He said he was from the District Attorney's office. He asked her if she realized that she would lower her social standing in San Francisco if she testified in the trials. Did she not think her husband's position would also be jeopardized? Mrs. Compton replied that her husband worked out of Chicago and would take care of himself. As for her social position, she said, she had been in San Francisco but a short time and had none. Several months later Mrs. Compton recognized her interviewer at Rena Mooney's trial. He was Martin Swanson.[64]

The defense made a more strenuous effort than before to show that the defendant was being framed and that Swanson had engineered the project. In Billings's trial, testimony about Swanson had been excluded as rigidly as the prosecution's testimony about conspiracy; in Mooney's trial Weinberg was permitted to testify about Swanson's alleged attempt to bribe him, and other evidence was admitted showing that the District Attorney had denied the defendants their right of counsel after the arrests. Cockran asked for a directed acquittal, on the grounds of the prosecution's irregular identifications, suppression and alteration of evidence, and Swanson's manipulations. The argument, unfortunately, was not entered into the record. Griffin made it clear when he denied the motion that he was impressed by Cockran's arguments, but he ruled that they went to the weight of the testimony and were properly the jury's to assess. The *Chronicle*'s account of the ruling makes it appear a close call for the District Attorney, and the *Chronicle* did not usually monger sensations at Fickert's expense.*

---

* *Chronicle*, February 6 and 7, 1917; *People v. Mooney*, III: 1647–48; *Bulletin*, February 6, 1917; and *Examiner*, February 7, 1917. The *Examiner* quoted Cockran in part: "We had the admission this morning from Captain Duncan Matheson that he willfully suspended justice in proceeding against the defendant. What a mockery, your Honor, that the law of California . . . may be set aside by a policeman at his own whim!"

The prosecution's argument after the close of testimony was presented once again by Fickert. He charged the jurors to render their verdict fearlessly, and asked for the death penalty. When he spoke of the connection of Billings's landlady with the Los Angeles *Times* bomb conspirators, Griffin admonished him to confine his remarks to the present case. Fickert assailed Dr. Moss again, accusing him this time of not attending to the wounded. Griffin upheld Cockran's objection that no such evidence was in the record. Fickert compared Mooney to John Wilkes Booth. Not excepting the trials of Lincoln's assassins, he said, Mooney's case was probably the most important ever tried in an American court:

> ... This defendant and his fellow-anarchists, in the time of peace, murdered ten men and women because these anarchists were bent on destroying the very government which Lincoln preserved and defended. The question which concerns you, gentlemen, here, as well as every other citizen of this great republic, is either to destroy anarchy or the anarchists will destroy the State.
>
> If the moral fibre of the people of this nation has been so weakened; if the seeds of anarchy have been so implanted in the body politic that we refuse or neglect to defend our citizens at home or abroad; when helpless women and children can be ruthlessly slain on the streets of our city, and those who murder them go unpunished, because those who have been sworn to enforce the laws have failed through neglect or fear to do their duty— we can then say farewell to the greatness of our nation; our boasted civilization is then only a self-delusion resting on the edge of a political abyss.[65]

Fickert ridiculed the idea that the United Railroads had anything to do with the case:

> The defense claimed and would have you believe that Jesse Lilienthal, president of the United Railroads, a man who does more charity than any other soul in San Francisco, one of the greatest attorneys in the state, and a man I am proud to call my friend, went out far and near and gathered in men and women to help in a conspiracy against Mooney.
>
> I know you men will not believe it. I know you men have plenty of nerve and courage. I want to tell you men of the jury there's been enough white feathers shown in this case to stuff a sofa pillow.[66]

Fickert also ridiculed Cockran: there were abler lawyers in San Francisco, he said, but not one of them was foolish enough to defend Mooney and his "frame-up" idea. "They had to go back to the Bowery of

New York—this gang of reds—and pick out Tammany's favored son to defend Mooney."[67]

The District Attorney apologized for his own shortcomings as an advocate; he lacked eloquence, he said, "but in my humble way I shall speak in behalf of the people of the State of California in language as simple as my belief is in the guilt of this defendant."[68] He concluded by asking the jury to do its duty fearlessly:

> For, with conscience satisfied with the discharge of duty, no consequence can harm you. There is no evil that we cannot face or fly from but the consciousness of duty disregarded. A sense of duty pursues us ever. It is omnipresent like the deity. If we take to ourselves the wings of morning and dwell in the uttermost parts of the earth, duty performed or duty violated is still with us for our happiness or misery, and if we say darkness shall overcome us, in darkness as in light our obligations are yet with us. We cannot escape their power nor fly from their presence. They are with us in this life, will be with us at the close, and in that scene of inconceivable solemnity which lies yet further onward, and when the memory of Mrs. Knapp has gone, we shall still find ourselves surrounded by consciousness of duty to pain us wherever it has been violated and to console us so far as God has given us grace to perform it.
>
> Gentlemen, I commit the honor of this city to your hands.[69]

Two *Bulletin* reporters, George P. West and Lemuel F. Parton, quickly discovered that Fickert's peroration had been lifted bodily from an address delivered by Daniel Webster at a murder trial in 1830. The relevant passages of the two speeches were printed late that day in parallel columns on the front page of the *Bulletin*.[70]

In addressing the jury, McNutt pointed out that it was not the defense's responsibility to discover who committed the crime. There was plenty of evidence to show that Mooney had not done it. The flag was not on trial, he said, nor had the prosecution shown the motive for the bombing; Cunha's promise in his opening statement to prove that the bomb was part of a conspiracy to bring on a revolution and to kill the President and the Governor was not substantiated by a shred of evidence. He charged again that the case was framed, that the frame-up was "the spawn of this slimy creature, Martin Swanson."[71] He pointed out that the prosecution had refused to put Swanson on the stand, and declared that Swanson was the only man who could disprove the frame-up. "We don't have to go to the Bowery or to any other street in New York . . . to prove the frame-up in this case." Oxman he dismissed as a "fool or a perjurer."[72]

The next morning, for the first time since the graft trials, admission to Griffin's courtroom was by card only.[73] The room was jammed for Cockran's final plea. His address was restrained, less oratorical and less personal than Fickert's, extensively theoretical, with occasional florid touches. He dwelt at length on the meaning of equality before the law. Would the authorities have seized and confined Mr. Spreckels or Mr. Crocker without warrant, without evidence, without arraignment befor a magistrate? Officers had testified to the state of affairs: "Matheson has avowed their principles of government; they suspend the law whenever they consider it necessary for justice." He discussed the meaning of reasonable doubt. The jurors should consider reasonable doubt of the evidence of Mooney's guilt as they would a doctor's word that their favorite child had leprosy. The lack of a known motive in the bomb case was grounds for reasonable doubt. Fickert attributed the crime to anarchism; his ideas of anarchism were distorted:

It does seem impossible even in the space of six weeks to get an idea through the head of the District Attorney. I must remind him that anarchy is opposed to every idea of violence. If I may be permitted to say so, he throws a fit at every mention of anarchy. . . .

To clear away the fog that the District Attorney is laboring under, I will tell him that anarchy is a theory of human perfection, that men are capable of living together in harmony without law.

It holds that government which is organized to preserve order is perverted to suit the purposes of the rich by individuals to whom that government is entrusted.

When the prosecution shows by its acts that the law treats Mooney in one way and the rich man in another has not the theory of anarchy been proved?[74]

Cockran compared the trial to the Dreyfus case. Was Mooney to be sacrificed to the honor of Fickert? Was Mooney to be "put on the end of a rope and sent spinning round and round and round that Martin Swanson may become more valuable to some corporation?" He concluded modestly, saying that he felt his own shortcomings.[75]

Cunha's argument was last. He analyzed testimony, attacked the frame-up charge, and stressed the anarchist theme. Cockran, he said, was only a visitor: "He is not concerned about San Francisco so much. He is not concerned whether the 'Blasters of San Francisco' are at work, and whether we cannot let our mothers and sisters go upon our main streets to watch a parade in safety."[76] Cunha defended the efforts of the police: they were unaccustomed to this kind of crime. He defended his witnesses: if they were not convincing, "we might as well abandon the city to 'the Blasters of San Francisco.' "[77] If the prosecution's evidence was defective in any way, the jury was not responsible: if a man is hanged on perjured testimony, the perjurer, not the juror, is guilty. To acquit Mooney of the bombing would be to convict Oxman of it.[78] As for Swanson, he was irrelevant: "We have shown you that Martin Swanson never had anything to do with a single witness in this case."[79] The frame-up idea was absurd: would the prosecution permit discrepancies in the testimony of its witnesses if it was framing the defendant? Then the climax:

Some day, when some of you gentlemen are gone, I may have to answer to a higher court than this. I may need you when one of these Van Loo children, grown up to be fifteen or sixteen years old, comes to me and says: "Are you Mr. Cunha? I want to speak to you about that bomb explosion. I can remember my mother—her hair, it was a beautiful golden color. I remember her smile. I have never seen a smile like that since. She knew what it meant. In her consciousness she grasped an American flag to her heart and said: 'I won't surrender a bit of my spirit. I will die bravely.' "

I hope I can say to him that you did your duty, gentlemen, that you walked out of this courtroom like American citizens.

I want you to return your verdict promptly in this case . . . kicking the props from under anarchy of San Francisco, kicking the props out of indecency and lawlessness in San Francisco, just as they kicked the head off of poor old Lawlor and blew his body to pieces.[80]

Jurors and spectators alike wept as Cunha concluded.[81]

Griffin's charge to the jury was prudent. Some thought it favored the defense. The judge told the jurors that they might take into consideration the manner of the arrests. If, in their view, the officials had willfully violated the defendant's rights, that affected the good faith of the prosecution; and the jury had the right to consider the prosecution's good faith in determining the credibility of its witnesses and the weight of their testimony.[82]

The jurors were out for six and a half hours. They decided quickly that Mooney was guilty of first-degree murder. After lengthy discussion they agreed on the death penalty. As they returned to the courtroom, a visiting attorney, Edwin V. McKenzie, saw the foreman glance toward Cunha and draw his finger across his neck. A moment later the clerk read the verdict. There was a pause, as if those who listened were waiting to hear a recommendation of life imprisonment. Then women

screamed and fainted. The crowd rose to its feet and wild disorder ensued. Rena Mooney's sister accosted Fickert and swore vengeance.
Police rushed to clear the court. McNutt was roughly handled by an
officer, who failed to recognize him, until Fickert and Cunha intervened. Mooney, pale but calm, was returned to his cell.[83]

VI

Fickert announced at once through the press that another co-con-
spirator, never before heard of in the bomb cases, had confessed committing 72 crimes, including murder and the dynamiting of property,
and had directly implicated most of the defendants.[84] "San Francisco
would be amazed to know the extent of the conspiracy of which the
Preparedness Parade bomb explosion was incidental," he said.[85] The
confession vindicated Mooney's conviction, and Mooney's conviction
would encourage other witnesses to come forward. "Heretofore we
have encountered much difficulty in securing witnesses, as people
everywhere are reluctant to come forward and testify."[86] The next
day Fickert revealed the conspirator's name. He was "Tex" Lefler, the
Oakland electrical worker convicted of dynamiting in the 1913 PG&E
strike.* Under questioning by reporters, Fickert conceded that prosecuting any of the defendants in the present case for earlier crimes on
the basis of Lefler's evidence was barred by the statute of limitations,
and that Lefler had vanished.[87] But there was even bigger news. "UP-
RISING IN S. F. PLANNED BY ANARCHS," announced the *Examiner*:
the Preparedness Day conspirators had "contemplated as a last resort
an armed revolt against law and order in San Francisco." On July 23,
1916, a "large number of rifles and ammunition were removed after
midnight from a secret hiding place in the office of 'The Blast.'" Fickert said that he had no direct evidence of rifles, but that he had "several
witnesses who saw long cases moved out of 'The Blast' office . . . and
they have told me that they had reason to believe arms were being
disposed of. These witnesses have been afraid to testify."[88]
    That was all. Rifles and witnesses, Lefler's confession and Lefler,
all quickly faded from the Mooney case, leaving a phantasmagoric resi-
due, and perhaps a firmer belief that Mooney's jurors had acted with
courage.
    Meanwhile Cunha reasserted the prosecution's long-standing claim

---

* See p. 100 above.

that Berkman was the "brains" of the bomb conspiracy. The grand jury might be asked to indict him for murder, he said. For the time being no indictment was requested. But for himself Cunha took no chances: police guarded his house 24 hours a day. Fickert had taken precautions earlier: at the beginning of the trial he sent his family out of town and moved into the Olympic Club.[89]

From the county jail Mooney reasserted his innocence and said that he could not stop perjury. "This verdict does not make me guilty. I am not guilty." He expressed his conviction that the labor movement would "assert its economic power all over this country to prevent the carrying out of any sentence that may be passed upon me."[90]

The first claim for the reward was made immediately after Mooney's conviction. It came from four members of the Sacramento police department, including Henry Balsz, on the grounds that they had advised the arrest of Mooney and Billings. But Captain Matheson announced that no reward would be paid. He said that the evidence was gathered piecemeal, and allocation of the reward would therefore be impossible.[91]

VII

William V. MacNevin, a San Francisco realtor, served as the foreman of Mooney's jury. He was personally acquainted with Cunha. The two had spent many weekends together with friends at Frank J. Murphy's ranch in Cupertino. (Murphy had been one of Abe Ruef's attorneys during the graft trials.)[92] In the pre-trial question of prospective jurors, MacNevin minimized his relation with Cunha; he claimed it was only a casual acquaintance. He also said that he was opposed to anarchy but believed he could give an anarchist a fair and impartial trial.[93]

Between 1922 and 1935, four persons testified that MacNevin was in collusion with Cunha during the trial: MacNevin's wife, who sued him for divorce in 1922; her brother, J. G. Denton, whose tale is fantastic and untrustworthy;* J. B. Zimdars, an attorney for MacNevin's business partner; and Edwin V. McKenzie, brother of Cunha's roommate at the Olympic Club and an attorney who joined the defense not

---

* According to Denton, MacNevin would get $5,000 for the conviction and $250 a month as long as Mooney was in prison, and Fickert and Cunha would make him president of the San Francisco Board of Police Commissioners. (Denton testimony, California Supreme Court, "Habeas Corpus," IX: 5518–25.)

long after Mooney's conviction. Zimdars alone was probably a disinterested party, but among the others McKenzie is a generally trustworthy source. Zimdars said that his information came from MacNevin in the fall of 1917; McKenzie's information came from Cunha through McKenzie's brother, shortly after the trial. According to Zimdars and McKenzie, meetings were arranged between Cunha and MacNevin at Frank Murphy's house and in Eddie Graney's poolhall on Market Street, where the men were inconspicuous in the evening crowds.[94] MacNevin denied the charges, and no proof of them was ever forthcoming. Ultimately MacNevin joined those who were trying to help free Mooney.[95]

CHAPTER THIRTEEN

Rigall Has an Idea

*Anybody taking a look at these letters ... , not
understanding all the facts of the case, certainly
they might get the wrong idea about the letters.*
—Ed Cunha

A little comedy doesn't hurt at all.
—Police Judge Matthew Brady
at preliminary hearing of Frank Oxman

THE STRAIN of the trial and the conviction left the defense weak.
Cockran returned east to appeal for labor's help. McNutt and Minor,
ill, were confined to bed for a fortnight. Lawlor was left to carry on
the "battle of the affidavits": half a dozen persons who showed up
shortly after Mooney's conviction swore out affidavits impeaching Oxman, Mellie Edeau, and the jury. With these statements the defense
supported its request for a retrial.[1]

The charges in the affidavits were sensational. Some of them eventually proved sound; others were erroneous or fraudulent. The most
remarkable affidavit was made by Mrs. Charlotte La Posee, a Portland
salesman's wife, who told defense attorneys a few hours after the conviction that she and her boy had watched the parade at Market and
Ellis Avenue (about five-sixths of a mile from Steuart), and that Oxman stood beside her until about 2 P.M. She recognized him, she said,
as a customer of the Portland clothing store where she had worked.[2]
In Oregon, Oxman denied the story. Cunha labeled it a defense frame-
up concocted to get a new trial.[3] Fickert stated that he had three witnesses now to corroborate Oxman, notably a "John Regal, an Oregon
business man, who was with Oxman on the day of the Preparedness
parade."* From other employees at the Portland store the prosecution
obtained counter-affidavits denying that Oxman had ever shopped
there.[4]

---

* *Call,* February 14, 1917. See also *Chronicle,* February 15, 1917. Fickert, questioned
about this in 1936, denied that he had ever mentioned Rigall's name as a witness. "In
fact, I am positive that no such statement appeared in the press at that time," he testified.
(California Supreme Court, "Habeas Corpus," XV: 9953.)

The La Posee statement was eventually to embarrass the defense, for it was contradicted by Earl Hatcher when Hatcher finally came forward. Post-trial affidavits were in any event frail reeds. The law gave little weight to the assertions of persons unwilling to declare themselves before the verdict. After Mooney's trial Griffin decided finally to ignore them all.[5]

Griffin denied the motion for a retrial and late in February sentenced Mooney to hang. He set the execution for May 17. It was Griffin's first death sentence. Mooney asked for permission to make a statement, but Griffin replied that it was not the custom; Mooney's attorney had spoken. The defense announced that it would appeal the verdict.[6]

II

Weeks before Mooney was sentenced, there began a long and outlandish sequence of events which led to the exposure of Frank Oxman.

Ed Rigall had Oxman's letters with him during his stay in San Francisco. He told no one about them. Before he left he mentioned casually to Cunha that he still had these letters, and Cunha asked whether he had them with him. He replied that he did not, that they were in Grayville.[7] Two weeks before the end of the trial, Rigall left San Francisco, convinced by the repeated assurances of the only people he knew there that Mooney and his associates were guilty.[8] He apparently had no reason to doubt the good faith of Fickert and Cunha, though he knew that Oxman was intending perjury. According to Rigall, Oxman once admitted as much, saying to him, "Hell, you were here as much as I was."[9] Between Rigall and the prosecution there had been at least a pretense of honesty. Fickert and Cunha never told him to invent testimony; they had accepted and reviewed the testimony he offered after repeated conversations with Oxman.[10]

On February 6 Rigall, back in Grayville, wrote Cunha a pleasant, sociable letter:

Dear Mr. Cunha:

I arrived home all O.K. and sure had a fine trip. Upon my arrival I found that Mr. Oxman had written my mother a letter the same as the one he wrote me. I have all letters, also telegrams. Shall I send them to you, or Mr. Fickert? Hope you are getting along with the case as well as when I left.

Yours truly,
F. E. RIGALL[11]

Cunha had not seen Oxman's letters and probably had little idea what was in them. He did not reply. Six days later, three days after Mooney's conviction, Rigall sent Cunha a startling, paradoxical wire:

Congratulations on your conviction. Think my evidence will get party new trial.[12]

Cunha wired back at once:

Cannot understand your telegram. You told me your friend was thoroughly truthful and reliable. We have plenty of other witnesses and conclusive evidence supporting his testimony. Am astounded at your suggestion that you have testimony to help defendant. It is your duty to reveal to me at once any and all facts which you have, because I certainly want this defendant to have a new trial if he is entitled to it. Wire me collect all details at once. Explain in detail your telegram and your attitude. Be careful and fair because any witness who has testified falsely in this murder case must himself be prosecuted for murder. You should have told me anything you knew before the witness testified. After wiring write me every slight notion even which you have on this case, and send all data. I am sure you know nothing to get defendant new trial, but I personally feel responsibility and would later on have Governor change penalty or pardon, if I developed any kind of a doubt. At present I am thoroughly satisfied even without your friend's testimony, just as jury was in first case, but I want every thing cleared up in my mind. Wire immediately to me at Olympic Club, San Francisco, California.

EDWARD A. CUNHA[13]

Cunha's telegram was disingenuous. He assumed that Rigall's "evidence" concerned Oxman, although Rigall had not said it did. His tone was high-minded, but he was already arguing that Oxman's testimony had not been crucial. Part of his telegram was pure bluff: he did not have "plenty of other witnesses" supporting Oxman; as he was forced to admit, years later, he had no other witnesses at all.[14] What Cunha wanted to know, without revealing his eagerness for the information, was what evidence Rigall had. Oxman's letters to Rigall —written evidence—might be dangerous. Oxman would know the truth; he did not have the letters but might have copies, and could at least help Cunha decide whether to take Rigall's threat seriously.[15]

Mrs. La Posee's affidavit was announced the day after Rigall's wire came. It gave Cunha an excuse to go to Oregon to see Oxman. The newspapers reported that Cunha went to obtain affidavits from Oxman and others to contradict Mrs. La Posee. Cunha did obtain a few such affidavits when he met Oxman in Portland a day later, but the real purpose of his visit was to find out what Oxman had written Rigall.[16]

According to Cunha's testimony much later, Oxman told him that he had merely done as he had been told. He had written to Rigall to get him to come out, and he had been mistaken in thinking that Rigall was the man he had seen on July 22; he had told Cunha so in San Francisco. (In this and other respects, Cunha's story differed from Rigall's.) Oxman, Cunha said, told him that his letter to Rigall had made it perfectly clear he was looking for the man he saw in San Francisco on July 22. When Oxman admitted he had also invited Rigall's mother, Cunha told him that he had not been authorized to invite her, and pointed out that he had never mentioned doing so. Uneasy, Cunha persuaded Oxman to return to San Francisco to be on hand in the event of trouble from Rigall.[17] Oxman arrived in San Francisco on February 17 or 18 and stayed for about five days, until the motion for a new trial was denied. The press reported that he was there to attend to cattle business and to refute Mrs. La Posee.[18]

Fickert knew no more than Cunha of what Oxman had written Rigall. All the testimony on this point, whether from Oxman, Rigall, Cunha, or Fickert, agrees; and reason sides with the testimony. Oxman's intent was too bald, too well recorded in the letters, for any attorney, no matter how unscrupulous, to condone it. Fickert was not and cannot be charged with conspiracy to suborn Rigall's perjury. Whether he condoned Oxman's own perjuries after reading the Kansas City affidavit is another matter.

Like Cunha, Fickert expected Rigall to return to San Francisco in time to exploit whatever nuisance value there was in Oxman's letters. Fickert proposed to solve the problem directly, without fuss. He asked Captain Matheson to station Lieutenant Bunner at the railroad terminal to intercept Rigall and relieve him of his papers. Matheson and Bunner refused to cooperate.[19] It was beneath their dignity to prowl around railroad stations on such a mission. Fickert later acknowledged the plan, and explained: "we became suspicious because it looked like he [Rigall] was making a demand for money or something, and thought it would be best to see if we could get him and follow him and see where he went to."[20] As it turned out, Rigall did not come to San Francisco as Fickert and Cunha expected. In fact, the prosecution did not hear from him at all. He never answered Cunha's telegram. Oxman went back to Oregon.[21] It was an ominous quiet, the calm before a storm.

III

Sometime not long after the trial, Mooney's attorneys learned from a Fresno woman who had known Oxman in his younger days that Oxman had come from Grayville, Illinois.[22] They decided that an investigation at Grayville might be fruitful. Ed Nolan accordingly wired Ed Nockels, secretary of the Chicago Federation of Labor, whom he knew personally: the prosecution would probably use Oxman at Nolan's trial, and the defense could not finance an investigation of Oxman in Illinois. Could Nockels handle it? Nockels telephoned John Walker, president of the Illinois State Federation of Labor, and asked him to send someone to Grayville.[23] Walker sent two investigators. They stopped at Rigall's poolhall during their inquiries. Rigall, supposing that they were San Francisco detectives, directed them to his attorney, Claude O. Ellis, ex-mayor of Grayville and once Oxman's attorney.[24] The two agents were shown Oxman's letters.[25] They reported their find to Walker, and Walker informed Frank Mulholland, the machinists' attorney assisting in Nolan's defense.[26] Ellis also wrote directly to Mulholland in Toledo on March 10: "I understand that you are one of the attorneys interested in the defense of Thomas Mooney. . . . I believe I can be of material assistance in securing the acquit[t]al of Mooney on this charge and I am willing to undertake the work on a contingent fee to be hereafter agreed upon."[27] (Ellis sent along a copy of an old local newspaper article, dealing with a land fraud in which Frank Oxman represented his swamp property as good farm land, showed his buyer a neighbor's farm, and made the sale.)[28] Mulholland left at once for Chicago, where he met Ellis and Rigall and examined the letters.[29]

Rigall was willing to let Mulholland have the letters for $10,000.[30] The price created serious difficulties. Mulholland conferred with Nockels, and Nockels promised to consult Cockran and Frank P. Walsh in New York. The three met in Cockran's office and concluded that Rigall's demands could not be met.[31] Meanwhile Ellis, having returned to Grayville with the letters, found his law offices broken into and thoroughly ransacked. So far as he could tell, nothing was missing. Apparently an attempt had been made to steal the Oxman letters. A few weeks later a second attempt, also unsuccessful, was made in San Francisco.[32]

Three weeks passed and the Oxman letters were still in the hands of Ellis and Rigall. Mulholland did not have the $10,000. Ellis did not insist upon cash; he was willing to accept a promise, but Mulholland was unwilling to give his word until he knew that he could make it good.[33] At this juncture a crisis was precipitated by the rumor that Fickert was leaving San Francisco for Chicago in connection with the Oxman letters. The negotiations would have to be settled by the time he arrived. Mulholland decided to go to Washington to see certain labor leaders, particularly William H. Johnston, the Socialist president of the International Association of Machinists, and Samuel Gompers. (Gompers had been informed by Cockran of the letters.) Mulholland needed at least guarantees of the money so that he could take possession of the Rigall documents and covering affidavits in Chicago before Fickert arrived.[34]

Meanwhile Edwin V. McKenzie had arrived in Chicago from San Francisco. McKenzie was an able, self-educated lawyer who had helped defend the anarchists Caplan and Schmidt in the aftermath of the Los Angeles *Times* case. He had recently joined the defense as Weinberg's attorney, along with Thomas O'Connor, a vigorous young criminal lawyer,[35] at the request of several San Francisco rabbis who were disturbed by press characterizations of Weinberg as a Russian Jew. The rabbis soon withdrew, persuaded by Fickert (with a flourish of an item or two from the Martinez arsenal) that Weinberg and Mooney were guilty; but McKenzie and O'Connor were kept on by the International Workers Defense League. According to McKenzie, the defense in San Francisco learned about the Oxman letters only on the first of April, an astonishing delay. Perhaps Mulholland had feared a leak to the prosecution. When the information came through, McNutt sent McKenzie east at once. The IWDL did not have $10,000. It was able to wire him $1,000 or $2,000 by the time he arrived in Chicago. McKenzie went on to Washington for the rest of the needed sum. He got it in a cash loan from William H. Johnston at Mulholland's request. He took the money back to Chicago and met Rigall and Ellis at the La Salle Hotel. There he examined the Oxman letters, compared them to an exemplar of Oxman's handwriting which he had brought from San Francisco, and confirmed Mulholland's belief that the letters were genuine.[36]

The three men argued all night over the ten thousand dollars. McKenzie acknowledged that he had the cash in his pocket and said that he would give it to them if he had to, but he pleaded for the use of the letters without payment. He said that the letters would lose most of their value if Rigall took money, that the prosecution would raise collateral issues and the transaction would be deemed equivalent to blackmail, that five lives depended upon those letters and the defense could not afford to compromise the evidence.[37] McKenzie later had this to say to the Assistant Attorney General of California at the 1935–36 hearings:

If you are trying to assume that I bribed somebody, why don't you ask me the direct question and give me a chance to answer you . . . ? I was dealing with a man who had at least come across the country to testify as to perjury in a case; I was not dealing with any sweet magnolia when I dealt with Rigall; I was under no illusions; I was dealing with a man who in the same kind of a case would want pay from me. Those men were trying to hold me up, but if the information that they had, if the letters that they had were authentic, then the fact that they were demanding money had nothing to do—was collateral to the writing of the subornation letters.

. . .

. . . Now, if those men were so without principle that they insisted on money for it, I would pay them the money rather than to see four or five people die because the money was not paid. That is my code. That is my principle. I want the record to show that I had quite a struggle on it, and that I believed it then and I believe [now] it would be absolutely cowardly not to have paid the $10,000 if I had been required to do so to get those letters.[38]

Rigall and Ellis finally relented. At eight o'clock the next morning McKenzie, according to his testimony, obtained the letters without paying a dollar. It was agreed that if necessary Rigall and Ellis would come to San Francisco, Ellis to be compensated for his time and Rigall to receive expense money. McKenzie immediately had the letters photographed for safety's sake and then returned on the Overland Limited to San Francisco.[39]

Was there nothing more to the arrangement than McKenzie described? The evidence is meager, but it is possible that Mulholland made a financial promise at some point to Rigall and Ellis: in 1935, when the defense was once again anxious to have Rigall's cooperation, Ed Nockels wrote Frank Walsh, who was then Mooney's chief attorney, that he had talked with Mulholland in Washington, "and he said something about having promised Rigall and his attorney Two Thousand Dollars upon Mooney's release. I mention this because I believe these fellows will want some dough before they go any further."[40] Walsh replied: "Of course, nobody has, or ever had, any authority either to pay any money or promise any money to either

Rigall or his attorney."* There is no evidence that Rigall at any time was paid more than his expenses.

IV

Rigall's depravity has been consistently overlooked or sidestepped in the documents and accounts of the Mooney case. In holding out the Oxman letters from the defense for a price, he prevented the letters from reaching Griffin in time for the judge to order a new trial, and so, as events unfolded, condemned Mooney to a 22-year search for justice. Still worse, until the Illinois State Federation of Labor's agents appeared in Grayville in March, about the time Mooney was sentenced to hang, Rigall had no intention whatever of showing the letters to the defense. What he wanted to do was to blackmail the prosecution.

Sometime during his original visit to San Francisco, Rigall decided that blackmail was more attractive than perjury. He may have calculated that there was more money in blackmail. His anticipated share of the bomb case reward, as a corroborating witness for Oxman, was perhaps $3,000; since a month later he demanded $10,000 for the letters from the defense, he presumably expected to ask at least that much from Fickert. And if money was the objective, why not? Oxman was rich and Fickert had wealthy contacts. Money was all on the side of the prosecution. Rigall's problem was to get at it. When he wrote Cunha he skirted federal laws against the use of the mails for blackmail: "shall I send the letters to you, or Mr. Fickert?" His subsequent wire was ambiguous. "Congratulations on your conviction. Think my evidence will get party new trial." The incongruity of these two sentences has always been apparent. Cunha protested before the grand jury in May 1917 (and again in the 1935–36 hearings) that he "did not know what to make of it."[41] Mooney's defenders had no such difficulty: they universally assumed that the telegram was, in McKenzie's words, a "piece of sarcasm."[42] That is, Rigall's congratulations were insincere, and Rigall, a man with a sense of fair play, wanted to give the villains a chance to undo their mischief before acting to save their victims. This interpretation is false.†

* Walsh to Nockels, July 10, 1935, Walsh Papers. McKenzie testified later that he "heard afterwards Mr. Ellis was paid $2,000." That may have been Ellis's legal fee. (McKenzie testimony, California Supreme Court, "Habeas Corpus," IX: 5292.)

† The explanation of Attorney Ellis was that Rigall's messages to Cunha were sent in order to get an admission from Cunha that Rigall was in San Francisco. (Ellis affidavit, November 8, 1917, paraphrased in Hunt, *Case of Thomas J. Mooney and Warren K. Billings,* pp. 264–65.) That may be true, but it is collateral.

It was not the congratulations which Rigall meant ironically. Rigall himself testified that he meant them sincerely, and he was probably telling the truth.[43] His irony was rather in his second sentence: he had no intention of helping Mooney to get a new trial. What he meant was, "Think my evidence *could* get party new trial." He was bidding for a bribe.

As Rigall understood the situation, there was little reason to care whether Mooney lived or died. He believed that Mooney was a dangerous anarchist, guilty of murder. By his own admission he had Oxman's letters in his pocket in San Francisco; he could have sounded out Cockran or McNutt for a sale then, had he seriously considered it. But he did not know the defense attorneys—he had no contact with them. He said afterward that he had been suspicious of them, and perhaps he was, though more likely he simply did not want to deal with them, as the following interrogation in the San Francisco police court in April 1917 indicates:

Q. [Oxman's attorney] You saw Mr. Bourke Cochrane [*sic*] seated at the trial table, representing Mr. Mooney?

A. [Rigall] Yes, sir, I knew him.

Q. You knew those gentlemen were counsel for Mr. Mooney, in that case, which meant life imprisonment, or death—you knew that, didn't you?

A. Yes sir.

Q. Why didn't you go to them and speak with them?

A. I was afraid they might think I was crazy, and maybe have me put in jail, or something, and frameup on me, and hang me, too.

Q. Why didn't you—you had the letters with you, and the telegrams you had received from Mr. Oxman?

A. Yes sir.

Q. Had them in your possession?

A. Yes sir.

Q. Why didn't you send them over to Mr. McNutt or Mr. Cochrane?

A. For the same reason.

Q. Afraid they might put some job on you?

A. They might think that I was crazy. I didn't know anybody in San Francisco, except Mr. Oxman.[44]

Rigall must have hatched the blackmail scheme before he left San Francisco; otherwise he would have had no reason to tell Cunha falsely that the letters were back in Illinois. He could not negotiate with Cunha while he was still in the city; Fickert's scheme for relieving Rigall of the papers on his return to San Francisco suggests what might have happened had Rigall started negotiations before he had left the state. There was plenty of time. Mooney's conviction would not change things. Even if Mooney were sentenced and hanged before an arrangement with the prosecution could be made, there were two more trials coming up. The problem was to inform the prosecution from Illinois, without leaving a trail of evidence, that the Oxman letters were valuable. In this respect Rigall failed. Fickert probably accepted Oxman's assurances that the letters were really quite harmless. There is no evidence that Fickert did go to Chicago in early April. As it turned out, the defense had found Rigall before any further moves between Rigall and the prosecution were made.

The question naturally arises why Rigall's blackmail attempt was kept quiet in subsequent proceedings by the men who became aware of it. The explanation probably lies in the fact that Rigall turned out to be everybody's witness. Fickert and Cunha had only limited circumstantial evidence to prove that Rigall had attempted to blackmail them. They could guess but could not prove that Rigall and Ellis had a price on the letters.* (That the defense was asked $10,000 for the letters was, of course, kept secret from the prosecution.) By making out a blackmail case against Rigall, Fickert might have helped Oxman, but he would also have embarrassed the prosecution, which had paid Rigall's expenses. As for the defense, Rigall became their witness. They naturally had no desire to discredit him, and he did not choose to defame himself.

V

If there was a turning point in the Mooney case, it came in the month of April 1917. The date is extremely early for a man who had been convicted for only two months and was not to leave prison for another 22 years. That contrast in time symbolizes the tragedy of the Mooney story. Juridically speaking, the climax came early; the rest was a glacial denouement. To be sure, there were many later crises, and for more than a year Mooney was on San Quentin's death row. But the defense came closer to justice in April 1917 than at any other time—for clemency in 1939 was hardly justice. In April 1917 the de-

---

* On August 20, 1917, a Chicago detective working for Oxman's attorney reported to him from Grayville that one William Halem "states that at the time Rigall was supposed to have received a letter from Oxman in San Francisco, he, Rigall, went to Halem and asked him what he thought would be the best way to sell or get money for certain letters that would help Mooney. . . ." Halem would not give the detective an affidavit, however. (Investigator No. 132, Special report, Shortridge file, California State Archives, Attorney General's Records, Box 226.)

fense obtained the Oxman letters, Fremont Older and Judge Griffin were converted, the police attitude softened, and Fickert almost conceded Mooney's right to a new trial. In April, too, a movement began to recall Fickert from office, Mellie Edeau was impeached, foreign protests commenced, and the case became a genuinely national issue. The foreign and federal aspects and the recall election will be discussed later. The remainder of the present chapter deals with the Oxman and Edeau affairs as they developed in the next few weeks.

When Edwin McKenzie returned to San Francisco, the defense took for granted that the Oxman letters would lead to a new trial for Mooney. As McKenzie said, "We had no thought . . . that prejudice would be enough to keep a man in, in the face of those letters."[45] The question was how to use the letters most effectively. The attorneys had two alternatives. They could go to Oxman and seek a confession from him, which might involve Fickert and Cunha in a charge of suborning Oxman's perjury; or they could go to Fickert and Cunha and bargain with them for a new trial, leaving Oxman to take care of himself. They chose the latter course, on the grounds that their objective was not to injure the prosecution, but to undo the results of the trial.[46]

Before approaching the prosecution, the defense sought out Fremont Older and won him over by showing him the letters. From the legal point of view this step was not particularly desirable. The case belonged in the courts, not in the office of a newspaper editor. But evidently Older already knew about the letters. Andrew Furuseth, the old sailor, had recently returned from Chicago, where he had seen or learned of the letters, perhaps through Nockels. Furuseth told Older about them. Shortly afterward Older was shown the originals.[47]

Older says in his autobiography that he believed Mooney was guilty until he saw the letters, which convinced him that Fickert had framed the Mooney case.[48] That was probably an oversimplification. Older did begin his long, arduous crusade for Mooney the day he saw the letters, but he must have had doubts of Mooney's guilt before then. A careful examination of his newspaper for the preceding seven months reveals a consistent avoidance of assuming Mooney's guilt. After all, he had never respected Fickert. His staff writers were familiar with the known circumstances of the bomb arrests and convictions, and in those circumstances were ample grounds for suspicion of more profound malfeasance than was yet known. Older himself knew that jury foreman MacNevin was a friend of Cunha's. Editorial policies suggest that he entertained doubts: the *Bulletin*'s ridicule of Fickert for his Webster speech did not reflect editorial sympathy with a District Attorney who might be trying his best to convict a guilty anarchist-bomber. It would probably be fair to say that Older did not know whether Mooney was guilty, that he distrusted Fickert, but that he had no conclusive evidence against the prosecution, and could not and would not do anything about the case without it. When Older saw the Oxman letters, he was not so much converted as galvanized. They provided him at once with the means to public leadership in defense of Mooney. It was a new crusade, one that was to develop dimensions as imposing as the graft prosecution crusade, and to prove much more prolonged and disheartening.

When Older was shown the Oxman correspondence, the defense attorneys probably did not intend him to publish the letters before they had acted on them. But others in the city had heard about them, too. Older learned that the *Examiner* was going to publicize them. The letters were therefore not only legal evidence, but also an urgent news scoop. With the attorneys' cooperation he published the story in a late Extra edition of the *Bulletin* on April 11, the day of McKenzie's return, under the banner headline "OXMAN FRAMED TO HANG TOM MOONEY."[49] The *Bulletin* charged that Fickert, Cunha, and the police had conspired with Oxman to convict Mooney. The next day Older published photographic reproductions of the letters and of Rigall's Olympic Club pass as the guest of C. M. Fickert. Rigall was quoted as saying that Cunha had told him his testimony would convict Mooney, bring Cunha a high state office, and elect Fickert governor. "The astonishingly bald and casual proposals of Oxman to Rigall with their undeniable revelation of a cold-blooded plot, constitute one of the most sensational chapters in the annals of criminal conspiracy." A lengthy article by McNutt presented Rigall's story, and concluded:

> We have conclusive evidence that the prosecuting authorities suggested to Rigall that if he would corroborate Oxman the large reward in this case would be divided between and among the Smith women, Oxman and Rigall.
> All of the documents bearing upon this matter are safe in our possession and the witnesses to prove every material fact are in readiness.[50]

In fact, the evidence McNutt referred to was not conclusive. It consisted of Rigall's testimony, which could be controverted. Moreover,

Rigall himself was to testify not that Fickert or Cunha made the offer, but that Oxman made it. What the defense had was conclusive evidence that Oxman had urged Rigall to commit perjury. The rest was debatable.

A statement from Cunha was published in the same issue of the *Bulletin*. Cunha said that he knew of the Oxman letters, though not their contents; that he was glad the matter was out in the open; that Rigall had been brought to San Francisco by a mistaken identification on Oxman's part; and that the prosecution knew during the trial of Oxman's mistake. He concluded:

> Despite this fact Rigall wanted to testify, but I would not stand for it. When I went to Portland to see Oxman, after Mooney's conviction, I asked him about these letters. He said to me that he had written some letters that might look bad on their face, but he believed that he had to write those kind of letters to get Rigall here, because he knew just how hard we had to work to get him [Oxman] to testify, and he believed it legitimate for him to pursue the same tactics with Rigall.
>
> I know there are some things in my conduct in this case that might be criticized. I know that the question might be asked, if I knew of all these things, why didn't I report it to Superior Judge Griffin when an effort was being made to secure a new trial for Mooney. My answer is that I didn't like the looks or actions of Rigall from the first; that I believed he was the bunk, and I put no faith in any of his statements.

There was also a statement—a call to arms—from defense attorney Thomas O'Connor: "This is but the entering wedge. The whole story will follow. The police department and District Attorney's office are on trial. Oxman should and must be returned to San Francisco. . . . There will be no discharge in this war. It must go on to the end."[51]

Fickert was reported in Tehachapi. He was not available for comment for two days. When he returned he read the Oxman letters and issued a prepared statement corroborating Cunha's: the frame-up cry was nothing new in bomb-throwing cases; Oxman would answer every charge against him; the trials of the other conspirators would go on, and Oxman would be called again to the stand in the next trial.[52] Meanwhile Oxman in Oregon reaffirmed his testimony and accused the defense attorneys of trying to frame him. Oxman and Rigall were both requested to come to San Francisco.[53]

At this point Matheson and Fickert fell out. The police were under attack from the defense attorneys and the *Bulletin,* and Bunner at least was implicated in the Oxman-Rigall affair. Matheson had had enough. He was more interested in rescuing his own department than in saving Fickert's reputation. He announced that the police would interrogate Oxman first, in an open session independent of the District Attorney. Fickert's office announced, however, that since Oxman was coming at the instance of the District Attorney, it was proper for the District Attorney to interview him first.[54] A day or so later Matheson urged Fickert to request dismissal of the charges against Nolan. Said the former chief of the Bomb Bureau, "I was opposed to the arrest of Nolan in the first place. I look upon it as a grievous wrong to spend public money in the prosecution of a case that to me seems hopeless."[55] Fickert refused to say what he would do about Nolan.[56]

VI

Before either prosecution or defense had acted on the exposé of Oxman, the public was treated to another sensation or two. The day after publication of the Oxman letters a group of defense leaders called on Mrs. Mellie Edeau at her home in Oakland. The visitors were O'Connor, McKenzie, Older, attorney Charles Brennan, and Detective William H. Smith of the Oakland Police Department. On information from Smith and from Walter J. Peterson, the Oakland police chief, together with information from a post-trial affidavit, the defense had put together the following story:

A few days after the Preparedness Day bombing, Mrs. Edeau, an Oakland seamstress, obtained temporary employment in the shop of an Oakland clothier. She told shop employees that she had been at the corner of Steuart and Market during the parade, had seen a couple of old men carrying a heavy black suitcase there, and had seen the explosion. One of the tailors urged her to see Chief Peterson. She did so, and was taken by Detective Smith to San Francisco to identify Mooney and Billings. On the way she told Smith of being at Steuart and Market with her daughter and of seeing two "middle-aged" men acting suspiciously there with a square black suitcase. At no time that day did she say anything to Peterson or Smith about having been at 721 Market Street.

Smith took Mrs. Edeau to the Bomb Bureau. There they saw a picture of Mooney wearing a moustache—evidently his Martinez photograph—and they were escorted by Sergeant Goff to see Mooney and Billings. Both prisoners were alone in their cells. Mrs. Edeau told Smith that she had never seen either of them before in her life. She returned to Oakland, and reported to her fellow employees, "Those was just boys they showed me over there." She said they did not look anything like the men she had seen. Later, however, she told them that she thought she would be a witness in the case. She said that there was a lot of money in it now. The tailor demurred: would she accuse men of committing a crime unless she were certain? She replied that she would be a good witness; she had already sent three men to the penitentiary. There were too many working people in the world as it was. "What difference does it make as long as you get paid for it?" she said.

After she had worked at the clothier's about a week, Mrs. Edeau left. The tailor read in the paper that she had testified in the Billings case, and again in the Mooney case, and he decided that she had gone far enough. He called a reporter for the San Francisco *Daily News* and told him his story. The reporter took him to defense attorney John Lawlor, and for Lawlor the tailor swore out an affidavit which was then published, one of many overshadowed by the La Posee affidavit.[57]

On the day of Mrs. Edeau's first trip to San Francisco, Detective Smith had made out for Chief Peterson a routine report stating that she had not identified the suspects, and the matter was forgotten by the Oakland police. When it appeared that Mrs. Edeau was going to testify, Smith called to Peterson's attention her original failure to identify the defendants. Peterson was dissatisfied with the handling of the cases, but he felt that it was none of his business and did not interfere. He did not inform the defense, either. As he later said, "you do not usually find police officers going and giving evidence to the defendants."[58]

While the evidence is not consistent, it appears that on January 30, 1917, after Mrs. Edeau had testified in Mooney's trial, Fickert sent for Smith and asked him to corroborate Mrs. Edeau's testimony.* Smith, in any event, told Fickert at that time of Mrs. Edeau's failure to identify Mooney and Billings, and showed him his diary entry for July 28, 1916, to prove it. According to an affidavit of Smith, Fickert then told him to keep his mouth shut; he told him that he would make a good witness for the defense.[59]

Smith returned to the Oakland City Hall. There he met Mrs. Edeau, who said she had come to tell him that she had been nervous

* Smith contradicted this in his testimony in *People v. Rena Mooney*, IV: 1904–5, quoted in *Mooney-Billings Report*, p. 151; but see Smith's daily report to Peterson, January 30, 1917, in California Supreme Court, "Habeas Corpus," VIII: 5024: "[I] went to San Francisco to see District Attorney Fickert; he wanted me to corroborate the testimony of Mrs. Sadie [i.e., Mellie] Edeau in the Thomas Mooney bomb case...."

and excited the day she went with him to San Francisco, and that she could not identify the defendants then but she could now. Smith reminded her that she not only had denied their identification before, but had also changed her story's location from Steuart to 721 Market. "Well," replied Mrs. Edeau, "they showed us an enlarged picture at the office of the District Attorney, and told my daughter and me that the picture of the two women in a group in front of 721 Market Street were our pictures. That's how it came about."[60]

It was no secret from the police of San Francisco that originally Mrs. Edeau had failed to identify the defendants. The fact was common knowledge around both the Oakland and San Francisco police departments. Word of it eventually reached the Mooney defense, and attorneys went around to see Peterson and Smith, but that was not until many weeks after Mooney's conviction.[61] It coincided with the Oxman exposé.

Older, McKenzie, and Smith stood at the door of Mrs. Edeau's house that day in April, while O'Connor questioned the seamstress about her part in the cases. She rambled incoherently, referred to her dead husband whose brown eyes were looking at her, and insisted that she had no part in any frame-up. Under close questioning she grew hysterical, ran to a small table, opened the drawer, and drew out a revolver. O'Connor caught her wrist and took the gun away. Smith removed the cartridges. Chief Peterson, whom Older had sent for, arrived at this juncture and took the revolver. The incident was considered closed as far as the visitors were concerned.[62] But not for Mrs. Edeau. The *Examiner* published her version of the visit, that Older bullied her and O'Connor tried to intimidate her:

I told him [O'Connor] that I would not perjure myself. Years ago a little child with brown eyes died and I told him that I wanted to meet her some day and that I was a Christian woman and would not lie for any consideration.

When I said that O'Connor jumped up and caught both my arms, bruising them. He began pushing me around the room, saying: "You lie—you lied at the trial. If you don't do what we ask we will arrest you and put you in jail for perjury and disgrace you by printing the story about you in the papers."

While we were struggling he pushed me up against a table in the drawer of which was a revolver. I got the drawer open and caught up a gun. When O'Connor saw that he broke away and ran to the door, crying:

"This Christian woman is trying to shoot me."

Then Fremont Older and the others came in. I ordered O'Connor out of the house, but he said he would not go until I was arrested. The others got him to go. In all the bunch Charles Brennan was the only one that acted like a human being and tried to protect me. My back is sprained, my arms bruised and I intend to take legal action against O'Connor.[63]

Since the *Examiner* published no account from Smith or Peterson, the visit appeared as an intrusion, unwarranted and indecent. Probably the *Examiner*'s article resulted from a grudge: two days earlier the defense had given the Oxman scoop exclusively to the *Bulletin*. Mc-Kenzie commented years later that the publication of the Oxman letters in the *Bulletin* had probably harmed the cause of the defense: "it is a terrible policy not to treat the papers against you with equal courtesy."[64] For the *Examiner,* the Oxman scoop was only the most recent irritation in long years of bitterness between the Hearst papers and the *Bulletin.*

Strange to say, the prosecution had not had enough of the Edeaus. Fickert put them on the witness stand again in the trials of Rena Mooney and Israel Weinberg. The defense put Smith and Peterson on the stand to impeach them. Peterson testified that Mrs. Edeau had declared in the April interview that on July 22, 1916, she stood at Steuart and Market streets in the flesh while she was at 721 Market Street in her astral body.*

Three days after the Edeau escapade a third bombshell was dropped when Estelle Smith, sometime star witness for the prosecution, signed an affidavit in which she swore that after Mooney's trial Oxman had offered her a "sum in five figures" to perjure herself in the forthcoming Weinberg case. She said that she asked Oxman whether Fickert had sent him, and that he answered: " 'No, the men higher up than Fickert sent me to you.' "[65] Perhaps the defense leaders suspected the affidavit of being a dud. Nothing significant ever came of it.[66]

The same day O'Connor announced that an interview had been requested of him by John McDonald. Was another major confession about to be made? O'Connor apparently thought so. "The only witness for the state who cannot be impeached," he said, "is Police Sergeant George Russell, who made the diagrams of the scene of the explosion."[67] But something went wrong, and the interview was not

---

* Peterson testimony, *People v. Weinberg,* II: 970–71. Mrs. Edeau denied it. (*Ibid.,* pp. 720–21.)

held. (In 1921 McDonald did retract his testimony, although it was not the end of his self-contradictions.)

VII

Two days had passed since the publication of the Oxman letters, and the defense attorneys had not yet approached the prosecution. The natural member of the District Attorney's office to deal with was Edward Cunha. Not only was Cunha Mooney's prosecutor, he also was a personal friend of Tom O'Connor and Edwin McKenzie.[68] As it turned out, Cunha made the first advances himself. Over the weekend of April 13–15 three conferences were held, involving Cunha, O'Connor, McKenzie, Charles Brennan, and Older. On the following Wednesday a fourth conference was held, at which Fickert was present.

Cunha called on Older Friday night. He explained that he had believed the defendants guilty, but that he did not desire their conviction on perjured testimony. The next morning he met with Older and the three defense attorneys at Older's office. He agreed to recommend a new trial to Fickert on the strength of the Oxman letters.[69] Cunha then consulted Fickert. In a second meeting with McKenzie and O'Connor that afternoon Cunha said that Fickert would recommend a new trial for Mooney, but that the prosecution wanted first to obtain from Oxman a promise that he would not accuse the District Attorney's office. Fickert, Cunha said, would then "throw Oxman to the dogs."[70] Cunha denied knowing that Oxman was a perjurer, but admitted having been suspicious of him. In a third meeting of Cunha, McKenzie, and O'Connor that night, in Cunha's room at the Olympic Club, McKenzie told Cunha that he knew of Cunha's conferences with jury foreman MacNevin during the trial. According to McKenzie, Cunha was now more worried about the repercussions of this than about the Oxman letters.[71] Cunha might avoid implication in Oxman's effort to suborn perjury, but his conferences with MacNevin, if proven, would ruin his career. McKenzie told Cunha that he was not free of complicity in the Oxman affair, either: his wire to Rigall had given him away.* The three interviews that day were intended mainly to consider ways of saving Cunha. Attorney Nathan Coghlan

* McKenzie testimony, California Supreme Court, "Habeas Corpus," IX: 5322. Cunha's version of the conferences can be found in *ibid.*, XIII: 7856–95. Cunha denied nearly everything that McKenzie, O'Connor, and Older claimed had been said in the conferences.

importuned McKenzie, who was his friend, to rescue Cunha, and so did McKenzie's brother, Cunha's roommate; they were Cunha's personal friends.[72] McKenzie was willing to go along, but Cunha would have to help bring Mooney justice. McKenzie refused to shake Cunha's hand: Cunha had attempted to hang an innocent man with perjured testimony.[73]

McKenzie was suspicious of Fickert. Fickert had said that he wanted time only to see that Oxman would not "round" on him. McKenzie believed that the defense should try to reach Oxman first, lest Fickert back down on the recommendation for a new trial after he had set Oxman in line. However, that possibility seemed remote; did the letters not speak for themselves? McKenzie supposed that every official who saw the letters would consent to a new trial.[74]

The plan tentatively arranged Saturday night between McKenzie and Cunha, according to McKenzie, was that on Monday morning Fickert, in the presence of the newspapermen at the Hall of Justice, would send for the defendant's attorneys, McNutt, O'Connor, and McKenzie, and would request them to produce the Oxman letters. After examining them Fickert would reappear and announce to the reporters that he had no choice in view of the letters but to recommend a new trial for Mooney.[75] As Cunha told McKenzie, "These Oxman letters are rotten; there is no possible theory upon which their lack of culpability can be shown."[76]

The public announcement thus scheduled did not occur. Fickert had not yet secured Oxman. Oxman and Rigall were both on their way to San Francisco. Rigall arrived in Los Angeles Tuesday afternoon, accompanied by his wife, his mother, and his attorney, Ellis, and was met there by O'Connor and McKenzie, who brought the four on to San Francisco. Oxman arrived the same evening. Avoiding Matheson's detectives, he met Fickert. Fickert secured an attorney for him. The next morning Rigall and the defense attorneys appeared before Judge Matthew I. Brady of the police court—an inferior, municipal court in which a felony suspect could be held to answer before a Superior Court—and presented charges against Oxman. Rigall repeated his story in all its sensational details before Judge Brady. McKenzie swore out a complaint against Oxman, charging subornation of perjury, a felony for which the maximum penalty was ten years. With Captain Matheson's approval, Brady issued a warrant for the arrest, over the objections of Fickert's representatives.[77]

Oxman surrendered to the police a few hours later and was

promptly locked up in jail. He protested vehemently. "After all I've done for the people of San Francisco, this is a mighty rotten deal!"[78] Fifteen minutes later he was out again, having cashed a check and put up $2,000 bail. Meanwhile Fickert had conferred at length with John D. Spreckels, Jr., the foreman of the grand jury. The District Attorney announced that he would place the Oxman affair before the grand jury.[79]

That evening Fickert and Cunha met with O'Connor, McKenzie, and Older in the bedroom of poolroom-owner Eddie Graney, at the Olympic Club. The defense attorneys said they would not stand for a grand jury investigation. The defense wanted a new trial for Mooney and strenuously insisted that the grand jury be kept out of the case, since it was closely allied with Fickert and Fickert was implicated in Rigall's charges.[80] A grand jury under Fickert's influence could whitewash Oxman in its closed sessions and persecute Rigall. As McKenzie later commented, "it was a political grand jury, in whom we had absolutely no faith; and we didn't want the delay of it and we didn't want any star chamber proceedings in a grand jury on this kind of matter; we wanted it in an open court room."[81]

The five conferees agreed that Fickert was to announce at once, in time for the morning papers, that he would ask the State Attorney General for a new trial. Fickert had consulted Assistant Attorney General Raymond Benjamin during the day. Benjamin was unsure of the legal procedure for instituting a new trial, but thought that if Fickert confessed error of fact to the Supreme Court, a new trial might be arranged. Older, McKenzie, and O'Connor went home believing that Mooney would have a new trial.[82]

When Fickert left the Olympic Club he did not prepare the promised statement. Instead he went to the grand jury in a midnight session and requested an investigation of Oxman. The request was granted. Fickert had made his choice: he was not siding with the defense against Oxman, but with Oxman against the defense.[83]

In their concern from Friday to Wednesday for rescuing Cunha, the defense attorneys lost their opportunity to force a new trial. They allowed Cunha and Fickert to put off announcing a new trial. By the time Fickert met with them at the Olympic Club, he had already made a rapprochement with Oxman, and had found for him a skillful, debonair attorney, Samuel M. Shortridge. (Shortridge had been a political protégé of M. H. de Young, a friend of Ruef, and one of Ruef's attorneys; in the 1920's he was a Republican Senator from California, whom old Progressives still heartily disliked.[84] George P. West described him as "a very Dickensian caricature of the cynically shrewd, unctuous, flowery-tongued legal servant of the rich.")* Fickert was almost ready to break off negotiations with the defense attorneys when he met them Wednesday evening. The meeting gained him a little more time, while the grand jury gathered.

According to Fickert, the grand jury invited him to make a statement before it. He went in and told the jury that it should have waited until after the police court hearing was through, but that if it intended to go ahead, a special prosecutor from the Attorney General's office should be requested.[85] The *Bulletin*'s version of the midnight session presents Fickert in a less innocent light: after the defense attorneys had gone home, Assistant District Attorney Aylett R. Cotton, Jr., told the grand jury that Fickert wished to make a statement. Fickert was admitted to the room. He made a strong plea for taking the Oxman inquiry out of the hands of the police court and making it solely the grand jury's concern, with Fickert himself, as defender of the law, presenting the matter to the grand jury and participating in its deliberations. To the suggestion that the Attorney General conduct the investigation, Fickert replied that he himself was in a much better position to do it, being familiar with all the facts; the matter was urgent and the Attorney General would take weeks to prepare. "After a long discussion, Fickert's request was refused and the agreement to submit the case to Attorney General Webb was reached."[86] Even the grand jury could not allow Fickert to run the show himself.

On Thursday Fickert announced that he had promised the defense attorneys a new trial only if they could prove to him that Oxman had committed perjury. He accused them of intimidation and attacked Older:

I don't mind saying that Mr. Older himself may yet have to answer questions as a witness in the trials growing out of the bomb plot cases. The Grand Jury would also be justified in calling him as a witness in inquiring into some of the occurrences prior to Preparedness Day, for Older knows more about them than he has ever published in his newspaper.

I say this with full knowledge of the facts. Older himself has on more than one occasion made the statement that he knew Mooney was a guilty man, but that is not the extent of his knowledge. He is apparently bent on saving Mooney at all hazards.[87]

* *Nation*, August 9, 1922. William Kent wrote of Shortridge: "Unless I am badly misinformed, his whole career has been discreditable. David Starr Jordan says that he is one of the worst men in the state, and I hear continual rumblings of his unconscionable legal practice." (Kent to Chester Rowell, May 5, 1920, Rowell Papers.)

Older retorted that if Fickert was telling the truth, he had failed his duty by keeping the information from the grand jury for the past nine months.[88]

Oxman was arraigned in the police court before Judge Brady the morning after Fickert's appearance before the grand jury. The hearing was set for April 23. In the afternoon the grand jury foreman requested U. S. Webb, the State Attorney General, to appoint a special grand jury prosecutor. Webb came from Sacramento and advised the grand jury the next day. On his recommendation it postponed its investigation pending the outcome of the police court hearing. Webb said he would decide after a few days whom, if anyone, to appoint as special prosecutor.[89]

Following Webb, Fickert reappeared before the grand jury to recommend the subpoena of Fremont Older. He said that Older might be able to tell the jury of correspondence between Alexander Berkman and Emma Goldman while the latter was Older's guest a week before the parade. He compared Older's editorials of those days to "the most violent literature connected with the Haymarket cases in Chicago."[90] A few days later Older, not having been summoned by the grand jury, went to its chambers himself and insisted on being interrogated. Fickert hustled him out into the corridor. An hour later a committee of jurors came to him there and said the jury would refer his request to Webb.[91]

In the alignment of newspapers over Fickert's squabble with Older, the *Examiner* spoke for Fickert, the *Bulletin* for Older; the *Chronicle* and *Call* were neutral, and the *News,* which was demanding a new trial, protested that the fight was irrelevant. The more serious questions, as Older himself insisted, were going unanswered. Where and how had Fickert acquired Oxman? The District Attorney's continuing refusal to clear this up, said the *Bulletin* and the *News,* indicated a deeper complicity with Oxman than had yet been revealed.[92]

VIII

Before the police court hearings opened, the defense made two further moves. Maxwell McNutt appeared before Judge Griffin and asked him to request the Attorney General to confess error in Mooney's trial and ask for a new trial. Since the case had long been out of Griffin's hands, it was doubtful whether the judge had the authority to make such a request. McNutt admitted that he knew no precedent for it.[93] Assistant District Attorneys Cunha and Cotton argued before

Griffin that he had no jurisdiction in the matter, although, under the judge's questioning, they did not dispute the authenticity of the Oxman letters. Griffin said that had he seen the letters in time, he would have granted the motion for a new trial. He asked the attorneys on both sides to join the court in asking the Attorney General to confess error to the Supreme Court and request from it a new trial, so that a jury judging Mooney might hear from Oxman himself his explanation of the letters. The prosecution attorneys refused. They would await the results of the pending investigation by the Attorney General, they said, before making any recommendations; anyway, they would petition only in the company of those whom they believed to be acting in good faith. Griffin rebuked Cunha for that remark. The grand jury delay was unnecessary, he said. The Oxman investigation was immaterial to justice for Mooney, "who now stands convicted of murder in the first degree without recommendation and is in danger of being hanged on that charge." Griffin concluded that he would draft his request to the Attorney General at once.[94] His letter is dated April 26:

. . .

In the trial of Mooney, there was called as a witness by the people one Frank C. Oxman, whose testimony was most damaging and of the utmost consequences to the defendant. Indeed, in my opinion, the testimony of this witness was by far the most important adduced by the People at the trial of Mooney. In confirmation of these statements, I would respectfully call your attention to the transcript filed on the appeal. Within the past week there have been brought to my attention certain letters written by Oxman prior to his having been called to testify, which have come to the knowledge and into the possession of the defendant's counsel since the determination of the motion for new trial. The authorship and authenticity of these letters, photographic copies of which I transmit herewith, are undenied and undisputed. As you will at once see, they bear directly upon the credibility of the witness and go to the very foundation of the truth of the story told by Oxman on the witness stand. Had they been before me at the time of the hearing of the motion for new trial, I would unhesitatingly have granted it. Unfortunately, the matter is now out of my hands jurisdictionally, and I am therefore addressing you, as the representative of the People on the appeal, to urge upon you the necessity of such action on your part as will result in returning the case to this court for retrial. The letters of Oxman undoubtedly require explanation and so far as Mooney is concerned, unquestionably the explanation should be heard by a jury which passes upon the question of his guilt or innocence.

I fully appreciate the unusual character of such a request coming from the trial court in any case and I know of no precedent therefor. In the circumstances of this case, I believe that all of us who were participants in the trial concur that right and justice demand that a new trial of Mooney should be had in order that no possible mistake shall be made in a case where a human life is at stake.

Respectfully yours [etc.][95]

The second move of the defense was to ask for Ed Nolan's release on bail. Attorney Nathan Coghlan appeared before Griffin to make the request, which was endorsed by Captain Matheson. The District Attorney went along with the request, and Nolan was set free. His bail was a nominal $2,500. He had been confined in jail for nine months, during which time his wife and child were supported by the machinists' union.[96] Although Fickert was not fully aware of it, Nolan's involvement had contributed materially to the District Attorney's difficulties, for it had brought to the defendants' aid the powerful International Association of Machinists and the funds with which the defense had approached Rigall and Ellis.

IX

Fickert changed his mind repeatedly during these days about the timing and sequence of the remaining bomb trials. Weinberg's trial had been scheduled next. Fickert decided that Rena Mooney's would be next instead, then decided to postpone it until after the Oxman investigation, and then announced upon Nolan's release that Rena Mooney's trial would begin the following day. Both sides accordingly went to court the next day, but no jury had been summoned. Mrs. Mooney's trial did not begin for several more weeks.[97]

The Oxman exposé was now twelve days old. These were dark days for Fickert. The press of northern California was demanding an investigation of Oxman and an accounting of Fickert's connection with him. If Mooney was framed, said the Sacramento *Bee,* then his prosecutor was as guilty as any dynamiter.[98] Enthusiasm for Mooney's punishment had died. Even the conservative weeklies of San Francisco were warming to the idea of a new trial: "today the doubters of Oxman are a majority instead of a minority," wrote Theodore Bonnet in *Town Talk.*[99] The San Francisco Labor Council was calling for the intervention of the Attorney General and a state investigation. In San Francisco and Sacramento there was talk of Fickert's recall.[100]

In this gloomy state of affairs Fickert appealed directly to the public. He published his convictions on the bomb cases with a lengthy

and eloquent argument in his accustomed manner: he offered no explanation or new information about Oxman, but dwelt upon the
anarchist menace and the menace of Fremont Older. He condemned
Berkman and quoted extensively from the *Blast*. He condemned the
IWDL, or "Murderers Defense League," which had defended Ford
and Suhr "for the murder of District Attorney Manwell" and Schmidt
and Caplan for the *Times* murders. "An adroit and heavily financed
effort," he wrote, "is being made to convince you, the public, that
Billings and Mooney are upright, conscientious citizens, loving their
country and their fellow men, who nevertheless have been made the
victims of an infamous conspiracy on the part of the officers of the
law to do them to death for a crime they never committed." He pleaded for help against Older's unscrupulous efforts to free Mooney: Older
and O'Connor, he said, had promised at their Olympic Club interview
to exonerate Fickert and laud and assist him in all his future under-
takings if he would dismiss the remaining bomb indictments and help
seek pardons for Mooney and Billings.

Once before Older succeeded in dominating absolutely the District Attorney's office of this city and county. The base use which he made of it, he
has confessed with groans of repentance. I shall save him from a second
shame. Neither he nor anyone else shall control that office while I am its
head.

> . . .

Whatever may be said of his methods, his motives, it may be argued,
were for the purification of the city and for the punishment of crime. Here
and now he is to the forefront, seeking the acquittal of red-handed murderers, the blood of whose innocent victims calls aloud not for vengeance,
but for the just retribution of the law. With him, in this malign work are
arrayed all the forces of evil in the city, all the anarchists of the United
States, and the time has come, my fellow citizens, for you to know these
things and knowing them to aid in upholding justice and seeing to it that
San Francisco is not made the home and refuge of anarchism under Older
and his criminal crew of Berkmans, Emma Goldmans and Mooneys.

Fickert included a few game thoughts about current anarchist death
threats to his family. He was not concerned for himself, he said, but
for his wife and children.[101]

According to Robert Minor, Fickert wrote his article after a conference with Frank Drew, attorney for the Chamber of Commerce,
and with the assistance of an *Examiner* editorial writer and a bottle
of good whiskey.[102] That Drew was involved seems likely enough,

since in acknowledged response to Fickert's appeal a "committee of citizens" met at the office of the Chamber of Commerce the day of the article, and adopted a set of resolutions backing the District Attorney.[103] The Chamber had not been involved in the Mooney case, with the possible exception, previously mentioned, that its attorney may have been the one who originally told Fickert about Oxman; its influence had rather been part of the environment in which the bomb prosecutions developed. It had not made any pronouncements on Billings and Mooney, nor had it explicitly attributed the Preparedness Day bombing to the labor unions. In December the Law and Order Committee published and circulated widely a handsome booklet reviewing the Committee's achievements and making it plain that the bombing was one of the reasons why the open shop was needed,[104] but apparently the Committee did not consider overt support of the prosecution against Billings and Mooney necessary until the Oxman crisis. Now Fickert needed help. The group at the Chamber resolved to ask the Committee to "investigate what assistance may be needed by the district attorney, and thereupon to offer to secure such special counsel and other services . . . as may be necessary . . . to the end that there may be no miscarriage of justice."[105]

The Law and Order Committee responded energetically. Through a full-page advertisement published in all the local dailies, the Committee reminded San Franciscans of their pledge at the Civic Auditorium nine months earlier to redeem the city from violence. Since then, the advertisement said, the citizens had subordinated the city's critical needs to those of the nation, but the anarchists had been spreading their doctrines and "their intimidation of courts and of elected officials." The Committee pledged itself to act on the adopted resolutions·

Coercion of courts, peremptory demands on elected officials that the law be arbitrarily set aside are a far more devilish expression of anarchy than was the bomb outrage itself; for this is striking at the very bulwark of our Americanism; it is striking at the very root of organized society and of the institutions of civilization.[106]

"The *Bulletin* cannot believe that these epithets stand for real mental processes," responded Older.[107] Defense attorneys pointed out that the Committee's concern for law and order evidently included no interest in the possibility that Fickert had known of a frame-up, in the truth of the charges against Oxman, or in the reason why Nolan had been denied bail for nine months.[108] The Law and Order Committee's action also angered the city's labor movement, which had begun to press demands for Fickert's removal and a new trial for Mooney. However, the Committee's advertisement and subsequent publicity undoubtedly strengthened Fickert's determination to stand pat on the Mooney trial at the only time when he might have been persuaded to agree to a new one.

X

To summarize the legal state of the bomb cases in late April: the District Court of Appeals had Billings's trial on review, the Supreme Court had Mooney's trial on review, Judge Griffin was requesting a new trial for Mooney, Judge Dunne was presiding over a delayed start against Rena Mooney, the Attorney General was faced with Griffin's request and the need to choose a grand jury prosecutor for the investigation of Oxman, the grand jury was temporarily biding its time, and the main theater of action was the court of a police judge.

A criminal suspect could be brought to trial in either of two ways: on indictment from the grand jury, or on "information" following a preliminary hearing in a police court. If both the police court and the grand jury examined a suspect, the grand jury normally took precedence; it alone of the two had the power of subpoena. In the matter of Frank Oxman, political and legal considerations sent the defense to the police court and the prosecution to the grand jury. As long as Webb kept the grand jury on leash, the police court could proceed with no other resistance than that of the prosecution and, of course, Oxman's attorney. The partisanship of the District Attorney's representatives for the man they were formally presenting to the police judge for prosecution placed the defense attorneys in an awkward and frustrating position, from which they were rescued by Judge Brady's determination to see the Oxman affair handled justly.

Matthew I. Brady was on the verge of an important role in the Mooney case. He was to become Fickert's political adversary and his successor as District Attorney. A Democrat and a Catholic, he had been a party leader in San Francisco's 39th Assembly District; in 1908 he was appointed by Mayor Edward Taylor to replace one of Abe Ruef's lieutenants as head of the city's civil service commission. In 1915 Mayor Rolph appointed him to the police court bench.[109] His career thus developed out of the graft prosecutions on the side opposing Fickert. It is not surprising that Mooney's attorneys went to

Brady with the Oxman letters, while Fickert resisted the move and went to the grand jury.

The police court hearing began April 23, in a room crowded with attorneys and spectators. Assistant District Attorney Louis Ferrari, accompanied by Brennan, requested a continuance until the grand jury hearings were completed or the Attorney General had acted. Ferrari also attacked the complaint against Oxman as illegal, because it had been sworn by McKenzie rather than Rigall. Attorney Shortridge, appearing with Oxman, moved for dismissal on the grounds that the police court had no jurisdiction. These objections were overruled.[110] The examination that followed was conducted by Ferrari, and there to prod him when he flagged or faltered were all the defense attorneys, plus Ellis. Ferrari began interrogating Rigall by reading him a section of the penal code, to the effect that his testimony might be used against him in a criminal proceeding. Since that section of the code was generally read to grand jury witnesses suspected of complicity in a crime and was rarely read in police court hearings,[111] the defense attorneys protested intimidation.[112] Bitter exchanges flew between the defense and prosecution attorneys—who ignored Shortridge—as applause burst from partisans in the audience. Violence ensued. At the end of the first session, as Brady left the bench, Rigall was cornered by Brennan and Ferrari. Rigall called for help. McKenzie rushed over and swore at Brennan. Brennan wheeled. His fist shot out and caught McKenzie on the cheek. McKenzie staggered, came back, and the two heavyweights went crashing to the floor, knocking over Oxman as they fell. The crowd jumped on chairs and tables and shouted them on. Matheson and Bunner pulled them apart while other policemen rushed the spectators out of the room. Now Brennan nearly came to blows with O'Connor. "We'll get you when we come to Estelle Smith," shouted O'Connor.[113] They were separated. "As to the fight," Brennan told a reporter, "I certainly did not get the worst of it. I have no black eye, and he has."[114] One editor pronounced the incident in keeping with the traditions of "little old San Francisco" and suggested that it would furnish a fine subject for a painting at the Civic Center.[115]

Under cross-examination by Shortridge, Rigall admitted his none-too-savory past. This affected his credibility as a witness, though it seemed to leave the Oxman letters untouched. Shortridge sprang the Nora Biford abduction charge on him, and it had undergone an interesting transformation: now Rigall had allegedly taken the girl across the Indiana border, and the charge was not simple abduction, but violation of the Mann Act.[116] Unknown to the defense, Burns detectives had approached Miss Biford and obtained from her a sworn statement, dated April 28, 1917, that Rigall had enticed her to New Harmony, Indiana. Why Shortridge never used her affidavit against Rigall is not clear, though he was probably responsible for procuring it.[117]

Shortridge urged upon Brady the worthlessness of the testimony of Rigall, "a characterless, miserable individual . . . whom your honor is certainly not called upon to believe." Brady replied, "If Oxman sent for a man to come here for this purpose, he would hardly have sent for a minister of the gospel, would he?" Shortridge denied that Oxman had sent for Rigall for the purpose alleged. "Then what about the letters?" interposed McNutt. "I will not allow myself to be diverted from my argument by such remarks," Shortridge replied—"nor by laughter from spectators."[118]

Shortridge did not put Oxman on the stand.[119] Apparently he anticipated defeat in the police court, and was saving Oxman and a surprise or two for the grand jury, in the hope of winning a grand jury dismissal, which might forestall the police court decision, if it could be delayed until then. As it turned out, he narrowly missed fulfilling his timetable.

Four days after the police court hearing began, Attorney General Webb appointed a special prosecutor to direct the grand jury investigation. The prosecutor was Robert W. Clarke, Deputy Attorney General at Los Angeles, former Superior Court Judge of Ventura County, and in 1912 a Progressive candidate for Congress. The announcement of Clarke's appointment was postponed until he had arrived in San Francisco and had begun to study the case.[120] Under his direction the grand jury took up its inquiry into the Oxman affair on April 30. Brady protested that the grand jury had stalled for twenty days and was now unfairly putting him in a difficult position. He asked that the grand jury suspend its investigation during the police court hearing, which, he said, would continue in any event. The grand jury declined to wait. Shortridge, having unsuccessfully demanded a continuation during the grand jury's inquiry, sought in various ways to drag out the police court hearing. His obstructive tactics continued for several days. The grand jury meanwhile subpoenaed Brady's witnesses, transcript, and reporter, but Brady arranged with Clarke to have them back part of the time. Only a few hours before the grand

jury concluded its investigation, Brady handed down his decision to
bind Oxman over to the Superior Court for trial.[121]

XI

The main difference in testimony betwen the rival hearings was
that before the grand jury both Oxman and Fickert told their stories
for the first time. Oxman explained nearly everything. He had come
to San Francisco on July 22 from Portland. (He did not mention Willows or Woodland.) On Market Street near Steuart he had met a young
man whom he thought at the time to be Ed Rigall. He had mentioned
the incident to Fickert and Cunha. They wanted him to bring the
fellow out: "we talked over the matter, and they wanted to know if
I could suggest any way to get him here, because you gentlemen probably don't understand that people don't like to come here and testify
to what they know about these people, because it is very annoying,
and I did write that letter, and I wrote it under Mr. Cunha's request
and instruction to write him and get him here." He said he did not
dare mention the bomb outrage in the letter.[122]

Oxman's crucial alibi was that in his second letter he had written
a postscript in his "rough way of doing" on a third, separate sheet of
paper. The alleged postscript said: "If you were not in San Francisco
on July 22nd cannot use you as a witness. Answer by wire. F. C. O."[123]

Oxman had many other explanations. He had invited Mrs. Rigall
to San Francisco "to blarney them along, to get the boy here." "Expert
witness" meant "character witness." He had advised Rigall to register
from Evansville, Indiana, for "a little more mileage" because it was
a big place and he thought the fare would be cheaper, and because if
Rigall registered from Evansville, "these anarchists couldn't trace him
as easy and poison his well, like they do mine."[124]

Oxman's account of his relations with Rigall in San Francisco during Mooney's trial was as follows: he discovered as soon as he saw him
that he had made a mistake; Rigall was the wrong man. But now
Rigall wanted to testify. Oxman was embarrassed; how was he to get
rid of him? Rigall was calling himself "Charles," which made matters
worse: "why, it looked like something was wrong on the face of it. See.
It didn't look right to me." So at the first opportunity he told Fickert
that he had made a bad mistake and was in trouble, and Fickert said,
" 'That will be all right. We all make bigger mistakes than that.' "

But Rigall was worried: " 'Now, if you aint going to use me,' he said, 'how the hell am I going to get my expenses?' " Oxman replied that he would personally make good Rigall's expenses up to $250, if the state did not pay them. Then Oxman went to Cunha and told him, too, of his mistake, and said, " 'Mr. Cunha, I think that probably we ought to let him go.' " Cunha said that that would be unwise; the defense had been shadowing Oxman, would know about Rigall's being in San Francisco, and would make a big issue of it if he left.[125]

Oxman denied to the grand jury that he had ever rehearsed testimony with Rigall in the presence of Fickert or Cunha. He swore once again to his original story of how he came to take down the jitney license number. He denied that he had offered a bribe to Estelle Smith. "I have never understood that there was any reward. I don't need any reward. I have lost more in this case now than all the reward ever will be. . . ."[126]

Fickert followed Oxman. He, too, explained nearly everything. He had learned of Oxman through Frank Woods in Durkee, though there had been "a rumor" before then about him. Subsequently he had talked with William Hough of the Western Meat Company about Oxman. He had not seen Oxman's letters when they were written. He had authorized Oxman to ask Rigall to come out, on the understanding that Oxman had seen him at Steuart and Market on July 22. He did not authorize any of the details in the letter except the state's willingness to pay Rigall's expenses.[127]

Fickert's biggest hurdle was to explain why he had kept Rigall in San Francisco for two weeks. Oxman had already prepared the way. The District Attorney now elaborated: he had not had the slightest intention of calling Rigall to the witness stand, but wanted him in court if the other side brought the subject up during Oxman's cross-examination. He had been surprised when the defense attorneys failed to mention Rigall, for his arrival as a prospective witness was known at the Terminal Hotel and among the police, and Oxman was "shadowed all the time." Fickert had extended to Rigall the facilities of the Olympic Club in full knowledge of the mistake: Rigall was eager to get away and needed to be entertained. He was in court only so that he could stand up to be identified. He was not under subpoena; "we had him here just to avoid the criticism of sending him away." Fickert acknowledged paying Rigall $150 for expenses when he left. The expenses had been promised him.[128]

Fickert had no quarrel with Oxman's letters. He explained that

Oxman had had the schooling of a "child about six." Oxman wanted to get the fellow to San Francisco without giving away why he was needed, "because it is very difficult to get people to testify in this class of cases." There was no doubt of Oxman's integrity. "He has the credit, I believe, of a million dollars on the Stock Exchange." Since Oxman had returned to San Francisco voluntarily, Fickert considered it a duty "to look after him and see that he had the same treatment as any other man would have," and hence had asked Shortridge to be Oxman's counsel.[129]

On request from Clarke, who was interrogating him, Fickert promised to produce Oxman's original Kansas City affidavit.[130] He never did so. As has been pointed out, the original document never same to light.

Cunha's testimony supported Oxman's and Fickert's. The grand jury then concluded its hearing. Clarke believed that there was ample evidence to indict Oxman, but the jurors voted overwhelmingly against an indictment.[131] Foreman Spreckels issued a public statement commending Fickert:

After a careful and conscientious investigation covering every phase of the charge of subornation of perjury, . . . we, the jury, find no cause for criticism of the District Attorney's office in connection with the bomb cases, and we unanimously commend the Hon. Charles M. Fickert for the able and fearless manner in which he has performed his duties to the people of the State of California in connection with these cases.[132]

There was still the police court. Brady stood fast. Shortridge, in an effort to forestall Oxman's commitment, sent the cattleman back to jail again for a few minutes while he obtained a writ of habeas corpus. Brady consulted the Appellate Court judges who issued the writ and with their approval committed Oxman. Oxman went back to jail again and Shortridge applied for a second writ of habeas corpus. Oxman was released again on bail.[133]

The Attorney General said he would await the outcome of the habeas corpus proceedings before acting on Griffin's recommendation that Mooney be given a new trial. Had the Appellate Court granted the final habeas corpus writ, Webb might have refused Griffin's request. But the court found otherwise. Fickert, Aylett Cotton, and James Brennan appeared before it in half-hearted opposition to the writs. The court called in McNutt as amicus curiae. The arguments were heard and the writs were dismissed. Shortridge walked across the hall and applied for a writ of habeas corpus from the State Supreme Court. The hearing on this writ resulted in another denial, and on May 24 Oxman and Shortridge were confronted with the settled fact that Oxman would have to stand trial. Oxman surrendered himself to the police for the fourth time and was released again on $1,000 bail. Meanwhile the day originally set for Mooney's hanging passed almost unnoticed. The appeal had automatically stayed his execution.[134]

Thus Ed Rigall had started a succession of unexpected moves in the direction of justice. Without his money-making schemes and the particular problems he encountered, the Oxman letters would never have reached the defense and Oxman would not have been found out. Without the Oxman exposé there would have been no conversion of Older and Griffin, probably no conversion of Samuel Gompers, no relenting of the San Francisco police, no releasing of Nolan on bail, no second thoughts in the press, no removal of Oxman as a witness in the later trials, no acquittal of Rena Mooney, no federal intervention, no commutation. In short, there would have been no breakthrough along the prosecution's front, but only impotent and outraged radical demonstrations, and scattered labor protests at home and abroad, followed by Mooney's execution and Billings's entombed oblivion: all this, had Rigall not calculated that blackmail was more profitable than perjury. In the Mooney case justice was born in corruption.

Justice was still a long way off. The defense had lost its initial assault on Mooney's conviction through the Oxman exposé. The prosecution had lost a decisive counterattack. Neither side was in a position yet to force final action through the Oxman issue; Oxman's trial was weeks ahead. Meanwhile, Rena Mooney's trial was at hand.

CHAPTER FOURTEEN

The Trial of Rena Mooney

If you see a good thing in the Blast, *cop it, friend,
cop it.*
—Alexander Berkman

Epsom salts means oxalic acid.
—Pickwick Papers

No public figure in San Francisco personified the change from the Progressivism of 1910 to the conservatism of 1920 better than Frank H. Dunne of the Superior Court. The judge who had been one of the important men in the prosecution of graft, who had offered no legal favoritism to the powerful and wealthy, came in 1917 and 1918 to see the great danger to American society as no longer irresponsible power, but radicalism. His changed outlook was manifested dramatically in the bomb cases. He had been Billings's trial judge. In April 1917, he was about to try Rena Mooney. His philosophy of law and society and his personal response to the cases started from about the same position as Griffin's and developed in the opposite direction. His position became as troublesome to the defense as Griffin's was to the prosecution. Like Griffin, he unavoidably occupied a position that proved increasingly political as the juridical aspects of the cases got further and further out of hand.

Dunne's shift from liberalism to reaction was attributable in part to the social climate, in part to the wartime patriotism of the wealthy, and ultimately to the specter of Bolshevism. His shift was also more narrowly personal, at least in connection with the bomb cases. The outcry against professional jurors reflected on his jury panels more than any others of the San Francisco Superior Court, and he naturally despised the attorneys who had made a prominent issue of it. The worst offenders, McKenzie, O'Connor, and Coghlan, were all associated with the bomb defense by the spring of 1917. Moreover, Dunne came to believe that the defense attorneys had imposed on his good faith. McNutt's presentation of a questionable affidavit after Billings's trial was one instance;* another arose when Weinberg's first attorney, J. G. Reisner, withdrew from the defense after six months and forced a postponement while McKenzie and O'Connor took over. Under other circumstances these irritations might have been ignored. But Dunne was growing increasingly apprehensive of radicals and impatient with attorneys who went to their rescue.

Every month the cases became more complex, the legal mechanisms designed to resolve the complexities more unwieldly, the repercussions more ominous, and a position of strict impartiality more difficult for a judge to maintain. In the spring of 1917 Dunne abandoned a position which had once been regarded on both sides as impartial. The Oxman letters did not deter him. They seem rather to have fixed his resolve, for he considered the Oxman affair an unfortunate distraction from the question of Mooney's and Billings's guilt, and from the deeper question of whether law and the social order could withstand determined anarchistic assault.

Dunne's first explosion from the bench occurred late in April. The case of Weinberg had come up on his calendar for trial. Things were looking very bad for the prosecution at the time, and the District Attorney's representative requested a continuance, which was opposed by McKenzie and McNutt. Dunne reminded the defense attorneys that the prosecution had been ready some time earlier and that the trial had then been postponed because Weinberg no longer had an attorney. Now the defendant had three. Said Dunne:

I think it is a good thing to let these cases continue. Perhaps in the meantime some of this poison gas that is being spread around in this community with intent to obstruct and injure the administration of justice may disappear, and the decent people, people who do not belong to any organization, the stay-at-home circle, will have a chance to wake up and see where they are and find out what is doing here; whether or not the atmosphere can be filled with all this poison. And the District Attorney's office might spend the next fortnight finding out who it is circulating pamphlets maligning and vilifying the administration of justice in this community. I found one outside my doorstep. On inquiry I found the town has been filled with these pamphlets. When I make further inquiry as to who the author is I

* One Neil McAuliffe gave McNutt a sensational affidavit naming the two supposed bombers of the parade, but repudiated it after McNutt had presented it to Dunne. McNutt believed that there had been foul play, since McAuliffe was arrested by the police prior to the repudiation. But McNutt was compromised, and Dunne was angry. (*Bulletin*, October 7, 1916.)

find out it is one Minor. When I make further inquiry I am told that he is crazy, and we ought not to pay any attention to him. And my answer is that it is just that kind of insanity that leads to murder and the illegitimate use of dynamite. How long the decent people are going to stand that condition it is up to them to say. . . . I find out also that every crooked, cowardly, blackguard lawyer who is going around in this community with a letter of marque in the shape of a license to practice can be permitted to obstruct the administration of justice.

He said he would request a Bar Association investigation. McNutt replied that he would gladly testify before the Association about the Mooney case. The following colloquy ensued:

THE COURT: Not the Mooney case, Mr. McNutt, but the Billings case was tried in this court and Billings was justly and properly convicted, and he was convicted not only by the case the State put in through its District Attorney, but by his own statement, which was perjury so palpable and plain it would not have deceived a jury of children. He was convicted properly, and that conviction should stand. . . .

MCNUTT: (Interrupting) Will your honor—

THE COURT: Let me talk. When there was nothing left to do but to abuse the personnel of the jury that tried the case and—

MCNUTT: (Interrupting) Are you addressing me?

THE COURT: I am addressing you. And I know of nobody who is more acquainted with the personnel of the jury panel than the counsel for the defense, and the counsel for the defense and the defendant were so well satisfied with them that they did not even avail themselves of all their peremptory challenges that they were permitted under the law. And if that state of affairs can be permitted to exist in this community, where are we at?

MR. MCNUTT: Does the Court not think I should have a right to investigate the testimony and the witnesses for the State, too?

THE COURT: In what case?

MCNUTT: In the case of The People vs. Thomas J. Mooney.

THE COURT: That case was not tried in this court. I am speaking of matters of which I know.

MCNUTT: May we have an order that the Court's remarks today be transcribed?

THE COURT: Why, certainly, transcribe them, certainly. I might say in addition that that—let me say this: That on the showing for a new trial in the Billings case the matters presented by the defendant in furtherance of his motion were so palpably perjured statements that I wonder that the district attorney's office did not go to work and have these people apprehended.[1]

Older was distressed. He hoped that Dunne's tirade was a passing outburst, but Dunne was irrevocably alienated. The loss was to be one of Older's most poignant regrets. In the months to come he was never able to bring himself to attack the judge satirically, as he attacked Fickert. He defended Dunne's integrity as long as he could make a case for it, but he felt keenly the weakened position in which Dunne left hopes for justice.[2]

The defense attorneys sought to replace Dunne with another judge for Weinberg's trial. The issue was not changed by the prosecution's substitution of Rena Mooney for Weinberg, since the indictments of both defendants had been assigned among three Superior Court judges, and in both cases Fickert elected to prosecute an indictment that appeared on Dunne's calendar. Fickert announced that he would fight the move to disqualify Dunne.[3]

Meanwhile Dunne, having warmed up, elaborated his warning to the public. An infamous defense organization was rushing the city toward internecine warfare through "an extremely subtle scheme" to cloud the real issue with the claim that the whole affair was a great battle between union labor and the Chamber of Commerce. The labor unions of the city had already been won over to this view, not by their own mature deliberation, he said, but by the most active propaganda; they were now raising money for persons who had never been a credit to organized labor. Fickert had acted in complete good faith. "Don't you see that all men should offer assistance to the district attorney?"[4] Responded Older: "Are you the only person in San Francisco who hasn't read the Oxman letters?"[5]

When the defense requested a change of venue, Dunne denied that he was prejudiced and refused to disqualify himself. He sought to make amends with McNutt: he said he had not referred to him as the attorney suborning perjury with the "letters of marque," but rather "to the jackal Lawlor, who appeared with you in the case." "His name is not jackal," replied McNutt, "and I don't believe he suborned perjury."[6] At the same time Dunne announced that he refused to preside at any more of the bomb trials. He said he would ask to be replaced by a judge from outside the county. When the trial finally got under way, a week later, Dunne's bench was occupied by Judge Emmet Seawell of Santa Rosa.[7]

II

By the time of Rena Mooney's trial both the San Francisco Chamber of Commerce and organized labor in the Bay Area had decided that the bomb cases were their vital concern. Frederick J. Koster at the annual banquet of the Chamber of Commerce pronounced intolerable "the propaganda which has been deluging the city for the past few weeks" and called for more "Practical Patriotism."[8] The Chamber fulfilled its pledge to give the District Attorney such support as he might need for the maintenance of law and order: Frank Drew, the Law and Order Committee's attorney, announced June 10 that the services of attorney Charles W. Cobb had been offered the District Attorney in the trial of Rena Mooney, and had been accepted.[9] Cobb appeared in the courtroom the next day and sat with the prosecuting attorneys for most of the trial. He had been one of Francis J. Heney's assistants in the graft prosecutions, and had also served as an assistant to President Taft's Attorney General. In Rena Mooney's trial he did not examine witnesses or offer argument, but he did give legal advice. He appears to have conducted himself discreetly.[10] It was never claimed that he did anything of particular significance for the prosecution, but presumably he served to bolster its morale. His presence at least signified the Law and Order Committee's misguided sense of its responsibilities, and was accordingly resented by friends of the defense.

At the same time the Central Labor Council and the Building Trades Council of Alameda County, more united in agitation against the bomb case frame-ups than San Francisco's Labor Council, chose a "labor jury" of twelve East Bay Union representatives to sit through the trial and report afterward their "verdict" on Mrs. Mooney to the organized labor movement of America.[11] It was an unusual device to publicize the concern of East Bay labor unions for a fair trial. The labor jurors met in a corridor of the Hall of Justice on the first day of the trial and swore before a clergyman that they would try the case impartially and render their verdict "in accordance with the law, the evidence, and the instructions of the court."[12] They sat quietly in the courtroom, but their presence was resented by many who believed that it compromised the dignity of a trial.[13]

The combined effect on conservative thinking of the Chamber's rally to Fickert and the labor jury's appearance may be surmised from the columns of the San Francisco *Argonaut,* a fashionable and influential weekly. In the issue of April 28, which went to the printer before the Law and Order Committee had made its move, the editor, Alfred Holman, was cautious and seemingly contrite: the public was "uneasy" about the Oxman affair; possibly the officials had shown insufficient self-restraint. "We may also remember usefully that the previous character of the accused [Mooney] has no direct bearing upon his guilt or innocence of the particular offense under trial." But the next week Holman's tone had changed: the Mooney-Billings defense and "the unsavory Older" were impeding justice with the Oxman letters. The guilt of Mooney and Billings was "a moral and legal assurance," properly proven in the courts with overwhelming evidence in the face of the defense's chicanery and unlimited funds. Oxman's possible subornation of perjury was "a minor issue involving nothing more serious than the integrity of a single witness—that witness being one whose testimony is not essential."[14] Five weeks later Holman lashed out at the labor jury:

It goes without saying that the "labor jury" will pronounce the defendant guiltless. It is for this purpose that it has been commissioned and instructed. For organized labor has chosen to take upon itself the "protection" of Mrs. Mooney and those associated with her in the bomb cases. . . .

Perhaps it is just as well that we should have this concrete evidence of the colossal pretension of organized labor in the arrogant form in which it presents itself in San Francisco. It seems to set itself up . . . as a superior authority in public affairs. . . .

It would be difficult to conceive an assumption more impertinent, or one tending more certainly to social demoralization. . . . The *Argonaut* has no question as to the outcome. The law, representing the authority of all the people, will prove superior to an attempted usurpation which seeks to establish the rule of a caste confessedly selfish, shamelessly arrogant, defiant of the constituted forces of society.

. . . The spectacle of a "labor jury" attendant upon a regular court and assuming a higher moral authority than the court itself is calculated to disgust rather than to edify men of sense—and men of sense ultimately control in every human society.[15]

As the United States District Attorney in San Francisco, John W. Preston, reported that month to his superior in Washington, "the community is at fever heat and deadly divided on the cases."[16] He added later: "The truth of this bomb situation here is that it was taken up by the Law and Order Committee of the Chamber of Commerce as a chance to suppress the Unions, and the Unions evidently took up Mooney's side of it in order to counter-move against the action of the Chamber of Commerce. In other words, it has become a bitter industrial struggle."[17] And Chester Rowell privately summarized the local conditions in the same vein: "There is a violent class war on in San Francisco," he wrote Theodore Roosevelt, "which is becoming nearly as bitter as was the schism over the graft prosecutions ten years ago."[18]

III

Jury selection for Rena Mooney's trial took three weeks and hundreds of veniremen. When twelve jurors were accepted at last, it was discovered that one of them had been irregularly summoned. His name had not been on the original list. The *Bulletin* accused Fickert of jury tampering, but the bailiff who was responsible evidently was only trying to get a job for a friend.[19] The bailiff was discharged, all peremptory challenges were restored to both sides, and the accepted jurors were reduced in number from twelve to seven. The box was then filled again.[20]

Rena Mooney was prosecuted by Assistant District Attorney Louis Ferrari, a Stanford-educated San Franciscan who had first been appointed to his post before the Ruef era.[21] Fickert examined some of the witnesses. The defense was now represented by six attorneys: McNutt, O'Connor, McKenzie, Coghlan, Charles Brennan, and John G. Lawlor.[22]

Ferrari, following the prosecution's established pattern, devoted most of his opening address to the alleged conspiracy of 1913–16. This conspiracy, he said, had been for "the accomplishment of a state of anarchy by violence, . . . by doing away with all religious, industrial and every kind of institution that we have, and . . . to bring about a state of anarchy and chaos with the Mooneys at the top of the heap." Mooney was its "master mind," Nolan its lieutenant, Berkman, Morton, and Mary Eleanor Fitzgerald its publicity department, and Billings, Hanlon, and Brown its handy team of dynamiters. "And, yes, this conspiracy also had its Lady Macbeth who was always at the elbows of the conspirators urging them to new and further acts of violence." He spoke of nitroglycerin, and promised to show that eleven days before the bombing, Rena Mooney and Weinberg purchased twenty pounds of niter from a newly arrived shipment at the city wharf for the manufacture of the bomb.

Ferrari also previewed the prosecution's version of Mrs. Mooney's reactions after the bombing: she returned with her husband to the Eilers Building, "looked down Market Street, saw the civilian marchers marching up Market Street notwithstanding the explosion of the bomb, and she was seized with rage to known [sic] that the object of the conspiracy had been frustrated . . . and she said . . . 'Oh if I only had a machine gun what a fine mess these marchers would make.' " He said that he would ask for a verdict of first-degree murder.[23]

Following the opening address Judge Seawell ordered the jury to be locked up for the trial—a stringent measure, provided by law but rarely invoked in San Francisco.[24] Seawell was determined to forestall as best he could any suspicion of jury tampering. Consequently the jurors spent their evenings playing poker or watching shows under the eye of the bailiff, complained about the length of the trial, and protested angrily of "being treated worse than criminals" when they found that the judge was opening their mail.[25]

The first half of the prosecution's case, presenting non-conspiracy testimony, was substantially like the case against Billings and Mooney, but much weaker. Ferrari's claim that Rena Mooney had obtained niter before the bombing was supported by the testimony of a longshoreman, Samuel Samuels, who stated that he gave her the niter when she requested it for her garden. Since Samuels had told his story to the police three weeks after the bombing, there was some question why he had not testified in the preceding trials. Also in doubt was his ability to identify people, for he was shown to have failed to recognize his own brother, a policeman, in Ferrari's company a week earlier.[26]

Estelle Smith resumed her place, unoccupied for Mooney's trial, as a witness to Billings's alleged presence at 721 Market Street. (Why she had not testified against Mooney was never explained. The defense charged that she had refused to take the stand because the District Attorney had not yet freed her uncle from prison.) Miss Smith was no longer the jaunty dental nurse she had been the preceding August. Weeping, she complained to the judge that a woman in the courtroom was making evil faces at her. The woman was Tom Mooney's mother, afflicted with a facial tic. Judge Seawell forbade such unmannerly questions on cross-examination as whether she had been a prostitute in Los Angeles, and threatened summary punishment of any spectator who snickered at the witness, but even so Miss Smith had difficulty finishing her testimony.[27]

John McDonald thought now that Billings had arrived at Steuart Street at perhaps 1:35 or 1:45. He admitted under cross-examination that the police had paid his board and room since the bomb cases began. The defense estimated that his expenses had amounted to $1,500 or $2,000.[28]

Oxman was never called. Three other witnesses testified that they had seen a small automobile turn into Steuart Street from Market before the explosion, but they could not identify any of the occupants.*

IV

About a week after testimony had started, a New York journalist, author, and educator, John A. Fitch, called on Edward Cunha at his office. Fitch was a labor research specialist and a staff member of *Survey*, a Progressive magazine for which he was covering the trial.[29] He explained whom he represented, and said he wanted to straighten out certain facts in the Mooney case. Cunha asked what facts. Fitch replied that he was principally concerned about Oxman. Cunha said that the record contained the facts and that he was not in the habit of talking. Fitch responded that the record did not contain the facts about Oxman. Then, according to Fitch, Cunha burst out:

If the thing were done that ought to be done this whole God damn dirty low down bunch would be taken out and strung up without ceremony. They're a bunch of dirty anarchists, everyone of them, and they ought to be in jail on general principles. I'm not speaking now as an officer, I am just speaking as a man and a citizen, to show you my attitude. I'm disgusted with all this outcry over Mooney,—making a hero of him by Older and all that bunch where he is an anarchist and a murderer. If he ought to be out of jail let him get out. The Courts are open to him. But I'm not going to help him get out. If I knew that every single witness that testified against him had perjured himself in his testimony I wouldn't lift a finger to get him out. I told him to get out if he could. . . .

And now people like Judge Griffin are going around saying he ought to have a new trial. Why, Judge Griffin almost cried there on the bench because we searched the Blast office without a search warrant. The Blast office, run by Berkman and that bunch of anarchists. Berkman's the man who shot Frick and he told me he did it on general principles because Frick is a capitalist. Berkman told me that he had no country and that he'd just as

---

* *Call*, June 21, 1917. One of them, J. W. Smith, saw a man and a woman in it, but he could neither identify them nor say "whether it was at 1 or 2" o'clock. (J. W. Smith testimony, *People v. Rena Mooney*, pp. 798ff., in California Supreme Court, "Habeas Corpus," XVII: 11,138–47.)

lief as not spit on the American Flag. I ought to have murdered him right
there for saying that. My only regret now is that I didn't. They'd talked in
the Blast about stopping the Preparedness parade. They urged a meeting
of protest and then they said that stronger measures should be taken. Do
you think I was going to wait around 2 or 3 days for a search warrant for
people like that? Now if it was your house or mine it would be different,
but I'm glad there was a dist[rict] att[orne]ys office here with guts enough
to [go] ahead and search those people without waiting for a warrant.[30]

All the while Cunha was shouting at Fitch, who was having no success
asking questions. Finally Fitch managed to inquire whether Cunha
did not think it endangered the rights of good citizens for the officers
of the law to override the law. Cunha said not when the law was disregarded in order to get at such people as Berkman and Mooney.
"These are the people who have defended the Los Angeles Times
dynamiters," he said. "And they let them talk on the streets. If I had
my way I'd get a bunch of cops and go after them and beat their God
damn heads off." Fitch reminded Cunha that it was not a crime to be
an anarchist. Said Cunha, "I consider that it is." Fitch replied, "It
isn't a question of what you consider it to be. You know as a matter
of fact that the law defines no such crime." "Well," Cunha replied,
"A man can't become an American citizen if he is an anarchist." Returning to Oxman, Cunha declared that the evidence was sufficient
to convict Mooney without him.[31]

After the interview, which lasted forty-five minutes or an hour,
Fitch walked back to his hotel and wrote out the interview, recount-
ing it as it substantially appears above, and using quotation marks
only where he was certain. The occasion so impressed him that years
later he said he could still quote Cunha.[32] In July 1917, *Survey* published his article on the cases, which incorporated most of these notes
verbatim.[33] Cunha did not publicly challenge or deny the article at
the time,[34] but at the 1935–36 Supreme Court hearings he denied
Fitch's account of the interview almost entirely. Without original
memoranda of his own, he related a completely different version,
which included in transcription some thirty pages of purported direct
quotation.[35]

V

After the prosecution had presented the direct testimony, argument was heard on the admissibility of conspiracy evidence. The trial

was now more than a month old. Seawell ruled that conspiracy evidence was admissible if its relevance to the case was subsequently demonstrated. Ferrari then offered extensive testimony about the activities of Billings and Mooney since 1913. The conspiracy evidence included testimony by detective Balsz of Sacramento, the Tanforan suitcase, pieces of the Martinez arsenal, Mooney's threatening note to Governor Johnson, testimony of David Milder that Mrs. Mooney had worked in behalf of Ford and Suhr and had once been an IWDL delegate, and information about her part in the URR car strike.[36]

For the first time in any of the cases the prosecution called Martin Swanson, to testify of alleged conspiratorial matters and to identify articles taken from the Mooneys' residence. His testimony and cross-examination revealed nothing new. He acknowledged that he had been Fickert's agent, with a specialist's knowledge of bombs and a personal knowledge of Mooney and Billings. He denied firmly all intimations that the defendants had been framed.[37]

Ferrari offered a mass of conspiracy documents. Among the papers seized from Mrs. Mooney's studio were some anarchistic books, to which the prosecution attributed special significance; they included Tolstoy's *War and Peace,* Austin Lewis's *The Proletariat,* Emma Goldman's *Anarchy and What It Stands For,* and *The Life and Works of Eugene Debs.*[38] For hours Ferrari read articles from the *Blast* to the jury, until finally one of the jurors arose and objected to further reading: "So far as I am personally concerned I would like to avoid being inflicted with it unless there is something that pertains directly to connect up the case."[39] Ferrari stopped, and the prosecution's case was closed. Judge Seawell then ruled that all the testimony relating to Sacramento, Martinez, and Tanforan, all the evidence concerning the alleged conspiracy prior to July 1916, excepting the car strike evidence, was irrelevant and was to be disregarded by the jurors.[40]

Seawell's ruling and Oxman's absence lightened the burden on the defense. It began by deluging the court with witnesses impeaching the Edeaus, McDonald, Estelle Smith, and the longshoreman, Samuels.[41] Captain Peterson, Walter J. Smith, and the traffic officers who had been stationed along Market Street on July 22 all took the stand for the first time. Other new witnesses assisted. One was a painter who had made himself known to the defense attorneys in response to a February advertisement in the *Labor Clarion,* appealing to the unknown passengers who had ridden in Weinberg's jitney on July 22 to come forward. He said he had entered Weinberg's jitney at Post and Fillmore (about two and a half miles from Steuart Street) at 2 P.M.[42]

The nature of explosives, of bombs, and of the probable construction of the Preparedness Day bomb was the subject of far more extensive inquiry and testimony in this trial than in either of the first two trials. The prosecution had no more evidence than before concerning the specifications of the bomb, but through expert testimony it sought to link the defendants to the crime by alleging a similarity between the Preparedness Day bomb and the San Bruno tower bomb, and by ascribing a sinister quality to the Epsom salts seized at Nolan's house. One powder expert testified that Epsom salts could be used in the manufacture of explosives, to slow down the combustion rate. The defense called its own powder expert, who testified that any inert matter would do, and that Epsom salts were in practice never used in the manufacture of explosives.[43] The defense also employed its expert, Arthur M. L. Eisert, to construct two time bombs with dynamite and nitroglycerin, according to such specifications as the prosecution had asserted earlier in the trial. The bombs were taken to the Berkeley hills in early July, placed beside a rock cliff in simulated Steuart Street conditions, and detonated. The effects differed from those of the Preparedness Day bomb in three important ways. First, the fragments of the clock, batteries, and wooden frame to which the infernal machine was attached were easily recovered. The clockface from the first bomb was intact, and half of that from the second was in one piece. Second, most of the debris, being of light weight, was distributed within a radius of six feet. The pipe caps were blown farthest, thirty feet. (Eisert explained that dynamite was a shattering rather than a propelling explosive.) And third, the lower part of the bomb, the part between the explosive and the ground, was relatively intact, so that it could be easily recognized as the bottom of a wrecked suitcase.[44] The implication was that the prosecution simply had not known what it was talking about. No parts of the Steuart Street bomb's alleged clock had been found, except for the three rings of doubtful origin. Perhaps the bomb had not been an infernal machine, but an aerial bomb, as the defense had contended all along.

Toward the end of the trial Rena Mooney took the stand and testified that she had no connection with the crime and no anarchistic convictions. She had once heard Emma Goldman speak but did not know her; she had never talked with Berkman; she did not subscribe to the *Blast* or even read it; she was a registered Socialist, and had voted for Socialist or Union Labor Party candidates since the introduction of woman suffrage. She said she had worked with the IWDL when it defended her husband in 1913. She acknowledged her part in the URR strike the preceding summer.[45] Ferrari asked her whether she and her husband had ever been comrades in any revolutionary movement. She asked if he was referring to her signing her letters "Yours for the Revolution." Ferrari said he was. Mrs. Mooney explained: "That is a saying with socialists. Eugene V. Debbs [sic] always signs his name 'Yours for the Revolution.' Jack London signs his books that way. That is a common expression of theirs."

Q. [Ferrari] You all exchange letters that way?
A. [Rena Mooney] Yes, and they always say "Dear Comrade."
Q. As I understand it, you got the saying or the habit from Eugene V. Debbs?
A. I don't know whether it was from him or not.
Q. But you have used the expression in your correspondence?
A. Yes, I think many socialists use that.[46]

The next day a headline appeared in the *Chronicle*: "MRS. MOONEY IN FAVOR OF REVOLUTION."[47]

Fickert's argument after the close of testimony followed the lines of his previous two summaries. He left out the Webster speech, but invoked the admonitions of Webster and Clay and Lincoln to preserve the country. Anarchy was now the great peril. Mrs. Mooney was the torch of the Furies. "In her handbag is contained no innocent powderpuff.... Instead, we find bullets of various caliber—the instrumentalities of murder." During the car strike "she brutally attacks the motorman and claws his face until it is bloody." He described her as the Mrs. Surratt of the case: "Mrs. Surratt paid the penalty of her participation in the murder of Lincoln, and so should this defendant pay the penalty for the blood she has shed, and for the orphans she has made." He asked for the death penalty.[48]

McNutt replied fervently: Fickert wanted vengeance. The defendant did not ask for sympathy as a woman; she asked only for justice. As for Mrs. Surratt, he said, she had been innocent of conspiracy to assassinate Lincoln; she was court-martialed and hanged in response to public clamor.[49]

When the jury withdrew, the labor jury withdrew also. It deliberated at Carpenters Hall for thirty-five minutes and returned a verdict of not guilty and a recommendation that the federal government investigate the prosecution: "We find that this is not a murder, but a labor, case; that the United Railroads and the Chamber of Commerce are the prosecutors, proven by the fact that the cross-examination of Rena Mooney was devoted mostly to her activities in attempting to organize the United Railroads, and that the Chamber of Commerce paid an attorney, Charles W. Cobb, to assist in prosecuting Rena Mooney."[50]

The regular jury found the going harder. Hour after hour passed. Through the doors of their guarded room could be heard high-pitched voices of the jurors, one of them calling another an anarchist. At 11 P.M., there being no decision, Seawell sent them to their hotel. The next day was no more conclusive. At 9:30 P.M. the foreman called the bailiff and asked him to tell Seawell that the jury was hopelessly deadlocked. Seawell's only reply was to lock them up for the night; the next morning there was still no verdict.[51] "Just picture us waiting 51 hours for a verdict," wrote Billings's cousin, Madeline Wieland, "everyone on the verge of breaking down, fainting etc. I can tell you that unless you had gone through that thing yourself, it can't be described. The tense faces of friends and relatives—poor Mrs. Hammerberg was worn down to a bag of bones—she looked frightful and we all believed she would go mad if Rena were convicted."[52]

At 3:15 the afternoon of the third day the bailiff returned from the jury room with word that a verdict had been reached. The courtroom quickly filled with an anxious crowd. The jurors filed into the box where they had sat for two months, a longer time than any case had lasted since the graft prosecutions. Their verdict was not guilty. A shout arose, quickly stifled by deputies, but caught up by the waiting crowds in the corridor. Mrs. Hammerberg laughed and cried with delirious relief. Rena Mooney embraced the jurors and rushed with her matron to the jail to tell her husband. Prisoners beat their bars and cheered. Then she was returned to her cell, for seven other indictments remained against her.[53]

Fickert said the verdict did not surprise him: "We have not been able to convict a single woman of murder since I have been in office." He was not sure at first whether he would prosecute Mrs. Mooney again. A day later he had decided he would: "Within a week it will be possible under the law to get women for jurors. I intend to get as many women jurors to try Mrs. Mooney as possible."[54] "Preposterous," said the defense attorneys. They predicted that Mrs. Mooney would be free in a few days, and that Weinberg would never be brought to trial.[55]

VI

Fickert opposed Rena Mooney's release on bail. She might or might not be tried on another indictment; in the meantime she should stay in jail. As it turned out, she stayed there for eight more months.

The defense claimed that Mrs. Mooney could not be tried again, and McNutt filed a motion for the dismissal of the remaining indictments on grounds of double jeopardy. But the double jeopardy claim was groundless; a separate indictment could be separately tried. The motion was denied by Superior Court Judge George H. Cabaniss.[56] The defense next argued the legal ethics of trying Mrs. Mooney again. As the *Bulletin* commented, "if the letter of the law were strictly adhered to she might be tried eight times more, found not guilty seven times and convicted and hung on the eighth. No one can twist such a possibility into the shape of justice or common sense."*

In an effort to publicize Mrs. Mooney's plight a stunt was organized by a local Socialist teacher, Malvina Milder. Two hundred children, followed by Mooney's mother, paraded down Market Street and along Kearny to the Hall of Justice and the jail. The children carried banners reading "We Love Our Music Teacher; Set Her Free," and "The Jury Has Acquitted Mrs. Mooney; Why Is She Not Free?" Gathering in the entrance of the building, they chanted:

> Rah! Rah! Rah!
> Whiskare-e-e!
> Rena Mooney shall be free.
> R-E-N-A M-O-O-N-E-Y
> That's the way to spell it,
> That's the way to yell it.
> Rena Mooney,
> Rah! Rah! Rah![57]

The police left them alone. But Chester Rowell, usually a fair-minded public critic, commented that the parade was "even more horrible than the original murders." The children, he protested, were being trained in class hatred rather than fair judgment.[58]

Formal argument on bail for Rena Mooney was postponed for three weeks, owing to the prosecutors' and judges' vacations.[59] Mean-

* *Bulletin,* July 27, 1917. It was commonly forgotten that the defendants were not indicted for nine or ten deaths, but for eight. Of course, the principle was the same.

while McNutt asked for Weinberg's release as well. Since the indictments against Rena Mooney had been distributed among three judges,
Dunne, Griffin, and Cabaniss, the consent of all three was necessary
for her release. To pay bail on the indictments before Griffin and
Cabaniss alone would have been a costly futility, since she could still
be confined on the indictments before Dunne. Cabaniss suggested that
the three sit *en banc* to hear the counsels' argument. Griffin agreed
but Dunne declined. After hearing McNutt, Cabaniss and Griffin set
Rena's bail at $20,000; bail for Weinberg was denied. Nate Coghlan
sought Dunne in his chambers and asked his consent for Mrs. Mooney's release, but to no avail. The question was then brought before
him formally; the prosecution opposed the motion. Dunne, comment-
ing on the heinousness of the crime, denied bail.[60]

Appeal to the higher courts was available. The way was slow, costly,
and of uncertain outcome. Across the country, labor papers published
a plea from Mrs. Mooney for help: "Don't let them bury us here!"[61]
But other aspects of the cases pressed more urgently. The question of
bail was delayed until November, when a sustained effort, ultimately
successful, was made to free both Rena Mooney and Israel Weinberg.

CHAPTER FIFTEEN

The Trials of Oxman and Weinberg

*When we find that a substantial injustice has
been done, we look through the record for errors,
and we damn well find them.*
—William Henry Beatty,
Chief Justice of California, 1888–1914

I'm trying to find an explanation for Oxman.
—Captain Matheson

THE JOY of the defense at Rena Mooney's acquittal would have been
more complete had there been any assurance by then of a retrial for
Tom Mooney. Attorney General Webb had delayed his decision on
Griffin's request, and it was not yet known whether the state would
formally confess error. Webb intended to take no action, or so he was
reported to have said the day after Rena's acquittal; but four days
later, perhaps in response to appeals from the California State Federation of Labor, he filed with the State Supreme Court a formal consent
to a reversal of judgment. He did not confess error, for on examining
the record he found no reversible error; but he agreed with the trial
judge that justice would be served by a retrial, and therefore stipu-
lated that the judgment entered by the trial court be reversed and the
case remanded for a new trial. He pointed to the Oxman incident
and the acquittal of Rena Mooney.[1]

Webb was adhering rigorously to the law. Oxman's effort to suborn
perjury was of course not in the record; the evidence of it had appeared after the trial was closed. Without some procedural flaw in the
record itself, some faulty ruling of Griffin's during the trial, on which
Webb could base a confession of error, the best he could do was simply
to recommend that the judgment be reversed. The *Bulletin* in 1917
and the *Mooney–Billings Report* in 1931 stated incorrectly that Griffin had asked Webb to confess error.[2] Had Griffin made such a request,
he would in effect have asked for condemnation of his own rulings.

Instead he left to Webb the question of how to secure a new trial. (As Robert Minor quipped, "Oxman did not commit error, he simply committed perjury.")[3] Whether the technicalities of Webb's action mattered would depend on the decision of the California Supreme Court.

Fickert declared at once that the only right Webb had was to confess error, and that since he had not done so, his action had no legal merit. Fickert said that the only basis on which strict justice would require a retrial of Mooney was a jury conviction of Oxman. If Oxman were acquitted, "the sole cause that Mooney now has for urging a new trial" would be removed, for the Attorney General had stated himself that the record contained no reversible error. Oxman's prosecution would be "honest and vigorous."[4] Fickert did not say who would prosecute him, though normally one of his own assistants would.

The Supreme Court responded unfavorably to Webb's recommendation. His request was novel, it said; there was serious doubt of the court's right to grant a new trial except for error; and it would not consider whether any other exceptions obtained without formal application from both parties involved.[5] In other words, Webb's stipulation was out of order, and if Mooney joined Webb, the stipulation might still be out of order, there was no telling. At once McNutt filed a motion with the Supreme Court to reverse the judgment by reason of stipulation by the parties in interest. A month later Webb and McNutt both defended the motion before the court. Fickert appeared in opposition. He called Webb's stipulation "vicious and irregular," a departure from proper procedure, and a way of presenting evidence not in the record, not under oath, and not tested by trial.[6]

The justices of the Supreme Court concluded that they lacked authority to order a reversal unless they found error in the record.[7] A few days later the motion was formally denied. The court stated that it was not authorized by the California constitution to go outside the record: its powers of review were limited. Where a substantive injustice occurred that could not be reached through the record, the remedy lay with the governor. He alone had the pardoning power.[8]

The defense thus suffered a harsh blow, however lawful. Still, the Supreme Court had yet to rule on error in the record. The court's "final" decision on Mooney's fate was postponed for six months, until his appeal came before it in the course of normal procedure, in March 1918.

1. Hawking Socialist literature with the "Red Special." Tom Mooney (2d from right) and his brother John (3d from right) with Eugene V. Debs (behind John) during Debs's 1908 Presidential campaign.

2. At the International Socialist Congress, Copenhagen, 1910. Tom and John Mooney are on the bottom step at the left. Directly behind Tom is Klara Zetkin, later one of the chief founders of the German Communist Party. At the lower right, joining hands, are Alexandra Kollontai of Russia and Luella Twining of California; between them is Morris Hillquit; four rows behind him, facing left, is Bill Haywood.

3. Mooney, "publisher" of the *Revolt,* with his wife, Rena, and a colleague, 1911 or 1912

4. Mooney, alias "Charles King," at Martinez, 1914

5. Charles M. Fickert and the future novelist Will Irwin in their undergraduate days at Stanford

6. Alexander Berkman at an IWW rally, 1914

The San Francisco Preparedness Day Parade, July 22, 1916. The white cross at lower right
marks 721 Market Street. Two vehicles are in the line of parade: a "Saxon" car with photographers
(above the banner) and an ambulance (beyond the intersection). The time, visible on the street
clock in the right foreground, is 2:14—eight minutes after the explosion, which occurred one
block from the Ferry Building, visible at the end of Market Street.

8. The alibi photograph: Tom and Rena Mooney (standing, hand on hat), watching the parade from 975 Market Street. The inset is an enlargement of the jeweler's clock across the street. The time was 2:01—five minutes before the explosion occurred over a mile away. This photograph was the second of Wade Hamilton's snapshots of the parade.

-10. The scene of the bombing: the south side of Steuart Street at Market after the explosion. he bomb exploded just to the left of the open sidewalk doors shown in the lower photograph.

11. Sergeant Charles Goff looks on as Officer Wilbur Pengally enters Mooney's name on the police blotter. This was about one week after Mooney's arrest on July 27.

12. Martin Swanson. The only known picture of the detective, this photograph was used by the defense for publicity. It seems to have been retouched to make Swanson's appearance more sinister.

13. Warren Billings (left) and his prosecutor, James F. Brennan

14. Fremont Older

16. Robert Minor

15. Lieutenant Stephen Bunner and Captain Duncan
Matheson examining the evidence

17. Judge Frank H. Dunne

18. Judge Franklin A. Griffin

19. Charles Fickert, a campaign portrait

20. Edward Cunha, Mooney's prosecutor

21. At Mooney's trial. Front, left to right: Cunha, Fickert, Maxwell McNutt, Mooney, Bourke Cockran. In the dock: Ed Nolan, Billings, Israel Weinberg. Directly behind Fickert are Rena Mooney and John G. Lawlor. Behind the police officer is John Mooney.

2. Rena, Weinberg's son Ernest, Mrs. Weinberg, McNutt, Mooney, and Cockran, during Mooney's trial

23. Mellie and Sadie Edeau

24. John Crowley

25. John McDonald

26. Estelle Smith

27. Commentary on Miss Smith's earlier
career by Robert Minor for a cover of
the *Blast*

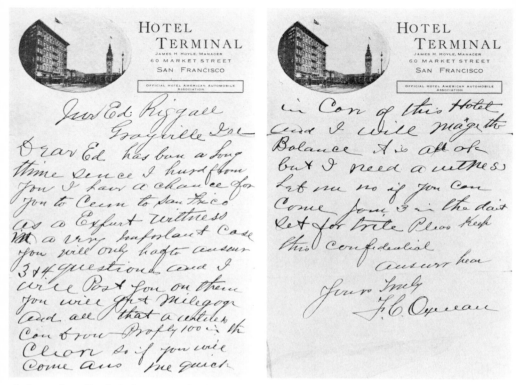

HOTEL
TERMINAL
JAMES H. HOYLE, MANAGER
60 MARKET STREET
SAN FRANCISCO
OFFICIAL HOTEL AMERICAN AUTOMOBILE
ASSOCIATION

Mr Ed Riggall
        Grayville Ill
Dear Ed has ben a long
time sence I hurd from
you I have a chance for
you to Cum to san frico
as a Expert wittness
in a very Inportant case
you will only hafto answer
3 & 4 questions and I
will Post you on them
you will get Mileage
and all that a wittness
can drow Proffy 100 in th
Cleor so if you will
come ans me quick

in Care of this Hotel
and I will maig th
Balance A is all ok
but I need a wittness
let me no if you can
come from 3 in the dait
set for trile Pleas keep
this confidential
            answer hear
Yours truly
        F C Oxman

28. Letter from Frank C. Oxman to Ed Rigall, December 14, 1916. Oxman claimed later that there was a third page with a postscript reading, "If you were not in San Francisco on July 22nd cannot use you as a witness."

29. Oxman (right) seated beside his attorney, Samuel Shortridge, at the subornation hearings

30. Ed Rigall

31. Oxman at the San Francisco County Jail

32. Mooney's wife, mother, and sister: Rena, Mary, and Anna
Mooney

33. Rena Mooney

Mooney on death row, July 1918

35. Mooney in the prison yard at San Quentin, 1920

Mooney and his wife at the Audita Querela hearing, San Francisco, 1921

37. Governor William D. Stephens

38. Governor Friend W. Richardson

39. Governor C. C. Young

40. Governor James Rolph, Jr.

II

About the time that Rena Mooney's trial began, the defense came within an ace of uncovering Earl Hatcher's story that Oxman had not even been in San Francisco at the time of the explosion. Agents for the defense talked with Hatcher in Woodland. There was only one hitch: Hatcher concealed his tale to cover up for Oxman.

Oxman himself provided the defense with its first clue about Hatcher. According to Edgar Gleeson, Oxman, following the publication of Rigall's letters, referred "as an afterthought" to the long-distance telephone call from San Francisco he had made on July 22 to Hatcher in Woodland.* Ed McKenzie went to Woodland to investigate for the defense, and turned up the fact that Oxman's signature was on the Byrns Hotel register for 8 A.M. July 22. The only train that Oxman could have taken from Woodland to get him to San Francisco by 1:30 was the 9:13 train. Had he taken it? The defense attorneys said they had found witnesses to testify that Oxman had driven a rig to a ranch six miles from town, and that he therefore could not have taken the 9:13 train, but must have come in on the afternoon train.[9] But the defense could get no assistance from Earl Hatcher or his wife. Hatcher was a friend of Oxman's. He acknowledged having seen Oxman that morning, and said that Oxman had taken the early train to San Francisco. "I have known Oxman for some time and have always found him square," he said.[10]

Hatcher knew of Mooney's conviction and knew from the newspapers of Oxman's role in the case. But he believed that Mooney was guilty anyway; the papers had quoted the jury foreman after the trial as saying that Mooney would have been convicted without Oxman's testimony. Hatcher did not want to get involved in the case, to get his friend in trouble, or to be known among other stockmen as a squealer. He kept quiet.[11] When Paul Leake, co-owner of the Woodland *Democrat*, asked him about Oxman's visit, he told him, too, that Oxman had left for San Francisco on the morning train.[12]

A short time afterward, Hatcher received a telephone call in Omaha, as he was passing through on business. The caller gave his name as Gilman or Gilmore—a name that has no known connection with the Mooney case—and said he was a lawyer calling from Denver.

* Gleeson to author, June 23, 1967. Hatcher's testimony in 1921, discussed on p. 167 above, confirms the fact of the call.

He offered Hatcher $5,000 if he would testify against Oxman. Hatcher told him to go to hell and hung up the receiver. He supposed that the offer came from the Mooney side.[13] The incident was never accounted for.

According to the later testimony of Hatcher, he also heard from Oxman. Oxman telephoned him in Woodland from Stockton one day and asked him to come down to discuss a cattle deal. Hatcher met him there, and Oxman said, "Earl, I believe they are going to put the old man in the pen unless you stand by me." Hatcher said that he replied: "Anything I can do to help you, you know I am your friend." Oxman probably took Hatcher's silence for granted from then on, or so Hatcher supposed.[14] For a long time Oxman was right.

III

Oxman's trial for subornation of perjury was postponed through the summer of 1917. After Rena Mooney's acquittal O'Connor declared that the defense attorneys and the labor movement would press for an early and vigorous prosecution of Oxman, and offered to prosecute the cattleman himself.[15] A few days later the San Francisco Labor Council offered to provide Fickert with an attorney to assist the prosecution. Fickert accepted, with the reservation that he would not have any attorney who served as counsel for anarchists. He specifically ruled out the defense attorneys, and suggested the president of the Labor Council, A. W. Brouillet. An acceptable attorney, he said, would be permitted to participate "to the same extent as did Mr. Cobb in the case of People vs. Rena Mooney."[16] Brouillet was regarded by the more militant members of the Labor Council as a reactionary labor politician, a betrayer of justice and of the labor movement. While all San Francisco newspapers except the *Bulletin* and the *News* were crediting Fickert with an open-minded offer to the unions, the Labor Council dallied three weeks and then declined to nominate anyone.[17]

Oxman's trial had been assigned to Dunne's court. Dunne granted so many continuances of the case that the *Bulletin* began to ridicule his solicitousness for the defendant. Oxman was at home in Oregon. He said that he was ill. Then his son was ill and in the hospital. Between times his attorney was in the hospital, too. The delays may have been justified, but at the same time Dunne was preventing the release of Rena Mooney, and tempers were growing ugly. (Four years later O'Connor contracted influenza while defending another radical in another notorious prosecution, the trial of Anita Whitney. The trial judge in that case refused postponement, and O'Connor, lacking an adequate substitute, drove himself to his death.)[18]

The date of the trial was finally set for September 12. Matheson reported that Rigall was holding out for $30,000 for his testimony, but Rigall arrived in San Francisco on September 3 with Ellis and stated that he was not being paid a cent. Meanwhile Oxman and a detective had spent a week in Grayville attempting to secure more information against him.[19] Oxman arrived in San Francisco September 5. His attorney was Shortridge, assisted now by James H. Nichols, Oxman's attorney from Oregon.

Oxman evidently decided that it would be well to take Earl Hatcher in tow during the trial. He invited the Hatchers to the city. They arrived a day before the trial, stayed at the Terminal Hotel, and dined daily with Oxman. During the trial Hatcher chauffeured him between the Terminal Hotel and the Hall of Justice. According to Hatcher, Oxman and his attorneys had a statement typed out, which Hatcher signed, declaring that he had met Oxman at the Byrns Hotel in Woodland shortly after 7:10 A.M. and that he accompanied Oxman to the station and saw him off on the 9:13 train. The statement was not notarized, and Hatcher later said he had not read it before signing, but it was an embarrassing document in later years, after he had told his story and was called to testify.[20]

As the opening of the trial approached, the question of who was going to prosecute Oxman remained unsettled. With the Attorney General's continued failure to appoint a special prosecutor, Fickert as prosecutor and a subsequent acquittal seemed inevitable. Fickert, however, announced that he was stepping aside; he appointed a substitute himself, the District Attorney of Tehama County, N. A. Gernon. "Fickert has chosen a friend to manage the acquittal business," charged the Bulletin.[21] However, the matter was not settled. The law governing the disqualification of district attorneys provided that a substitute be appointed by the Attorney General. On the day before the scheduled opening of the trial, Chief Deputy Attorney General Raymond Benjamin announced that Webb had appointed him to prosecute. Gernon was invited to remain as an adviser.[22]

Raymond Benjamin was one of California's many conservative Progressives who abandoned the Progressive Party in 1916 for Republican reunification and Charles Evans Hughes. He became Republican state executive committee chairman. He was also a past national

Grand Exalted Ruler of the Elks. His appointment as Oxman's prosecutor was received without enthusiasm from the Mooney defense.*

Oxman's trial lasted two weeks. From the first day it was obvious that he would be acquitted. Dunne's bias was apparent. He tendered Oxman "the protection of the Court," but to Rigall he made shadowy threats of prosecution for perjury.[23] Benjamin showed little enthusiasm for the case, made little effort to protect his major witness during Shortridge's cross-examination, and avoided any suggestion that the District Attorney might be implicated in the charges against Oxman: it was Shortridge, not Benjamin, who told the jury that Fickert's "honor and good name are involved here."[24] The police were indifferent. Mayor Rolph had ordered a police investigation of the Oxman affair weeks before, but Matheson disregarded the order: it was one thing to refuse further cooperation against the bomb defendants; it was another to expose Matheson's own department's role in the first two cases. Before Oxman's trial began, Police Commissioner Theodore J. Roche assigned three detectives to assist Benjamin in securing evidence; Matheson withdrew them before the case was over. The two policemen who testified, Lieutenant Bunner and Detective Draper Hand, offered nothing that would reflect on Fickert and little that would embarrass Oxman. Hand did not come out for another three years with his story of police malfeasance in the Mooney case.[25]

Dunne properly excluded the Mooney case from Oxman's trial, though he pricked up his ears when Fickert testified that Rigall had been kept in San Francisco because the Mooney defense had men following him:

THE COURT: Q. Following whom?

A. [Fickert]: Every witness they could find, if they thought they were witnesses of ours they would follow them, and they had assaulted some of them.

---

* *Chronicle*, October 22 and January 12, 1916; *Bulletin*, April 14 and 19, 1916, and April 26, 1918. Benjamin's qualifications and conduct were disputed. According to the *Bulletin* he was a personal friend of Fickert and chatted with him daily during the trial. (*Bulletin*, April 26, 1918.) In direct contradiction was the statement of another qualified observer, attorney G. S. Arnold:

"The fact is that Mr. Benjamin was Prosecuting Attorney for Napa County for many years prior to his appointment as Assistant Attorney General, and since his appointment has handled the bulk of all appeals in criminal cases for the Attorney General in the higher courts of this State. Of all the attorneys in the Attorney General's office, he was undoubtedly best equipped to handle this exceedingly difficult case." (G. S. Arnold to Felix Frankfurter, December 31, 1917, in National Archives, RG 174, file 20/473.) Arnold investigated the Mooney case for the Federal Mediation Commission in the fall of 1917.

Q. [Dunne]: Scaring witnesses, do you mean scaring witnesses?

A. Yes, and they were following witnesses.

MR. BENJAMIN: Now, your Honor, I don't think that this is right, that this is relevant.

THE COURT: I think it is. He is telling you what the condition was, what put this in his mind. That is relevant, is it not?

THE WITNESS [Fickert]: In fact some of the fellows here in Court now were following.

MR. BENJAMIN: I move to strike that out as a volunteer statement.

THE COURT: I don't know. I wish I knew who they were.

THE WITNESS: Mr. Schulberg, who was here this morning, he took a very active part.

MR. BENJAMIN: May I have a ruling?

MR. SHORTRIDGE: I have no objection.

THE COURT: Well, it may go out.[26]

Selig Schulberg, the accused sleuth, an officer of the IWDL, was in the corridor of the Hall of Justice the next evening, on subpoena from the grand jury, when Fickert passed by. Fickert struck him in the face and knocked him to the floor, smashing his glasses and cutting his face. The District Attorney explained that Schulberg had made a face at him and had said, "You will get what Manwell got." (Manwell was the Marysville District Attorney killed in the Wheatland riot.) Fickert said that Schulberg "made a pass with his right hand to his hip pocket. I decided to get him first. I will kill him if he comes within four blocks of my house. He is a red-handed anarchist." Schulberg denied that he was carrying a gun. He asked for police protection, and was assigned an officer while the grand jury hearing was continued.[27]

Rigall, the only significant witness for the State, was unimpressive. He avoided admissions of having attempted blackmail or bribery, but he detailed his own unsavoriness and untrustworthiness, while Short-ridge probed and Benjamin stood by. Shortridge even conveyed to the jury the impression that Rigall was too cheap to bathe.[28] Rigall plainly did not convince the jury that there had been no postscript to Oxman's letter, or that Rigall had genuinely been intended as a witness against Mooney.[29]

In contrast to Rigall's past, Oxman's was not discussed. The jury did not learn that once before, in the Spain case, Oxman had proposed to suborn Rigall, for that case had not yet come to light.

Oxman's defense echoed his explanations to the grand jury. There was the postscript alibi, and there was the contention of Shortridge, supported by Oxman and Fickert, that Rigall had been neither a witness nor "about to become a witness" in the Mooney trial, and that therefore Oxman could not be regarded as having committed an indictable crime when he wrote Rigall; for one cannot be guilty of suborning perjury if the allegedly suborned does not come within the legal definition of "witness" as applied to subornation of perjury.[30] Shortridge had a point, but the law was less clear than he implied.* In any case, the question of Oxman's guilt would have been a difficult one under the best of circumstances.

Under strenuous cross-examination by Benjamin, Oxman became confused. He was describing his preparations to write Rigall, and said: "I remember Mr. Fickert asked me if I knew any way I could frame up a letter."[31] Spectators laughed and Dunne interrupted to clear the court. Oxman regained his composure, consulted Shortridge, and explained that "any letter that is written is framed up."[32] Commented the *News*: "Prosecutors believe that Oxman would have completely collapsed had not the judge rushed to his rescue."[33]

OXMAN WHITEWASHED. VERDICT NO SURPRISE. TRIAL PROVES FARCE. So ran the *Bulletin* headlines when Oxman was acquitted.[34] From an acquittal there was no appeal, except to the public. Oxman's letters, exorcised and interred by legal rite, were to reappear time and again to haunt the Mooney case.

* The California Penal Code at the time stated: "Every person who wilfully procures another to commit perjury is guilty of subornation of perjury, and is punishable in the same manner as he would be if personally guilty of the perjury so procured." (*West's Annotated California Codes: Penal*, Sec. 127.) This left unclear whether the procurement for the purpose of perjury constituted in itself an act of subornation: the first clause implies that it does, while the second plainly assumes that the perjury is actually committed. However, from *West's Decennial Digest, 1906–1916*, citing a Delaware case of 1908, it appears that the attempt itself was held to be criminal: "An attempt to instigate or persuade another to commit perjury is an offense at common law, even though the perjury was not afterwards actually committed." (*West's Decennial Digest, 1906–1916*, XVII:1657, citing *State v. Schaffner*, 69 A. 1004, 6 Pennewill 576.) In California criminal law the attempt to commit a crime is chargeable as the crime. Nevertheless, the delimitation of "attempt" is difficult: at what point may the accused leave off an attempt and still be guilty? If Oxman ceased urging Rigall to commit perjury before the trial—and whether he did or not was largely a matter of Rigall's word against Oxman's—was he still guilty?

IV

Upon his acquittal Oxman was immediately rearrested and charged with perjury.[35] The Mooney defense, frustrated in the attempt to convict Oxman for subornation, was contemplating the more drastic step of prosecuting Oxman for his own testimony against Mooney. It was a long shot, and one that required, at the very least, the cooperation of Earl Hatcher. That cooperation was not forthcoming. The warrant for the arrest was signed by Griffin, on the understanding that a witness in Woodland would testify against Oxman. The press reported that a witness of unrevealed identity would testify that Oxman was in Woodland on July 22, looking at sheep until past noon.[36] When the defense attorneys failed to produce their secret witness in court, Griffin dismissed the new case for want of evidence.[37]

Oxman went back to Oregon protesting that he was $30,000 out of pocket for his own defense. His difficulties in San Francisco probably had cost him heavily. Around the Bar Association it was rumored that Shortridge received $10,000 as his fee. Radicals charged that it was paid by the Chamber of Commerce, but according to Shortridge neither the Chamber nor anyone connected with it paid him for defending the cattleman. Oxman announced that he was going to bring suit in the federal courts for $250,000 against his persecutors, but nothing ever came of the threat.[38]

That was the last seen or heard formally of Frank C. Oxman in the Mooney case. Members of the Mooney defense committee went to Durkee two or three times in the 1920's in the hope of obtaining a retraction, but failed even to see him. In his last years Oxman was an invalid, and a convert to Catholicism; in 1929 Mooney made an artificial, pathetic appeal to him to confess his perjury while there was yet time, "that the rest and peace that comes of cleanliness might descend upon you." Without confession, "when you eat and drink of the sacrament unworthily, you eat and drink damnation to your own soul."[39] In 1928 Mary Gallagher of the defense committee tried to reach Oxman through his priest, but found Mrs. Oxman an insurmountable barrier. "Father D[ominic O'Connor] says that Mrs. would prevent a clean breast as we would desire mostly because she wants to retain some shred of respect in this community, though it is a very small shred now."[40] Few neighbors saw Frank Oxman, but according to one who knew his nurse, he was a despairing and pitiful man, "praying and carrying on at night," and ill-treated by his wife and son.[41] He died of a heart attack in his home on July 22, 1931, the fifteenth anniversary of the Preparedness Day bombing.[42]

No one seems ever to have learned why Oxman testified in the Mooney case. The common view was that he wanted the reward or the limelight. Perhaps he wanted both, but he certainly did not need the money; and in the beginning, at least, he pretended quite convincingly that he did not want the nuisance of testifying. The defense committee always hoped "that something might reveal the real reason why Oxman was brought here," as Rena Mooney expressed it in 1922;[43] but the answer never came.

V

Alexander Berkman was indicted by the San Francisco grand jury in July 1917 for complicity in the Preparedness Day bombing. The indictment came almost a full year after the crime. Berkman had remained in the city for three months after the original arrests, and had been left alone during that time, apart from one *Blast* raid by the police and District Attorney. He went to New York with the intention of continuing the *Blast* there, although publication was suspended soon after it began. He joined Emma Goldman in the radicals' fight against military conscription, and in June the two were arrested for draft interference. They were tried and convicted. Berkman was sentenced to two years in the federal penitentiary and was taken briefly to Atlanta. His release on bail was pending at the time of his indictment in San Francisco.[44]

Fickert obtained the indictment at the same time that the prosecution was pressing its conspiracy testimony against Rena Mooney in her trial. He called a special meeting of the grand jury and stated that he had a mass of evidence, including a large quantity of material that the United States District Attorney in New York had sent him after the raids on anarchist headquarters there. He called only five witnesses: Matheson and four local radicals, Minor, Morton, Milder, and Ernst. The grand jury minutes, which came to light in 1936, contained articles and editorials from the *Blast,* letters from Mooney, and the witnesses' testimony, none of which warranted the indictment. Nevertheless, the indictment was returned, about ten days before the end of Rena Mooney's trial.[45] That it was a move to support the prosecution's conspiracy thesis and buttress the other cases is apparent.

Fickert wired the prison authorities in Atlanta to hold Berkman; he said that extradition papers would be filed and a detective sent to bring him back. But Berkman was returned from Atlanta to New York and freed on bail September 10. He was rearrested on a warrant issued by the Superior Court of San Francisco, there being as yet no extradition papers.[46] By this time, however, a campaign to oppose Berkman's extradition to California had been organized by the left-wing Jewish labor unions in New York City. They had come to Mooney's aid at Berkman's request; now it was Berkman who needed help. Mass meetings organized by the New York publicity committee of the IWDL were addressed by Mooney defense leaders from San Francisco. The campaigners were encouraged by the announcement from Washington that a federal commission would investigate the Mooney case. A large delegation led by Morris Hillquit went to Albany to protest the extradition.[47]

The response of the Governor of New York, Charles S. Whitman, was encouraging. Fickert's agent had arrived with the extradition papers but had been put off. Whitman accepted Hillquit's suggestion that he request a transcript of the grand jury minutes from California, so that he might review the basis of the indictment. The Governor also indicated that he was willing to await the federal investigators' report on the Mooney case before he acted.[48]

Fickert accepted Whitman's decision and said he would wait until after the federal investigation to press for extradition. He requested more time to prepare the grand jury minutes, but in the end they were never sent. Fickert never resumed his attempt to extradite Berkman. The federal report on the Mooney case was published in mid-January, and by that time the bomb trials were over.[49]

VI

Weinberg was brought to court in October 1917, and subjected to a long and tedious trial in which old evidence was rehashed, some of it abandoned, and nothing of importance added by the prosecution. The indictment which the prosecution selected for trial was one before Dunne. Again the defense protested Dunne's prejudice. Dunne denied a motion for a change of venue, but at the last minute gave over the bench to Emmet Seawell. Jury selection took two weeks. Most of the talesmen wanted to be excused. Seawell ruled that both Chamber of Commerce and labor union members were ineligible. A number of prominent San Franciscans, including Herbert Fleishhacker, Marshall Hale, and Homer Curran, were excused on the basis of this ruling.[50]

Ferrari prosecuted. The general fiendish anarchistic conspiracy of 1913–16 was predominant again, over defense objections. Weinberg was accused particularly of subscribing to the *Blast* and of driving the Mooneys to three anarchistic destinations: the car strike meeting of June 10, 1916, the anarchist picnic of July 4, 1916, and Steuart Street on July 22.[51] Jurors slept as the corpus delicti evidence droned on. They were shown motion pictures of the scene shortly after the bombing, which had been barred from Rena Mooney's trial. The prosecution also put on the stand Mrs. Rose Lawlor, widow of the most horribly mangled victim, who was asked to identify her husband's clothing. The defense hastily conceded the identification as Mrs. Lawlor, seeing the riddled hat, verged on collapse.[52]

Neither Oxman nor Estelle Smith was called. Neither was available, according to the District Attorney. Fickert claimed that he had asked Oxman to come and had received no reply. As for Miss Smith, he said that she had come under Older's influence, which in fact was true.[53] Mrs. Edeau cried out on the stand that McKenzie had attempted to bribe her. Spectators laughed and Seawell cleared the court.[54]

McKenzie charged to Ferrari's face that the case was framed. Ferrari thereupon protested that the defense attorneys were constantly insinuating improper matters before the jury. McKenzie denied that he was insinuating anything; he was openly charging frame-up. Seawell silenced the two with threats of punishment.[55]

Once again Ferrari offered the extensive Berkman-Mooney-Morton correspondence and articles from the *Blast*. Again Seawell tentatively admitted them.[56] The defense pointed out that Weinberg had neither written nor received any of the letters, nor had he written any of the *Blast* articles that Ferrari was reading to the jury. Said McKenzie:

The admission of this kind of evidence absolutely tears down every safeguard a defendant has in a Court of Justice. It is the rankest sort of hearsay, three or four degrees removed. [A letter] From Morton to Nolan. Weinberg? No. Did he receive a letter? Never. He never had anything to do with The Blast.

MR. FERRARI: I am glad if it is dangerous testimony for the defendant, because anybody who would associate himself with The Blast ought to have some responsibility in the things that The Blast accomplished.

MR. MCKENZIE: That means lynch law?

MR. FERRARI: Not lynch law. It is the law of the State of California. When a man subscribed for an anarchistic paper it is some evidence he is an anarchist.

. . .

MR. MCKENZIE: . . . It won't be assumed that the prosecution can retroactively charge that the issues prior to his becoming a subscriber to The Blast are binding upon him?

MR. FERRARI: . . . The issues before as well as the issues after would be just as binding.

MR. MCKENZIE: You would then make the acts and every statement in The Examiner binding upon me thirty years ago.

MR. FERRARI: . . . The Examiner and The Blast are two different things.

MR. O'CONNOR: . . . the principle is the same.

MR. FERRARI: . . . No. Here is one which we shall contend is an unlawful paper having for its object an unlawful purpose. The other is a lawful paper.

MR. MCKENZIE: A lawful paper having some unlawful object, as some people say. It all depends upon how you feel.

MR. FERRARI: Everybody I think will feel the same.[57]

The reading from the *Blast* continued until the court had had its fill, and the prosecution rested.

Weinberg's trial closed at the end of its seventh week. The jury deliberated for 23 minutes and returned a verdict of not guilty.[58] Commented one of the jurors: "The jury did not discuss the evidence at all. . . . There seemed to be no case against Weinberg. I waited patiently, day after day, for the State to make some guilty connection between Weinberg and Mooney and Billings; but none was produced."[59]

The defense was encouraged. If Weinberg were freed, could the others be far behind? Fickert thought that Weinberg would probably not be subjected to "more than one more trial," since Weinberg was "not so definitely connected with the anarchistic conspiracy." The other defendants would each be tried on "at least two other indictments."[60] Ferrari announced that Nolan's trial would begin, if possible, the following Monday.

The following Monday there was no trial. Though the District Attorney blustered and bluffed for months, he never brought any of the defendants to trial again. With the acquittal of Weinberg the bomb prosecutions had come to their tardy and inconclusive end. Henceforth the concern of Fickert in the Preparedness Day cases was to prevent the retrial of Mooney, to oppose executive clemency, to sustain public concern about radicalism and prevent his own recall from office, and to deny Rena Mooney and Weinberg either bail or the dismissal of their remaining indictments.

VII

Weinberg had been in jail sixteen months. His savings were wiped out, his customers gone, his wife and son dependent on friends. He had been acquitted without debate. Yet Fickert opposed bail.[61] Judge Seawell left the question to Dunne. Dunne had been keeping Rena Mooney from bail for the past four months, and the same fate apparently awaited Weinberg. Dunne postponed decision. The defense enlisted the moral support of the jurors. All twelve petitioned the judge to grant bail: "We do not believe any good can come of holding him in durance longer."[62] One of them spoke more strongly: "I'm against anarchists; and I went into this case with an absolutely open mind, and I was ready to convict on any kind of adequate evidence —but not on a wild-eyed, astral-bodied, wine-bum case like that— never!"* Labor unions, led by Weinberg's and Nolan's locals, passed resolutions demanding Weinberg's release.[63]

McNutt appeared before Dunne and argued for bail. Dunne said that he would admit Weinberg to bail only on the indictment for which he had stood trial, and not on the others. "Ridiculous," said McNutt.[64] The following colloquy ensued:

THE COURT: It's a significant fact that since the incarceration of these defendants there has been no dynamiting in this city.

MCNUTT: Yes, and there was none before in this city either.

THE COURT: I want to say so far as the prosecution is concerned that it has been hampered by the activities of the defense and the kind of activities that the defense has seen fit to resort to.

MCNUTT: My answer to that is this; that these defendants, every one of them was framed against, and I have the proof.

---

* Juror A. P. Happ, as quoted in the *Bulletin*, November 29, 1917. "Astral-bodied" refers of course to Mellie Edeau, and "wine-bum" to McDonald. This reaction points up the key role of Oxman's testimony in the conviction of Mooney.

THE COURT: And every crook and every anarchist and every I.W.W. thinks as you do, Mr. McNutt. Every vicious anarchist and every vicious crook hollers "frameup."

MCNUTT: I have the statement of some of the witnesses who indicted them.

THE COURT: You ought to know all about perjury, Mr. McNutt.

MCNUTT: I have been around here long enough to know all about it.

THE COURT: You and Mr. "Jackal" Lawlor, Mr. McKenzie, Mr. O'Connor, and Mr. Brennan ought to know all about it.

MCNUTT: Yes, and we possess the proof of it.

THE COURT: You ought to know all about perjury and juries.

MCNUTT: And judges included.

THE COURT: Well, the motion is denied.[65]

Weinberg went back to jail.

McNutt went to Judge Griffin and applied for a writ of habeas corpus. Fickert and Ferrari opposed it. Griffin agreed to admit Weinberg to bail on all the indictments pending before himself and Judge Cabaniss, but refused to interfere in Dunne's court. McNutt went to the Appellate Court, lost there, and went on to the Supreme Court, where his habeas corpus petition waited its turn for another two months.[66]

Meanwhile Cabaniss and Griffin lost all patience with the district attorney who talked incessantly of trying another bomb case and never commenced. Early in February 1918, Cabaniss ordered Fickert to try Weinberg before him on the 13th of that month. The prosecution responded that it preferred to retry Mooney first, if he were granted a new trial by the Supreme Court or the Governor. (That, as it turned out, would have delayed things for another ten months.) When the appointed day arrived, Ferrari requested postponement. Cabaniss angrily refused. Fickert complained that Cabaniss was opposed to capital punishment. He said he wanted more time to get witnesses, to get Oxman. Cabaniss ordered the jury impaneled. A week later the veniremen showed up. Ferrari was still unprepared, but Cabaniss was adamant: Ferrari might have until 2 P.M. to begin. Ferrari returned at 2 P.M. and moved for the dismissal of the two indictments against Weinberg in Cabaniss's department. Cabaniss granted the motion and Weinberg's second trial was a victory by default. Weinberg went back to jail. He had five indictments to go.[67]

Griffin now set an early date for Weinberg's trial, and it was Cunha's turn to think of excuses and be the reluctant dragon. Griffin refused to postpone; Cunha moved for dismissal; Griffin dismissed all the indictments before him. The remaining indictments came up before Dunne and he postponed them for five weeks; that postponement was on motion from the prosecution, which did not want another trial before Seawell.[68]

The Supreme Court overruled the Appellate Court and admitted Weinberg to bail.[69] Fifteen thousand dollars cash was secured and Weinberg went free, twenty months after his arrest. Friends and reporters greeted him in the lobby of the city jail. He was asked if he would run his jitney bus again, and he replied—unless the remark was invented by a waggish reporter—"I can't; Oxman has the license."[70] Weinberg took his family back to Cleveland, to a carpenter's living and obscurity, from which he was but occasionally called during the next twenty years on behalf of the Irishman who had once been a passenger in his jitney bus.[71]

Rena Mooney was still in jail. Weinberg's release paved the way for hers. McNutt and Cunha had agreed in Griffin's department that her trial would follow Weinberg's. Fickert said he was ready and did not expect to dismiss any charges. But a day later an agreement was reached between the defense and the prosecution in Griffin's chambers that the trial would not proceed; neither would the District Attorney oppose Mrs. Mooney's release on her own recognizance (that is, without bail) from the courts of Griffin and Cabaniss. That left the indictments before Dunne to settle. McNutt filed petition for habeas corpus directly with the Supreme Court and then went to Dunne. Dunne capitulated. He said that the defendants all belonged in jail but that in view of the Supreme Court's ruling for Weinberg, he did not wish to appear stubborn. Another $15,000 cash for the bail was immediately raised, and at last, on March 30, 1918, Rena Mooney went home.[72]

CHAPTER SIXTEEN

Fickert Faces Recall

Astral bunk and astral gall
That's why the people demanded recall.

Just then the barfly chorus struck up the Fickert
campaign anthem: "You're an anarchist, he's an
anarchist, they're all anarchists, too."
　　　　　—*Bulletin*, December 8 and 10, 1917

THE OXMAN LETTERS had scarcely been published in April 1917 when a movement began to recall Fickert from office. Rumors circulated in the state legislature that recall petitions would be circulated before the end of the month. Efforts were made in Sacramento to have Attorney General Webb appoint as Oxman's special prosecutor someone who would run against Fickert in a recall election. Among those mentioned were John Francis Neylan of the Board of Control; O'Connor's law partner, William A. Kelly; and Charles A. Sweigert, a former police commissioner who had run against Fickert in 1915. Neither Neylan nor Kelly was interested. Sweigert parried inquiries, but one of his friends, the Progressive county committee chairman, was the leading proponent of the recall. When Webb appointed Robert Clarke as the special prosecutor, the movement was slowed but not stopped. "The finger of recall already points at him," said the *Bulletin*. "The important thing is to give the bomb case defendants . . . as fair a trial as an honest prosecution can give them. This requires a preliminary housecleaning, and among the debris to be swept out is Fickert."[1]

Before the end of April a small group of San Franciscans who were not directly connected with the bomb cases organized the Fickert Recall League. Half of its founders were minor labor officials; another was Sara Bard Field; the chairman was J. H. Young, an active member of the anti–capital punishment league. To set a recall in motion they needed 11,800 valid signatures of registered San Francisco voters. They opened an office on Market Street, circulated petitions, and by early June announced that they had over 17,000 signatures and would soon file with the city registrar.[2]

The prospects, however, were dimmer than they looked. Building a strong movement proved difficult. Through May and June the Fickert Recall League received little publicity. Sweigert's candidacy went unannounced. (Unfamiliar with the election laws, the League at first intended to recall Fickert without electing anyone in his place.)[3] The Labor Council was divided. The *Bulletin* and *News,* predictably supporters of the movement, were almost silent on the question. Older and the Mooney defense were preoccupied with the Oxman imbroglio and the trial of Rena Mooney, from which the recall proponents undoubtedly expected additional ammunition. And it was hoped that Governor William D. Stephens (Hiram Johnson's successor) or the Attorney General might remove Fickert from office, as some of the labor unions were demanding. Privately, defense attorney Lawlor remarked that the recall movement lacked drive and would fail.[4]

Two days before Rena Mooney's case went to the jury, the Fickert Recall League filed its petition with 15,000 signatures and a statement that the District Attorney had "prostituted his office at the behest of certain interests for the purpose of bringing discredit to the ranks of union labor." At the same time the League announced Sweigert's candidacy.[5]

Fickert, who had said little, declared that his enemies were seeking his recall because he had performed his duty: "The people leading this fight against me are the anarchists. Their main reason in wanting me out of office is that they fear prosecution."[6] He sought to block the election by challenging the validity of the petitions in a variety of court actions. He accused the petitioners of fraud, and obtained indictments for perjury against several of them; when these indictments were voided by Judges Cabaniss and Griffin for flaws and insufficiency, he went back three times to the grand jury and obtained additional indictments until some were accepted in Dunne's court; then he prosecuted. (One man was convicted, after the election was over.) His representatives stood by the registrar's clerks as they checked signatures and successfully challenged thousands; when the League brought 5,000 reserve signatures, enough of which passed muster to force the issue, Fickert went to court with renewed allegations of wholesale fraud, and obtained a temporary restraining order to stop Registrar Zemansky from certifying the recall lists to the Board of Election Commissioners. He also filed for an injunction as a taxpayer, alleging that the election would be unnecessary and would cost the city over $50,000.[7]

The League fought back in the courts. It asked the State Supreme

Court for a writ of mandamus to compel Zemansky and the election commissioners to proceed with the election. Hearings were set and the matter dragged on through October.[8]

The prospect that an elected official might thwart a recall movement by appealing over the registrar to the courts, and that the courts might review the lists or prohibit their certification, alarmed the Progressive authors of direct legislation in California. Dr. John R. Haynes of Los Angeles, president of the Direct Legislation League of California, denied that the courts had any authority to review Zemansky's findings. The Direct Legislation League took no side in the recall effort against Fickert, he said, but the recall laws had intentionally been formulated to preclude the review of county registrars' decisions by the courts; if the Supreme Court decided that the petition for Fickert's recall was subject to court review, the effect would be to nullify the direct-legislation provisions of the state constitution. "If these matters can be delayed in the courts it means that an official may stall a case until his term of office ends or he dies of old age." The issue, Haynes said, was whether the people or the courts would rule.[9] He called a conference in San Francisco of his League's executive committee, which included William Kent, former governor George C. Pardee, Senator James D. Phelan, Rudolph Spreckels, and other prominent Progressives. At the meeting resolutions were adopted condemning Fickert's actions. Returning to Los Angeles, Haynes continued to spread the alarm of impending "disaster."[10]

A week later the Supreme Court ruled Fickert's temporary restraining order invalid, and directed Zemansky to fix a date for the recall election. But Fickert was not through. He went to Los Angeles, where the Supreme Court was in session, and charged Zemansky with fraud: he alleged that the registrar had corruptly refused to allow him to file proofs of fraud and irregularity in the recall petition. This was another matter. The court issued a temporary restraining order against the San Francisco Board of Election Commissioners just as they were convening to set the election date.[11] Milton T. U'Ren, attorney for the Fickert Recall League, was indignant: "It is a clear indication of the desperate straits Fickert is in when he makes such an attack as this upon an official like Zemansky, whose honesty and efficiency have long been unquestioned throughout his long career in the service of the city."[12] The election commissioners had intended to put the recall contest on the general November ballot, but the restraining order made it impossible. Amid public confusion a hearing was set for early

November. Attorneys appeared before the court for Fickert, Zemansky, and the Recall League and offered familiar arguments. Two days later the court denied Fickert's appeal. The special election was set for December 18.[13]

II

Sweigert campaigned for District Attorney on two issues, impartial justice and the suppression of vice. The vice question had developed since August, when a leading minister of San Francisco, Paul Smith, announced that he was joining the recall campaign and would supply additional signatures for the petitions or begin again if the Fickert Recall League failed. He did not join the League, but organized his own movement, which, he said, had no connection with the Mooney case.[14]

Fickert's accommodation of the demimonde had been a more or less accepted condition of San Francisco life. There had been scandals and outcries but no successful opposition. When the Red Light Abatement Act against brothels was passed in 1913, San Francisco's prostitution was wide open. Fickert turned over enforcement of the act to the attorney for the property owners who were its leading opponents; needless to say, the law was laxly enforced.[15] In 1917, with Sweigert campaigning against him, Fickert filed some red-light abatement suits to close disorderly houses, but the tenderloin had already taken cover.[16] "I passed through the Barbary Coast last night for the first time in years," Rowell remarked. "There was not a drunken or disorderly person in the whole region and it was so quiet that it was ridiculous."[17] According to the *Bulletin,* the uptown tenderloin along Mason Street was solidly behind Fickert. A reporter visiting the dance halls encountered only one Sweigert supporter. "The cabaret girls, many of whom admitted that they didn't know what the election was all about, all had instructions to vote for Fickert. So had the male entertainers, the bartenders, and the beer slingers."[18] The vice question was secondary to the bomb cases, but it was a fighting issue.

III

Charles F. Hanlon, a well-known San Francisco attorney and the chairman in 1916 of the Pacific Coast Defense League, which had sponsored the Preparedness Parade, was an ardent trotting-horse racer, bon vivant, and theater patron. During the Panama-Pacific International Exposition he had entertained the actress Lillian Russell and her fourth husband, Alexander P. Moore, when they visited San Francisco. Moore, a millionaire, was the editor of the Pittsburgh *Leader*. He had taken an active part in the formation of the Progressive Party in 1912 and was a close friend of Theodore Roosevelt. A few days after the San Francisco election commission had set the date for Fickert's recall election, Hanlon wired Moore to ask him to intercede with Roosevelt for an endorsement of Fickert, who had "successfully prosecuted the biggest bunch of anarchists in the United States." Might not the Colonel commend Fickert's stand? Moore was obliging.[19]

Roosevelt took up the challenge. He hated anarchists. In the Haymarket affair he had applauded the executions, and later proposed exclusion laws: "If Anarchists do come, they should be . . . shot down."[20] (It was a fixed conviction. "I treated anarchists and the bomb-throwing and dynamiting gentry precisely as I treated other criminals," he wrote in 1913.)[21] Roosevelt wired Fickert that if the information was correct,

. . . I not only feel that the issue betwen you and your opponents is that between patriotism and anarchy, but I also feel that all who directly or indirectly assail you for any such reason should be promptly deprived of citizenship.

Anarchist bomb throwers are murderers, worse than ordinary murderers, and all men who sympathize with them or give them aid and support are enemies of the country and should at least be disfranchised and furthermore punished to any extent that is necessary.[22]

The message was published, to the elation of Fickert's supporters, and Fickert replied with gratitude.[23] But Sweigert wired Roosevelt that his information was erroneous; Fickert had "suppressed testimony, manufactured evidence, and suborned perjury" in the bomb cases:

The fight against Fickert is the same old fight we have been waging here against corruption and vice which received your endorsement [in] 1908. Fickert is supported by the same old crowd. My candidacy is backed by Rudolph Spreckels, Paul Scharrenberg, Daniel C. Murphy, . . . William Kent, Franklin Hichborn, . . . Fremont Older, all known as highest type of California citizens, and many known to you personally.

He asked Roosevelt to switch the endorsement.[24] Commented Fickert: "many of the persons mentioned . . . are either openly or otherwise in

sympathy with Alexander Berkman, Emma Goldman, and other anarchists."[25]

When Moore's part became known, he explained that he had appealed to Roosevelt because he had been told that opposition to
Fickert sprang from his prosecution of the IWW: "Colonel Roosevelt's compliance with the request was only because he believed that
he was helping to stamp out sedition."[26] "Right," said Fickert, "so am
I."[27] Then Hanlon's role came to light. Moore acknowledged that all
he knew about the case was what Hanlon had told him: "I know nothing about the merits of the case. If what Fremont Older telegraphs me
is true about the District Attorney he is the arch criminal of the
United States. If what I hear from the other side is true he is probably
the most abused man in the United States."[28]

Many San Franciscans wired Roosevelt their approval of his stand.
"A villainous and well-financed publicity bureau has poisoned the
nation with lies and libel," Judge Dunne told him.[29] Joseph R. Tobin
of the Hibernia National Bank asserted that Max Eastman was behind
the recall movement.[30] Roosevelt privately wrote Rowell that he did
not know Dunne but that Tobin was straight and clean,[31] and that
Older, Spreckels, and Kent were hopelessly unsound: "I feel they have
gradually grown to be downright sympathizers with anarchy and
murder, and this to the extent in the case of Older at least of becoming
an accessory to the gravest wrongdoing." Mooney and Billings, if
necessary, should be executed under martial law, which was the proper
way of dealing with outrages of this character when civil law proved
inadequate, "and when failure to get at them means grave menace to
the country and indeed to the foundation of civilized society." The
very agitation of the Bolsheviki and anarchists for Billings and Mooney, he said, showed that the radicals themselves thought the pair
guilty: "If Billings and Mooney were not anarchists, were not bomb-
throwers, were not murderers and were really entirely innocent, well-
behaved, law-abiding men, then the Bolsheviki people at home and
abroad would be utterly indifferent to their fate."[32]

Fickert advertised Roosevelt's endorsement widely in his speeches,
in the newspapers, and on billboards. He was also assisted by endorsements from the Downtown Association, the Civic League, and the
Chamber of Commerce.[33] The Chamber's attitude was expressed
graphically in a private letter its manager wrote a prominent businessman in Paul Smith's congregation:

While it may seem to you to be tough that good men are trying to prevent the recall of such an officer as you believe Fickert to be, it is more than tough that good men like Paul Smith and others are lined up with the worst I.W.W. and anarchistic elements in the country to give aid and comfort to the worst enemies of our government within our borders. If the ministers and others want to recall Fickert on purely moral grounds, it would be perfectly proper for them to institute their own petition and have the recall based on these reasons. [But] both Fickert's personal character and his failure to prosecute vice in this town pale into insignificance compared with the great question as to the support of or non-support of constituted authority in the prosecution of diabolical crime.

The writer, Robert Newton Lynch, added that if law and order surrendered to the anarchists, the ministers would have no protection except by appeal to the office of the *Bulletin*.*

Sweigert had endorsements from the California State Federation of Labor and a large number of ministers. He also had the active support of Mooney, who went $3,000 into debt for 100,000 copies of "Justice Raped in California," the fourth edition of the IWDL pamphlet, which was distributed free during the campaign.[34]

The campaign was abusive on both sides. Sweigert called Fickert the "astral body of Patrick Calhoun"; "his last act was to sprinkle chloride of lime upon the oozing Oxman"; "now he is wrapping the draperies of the flag about him and lying down to patriotic dreams." He charged that Fickert, supported by "the putrid precincts," had "made rape safe in San Francisco."[35] Fickert, for his part, adhered to the anarchist theme. The two candidates, addressing one organization together, nearly came to blows.[36]

Since the turnout for special elections was usually light, and since the war had taken away 10,000 voters, Registrar Zemansky predicted that only about 40,000 of 140,000 qualified voters would go to the polls. Betting was reported light, with even money posted that Fickert would win by 6,000 votes.[37]

IV

Late election eve a bomb exploded at the Executive Mansion in Sacramento. The back porch and basement were badly damaged, al-

* Robert Newton Lynch to Rolla V. Watt, in Franklin Hichborn, "California Politics, 1891–1939" (typescript, University of California Law School, Berkeley), III: 1591–93. Watt remained away from the polls: "I would not dirty my fingers with a vote for Fickert under any circumstances," he wrote Smith, "but I feel that I cannot conscientiously vote for his recall under existing circumstances." (*Ibid.*, p. 1954.)

though no one was injured. The bombing occurred at 11:55, before the San Francisco papers went to press.* The next morning San Franciscans read that an attempt had been made to assassinate the Governor, and turned out heavily at the polls to defeat the recall. Women organized into groups and combed their districts to get out the votes, according to Zemansky. "The feeling was everywhere pronounced, and that it played a large part in the heavy vote cast is unmistakable." Of the more than 74,000 ballots cast, 46,460 were for Fickert, 26,983 for Sweigert.†

"Patriotism has triumphed over anarchy," Fickert wired Roosevelt. "Your timely message brought thousands of loyal citizens to a realization of the true issue." He urged that San Franciscans "all help to suppress anarchy and sedition wherever it exists, so we may enjoy security and happiness protected by law."[38] Moore sent Fickert his congratulations: "I was accused by these red shirts of deceiving Colonel Roosevelt."[39] The *Chronicle* stated that the recall movement had been inspired only by anarchism. Another journal declared: "there are not so many undesirable citizens in San Francisco as some folk believed." And the San Francisco *Retail Grocers' Advocate* said, "The manner in which the housewives voted for Fickert once more proves the political influence of the Retail Grocer with his customers."[40]

Among the other factors in Fickert's victory were his record on radicalism, his patriotic stance, the conservative opposition to the recall process as an expensive device of the Progressives, and the bombing of the Governor's residence. That the bombing affected the election was conceded at Fickert's headquarters, but his supporters claimed that he would have won anyway.[41] Probably that was so.

Surveying the outcome, the *Bulletin* reflected: "Fickert's reelection is only a reprieve. In calmer times his record will be understood in all its sordidness and it may be that justice will ultimately be done Mooney and Billings."[42]

---

* According to an IWW source, girls were put on telephones that night, calling voters out of bed with the message: "Vote for Fickert and your own preservation. Stop dynamiting in California." (Harvey Duff, *The Silent Defenders: Courts and Capitalism in California* [1919], p. 17.)

† *Call*, December 18, 1917; Zemansky, as quoted in *Examiner*, December 19, 1917. See also Hichborn, "California Politics," III: 1594–95. These were first-preference votes in a preferential balloting. Few voters entered second or third choices. A third candidate, Frank P. Haynes, received fewer than 2,000 votes; Haynes allegedly had been put up by Fickert's backers to draw votes from Sweigert. Like Sweigert, he was a Catholic, an attorney with labor affiliations, and had run for office in San Francisco; he could also have been easily confused with John R. Haynes. (*Chronicle*, December 14, 19, and 25, 1917; Mooney to Bourke Cockran, November 16, 1917, in Cockran Papers.)

V

Some of Mooney's friends suspected that Fickert had instigated the Sacramento bombing, but the crime was never solved.* Sacramento detectives, abandoning the theory that assassination was the motive, suspected intimidation; they considered it significant that the bomb had been placed on the side of the house away from the Governor's bedroom. The Sacramento police chief announced that he suspected the IWW.[43]

In some respects the Sacramento case was the Preparedness Day case all over again. Sacramento newspapers had condemned the IWW for years. Feeling in the city ran high. The police department was under great pressure; the City Commissioners and the Sacramento Chamber of Commerce demanded action; a reward was offered; the leading newspaper favored vigilante action.[44] The crime was constantly ascribed to radical, pro-German, IWW terrorism. One reporter wrote: "The detectives are at sea for a motive, but not for the perpetrator. Swarms of investigators trampled over the Governor's lawn all day, dividing their time seeking shrapnel from the thing that exploded and blaming the I.W.W.'s."[45] Pieces of a suitcase were found. Numerous arrests were made without evidence. The accused were held incommunicado; witnesses came forward and offered identification; the police chief made confident predictions.

On December 22, thirty members of the IWW were arrested in Sacramento, and others were picked up in the days following. One of the Wobblies, William Hood, was arrested with a companion on the street while carrying a box of explosives. He denied complicity in the bombing, but pleaded guilty on a federal charge of transporting dynamite illegally.[46] According to IWW correspondence seized by the San Francisco police, the Wobblies considered Hood "on the square, but a good deal of a pinhead and a blatherskate," and "some crack-brain" for having taken dynamite into Sacramento at that time.[47]

Apparently local authorities, supported or encouraged by Deputy United States Marshal Thomas Mulhall of San Francisco and Assis-

* Louise D. Harding to Bourke Cockran, January 9, 1918, in Cockran Papers. Franck R. Havenner of the *Bulletin*, investigating the case, unearthed evidence that the watchman might have been responsible, and that "not long before the night when the dynamiting took place, the watchman and Martin Swanson ... were seen together in Sacramento." (John D. Barry to Felix Frankfurter, January 12, 1917, in National Archives, RG 174, Box 176.)

tant United States Attorney P. H. Johnson, wanted the federal government to take over the prisoners and prosecute them. According to
newspaper accounts, a special agent from the office of the Department
of Justice in San Francisco, Don S. Rathbun, examined the evidence
with Mulhall and announced that nothing had been found to justify
placing any charges against any of the men held in Sacramento except
Hood and his companion for unlawfully transporting dynamite. But
Johnson, after conferring with United States Attorney Raymond Benjamin, swore out complaints on charges that were similar to those
made against William Haywood and other IWW's on trial in Chicago.
The charges included obstruction of military enlistment by such
means as "urging disloyalty to the United States" and by "execrating
the President of the United States." ("Since their arrest," reported the
Chronicle, "the prisoners have cursed the Government and President
Wilson in songs and hymns which could be heard for blocks.") In February 1918, the prisoners were indicted by the federal grand jury in
Sacramento on charges unrelated to the bombing, and so were nine
other California IWW's, four of whom had just been released by the
United States Commissioner in San Francisco for lack of evidence
against them. Nearly a year later 46 were tried for violation of the
Espionage Act.* Most of them in protest and contempt refused to
defend themselves; this became the celebrated case of the "Silent Defenders." They were convicted, and many were sentenced to ten years
in prison.[48]

* George Bell, attorney for the California Commission on Immigration and Housing,
observed before the trial: "the Government has practically no evidence to hold all or any
of these people under the espionage or any other law—therefore the Federal Government
is in a fair way to creating some forty-five new martyrs to the cause." (Bell to Felix
Frankfurter, undated memorandum, National Archives, RG 174, Box 193.)

CHAPTER SEVENTEEN

The Labor Defense Movement, 1917

At a regular meeting of Beer Bottlers Union No. 293, held July 17th, the undersigned was instructed to communicate with you, and ask you to give Tom Mooney a new trial.
—Petition to the State
Attorney General, 1917

WITH MOONEY'S conviction and Oxman's exposure the demand for justice mushroomed from the special concern of radicals and defense attorneys into a nationwide movement of organized labor. This movement, representing primarily the militant components of the American Federation of Labor, involved dozens of AFL state federations, scores of city and district labor councils, and hundreds of local unions across the country. As a result of organized labor's diverse efforts for Mooney in 1917, Mooney's name became a household word, and his case a fixed feature of the American labor scene for the next generation.

The defense received early and valuable support from the Chicago labor movement, particularly the Chicago Federation of Labor, which began a long, dedicated affiliation with Mooney's cause before he went to trial. Chicago was a stronghold of organized labor. Its labor council was the country's largest and probably most important city central. Although it had little direct influence on the national policy making of the AFL, since the international unions rather than the city centrals or state federations held the AFL's reins, in labor circles the Chicago Federation of Labor was nationally prominent and locally powerful. Led by President John Fitzpatrick and Secretary Ed Nockels, it was a militantly progressive body, radical—though not doctrinaire —in comparison to the moderate, trade-union norms of the AFL.[1] Chicago was also a center of radical movements, the home of national headquarters of the Socialist Party, the IWW, and later the Communist parties; Haymarket Square was hallowed ground for anarchists.

The city was a natural choice for national left-wing conventions. Size, location, radical activity, and the role of the Chicago Federation of Labor all helped make Chicago the key city in the nationwide labor defense of Mooney.

Late in December 1916, the Chicago Federation of Labor sponsored a mass meeting to protest the "legal farce" in San Francisco, the manipulation of courts and jury by the Chamber of Commerce, and the "frightful conspiracy of Big Business which has no other purpose than to convict Union men and then use their conviction as an indictment of Organized Labor." Ed Nockels pointed out to the assembly that Bourke Cockran and Frank P. Walsh were donating their services to the defense. He said it was time Chicago woke up.[2] Chicago radicals, of course, were already awake; some anarchists rented a small auditorium for their own protest meeting, which was addressed by William Z. Foster, Bill Haywood, Alexander Berkman, and the famous Sinn Fein rebel Jim Larkin. (Together the Syndicalist, Wobbly, anarchist, and Irish Socialist symbolized the radicals' common concern for Mooney and Billings. According to Lucy Robins Lang, the audience was warmly pro-Irish, and entertained the speakers afterward in the saloon downstairs.)[3]

Cockran spurred on the Mooney cause in Chicago as part of a defense publicity tour he undertook at Mooney's request. He laid plans with the Chicago Federation of Labor to hold a mass meeting in the Chicago Coliseum on March 25, 1917—an ambitious project, since the Coliseum seated over 12,000 and for best effect it needed to be filled.[4] Before the meeting he returned to New York to address another rally at Carnegie Hall, under the auspices of the United Hebrew Trades and other labor groups. There, reviewing the prosecution's charge that the bombing was part of an organized conspiracy to assassinate the President and the Governor of California and obstruct preparedness, Cockran urged a federal investigation of the case. Resolutions supporting the proposal were adopted.[5] Eleven days later an audience variously estimated between 8,000 and 20,000 gathered at the Chicago Coliseum to hear Cockran, Fitzpatrick, and Nockels. The meeting adopted the same resolutions, which were sent to Congress and the President. Mooney's friends distributed copies to the local unions of molders and streetcar men across the country, with the request that they, too, adopt them and send them to Washington.[6]

Cockran received a flood of requests to speak at other mass meetings, but he decided to discontinue public speaking for the defense lest the movement appear to be a one-man performance. "Unless labor men themselves take up the discussion now," he wrote Mooney, "the whole movement is likely to show a lack of spontaneity that will probably be fatal to its success." Mooney disagreed. He wanted Cockran to tour the country as the principal speaker for a series of great labor protest meetings: "We need publicity, and funds, and we can not get either until the case is understood, and the very best way to prepare an understanding is to have a man who knows all angles of the case to take up at least the preliminary work." But Cockran stuck to his decision.[7]

II

Immediately after the Coliseum meeting Cockran entrained for Washington and met Samuel Gompers, who had asked to see him. Gompers approved of the resolutions adopted in New York and Chicago. He promised to take the matter up at once with the federal authorities. Since he was not only president of the AFL but also an adviser to the Council of National Defense, the highest civilian war-planning board of the Wilson administration, Cockran was greatly encouraged.[8]

With the discovery of the Oxman letters, Cockran proposed to Gompers and others that a federal investigation be requested on the basis of Oxman's use of the mails to commit fraud. He believed the best approach would be to ask for a Post Office investigation. "Its inspectors are by far the most skillful of the Secret Service men, and the letter sent to Rigall brings the whole matter within the jurisdiction of that department."[9] A federal charge would be far better than a local San Francisco prosecution: "I have little doubt that if he [Oxman] found himself pursued—not by officials who had been abettors of his crime, and who are therefore bound to protect him from serious consequences, but by honest, independent officials . . . he could be made to disclose all the ramifications of this dark transaction."[10] Gompers agreed that the Rigall letters were sufficient to set the government in motion, but preferred to go to the Department of Justice. His strategy was probably based on Postmaster General A. S. Burleson's hostility to organized labor.[11] But the Justice Department contended that it had no right even to express an opinion on the case.[12] So far as the perjury question was concerned, its position was correct: according to Frank Walsh, the laws protected the mails only against their use to defraud persons of their property.[13] The Attorney General, Thomas

W. Gregory, did consult United States District Attorney Preston in San Francisco on the whole question. Preston advised him that Oxman's scheme of fraud had involved "about Three dollars in mileage. This seems not to be of sufficient moment to require this office to arrest him, especially in view of the fact that on the main charge, to wit, subornation of perjury, he has been held to answer."[14]

A demonstration for Mooney in Petrograd gave Gompers another line of approach. He urged the Secretary of State, Robert Lansing, to intervene for the sake of better relations with Russia. Lansing was interested, but for the time being there were no noticeable results.[15] Cockran was annoyed because he thought that Gompers had compromised the main point: it was not enough for the federal government to ask the state executive for a commutation of Mooney's sentence in order to improve relations with a wartime ally. "I did not propose," he wrote Mooney, "that he should ask clemency for a guilty man. I wanted him to demand justice for an innocent man."[16]

Yet another way of involving the federal government was to stir up a Congressional investigation by proposing federal legislation that would bear indirectly on the case. Walsh conferred with labor friends in Washington and drew up a bill "to prevent the use of the mails for the purpose of securing false witnesses, suborning perjury, and procuring false testimony in civil or criminal cases." The bill provided for a fine of $1,000 or up to five years' imprisonment.[17] Walsh intended that it be introduced by one of the California Congressmen.[18] He also drafted a resolution for a House of Representatives inquiry into the use of the mails for the solicitation of perjury "and especially the charges that the mails have thus been used in procuring false and perjured testimony in the case of the State of California against Thomas J. Mooney, . . . with full power to compel the attendance of witnesses, the giving of testimony and the production of books, papers and documents before such special committee."[19] Walsh's resolution, if followed through, would have given handsome publicity to the Oxman affair, for whatever advantage might develop for Mooney. Congressman John I. Nolan of San Francisco, a member of Mooney's union, seemed the logical person to introduce the bill and resolution. Walsh, Nockels, and Andrew Furuseth talked to him about it. Nolan disliked Mooney but agreed to cooperate, provided that he were asked to do so by California labor organizations. Requests were promptly sent by the San Francisco Labor Council, the San Francisco Building Trades Council, and the California State Federation of Labor, but Nolan changed his mind: he would introduce only the bill. He put it into the House hopper on June 2. It was buried in the Committee on the Post Office.[20]

Nockels returned to Chicago in disgust. Two weeks later he was back, buttonholing Senators to introduce the resolution in the Senate. He obtained the help of the private secretary of Senator Harry Lane of Oregon, but everywhere they ran against the opinion that the resolution should be introduced by one of the Senators from California. "You know the senatorial courtesy stuff, etc.?" Walsh wrote Mooney.[21] Senator Johnson refused to help; Senator James D. Phelan was less blunt but no more accommodating. And so the project for a Congressional investigation of the Mooney case faded from sight.[22] Not until 1938 was one undertaken.

III

The San Francisco labor movement began to show a change of heart in the spring of 1917. Prior to the conviction of Mooney the Labor Council and the State Federation of Labor had been little concerned for the defendants. Labor leaders believed that the defendants were not receiving due justice, but they ascribed this to an unsatisfactory jury system, and felt that the cases had nothing to do with organized labor. After Mooney's conviction this view was abandoned. The key labor officials leading the change were liberals, notably Daniel Murphy, Andrew Furuseth, Walter Macarthur, and above all, Paul Scharrenberg. With the support of the moderate and radical labor delegates, they instituted a new policy in the Council and Federation on the Mooney case, despite opposition from the Council's conservative president, Arthur W. Brouillet, and secretary, John O'Connell.

Paul Scharrenberg was the secretary of the State Federation and a leading figure in the California labor movement. In 1916 he had assailed the Chamber of Commerce for its open-shop campaign, ridiculed Captain Robert Dollar, denounced the Law and Order Committee, and fought the preparedness movement. Like Fremont Older, however, he was slow to charge that the cases were framed; for more than six months he made no public claim that they were an effort to discredit organized labor.[23] As late as mid-January 1917, he assailed the Chamber of Commerce without reference to the cases—an omission that was the more significant because the Chamber's booklet, "Law and Order in San Francisco," which he was attacking, insinuated that the Preparedness Day bombing, like the waterfront violence, was proof that the unions were a menace.[24] Scharrenberg's first intimation that he considered the Chamber improperly involved in the cases appeared but a few days before Mooney's sentence. Then, following the Oxman exposure, he became a leading proponent of a new trial. The information that Fickert had sponsored Rigall's original visit to San Francisco convinced Scharrenberg that the District Attorney had framed Mooney.[25] And when the Chamber of Commerce went to Fickert's rescue, Scharrenberg also became convinced—as only the radicals originally had been—that the Chamber had helped frame Mooney to "get" organized labor. The Law and Order Committee and the Chamber, he said, "have been smoked out of their hole and are now openly aligned with those who would prostitute justice." Organized labor would repulse the Chamber's effort to brand union labor with the ghastly crime of Preparedness Day.*

The San Francisco Labor Council reacted similarly, for similar reasons. In November 1916 it had passed a resolution asking for a fair trial and mentioned that the four male defendants were union men, but said nothing about "labor cases."[26] At the Council's meeting of February 16, a week after Mooney's conviction, President Brouillet, who was a salaried officeholder in the state's Republican administration, and Secretary O'Connell, an old supporter of the Ruef regime, opposed the adoption of resolutions calling for new trials; O'Connell argued that Mooney had probably dynamited the URR power towers, and that Mooney and his men had gone armed to the URR organizing meeting of June 10. He said that the trial had been fair and that the judge would ignore a Labor Council resolution in any event.[27] Although the Council adopted the resolutions anyway, it did nothing further for weeks, despite pressure from its own left wing and other labor organizations. But as the events of April unfolded, the Council began to stir. A committee was set up to collect funds for the defense. Every affiliated union was asked to contribute an hour's wage for each member. The Council brought pressure on Attorney General Webb to adopt Griffin's recommendation for a new trial, and demanded Fickert's recall.[28]

---

* *Coast Seamen's Journal,* May 2, 1917. See also April 25, 1917. The California State Federation of Labor's executive council stated in a circular letter, July 9, 1917: "those who would secure the conviction of these particular men and then attach their conviction to the name of organized labor would actually resort to . . . perjured testimony to gain the desired end." (*Ibid.,* July 11, 1917.)

Yet even after the Oxman exposé, the Labor Council's performance was tepid. The conservatives' resistance continued. The defense assessment was indifferently met: had the full sum been raised, it would have amounted perhaps to $30,000, or as much as the IWDL had been able to raise throughout the country in the first eight months, but no such sum was raised.[29] Nor did the Council sponsor mass meetings. As Older wrote Nockels, "Labor here seems paralyzed. It is the greatest case for labor in the history of the world and labor here doesn't realize it." He believed that the linking of Mooney with the *Blast*'s anti-Catholic articles had alienated Irish-Catholic labor leaders.[30] When Fickert invited the Council to appoint Brouillet as its special prosecutor at Oxman's trial, Older accused Brouillet of siding with Fickert. Denying the charge, Brouillet replied that he was proud of his disagreements with the *Bulletin*:

If you can find comfort in aligning yourself with I.W.W. or anarchist tendencies or practices, you are welcome to the company; but, personally, I believe and always have believed that labor never did and never will accomplish anything by destruction of life, limb, or property and that the Goldman, Berkman, Billings, et al, coterie have done more to discredit labor than any single agency that I know of. When the bomb cases were first discussed in the Labor Council, I took the position then that they were not labor cases, as they did not arise out of any dispute between employer and employees concerning wages, hours, or conditions of employment and that the people who, through their past actions, had centered suspicion upon themselves should clear themselves as best they could. I protested then and protest now against the labor movement of this or any other community being bled by assessments to support mountebanks, disturbers and destroyers of the American labor movement.[31]

The conflict between Brouillet and his labor opponents erupted at the annual convention of the State Federation of Labor at Sacramento in October. Selig Schulberg introduced a resolution pledging the Federation's assistance to the federal commission that Woodrow Wilson had just appointed to investigate the Mooney case and other Western labor disputes. Brouillet took the floor in opposition, and a tempestuous scene followed. He asserted that Mooney had set the bomb; "Tom was peeved and sore" because the Labor Council had spurned his car strike. "The bomb explosion was a dastardly, mean, contemptible way of venting his spite. You can't afford to give support to these vipers who are sucking your blood."[32] He announced that he intended "to finish the job that Fickert started last week" on Schulberg, and headed toward him. Delegates intervened.[33] Brouillet then lashed into Fremont Older, "a dirty skunk. He told people of high repute that they had the right men. I will see that he and they are brought before this Federal investigation committee."[34] He declared that there were delegates "in this convention hall now who know in their craven hearts that these defendants are guilty."[35] Scharrenberg retorted that he would be happy to accommodate him if he were looking for a fight. Daniel Murphy emphatically reasserted the innocence of the bomb defendants. Schulberg defended Older: "Labor knows full well what his attitude has been toward its cause. The San Francisco Bulletin has been a beacon of light for every thinking man in California."[36]

Brouillet had overplayed his hand. Member unions in the San Francisco Labor Council demanded his resignation. Formal charges were soon brought, and two committees were appointed to try them. The first exonerated Brouillet, but Furuseth and George Kidwell, two opposition leaders in the second, prepared a minority report, which was adopted by the delegates 95 to 46.* The president was declared suspended. A formal request by his local, the retail shoe clerks, that he be reinstated was rejected, 74 to 71. Vice-president Daniel Haggerty, whose attitude toward the bomb cases resembled Scharrenberg's, was then elected president, and the way was open for more energetic action.[37] Meanwhile other labor organizations across the country had taken up the issue.

IV

During the spring of 1917 the Mooney case became a national labor cause. Protest meetings were held in cities from coast to coast and appeals were made to the federal government. They commenced a month after the conviction. On March 7 the Detroit Federation of Labor asked President Wilson and Hiram Johnson (who was still Governor) "to use their efforts to influence the courts of California to grant a new trial."[38] In New York the same day Eugene Debs at Cooper Institute attacked working-class victimization:

---

* Kidwell was head of the Bakery Wagon Drivers Union in San Francisco. He was "a mildly radical, adroit leader with leanings toward industrial unionism." (Robert E. L. Knight, *Industrial Relations in the San Francisco Bay Area, 1900–1918* [1960], p. 335. See also Matthew Josephson, *Union House, Union Bar* [1956], p. 112.)

"There is Tom Mooney," he said, "sentenced to be hanged on May 17—"

"He won't be," shouted a voice in the audience.

"No, he won't be," answered Debs, his voice rising. "We'll see that he won't be. I am going out there in April, and if they hang him they'll have to prepare another noose for me."[39]

In Salt Lake City four days later a mass meeting endorsed the action of the city's federation of labor "recommending the general strike and the placing of all California products on the unfair list, as a means whereby the workers will use their economic power; which is practically the only . . . powerful weapon whereby they may secure justice for our imprisoned victims." The resolution was sent to President Wilson. It favored May Day as the appropriate date for a general strike on behalf of Mooney and Billings.[40]

Many state federations of the AFL protested. In West Virginia, where conflict with employers was a harsh reality in the coal-mining towns, the State Federation of Labor and district councils of the United Mine Workers, the IAM, and other international unions commended Fremont Older for his services in "preventing the criminal effort of the capitalists of [San Francisco] to railroad" Mooney and his wife to the gallows.[41] The Maine State Federation of Labor, meeting at Bar Harbor, commended Cockran for his efforts to obtain justice.[42] The Missouri State Federation of Labor recommended that all members be assessed twenty minutes' wages for support of the defense.[43]

Among the many local labor councils that helped Mooney and Billings in 1917, two of the earliest were the Essex Trades Council and the Essex Building Trades Council, of Essex County and the city of Newark, New Jersey. The history of their efforts illustrates some aspects of the Mooney labor defense movement. As early as January 1917, the official monthly journal of the two councils carried news of the bomb cases. In February the journal published an analysis of the cases by George P. West. By the time of Mooney's conviction, therefore, the Newark labor movement had a description of Mooney's role in San Francisco's labor struggles and an analysis showing that the cases were framed.[44] In April the Trades Council remitted money to the IWDL for 100 copies of Minor's "Frame-up System."[45] In May the journal published an article on the Oxman exposé by Dante Barton, a member of a private industrial relations organization headed by Frank Walsh: "Let labor get this whole business 'exposed to the sun and the air,' so that not only the innocent men now facing the gallows shall be set free, but *the habit* which vindictive employers have of dragneting labor leaders into false prosecutions and false convictions shall be stopped definitely and for all time."[46] A Bayonne worker who had met Mooney at Richmond, California, in 1914, wrote that Mooney was framed at Martinez because the employers considered him dangerous. If Mooney was now to be hanged, he said, his martyrdom would result from the apathy of those for whom he died: "Consecrated to the emancipation of labor, he could not be bluffed nor bought, neither could he be swayed from the course of duty. No cleaner souled Irishman ever left 'the old sod.' "[47]

The Essex County Building Trades Council received an IWDL appeal for funds in mid-May 1917. A motion was made to donate $25, but during the discussion the defendants were accused of disrespect for the government and the motion was defeated. At the next meeting J. Edward Morgan, appearing officially as a representative of the Alameda County Building Trades Council, explained the case in detail. The New Jersey council reconsidered its previous action, donated $50, gave Morgan credentials to visit affiliated locals, and instructed its delegates to take up the case in their locals. Meanwhile the Essex Trades Council heard Morgan and suspended its constitution in order to contribute $25. It likewise granted him credentials to solicit funds among the member unions. Within a few weeks the unions in and about Newark had contributed several hundred dollars to the defense. A mass meeting was organized by the two councils and the local Socialist Party organization.[48]

The Essex Trades Council was visited early the following year by Anton Johannsen, who was touring the East to solicit IWDL support. He denied reports that the defendants were IWW's, and said that Mrs. Mooney was guilty of nothing more than marrying Tom Mooney without the consent of the San Francisco Chamber of Commerce. The Council gave him credentials to visit local unions.

Newark was one of at least 25 cities in which the labor movement formally observed "Mooney Day," July 28, 1918. Johannsen returned for the occasion and addressed a mass meeting, at which resolutions urging a new trial were passed and sent to President Wilson and Governor William D. Stephens. A month later the New Jersey State Federation of Labor, at its annual convention, passed similar resolutions. At a single meeting in November the Council received messages on the Mooney case from labor bodies in Seattle, Milwaukee, Schenectady, and San Francisco. Among these probably were requests to join a general strike in December. The District Council of the machinists union for northern New Jersey took a strike vote on the plan, but the Essex Trades Council did not; it even refused a personal appeal from J. Edward Morgan to hold a mass meeting, for its committee believed that such a meeting could not succeed. But the Council sent another resolution to the Governor of California.[49]

The experience of the two Newark labor councils was repeated with variations in scores of others throughout the country. In all these organizations the feeling of a crusade, the belief in Mooney as a labor martyr, was a strong emotional force, but extensive publicity was necessary for its effective expression. Apart from the many local labor organizations, the primary agency for this publicity was the International Workers Defense League of San Francisco.

V

"Minor is conducting the Defense League along the lines of a modern publicity bureau," observed the *Examiner* barely two weeks after Robert Minor came from Los Angeles to San Francisco to reorganize the IWDL.[50] Like Berkman, Minor believed that publicity was more important than legal work. "I have learned long ago," he wrote Cockran, "that law cases are not tried in court, but in the street and the voice of the street—the newspapers."[51] Publicity was necessary to arouse labor and to raise funds for the legal defense.

The IWDL worked from week to week with whatever funds were available. They were usually insufficient. On the day Mooney went to trial, there was but $250 on hand, enough for one day's expenses. But money did come in. The total receipts of the League from August 1916 to the end of 1917 amounted to $108,226. Donations constituted $97,746 of the total; the rest, $10,480, came from the sale of the "Frame-up" pamphlet. The fluctuations in monthly receipts reflected the extent of knowledge and concern about the case: from August 1916 through February 1917, the receipts fairly steadily averaged about $3,400 per month. From March through May the figure climbed steeply, reaching its peak of $14,573 in the month after Oxman's exposure. From then to the end of the year the amount settled around $7,500 per month, more than twice the average of the first period. Among many contributing organizations the increase in support was very pronounced. The California State Federation of Labor, for instance, collected only $350 for the IWDL before March; in the next ten months it raised $7,640.[52]

The AFL did not contribute funds as an organization, nor, with just one exception in 1917, did its international unions. Most of the money came from trade-union locals and city and state labor bodies across the country. Contributions also came from Socialist locals, IWW locals, Workmen's Circles, and many other radical organizations. San Francisco's International Radical Club and the Gruppo Anarchico Volontà contributed. The Chicago Federation of Labor sent $2,000 by the end of 1917. An "All Prisoners Ball" held in New York City netted more than $1,000 for the Mooney defense in May. Most sums, however, came in amounts ranging from $1 to $25, and occasionally $100 or $500, from hundreds of union locals. United Mine Workers Union locals contributed by the dozens, and the UMW was the only trade union to contribute from its national treasury. The building-trades unions also contributed heavily. The strongest support from the carpenters' locals came in the month of Weinberg's trial, when 95 of them donated $1,973. Very few locals of Mooney's own molders' union contributed to the IWDL, however, and their failure to support him galled Mooney.[53]

The largest sums spent by the IWDL were for legal work. Legal expenditures amounted to $58,984, or 54.5 per cent of the total IWDL's receipts to the end of 1917. These expenses included attorneys' fees, briefs and transcripts, investigations, photographs, and dynamite experiments. Of the attorneys' fees Maxwell McNutt received a total of $11,647 for a year and a half's work. Lawlor, McKenzie, O'Connor, and Coghlan received about $7,000 each. Charles Brennan received $2,855, and Cockran received his expenses, $1,044. The official report of the IWDL's finances may have failed to stop rumors that the defense attorneys were highly paid, but the audited accounts corroborate what anyone might reasonably expect, that labor defense was no way for a lawyer to get rich.

Of the other expenses the largest by far was publicity, which accounted for $37,583, or 34.7 per cent of the receipts to the end of 1917. The major items were $14,434 for publicity salaries (for field representatives and writers), usually seven to nine of them at any one time; $9,791 for printing and postage; $3,023 for mass meetings and related costs; $3,601 for the filming and showing of a motion picture, "The Frame-up in the San Francisco Bomb Trials"; $1,462 to bolster circulation of Oakland's two left-wing papers; and $1,201 for telegrams. Robert Minor, Selig Schulberg, J. Edward Morgan, and Ed Gammons were among the fifteen paid publicists. None of them received more than a bare minimum. Minor took $1,300 for seventeen months' work, an average of about $19 a week, paid irregularly because of the demands made on the available funds. Office expenses, prisoners' personal expenses, and incidentals during the same seventeen months amounted to $9,193, or 8.5 per cent of the receipts. On January 1, 1918, the IWDL had a balance on hand of $2,465.[54]

Publicity work was a struggle. Minor worked like "a faithful old horse," wrote Mooney. Cockran paid him tribute too.[55] The administrative difficulties Minor faced were great. Apart from the uncertainty of funds, there was need for effective general management. "We have all been overwhelmed with more than we could do," he wrote Cockran, "and there is none too much executive ability among us."[56] He was distressed by the extent of discord within the organization: cooperative effort was nearly impossible; the "amazing bickerings in the ranks of men engaged in behalf of the sacred cause make it easy to see and forgive the bickerings and many horrible mistakes of the members of the bigger groups of human society."[57]

The IWDL ordered a carload of paper for the second edition of the "Frame-up System."[58] Publication and distribution of the pamphlet were turned over later in the year to the Tom Mooney Molders Defense Committee. Copies were sent to editors and labor unions all over the country, as were fortnightly editions of Minor's newsletter.[59] By August 1918, according to Mooney, the Molders Defense Committee had issued 1,300,000 pamphlets during the preceding twelve months. Mooney directed the pamphleteering work from his cell. The labor was contributed by his friends and by Rena Mooney after her release.[60]

The defense film, "The Frame-up in the San Francisco Bomb Trials," was prepared in the spring of 1917. Ed Nolan wrote the scenario. The film was shown in a dozen major cities from the West Coast to Chicago in the next few months, and at the annual convention of the Illinois State Federation of Labor in October.[61] Another form of visual publicity was the stereopticon slide lecture. This was a specialty of field representative William D. Patterson, an Oakland carpenter, advertising manager for the Oakland *World,* and state organizer for the Socialist Party. Patterson, accompanied by Mooney's brother John, toured California with the show. Labor papers and the daily press publicized the exhibit and lectures, which helped to raise funds for the defense.[62]

The field representatives for the IWDL occasionally met with violence or the threat of violence. Leon Green, the agent on tour with the film, was arrested in Chicago in November 1917 as an alien and an anarchist, and was beaten by an agent of the federal government's Bureau of Investigation.[63] A few months later in southern California, J. Edward Morgan, arriving in El Centro to address a Mooney meeting, was met by a committee of ranchers. After threatening to tar and feather him, they hustled him fifty miles out of town and left him near an Army camp at the Mexican border. He went on to San Diego, where the mayor and police chief promised protection from the local vigilantes and contributed $30 to the defense.[64]

In summary, state and local labor organizations broadened the early radical base of the defense movement after Mooney's conviction. The union elements supporting the defendants' cause tended to be the militant groups, both in and out of the AFL; the strongest support came from those cities and mining communities where rebellion against the traditional, conservative policies of the AFL was strong. Official AFL concern was very limited. The national organization, which had helped finance the defense of the McNamaras in 1911 and had been humiliated by their confession, declined to give vigorous support to Mooney and Billings. Formal action at the annual AFL convention in 1916 was forestalled by the resolutions committee, and at the 1917 and 1918 conventions was limited to the passage of resolutions appealing to California and federal authorities. The AFL Executive Council made similar appeals in 1918 and later, but did not raise funds or countenance coercive labor measures, such as a general strike, on behalf of the defendants.[65] However, formal action was not the whole AFL story; while the conventions, the Executive Council, and the international brotherhoods paid the issue relatively little heed, Samuel Gompers was working quietly behind the scenes in Washington to see what could be done. As will be seen, it was partly because of Gompers that a federal investigation of the case eventually was undertaken.

CHAPTER EIGHTEEN

Petrograd and Washington

How can our laborers make sacrifices for American democ-
racy, if justice be denied one of their number? The execution
of Mooney would be a tremendous help to German or to Bol-
shevist propaganda.
—Samuel E. Morison to Governor
Stephens, April 5, 1918

Unless speedy action is taken, America will have another Drey-
fus case and California will have been the perpetrator.
—Paul H. Douglas to Governor
Stephens, August 26, 1918

THE MOONEY CASE became an international cause célèbre in the spring of 1917, when anarchists in Russia conducted public demonstrations in Mooney's behalf. As a result of these demonstrations, the Wilson administration was moved to intervene in the case as a wartime measure to support the image of American democracy at home and abroad; and its action helped to save Mooney's life.

When word of the Russian revolution of March 1917 reached the United States, several hundred Russian immigrants and aliens, including Leon Trotsky—a temporary visitor in exile—returned home to aid the revolutionary cause.[1] The repatriates took with them news about the Mooney case, which they apparently obtained first-hand from Berkman and William Shatoff, an anarchist and former IWW speaker who served as Berkman's bodyguard during his tour of the East for Mooney. (Shatoff, who later became Petrograd's police chief, made the traveling arrangements for many of the returning Russians.)[2] Some of the Russians who sailed from San Francisco visited Mooney personally in the county jail before they left.[3] Even before the first group of repatriates arrived home, news of the case reached Petrograd and prompted a demonstration of anarchists there on Mooney's behalf.*

* Emma Goldman claimed that the anarchist demonstrations in Petrograd were held in response to messages that she, Berkman, and their associates "sent to the councils of workers, soldiers, and sailors by the refugees that had departed in May and June." This may account for later demonstrations, but the first one occurred on April 22 (all Russian

On April 22, 1917, just two months after Mooney's sentencing, a Marine officer of the Provisional Government in Petrograd telephoned the American Embassy to warn the American Ambassador, David R. Francis, that an anarchist mob was gathering to attack the Embassy. Francis thought that anarchists had nothing against America and discounted the report, but a few minutes later the officer called back to confirm it. The mob was forming on Nevsky Prospect, about six blocks from the Embassy. Revolver in hand, the Ambassador went down to the entrance, where he found a squad of Russian soldiers stationed to defend the Embassy. The object of the mob was reportedly to avenge the execution in San Francisco of an Italian named "Muni." The name meant nothing to Francis. The anarchists were dispersed, reportedly by Cossacks, before they reached the Embassy. Francis was told at first that Lenin had incited the protest, but the next day the foreign minister, Paul Miliukov, telephoned to report that the instigator was an Italian anarchist.[4]

Francis cabled to Secretary of State Lansing: "Who is Muni? What crime committed? Wouldn't cable this insignificant incident but fear sensational reports may create impression that order not enforced here where quiet prevails and life and property are safe."[5] Lansing, on information from the Department of Justice, wired back identifying Mooney and reporting the status of his case in the California courts.[6] Two days after the attempted attack Alexander Kerensky, head of the Provisional Government, called and expressed regrets.[7]

Newspaper correspondents cabled reports of the demonstration to England and the United States. Eastern newspapers published front-page accounts of the incident, usually with the statement that Lenin had aroused the mob.[8] However, Arno Dosch-Fleurot, Petrograd correspondent for the New York *World,* reported that the demonstration was set off by an account of Mooney's trial given by a returned

dates in this chapter follow the Western calendar), before any of the refugee groups had arrived. Of the six hundred radicals said to have left New York, the first party, which included Trotsky, sailed on March 27, and was interned in Halifax for a month by the British; Trotsky did not reach Petrograd until May 17. The second party left New York on April 3 by the much longer route of Vancouver, Japan, and Siberia. Evidently these groups were preceded by isolated radicals or by publications describing the Mooney case. That Mooney literature reached Russia is indicated in the 1918 newspaper report from San Francisco of a Dutch steamship quartermaster, who was found in possession of two large bundles of IWW propaganda, allegedly destined for Siberia; according to police, he visited Mooney in jail whenever his ship docked in San Francisco. (Emma Goldman, *Living My Life* [1934], II: 637; Thomas J. Tunney, *Throttled! The Detection of the German and Anarchist Bomb Plotters,* p. 267; Isaac Deutscher, *The Prophet Armed: Trotsky, 1879–1921,* pp. 246–48; *Examiner,* July 9, 1918.)

exile to his fellow anarchists, mostly students, at a college meeting.[9]

This was the first many Americans had heard of either V. I. Lenin or Thomas J. Mooney.* After the original reports in the eastern press of the Preparedness Day bombing, the case was almost completely ignored. The New York *Times* had mentioned it occasionally. It was often claimed—for instance, by Upton Sinclair in *The Brass Check*— that the capitalistic newspapers in the East deliberately suppressed news of the Mooney case until the Petrograd demonstrators forced them to publish it.[10] Since the northern California newspapers, no less capitalistic, were publishing regular accounts of the trials, it seems more likely that the case had simply failed to strike eastern editors as important. As the cause of an attack on the American Embassy in Russia, however, the Mooney case became newsworthy from coast to coast. Before long, eastern papers such as the New York *Tribune* were carrying extended accounts of the case, and were discussing the class tensions behind it. At the same time the significance of the Petrograd demonstration was recognized. The New York *Tribune* said that it had presented a deserved indictment of American government in one of its worst aspects: the Mooney case is "a political issue in the truest sense of the word, and it is inextricably interwoven with the somewhat sinister political history of California."[11]

On April 26, the same day the official report of the Petrograd demonstration was released in Washington, the federal government announced that Elihu Root, the former Secretary of State, had agreed to lead a mission to Russia to strengthen ties with the Provisional Government and encourage continued Russian participation in the war.[12] Because of the Petrograd protest, the administration realized that the Mooney case might hinder the mission's efforts, and it took steps to intervene directly in the case. Lansing learned more of the facts from Gompers, who provided him with photocopies of Oxman's letters.[13] Gompers wrote Cockran of this on May 10. On May 11 Woodrow Wilson privately sent Governor Stephens of California a telegram asking him to intercede for the sake of the country's foreign relations:

I hope that in view of certain international aspects which the case has assumed you will not deem me impertinent or beyond my rights if I very warmly and earnestly urge upon you the wisdom and desirability of commuting the sentence of Mooney or at least suspending its execution until

---

* Lenin had arrived in Russia from Switzerland just ten days earlier. He was first mentioned in the New York *Times* on April 15, 1917.

the charges of perjury lodged against the witnesses in the case are judicially probed to the bottom. Such an action on your part would I can assure you have the widest and most beneficial results and greatly relieve some critical situations outside the United States.[14]

Stephens replied the same day that Mooney's sentence was stayed indefinitely by the appeal pending in the State Supreme Court. He added that the subornation of perjury charges were pending in the Superior Court.[15] The President wrote a note of thanks on the 14th: "It relieves a rather serious anxiety."[16]

Neither Wilson nor Stephens released the correspondence to the press. The Governor made it public only in late August. Its announcement caused great excitement in San Francisco, and some irritation as well: John G. Lawlor wrote Cockran that Stephens had tried to help Fickert convict Mrs. Mooney by concealing the fact that the President had interceded on her husband's behalf.[17] Whatever Stephens had in mind, when he published the telegrams it became clear that the President had intervened for diplomatic reasons. And it is likely that Wilson had seen the copies of the Oxman letters before he acted.

The President's first appeal had no effect in Russia while the Root mission was there. The mission left before the message was made public. After returning, the mission reported informally that Russian radicals and pro-German propagandists were using the case to destroy Russian confidence in the United States and impair the war effort.[18]

II

With the President's wire to Stephens, federal intervention in the Mooney case began. The second step, a more important one, came with the federal investigation in November. The decision for a federal investigation was made not in response to the Petrograd demonstration,* but almost as an afterthought amidst efforts to cope with the acute labor troubles that threatened the American war effort in the summer of 1917.

* Robert Minor and Emma Goldman, among others, considered the Petrograd anarchists responsible for the investigation. (IWDL Newsletter #25, Scrapbook, Mooney Papers; Emma Goldman, *Living My Life*, II: 638.) But the timing does not support that interpretation: after the demonstration in April, no further protests were reported until October 1917; the federal decision to investigate the Mooney case was made in September, five months after the Embassy was first threatened and too late to be useful to the Root mission.

Two critical industries in the western states, copper mining and spruce lumbering, were disrupted by IWW strikes. In Bisbee, Arizona, the copper miners struck on June 26. They complained of low wages and the "rustling card" system, a refinement of blacklisting. The managers responded by calling the strikers pro-German. The sheriff and a posse herded the miners into cattle cars, took them across the New Mexico border, and left them in the desert. In Montana other miners were on strike and the Anaconda Copper Mining Company mines were practically closed down. An IWW organizer, Frank Little, was lynched in Butte. Meanwhile logging operations in Washington, Idaho, and western Montana had ceased, thereby threatening the production of airplanes, which were built with northwestern spruce.[19]

With the state governments helpless to intervene, federal action appeared necessary. Early in June the administration's Council of National Defense approved a plan to create a labor arbitration commission with jurisdiction over industries with government contracts. For some reason this plan was shelved; the Council marked time, although urged to act by the governors of eight western states, by western organizations of the AFL, and by Gompers, who was a member of the Council's advisory commission. He protested directly to the President about the violence and asked for an investigation. Wilson heard him sympathetically and arranged late in August for the matter to be pressed in the Council by the Secretary of War, Newton D. Baker. Baker proposed that a commission visit the affected localities and confer with both sides in an effort to compose differences and make clear the national government's active interest in settling the disputes. The Council voted to request the President to appoint such a commission.[20]

The proposed "mission of inquiry and reconciliation" was far more moderate than the previously proposed commission of arbitration. Yet even the milder plan was temporarily set aside; attorney Felix Frankfurter, whom Secretary Baker offered from his staff to serve as the Commission's secretary,[21] wired Colonel E. M. House, the President's personal adviser, on September 4 that the proposal had been suspended: "The wisdom of dealing with the western labor unrest by a public commission is very doubtful and the project is, therefore, being reconsidered."[22] The reason is not clear, but three weeks later the President decided to go ahead. On September 19 he drew up an order creating the Commission and naming its purposes and members—two employers, two labor union officials, and two government officials. It came to be known as the Federal Mediation Commission. Gompers had played a major role in the creation of the Commission: he nominated the labor members and was consulted about at least one of the employers; he had also recommended that the Commission consist of six men.[23]

The President did not mention the IWW in his directive, or name the places the Commission should visit. His written instructions were general: the mission, he said, was to deal with both sides "in a conciliatory spirit" and to seek a working arrangement between them for the duration of the war. The Commission was instructed to learn the real causes of discontent not through public hearings but through conferences and personal conversations.[24]

Nothing suggests that the President originally wanted the Commission to investigate the Mooney case. Neither the correspondence of Gompers in the summer of 1917, nor the minutes of the Council of National Defense, nor the Presidential order mentions the case. Gompers may well have had Mooney in mind, since he sought federal intervention in the case both earlier and later. But so far as the government was concerned, the Mooney case was an afterthought. And the afterthought came from Colonel House, who interceded for friends of Mooney and Berkman in New York.

House was in New York when a group of labor leaders called on him on September 20 to ask his help in preventing Berkman's extradition to California. House did not record what they said about Berkman, but he did note in his diary that they "were after me today to use my good offices in behalf of Thos. J. Mooney."[25] One of his callers was J. Edward Morgan of the IWDL. Morgan left with him a memorandum reviewing the case, the Oxman fraud, and the views of Cockran, Walsh, and Griffin, and asking House to help obtain a federal investigation:

Labor throut the land has been tremenduously aroused over these judicial atrocities. The Mooney Case is famous even across the seas. Thousands of Russians and Russian Jews who were active in many American cities in spreading the news of these unjust convictions, many of them who were personal friends of the Mooneys of Nolan and Israel Weinberg, returned to Russia and spread the story of the Mooney Case far and wide in their native land.[26]

House was impressed. He wrote the following day to the President:

I have never brought to your attention such matters as that of the death sentence of Thos. J. Mooney of San Francisco, but in this instance I feel it is important for you to give it some personal attention for the reason that it has a bearing on the labor troubles in the West and has encited such nation wide interest.

Federal investigation of the methods employed in securing conviction is all that is asked and that I think in the circumstances, should be done.[27]

At the same time Morgan went to Washington. He sought out department heads and Congressmen in an effort to bring the case directly before the President. He did not see Wilson, but he did create some favorable newspaper publicity. The Philadelphia *Public Ledger* reported his activities, recalled Gompers's earlier efforts for a federal investigation, and editorially urged the President to investigate in order to convince revolutionary Russia that the United States was a liberal, democratic, justice-loving nation.[28]

Wilson referred House's letter to Attorney General Gregory, "along with the enclosed editorials in order to ask if you will not be kind enough to have the investigation suggested by House made with as much thoroughness as possible. We cannot leave any stone unturned to prevent or soften labor troubles."[29] The following day newspapers announced that the President had asked both Gregory and the Mediation Commission to investigate the case. Eastern newspapers commended the decision,[30] but in San Francisco the defenders of law and order protested the President's meddling in local affairs. The *Chronicle* asserted that any investigation of "individuals under judicial inquiry or sentence" would be an impertinence.[31] The *Argonaut* reacted more strongly: "If the President thinks he can accomplish any good by coddling the nihilists of Russia and playing up to the anarchists of the United States he is due for a rude awakening."[32] Radical bugaboo aside, the issue of states' rights was adding another dimension of conflict to the case.

III

Of the two announced investigations, the one by the Department of Justice amounted to very little. Gregory conferred with the President and agreed to get some informal information on the case from a reliable source. It was rumored that he would send an assistant to San Francisco,[33] but instead he referred the problem to United States

District Attorney Preston in San Francisco, who in turn consulted G. S. Arnold, a San Francisco attorney serving the Mediation Commission in its own investigation. Preston and Arnold saw the case the same way. Preston therefore simply forwarded a copy of Arnold's voluminous memorandum for the Commission to Gregory in November. The Attorney General thus obtained an early report, but had nothing to offer the President from a separate inquiry.[34] The important investigation was not his but the Mediation Commission's.

The Commission consisted of six well-qualified though not impartial men. Its composition was Wilsonian. William B. Wilson was chairman, John H. Walker and Ernest P. Marsh were the labor commissioners, and Jackson L. Spangler and Verner Z. Reed the employer commissioners; Felix Frankfurter was counsel and secretary. The character and convictions of these men might inspire a warm welcome from the San Francisco liberals, but not from the friends of the prosecution. Wilson was a former trade-union official and known to oppose private detectives.* Walker was president of the Illinois district of the UMW, and Marsh was president of the Washington State Federation of Labor. Walker had helped the Mooney defense uncover the Oxman letters, and the unions in his state were vociferous supporters of a new trial. Marsh had been less directly involved in the case than Walker, but in his state, too, especially around Seattle, the radical labor movement gave active support to the defense. Marsh was known to believe that the shortcomings of society were responsible for the IWW.[35] Both men were thoroughly loyal to the government and had worked vigorously to cope with wartime labor problems in their states,[36] but that did not make them disinterested observers of the Mooney case—quite the contrary.

Spangler and Reed were wealthy, independent mining operators with records of service in mediating labor disputes. Spangler, who came from a Pennsylvania Dutch background, was an old friend of William B. Wilson and an admirer of the President. He considered himself a "good neutral" who played a "fair game" in helping Secretary Wilson conciliate stubborn parties and determine wage scales in the Pennsylvania coalfields. At Secretary Wilson's suggestion Gompers had asked Spangler to serve on the Commission.[37] Reed was an author, traveler, and Roman Catholic, a Colorado capitalist engaged

---

* He had called them an instrument of private warfare in labor disputes and had urged Congress to outlaw them in interstate commerce. (Martinez *Standard*, February 6, 1914; *Labor Clarion*, February 13, 1914. See also *Who's Who in America, 1916–1917*.)

in ranching and metal and petroleum mining in several western mountain states. Frankfurter described him as a man who looked "every bit like one of the old Popes, and who is an amazing combination of uncanny money-making and spiritural [sic] order." He had cosigned a $35,000 bail bond for the release of John R. Lawson, the UMW's organizer in the Colorado minefield strike of 1913 who was persecuted with a murder charge. Reed had also successfully mediated mining strikes at Leadville, Colorado, as a government conciliator.[38]

Frankfurter in those days was an assistant to the Secretary of War. He was on leave from the faculty of the Harvard Law School. A close student of labor legislation and labor relations, he had helped Louis D. Brandeis draft his famous brief for the Supreme Court on the Oregon ten-hour law. Although Frankfurter had many friends in San Francisco, he recalled long afterward that he had not heard of the Mooney case until the Mediation Commission was assigned to investigate it.[39]

Obviously, the Commission did not represent a cross-section of business and labor opinion. Reed and Spangler did not "balance" Walker and Marsh. The commissioners had not been selected on the theory that equal numbers of dedicated partisans made an impartial body, or, conversely, that disinterestedness was a prerequisite for quasi-judicial service. The Commission was set up as a working team, to investigate—preferably with open and flexible minds—to conciliate, and to get results. In the strike controversies of Arizona, California, and the Northwest, results were at least conceivable.[40] In the Mooney case they were not, for the antagonists were legally incompetent to compromise. The mediating of contractual disputes between employers and employees was possible, but not the mediating of a duly processed murder conviction.

The Commission arrived in San Francisco from Arizona on November 9, established headquarters at the Palace Hotel, and stayed for two weeks. Reed had arrived earlier. Walker was absent, attending the Buffalo convention of the AFL.[41] The Commission's primary concern in the Bay Area was a telephone strike; the Mooney case was secondary. Secretary Wilson was noncommittal about investigating the case: "We shall make some effort in that direction," he said, "but it will be entirely incidental to the labor investigation."[42] Evidently the Commission asked the newspapers to suspend publicity; on the second day after their arrival a news blackout in the San Francisco press commenced which lasted for the rest of their stay. Even the IWDL biweekly newsletter withheld comment. The commissioners may have wanted to avoid publicity because Weinberg was on trial. In any event the public was not informed of their methods, or, for the time being, their views.

Part of the time Secretary Wilson was ill. The burden of the Mooney investigation fell on Frankfurter and the Commission's special counsel for the occasion, G. S. Arnold. Arnold had not committed himself to either side of the case. He was a son-in-law of United States Tariff Commissioner William Kent, who was a Wilsonian Progressive. Preston considered Arnold "a man of the highest integrity, thoroughly impartial, and of excellent judgment."[43] Arnold reviewed the trial records carefully and prepared a brief for Frankfurter on his arrival. Also awaiting the Commission were briefs prepared by McNutt and Cockran, which dealt with both the legal merits and the social and political background of the cases.[44]

District Attorney Fickert offered to put the records of his office at Secretary Wilson's disposal.[45] Arnold arranged a meeting at which Fickert, Ferrari, Frankfurter, and he were present. It lasted about an hour. Frankfurter set forth the Commission's purposes, explained its intention not to hold formal hearings, and named persons he intended to consult. Fickert appeared agreeable. He and Ferrari said all they wanted to say and made no suggestion for another meeting. Or so Arnold reported;[46] Fickert was shortly to publicize a wildly different account of the situation.

Frankfurter saw a number of other people about the case. He spent a morning discussing it with members of the State Supreme Court, including Frederick W. Henshaw, M. C. Sloss, and Chief Justice Frank M. Angellotti. He talked with Attorney General Webb and with members of Webb's staff. He conferred with McNutt, with Preston, and also with the Archbishop of San Francisco, the Most Reverend Edward J. Hanna.[47]

The Commission left San Francisco on November 24 for the Northwest and Chicago, and then returned to Washington. A report on the Mooney case was prepared by Frankfurter and signed by all the members January 16. On January 22 Secretary Wilson submitted it to the President.[48] The report was brief. The Commission questioned the justice of the convictions, pointed out the broader implications of the case, and recommended presidential intervention.

Mooney, said the report, was a labor radical, a believer in "direct action" who had associated with anarchists. The San Francisco utilities regarded him as a malevolent labor agitator. They sought to "get" him, through activities directed by Martin Swanson. Because of Mooney's association "with views which justify violence at least in industrial conflict" and because of San Francisco's labor strife, the public was easily persuaded that the defendants were guilty. All the arts of modern journalism inflamed public prejudice. Irrespective of his personal merits, Mooney had come to symbolize the labor movement for workers and their sympathizers. The case was "a new aspect of an old industrial feud." The Commission said that the trial juries were not to blame; they had acted in good faith on the evidence submitted. But the Oxman letters and the acquittals of Rena Mooney and Weinberg cast doubt on the prior convictions of Billings and Mooney. Oxman's acquittal was irrelevant; his letters discredited his testimony, and "when Oxman was discredited the verdict against Mooney was discredited."

The Commission did not comment on Mooney's guilt or innocence. "We conceived it to be our duty merely to determine whether a solid basis exists for a feeling that an injustice was done . . . and that an irreparable injustice would be committed to allow such conviction to proceed to execution." The State Supreme Court might find error in the record and grant a new trial, but if it did not, the Governor alone could supply relief.

Such relief it is hoped will be forthcoming. It is now well known that the attention to the situation in the East was first aroused through meetings of protest against the Mooney conviction in Russia. From Russia and the Western States protest spread to the entire country until it has gathered momentum from many sources, sources whose opposition to violence is unquestioned, whose devotion to our cause in the war is unstinted. The liberal sentiment of Russia was aroused, the liberal sentiment of the United States was aroused, because the circumstances of Mooney's prosecution, in the light of his history, led to the belief that the terrible and sacred instruments of criminal justice were consciously or unconsciously made use of against labor by its enemies in an industrial conflict.

However strange or however unexpected it may be, the just disposition of the Mooney case thus affects influences far beyond the confines of California, and California can be depended upon to see the wider implications of the case. With the mere local aspects, with the political and journalistic conflicts which the case has occasioned, neither the commission nor the country at large is concerned. But the feeling of disquietude aroused by the case must be heeded, for if unchecked, it impairs the faith that our democracy protects the lowliest and even the unworthy against false accusations. War is fought with moral as well as material resources. We are in this war to vindicate the moral claims of unstained processes of law, however slow at times, such processes may be. These claims must be tempered by the fire of our own devotion to them at home.

Your Commission, therefore respectfully recommends in case the Supreme Court of California should find it necessary (confined as it is by jurisdictional limitations) to sustain the conviction of Mooney on the record of the trial, that the President use his good offices to invoke action by the governor of California and the cooperation of its prosecuting officers to the end that a new trial may be had for Mooney whereby guilt or innocence may be put to the test of unquestionable justice. This result can easily be accomplished by postponing the execution of the sentence of Mooney to await the outcome of a new trial, based upon prosecution under one of the untried indictments against him.[49]

That California could be "depended upon to see the wider implications of the case" was an untested hope. The President wrote Stephens at once:

Will you permit a suggestion from me in these troubled times which perhaps justify what I should feel hardly justifiable in other circumstances?

The suggestion is this: Would it not be possible to postpone the execution of the sentence of Mooney until he can be tried upon one of the other indictments against him, in order to give full weight and consideration to the important changes which I understand to have taken place in the evidence against him?

I urge this very respectfully indeed but very earnestly, because the case has assumed international importance and I feel free to make the suggestion because I am sure that you are as anxious as anyone can be to have no doubt or occasion of criticism of any sort attach itself to the case.[50]

The Governor replied that if the case came before him he would consider the suggestion.[51] He was unwilling to act as long as the case was before the Supreme Court.

For the President there remained the question whether to publish the report. He asked his secretary, Joseph Tumulty, to find out the Secretary of Labor's opinion, and added, "The effect on Mooney himself must be considered."[52] Tumulty consulted Secretary Wilson and reported that the Commission was willing to have the report publicized. The Secretary was less sensitive than the President to Mooney's personal fate. "He stated that the Commission felt that the effect on Mooney was of less importance than the effect on this country and the effect on our foreign relations. . . . The Commission thought that either the beneficial or injurious effect on the individual was of less consequence."[53] Tumulty looked over a copy of the report and the next day handed it to a member of the Committee on Public Information.[54] It was published in the Committee's *Official Bulletin* a few days later.

The President's advisers were thus more concerned about the wartime effects of an injustice than about the personal injury it caused, but the President himself was still moved by an injustice because of its individual harm. There, still, was the moral leadership of the New Freedom.

IV

While the federal administration looked into the case, protests began again in Russia. A giant rally was held in Petrograd on September 30 to protest the way America dealt with its revolutionaries, particularly Berkman, though Mooney, too, was mentioned. The rally was held in the Cirque Moderne, a great, low, rambling structure, which Albert Rhys Williams called "the new Cathedral of the proletariat." Thousands heard Shatoff, John Reed, A. R. Williams, and perhaps other American revolutionaries who had reached Petrograd.[55] Elsewhere in Russia Americans encountered expressions of interest in Mooney. John Reed, riding to the Russian front in an ammunition truck, was questioned by a Red guard about Mooney and Berkman. A YMCA worker who traveled through Russia during the war reported that the Mooney case was widely discussed. On one occasion fifty Kronstadt sailors, anarchists by conviction, called on the American Embassy and demanded that the Ambassador intercede for Mooney.[56]

The Mooney protests in Russia were almost entirely the work of Petrograd anarchists. The Bolsheviks took power in November, and in those chaotic days tolerated the local anarchists, who baited Ambassador Francis. They threatened him repeatedly in January 1918, at the same time that two ex-ministers of the Kerensky government were assassinated by sailors not far from the Embassy.[57] On January 19, a menacing article appeared in a Petrograd anarchist newspaper:

Mr. American Ambassador, kindly take notice of the following statement.

The leading fighter in the cause of liberating mankind, our comrade Thomas Mooney, has been sentenced to death by your Government. The Government of the United States has also put into prison our comrades Alexander Berkman, Emma Goldman and others.

At numerous meetings regarding this the Russian workmen, peasants, soldiers and sailors have expressed their energetic protest regarding atrocities perpetuated by your Government towards honest revolutionists and demanded their immediate liberation. In numerous resolutions regarding this the Russian soldiers, workmen and sailors pointed out that to violence they will reply by violence, to death by death.

Owing to the fact that neither you, Mr. Ambassador, nor your Government have given due attention to these resolutions we are authorized to officially announce to you that if in the shortest time possible our comrades Thomas Mooney, Alexander Berkman, Emma Goldman and others will not be liberated then we shall consider you personally responsible for their lives and liberty. You defend one of the members of the Diplomatic Corps as its *doyen* which means that you have diplomatic mutual responsibility. Know then that with us revolutionists there is also our own international mutual aid.[58]

News of this threat reached the State Department on January 24, the same day that the Mediation Commission's report went to the Government Printing Office.[59] In Petrograd, Francis requested troops from a Bolshevik garrison to guard the Embassy. On January 19 he took shelter for the night at the lodgings of his private secretary, after being told by a Russian-American woman that the soldiers were planning to loot the Embassy and kill him.[60]

A few days later another threat was transmitted to Francis by the Soviet Foreign Office, this one from a group of anarchists who met January 11 at the Mikhailov Artillery School in Petrograd. They demanded the release of Berkman, Emma Goldman, and Mooney: "if measures are not taken to save the lives of our comrades in America, then we, the revolutionary workers and soldiers of the city of Petrograd, will take energetic measures in the line of demonstration before the American Embassy." This was a milder threat than the other, but since the Foreign Office seemingly endorsed it, it made Francis angry.[61] According to Edgar Sisson, who was in Petrograd for the Committee on Public Information, the Soviet Foreign Office was trying vainly to get visas from Francis to enable Bolshevik officials to go to America, and, getting no response from him, the assistant Foreign

Commissar, Zalkind, "vented his feelings harmlessly by sending . . . a copy of new resolutions, adopted at a public meeting, calling for the release of Mooney from [a] California prison."[62]

The President wired Francis the Mediation Commission's report to mollify the anarchists,[63] but evidently the Ambassador considered its publication unnecessary. There were no more Mooney demonstrations in Petrograd, and before long it would not have mattered anyway. The Treaty of Brest-Litovsk in March ended whatever hopes remained after the Bolshevik Revolution that Russia might resume the fight against Germany. Francis abandoned Petrograd on February 24. By the middle of March the Wilson administration no longer cared what the Russians thought of the Mooney case.[64]

V

Early in March 1918 the California Supreme Court denied the regular appeal of Mooney's conviction that had been filed a year before. Shortly afterward President Wilson wired Governor Stephens again. His action this time was prompted by Secretary Wilson, who brought the case up in a Cabinet meeting March 26,[65] and by the Secretary of the Interior, Franklin K. Lane of California, who wrote the President the same day:

Some time ago I made inquiry regarding the Mooney case, when I first heard you speak of the effect in Petrograd of his conviction. While I have not communicated with Governor Stephens, I found that the feeling among his friends was that he was committed to the proposition that whatever the courts decided he would abide by. There are a lot of men whom I could name in California who are his friends, but in my judgment there will be no use in appealing to him through them. If you cannot by your direct personal telegram cause him to take the course which you advise, there is nothing that can be done.

The next day the President wired Stephens: "With very great respect I take the liberty of saying to you that if you could see your way to commute the sentence of Mooney it would have a most helpful effect upon certain international affairs which his execution would greatly complicate." Stephens replied from Los Angeles, "You can rest assured Mooney case will have careful consideration." The Supreme Court, he said, might order a rehearing.[66] The time in which it could do so, however, had nearly passed.

For some reason the President had shifted the question; he asked only for a commutation, not for a pardon or a new trial. Perhaps Lane's discouraging memorandum made him feel that the most he could hope for was half a loaf. Whatever his reasons, this change of a single phrase was to cause much bitterness in California eight months later.

VI

Foreign protests came from other countries besides Russia. For the most part these remonstrations followed Wilson's third appeal to Stephens in March 1918. However, as early as May 1917, the national labor organization of Holland protested to the American Ambassador at The Hague, and J. Edward Morgan pointed this out to House in his appeal for intercession with Wilson.[67] From England, George Bernard Shaw wrote the critic and author Frank Harris, then living in New York: "That sort of thing is always going on in America. . . . I have no illusions about the Golden West; probably, however, it only appears to be the worst place in the world politically and judicially, because there is less hushing up; that is, less solidarity among the governing class than in England and Russia."[68]

By May 1918, protests from British and Continental labor organizations were reaching the State Department and the American press frequently. That month Lansing received a resolution from the British Labour Party on the Mooney case. He forwarded it to the President, who asked him to have Ambassador Walter Hines Page in London acknowledge it.[69] Similar resolutions were passed by the London Trades Council and the Parliamentary Committee of the Trades Union Congress.[70] During the next twelve months other English protests came from labor organizations in London, Hull, Coventry, Birmingham, and Manchester.[71] Protests came from Scotland too. The Scottish Ironmolders Union asked the British cabinet to press Wilson for a new trial. A mass meeting of miners and citizens of Glencraig, Fife, protested Mooney's imprisonment.[72] A Glasgow branch of the Independent Labour Party condemned the "barbarous and inhuman sentence of death . . . as being contrary to all the principles of Liberty, Justice, and Democracy, for which the Allies are fighting. [Mooney's execution] will be a crime equal to any of the atrocities committed during the War."[73]

Labor bodies protested in Ireland, Australia, Italy, and again in Holland. In Ireland the Dublin Trades Council and the Socialist Party censured Mooney's sentence. In Australia the labor councils of Sydney and Melbourne and the South Australia Labour Party and Trades Council did likewise.[74] In Rome the American Socialist Mission to the Allied countries cabled the Committee on Public Information that German sympathizers in Italy were using the case against America and particularly against Wilson. The Committee thereupon obtained a statement from the IWDL that the President was doing his best and that Mooney wanted no German support.[75] Two months later the secretary of the General Federation of Labor of Milan wrote Gompers that Italian unions had held countless demonstrations for Mooney; he enclosed a list of labor resolutions on the case.[76] In September, Lansing told the President that the American Legation at The Hague had received threats from revolutionary socialist organizations in Holland:

Threats of these organizations have been considered by the Dutch authorities of sufficient importance to establish special guards in front of Legation buildings to prevent any demonstration or act of violence and to issue several warnings to the Legation. The Legation would like to be informed by the Department of the present status of the Mooney case with a view to using this information to contradict rumors and possible disturbances.[77]

At that time the best the government could say was that Mooney had been reprieved and that the President was still trying to persuade Stephens to forestall the execution.

VII

While national and international concern over the Mooney case heightened, a delayed and contentious response to the Mediation Commission's report emerged from the office of District Attorney Fickert. Fickert had appeared cooperative when the Commission visited San Francisco in November. After the Commission left, Ferrari told Arnold that the prosecution wished to file a brief, and asked for ten days' time. Arnold made the necessary arrangements. When the District Attorney's office asked for another ten days, Arnold urged haste. Two weeks later he was informed that the brief was almost ready. Then, on December 26, Ferrari wired Washington asking Frankfurter for another extension. Frankfurter, in Chicago, did not see the wire. About three weeks later Ferrari told Arnold that the brief was still not ready. By then the Commission had already reported to the President and disbanded. Commented Arnold: "the Commission, after over two months delay during which the District Attorney's office had neglected to fulfill its promises, was certainly justified in assuming that Mr. Fickert had no bona fide intention of filing any reply to the briefs submitted by the defense."[78]

When the report was published Fickert immediately denounced the Commission. He said that he had offered it his office and records, that no member of the Commission had ever called, and that no person connected with the prosecution was asked or permitted to appear before it. After the Commission left, he had received copies of Cockran's and McNutt's briefs, and, needing time to answer, had wired Frankfurter for an extension, but received no reply. The Commission submitted and published its report before hearing from him. Its findings were vicious: "I do not mean to become a party to turning loose upon the community in this crisis a band of guilty murderers, anarchists and traitors on the recommendation of any commission that has made absolutely no investigation."*

The District Attorney had strong supporters in California.[79] Judge Dunne commented that the report was just what he had expected of Frankfurter: "He did not come to me for information, and he got all his facts from those who saw only one side. What he has written is intended to make trouble." Frankfurter, he said, was a "Bolshevik."[80] C. K. McClatchy of the Sacramento *Bee* similarly condemned the investigators, the report, and the defendant, whom he habitually referred to as a "professional dynamiter." The Commission, he said, admitted that Mooney and Billings were associates of anarchists and had been in trouble before because of possessing dynamite; yet it rebuked the San Francisco utilities for defending themselves. The utilities were rather to be commended for doing their share toward the conviction of "such enemies of all mankind." The Commission had blamed the newspapers for arousing public passions, but the component of the press that really deserved reproof was the one that "always knuckles down to the crazy Anarchist and the professional dynamiter, claiming that not he but Society is to blame." Woodrow Wilson, said McClatchy, had as much right to interfere in a criminal trial in the Balkans. If California granted Mooney a new trial, it would be forced on her by an enormous campaign of lies. "In fact, the one gigantic

* As quoted, *Examiner*, January 27, 1918. In 1930 Cunha testified that the Mediation Commission "made that decision without coming near the prosecution at all." (California Supreme Court, "In re Billings," II: 1121.)

'frame-up' in this whole matter has been the international 'frame-up' to get a new trial for this professional dynamiter."[81]

Three weeks after the Commission's report was published, Fickert wired the President asking him to take no action before reading a statement that he would send shortly. A month later Fickert was ready. According to the IWDL, his brief was presented to the Department of Justice about April 5 by Frank Drew, attorney for the Law and Order Committee, and Edward Hurlbut, the Committee's publicity agent. The brief was refused. Its important circulation was in California, where it was released in mid-April.[82]

In his brief Fickert challenged the Commission's right to investigate the case. He denied that it was a labor case; Mooney had joined the molders union just to spread anarchism and to obtain union aid in case of "trial for any of his many crimes." The *Blast* was proof of Mooney's indifference to the bona fide labor movement. And the threatening notes at the time of the parade were "all so identical with the same found in the 'Blast' that no reasonable mind can doubt but that the persons responsible for the one are also responsible for the other. The letters were not written in the ordinary handwriting but each letter was printed or drawn and that character of writing is found on many of the cartoons in the 'Blast.' " (Fickert did not say why he had never arrested Robert Minor or Lydia Gibson for having sent the notes. There was in fact only a crude resemblance between the lettering in *Blast* cartoons and that in the notes.)[83] As for his witnesses, Fickert conceded nothing. The testimony of the Edeaus, McDonald, and Oxman was sound and unimpeached. Judge Dunne he praised as the foe of lawlessness and corruption during the graft prosecutions; Dunne had "won praise of all decent citizens not only of San Francisco and of California, but all over the United States for his manly, his courageous, his fearless and uncompromising stand."[84]

For Fremont Older, Fickert had a special word. "It is difficult for us to believe that there are men of apparent intelligence who have themselves no reason for dissatisfaction with either the social or economic system under which we live, who find justification for the commission of crimes similar to that of July 22, 1916. We have such a person in Fremont Older." Older, he said, had done everything possible to poison the public mind in the Los Angeles *Times* case; he had sided with Ford and Suhr; guilt and innocence did not count. He was an "intimate friend" of Berkman and a friend of Mooney, "and the reason why justice was cheated in the trial of Mooney at Martinez was not by reason of the jury system, but by reason of the tremendous influence wielded by Fremont Older in his behalf." In the bomb trial Older had intimidated and contaminated witnesses, notably Oakland's Police Chief Peterson. "Can it be that if these defendants had been left to their fate, a confession would have been forthcoming implicating Fremont Older?"[85]

Early in April, Frankfurter compared notes with Arnold on this incredible document. Arnold agreed that Fickert had not asked Frankfurter to see Dunne or Matheson. He wired Frankfurter: "Statement attributed to Fickert which most astounded me was that he had been given no opportunity by Commission to reply to briefs of defense. . . . I withdraw the assurance hitherto given you concerning my opinion as to his good faith and integrity. You are at liberty to use this wire in any way you choose and to call upon me to substantiate." Frankfurter sent the telegrams to Secretary Wilson, with the suggestion that he might show them to the President. Secretary Wilson considered Frankfurter's evidence conclusive, but declined to give the matter further publicity.[86]

Because the *Chronicle* and *Examiner* gave wide circulation to Fickert's story of being snubbed by the Commission, Arnold wrote Governor Stephens setting forth the relations between Frankfurter and Fickert. He denied that Fickert had suggested Frankfurter see Dunne; to be sure, Ferrari had discussed Dunne's attitude, but no one had proposed that the Commission could learn anything from Dunne which could not be learned just as well from Fickert.[87] The District Attorney countered this letter with a fantastic one of his own. The Commission had wholly neglected him; Arnold did not attend any conference with him; Frankfurter had conceded the legal indefensibility of the investigation; and Frankfurter had failed to keep an appointment with Dunne arranged by Justice M. C. Sloss of the State Supreme Court.[88]

A few weeks later Fickert submitted to the Governor a brief opposing Mooney's application for a pardon. In it he reiterated his charges against the Commission. Six weeks later he followed this up with an affidavit to Stephens, in which he attacked the Commission as a "whitewash" body and charged that Frankfurter had said to numerous citizens in San Francisco and to members of the State Supreme Court that he, Frankfurter, was convinced of Mooney's guilt, was satisfied that Mooney had had a fair trial, believed that Mooney's rights had been fully protected, and attributed the demand for a new trial to the desire to placate American radicals and the Bolshevik government.[89]

Frankfurter had refrained from entering the controversy, but Fickert's latest asseverations were too much. He wrote Sloss for a statement. Sloss conferred with Chief Justice Angellotti and wired back that neither of them had heard Frankfurter make the alleged statements. The other three Supreme Court justices whom Frankfurter had consulted also denied the charge.[90] Frankfurter wired Stephens:

I cannot believe that a district attorney, who is a judicial officer, acting under one of the most solemn oaths imposed upon any official, should wilfully or recklessly charge others with facts which he must know to be untrue. I therefore am loath to believe that the report which the eastern press attributes to Dist. Att'y Fickert is true, but I burden you with this telegram of denial in order to avoid even the most remote possibility of misunderstanding.[91]

Commented the *Bulletin*: "It is too late in the day for District Attorney Fickert to dam by a cheap lie the flood of indignation which has slowly risen, all over the civilized world, against his perversion of justice in the Mooney case."[92] And in the East the *New Republic* remarked: "American judicial history can hardly afford a better instance of the public prosecutor . . . degenerated into a passionate, primordial hunter of men."[93]

Thus federal intervention, prompted by the war, came up against states' rights, the radical bugbear, evasion, and acrimony. Yet the foreign repercussions, the Mediation Commission's investigation, and the Presidential appeals helped to save Mooney's life. They bolstered the defense movement and increased the pressure on Governor Stephens. Stephens was the key figure, for after the courts had ruled, no one but the Governor of California stood between Mooney and the gallows.

CHAPTER NINETEEN

From Intervention to Commutation

~~To be executed.~~
—San Quentin Prison record card for Inmate 31921

THE DECISION of the California Supreme Court in March 1918 to uphold Mooney's conviction was an event long expected. The Court found no error in the record. Conceivably, it did not try very hard; it might, for instance, have accepted McNutt's argument that there was reversible error in the prosecution's failure to establish the corpus delicti adequately (for, as McNutt said, "the *criminal agency is still subject to conjecture*"), and in the trial court's admission into evidence of such articles as the so-called clock rings and the ball bearings found in Steuart Street, which were connected with the explosion only by "guesswork."[1] But if one assumed that the Court's reasoning was sound, and that the record contained no reversible error, there appeared to be nothing further it could do; for according to the law and the construction placed on it at the time, the Court was powerless to set aside the judgment on any other grounds. At least one of the justices reviewing the case, Victor E. Shaw, realized that the conviction was unjust, but even he believed that the bench could do nothing to change it. Long afterward Shaw wrote privately:

As a juror I would never have convicted him upon the record presented, nor do I believe for one moment that if tried now or at any time after the intense feeling against him resulting from the accusation based upon the terrible crime had subsided, that the result would be a conviction.
...The character of those purporting to be eye witnesses to the alleged fact that Billings and Mooney deposited the satchel wherein the bombs were contained was and is not such as to carry conviction to an unprejudiced mind.... Moreover, there was to my mind conclusive circumstancial [*sic*] evidence that at the hour of and immediately before and after the ex-

plosion Mooney was more than one mile from the location. However, . . .
Mooney was in ill repute on account of his anarchistic activities and the
public demanded a conviction. . . . I *do not believe* him guilty of the crime
of which he was convicted.

Nevertheless, said Shaw, "the Supreme Court could do nothing other
than to affirm the judgment of the conviction," even though it was a
capital case.[2]

California law has come a long way since 1918. Justice Raymond
E. Peters, a legal scholar and member of the present California Supreme Court, holds that the Court was at fault in regarding criminal
procedure as an end in itself. Supposing another man had confessed
the bombing, he asks, would the Supreme Court nevertheless have
allowed Mooney to hang? He considers the Mooney decision absurd,
and contends that if no procedure existed for setting aside the judgment, the Court should have invented one.[3]

The defense was entitled to ask for a rehearing, but did not consider it worthwhile. The time had come to approach Governor Stephens with a formal request for a pardon. McNutt filed a petition for
executive clemency in early April, shortly before Mooney was resentenced. Against the petition Fickert filed an opposing brief, in which
he reiterated the anarchist evidence and contended that Mooney had
been paid for the Preparedness Day bombing with German money.[4]
"Chops and tomato sauce," said Older: the brief resembled the address of Serjeant Buzfuz in the memorable case of Bardell against
Pickwick. But the reaction of Stephens in the case of People against
Mooney was not disclosed.[*]

The defense hoped that Stephens would accept the recommendation of the Mediation Commission that Mooney be pardoned and retried. It was widely rumored, however, that the Governor would do
no more than commute the death sentence. Stephens gave no hint of
how he would act.[5] Mooney's friends petitioned the President for renewed intervention. The President's letter of January 22 to the Governor was made public in Washington in late April, and the text
showed that Wilson had asked for a new trial. At the same time the
President said that he could do no more, and expressed confidence
that Stephens would act justly.[6] (Five weeks later he changed his mind
and sent another appeal, his last.) From the county jail Mooney de-

* *Bulletin,* June 12, 1918. Throughout his life Older was devoted to Dickens's novels.
He literally read them to tatters. (Evelyn Wells, *Fremont Older* [1936], pp. 370, 389.)

manded that he be given a fair and honest trial or else be hanged. If there was not justice enough in California to obtain his liberty, then there was only one fitting penalty for the crime. "I refuse to buy my life by a lie and a compromise," he said.[7]

II

"I am loath to resentence this man to death," said Judge Griffin, but under the law, there was seemingly no alternative.[8] Mooney's attorneys disagreed; they had unearthed another possible course. McNutt petitioned Griffin for a writ of error *coram nobis*.

Coram nobis was a rare, ancient writ, designed to remedy duress or fraud external to the legal record. One modern authority has defined it as

a common law writ, issuing out of a court of record to review and correct a judgment of its own, relating to some error in fact, as opposed to error in law, not appearing on the face of the record, unknown at the time, without fault, to the court and to the party seeking relief, or not made known because of fraud or duress, but for which the judgment would not have been entered, and for which the statutes in force provide no remedy.[9]

The writ had never been issued in California, and the statutes of the state made no provision for it. It was a peculiar remedy, available, if at all, for an action of equity in civil rather than criminal cases. However, it had been used in criminal proceedings in other states, as McNutt pointed out. He cited several precedents, particularly an Indiana murder case of 1878, in which the defendant had pleaded guilty because mob violence was imminent; after being sentenced the defendant was granted a writ of *coram nobis*, and was permitted to withdraw his plea and be duly tried.[10] McNutt contended that the power to grant the writ was inherent in the court. Fickert's representative, Assistant District Attorney Cotton, contended it was not.[11] Griffin was skeptical. He considered their arguments, their authorities and documents, and finally ruled that he did not have jurisdiction to consider McNutt's motion.

So far as the alleged perjuries of Oxman and Mrs. Edeau were concerned, said Griffin, their testimony was in the record and therefore could not be readjudicated by a writ of *coram nobis*. "In this state it is the settled law that a judgment cannot be set aside because it is predicated upon perjured testimony or because material evidence is concealed or suppressed. The fraud which is practiced in such cases [is not] extrinsic to the record." He held, further, that *coram nobis* was inapplicable because there were statutory remedies available, namely, the right to appeal and the right to ask for a new trial. If the District Attorney had violated his oath that he would present only competent and legitimate evidence, "in so far as the judgment is concerned, the injured party is without remedy."[12]

The decision was probably distressing as well as difficult for Griffin. "With all the harshness and severity of this rule," he said, "and with a knowledge that injustice must at times be done in its application, it is the law defined by the Supreme Court of this State."[13] His opinion was adopted almost verbatim two months later by the Supreme Court, when it denied McNutt's application for a certificate of probable cause. In upholding the lower court's decision against *coram nobis,* the Supreme Court added something that Griffin had not said: "the showing of fraud or misconduct on the part of the district attorney and his assistants in conducting the trial is of the weakest character."[14]

The contention that statutory remedies were available to Mooney was specious. Oxman had been exposed after the time during which a motion for a new trial was allowed. McNutt's motion, filed before the Oxman exposé, had been denied. As for the right of appeal, it had resulted in a denial of a new trial on the very grounds on which *coram nobis* was supposed to provide a remedy—that is, the evidence was external to the record. Whether or not the District Attorney had committed fraud, fraud there had been. Yet taken together, the rulings of Griffin and the Supreme Court left Mooney with no recourse but executive clemency.

The Supreme Court's ruling dismayed at least one Californian who favored the suppression of radicalism and had not the least interest in Mooney. He was a Modesto attorney, Jay A. Hindman, an elderly, prosperous, civic-minded, middle-of-the-road Democrat.[15] Hindman was alarmed by the Court's decision because it amounted to an abdication of judicial responsibility. He wrote an article for the *American Law Review* forcefully denying that a legal wrong could exist without a legal remedy: according to the Court's ruling, he said,

if by means of fraud and perjury, a concededly innocent person is convicted of a crime and is condemned to death, the courts of this State, under the conditions stated, are so manacled and fettered by their own arbitrary rules and precedents as to be without power to undo the wrong. . . . This is murder—judicial murder—and nothing less.

Nor does it mitigate this wrong one whit to say that its consummation may be averted by executive clemency. The pardoning power was never intended to be put to any such use. And for a court to condemn a man to death, knowing his conviction to have been procured by fraud and perjury, even though the governor may have power to nullify the sentence, is un-American and contrary to the genius of free government.

... we have this humiliating spectacle of the highest court of a State proclaiming to the world that under certain conditions of its own making, its arm is too short and too weak to rescue a victim of fraud and perjury, committed within its own precincts. ...

As a lawyer, I cannot subscribe to the doctrine that our courts are not able, within themselves, to administer full and complete justice in every instance, without the aid or consent of any other department of government. Such a confession of impotency will not command respect for, nor inspire confidence in our courts, but on the contrary, will breed contempt for law among the very classes it is intended to restrain.[16]

III

Before he became Governor, William D. Stephens was a progressive, public-spirited wholesale grocer in Los Angeles, who served for many years as a director of the Los Angeles Chamber of Commerce. After a brief period as interim mayor of his city, he ran as the Progressive candidate for Congress, where he served three terms. He became Governor of California by a process of negotiation: Hiram Johnson, who wanted election to the Senate in 1916, reluctantly appointed him Lieutenant Governor after the death of John Eshleman, the incumbent, in order to have the support of a powerful group of southern Progressives for the Senatorial race. Johnson won, and Stephens inherited the governorship in March 1917. He was a less vigorous, less colorful executive than Johnson, who called him another William Howard Taft: an apt comparison, for Stephens, as William Kent said, was "unaggressively right-minded." Chester Rowell appraised him as a fine, likeable fellow of no great ability. Although Stephens was to defend Progressive policies after the war, when Progressivism was a rapidly declining force, in 1918 he devoted most of his time to the war effort and his own reelection.[17] In the midst of these cares, like an unwanted child, arrived the Mooney question.

Griffin had resentenced Mooney to hang, and the stay of execution expired with the Supreme Court's decision. Execution was scheduled for August 23. From the San Francisco county jail, where he had spent two years, Mooney was transferred to San Quentin's death row.[18] More clearly than ever before, Stephens alone stood between him and the gallows. The Governor had said for months that he would consider the case when it was wholly free of the courts. It was time for him to act.

During the months that had passed since the filing of the pardon petition, the question of a pardon had become an issue in the Republican gubernatorial primary. In May Fickert announced his probable candidacy. In June he entered the race and published his platform, which consisted mainly of ways in which he would suppress radicalism. "Americanism or anarchy, that is the issue," said the District Attorney.[19] Stephens probably took Fickert's candidacy about as seriously as the *Bulletin*, which observed that Fickert's vote would serve "as a sort of boring-rod to show how deep the mud is."[20] The Governor had more serious rivals, notably Mayor James Rolph, Jr., of San Francisco. But Californians were deeply divided over a pardon for Mooney, and any decision was certain to alienate a large group of voters. Stephens resolved his dilemma, late in July, by reprieving Mooney until December. He explained that he wanted time to give the case the fullest possible consideration.[21]

IV

In the spring of 1918 William Randolph Hearst changed his mind about the Mooney case. He withdrew his support of Fickert, and published a somewhat supercilious retraction in the New York *American*. The evidence against Mooney was not convincing to a fair mind, he said, and Mooney should not be executed, although he might have had prior knowledge of the crime.[22] Older responded bitterly:

the public tolerated the trial methods because the lies knowingly given currency by the Hearst papers had convinced it that Mooney and his fellow prisoners were guilty. When Hearst denounces those methods he denounces himself. When he asks clemency for Mooney he asks that a wrong be undone which could never have been done without his conscious aid.

. . .

There can be no excuse or evasion for Hearst. All that he or his New York editor knows now about the trial of Mooney he and his San Francisco editors knew a year ago. If it appears now that Mooney has been unjustly treated it appeared so then.

The only difference is that a year ago it took courage and a willingness to make sacrifices, to demand justice for Mooney and that now it is dangerous for a newspaper to stand out against that demand.

Fickert's ship is going down. And the rats are leaving it.[23]

While the Hearst papers were taking a softer line on Mooney, Older's troubles over the case within the *Bulletin* office were growing. The owners of the paper had been pressing him since the spring of 1917 to give up the fight. R. A. Crothers and Older had not seen eye to eye since the graft prosecution days, and the tension grew after Crothers's nephew, Loring Pickering, joined the *Bulletin* as part owner. Pickering neither understood nor accepted Older's policies, and harassed the editor in every possible way. After the *Bulletin* published the Oxman letters, the Law and Order Committee called in Crothers and Pickering and asked them to stop interfering in the case. Laying the blame on Older, the owners promised that the paper would reform. But Older refused to comply. The *Bulletin* suffered heavy losses in advertising. Tension grew.[24]

Hearst had long had his eye on Older. The newspaper war that had raged between them he looked upon as part of the newspaper game. Older was an unusually good editor with a strong labor following, and Hearst wanted him. Several times since 1907 Hearst had approached Older and had been refused. When he learned of Older's difficulties with Crothers and Pickering, his hopes revived. He had in mind assigning Older to the *Call,* a languishing paper which he did not yet own but which he controlled and could buy any time. Before taking up his option on the *Call,* Hearst renewed his offer to Older, on very attractive terms: Older could bring the Mooney cause with him and have a comparatively free hand in running the paper.[25]

Older loathed Hearst, but Crothers and Pickering were becoming increasingly difficult. He did not want to leave the *Bulletin;* "he *was* the *Bulletin*";[26] but he had to give up either his paper or his causes. Another consideration was his need for security. He had asked Crothers and Pickering to assure him of his job on the *Bulletin,* and they had refused.[27] Older himself had never cared much about security or a large income, but apparently his wife did, and urged him to accept Hearst's offer.[28] He was 61 years old and could not even call his ranch entirely his own.[29] Hearst's conditions were liberal and the financial terms lucrative. Older swallowed his pride, went to New York, and saw Hearst.[30] Shortly after he returned he appeared at the house of Colonel C. E. S. Wood and his wife, Sara Bard Field, his neighbors in Cupertino, and asked: "Do you allow in Hearst's prostitutes?"[31] To the distress of his admirers and the disdain of his critics, Older had accepted the editorship of the *Call.*[32]

The Mooney fight continued from the *Call,* as Hearst had promised.[33] Some of the most spectacular revelations in the case were made by the *Call* under Older's editorship. Yet posterity may endorse Older's initial judgment: nothing Hearst did from 1918 on could strike one line from what he had published in the week of the arrests and for eighteen months afterward.

V

The imminence of Mooney's execution led to a concerted national demonstration in his behalf on July 28, 1918, "Mooney Day." Hundreds of mass meetings, parades, and demonstrations were held in more than forty American cities from Seattle to Miami, Florida. Many prominent labor leaders and liberals associated with the cause spoke that day: Frank P. Walsh in Chicago; Clarence Darrow in Philadelphia; James Duncan, vice-president of the AFL, and John D. Barry in Boston; John A. Fitch in Rochester; Dudley Field Malone in New York; William Spooner, president of the Alameda County Central Labor Council, in Seattle; and William Patterson of the IWDL in Denver.[34] In San Francisco a giant rally in the Dreamland Rink was addressed by John H. Walker. It was a day of fiery talk. Walker blamed the bombing on those who were responsible for Mooney's conviction; the crowd roared with approval and pledged allegiance to "one nation indivisible with liberty and justice for all, including Tom Mooney." In Chicago Walsh proposed to send federal troops to California to ensure a pardon. The mayor of Butte proclaimed that "Almighty God would look down smilingly on a bunch of men who would burn Fickert at the stake."[35] When the speeches were read in California, the Sacramento *Bee* declared: "Is there any wonder that the people of the East are unable to comprehend California's righteous stand in the Mooney case when they are forced to hear such lying rot?" "In asking for Federal troops, this man Walsh reveals himself as one of the [IWW] type, willing to ravish an orderly State of its inherent rights, and to cause bloodshed, if necessary to save the life of a wretch like Mooney."[36]

The most ambitious Mooney Day demonstration was in Washington, where nearly a thousand labor representatives convened to hear speeches and select a delegation to call on the President. Bourke Cockran set aside his objections to his own participation in Mooney meetings and went to Washington to address the group and lead the delegation. Arrangements had been made with Tumulty for the President to receive a small group and hear their request. After Wilson had approved the appointment, however, he changed his mind, and the delegation was asked to submit its statement in writing.[37]

Supporters of Governor Stephens approved the reprieve in July on the grounds that it removed the case from politics.[38] Others were skeptical. "The Mooney case IS in politics and it cannot be kept out," said the *News*.[39] After the Republican primary, in which Fickert was resoundingly defeated, Stephens continued to campaign for the November election. Mooney's pardon petition stayed on the shelf. Partisans on both sides of the case taunted the Governor. "No doubt," said the Sacramento *Bee*, "in all his gubernatorial perambulations, Stephens steadfastly ponders this Mooney question; studies the mass of testimony . . . to the exclusion of politics and all other non-essential matters."[40] Harrison Gray Otis regretted that a man of Fickert's caliber did not occupy Stephens's place: the Governor was temporizing with crime and allowing the probity of the judiciary to be called into question.[41] Fickert himself took a neutral stance: he would not try Mooney again, and if the Governor wanted to pardon him, that was his business.[42]

During the spring and summer of 1918 the left-wing labor movement made sporadic efforts to call a general strike on behalf of Mooney. May Day and Mooney Day were both suggested. Mooney himself did not urge such an extreme measure, and on one occasion he wrote President Wilson to say that he disapproved of it because it would hamper the war;[43] but as the fall wore on and December 13 loomed larger, the idea spread. The movement was spurred by the refusal of the United States Supreme Court in November to review the case.[44] ("Then they wonder why some workers become infected with Bolshevikism," said Mooney.)[45] On November 19 the Alameda County Central Labor Council recommended December 9 as the starting date for a general strike against the execution.[46] Seattle's Metal Trades Council and Central Labor Council endorsed the project enthusiastically, and scattered support came from San Francisco, Portland, Salt Lake City, Chicago, Dallas, and Brooklyn. No major labor councils outside of Oakland and Seattle approved it, however, and Seattle was itching for a general strike anyway; the unions there went ahead with one on their own account, for a different purpose, the following January. The IWDL claimed that 500,000 American workers had taken action in favor of the protest strike, but the estimate was certainly exaggerated.[47]

Late in November Judge Griffin wrote Stephens, by then reelected Governor, and asked for a pardon and retrial. "Simple justice and fair play" required that action. It was a matter of public record, he said, that the testimony of Oxman, McDonald, and the Edeaus was worthless. The Attorney General had agreed that Mooney deserved a new trial; the courts were powerless to grant it. To execute Mooney without a new judgment would be "a blot upon the administration of justice which this State cannot afford to bear."[48] The Governor did not comment. At the end of the month a delegation of state labor leaders, including Paul Scharrenberg and Daniel Murphy, called on Stephens and repeated Griffin's request. The Governor heard them out in silence. His callers felt that he had made up his mind. What he had decided they did not know.[49]

VI

Late in November an extraordinary new development was spread across the front page of Older's *Call*. Sensational discoveries about Fickert had been made secretly by John B. Densmore, head of the United States Employment Service, and were revealed to Older for publication. This was the celebrated "Densmore Report."

Densmore had been in San Francisco in 1917 to investigate some criminal cases connected with the Immigration Service. At that time he was the Department of Labor's Solicitor. While he was there he inquired briefly into the Mooney case at the request of the Secretary of Labor, William B. Wilson, for the Mediation Commission. His curiosity whetted, he subsequently requested and was granted permission to investigate the case further. On his instructions two immigration inspectors, George Parson and Ignatius H. McCarty, assisted by Charles Goff, planted a dictaphone in Fickert's private office on the fourth floor of the Hall of Justice. For two months in the fall of 1918 stenographers recorded the telephone calls and office conversations of the District Attorney.[50]

Densmore submitted the transcript and his comments to Secretary Wilson on November 1. What Wilson would have done with the report had it been kept secret is uncertain, for the news was out. Goff had told Older about the investigation and had introduced Parson to him.* According to Older, Parson gave him the report when it was nearly completed, with the comment that it ought to be published: "I think the American people ought to know what has been going on in this town. I thought perhaps you might print it. There is some hot stuff in it."[51] Older published the report in the *Call* on November 23.

The revelations in the Densmore Report were sensational. The conversations of Fickert and his associates did not for the most part directly concern Mooney, but they revealed much about the operations of the District Attorney. Rena Mooney was mentioned from time to time, for Fickert was thinking about bringing her to trial again. On one such occasion, when he was discussing the matter with Cunha, Cunha exclaimed:

"Chief, if you can get a witness who will put Mrs. Mooney at Steuart and Market Streets, I don't give a damn if you put her there in a balloon."

Fickert said, "I think I can put her there in a taxicab. It looks as though we had the witness."

"If you have, Chief," said Cunha with real enthusiasm, "I will put that s—— of a b———— [*sic*] Mrs. Mooney on trial again and I will convict her by every rule of the game."

Two days later Fickert declared: "That s—— of a b———— Griffin if it wasn't for him we would have had Mooney shoved right off at the end of the trial."[52] A few days later an unidentified man telephoned to ask Fickert about Mooney:

MAN. "We have an inquiry from some up-State people in New York asking whether the Mooneys are Russians. Is Mooney his right name?"

FICKERT. "I'm inclined to think it is. We first got track of him in 1907. I think it's unlikely he's a Russian.

MAN. "Is she a Russian Jew?"

FICKERT. "No. I'm inclined to think she's of Irish descent. The mother's name was Brink, before she married Herman[n]. Mooney went under a Russian name in Chicago—why, I don't know."

---

* Fremont Older, *Growing Up* (1931), p. 159. According to Edgar T. Gleeson, Goff had tipped Older off that detectives were trailing Fickert. Gleeson tried to discover who they were, but was able to determine only that they were not police detectives or local private agents. Goff then told Parson that Older knew about their work—which was scarcely true—and so Parson, fearing that Older would give their work away, consulted Densmore and went to Older. (Author's interview, Edgar T. Gleeson, February 6, 1960.) Apparently Goff's long-standing dislike of Fickert was the motivation behind all this.

MAN. "Is it true that he belonged to the Russian, German, and American I.W.W.'s?"

FICKERT. "Yes; he was the king-pin of them all."[53]

On another occasion a Burns agent called on Fickert and discussed new witnesses in the case. The detective said: "There is only one way to handle cases of this kind. You've got to have three or four fellows working on them [the prospective witnesses]—one to do a little missionary work and the others to follow up. . . . You could get up a real thriller. . . . I can frame the damndest lot of stuff you ever heard of."[54]

The Densmore Report revealed that Fickert was working to obtain witnesses against Rena Mooney. Specifically, he was trying to persuade Mrs. Virginia Judd and a Mrs. Barlow to identify Rena Mooney at Steuart Street. Mrs. Judd, he said, had stated that Rena Mooney got out of a taxicab and waved at her.[55] Mrs. Judd was reluctant to testify, and Fickert devised ways of encouraging her. Mrs. Judd stated subsequently to Edgar T. Gleeson that she had not seen the parade and knew nothing about the case, that she was taken unwillingly to Fickert's office for questioning, and that on another occasion one of Fickert's detectives asked her to go with him to Buena Vista Park to be in some moving pictures. "It was all very peculiar," she said. "They must have been trying to use me in some way, to do something with me."[56]

Apart from the bomb cases, the Densmore Report revealed that Fickert was making illicit bargains with Pete McDonough, the local bail bond broker, to fix cases and release arrested persons, and that Fickert was closely associated with Justice Frederick W. Henshaw of the California Supreme Court. Through collateral documents provided by Older, the Report showed that in 1901 Henshaw had taken a $410,000 bribe to change the decision in a famous case contesting the will of James Fair, the California mining magnate. Older had obtained the documentary proof in 1917. He had planned to publish it then, but Henshaw learned that it was in his possession, and, according to Older, had offered to resign from the Supreme Court, to use his influence with the Governor to secure a new trial for Mooney, and to sever his connections with Fickert if Older refrained from publishing the story. Older agreed. Henshaw resigned from the court, but reneged on the rest of the agreement. When Densmore's dictaphone transcript showed that Henshaw and Fickert frequently conferred about the Rena Mooney case, Older gave Densmore his documents, the ledger and the confession of Henshaw's intermediary in the bribery, and these were published as part of the Densmore Report.[57]

The Report shocked San Franciscans and created demands for an investigation of the District Attorney's office. (A subsequent grand jury investigation eventually produced another whitewash.) Attorney General Webb was asked to suspend Fickert from office. A copy of the Report was submitted to Governor Stephens. It added materially to the public impression that Mooney's sentence was unjust. "Will Governor Stephens let Mooney hang now?" asked Older, and through the city the question was repeated. Stephens said nothing.[58]

Fickert commented that the Report was a desperate attempt to divert public attention from Mooney's guilt, and that the transcript merely proved that he was making every effort to follow up new clues in the case.[59] The next evening, encountering Older in the lobby of the Palace Hotel, the District Attorney punched him in the head, knocked him down, and was apparently about to kick him when he was pulled away by his companions. Older declined to bring charges. Fickert offered the familiar excuse that Older had made a move toward his hip pocket.[60]

The Densmore Report angered many people. It did not prove that the District Attorney had framed Mooney. In fact, it did not really prove anything about the trial and conviction of Mooney and Billings. The dictaphone transcript amplified the evidence about Fickert's character, his associates, and his methods. But Densmore did not stop there. He was far less scrupulous than Felix Frankfurter had been about expressing personal opinion in a government report. Fully convinced that Fickert had framed Mooney, he interspersed the dictaphone transcript with his own comments, which the evidence in the transcript did not substantiate. These comments were partisan and inflammatory. A few of them could not have been proved from any source. Henshaw, he said, was

one of the leading attorneys of the corporate interests behind Fickert in the Mooney case. Henshaw and Frank C. Drew, the latter an attorney for the Chamber of Commerce in San Francisco, are the real brains of the antilabor forces arrayed against Mooney. These two attorneys either prepare or review all the briefs presented by Fickert in the Mooney case, Fickert himself being a man of no intellectual powers whatever.[61]

If Henshaw and Drew did prepare or review the briefs, it was never proved. It was simply an inference based on Fickert's known connection with the two men and Densmore's low opinion of his intelligence.*

When Densmore commented on "the easy adaptability of some of the star witnesses," "the sorry type of men and women brought forward," and the "sang-froid with which the prosecution occasionally discarded an untenable theory to adopt another not quite so preposterous,"[62] he wrote of matters which had been substantiated from other sources but to which the dictaphone transcript added nothing new. His reference to the Petrograd demonstrations as expressing "the liberal sentiment of Russia"[63] followed an interpretation that had been standard among American liberals a year before and had subsequently been proved naïve. Altogether, Densmore's commentary was distinctly vulnerable.

The Densmore Report raised a greater storm than the Mediation Report. In part, this was the effect of accumulating reactionary influence; the Red Scare was to begin only a month later. In part, it was the cumulative effect of widely disseminated falsehoods about the bomb cases; any unfavorable report by a federal agency would have been widely denounced. But also responsible were the opinionated character of Densmore's comments and the impropriety of a federal bureau chief's wiretapping the office of a city official—particularly when the results were scurrilous rather than conclusive. Densmore may have harmed the Mooney cause considerably. When the Sacramento *Bee* dissected the Report and exposed its many flaws, McClatchy provided Mooney's enemies with more sound reasoning than Fickert ever had. If the District Attorney was guilty of malfeasance or Henshaw of bribery, he said, they should be punished; but their guilt in matters unrelated to Mooney's trial was irrelevant to the fairness of his sentence, and "should not be permitted to cloud the truth therein, any more than the fact that every dynamiting thug, murderer, I.W.W. and Bolshevik . . . clamors for Mooney's pardon should be urged [as a reason] why Justice should be denied even to such as he." McClatchy urged people to read the Report. He held that it presented no facts of any character that would entitle Mooney to leniency.[64]

---

* In the habeas corpus hearings of 1935–36 the defense offered no other evidence against Henshaw, and the matter was not prominent in its charges against Fickert.

VII

Two weeks before Mooney was scheduled to hang, Governor Stephens commuted his sentence to life imprisonment. He said he was doing so because of new evidence in the case and because of President Wilson's repeated requests. He did not mention that one of them had been for a pardon. He quoted the President's March telegram and the final one of June, which read:

> I beg that you will believe that I am moved only by a sense of public duty and of consciousness of the many and complicated interests involved when I again must respectfully suggest a commutation of the death sentence imposed upon Mooney. I would not venture again to call your attention to this case did I not know the international significance which attaches to it.[65]

Stephens remarked that commutation would give Mooney the same status as Billings: "The logic that a man is either guilty or innocent and that necessarily if the maximum punishment is not justified pardon should follow does not hold either in theory or practice." He declared that the propaganda representing Mooney as a labor martyr was absurd, and that Mooney had never been identified with labor; "his connections have been with a small group of agitators of pronounced anarchistic tendencies." Mooney's previous record was "not such as to enlist faith in him among law abiding citizens." The sentence was therefore commuted to life imprisonment in the state prison at San Quentin.[66]

"A solemn document that, from beginning to end, rises superior to reason or logic," said John D. Barry in the *Call*. "I find myself lingering over its phrases, fascinated and amazed."[67] Indeed, logic had no part in it. Stephens had emphasized the President's urgent requests, but Wilson had been sending them for a year and a half. He spoke of international repercussions, but the war was over. He accused Mooney—by quoting Berkman. He called the crime "German" and the convict dangerous, and refused a hanging. He mentioned new evidence, and neglected to say what it was. "Justice is tempered with mercy," said the Stockton *Record*.[68] More accurately, it was tempered with expediency. The commutation, as Barry said, was "a model for those politicians who thrive by dodging."[69]

Many Californians unsympathetic to the defense were satisfied with Stephens's "disposal of the matter," as one of them told him. Fickert voiced no objection to it; Matheson thought that Stephens did "absolutely right"; pro-Stephens newspapers commented similarly.[70] Stephens himself was content with what he had done. "The Mooney case was indeed a difficult problem but I solved it as my conscience dictated and I can at any time go to my Maker so far as the commutation of Mooney is concerned."[71]

Mooney's friends were understandably bitter. "The Governor's action in the Mooney case embraces so completely every stupidity for which any opportunity was afforded him that it amounts to inverted genius. Surely never before has a public officer written himself down an ass so conspicuously and with such complacency." So Cockran wrote McNutt.[72] John A. Fitch supposed that Stephens felt he was avoiding the wrath of both labor and business in San Francisco. "His act is an exhibition of weakness and cowardice." It would go far, he said, toward undermining respect for law and government, especially in the eyes of labor.[73] Walsh wrote Mooney: "Of all the crimes committed against you in the name of justice, in my opinion, this last is the worst." Mooney thought so, too. He wrote Stephens: "I prefer a glorious death at the hands of my traducers, you included, to a living grave."[74]

On Mooney's prison record card a red line was drawn through the words "To be executed." But San Quentin was to be his living grave for another twenty years.

CHAPTER TWENTY

Mooney and the Red Scare, 1919

> *It is barely possible that his case can be reopened*
> *but why spend any more money fooling with the*
> *damned courts. Lets have a nationwide strike and*
> *serve notice on the master class and the courts*
> *that a repetition of the Mooney case will not be*
> *tolerated.*
> —Letter to William B. Wilson, June 16, 1919

> *The syndicalist utters the words, "The general*
> *strike," as a finality. But the trade unionist asks,*
> *"Well, then what?"*
> —*Labor Clarion*, 1913

THE COMMUTATION demoralized Mooney's left-wing supporters across the country. The sense of emergency had dissolved. "I felt, I think everybody felt," wrote Max Eastman's sister, Crystal Eastman, "that when the Governor of California . . . saved Mooney from hanging and condemned him to life imprisonment, he had taken the dramatic force out of the Mooney agitation and it would be impossible to revive it."[1] On the advice of the International Workers Defense League the general strike planned for December 9 was called off, to the disappointment of many of its advocates.[2] In its place the IWDL proposed a national Mooney labor convention. This idea, which originated in the Alameda County Central Labor Council, was taken up by Ed Nolan, who had succeeded Minor as secretary-treasurer of the IWDL. He wired union organizations in all the industrial centers of the country early in December, urging that they meet in Chicago six weeks later to consider a labor program for liberating Mooney and Billings, and to lay plans for a national general strike as an ultimate measure in their behalf. The city labor councils in Oakland, Chicago, and Seattle took up the proposal enthusiastically; they assisted in spreading the call. Many other labor organizations responded favorably. On January 14, 1919, more than a thousand delegates convened at Turner Hall on Chicago's North Side for four days of deliberation, resolutions, and noisy debate. This was the Chicago Mooney Congress.[3]

The Mooney Congress was a national convention of trade-union radicals. Its members represented neither a cross section of organized labor nor the national leadership of the AFL. Nor did they represent a cross section of American radicalism, since only trade-union representatives were accredited as delegates. Ignored or condemned by most state federations of labor, by the executive council of the AFL and President Gompers,[4] the congress consisted overwhelmingly of delegates directly representing local unions and city central labor bodies where radicalism was flourishing in 1919. The roster of delegations comprised an index of American trade-union radicalism on the eve of the Red Scare.

The congress was also an engagement of radicals for and against Bolshevism more than half a year before the birth of the American Communist and Communist Labor parties. The "ultra-radicals," inspired by the Bolshevik revolution, sought to exploit the Mooney Congress as a forum for a new American revolutionary movement. Led by delegates from the Seattle and Butte labor councils, with strong support from the Illinois miners, they comprised a substantial minority faction. The convention, however, was not in their hands but in those of the old-style radicals, inspired by prewar left-wing labor ideals. Led by the IWDL and the Chicago Federation of Labor, the majority faction included John Fitzpatrick, John H. Walker, Nockels, Nolan, Schulberg, and Johannsen—men who were determined to restrict the Mooney Congress to the Mooney case, and to treat it, as one of their resolutions stated, "not as an issue of class war particularly, but as an issue of the broad fundamentals of human rights and liberty."[5] From the outset they had to fight to retain control. At the first meeting of the organizing committee they prevailed only when Fizpatrick threatened to withdraw the support of the Chicago Federation of Labor. The new radicals bided their time, believing they could capture the convention from the floor; when they discovered at Chicago that they could not, they were enraged.[6]

For all the factional bickering, union men in various parts of the country believed that the Chicago Mooney Congress deserved support because it would give voice to genuine rank-and-file beliefs. Few professional labor leaders would be present. As a Virginia labor paper declared,

It will be a spontaneous assembly of delegates chosen by men who are working in the shops and factories of the nation, and who will not face a convention machine that prevents progressive action. As the first time that individual locals of America have sent their delegates to a national convention of all crafts and trades, it will give an opportunity to see how labor really feels back home. . . . So many of the international officers are considered reactionary by the rank and file that it is a wonder how they ever get re-elected.[7]

The delegates of both factions were bona fide representatives of their locals and councils, which bore the costs of sending them to Chicago.[8]

The delegates at the congress represented nearly twelve hundred labor organizations in 37 states. According to Anton Johannsen, every craft in every industry had at least one member present. Eight state federations and seven international unions sent delegates. The latter included the machinists and three left-wing clothing trades unions (the ILGWU, fur workers, and journeymen tailors) but not the molders or other leading AFL internationals such as the UMW and carpenters. On the other hand, 114 city centrals in 28 states were represented (as compared with 143 at the AFL national convention later in the year). San Francisco's labor council refused to participate, but the labor councils of Oakland, Chicago, Seattle, New York, Detroit, Minneapolis, Portland (Oregon), and Butte, among others, all sent delegates. These cities were all centers of radical labor movements.

Most of the delegates represented union locals. Two hundred UMW locals in left-wing districts, particularly Illinois, were represented, as were about 75 machinists' locals and some 50 garment trades unions, particularly in New York and Chicago. Chicago trade unions were heavily represented with 171 delegates; Seattle sent 30—of whom, according to Crystal Eastman, 28 belonged to the Socialist Party or IWW as well as the AFL; New York was third with 23. The unions of the San Francisco Bay Area sent only 18, most of whom were associated with the IWDL, including Schulberg, E. B. Morton, William D. Patterson, and President William A. Spooner of the Alameda County Central Labor Council.[9]

The two factions clashed at once over the chairmanship. John Fitzpatrick, who welcomed the delegates, attempted to introduce Ed Nolan as permanent chairman; the ultra-radicals insisted that the convention elect its own chairman. James H. Maurer, president of the Pennsylvania State Federation of Labor, was their candidate. Their other leaders included Frank Turco, vice-president of the Seattle Metal Trades Council; William F. Dunne, leader of the left-wing labor movement in Butte; and Dennis E. Batt of Detroit.* In com-

* Turco was a flamboyant, fist-swinging Italian immigrant with a large following and many enemies in the Seattle labor movement. A free-wheeling, undoctrinaire radical, friendly to the IWW, he believed in working-class solidarity and industrial union-

promise, Nolan was recognized as temporary chairman pending settlement of the credentials question. Many of the participants had come as Socialist and IWW representatives without invitation. After an hour of riotous disorder Nolan put the question to exclude those who did not present trade-union credentials, and declared the motion carried by voice vote. With a roar of disapproval, the ultra-radicals tried to appeal the ruling, but were cried down. The left wing threatened to hold a rump convention. However, most of the Socialists and Wobblies also bore credentials from AFL unions and so retained their seats. The others withdrew to the gallery, where they continued their raucous demonstrations. Nolan was elected permanent chairman and Maurer vice-chairman. They retained the support of the majority.[10]

The brief agenda of the Nolan faction was concerned only with the Mooney case. At the urging of Bourke Cockran and Frank Walsh, the faction proposed to appeal for renewed federal intervention and to seek the revision of California law—cautious measures that elicited no enthusiasm. If neither of them succeeded (and there was little expectation of success), the majority faction proposed to take a national referendum on a general strike. This was their pièce de résistance.[11]

In contrast, the ultra-radicals, seeking action on a broad left-wing front, were armed with resolutions for a national soldiers' and sailors' council, recognition of Soviet Russia, withdrawal of all Allied troops from Russia, Bolshevik representation at the Paris Peace Conference; for industrial unionism, withdrawal from the AFL, and a six-hour day: a program, said Dunne, "to free ourselves from the chains of industrial slavery." All these proposals were rejected. Dunne voiced the resentment of his faction. The "conservatives" were using steamroller tactics; the convention was not the property of the IWDL, and might

---

ism, and was shortly to have an important part in the Seattle General Strike. At the Chicago Mooney Congress he introduced many of the ultra-radical resolutions. Dunne was chosen in caucus at the congress as the left-wing floor leader. An acidulous, colorful orator, he called the other faction "anarchists," but said he did not know what he was himself: "Craft unionism is out of date, it's too late for industrial unionism, —mass action is the only thing." Later that year he led the Butte branch of the Socialist Party into the Communist Labor Party. Eventually Dunne became editor of the *Daily Worker*. Batt became a leader of the Michigan faction of the Communist movement and a founder of the Communist Party. Communist leadership, however, was drawn but slightly from the ultra-radicals attending the Chicago congress.

(On Turco, see Robert L. Friedheim, *The Seattle General Strike* [1964], pp. 42–44; *Call*, January 16, 1919. On Dunne, *Western Socialist*, January 30, 1919; Joseph Freeman, *American Testament* [1936], pp. 292–94; *Liberator*, March 1919; Theodore Draper, *Roots of American Communism* [1957], pp. 316, 317; George Hardy, *Those Stormy Years* [1956], pp. 156–57; Daniel Aaron, *Writers on the Left* [1961], p. 326. On Batt and Communist leadership, Draper, pp. 160, 173, 182, and *passim*; and Irving Howe and Lewis Coser, *American Communist Party: A Critical History* [1957], pp. 36–40.)

discuss any subject it pleased. The left wing, he said, was entitled to discuss international questions after planning for Mooney.[12]

Although the left wing shared the majority's commitment to a general strike for Mooney, intense controversy arose over the project. The left wing scorned preliminary appeals to the government: legal means had been exhausted; funds should be used for organizing the strike. "I understand the A. F. of L. maintains a lobby at Washington —let them take up the legal end," said Dunne. His faction wanted the general strike to be for all political prisoners—for Emma Goldman, Eugene Debs, William Haywood, Rose Pastor Stokes, Victor Berger and others convicted since the beginning of the war, as well as for Mooney and Billings. The left wing also wanted the general strike to begin on May Day, which the majority faction rejected in favor of the Fourth of July.[13]

The clash over this issue was lengthy, symbolic, and tumultuous. The left wing taunted the Nolan crowd. "If we were ready for a general strike on December 9th to keep Mooney from hanging, why wait till July 4th to call a strike for his freedom?" demanded Kate Greenhalgh, a fiery Socialist and popular Seattle orator. "Why stop work on the one day in the year when you're allowed to stop work?"[14] (Fitzpatrick retorted, "If we want an international day let us select St. Patrick's Day.")[15] After five hours' debate the majority's resolutions were adopted without amendment. As a minor concession to the ultra-radicals, a resolution was passed favoring amnesty for all political and industrial prisoners and the withdrawal of American troops from Russia. A voluntary assessment of 50 cents on all union members for strike publicity and organizing was also approved.[16]

The left wing expected plans to be laid for a second radical congress, but the convention was abruptly adjourned over its protest. A few days later the Seattle radicals, disgusted with the IWDL and the outcome at Chicago, began their own general strike, led by the Seattle Central Labor Council and its president, James A. Duncan, who had attended the Mooney Congress. (The radical labor movement in Seattle, restless and independent, had been itching to try out a general strike—a militant labor weapon often discussed but hardly tested in the United States.) The Seattle general strike was in support not of Mooney but of the Seattle shipyard workers, who were striking for higher wages.[17]

After the Chicago Mooney Congress was over it was misrepresented on all sides. The American Civic Federation, which supported conservative trade unionism, called it an ambitious scheme to break up the AFL; conservative labor journals and some of the daily papers treated the congress as a Bolshevik-IWW gathering; left-wing journals described it as a typical AFL gathering which had called a general strike only because of left-wing pressure; the journals of the majority faction minimized the chaos and dissension at Turner Hall. The achievements and proposals of the congress were debated in labor unions all over the country.[18] However, the aftermath of the Seattle general strike and other events that spring crowded the congress and its program from public attention. The IWDL was left alone to prepare its general strike as best it might.

II

Setting up the general strike referendum was a herculean task. The IWDL expected to have the vote taken through the machinery of the international unions. When these unsympathetic organizations declined to cooperate, the IWDL sent out its own ballots.[19] At the same time it arbitrarily changed the plans: there would be not one but three general strikes, the first two to begin Independence Day and Labor Day, and each to last five days. If neither of these secured freedom or new trials for Mooney and Billings, a third general strike, lasting indefinitely, would start on November 19, one year after the commutation.[20] According to reports, four million ballots were distributed to 20,000 union locals; it was America's first direct national labor referendum on any issue.[21]

The IWDL's persistence prompted one of the AFL leaders, Matthew Woll, to declare that a general strike would be revolutionary, would harm Mooney's cause, and could result only in the destruction of the trade unions. He attributed the general strike impulse to the enormous growth of unions since 1917 and to the effect of "pernicious" radicalism on the newer immigrant members.[22] Ironically, the pernicious radicals of the IWDL had embraced a democratic reform of the Progressive era, the direct referendum, and were imposing it for their ends upon the AFL, whose national officers were no more democratically elected—as Crystal Eastman pointed out—than United States Senators before the Sixteenth Amendment.[23]

In the meantime, little came of the IWDL's efforts to free Mooney by other means. In the California legislature Ed Hurley of Alameda introduced a bill to permit a convicted man to re-appeal for a new trial on grounds of newly discovered evidence. He also introduced a resolution calling for a legislative investigation of Fickert's office. Fickert assailed the proposal by attacking Hurley as a friend of Mooney's who had testified for him at Martinez and who knew he was guilty of the Preparedness Day bombing. This put Hurley on the defensive. Both the bill and the resolution died in the Judiciary Committee.[24] The San Francisco Labor Council continued to deride the IWDL and predicted that the general strike would fail: "The workers of the country are not as insane as some of the lunatics believe them to be."[25] In April, James A. Duncan came to San Francisco and defended the Mooney Congress and the Seattle general strike. His reception was cool.[26]

Elsewhere there was greater activity on Mooney's behalf. The American minister at Stockholm received indirectly a proposal from the Soviet government to exchange an American citizen, one Kolomatiano, imprisoned in the Kremlin on a commuted death sentence, for Mooney or Debs. In Washington the State Department also reported that the Bolsheviks had offered to free an American consul held by the Russians if Mooney or Debs were pardoned. President Wilson, speaking at the Metropolitan Opera House in New York, was picketed by workers demanding freedom for Mooney and Ireland. New York City's central labor council (the Central Federated Union) requested Governor Al Smith to bring the case before the national conference of governors. In Peoria, Illinois, the miners announced that every UMW local there had adopted the Chicago congress program, in spite of UMW rules. Altogether, the Mooney case and the Chicago Mooney Congress were part of the new, postwar ferment.[27]

Regardless of the Chicago congress, the left wing was bent on May Day action. The Seattle group was dissuaded from severing connections with the IWDL only by Duncan's appeal for cooperation against conservative unionism ("the labor fakirs of San Francisco") and "the Fickert gang." In New York the left-wing unions went ahead with plans for a one-day general strike on May 1.[28]

The prospects for peaceful May Day demonstrations in New York were dim. The city was the port of debarkation for thousands of soldiers and sailors, who had already clashed with local radicals: the first riot of the Red Scare era occurred there on the day after Armistice Day, 1918, between soldiers and Socialists parading up Fifth Avenue to a Mooney rally. Riot squads with free-swinging night sticks had quelled the disorder. (One of the injured was J. Edward Morgan.)[29] On May Day, 1919, New York was the national center of Mooney demonstrations. Three hundred thousand workers took the day off; many of them joined in Mooney parades and rallies organized by Socialist leagues, radical unions, and the General Mooney Committee of the New York Central Federated Union. Under dark clouds and rain, orators and manifestos proclaimed friendship for Soviet Russia and demanded a general strike for the labor prisoners in America.

That evening the New York City police defended free speech and free assembly in a maneuver which, though long since forgotten, is a memorable exception to the indifference or hostility toward radicals on the part of most law-enforcement authorities during the Red Scare. The General Mooney Committee and the United Hebrew Trades had arranged a Mooney protest meeting in Madison Square Garden. Nolan and Walsh addressed the meeting, and so did Rena Mooney, who came from Seattle for the event. Fifteen thousand people were jammed into the old building, which stood between Fourth and Madison Avenues at 27th Street. Word had gone out to the soldiers' and sailors' clubs that this was a Bolshevist demonstration. About 9 P.M. a crowd of about a thousand servicemen and veterans gathered a few blocks away on Broadway. Led by a bugler, a Canadian veteran, and a Marine carrying an American flag, they headed east toward Madison Square Garden. Waiting for them were seventeen hundred policemen, reportedly the largest force ever assembled to protect a meeting in New York. Police outriders were stationed two blocks from the Garden in every direction. When a sentry reported that the mob was approaching, mounted troops were dispatched to disperse it. The soldiers were pushed back to Broadway, but regrouped at the bugle's call and advanced again. Shouting and jeering, the multitude surged out of 29th Street onto Madison Avenue. Mounted policemen, lined from curb to curb, met them and ordered them to disperse. They threatened to rush the police. Suddenly a company of foot patrolmen with drawn batons swung up Madison Avenue and joined the mounted officers, and together mounted and foot patrolmen swept back the mob to 29th Street, where they broke it up. The most serious threat of the day thus passed without violence.

Attempts to storm the Garden, however, were not over. In later encounters that evening, bottles and stones were hurled at policemen, and bricks were thrown at them from rooftops. Then the officers began clubbing, and felled half a dozen rioters. Police reserves in company formation poured from the basement of the Garden, and eventually the rioting was quelled. None of the protesters got closer than a block from the radicals' meeting place. The thousands at the Garden voiced approval of the Mooney general strikes beginning July 4, and listened to a number of comparatively mild speeches.[30]

Several New York dailies expressed indignation that American servicemen had been ridden down by mounted police protecting a radical Mooney rally. But it was to the credit of Mayor John F. Hylan and the city police that the beatings of November were not repeated. Meanwhile that day, police officers, soldiers, and private citizens in other cities were battling Socialist demonstrators in bloody riots. These have been remembered as fragments in the Red Scare mosaic, but averted riots have a way of fading from memory.[31]

May Day, 1919, was the occasion of another contribution to the Red Scare: three dozen bomb packages were mailed to prominent public men. Ole Hanson, the mayor of Seattle and a strident opponent of the general strike there, received the first such package on April 28, but it arrived in a damaged state and did no harm. The next day former Senator Thomas W. Hardwick of Georgia received a similar package, which exploded when the maid opened it. It blew off her hands and burned his wife about the face. At the same time, bomb packages were delivered to Fickert and Cunha. Both happened to be in the hospital at the time. Fickert was seriously ill and not receiving mail; Cunha, according to report, had been in a Mission Street barroom fight and was in for stitches over his eye. His package was delivered to him on the 29th, when the Hanson parcel was in the news. Realizing that his own package fit the description of Hanson's, being marked as a sample from Gimbel Bros., he had it removed. The bomb had been constructed of a wooden tube with an acid detonator and nitroglycerin. Fickert's was also removed, although not disposed of until several days later, when someone realized that the acid was eating through the container.

Other intended recipients of these bombs included the new United States Attorney General, A. Mitchell Palmer, John D. Rockefeller, and J. P. Morgan, as well as persons such as William B. Wilson, who were less likely targets of a radical *attentat*. None of the intended recipients was injured; sixteen of the bombs were held up in the New York post office for want of postage. Altogether it was a vicious, bungled, frightening episode.[32]

Fickert adjudged the bombs part of a well organized terrorist campaign. "I don't believe that it springs directly from the Mooney case. It appears to be nation-wide in scope."[33] He announced that he had intended to give up his office because of poor health, but now would run for reelection. His life had been threatened many times, he said, and the latest attempt made him determined "to notify the anarchists and 'reds' throughout the country that I am not going to quit on them."[34] He added later that the radicals were planning to dynamite the Pacific Union Club in San Francisco, and that their leaders were parlor Bolsheviks, wily students of crime who planned their bombings so carefully that the police could find no clues.[35] He appointed James Brennan as a special bomb investigator; Brennan announced that anarchists, Bolsheviks, and IWW's would be rounded up and prosecuted under California's new criminal syndicalism law.[36] The bombs were also attributed to the IWDL: Captain John J. O'Meara of the San Francisco police said that the police had information indicating that the IWDL had helped finance the May Day bomb conspiracy, and urged labor unions not to support the IWDL and its "inner circle of anarchists." Captain Matheson, however, told reporters that the San Francisco police were stymied. "We will have to depend now upon the New York authorities for discovery of the men behind the conspiracy, for we haven't a single thing on which to work."[37]

III

Undeterred by the May Day events, the IWDL continued to prepare for the general strike. For months their representatives visited central labor councils and local Mooney defense committees, addressed rallies and labor organizations, and urged unions to participate in the referendum and support the general strike. J. Edward Morgan, Rena Mooney, William D. Patterson of the IWDL in San Francisco, and Norman H. Tallentire, a Leninist carpenter from Denver, were particularly active throughout the East. Except for Chicago, participation in the referendum was disappointingly light, but the thousand union organizations that did respond endorsed the general strike overwhelmingly. The IWDL therefore went ahead with its plans, to the public's alarm.[38] In California, the official organ of the Native Sons and Native Daughters of the Golden West proposed that the radicals be rounded up, the aliens among them deported, and the citizens shot to save the cost of keeping them in prison. The West Coast insurance trade journal proposed that Wobblies be branded on the forehead, and that property owners take out dynamite insurance. Seventh Day Adventists saw the threatened Mooney general strike as one of many cataclysmic events at home and abroad that portended the Second Coming of Christ. And the New York *World* published a macabre description of New York under Soviet dictatorship, ruled by Emma Goldman, Berkman, and Bill Shatoff from the New York Public Library.[39]

In Atlantic City that June, the American Federation of Labor debated the Mooney question more fully than at any of its preceding or subsequent national conventions. Among the delegates were many radicals who had attended the Chicago congress, including James A. Duncan, Anton Johannsen, Ed Hurley, and William D. Patterson; Duncan was their leading spokesman. Although exceedingly vocal, they had little weight in policy making, because voting was weighted in favor of the conservative-led international unions as opposed to the more radical city centrals. (Radical voting strength was at most about one-tenth of the total. Had the convention been more representative of rank-and-file opinion, it would have been greater: in this time of radical ferment, optimism, and activity, in Chicago, the Northwest, the coalfields, the garment industry, it seems likely that radical ideas permeated a third or a fourth of organized labor.)[40] Radical delegates introduced a variety of their favorite proposals: recognition of the Soviet government, withdrawal of troops from Russia, One Big Union, the six-hour day, substitution of May Day for Labor Day, and the Mooney strike.[41] The AFL leaders opposed most of them. Secretary of Labor William B. Wilson urged the convention not to support a Mooney general strike: "no one who belongs to the great masses of our people can afford to undertake to try Mooney by the process of a strike."[42] When the radicals' resolutions were taken up, acrimonious debate and a general uproar ensued. The Mooney strike controversy provided the "real fireworks," with delegates nearly coming to blows over it. Gompers and other organization leaders attacked the strike and the IWDL.[43] The resolutions committee submitted a report repudiating the strike and favoring instead the exertion of every effort "through recognized processes" to bring about a new trial; it also censured the IWDL for having usurped the authority to poll members of international unions. The report was adopted by an overwhelming vote.[44]

Most of the other radical proposals were also rejected. The convention refused to endorse recognition of the Soviet regime, but did urge withdrawal from Russia of American troops. In certain other respects the convention was hardly conservative: most notably, it supported the so-called Plumb Plan for government ownership of the railroads, demanded the removal from office of Postmaster General A. S. Burleson, and attacked the federal courts for granting anti-union injunctions. But for 1919 the general tone was one of caution. "Reason Rules American Labor," stated the New York *Times*: "Under its present officials . . . the Federation is a valuable force for the preservation of our institutions."[45]

The day after the general strike resolution was rejected, the IWDL announced that it would go through with its plans. Eighteen convention delegates published a statement defending the IWDL. Duncan predicted that 60,000 workers would participate in Seattle; Julius Deutelbaum, radical Central Labor Council delegate from Detroit, said that 25,000 would strike there; William D. Patterson said that thousands in California would walk out. There were other signs: Rena Mooney continued to draw sympathetic crowds on her tour through the East; the Detroit Auto Workers voted for the strike; the Washington State Federation of Labor endorsed it; so did the national executive committee of the Socialist Party.[46]

Nevertheless, the general strike movement faltered before July 4, as it became increasingly evident that the movement was insufficiently general. Even in Chicago and Seattle enthusiasm declined. In Chicago, Nockels indicated that the strike for Mooney would be combined with demands for city employees—including policemen—who were considering a strike for better wages; in Seattle only two-fifths of the local unions voted for participation. William Z. Foster, whose AFL committee was organizing for the steel strike, refused to be sidetracked. And Anton Johannsen, IWDL manager in Chicago and one of the strike's key organizers, declared that it should be postponed for lack of support, and quit the post and the program.[47]

IV

The futility of the general strike cause was predictable at the time, even from newspaper items. Nevertheless, fear of the impending event spread. A rumor circulated that July 4 would mark the beginning of the Bolshevik revolution in America.

The origin of this rumor appears to have been an article in the New York *Evening Mail* on May 14 by Rheta Childe Dorr, a former Socialist, suffragist, labor-reform journalist, and war correspondent, who had visited Russia for three months in 1917 and written superficially about the revolution ("Another thing Russia needs is the soda fountain").[48] Miss Dorr alleged that hundreds of radical agents were organizing the strike in every city and industry throughout the nation, that public school teachers and newspapers in nearly every language were spreading strike propaganda. It was to be the first Bolshevist demonstration, "a beginning of revolution," and if successful, "the slogan, 'All the power to the Soviets,' will be raised here as it was in Russia in July, 1917." The plans had been formulated by the Socialists and IWW's at the Chicago Mooney Congress; information about the conspiracy abounded in propaganda literature and at public lectures, she said, quoting extensively from the *Liberator*: "I am taking Crystal Eastman's word for it."[49]

When Miss Dorr's article appeared, the New York City Central Federated Union challenged the writer and the *Evening Mail* to produce "the least tithe of evidence" in support of her predictions. There was no response. By early June other newspapers were playing up the story of a gigantic Red plot to terrorize the nation on July 4 and to attempt the "destruction of civilization."[50] These rumors took on ominous substance: on June 2 the residence of Attorney General Palmer in Washington was damaged by the explosion of a bomb, set off by an unknown person who was blown to bits in the blast.[51] Homes of prominent men in eight other eastern cities, including that of the mayor of Cleveland, as well as a Catholic church in Philadelphia, were also dynamited.[52] These depradations heightened expectations of violence on July 4; further explosions were forecast. In Philadelphia, the supposed home town of Palmer's bomber, the police issued orders for the arrest of persons publicizing the July 4 strike.[53] The IWDL protested against "this sensational newspaper-invented 'reign of terror' that is now being screamed about in the press." But the fears were given official sanction by the Department of Justice, which alleged that a third series of bombings was scheduled for July 4.[54]

The Department of Justice claimed to have secret information of such a conspiracy. Although the Bureau of Investigation subsequently dropped the claim, there was more to it than that. The department was under pressure to solve the recent bombings, and its new head, A. Mitchell Palmer, was politically ambitious. Moreover, his own appointment had not yet been confirmed, and he was under fire in the Senate.[55] The department had previously requested a Congressional appropriation of $1,500,000; on June 12 Palmer asked the House

Appropriations Committee for an additional half-million dollars to combat the anarchists behind the recent bombings.[56] At the same time a report circulated that the department had inside information of a band of terrorists based in Chicago who were planning to explode bombs in more than twenty large cities on July 4. A few hours later, nine hand grenades were found in a coal car in Chicago. The Chicago police chief said they might have been part of the intended July 4 demonstration, but also said he doubted that a terrorist conspiracy existed in his city.[57]

The Department of Justice set about expanding and reorganizing the Bureau of Investigation in anticipation of a $2,000,000 Congressional grant. The Republican House Steering Committee was not sympathetic, however, and following its instructions, the Republicans on the Appropriations Committee cut the appropriation for the Bureau to $1,400,000. Officials of the department protested vociferously. The department renewed its appeal and carried the fight to the public. Palmer's testimony before the Appropriations Committee was released, and the press seized upon a statement in it that the Department of Justice knew almost positively that "on a certain day in the future, which we have been advised of, there will be another serious and probably much larger effort . . . to rise up and destroy the Government at one fell swoop."[58] The plot, Palmer had said, was nationwide, and the Department of Justice hoped to prevent as well as punish revolutionary crimes. He had named no date. William Flynn, the recently appointed chief of the Bureau of Investigation, alluding to the plot, disclaimed knowledge that it was set for Independence Day; but the New York *World* named July 4 as "the date most generally accepted." Flynn said police were taking all precautions for that day.[59] Another Department of Justice official, Francis P. Garvan, testifying before the Senate Appropriations Committee a few days later, declared that an organized nationwide effort to overthrow the government was under way, and that conditions were particularly serious in New York, Chicago, and Paterson, New Jersey. Asked whether an outbreak of bombing was planned for July 4, he replied, "There is a great deal of talk to that effect."[60]

Thus the July 4 scare was official. The public was offered no specific evidence, but its apprehensions were reinforced by news reports of the Winnipeg general strike, allegedly supported with Bolshevik funds from Chicago, and by an impending general strike in France.[61] The American Defense Society and the National Security League

helped spread the July 4 scare with warnings of "anarchist mass terror."[62] Arthur Guy Empey, war veteran and author of *Over the Top*,
recommended that the July 4 "attempt at revolution" be met with
force.[63] In San Quentin, Mooney denounced the scare as the propaganda of big business.[64]

William Flynn put his Bureau's views before a conference of police
chiefs from a number of eastern and midwestern cities on June 29.
They met in New York to discuss cooperative measures to track down
bombers and revolutionists. He assured the officers that the bomb
plotters of early June would be found, and was assured in return of
the assistance of police departments. In the next few days most of the
departments represented took strenuous measures to thwart the anticipated July 4 outbreak. The Chicago chief, though still skeptical, denied parade permits, canceled police furloughs, and supplemented the
regular force with volunteers; two infantry companies were brought
into the city. Seventeen more unidentified hand grenades were found
in the first days of July. (Nevertheless, two practical jokers in the Chicago detective bureau rigged up a dummy bomb and left it in the
office for their chief!) In Philadelphia the full police force was on duty.
In New York all policemen were under orders for emergency duty,
and regiments of the state guard were called to their armories; a patriotic meeting in Carnegie Hall was canceled for fear of violence. A few
people even left town to avoid the bloodshed. On July 2, Flynn declared that the Department of Justice had no reason to anticipate any
nationwide bomb plot, but the sorcerer's apprentice could not stop
the flood.[65]

Police departments of western cities, which had not participated
in Flynn's conference, escaped the July 4 jitters. California newspapers represented the bomb plot scare as an eastern affair. Although
the Oakland police seized half a dozen radicals under the new criminal syndicalism law, Oakland had no bomb scare. In San Francisco,
when two small boys found some sticks of dynamite hidden in a park,
Captain Matheson said that the dynamite had probably been hidden
by robbers.[66]

The Fourth of July passed quietly. In Chicago, Mooney protest
rallies were held in vacant lots; one revolutionary orator was hauled
off in a patrol wagon. The hottest Fourth on record drove New Yorkers to the beaches and left the pavements to the police. In the whole
country only two explosions were reported: a pay office in Butte and
a colliery engine in Wilkes-Barre were dynamited. The Department

of Justice claimed that the absence of outrages was due to widespread publicity, but as the *Nation* pointed out, that claim would have been more impressive had the authorities caught the miscreants of the May 1 and June 2 bombings.[67]

As for the scope of the general strike, no one could say on a holiday how the numbers stood. And since the 4th was a Friday, the picture did not take shape until the 7th: in Chicago a few thousand were out; in New York, a few garment workers; in Butte and Peoria, some miners, but the Butte effort was an acknowledged failure; in Seattle and Detroit the central labor councils had backed down at the last minute, and only a handful of workers were out. Minneapolis unions switched to a "Mooney Protest Picnic." The general strike was a fiasco.[68]

On July 19 Congress appropriated $1,600,000 for the hunting and prosecuting of radicals. The grant helped make possible the arrest and deportation of many Reds that winter, including Emma Goldman and Alexander Berkman.[69]

The Mooney case as a national, radical cause declined sharply in the remaining months of 1919. As the Red Scare moved into high gear with the great eastern strikes and radical deportations, the Mooney issue subsided, leaving its mark in prejudices and anxieties. Not for a decade or more was it to attract so much national attention again.

For several months Rena Mooney continued on a national tour, drawing large and sympathetic crowds. John L. Lewis introduced her at the national convention of the United Mine Workers. In most of her speeches she said little or nothing about another general strike.[70] The IWDL still wanted the second strike, planned after the Chicago Mooney Congress, but the prospects were hopeless. It postponed the Labor Day general strike for a month and then canceled it. A handful of Seattle workers who struck anyway were fired for "irregularity."[71]

The IWDL itself was on the skids. Weakened by its own grandiose schemes, despised alike by conservative labor and the left wing, it never drew much attention again. In the changing times it offered neither chauvinism nor left-wing militancy. A rival organization, the Labor Defense League, was set up in San Francisco during the summer of 1919 by the left wing to defend Californians accused of criminal syndicalism; David Milder, formerly of the IWDL, was its president, and Charlotte Anita Whitney, of the new Communist Labor Party, its treasurer.[72] The old patterns of radicalism were fading. The

Socialist movement was rent by Communism, the IWW by prosecutions in Chicago and Centralia, Washington. The new Communist movement had its own way of doing things; the Communists regarded the Mooney case as a useful piece of class-war evidence.

V

The Mooney case in 1919 was also part of the anti-radical crusade in Congress. The Department of Labor, and particularly the United States Employment Service, came under attack that summer for alleged radical sympathies. The USES smacked too much of postwar Socialism and public welfare for conservatives and private employment agencies. Congress had cut off virtually all funds for the USES in the spring, but the Employment Service was still in existence, and the pending Kenyon-Nolan bill might have rescued it. To head this off, its opponents brandished the Densmore Report on the Mooney case, for John B. Densmore was the USES chief. Democratic Congressman Thomas L. Blanton of Texas led the attack.

Blanton was an eccentric, petty demagogue, who had come to the House in 1917 from a Congressional district that extended 566 miles from Mineral Springs across the Pecos River to El Paso. John Nance Garner described him later as "a disgrace to the House and a humiliation to the State of Texas."[73] He was a buffoon who eventually exasperated his colleagues with his charges of Congressional graft and salary grabs, a fist fight in a committee hearing, and demands for roll calls before the chaplain's prayers; in 1921 he was formally and unanimously censured for inserting profanity into the *Congressional Record*.[74] But in 1919 he was building a reputation as an outspoken enemy of radicalism and organized labor.

Blanton denounced Gompers, William B. Wilson, and Densmore in the House that summer for defending the anarchist Mooney; he called the Densmore Report a frame-up, and charged that Densmore had wasted thousands of dollars trying to release Mooney from California law. He blamed the recent bombing atrocities on the labor unions, and connected Rena Mooney with the dynamiting of Palmer's residence. Through his efforts the Densmore Report was published by the government and widely circulated. By stressing Densmore's connection with Mooney, Blanton kept up his pressure on the Department of Labor. His charges were spread by such organizations as the National Association of Manufacturers, and in the end the anti-labor forces successfully administered the *coup de grace* to the dying Employment Service.[75]

In and out of Congress, 1919 was a good year for anti-Red rumors. Professional patriots helped spread them. One who specialized in the Mooney case was a Philadelphia broker and Union League member, Francis Ralston Welsh, who had investigated subversive activities for the Department of Justice during the war. Welsh's pamphlet, "America's Greatest Peril: The Bolsheviki and the Mooney Case," was published early in the year and circulated by the American Protective League.[76] Among Welsh's many fictions was one of the most preposterous of all the myths of the Mooney case, that Leon Trotsky had been Mooney's companion in San Francisco. Welsh sent his pamphlet to Blanton, who spread the story in the House of Representatives and inserted the pamphlet, Trotsky and all—except for a libelous passage on United States Tariff Commissioner William Kent—in the *Congressional Record*. Welsh claimed later that it was he who had inspired Blanton to investigate the Densmore Report.[77] As for Trotsky, he had in fact remained in and about New York during his brief visit to the United States in 1917. It appears that a Russian immigrant named Trotsky ran a movie house on Kearny Street in San Francisco from 1912 to 1914; imagination took over from there. Welsh must have picked up the tale from Fickert, for the dictaphone transcript of the Densmore Report shows that Fickert had talked about Trotsky and had corresponded with Welsh before Welsh's pamphlet appeared.[78] Fickert to Welsh to Blanton: it did not take much to set absurdities into national circulation. But as Fremont Older said, "There isn't any tolerance to speak of, there isn't any humor where humor is most needed."[79] The nation, Walter Lippmann observed, was suffering from a case of bad nerves.[80]

Fickert ran for reelection as District Attorney in the fall of 1919. The campaign was uneventful. He was handicapped by a long and critical illness, involving an operation for a spinal tumor, from which he recuperated slowly. Reports on his progress conflicted as the election approached. His opponent was Judge Matthew Brady of the municipal police court. The issues and alliances differed little from those of earlier elections, except that the declining Union Labor Party endorsed Brady rather than Fickert. Fickert had the endorsement of the Civic League and the *Chronicle*.[81] His platform was anti-radicalism: "My position is unchanged." A week before the election he announced that he was sitting up, and would soon be resuming the battle against Reds and dynamiters.[82] But he lost: Brady received 47,000 to Fickert's 40,000 votes. Chester Rowell attributed the outcome to the revelations about Fickert published in the Densmore Report.[83]

A week after the election Fickert returned home from the sanitorium. His retirement from office occasioned little rancor from either side. For several years he remained a popular figure in San Francisco. Early in 1921 it was rumored that he might be appointed United States Attorney in San Francisco after Harding's inauguration, with the support of such prominent Republicans as Herbert Hoover and David Starr Jordan; but if such an effort was made, nothing came of it.[84] In 1923 Fickert ran again for District Attorney against Brady and was overwhelmed, 71,000 to 27,000.[85] He subsequently moved to Los Angeles, and for a number of years practiced law there in obscurity, from which he occasionally emerged to defend his record in the Mooney case.

CHAPTER TWENTY-ONE

New Discoveries and Eclipse, 1920-1927

> *Q. You testified against these men, knowing they*
> *were charged with a capital offense?*
> *A. Yes, sir.*
> *Q. And lied, and lied, and lied, and lied, is that*
> *right?*
> *A. Yes.* —McDonald testimony, 1930
>
> *Blessed be McDonald. I hope he lives for six gen-*
> *erations, grows a patriarchal beard, and develops*
> *a real conscience.*
> —Letter to Mary Gallagher

THE DEFEAT of Fickert in 1919 gave Mooney's friends new hope. They looked forward to Brady. Documents might be unearthed in the District Attorney's office that would further expose Fickert's methods; Brady might intercede with the Governor; a new trial might at last be arranged on one of the remaining indictments.

In the last few days before leaving office, Fickert and his staff sought to have these indictments dismissed. "We would not have time to try any of these indictments," said Cunha. "I have had plenty of trouble with my good friends over this case, and I don't want to have any more. . . . I believe a new trial would be a farce."[1] At Mooney's request Maxwell McNutt objected to the dismissals, but he was unsuccessful save in Griffin's court: Griffin agreed to retain one indictment each against Mooney and Billings, in the event that a new trial might some day be possible. The rest were dismissed.[2]

Fickert's entire staff left office with him. "Brady is a good politician," said one of the departing clerks with a laugh. "He is cleaning out one bunch of crooks and putting in a new bunch of crooks."[3] The cynicism was unwarranted. Brady's new staff included Milton T. U'Ren, an associate of Progressive reformers Francis J. Heney and William Kent; Joseph T. O'Connor, one of Brady's political sponsors; and Isador Golden, a close friend and supporter of Hiram Johnson and formerly a justice of the peace.[4] Encouraged, the IWDL started a movement at once to persuade Brady to grant Mooney a new trial. "The opinion is that he is on the square," said Nolan.[5] Rena Mooney and others circulated petitions to prod the new District Attorney. In May 40,000 signatures were presented to him at the Hall of Justice by a large delegation. There the matter rested for six months.[6]

Presenting the petitions was the IWDL's last action for Mooney. The organization disbanded shortly thereafter. It had been hampered by enmities arising from the Chicago Mooney Congress, and for a year it had accomplished little in the way of propaganda.[*] Mooney had grandiose publicity ideas, which Nolan evidently disapproved; he also had a tendency to alienate those who worked for him by ordering them around. Hence mutual dissatisfaction had arisen.

Mooney reorganized his old Molders Defense Committee and put his wife in charge. For several years thereafter she was the defense organization's secretary-treasurer, the successor to Robert Minor and Ed Nolan, who had both left the defense group.[7] Mooney's grand design was to publish a journal, *Tom Mooney's Monthly*, which would renew publicity on the case, assail his enemies, and serve more generally as a militant organ of nonsectarian radicalism. It commenced publication in August 1920, achieved a circulation of 7,000–13,000 or more, and lasted for nearly three years. It helped, as Nockels said, "to keep up the agitation." Mooney supervised it as best he could from prison. Rena Mooney, Schulberg, and other friends assisted outside. Among the heaviest subscribers were the mid-western coal miners. Subscriptions were sold at labor meetings and Mooney rallies by field representatives of the defense committee; thousands of copies were given away. Low as publication costs were, they exceeded the journal's income and strained the finances of the defense committee. After a year of publication $1,400 was due the printer, and on at least one occasion there was no money to mail the latest issue.[8]

The most remarkable thing about *Tom Mooney's Monthly*, after the fact of its existence, was that it regularly had new developments in the case to publicize. For a string of unexpected events occurred, beginning in the fall of 1920, that bolstered Mooney's claims of innocence and intensified the demands for his freedom.

---

[*] Rena Mooney to S. A. Nelson, October 17, 1922, Mooney Papers. In the Northwest the radicals had refused to contribute funds for Mooney to the IWDL, but formed their own Mooney defense committee. They collected nearly $10,000 and spent all but $900 of it on salaries and expenses. (Rena Mooney [?] to T. Wright, May 16, 1921, Mooney Papers.)

II

One day in November 1920, Officer Draper Hand of the San Francisco Police Department went to Mayor Rolph, at the instigation of Fremont Older, with a remarkable story about his own part in the bomb cases.* According to Hand, who had been assigned during the cases to handle prosecution witnesses, Oxman had never seen Weinberg's jitney until Hand showed it to him:

Swanson sent for me and asked me to take Oxman to the North End station and show him Weinberg's auto. They had taken the car out there. . . . I took Oxman to see the car. It was his first and only sight of the car. . . . Oxman was very much concerned, when he saw the car, to find out if it were possible for a man to sit in it and hold a suitcase as he was going to describe in court. He had me get in the car and let my hand hang down over the side, as if I were holding a suitcase. He wan't satisfied till I got in and did as he wanted; after that he thought his version was all right— that the defense wouldn't prove it impossible. . . .

There wasn't any license plate on the car when I took Oxman to see it. . . . If the plate had been there it would be bad for the prosecution if Oxman were asked if he hadn't got the number when he saw the car at the police station. Cunha had had the plate taken off that car. It was in a drawer in an inner office at the station. Cunha told me to copy the number. I did that and gave it to him. As far as I know Oxman never saw the license plate itself.

Hand said that he had had to bolster up John McDonald when he was "on the verge of breaking down":

McDonald said to me, "Unless I get a job I'm going to spill everything to Fremont Older."

I went to Lieutenant Goff and warned him to arrange a job of some kind for McDonald. Then he was given a job—in Tracy or somewhere in the interior of the state.

He didn't tell everything then, but I'm sure that he'd tell the truth if he were brought here now.

---

* Hand's motive for going to Rolph is not clear. Hand said later that Older offered him no inducement other than his conscience. Older had known something of Hand's story for a year or more. He persuaded him to tell it fully at this time in order to prevent the appointment of Captain Duncan Matheson as the new police chief. Matheson had been closely associated with the bomb prosecution, and Hand's story reflected very unfavorably on him. (Hand testimony, California Supreme Court, "Habeas Corpus," XI: 6816–17, 6888, 6890, 6916. See also Mary Gallagher to Traverse Clements, February 11, 1929, in ACLU Papers, v. 371.)

The Edeaus, Hand said, he took to the prison, where he pointed out Mooney and Weinberg.

When I first met Mrs. Edeau and her daughter, they told me they had seen nothing at all—absolutely nothing—that would help the prosecution. The bomb bureau had located them and had sent me to talk to them. I went back and told what the women had said. But the bureau wasn't satisfied with that. Matheson wasn't satisfied till he had their identification of the prisoners.

Hand also alleged that Brennan had quarreled with Matheson over some of the evidence; that Matheson had accused Brennan of selling out to the defense; and that Brennan "smelt a rat in the Oxman story before Oxman came here."[9]

Older published Hand's story in the *Call,* and other papers took it up. The *Chronicle* was scornful: "San Francisco has had so many 'Mooney frame-up' stories that this one told by Hand is causing more mirth than excitement, and the general impression appears to be that the only 'frame-up' in the case is a frame-up on the public."[10]

Hand's most important allegation, that Oxman got the number of the jitney license from the authorities, cast new light on statements made by Ed Rigall and Officer Steve Bunner to the grand jury in 1917. Rigall had testified that he and Oxman were shown Weinberg's jitney together and that Oxman examined the plates closely.[11] Bunner had testified:

Oxman said one afternoon that he would like to go out and see the automobile, and I made an appointment with him. . . . I went out to the North End Police Station to where Weinberg's machine was, and there both men looked over the machine very carefully and looked at the two tags that was on it containing the number of the machine, that is, the state license number, it was on two tags. I then left them and went into the North End Station noticing the jitney tags and license and permit was off. I asked the station keeper what became of the jitney tags, license and permit. He said "We have them here." I said "Let me see them." He brought them out and I was looking at them. As I was looking at them in came Oxman and Regall [*sic*], and either one of them picked up the City and County license permit.

Bunner had also testified that he did not notice Oxman making any notations there.[12]

Matheson at once denied Hand's charges. "It looks as if Mr. Hand might be flirting with the penitentiary, unless the statute of limitations lets him out of a perjury charge." McDonald was in the East, Matheson said, but he refused details: "Every effort has been made to get McDonald out of the way, by certain persons interested in the defense."[13]

At a police inquiry the next day Hand denied or withdrew some of the statements attributed to him in the *Call*. He repudiated in particular the sentence, "It was his [Oxman's] first and only sight of the car," which, he explained, had been only his inference; he could not have sworn to it. But he stuck to the charge that Oxman obtained the license number from the prosecution, and confirmed many other essentials.[14] The Police Department reacted by bringing formal charges against Hand for filing false reports, neglect of duty, and conduct unbecoming an officer. (The department held that officially it was still investigating the Preparedness Day crime, and therefore that Hand's unauthorized public comments were improper.) Matheson drew up the charges and submitted them to the new police chief, Daniel C. O'Brien. They were heard by the Board of Police Commissioners in 1921 and were eventually dismissed.[15]

Hand never gave his story under oath. Mooney asked him later to put it in an affidavit, "and he beat around the bush for some time and finally said No."[16] In 1924 Matheson became a supporter of Mooney's freedom, and Hand's story was dropped by the defense committee "as a matter of courtesy."[17] Hand eventually fell on evil days. After two additional charges of conduct unbecoming an officer, he resigned in 1925. Six years later he was indicted for grand theft and put on probation. (The judge who took Hand's bail remarked to Mooney on a visit to San Quentin, "None of them that had anything to do with your case have ever had any luck.") Mooney himself came to believe that Hand was "a ruthless, unscrupulous scoundrel."[18]

Hand's accusations, however, prompted other disclosures to the defense in the six months after his visit to Rolph. Brennan was the first to speak his mind. The day after Hand's story came out, he was interviewed by Edgar T. Gleeson for the *Call*. Brennan was in a reflective mood. He said that had he been a juror in Billings's trial, he would not have voted for conviction: "The chain of evidence was not complete." He denied that he had been a party to any fraud, regardless of what Hand might have done, but he regretted his own part in the case:

Like all prosecutors, I was blind to all but the pursuit—the chase which would end with the conviction of my quarry.

.   .   .

Unconsciously, and with no wrong intent, the prosecutor retains the facts which further his case. Others, perhaps vital to the proof of innocence of the accused, are cast aside. He is a keen-scented hound on a trail. He has become obsessed with his case. Given the slightest evidence supporting his theories, which he has already framed in his own mind, he weaves these into a web of circumstances which are ofttimes damning to the accused, and against which even the innocent may not be able to stand.

Witnesses whose testimony is wholly false or founded on little fact can make almost any case for such a prosecutor. The fair minded district attorney constantly has to guard against them.

I would say that, as a general rule, no man wants to put an innocent person in prison. The prosecutor's motives can not in a majority of cases be questioned.

But he is biased toward conviction, and this is uppermost in his mind. Every public prosecutor wants to make a record. He sees as his goal political preferment, applause of his constituents, his personal aggrandizement. This can be gained only by conviction of the accused, against whom the public mind in sensational cases has already been poisoned.

.   .   .

The case has been a nightmare since the date of the trial. My motives have been misconstrued, and in view of my own personal doubt as to the guilt of Billings, I regard it as an evil day in my life that I was given charge of the prosecution.*

Following the statements of Hand and Brennan, Mooney appealed to Brady and Griffin for a new trial. Brady said he was powerless to act; he could not prosecute Mooney in good conscience. "We could not use the old witnesses, and moreover, I have no confidence in their credibility."[19] The case was up to the Governor. But Griffin declined to appeal to him again: "I have said everything to the governor that I can say."[20] Shortly afterward Brady announced that he would take the case to the grand jury for a thorough investigation.[21]

The grand jury met at the end of the month and heard the testi-

* As quoted, *Call*, November 13, 1920. In 1930 Brennan testified that Gleeson had garbled this account, but Gleeson responded that Brennan had never complained of it to him or to the *Call*: "At that time Brennan thought that this was a way out for him." (Brennan testimony, California Supreme Court, "In re Billings," II: 1069–70, 1075–76; Gleeson testimony, *ibid.*, III: 1898, 1900.) Brennan acknowledged later that Gleeson was "probably one of the most respected men of the newspaper fraternity." (California Supreme Court, "Habeas Corpus," XVI: 10,383.)

mony of a single witness. W. H. Taylor, a crippled old sailor, had come to Brady a few days earlier with a story that he had been at Steuart and Market streets shortly before the bomb exploded, and that he had sat on a suitcase and been shooed off by "a big man, apparently a Mexican." He testified that he had tried to tell this to the prosecution soon after the explosion, but that no attention was paid to him, and that when he went to court as a spectator during Billings's trial, he was taken out and sent home to Stockton.[22]

The investigation was adjourned. Two months later a delegation of churchmen interviewed Brady in an effort to prod him, but nothing further happened until the appearance of John McDonald.[23]

III

John McDonald had never received the reward that was to have taken him back east on the cushions. In October 1919 he returned to Baltimore anyway, and later moved to Trenton. Late in 1920 Bourke Cockran, having learned that McDonald was no longer in California, wrote Ed Nockels to suggest that he look for him. California law set a three-year limit on prosecution for perjury; with the expiration of this limit, McDonald might have something to say. Nockels agreed. "We had secured the Oxman letters of one witness, then it was our idea that it would be well to look up the others," he said later.[24] He circularized local labor organizations and sent out to them about a thousand photographs of McDonald. He made personal investigations in cities from St. Louis to Baltimore, "wherever we got a lead." Meanwhile, Cockran heard that McDonald was living at a certain hotel in Trenton and working as a strikebreaker. Nockels went there, secretly identified McDonald, and about January 1, 1921, assigned a friend from the Chicago Federation of Labor, Jack Johnston, to observe him and "see if he said anything about the Mooney case." The Federation paid Johnston his expenses and about $5 a day. Several times a week he reported to Nockels, who was in New York. For a month or two he had nothing conclusive to pass along.[25]

McDonald had not forgotten about the case. In May 1920 he had written Matheson asking about the unpaid reward. After Johnston's arrival he wrote Matheson again, on January 11, 1921:

Well Capt. what is all the fuss about Mooney again   I just seen a little peice in the paper it said Draper Hand told Rolph that he knew it was a frame up, has Draper Hand gone crazy, I will say if I was on my death bed and the last words from me, would be that he is guilty, and that what I swore to was nothing but the truth, and I am willing to take the stand tomorrow and swear to the same things Do you think Brady will open up the other case against him. If they want me they can get me any time, and I will swear to what I swore before, the truth.[26]

Matheson attributed the letter to all the newspaper publicity.[27]

Several weeks later Johnston called Nockels to report that McDonald had made a full confession, and would come to New York to sign an affidavit for Bourke Cockran.[28] It was a sudden shift for McDonald. Said Matheson later: "I couldn't understand why he would write me this kind of a letter, and then later, within a month, change his story completely, unless somebody, as we say, was 'working on him.' "[29] McDonald himself explained in 1930 that he had become deathly ill one night and had wished to make a "death bed" confession to his friend Max Kesselman, the proprietor of the hotel.[30] Kesselman corroborated this:

... he became very ill one night and called for me. I called for a doctor and gave him all the attention I could. He looked to me to be in a very dangerous condition. . . . During the night he told me he had something on his mind which he had never told to any person yet.

. . .

He said the reason he wanted to tell me was that this had been on his mind for a long time and it worried him always. He said that he was afraid that he might die in one of these attacks that he had and the men would remain in prison forever.[31]

(McDonald said that he could not remember whether the night of the "deathbed" confession was before or after January 11! "I was sick practically all the time.")[32] Kesselman told his nephew, an attorney, about McDonald's confession, and the nephew called Cockran's office.[33]

Shortly thereafter McDonald accompanied Johnston to New York. Since Cockran was out of town, they went to Frank Walsh's office, and there he made his confession. "I told Mr. Walsh I wanted to make a clean breast of it. . . . So he says 'Is this the truth.' I told him it was. . . . And he said 'All right.' So they called the Secretary in to sit down there and take my statement."[34] In this affidavit McDonald stated that he had seen a man set down a suitcase on Steuart Street and talk with another man in front of the saloon, but that "I could not identify the man"; that when he went to headquarters at the urging of a friendly policeman, Fickert said to him, "Do you know Tom Mooney?" "He is the —————— we want. He is a dynamiter." "We want you to stay around where we can get you any time, because I want the lieutenant to show you Mooney." He stated that Lieutenant Goff took him to Mooney's cell ("I had no recollection of ever having seen the man before, and of course could not have identified him"); that Goff also showed him Billings, whom he likewise did not recognize; that Fickert said, "Now Mac, we'll take good care of you; we'll pay for your hotel expenses," and "I will see that you get the biggest slice of the reward." He said that Fickert repeatedly coached him in his testimony, and that Cunha had also coached him:

About a week before the trial of Thomas J. Mooney, Assistant District Attorney Ed Cunha sent for me and I went into his private office. He read over the testimony which I had given in the Billings trial. He said to me: "You had better make the time that you saw the man set the suitcase at 1:30 instead of 1:50." I said to him: "Mr. McNutt will grab that right away; he will see that I changed my testimony from what it was in the Billings trial."

He said, "Oh, hell, we will beat him on that. You can say that you were not positive about it at the time of the first trial." He said, "You see, if that suitcase was set at 1:30 that would give them time to get back up Mission street on top of the Eilers' building". . . .

I followed the instruction of Mr. Cunha, and said that I was not positive, that it might be between 1:30 and 1:45.[35]

Walsh believed that McDonald had finally told the truth.[36]

The affidavit, published in the *Call*, created a stir. Fickert denounced it. Goff challenged McDonald to show that he had attempted to influence witnesses' identifications. Matheson released McDonald's letter of January 11 and accused him of perjury. Only Brennan—whom McDonald had not impugned—suggested that the convictions might have been unsound.[37]

Brady announced that every effort would be made to bring McDonald to San Francisco to appear before the grand jury. That was what the defense wanted. Nockels made the necessary arrangements: with funds from the Chicago Federation of Labor, he bought a round-trip ticket for McDonald, who was to be accompanied by Johnston, and gave each of them $500 for expenses.[38] Nockels later explained:

"I estimated that probably it would consume all of two months time and I thought that was a reasonable amount for expense." He did not say why he thought that so much time would be needed, or why McDonald should have received his expenses in a lump sum before departure. To McDonald the sum must have looked very large. It had the earmarks of a bribe.[39]

McDonald and Johnston left at once. They detrained at Sacramento and, accompanied by two *Call* reporters, motored to San Jose, where McDonald remained in seclusion while arrangements were being made for the grand jury hearing.[40]

The next few days were filled with confusion. It developed that because McDonald had left California before the end of the three-year period during which he might have been prosecuted for perjury in the bomb cases, the statute of limitations did not yet apply to him. Therefore a guarantee of immunity was demanded. Brady was willing to give it but the grand jury was divided. Newspapermen noted that William McNevin, the foreman of Mooney's trial jury, was openly boasting in the corridors of the Hall of Justice that thirteen members of the grand jury were ready to indict McDonald. The jurors finally decided that they would not indict McDonald for what he had said in 1917, but that they reserved the right to indict him for what he might say now.[41] Said the jury foreman: "If the threat of prosecution is removed there would be no object in having a witness take an oath before testifying before the grand jury." The jurors wanted to hear McDonald, he said, but "saw no use in taking his testimony if he were not bound to tell the truth on the stand."[42] Brady pointed out that immunity did not bind them to believe McDonald; but the grand jurors felt that the exemption of one witness would entitle others to the same privilege, and that the hearing would degenerate into a debate for the sole benefit of the press.[43]

Rena Mooney, who had been awaiting McDonald's appearance hopefully, went home from the courthouse crushed and dispirited. There was nothing left to do. McDonald returned to Baltimore. Brady expressed his regrets and blamed the grand jury. Matheson declared that if McDonald had lied in the bomb trials, Mooney and Billings should be free and McDonald in jail: "The police department, the district attorney and the court can not tolerate a man's coming into court under oath and swearing away the liberty and life of another man. I never put much faith in Oxman. McDonald was the chief witness."[44] McDonald remained in Baltimore. Nine years later he would be called back to San Francisco on better terms.

IV

The Mooney case in 1921—as in years afterward—had a professional fascination for attorneys. Widely known and immensely complex, the case lay beyond their reach. It defied the old legal maxim, recognized in California law, that for every wrong there was a remedy. If one believed the principle, a solution had to exist that lay within the power of the courts. It seemed that one had only to find the key— the motion or writ that the courts would recognize as a legitimate basis for reopening the case. The key was not *coram nobis*; that had been tried. It appeared not to be a federal writ of *habeas corpus*; as Bourke Cockran pointed out, the United States Supreme Court had ruled in the Leo Frank case six years earlier that after the state courts had held that a trial was fair, their decision was not subject to federal review.[45] Cockran said California would never be a civilized state while Mooney was denied a new trial, but he could not suggest how such a trial might be arranged.[46]

A San Francisco attorney named Byron C. Parker had an idea. He took it to Mooney, who authorized Parker to act as his attorney. Not long after the McDonald episode had closed, Parker went to court and asked for an old and obscure common law writ called *audita querela*.[47]

The traditional purpose of *audita querela* ("the complaint having been heard") was to quash a judgment already issued, on the basis of a defense that had arisen after the judgment. According to Blackstone it was "a writ of a most remedial nature, and seems to have been invented, lest in any case there should be an oppressive defect of justice, where a party, who hath a good defence, is too late to make it in the ordinary forms of law."[48] Most states, including California, made no statutory provision for its use, and its use was negligible. Among lawyers it was perhaps the least known of any of the common law writs still available under modern legal practice in the United States. Parker could not find any precedent for its use in California, or for its use in a criminal case in any state.[49] His motion was said to have been the first of its kind ever made in a San Francisco court. Understandably, Brady's first response was that he did not know whether Parker's writ was good law.[50]

Argument was held in May before Superior Judge Harold Louderback. Parker, accompanied by Thomas P. Wickes, appeared for Mooney; Milton T. U'Ren appeared for the District Attorney's office. In an unusual arrangement Mooney was permitted to attend. Tanned and graying, dressed in a business suit, and handcuffed, he was brought by limousine and ferry from San Quentin to the Hall of Justice. ("It was good seeing the bay and the city again," he told reporters.)[51] Parker and Wickes held that Mooney had been wronged by perjury and conspiracy to commit fraud on the part of McDonald, Oxman, the Edeaus, Swanson, Fickert, and members of his staff and of the police force; that in the absence of a statutory remedy, the defendant was entitled to go to the common law; that the court had the authority to issue the writ; and that it should do so in order that Mooney's sentence be vacated and he be retried.

U'Ren responded that although fraud and conspiracy to defraud might have been committed, the writ was not available and the court had no authority to grant it. The issues, he said, were the same as those passed upon when Mooney applied for the writ of *coram nobis*; the state's Penal Code provided a complete system of jurisprudence, and therefore common law remedies were not available in California: "the District Attorney and the Court must take the law as they find it; neither the District Attorney nor the Court is the Legislature or the Governor."[52] U'Ren contended that the remedy lay with the Governor. Wickes replied:

We have gone to the Governor. The Governor has said, "Stay there in San Quentin for the rest of your natural life." It is no remedy to go to some official and say, "Please do this as a favor." If there is a remedy for every wronged person, including Mooney, we are entitled to a remedy which the courts can enforce. . . . The remedy we are entitled to is the remedy of acquittal.

· · ·

Remedies are only enforceable through the instrumentality of courts of justice. He [Mooney] cannot enforce a remedy of acquittal from the Governor. The Governor has no more right to acquit him than you[r] Honor has a right to pardon him.[53]

U'Ren countered:

Counsel seems to think that the term "remedy" means successful litigation. . . . Remedy just merely means an opportunity of presenting the matter and having it passed upon, and the courts have held that the Governor in entertaining applications of this kind is ex judicio. . . . Because the Governor did not extend a pardon does not mean that there is no remedy. . . . It may be that no successful remedy lies.

· · ·

MR. WICKES: I say that the result of this case shows that the Governor is capable of capricious and arbitrary action in this case, and in going to the Governor for a remedy in the case there is no remedy at all.[54]

The issuing of the writ, said U'Ren, would establish a precedent that would flood the courts with petitions and swing open the prison gates for the guilty as well as the innocent. The rules of law might seem harsh, but they existed because somewhere there had to be an end to litigation.[55]

Judge Louderback, like Griffin before him, believed that his hands were tied. He said that he would have granted the application had he been able, but that he lacked the power. The only course open, he said, was to apply for executive clemency.[56] Parker appealed the decision. The matter was still pending in May 1922, when Mooney requested that it be dropped in favor of a pardon appeal.[57]

V

One of the witnesses whom the defense had intended to call, had the writ of *audita querela* been granted, was Earl Hatcher.

Hatcher had remained loyally silent throughout Oxman's trial for subornation of perjury. Sometime during the following year he asked Oxman for a $10,000 loan. Oxman replied in July 1918 that he could not help, that he had suffered losses on cattle shipments and had no more credit in California. He offered a tip on hogs, but no loan.[58] Hatcher brooded over this ingratitude. In October 1918 he unburdened himself to Oxman's attorney, James Nichols, in Baker City:

Jim I lied to you in S.F. last year when you asked me if Oxman was down there when that explosion took place. He was'nt there at that time any more than you was. He ate dinner at my house that day and never left Woodland until after 2 oclock. He never got to San Francisco until after 5 oclock that evening.

I have stood up for Oxman and been loyal to him because I considered him one of my best friends, but he has turned me down cold. It hurt me like the devil Jim to think he would treat me the way he has. Have written him several letters reminding him of his moral obligation to me. Some of them he doesnt even answer. He has made me lots of promises to help me out and every appeal I have made to him he has evaded. Jim I got my little wife to stand by the old man when he was in trouble, She lied to those attorneys when they came to Woodland, just to help Oxman.

Every thing has gone wrong with me this year and I could'nt make a dollar. When I asked Oxman for a loan to help feed and clothe my wife and babies he turned me down. Does that look right. If I had gone on the stand and told what I know, Oxman would be in the State Prison today.

After that trial of his was over he put his hand on my shoulder and said "Earle [sic] you and your wife have been my best friends and I am going to help you make some money." I guess he thinks that because he was acquitted he does'nt owe any obligations to any one. I consider that he owes me a debt that money alone cannot repay. If you will think back you will remember how anxious he was to get my wife and I to sign those affadavits. Am glad now they were never witnessed before a notary public. You know Mr. Oxman better than I do so you know he likes notoriety. That was all he wanted when he testified that he was in S.F. at the hour of that explosion. . . . We can recall every part of his stay in Woodland that day, even to what we had for lunch. . . .

Now Jim I asked Mr. Oxman for a loan of enough money to give me a start in the sheep business. It will take $10,000.00 I will pay him back with interest. He is a big man in financial circles and can get this money for me. I cant get it here or I would'nt ask him.

He never made any answer what he would do. Jim you know what my information would be worth to the other people, but as I have stood by Oxman so long I dont want to get mixed up in that affair again. I want you to talk it over with Oxman, and try and show him where he owes me a favor. Have been sorry a thousand times I ever persuaded my wife to lie for Oxman. . . . His son Frank J. came down here this summer and beat me out of $77.00 so I am pretty much disgusted with the Oxmans.

Have never told a soul what I have written you. . . .[59]

Nichols shortly wrote to Cunha about this letter, and gave "a general indication of its contents," but there the matter rested. Cunha did nothing. Hatcher's letter was torn to bits—but instead of being thrown out, the pieces were put in an envelope and tucked away in a safe.[60] There it remained, unknown to others, until 1936.

Hatcher did not go to "the other people" or to the authorities. Sometime in 1918 he did tell his story to an acquintance, Charles H. Sooy, a San Francisco attorney. (The evidence, although not conclusive, indicates that he did so several months prior to Oxman's refusal in July to give him the loan.)* Eventually Sooy told Brady. In April

---

* Hatcher testified in May 1921 that he told Sooy in February 1918, "It wasn't through any malice for Oxman because I had business relations with him afterwards the following summer." (Hatcher testimony, San Francisco Grand Jury, "In re Thomas J. Mooney," May 28, 1921, p. 12.) On the same occasion Assistant District Attorney U'Ren said: "There is no question but that this story was told three years ago." (Ibid., p. 24.) The records show no contradiction of Hatcher in this matter.

1921 Brady, accompanied by George Parson and Ignatius H. McCarty, the Densmore investigators, went to Hatcher. Hatcher refused to talk. "I told him . . . that I was going to talk to an attorney, that he could find out for him." He also refused to talk to Edgar Gleeson.[61] In May he was subpoenaed to appear at the *audita querela* proceedings, where Mooney asked the court to hear him. The dismissal of the defense motion made this impossible, but Brady subpoenaed him to testify before the grand jury.[62]

Hatcher told the grand jury of Oxman's visit to Woodland on July 22, 1916, of their livestock business that day at the Byrns Hotel and lunch with Mrs. Hatcher, and of Oxman's departure for San Francisco.

Q. You saw him get on the train?
A. Yes sir.
Q. And what time was it about that that train left Woodland for San Francisco?
A. Shortly after 2, 2:15, or something like that.*

Hatcher said that he had not come forward previously because Oxman had been his friend, and because he had always thought that Mooney was guilty; "they had a world of other evidence besides Oxman." "I didn't want to get mixed up in it if I could possibly get out of it . . . , I felt that way, and still feel this way." He testified as a reluctant witness. His testifying, he said, would hurt his livestock business. He did not mention having sought a loan from Oxman.

Q. Are you and Oxman friends today?
A. I don't know, I haven't saw Mr. Oxman for some time.

. . .

A JUROR: Q. Is it not common knowledge, however, you and Mr. Oxman are at outs now?
A. I would not say really at outs, because we have never had any.

---

* Hatcher testimony, San Francisco Grand Jury, "In re Thomas J. Mooney," 1–11. He described the time again as "2:15 or 2:08." (*Ibid.*, 35.) This train was the next one to San Francisco after the 9:13 A.M. train. It was in fact scheduled to leave Woodland at 2:55, and the train dispatcher's report showed that it left that day at 2:55; these facts came out in 1936 and were offered at that time as impeaching evidence against Hatcher. (California Supreme Court, "Habeas Corpus," XVI: 10,217–22; Southern Pacific R.R., "Shasta Route" schedule, June 1916, courtesy of J. G. Bell.) The afternoon train from Woodland was changed in 1917 to 2:08. (J. G. Bell to author, March 30, 1962.) If Hatcher's error was due to faulty memory, this change was probably the basis of it.

He had not seen Oxman for three years, he testified in conclusion.[63]

Hatcher's wife corroborated his story. The time of Oxman's departure from Woodland, she said, was "somewhere around 2 o'clock."[64] The grand jury also heard the testimony of Paul Leake, editor of the Woodland *Democrat,* who confirmed an interview he had published in June 1917, in which Hatcher told him that Oxman "left Woodland on the 9:08 [i.e., 9:13] train."[65]

Brady announced that he would appeal to Stephens for a pardon. At Sacramento, officially inspired rumors circulated that Stephens would reject the appeal. Brady, occupied with other pressing duties, let the matter rest. The defense kept after him—"that spineless jelly fish Brady," wrote Mooney in a letter smuggled out of San Quentin; the California State Federation of Labor prodded the District Attorney, too. After eleven months he got around to writing Stephens, and did so then, according to Rena Mooney, only because Older threatened to break him politically.[66] Brady did urge Stephens to pardon Mooney and Billings: "The only reason for keeping them in prison is that they are undesirable citizens and, if they have not committed the offenses charged, [that] they have been guilty of other activities that justify restraining them. I am convinced that such reasoning is most insidious and, ultimately, most destructive."[67] According to the *Bee,* this was just Brady's personal opinion, in which the "Bolshevist" frame-up cry could be detected.[68] There, once again, the matter rested.

VI

Californians were tired of the Mooney case—"sick and tired," the *Call* regretfully noted. The decline of public interest was evident. Observing it from the sidelines, G. S. Arnold wrote Felix Frankfurter shortly after Brennan's self-revelation:

The composit[e] mind of San Francisco has to be interpreted in the light of its habits—it likes a sensation like the Mooney controversy, only so long as it has a good kick,—but after the cork has been out for a year or two the thing has gone flat, and all the kings horses and all the kings men cant make it worth talking about again. Then too—relict of the Vigilantes— relative justice gives more satisfaction than the vindication of the law— the law having been a notoriously loose jade here since the beginning.

People wanted Mooney kept in prison so as not to "have him around urging dynamite as a tonic for the body politic. I doubt whether this sentiment, which is the majority sentiment, will ever change," he added.[69] It did not change in the 1920's.

The Mooney case passed into an eclipse following the developments of 1920–21. Sensational confessions, front-page headlines, organized publicity, and fund raising declined and virtually disappeared until late in the decade. Legal action was limited to petitions for executive clemency. The death of Bourke Cockran in 1923 symbolized the end of a major phase of the case. *Tom Mooney's Monthly* ceased publication in April 1923. The defense committee itself became dormant that year, and stopped issuing publicity. Both Mooney and his wife were in poor health. Labor organizations passed routine resolutions; in an era of conservatism, the AFL drifted on an ebbing tide.[70]

The times had changed. The business of America was to seek other good things of life than a free and just society. ("The trouble with this country," said Mother Jones at the age of 93, "is that there is too much four-flushing and not enough real leaders.")[71] For those who cared about social causes, the harvest was plentiful but the laborers few. Movements that had come to Mooney's aid were declining; for instance, the Socialist Party, which called once again in 1923 for the release of Mooney and Billings, had declined in membership from 118,000 in 1919 to 12,474.[72] In the East the Sacco–Vanzetti case and in California the Anita Whitney case had special appeal to liberals; both cases were terminated in 1927, the one in execution and the other in clemency, but meanwhile they overshadowed Mooney and Billings.

Editors changed with the times. Even Fremont Older found little to say, for an editor needed fresh events and receptive readers. His leading social cause became the abolition of the death penalty.[73] In these years he returned occasionally to the Mooney case, but the general nature of his editorial page had changed: his editorials had less bearing on current affairs; they tended rather toward belles lettres and moral homilies. The one social campaign of the *Call* in the 1920's was Older's struggle to change popular concepts of crime and justice. Yet he went along with the times in playing up violence; murders dominated the front page. The *Call* was not the paper the *Bulletin* had been. Older may have felt this himself, for neither of his autobiographical books covered the years after 1920.[74]

Politicians changed, too. In Washington one of the defense committee's workers, Leonard Craig, visited President William H. Johnston of the machinists' union one day in 1923 to see if he would make a date with President Coolidge. Johnston told him it was useless; Coolidge "would sidestep it as he sidesteps everything."[75] Perhaps Craig was the only one who seriously thought that Calvin Coolidge might intervene in the case.

Still, in Sacramento there was Stephens and his successor.

VII

In May 1922, Mooney abandoned his reluctance to apply for a pardon. Before then he had pinned his hopes on a new trial, but the unwillingness of Brady to prosecute on the remaining indictment and the failure of the *audita querela* proceedings convinced him of the futility of legal action.[76] "I maintain that the courts are the instruments of the rich and for the subjugation of the poor," he said.[77] The prospects for a pardon from Stephens were as bleak as before, but an election was coming and another governor might respond more favorably. The defense made preparations to oppose Stephens's reelection with such limited influence and resources as it had. In the meantime the *audita querela* appeal was dismissed "to take this excuse away from him."[78]

Since California was a Republican state, the important hurdle for Stephens was the Republican primary. His challenger was the State Treasurer and former publisher of the Berkeley *Gazette,* Friend W. Richardson, a homespun Quaker with a walrus mustache. Richardson, a former Progressive, had a strong "dry" following and a reputation for economy—having, as State Printer, cut the costs of publishing state schoolbooks by a third. His candidacy did not arouse the Stephens forces, who expected to remain in power on a moderately progressive record, but Richardson had the backing of the Los Angeles *Times,* the small-town press, the Better America Federation, "and all the reactionary forces."[79]

That Mooney should support Richardson was a source of political mirth and a sign of the prisoner's despair.[80] "Richardson certainly can't be any worse than Stephens," said one of his defense workers, but much earlier Mooney had observed: "To hope for different results from some future Governor is to look for the impossible. In California they are getting worse instead of better. If Stephens does not succeed himself in office he will make way for a successor far worse than he ever dared to be."[81] Vindictiveness led Mooney to oppose Stephens: "if we can defeat him it will be a lesson to some of the others." Vanity, too, was a factor. It was presumptuous of Mooney to suppose that he had some weight in California politics, particularly on behalf of such a candidate; but Brady's pardon recommendation had been somewhat embarrassing to Stephens, and, as Edward Hamilton of the *Examiner* remarked, the Mooney case remained a live political issue.[82] A special issue of *Tom Mooney's Monthly* endorsing Richardson was widely circulated, and support was sought from labor.[83] "We got Fickert and we will get Stephens," Mooney's brother told the San Francisco Labor Council. California labor leaders and Fremont Older sensibly endorsed Stephens; Mooney reacted bitterly. But the California Socialists were bitter, too, because Mooney was not supporting their ticket. "The Mooney group," said the *World,* had "demanded 'general strikes' and 'mass action.' Now we find them supporting the worst capitalistic reactionaries on the ballot."[84]

To the surprise of many, Stephens lost. Richardson, campaigning on the issue of economy,[85] received the nomination by a slender majority.* In the successful election contest that followed, he took no stand on the Mooney case: "I haven't thought about it enough to make a statement."[86] The defense committee had no information on Richardson's intentions. Before Stephens left office, Older appealed to him to release the two prisoners, but Stephens declined.[87]

Richardson was a conservative governor. His policies included economy and the restriction of public services, antipathy to organized labor, and the upholding of "law and order."[88] He disapproved of pardoning prisoners. A governor, he held, ought not to pardon anyone duly convicted by a jury and sentenced by a judge. For a long time he extended clemency to no one; after two years he had commuted one death sentence, that of a seventeen-year-old boy. In the Anita Whitney case he said that he could not "respond to popular clamor."[89] The prospects for Mooney were bleak indeed.

Preparations for submitting a formal petition for clemency had begun by the time Richardson took office. The rules governing clemency applications required statements from the judge, the District

---

* The vote was 286,442 for Richardson, 261,521 for Stephens. One lone labor journal commented that Stephens's defeat might be ascribed "in part to his vacillating policy on the Mooney case and his fathering of criminal syndicalism." Mooney himself considered his case the main cause of Stephens's defeat. (*California Bluebook* [1924], p. 470; Contra Costa *Labor Journal*, September 13, 1922; Mooney to Nockels, September 18, 1922, Mooney Papers. See also Richard H. Frost, "The Mooney Case in California Politics" [M.A. thesis, University of California, Berkeley, 1954], 115–17.)

Attorney, and the jurors. For Mooney this was only a beginning, since he had no intention of throwing himself on Richardson's mercy; he aimed rather to prove his innocence. As one of the regulations stated, "In applications based upon newly discovered evidence, the evidence must be such as would probably have produced an acquittal on a second trial." It might have been written for him. But in assembling the voluminous materials, Mooney and his wife, working under handicaps, encountered many delays and disappointments. Rena Mooney supposed that the petition might be completed by the end of 1923, but work went on slowly throughout most of Richardson's term of office.[90]

One of the major projects was an investigation of Oxman. In 1920 Claude Ellis reported that Oxman had moved to Baker City and was partially paralyzed. Rena, though not optimistic, went to Oregon in 1924 in the hope of obtaining a sickbed confession. Failing this, she interviewed people in Baker City, Pendleton, and Spokane who had known Oxman. From B. C. Wilson (the railroad claims agent) and others she learned about Oxman's earlier local reputation and particularly about the Spain case.* Wilson had privately written about the Spain case to Governor Stephens in 1918, but the defense did not know this until Rena's trip to Oregon.[91]

Oxman's Kansas City affidavit was also the object of extended inquiry. Mooney had known of its existence since 1917, but had never seen it. No copy was at the District Attorney's office. Fickert gave no assistance. Cunha said that he did not recall the affidavit, but was willing to help. He wrote the local Burns Agency that so far as he was concerned, Mooney might have the benefit of any affidavit made by Oxman. The office had no copy, but one was located at the agency's Kansas City branch, which refused to release it without an order from the San Francisco branch, which in turn denied any jurisdiction. Eventually this pettifogging was overcome and Mooney obtained an uncertified copy. He then appealed to Frank Walsh in New York to have it certified by the Kansas City notary public before whom the original had been sworn, and at last, in 1926, the document could join the 342 other exhibits attached to the pardon petition.[92]

Fickert and Cunha declined to support the petition. Oxman's testimony, said Fickert, had not been indispensable; the Hatchers' testimony was worthless because they had made "affidavits" both ways;

---

* See pp. 166–67 above.

McDonald had told the truth at the trials, and later yielded to the temptations of money, but had refused to testify to the grand jury under oath, "notwithstanding the fact that District Attorney Brady offered him immunity from punishment." Fickert also cited the writings of Mooney and Berkman as evidence of Mooney's guilt. "Notwithstanding the fact that on several occasions some of your sympathizers have attempted to take my life by the use of bombs and other methods, I have nevertheless tried to act impartially in your case."[93] Commented McNutt: "His attitude does not surprise me in the least. Evidently, he still believes that somebody is trying to murder him."[94]

Letters supporting the application were written by Brady, Griffin, and nine of the ten surviving jurors. (The tenth was not opposed to a pardon, but said he would not presume to tell the Governor what to do.) Wrote Griffin: "as time passes, the suspicion later surrounding the conviction of Mooney, instead of diminishing, actually increases." He reminded Richardson of the remaining indictment, on which Mooney might be prosecuted after a pardon if sufficient evidence of guilt were uncovered. Matheson, Goff, and Brennan also endorsed the application. Matheson had changed his view of the case by 1924—a magnanimous step, considering what McDonald, Hand, and the defense had said about him. Oxman, he wrote, was "a romancer, pure and simple."[95]

Not until December 13, 1926, was the pardon application, filling nine volumes, submitted to Richardson. Richardson had about three weeks left in office. On the 29th he announced that because of insufficient time, he would not pass judgment on the application. "I desire to be fair in this matter and will not deny the application," he said.[96] The question was left to his successor, Clement C. Young.

CHAPTER TWENTY-TWO

San Quentin

We have done a lot in America to make prison life pleasant.
　　　　　　　—*Chronicle*, September 12, 1933

The matter of Tom's character is delicate.
　　　　　　　—A Palo Alto Quaker

TWELVE MILES north of San Francisco on a hook of land running into San Francisco Bay stood San Quentin Prison, which looked from a distance like a romantic old gray fortress. The prison was established by the state in 1852 and named, like the point on which it stood, after a local Indian warrior, Quentin, whom early Americans had canonized in their enthusiasm for Spanish California place-names.[1] The setting by the water's edge was remarkably beautiful: to the west rose the wooded slopes of Mount Tamalpais; opposite, the hills of Contra Costa; to the south, islands of the Bay and the distant skyline of San Francisco. Inside the main entrance was a colorful, well-kept flower garden. Sea gulls drifted overhead, and cattle grazed beneath great live oak trees on the hills overlooking the prison blocks.[2] "I'd rather be in prison in California than free anywhere else," a California novelist wrote. "San Quentin is without doubt the most delightfully situated prison in the whole world."[3] But she had never tested the option. As a former San Quentin convict remarked, "There is something strange and bitter in all sweet pastoral things seen from a prison cell."[4]

Mooney occupied a small stone cell on San Quentin's death row from mid-July to the end of November, 1918. His contacts there were limited to other condemned men, the guards, and the cell tender for the row, J. B. McNamara, who was esteemed at the prison for his good nature and undefeated spirit.* Prison regulations forbade any visitors

---

* David A. Lamson, *We Who Are About to Die* (1936), p. 40. McNamara was serving a life term for the Los Angeles *Times* bombing. He died in San Quentin in 1941, after the longest confinement of any labor prisoner in the country. (*Chronicle*, September 24, 1938; New York *Times*, March 9, 1941.)

other than relatives and attorneys. The warden permitted Mooney's wife and mother to visit as often as they wished. Condemned prisoners were not required to work; they were taken outdoors one hour a day for exercise.

Mooney did not believe he would be executed. Shortly before his arrival he wrote privately: "If the worst comes to the worst, I feel that I am physically and mentally able to meet the occasion; but I am confident, beyond all doubt, that the workers of this nation . . . will never permit the consummation of this judicial assassination."[5] When the wartime influenza epidemic swept through San Quentin, other condemned men refused face masks, but Mooney wore one faithfully. He later said that he slept like a rock, and that he got along well in the routine of death row, where the food was good and his time was his own. He was reported as saying that he had suffered intensely only in the county jail, when the jury was deliberating his wife's verdict. "Then for 56 hours I endured the tortures of the damned."[6]

After his commutation he was moved to the old prison section. His cell was four feet wide, eight feet deep, and seven feet high. The ceiling was arched like a tapped wine cask, which made the space smaller, though it did not affect the standing room. The walls and ceiling were of stone. In the cell was a small iron cot with a straw pillow and a thin mattress, which was replaced every six months, or on request if infested with bedbugs. A small green wooden table and a stool, two bookshelves over the cell door, and a water pail and chamber pail completed the furnishings. All light came from a 40-watt bulb overhead; there was no window. In the heavy iron door, equipped with a double bolt and two locks, was a small wicket through which Mooney could see the opposite tier of cells and a patch of sky. The cell was ventilated through a pipe at the back, connected with a motor on the roof. The ventilation worked satisfactorily in warm weather, although Mooney sometimes plugged the vent with newspapers or rags to stop the distracting noise of rushing air. He also plugged it in chilly weather, since the cell was unheated; and when too many vents in the tier were plugged, the air pressure built up and the weaker plugs popped. The plug had to be removed from time to time in any event, because the air became stale. In the winter he often wore his outdoor clothing and even a blanket while reading or writing.[7]

Mooney's first prison job assignment was in the machine foundry, where he worked for two years. Most San Quentin prisoners were required to work for at least three months in the hated jute mill; Mooney worked there for three months in 1920 and then went to the prison laundry for a year. Beginning in April 1921, he received more desirable assignments. For three years he ran the donkey engine on the prison wharf, outside the main walls, where he loaded fuel and construction materials into the warehouse, and also raised vegetables in a small plot. This was a "bonarue" job with the privileges of a trusty. The number of such privileged jobs was limited, but Mooney never got into trouble with the prison authorities, and he held bonarue jobs consistently until 1937.* For eleven years he was assigned to the Officers and Guards Mess.[8] During these years a typical day went as follows:

At 3:45 A.M. a trusty woke him and unlocked his cell. Washing and dressing rapidly in the cold, he put on white ducks and a white coat, the regulation uniform of convict workers in the O&G Mess. He joined a line of prisoners from his lock-up, went to the toilet dump in the court, washed his toilet pail and put in a spoonful of lime, and returned the pail to his cell. He then went down to the court and out an iron gate, through the "Garden Beautiful" to the main entrance. There he showed his pass and was let outside the main walls to the Officers and Guards Mess, where he set to work peeling potatoes. For two or three hours in the early morning and intermittently thereafter, for about six hours a day, he peeled about two hundred pounds of vegetables, according to the convict cook's instructions. He ate the same food as the guards, which was better than the "main-line" convict fare. Moreover, unlike most prisoners, he was allowed a daily shower and change of clothes. On those rare early mornings when the air was warm outside, he took his work outdoors and watched the ferryboats ply between San Francisco and San Rafael, or, in clear weather, the outlines of San Francisco and Oakland.

After work he returned through the entrance to the Main Yard and walked about for exercise, often in the company of an acquaintance or two. An hour later he went to the turnkey's office for packages, books, or stamps. (Letters came directly to the cell.) He was then free to remain in the Yard or go to the library, but he usually returned to his cell, because there he could be alone and read while the door was still open.[9]

Mooney regularly received about a dozen newspapers and periodicals, including the New York *Times,* New York *Call,* Portland *Oregonian,* Baltimore *Sun,* the *Nation,* and the *New Republic.* (Califor-

---

* Mooney's prison record card shows not a single infraction.

nia papers were forbidden to prisoners.) Some of the subscriptions were contributed by friends. The *Times* he considered "the BEST *newspaper* in the U.S."; it kept him well informed, he said, "more so than any other units of the KEPT PRESS."[10] He read his mail and wrote letters on his old typewriter—one letter a day, according to prison regulations, although the turnkey often let him send several letters in the same envelope. Books that were not from the prison library had to come directly from the publishers; those which bore a "revolutionary title" or for other reasons were considered subversive at the turnkey's office were withheld: as one of the wardens explained, "no class articles or anything that is even suggestive of strife is to be allowed, as we have enough to contend with inside without borrowing trouble from the outside." Nevertheless, Mooney read Theodore Dreiser's *American Tragedy* at San Quentin.[11]

Most prisoners were locked in their cells at 4 P.M. and their lights turned out at 9:30, but Mooney was on "late lock-up"—6 P.M.—because of his job, and was permitted to read as late as he wished.* For a time, at least, he had both a radio and a phonograph in his cell, and was allowed to use them after lock-up.[12] Altogether, as prison life went, he was favorably treated, and he knew it: the prison officials, he wrote Older, "have been just fine—always willing to extend to me every consideration that I ask for—I could not expect more."[13] The wardens regarded Mooney as a model prisoner and at least one of them believed he was innocent: Frank J. Smith, who was Governor Richardson's son-in-law, publicly enlisted in the movement to free Mooney after he left office. Having a celebrity on their hands was to cause some headaches for prison officials in the 1930's, but the wardens sanctioned Mooney's privileged status. "Knowing him to be innocent," said Frank Smith, "I placed Mooney in the position of steward of the officers' and guards' mess, a position formerly held by a free man. He rendered better service than the civilian before him. . . . He has been the victim of a terrible mistake."[14]

II

Mooney was an indefatigable correspondent. He wrote thousands of letters from prison, and kept copies of them, together with thou-

* *American Spectator*, February 1933. Early lock-up was well before dusk so that there would be time to search for any missing prisoners before nightfall. (Lamson, *We Who Are About to Die*, p. 55.)

sands of letters he received. They accumulated in disorganized piles around his cell.[15] Although very few letters written before 1926 have survived, the subsequent ones are extant. Mooney kept them because he considered himself a significant historical figure, "the symbol of the oppressed and down-trodden workers."[16] Eventually he willed his papers to the University of California, where they fill row upon row of shelves at the Bancroft Library.

From these personal records the character of California's famous prisoner emerges clearly: cantankerous, self-centered, self-pitying, and obsessed by the injustice that had wrecked his life. He submitted to the prison routine, but, unlike Billings at Folsom Prison, he never adjusted to it. "It may as well be admitted that Mooney is not a gentle, tolerant saint," wrote Miriam Allen de Ford. "I have been rather amused to find that people outside California, who are indignant at the injustice done him, picture him as a mild-eyed martyr. Mooney is an aggressive, stubborn fighter; a sensitive, self-willed, touchy individual, not broken but embittered."[17] He was determined to direct his own defense efforts, regardless of the handicaps. He conciliated neither friend nor enemy, and the demands he made on his closest supporters alienated, one after another, all but the most patient and understanding.

"Mooney is daily becoming more of a fathead," declared one of his lawyers. Roger Baldwin, national director of the American Civil Liberties Union, remarked more tolerantly: "I am used to Tom's language and don't mind it a bit. I think I would speak a good deal stronger if I had done thirteen years on a frame-up." But Baldwin, unlike the members of the defense committee, did not take orders from Mooney. Even Frank Walsh, patient and courteous, occasionally became exasperated. "I marvel that you have retained your sanity," he wrote Mooney; but to Baldwin he confided that freedom might be obtained more easily: "I only wish I could chloroform poor Tom." And Fremont Older reacted similarly: "he is just as inflexible to me as he is to you," he wrote Baldwin. "He is, as you must have discovered, a monumental egotist and feels that he is a great figure in the civilized world. Of course he is difficult to deal with."[18]

In prison Mooney got along with the other inmates: he usually left them alone. He carefully avoided cliques and quarrels. Occasionally he befriended another inmate and went out of his way to lend a helping hand, as in the case of a penniless Greek waiter who was eligible for parole, for whom Mooney sought work among outside friends. The prison surgeon and certain others reported that Mooney was a cheerful prisoner. Altogether, however, he lacked the compassion of Debs, or the humanity of J. B. McNamara, who "understood and loved" Mooney, and enrolled him at San Quentin as an honorary member in "Dynamiters Local No. 1." "Tom is a great guy, but too selfish," wrote a convict who had served twelve years in a nearby cell. "It has been Tom for so many years that no one exists but he." And another inmate summed it up: "Hell, Mooney don't know he's a con. He's a martyr!"[19]

San Quentin did not form Mooney's character. He was bumptious before San Francisco had ever thought of preparedness. But the injustice of his imprisonment undoubtedly eroded his gentler traits, leaving him suspicious, brusk, and embittered. Repeatedly he turned against the very persons, like Older, who worked hardest for him. "Older is getting very old," he wrote Nockels, "—lacks his old time fighting spirit and pep." In a letter asking for financial help from his own union, Mooney charged, "250 will not break your local." Again: "Please Mother . . . fork over the LOAN." To Baldwin he wrote that if he were in a heated and well-lighted room on Fifth Avenue, he might be more civil in his correspondence. His defense committee friends protested his dictatorial treatment ("I receive a letter every day, a do-this-do-that letter." "If Tom would just keep hands off and rest his case ENTIRELY in the hands of his friends, his chances for release would be far better"). To their protests he rejoined that he was directing the defense committee because he was the sufferer, and he thought well of his own plans: "in this solid ivory dome of mine I do get an idea once in a while and it is such a sensation for me that I have to let others know about it and pass it along." To his sympathizers Mooney's bitterness and ingratitude were part of the tragedy of the case. As the *Nation* observed, "It is proof of the terrible truth that stone walls *do* a prison make, and iron bars a cage."[20]

Prison ruined Mooney's health. He entered San Quentin in excellent condition and with no unhealthy habits, according to the prison surgeon.[21] During his first years at San Quentin he looked well, and seldom reported for sick call. But years of worry and poor prison fare took their toll. For a long time he had the same monotonous, starchy food as most of the other inmates. In consequence he developed stomach ulcers. Seriously ill, he lost fifty pounds in 1924 and "felt like 90 years old with one foot in the grave and the other on a banana peel." Fortunately, he was able to get transferred to the Officers and Guards

Mess, where he could have milk and eggs. (For a while he was required to work there sixteen hours a day; the rest of the day he was in bed.) After a year and a half he was hospitalized with a hemorrhaging duodenal ulcer. The doctor put him on a soft diet and told him that a recurrence of the bleeding might prove fatal. For about three weeks he carried on his pardon petition correspondence from the hospital bed; then he returned to the O&G Mess, although he was back in the hospital twice before the year was out. For three years he lived on a liquid diet, "for fear of opening up those old ulcers."[22]

Mooney had the best treatment available, but compounding his other anxieties was now the fear that he would die in prison. Inspired by Bernarr Macfadden's Physical Culture books and magazines, he began to experiment with fasting and sunbathing. Four fasts lasted for periods of up to 24 days, during which he took only water and diluted orange juice, while he continued on his prison job. He claimed that he felt better after them, but in the spring of 1929 he was back in the prison hospital, wracked with abdominal pains and suffering from extreme exhaustion. "He is living on his nerves and if something does not happen soon it will be too late," said Mary Gallagher. Baldwin wished Mooney would give up directing his own defense, but he knew there was little hope of that. Though he might die in prison, Mooney would struggle to the last. "I need a rest," he said weakly on his discharge from the hospital: "rest from doing time and everything only rest."[23]

The ulcers never properly healed. They compelled his hospitalization again in 1937, and after his release from prison they hastened his death.

III

San Quentin was conveniently located for visitors from San Francisco. The trip took an hour and a quarter from the Ferry Building— by ferry to Sausalito, train to San Rafael, and omnibus from there to the prison. "You tell the ticket agent in San Francisco that you want to go there, and he says, 'One way, or 'round trip?' and laughs. You perceive that this is his standard joke, made to everyone who names this destination and is not accompanied by a sheriff's deputy." The train ran past suburban villages with charming Spanish houses half-hidden by trees and gardens, "little paradises of the comfortable middle class which, in California, is so violently conservative," as Bruce Bliven of the *New Republic* observed. At the prison, visitors went to the office of the captain of the guard and waited. "All day long one pitiful woman's face after another appears before the little grilled window, asking always to talk to a prisoner." Callers and inmates sat on either side of two long counters in the visiting room and talked through a screen over a low partition.[24]

Mooney had many visitors. For the most part they were relatives, friends, and defense committee members; occasionally they were prominent radicals. Most of the time newspapermen, including Older, were prohibited. Debs called on Mooney after his own release from the Atlanta penitentiary; Norman Thomas, William Z. Foster, James P. Cannon, Ella Winter, Lincoln Steffens, Upton Sinclair, Theodore Dreiser, and Sinclair Lewis came, too. Steffens was more interested in McNamara and Matt Schmidt than in Mooney, whom he considered a righteous bore: "I'm not interested in your case," he quipped, "you're innocent." But Dreiser, among the others, was keenly interested: "you are not forgotten," he wrote him, "you are the essence of a great issue."[25] These special visitors encouraged Mooney's belief that he symbolized a great cause. But his most faithful visitors were not celebrities or political allies; they were his wife and mother. Rena made the trip regularly once a fortnight.[26]

Through the early 1920's Rena Mooney worked industriously for her husband's freedom. She toured the continent to address labor organizations and public meetings, and to raise defense funds. On one trip she was injured by a collapsing Pullman berth; from the compensation paid her by the railroad, she lent the defense committee $1,300, probably in the realization that she would never be repaid.[27] In San Francisco she managed the office of the defense committee, kept the committee's voluminous records, and helped publish *Tom Mooney's Monthly*. Ed Nolan paid her a moving tribute in those days: "every time I have seen you so courageously hoping on, a most depressing feeling of sorrow has been with me for days. Dear woman if I might have one wish in this world satisfied, then it would be to know that your battle for right and justice and love was won and the terrible dragging uncertainty of hope deferred ended in a glorious reunion."[28] Six years after Mooney was transferred to San Quentin, her loyalty won the grudging admiration of Edward H. Hamilton in the *Examiner*: "It can be said for Mrs. Rena Mooney . . . that she has completely upset the dictum of former Warden Hoyle that the limit of a woman's constancy is three years."[29]

Working with labor and radical organizations did not come easily to Rena. The causes of radicalism and militant labor, which meant so much to Mooney, had never won her wholehearted support. She had belonged to the Socialist Party before 1916 for her husband's sake. Apart from him, her main interest was music. Music had been an early passion of her childhood in Missouri, as an autobiographical fragment written in the San Francisco jail reveals: at the age of four she had wanted to play the bass viol; at eight she made a violin out of a cigar box. Her father, a carpenter, and her mother tolerated but did not encourage her musical ambitions. As a young woman she studied at a San Jose conservatory, and later taught music. Her first marriage, to a man named Will Hermann, ended in divorce; after her marriage to Mooney in 1911, she continued giving private piano and violin lessons, the income from which made possible some of Mooney's labor activities. She resumed her teaching after her acquittal in 1917.[30]

The strain of working for her husband's defense eventually took its toll. Unable to do all that he demanded, week by week, and depressed by the uncertainty of hope deferred, Rena turned to drink. Eventually it became chronic: by the early 1930's she was an alcoholic.[31] She gave up working for Tom's release in 1925. The circumstances are not altogether clear, but it was a time when defense efforts had nearly ceased. She did not abandon hope for his freedom, nor does she appear to have been faithless to him, but she did abandon defense work, and never returned to it. On several occasions Mooney asked her to resume working for him, but she said she could not give up her pupils.[32]

Mooney still professed to love his wife, but their relationship changed. In the absence of sufficient evidence one can only speculate. Mooney probably came to believe that his wife no longer loved him because she would no longer work for his cause. Prison is a breeding ground for suspicion, and he was suspicious at one time or another of practically everyone. Yet Rena continued to visit him, and her surviving letters reveal undiminished affection:

it seems to me more than 9 years since we were together on the [Russian] river, I will never forget our happy times together and I hope it will not be long until we can have our 3rd honeymoon....

Darling if my undying love will make you well, you will surely recover rapidly.

... one of my birthdays I will never forget when you were out of work, but hadn't forgot, there was on my plate a little red rose....

This is just another birthday of the many passed since we were together to fold our arms about each other, but the years may be many [yet] you have one faithful little "girlie" as you used to call me.

I wish I could have placed a red rose on your plate this morning not over there but over here, where I could have given you the love which goes with such a token.

My darling its coming Xmas and N.Y. mabe the Gov. will see right and send you to me for all our remaining birthdays. All my love to you only.[33]

IV

By 1928 Mooney was anxious to revive his defense committee, in order to renew agitation for his release and prod Governor Young for a pardon. He sent documents on the case to friends and prominent Californians and asked for their help. One of the recipients was Mary Gallagher, a Los Angeles radical whom Mooney had known for many years. Not long afterward, on a visit to San Francisco, she called on him during one of his fasts. Other visits followed, and she agreed to reestablish the committee.[34]

Mary Gallagher came from a midwestern Irish laboring family. As a young woman she had heard Debs speak in Chicago during his Presidential campaign of 1908, and became "a confirmed socialist right on the spot." She met Mooney in Chicago the same year. Thereafter her associates were radicals, particularly IWW's, whose belief in non-political "direct action" appealed to her. In 1914, the year before Joe Hill's execution, she began doing public work for them; and from 1918 to 1924 she worked for the IWW's General Defense organization in behalf of the indicted and convicted Wobblies. She was never attracted to the Communist movement. To the IWW she rendered fine service, according to the chairman of the Los Angeles branch of the ACLU: "We regard her as very efficient and reliable," he wrote Roger Baldwin, "and I think you may trust her judgment in almost anything that comes up. In short, we like Mary."[35]

Mooney liked Mary, too. She brought him feminine enthusiasm, attention, and cheer. Misery lost its grip: "my hopes are higher now than at any time in twelve years," he wrote Older, "why I don't know, but for the past three or four weeks, I have had a sort of premonition that good things are in store for us. I have just felt jubilant, my spirits are the best—my hopes high." He wrote Mary that he had been like a sinking ship with no wireless to call for help, and when she "hove in

sight without a convoy—then real help became possible." She was his
rescuer, and with her coming, "happiness too came and also love."[36]

Mary expressed surprise at Mooney's thoughts. "I thought you
were immune to such experiences, that your struggles had separated
you from that part of life and that you accepted people quite imper-
sonally," she said. But the quickening of his spirit delighted her. Her
own marriage of eleven years to Douglas Robson, a vaudeville singer
and labor song composer, was not a happy one. "My whole life has
been an endless quest for some exquisite and beautiful thing. . . . Perhaps this is the way at last."[37]

Mooney was overjoyed. In his letters a quality of delight appeared
that had not been there before—and never was again. Hour by hour
after lock-up he played records on his "Grafonola," and after prison
taps, when the sound of phonograph or typewriter was forbidden, he
took his pen and wrote out the words and titles of popular tunes that
"thrilled me to the depths," and sent them to Mary; he urged her to
go to a record shop and ask to hear them, as though she intended to
purchase them. "Then you will know some of the beauties of my Sunday Evening."[38]

He became more conscious of San Quentin's natural beauty. "The
last few nights have been exceptionally lovely evening[s], clear and
calm with the warmth of spring in the evening air and the Moon
shinning and the stars glistining in their orbit. . . . Your dreams make
me real happy." From the prison yard he appreciated the view of
Mount Tamalpais, and from outside the walls, the view of the Bay.
"Last Night as the Great large ball of gold the Moonn came stealing
over the hills of Oakland and laid its path of gold across the Bay and
later turning it to silver, . . . I threw my hand up and out into the air
as if reaching for it." He rarely wrote of these things except to Mary.
"Your presence is the most desired thing in the world to me—nothing
is so lovely and wonderful." The year of imprisonment past was the
"sweetest year in my life. . . . There is only one other who knows what
made this my happiest year of my life."[39]

With Mooney behind bars for life, the future for such sentiments
was dim. Mary might have been willing to wait for his pardon; she
was working for it, and there was reason to hope that Governor Young
would free him. But Mooney, lamentably true to form, was so incorrigibly conceited that he stifled Mary's affections. He tried to hold her
through the bars in an unyielding grip. His love for her stemmed partly
from her willingness to serve him: she was, he said, "some one who

understood him and was willing to carry out his orders—I should say instructions, that some day he might be free again." He instructed her in nearly everything: whom to see, what to write, what trains to take; he admonished her for working too hard ("I dont want to be charged with any more *murders*"); he lectured her for being "so 'VULGAR' as to smoke a 'coffin nail' in public." This provoked Mary, "one of the 'Micks' "; she turned on the "big boss" and took him down a peg. "Say, Dear," he demurred, "That was an awful slam—to a certain dreamer. I would not slam a S. house door that hard." But his contrition did not last. "Who has a better right to love you may I ask? Who have you done more for?"[40]

The despoiling of Mary's quest for the exquisite and the beautiful was not accomplished all at once. Initially, her own loneliness was offset by confidence in him and in his liberation. "Had my fortune told the other night and the banshee said 'All your work this winter will be brilliantly successful.' " "I feel enwrapped by an ecstatic cloud of tenderness and protectiveness." "I am but a priestess at the temple, and your happiness is the altar where I serve." En route to Portland in a vain effort to see Oxman, she thought of Mooney in his white coat against the gray prison walls:

Every tree is covered with snow frozen on every branch, like a decorated Christmas tree.... Anything in white against a gray background will always remind me of how you stood yesterday watching me walk away from you.

One thing I thank God for tonight, Tom, is your character. You are not selfish in spite of your great need. Men are such vultures, generally, even the best of them, seeking only what they can devour.[41]

Though she absolved him of selfishness, Mooney's demands exhausted and depressed her. "Now, just don't scold me any more, give me a chance to pull myself together and we'll both work hard again." Within a few months of the initial encounter there came the agonizing reappraisal:

I wish you were more generous in your attitude to people, you do allow a narrow feeling to possess you which interferes with your happiness and with your own development. That is one thing I fear about you. Your strength is the strength of the unforgiving and once I thought it was the strength and courage of the tenderhearted.... Of course, very few persons have been put to the test of endurance that you have and you have not failed so far in the big things, but sometimes in the nonessentials in your own life I think you make a mountain out of a molehill. If you were once impersonal, it might be a good idea to sort of mix a little of that with your present extremely personal and self centered attitude.

One idea of mine is to rush out right now and drown my sorrows but My opportunities are limited so I guess there is nothing for me to do but drown them in tears. . . .

I've just been thinking of all the different ways there are of finding happiness in life. . . . Mine for a long time has been to go in spirit to the place where *one* is lonely and share his sorrow. But I am afraid I have been banished. Still faithfully I go.[42]

Thereafter her attitude became increasingly impersonal. She worked as hard as ever for him, but her steadfastness was now nothing more than dedication to a worthy cause. She continued for two years in spite of Mooney. "I am ready to scream at your waste of time and paper in giving me orders. You are driving me to death and if you want me to continue you have got to stop."[43] But he did not.

Mooney never saw what he had done. For a time his expressions of endearment continued, but prison life closed in once again. "I am just dragging my self along on my nerve alone—that['s] all—nothing else." He continued to dictate on his battered old typewriter to his defense committee. "Say it is cold enough this morning to freeze the B. off a brass monkey. Here I am blowing off steam over this typewriter so thick and fast that I can hardly see the machine in front of me. . . . It is too cold to peck away any longer." The constant letter-writing was misplaced effort. Perhaps its greatest value lay in diverting him from misery, pain, and void. "All my life has been chuck full of sorrow and unhappiness—want—deprivation and suffering and this had to be capped with thirteen years of cruel and unjust imprisonment—with, it seems, more torture at the end." "I am so lonely—never was I so lonely."[44]

There were always visitors—a diversion, at least. "John was here with Mother and two of his carmen friends, an ILD, and a German 'Nut'. . . . He said he would touch my 'FLESH' then look into the sun and I would go out of this place—but the building prevented him carrying out his mystic powers." And there were always the sympathetic letters from distant well-wishers offering comfort and advice: horoscope readings, herbal remedies, homilies . . . "Greetens: I pray the Lord Jesus Christ and his Father Jehovah If you are real inocent of the crime that men claim upon You, That God by some means releace You." "I am sure sorrow to Know you are in prison."[45] The walls remained a tomb.

Mooney had compensations for his imprisonment, as Theodore Dreiser pointed out to him. The world was not indifferent to his plight; he was not forgotten; he was a symbol of class inhumanity. "I actually think that there are thousands of people in that active, militant world . . . who would gladly step into your shoes. . . . You are going to look back on this period possibly with regret. Life, excitement, public interest, is certainly worth something."[46] More perceptive, however, was the observation of Asa Keyes, a former District Attorney of Los Angeles, who served nineteen months in San Quentin:

The mass resentment and hatred of 4000 men which seems as tangible as the prison walls, the monotony of endless days without hope, the association with the dregs of humanity, all combine to turn the average prisoner into a worse man instead of a better one.

I don't know what to suggest in place of prisons. . . . It is a thing far more terrible than most people realize.[47]

Mooney's prominence did not exempt him from these oppressions. On his behalf a defense committee member wrote privately:

There is something about prison life that never can be described. It is the force, the vividness, of one's sentiments. A monastery will do that too, but in the unholy claustration of a jail one is drawn back wholly upon oneself, for God and Faith are not there. The people outside disperse their affections; we hoard ours. What they let slip, what they forget in the movement and changes of free life, we hold on to, amplify, exaggerate into a monstrous growth of memories. They can look with a smile at the troubles and pains of the past, but we can't. Our pains keep on gnawing at our hearts. Old desires, old deceptions, old dreams assail us in the dead stillness of our present when nothing moves except the irrecoverable minutes of our life.[48]

In the simple words of Sherwood Anderson: "He should be turned loose. They should quit it. There should be a limit, even to our human cruelty."[49]

CHAPTER TWENTY-THREE

The Pale Cast of C. C. Young

*Well, you cannot expect the same leadership from
me which you had from Hiram Johnson.*
—Governor Young

*We don't even care any more whether there was a
Preparedness Day Parade. Pretty soon some wit-
ness will come along and deny it, anyhow. Let
Boolings and Mibbey stay in prison. Let them
out. Particularly Millooney. We are tired.*
—University of California
Daily Californian, 1930

MOONEY'S FORMAL PETITION for an executive pardon had aroused
little comment when he submitted it to Governor Friend W. Richardson in December 1926, shortly before Richardson left office. Not
even the *Call* ran an editorial. Mooney complained that the newspapers paid less attention to his petition than they would to "a yellow
dog being run down by an auto."[1] But he was fully aware that his
hopes now lay with C. C. Young. "Here is hoping that a little justice
will creep or sneak into California during 1927," he said.[2]

The inauguration of Governor C. C. Young heartened progressives
in California. A Phi Beta Kappa graduate of the University of California, Young had taught English at San Francisco's elite Lowell High
School, coauthored a poetry text, turned to the real estate business in
Berkeley the year of the great earthquake and fire, entered politics
as a precinct organizer with the Progressives' new Lincoln-Roosevelt
League, and won election to the State Assembly. He was the original
Hiram Johnson man, according to Franklin Hichborn—the first Progressive, after Mrs. Young, to propose that Johnson run for the Governorship. At Sacramento, Young sponsored the direct primary law, became the Progressives' leader in the Assembly and Speaker of that body,
and was twice elected Lieutenant Governor. Consistent and depend-
able, he remained loyal to Johnson and the "moral issues" of earlier

Progressivism, particularly in opposing liquor, gambling, and prostitution. In 1926 John R. Haynes, Rudolph Spreckels, William Kent, and others like them considered Young the only politician of their bent who could defeat Richardson in the Republican primary. After winning the primary by a slender margin, he easily won election in Republican California. Young's supporters hailed his victory as the return of progressive reforms.[3]

Unfortunately, Young was not Johnson. He was not a fighter. Reserved in manner, he was dedicated, intelligent, and judicious, but he was also mild and indecisive. He wanted a quiet administration. He had not campaigned on a liberal Republican platform, he refused to fight for Progressive control of the legislature, and he rekindled little of the old, militant Progressive enthusiasm. George P. West noted that Young had never spoken out against the state Criminal Syndicalism Act, "and as presiding officer has honorably escaped so many votes on important issues that in spite of his long public career his course is a matter of guesswork. . . . California is getting . . . a representative of left-wing Babbitry."*

Shortly after taking office, Young said he would give fullest consideration to all applications for clemency. Mooney wrote and asked him to consider the application to Richardson as though it were to him, and Young's secretary replied that the Governor would take up the pardon petition after the legislature adjourned.[4] There the matter was left for several months. In April, Mooney prodded Older and Older prodded Young; the reply came back that the Governor would give the matter his attention after the 30-day bill-signing period.[5] That meant June. The delay was reasonable, but Older already doubted Young's intentions toward Mooney and Billings: "He may have the same timid attitude toward releasing them that other Governors have had in previous years."[6]

Among the clemency cases facing Young, the first to claim his attention was not Mooney's, but that of Charlotte Anita Whitney. Miss Whitney, a graduate of Wellesley College, niece of former United States Supreme Court Justice Stephen J. Field, and a social worker for many years in Oakland, had been convicted of violating the Crimi-

---

* *Nation,* November 17, 1926. On the eve of the new legislative session two leading progressive Senators, Herbert C. Jones and J. M. Inman, met in the lobby of the Senator Hotel in Sacramento. "Where's Young?" asked Jones. "In his cyclone cellar," Inman replied. (Hichborn, "California Politics," IV: 2384.) For a more favorable view of Young see H. Brett Melendy and Benjamin F. Gilbert, *The Governors of California: Peter H. Burnett to Edmund G. Brown* (1965), pp. 349–60.

nal Syndicalism Act in 1919 on the grounds of her membership in the
Communist Labor Party. She had been free on bail during the many
years her case was on appeal. When the United States Supreme Court
denied appeal for the second time, in May 1927, the only alternative
to her imprisonment was executive clemency. Support for it was widespread and highly respectable: state legislators and other officials favored it, and so did hundreds of prominent educators, publishers,
businessmen, and jurists.[7]

Miss Whitney had never applied for a pardon. She held that such
a request would be a tacit admission of guilt. But a petition from her
was not necessary, and in June, Young pardoned her without one. He
pointed to prejudicial testimony about the IWW at her trial, and
added that Miss Whitney—whom he had known personally for many
years—was "a lady of culture and refinement."[8]

Mooney was envious of Anita Whitney's support. She had had a
"Rolls-Royce" protest, whereas he and Billings had only a "Ford"
protest.[9] He protested to Older and Rowell that no one had interceded personally with Young for them. Older replied: "You are quite
mistaken in bringing your case on a parallel with Anita Whitney's.
. . . 90% of the people in Northern California were for her pardon.
Even with that big factor, the governor did not want to do it, but he
did it really because he felt he had the backing of a large majority
of the people of California."[10] Rowell told Older that he would see
Young if it would help, but said that inasmuch as Young had

made good with the "soft hearted," like you and me, in one decision, I
have a notion that the Governor's impulse would be to make good with
the "hard boiled" in his next decision. A cynic like you should not criticize a politician for these motives.

                                    .   .   .

As a newspaper publisher you will realize that, having offended the
second most important of his newspaper supporters, the McClatchy family,
by his action in the Whitney case, and having placated your own paper and
its associates by the same action, the Governor would have to rise above
political motives if he were now to repeat that offense in the Mooney case.[11]

Older deferred to Rowell's analysis but refused to concede the issue.
"My interest in the Mooney case is not personal. It is the injustice,
and the smear upon the State that lies back of it."[12]

II

Young wanted Mooney to apply for a parole. For the Governor a parole had attractions that a pardon lacked. He made the suggestion to Older and McNutt,[13] and later rationalized it to Chester Rowell:

I am impressed with the fact that whatever appeal may be made for Mooney is largely because of his prominence in former years as a rather militant dissenter from the established order of things, rather than for causes immediately connected with his trial. Of course I know the latter will always be alleged reasons for appeal to clemency, but it seems to me that that matter has been thrashed over so frequently that it would be unwise to open it just now.

I have always taken the attitude that in a state such as ours, with the very liberal parole system we possess, the ordinary procedure of release from prison should be first through parole, and later, after the parole term had been served, and the prisoner had subsequently demonstrated his right attitude toward the social order, that a pardon and restoration to citizenship should follow.

It would please me very much if you could aid me in getting this idea across to the friends of Mooney. I should hate to see a request for a pardon which I cannot grant, but I believe that at the proper time the other avenue of release may properly be invoked.[14]

Older read this and took issue with the Governor:

I certainly know of no one who is interested in the injustice being done to Mooney who has been influenced by their admiration for Mooney's activities prior to the bomb explosion. Certainly President Wilson could not have been so influenced. . . .

. . . You also say that even parole should not be invoked except at the proper time, whatever that may mean. I am sure the Prison Board will not parole these men unless they know you are favorable to it.

Will you kindly let me know at what time I may file the petition for parole of these two prisoners, with the assurance that the Board will grant the petition?[15]

Young replied that he would not dictate to the Board. He had never intervened against a parole, he said.[16]

Mooney scorned the proposal. As early as 1922 he had declared, in connection with the efforts of his sister-in-law, Belle Hammerberg, to obtain his jurors' support for a pardon, that he would not seek a parole. "If I am to be a prisoner of the State of California I want to be

a real one, with all the trapping[s] that go with it—not on parole."
He might die in prison, he told Older, but his mind was fixed. "No
parole."[17]

His advisers objected. Older and Nockels warned that parole
might be all he could get, and that if he spurned it, labor might
lose interest in his case.[18] From Baltimore, H. L. Mencken later chided
Mooney:

... I can't get rid of the feeling that it is rather quixotic. After all, the
important thing is to get out of prison. It seems to me that pardon is just
as patronizing as a parole. There should be some machinery for getting
you a rehearing and turning you loose at once, without either pardon or
parole. But our legal system is so medieval that it offers nothing of the
sort and so you are forced to take the best you can get. It seems to me that
a parole is better than nothing. Once you are out, no one would dare propose sending you back.[19]

Mooney insisted his objections were practical. A paroled convict had
to be off the streets before 10 P.M.; he could not enter a poolroom or
dance hall, drive an automobile, sign a contract or go into business
for himself; he could not change his job or residence without permission; he could not leave the county without permission; he had to
report once a month to the parole officer and give personal details of
his life. Worst of all, he could not participate in any union or political
activity. In short, Mooney felt that on parole he would only be doing
time outside prison. If his enemies so arranged, he might be arrested
on false charges and promptly returned to prison by authorities hostile to left-wing labor. To apply for a parole, he said, would be to
abandon his responsibility to the labor movement: his case was a "symbol of the times," and he was "one of the actors"; he must not be considered personally.[20]

Rowell washed his hands of Mooney, but Older was sympathetic.
He said that a parole was absurd "when they are both wholly innocent
of the crime for which they were convicted and sentenced." He declared editorially, "there is no more legal reason for them to go on
parole than for Mr. Rowell or for Governor Young himself to do so."[21]
And Judge Griffin, who had not been a party to this controversy, advised the Governor early in 1928 that a parole would be unsatisfactory:

... Mooney's case is no different from any other man who has been wrongfully and upon perjured testimony convicted of a crime of which subsequent developments absolutely demonstrate his innocence. Speaking very

frankly, it seems to me that the great obstacle in the way of Mooney's pardon has been his alleged bad reputation. In other words, he has been denied real justice because the opinion seems to be prevalent, that he is a dangerous man to be at large and therefore should be, innocent or guilty, kept in prison. Conceding, for the sake of argument, that Mooney has been all he is painted, it is, to say the least, most specious reasoning; indeed, no reason at all, why Mooney should be denied the justice which, under our system, is due even the most degraded. Moreover, such a doctrine is more dangerous and pernicious than any Mooney has been accused of preaching.[22]

These were the views of Young's political friends. They had no apparent effect. A year and a half later the Governor was still talking about a parole.[23]

III

The pardon issue drifted through 1928. Older had a long conference with Young in January and came away feeling that there was no hope at the time for a pardon. "He did not say definitely that he would not but his talk convinced me that he would not."[24] California labor leaders appeared to be indifferent toward a pardon, and their indifference was critical. The labor movement had benefited from Young's election: Scharrenberg held office in the administration; the legislature was more receptive than previously to bills favored by the State Federation of Labor; in general, it was not a time for militancy. Nockels informed Mooney that no labor leaders on the Pacific coast were demanding his pardon.[25] They considered a parole adequate, and Young knew it.[26]

Nevertheless, many of Mooney's supporters regarded a parole as inadequate, and no hearing had been held on the pardon application. Mooney wanted a delegation of prominent sympathizers led by Frank Walsh to visit Young and make a strong appeal for a pardon. Older concurred, and invited a small group to participate. Walsh made the trip at his own expense.[27] ("Your case . . . makes my blood boil, every time I think of it. It is absolutely incomprehensible how any such thing could take place in America any place.")[28] However, he could not leave New York until July 1, and Young was going on vacation that day. Mooney was distraught: "it will be more delays, vacations, campaigns, trial, etc and we will never get anywhere. This takes the heart out of a fellow."[29] The date was finally arranged for August 28. Older in the meantime saw Young again, and this time got the impression that the Governor believed that Mooney and Billings were innocent. Young later denied that he had implied anything of the kind.[30]

The delegation included Walsh, Older, Griffin, Scharrenberg, Furuseth, and William MacNevin, the jury foreman. Their reception was chilly. Walsh found that Young had not read the record and inferred that he had no intention of reading it or doing anything for Mooney. However, the Governor did warm up during the interview, and seemed impressed by Walsh's remarks about Oxman and McDonald. He promised nothing, but everyone left in a hopeful mood. Walsh was so pleased with the conference that he went directly to San Quentin to tell Mooney about it.

The danger was that the effect of the hearing might wear off and things go on as they had before. Walsh was convinced that pressure from organized labor could prevent this from happening. On his return trip east he stopped in Chicago and urged Nockels to organize a campaign of resolutions from local labor unions across the nation. "Walsh says the labor movement is charged with the throwing of the bombs, regardless of what labor may say to the contrary," Nockels reported to President Michael J. Keough of the International Molders Union, "and back of this whole conspiracy are the 'open shopper' employers of California."[31] Resolutions and petitions subsequently flooded Young's office. Young objected. "No self-respecting governor would relish appearing to be pushed into an action which he may decide to be right, and no honest governor could permit himself to be pushed into an action which he may decide to be wrong," he told Scharrenberg.[32] And he implied that a pardon would be wrong: "Whatever our sympathy may be for an individual, it would manifestly be bad for society as a whole to show such lenience to one whose act has destroyed many innocent lives." ("Whose act?" Mooney demanded.)[33]

Young claimed by this time to have studied the case at length, but he was still shirking a decision. He called on Older in October and suggested that the editor propose that a commission of prominent men be appointed to investigate and make a recommendation. This idea had been suggested previously by Professor Guido Marx of Stanford, a civil rights advocate highly sympathetic to Mooney's cause.[34] Mooney, however, was firmly opposed:

We have a very fine example of the Sacco and Vanzetti case....

If the Governor is not favorable to the idea of pardon, he surely will not appoint a commission favorable to that idea. And in the event that he should appoint one, and they recommended that the pardon ... be denied, he could say that he was in no way responsible for their report, except that he was bound to be governed by their recommendation and deny my application for a pardon. Where if he reviews the case himself and refuses to grant a just relief, he can at least be held responsible to his constituitents on his return for their suffrage [sic]. This is our only hope now. SMOKE THEM OUT.[35]

Young probably did not recognize Mooney's point as a lesson in government administration, but the commission project was dropped.

IV

By the summer of 1928 Mooney was convinced that he needed his own defense organization once again. For a year and a half following Young's inauguration, he had sought neither publicity nor funds, and had worked only through a few friends, "and I am very sorry to say that it does not seem to have gotten us any where."[36]

The Tom Mooney Molders Defense Committee had long been moribund. As a first step toward reviving it, documents relating to the case were mimeographed secretly in San Quentin for private distribution outside. One result, previously noted, was the attraction of Mary Gallagher to Mooney's cause. Clarence Darrow also came to his aid: he urged publication of the documents, and sent Mooney $500. Until this boon, Mooney had had "not a dime" to reestablish his committee.[37] (Darrow, Walsh, and Older, he said, "are a holy trinity to me.")[38] He wanted to publish and distribute the documents to the voters of California—all 2,300,000 of them. The cost would be $50,000, a prohibitive sum, but Mooney meant to raise as much as he could. For the time being, Walsh, Darrow, and Nockels all disapproved, since the pardon petition was still pending; but the defense committee was reestablished.[39]

December 8 was Mooney's forty-sixth birthday, his tenth in San Quentin. His mother went to Mission Dolores to pray for him at high mass. Mooney wrote the Governor and asked him for a meeting face to face at prison: he was sure, he said, that he could convince him of his innocence. The Governor's secretary, Keith Carlin, having business at San Quentin, called on Mooney shortly afterward, and told him that the Governor took exception to his intention to circulate the documents; that Young would study the pardon petition during his next vacation, following the close of the next legislative session; and that there would be a decision within the next twelve months. Mooney was wroth. Young was offering "only a subterfuge for time to pass"; he had already had two vacations without reviewing the petition; "what assurance have we that it will be reviewed next vacation?" He had said nothing about a vacation to Walsh in August, "for he had just returned from one." Five months had passed and, by Carlin's admission, Young had not yet looked at the petition. Mooney was certain what Young's eventual decision would be. He himself could write it for the Governor, he said bitterly.[40]

On January 10, 1929, Young stated to the legislature that he would take up the Mooney case during his vacation. "As I have said, I intend at my earliest opportunity to study very thoroughly this case." He added a warning against undue influence.[41] Max Stern, editor of the San Francisco *News,* asked him whether a strong, respectable committee building up sentiment for Mooney's pardon might not make it easier, and Young replied that it would embarrass him. Stern thought otherwise. "He is essentially a timid person and hates to make up his mind, especially in an issue that is bound to have political reverberations."[42] But even greater difficulty lay in forming such a committee: there were not enough prominent Californians—"the 'sacred cow' element," as Older called them—who cared, and a committee of liberals without them would do no good at all. Since respectable California businessmen would not support efforts for Mooney's pardon, the project was dropped.[43] As Austin Lewis reported from his own experience:

There is . . . the feeling among the upper bourgeoisie which is malignantly and bitterly against the men. I had an instance of that the other day which beats anything that I have had hitherto, in all the years of my fighting. At the First Presbyterian Church Men's Club at Berkeley, I was driven from the platform among cries of "Liar" when I told them that Mooney was innocent a few weeks ago. . . . I have had apologetic letters but the feeling is there.*

The feeling was there, whether Young liked it or not, in his own daily mail.

* Lewis to Baldwin, April 27, 1929, in ACLU Papers, v. 371. Five weeks later he added: "the man who led the attack on me . . . is comfortably and naturally dead. After many years in the California labor movement the . . . term 'naturally' has an element of strangeness and would seem to point to the existence of an active Providence." (Lewis to Baldwin, June 4, 1928, same file.)

V

"My Dear Governor:" "Honorable Sir:" "My Dear Governor Young:"

"Stand firm, Mr. Governor." "Too many criminals in the whole United States are having leniency extended to them." "I remember, and so do you, the agitation that was gotten up on behalf of the McNamara brothers who destroyed the Times Building in Los Angeles. It was claimed that they were the innocent victims of capitalistic conspiracy under the direction of Harrison Gray Otis. The agitators knew nothing more about the facts of that affair than do the present excitable friends of Mr. Mooney." "[Mooney] was caught out in Suisun Bay with a boatload of dynamite." "If Mooney was not a strong union radical there wouldn't be all this fuss made over him to liberate him."

"Pardoning Mooney would mean that the preparedness parade [was] unpatriotic and wrong and should not have been held." "One of my childhood friends was killed in that frightful affair." "Emma Goldman was in the city at the same time, and I regard them all as accessories to crime." "The Department of Labor during the Wilson administration seems never to have missed a single opportunity for unwarranted interference with due process of state law where agitators were involved." "We hope you will be courageous enough to hold your own ground (as Calvin Coolidge did when the Police and Firemen of Boston wanted to unionize) and not be politically influenced by the murderers and rough necks of the country." "None of these petitioners have suggested who might have been guilty of this crime, and some doubtless have inside information. In my judgment his sentence should be relentlessly carried out."

"These men are not Savanarolas. The class to which they belong is entitled to the same consideration we give mad dogs, hydrophobia skunks, and rattlesnakes." "Sympathy should not thwart the purpose of our people in meting out appropriate punishment to a misguided Russian, posing under an Irish name." "If Tom Mooney ever be Pardoned or released, He should by all means be deported because every body knows, he has been working against our flag. Tom and his Brother has allways been an I.W.W." "Mrs. Mooney was also as vicious as her husband." "Many of the anarchist–Communist–American Civil Liberties Union crowd would like to see them released." "The Communists wish to get these prisoners out of jail to advance the

*cause of communism, which is exactly what their pardon would do."
"I commend you for not allowing the Hearst mud slinging machine
to rail Road you into making a decision on the Mooney Billings
cases." "I have just been talking to a few spies and if the Mooney
methods of political threats are successful the whole state will soon
be worse than Chicago."*

*"Have you noticed since Mooney and Billings have been locked up
that there has been no dynamiting of buildings?"* "Do you believe
for one moment that money in great sums has not been used to bring
about their release?" "Dont be a 'jellyfish' again by liberating this convicted assassin. You were fooled as to the Whitney female but dont
repeat that mistake in the Mooney case." "The idea of such notariety
hunters such as Sinclair Lewis going out and retrying the case and
playing Judge and Jury and declaring him innocent." "They cry for
his release like those of old cried for Barabas's release."*

*"Stick to your guns like the good soldier that the people of this
great State believe you to be." "If I have helped just a little to stiffen
your backbone I'll feel repaid." "This republic would crumble to
peices if it wasnt for the courageous fellows like you." "It is unfortunate that the matter came up now, but I am sure you have the
approbation of our best people."*[44]

VI

Young went on vacation in July and took along his Mooney papers. He spent six or seven hours a day examining the evidence, four
days a week. When he returned he had not finished. He indicated that
he would reach a decision about the middle of September. A few
weeks later he announced that he would not be able to give his decision for at least three months.[45] "That is all he has done in the Mooney case since taking office 33 months ago," said Mooney. "Postponement after postponement." Young, not Fickert, he said, was the "real
criminal" now.[46] Yet despite the Governor's evasions there was growing opinion at Sacramento that Mooney would be fully pardoned.
John R. Haynes, John Francis Neylan, and Hiram Johnson all told
Older that Young did intend to pardon him.[47]

That fall C. C. Young discovered the case of Warren Billings. After
receiving—and presumably studying—a copy of the Billings trial tran-

* During the 1920's the Church of Saints Peter and Paul in San Francisco was
bombed several times, and in 1925 a bomb exploded in the main corridor of the Hall of
Justice, without causing personal injury. (See *Call*, January 12, 1925, and August 6, 1927.)

script, he announced that the Billings case closely paralleled Mooney's, and that he wished Billings would apply for a pardon, too, so that both cases could be considered at the same time.[48] This seemingly constructive suggestion precipitated a crisis in the ranks of the defense.

Billings's chances for clemency were inherently poorer than Mooney's. He was serving his second prison term at Folsom, the first having been for carrying dynamite in Sacramento in 1913. According to the state constitution of 1879, the Governor could pardon a recidivist only if a majority of the State Supreme Court justices recommended that he do so.* This meant that any pardon request by Billings would have to be referred to the Court for its approval. Billings's case for a pardon, moreover, was considerably weaker on its face than Mooney's. Billings had not had a strong alibi at his trial; he was not in the Eilers Building photographs; Frank Oxman had not testified at his trial; his judge, Frank Dunne, did not believe he had been unfairly tried; and of Billings's six living jurors, only three had consented to join in asking for his pardon, whereas the one holdout of Mooney's ten surviving jurors had joined the other nine in favoring his.[49] There was hardly any respect in which a stronger case for pardon could have been made out for Billings than for Mooney.

Mooney and Billings had made an agreement through a third party in 1922 that Mooney's case should be presented for clemency first, and that Billings would await the outcome. Billings's prospects would of course be enormously improved if Mooney were pardoned, and, as Mooney said, "almost all of the most favorable outstanding material discrediting the state's case was directly used in my trial."[50] Later he was accused of deserting Billings and concentrating selfishly on his own cause, but his strategy was essentially sound. Young's proposal now jeopardized the arrangements. Mooney was suspicious. He wrote Billings:

it is not done out of any real desire to see you out with me, but to prevent my becoming active in your behalf. . . .

There is still room for danger to us through your filing of your own petition. They could act upon yours first—deny it—then use that as an excuse to base their denial on my own. You know that Dunne is hostile, he would talk against you as Griffin talks for me. With Fickert and Dunne

---

* This restriction had been adopted at a time when the feeling in California was widespread that the Governors were too easily reached and were too lenient in granting pardons to convicted felons. (*Debates and Proceedings of the Constitutional Convention of the State of California . . . 1878* (1880), I: 274, 372, and *passim*, III: 1478.)

he could make a very good showing on the surface against you—this would
be passed on by the Supreme Court then the Executive would throw in his
kick and add . . . his denial of my own petition.[51]

To Older he added: "I know you will laugh yes even sneer at this
sort of reasoning, but I well [remember] all that we have gone
through and there is hardly a single thing that has happened politically or that politicians were a part of that give[s] me the slightest
reason to have respect for their word."[52]

But Older, who had seen Young again, was positive that the Governor was going to pardon Mooney. He disapproved of anything that
looked like balking, and was much put out that Mooney opposed Billings's application. Scharrenberg felt the same way; and the California
State Federation of Labor, in convention at Long Beach, made an
urgent request that Billings file his application. Others close to the
defense bore the same view: Young would not go out of his way to ask
for Billings's application only to turn around and deny it. As a friend
of Billings said, "Such a course would be suicidal, politically speaking."[53]

Under this pressure Mooney and Billings decided to relinquish
the old agreement and "throw all their chances in this final gamble
for liberty." Billings promptly prepared his petition and submitted it
to the Supreme Court in early November. Rumor had it that the
Court was prepared to act favorably, but not in haste. "Now," said
Mary Gallagher, "we can only hope that Governor Young has not
spiked our guns." Young asked the Court to be as expeditious as possible, and offered his own files. He also announced that he would make
no decision meanwhile on Mooney's application. "Whatever action
affects one should naturally affect the other. Either they were both
innocent or both guilty." Everyone agreed about this, he said.[54]

Before long a small, dark cloud appeared on the horizon: late in
November, Young passed the Mooney case to the State Advisory Pardon Board. He wanted its opinion on the case, and with the Billings
pardon before the Supreme Court, no time would be lost, he said.[55]
The step drew fresh skepticism. "There is something queer somewhere and I dont think that Older with all his shrewdness and knowledge of the game has smelled it out," Austin Lewis confided to Roger
Baldwin. "Has the Governor shifted responsibility because after all
there is going to be an auto-da-fe? . . . I am not at all so positive about
this thing coming out well as I was a week or two ago." The Board,
Lewis pointed out, was only a creature of the Governor anyway.[56]

Older was still confident. "I have just received absolute information that everything is all right. The Board of Pardons will render a
favorable decision; so will the Supreme Court. So it is only a matter
of a short time."[57] But in that short time he grew troubled. He
learned from a member of the Board, H. L. Carnahan, that the Board
did not expect to make its decision until the following April—four
months away. "What is there to 'study' that should take more than two
days?" Older asked Young.[58] And, for the first time since the inauguration, he assailed him publicly:

What is HIS decision about the Mooney and Billings cases?
And why does he need the support of any group, any board, any organization of men who are, themselves, part of his official family? ... Never,
in all the months he was studying the Mooney case, did he even suggest
that when he was finished he would NOT be finished, but would ask for
more delay and more investigation. Yet that is what he has done![59]

Privately, Older said over and over that Young had no escape—that
he had to pardon Mooney, and very soon.[60]
Mooney was disgusted. Older, he said,

has been used USED USED by the governor to get away with Murder. . . . He
pleaded for five weeks . . . August 9th. now five months have passed and
we are told that four more months is necessary and then the Campaign
will be in full bloom and then [Young] can say he does not want it to become a political issue and will ask that the matter be held in abeyance. . . .
No one wants to expose the sham of the whole thing.[61]

Billings was bitter, too. "I'm thoroughly satisfied that the bubble has
burst . . . so what the hell difference does it make?" He wrote Mary
Gallagher that he was thinking of withdrawing his application, in
order to prevent Young from obtaining an excuse from the Supreme
Court to deny Mooney a pardon. "And I am damned tired of waiting,
too." The prison censor at Folsom evidently informed the administration of this letter, for a few days later Young wrote Older to urge
Billings to do no such thing.[62]

VII

The Quakers of the Bay Area were among the minority of Californians actively concerned about the case. Several Friends visited

Mooney in San Quentin, were favorably impressed by him, and felt that he would make a useful citizen if freed. They doubted that he ought to request a pardon; "violence to conscience" was involved, Arthur Heeb of the Palo Alto Meeting wrote Young. Young was the third Governor whom they had petitioned for the pardons of Mooney and Billings. ("Once we turn our hands to the plow we are not apt to look back.") Mooney suggested that they hold a mass meeting, but, as Heeb replied, "Somehow a mass meeting is not the way of Friends." It was the sense of four Meetings that the Friends should seek an interview with Young. Some of the older members thought it a bit too romantic to go and "stand before Governors," although they did not oppose the step.[63] In June 1929 an interview was requested with Young, but not granted. The Quakers were put off repeatedly by the Governor's office. However, their persistence eventually bore fruit. On March 9, 1930, a delegation of six, including Professors J. Murray Luck and Frederic Anderson of Stanford University, Professor Howard Brinton of Mills College, and Arthur Heeb, an editor, called on the Governor on behalf of Mooney and Billings.[64]

Young said that he was personally inclined to consider the men guilty. He challenged the Friends' knowledge of the case. He contended that very few people had examined the court records, and that such a study would shake the confidence of those who regarded Mooney and Billings as the victims of a miscarriage of justice. He pointed to Dunne's belief in their guilt. He said he had evidence against Mooney and Billings that had never been presented in court. (Griffin had challenged a similar statement of Young's a year or two earlier, but had elicited no details.)[65] He spoke of large amounts of money behind the defense, asserted that a great deal of it had not been accounted for, and insinuated that some of the affidavits of witnesses and jurymen had been secured by Mooney's supporters through bribery.[66] And as evidence against Mooney's present character, he offered a harsh letter that Mooney had recently written to Rena. (Heeb demurred. Any man in Mooney's situation would be "getting pretty crabby.") But he said that he would "depend entirely upon the evidence" in making his decision.[67]

Young did make two important admissions. He acknowledged for the first time that Oxman's testimony was completely discredited, and he agreed that practically all of the witnesses for the prosecution were very unsatisfactory. The Quakers were deeply troubled. "In the light of these two admissions it is almost impossible to understand why the

Governor does not feel free to pardon Mooney at once," concluded Luck.[68]

VIII

"Honored Sir:"   *"Excellency:"*   *"Dear Governor Young:"*

"Is this California?" "Can't justice be done the man? Is there any shadow of doubt that the man is innocent?" "What's the matter with pardoning these men?" "I am shocked to learn that . . . we are without remedy in our courts to grant relief." "The commutation was an impossible middle way. He was either guilty or he was innocent." "War Insanity had a great deal to do with his conviction." "There is a suspicion abroad that you are keeping them in custody because you consider them undesirable citizens." "The principle I have heard expressed, that the person may or may not be guilty as charged but 'whatever he gets is coming to him,' I consider one of the most dangerous affecting criminal practice. It is the spirit of the inquisitions of the Dark Ages."

"There is enormous interest throughout the east in your probable action on the Mooney case." "There is a strong feeling among men whose opinions are worth while, independent publicists, professors of law, leaders of economic and political thinking, that the verdict of the Mooney jury was secured by perjured evidence; and that Mooney is in jail not because of the exercise of justice but because of the deliberately contrived victory of injustice." "We people of the Carolinas have our Marion and Gastonia to grieve us. . . . May God's spirit prevail upon you to do justice."

"The admission of Estelle Smith that she perjured herself in my mind clinches the case against Fickert and the other perjurers who sent these innocent men to prison." "I knew Frank C. Oxman personally and in my opinion he was a damned rascal and I wouldn't believe him under any circumstances." "I do not think that the influence of men such as Ed Cunha, who do what they can to influence sentiment in an adverse direction, should have any weight." "But if, as I understand, the trial judge wishes the pardon of Billings and Mooney . . . the refusal to release them would be a severe blow to the principles on which the Republic stands, 'liberty and justice for all.' " "How can we honestly teach our school children to repeat that this is a land of 'liberty and justice for all,' when such a notorious denial of that ideal exists?"

"Thousands of right-thinking people voted for you because they were heartily ashamed of the Anita Whitney episode, and expected you to grant her pardon. These same people feel as strongly about Mooney. Why should California be a scorn and a hissing for the rest of the world?" "I would not bet a peanut that you will be reelected." "Is it as some people believe, you are afraid of the P. G. and E. Company?"

"I am for peaceful action and dislike to see so many driven to direct action, 'bolshevism.'" "I call it poor business to place before Communists, Socialists and others who would destroy belief in American institutions, such corking good propoganda."

"This outrage has gone on long enough. It makes me ashamed to admit California is my native state." "How is it that you people of Scotch or English descent simply cannot live without making it hot for every other race in the world." "You are procurator of California. You cannot wash your hands of this affair without wiping them on the white towel of the nation's good name." "I wish you would go out on the street, incognito, and listen to the things that are being said about Governor Young." "Your excuses are so shallow that most Americans are ashamed of you and California." "Even if you were a school teacher you should still have some manhood left." "In short your progressiveism is very largely bunk." "You Pardon these men or I will put 7 bullett hols thro your guts." "As you will notice I at least have backbone and say what I think."

"Sinclare corrupts a great government and goes free, . . . Pantages in your state commits a felony, and by hokus pocus . . . it is not considered a crime in your state to rape a girl.* Nearly all the people who think are convinced that there are two laws in our country, one for the poor and one for the rich. When that sort of thing goes far enough there will be a whirlwind." "And you, dear Sir, why do you not rise above this moth-eaten system of judicial precedent and deal out truthful, honest justice to these two unfortunate men."

"I have just returned from several months in Europe and it is amazing how strong the feeling is in other countries that American justice is a matter of class." "I was asked about this case when I lived in China and worked in India with students in the Y.M.C.A. move-

---

* These references are to Harry F. Sinclair of the Harding scandals, and Alexander Pantages, a California motion picture theater magnate, who was convicted in 1929 of criminal assault on a dancer; Pantages was retried and acquitted in 1931. (*Examiner,* July 11, 1930, and December 4, 1931.)

ment, and the soldiers in the British Army up at Peshawar used to twit me about it."

"The late John P. Altgeld became immortal because he defied the poisoned fountains of malice when he freed the men wrongfully sent to prison in Illinois in 1886." "I beg of you to delay no longer in pardoning Thomas Mooney & Warren Billings." "Such an act would be a refreshment to believers in democracy the country over." "Of course such a pardon will not restore to him the wasted years that he has spent in the penitentiary, but it will at least be one step toward rectifying the terrible wrong." "The best years of their life, old before their time. And they say God sees all, it makes me doubt there is a God. And I am an old Woman. I have seen so much Injustice of all Kind done."*

One of Young's secretaries scribbled an office memorandum: "More and yet more Mooney—looks as though the people are all looney."[69]

IX

Months passed and no recommendation came from the Supreme Court. The heavily burdened Justices had fallen far behind in their regular duties,† and it later appeared that they were "sore about this law that allowed Young to shift the responsibility in this matter onto them."[70] In January 1930, Older confided to Mooney that the Court would hand down its recommendation about March 1. By the end of March, Mooney's friends predicted that no recommendation would be made before the August primaries. In April the newspapers said that the Court had hit a legal snag in investigating affidavits, and that final action would be considerably delayed. In early May there was "confidential information" that the Court was ready and that pardons might be granted within a week. Two weeks later Older was saying that the case would be decided soon and favorably.[71]

---

* Excerpts from about forty letters to Young, 1927–30, in Mooney file, Transcripts and Prison Records, Governor's Office Record Group, California State Archives. (Misspellings are in sources.) An anonymous letter of December 6, 1931, to Young's successor, stated: "I am a Negro and as such living in a country where Negroes are roasted alive for offenses they did not commit I should not be interested in a white man getting a little of the medicine which his race has for years given mine. But I am. I forget that Mooney is a white man. I think of him only as a victim of injustice."

† Justice John W. Preston told the California Bar Association in 1931 that the Court was two and a half years behind in its work. (*Chronicle,* October 6, 1931.)

Meanwhile the Governor waited for the Court. He announced his candidacy for reelection. His wife reportedly told friends that she and her husband were getting tired of the Mooney case. ("I'll bet they are," commented the newsmonger.) Late in June the daily papers reported that the Court was ready and that, according to sources close to Young, pardons were expected; but a rumor also ran that three of the seven justices were opposed to Billings's pardon. Billings told friends that he had put on his slippers and was "in for the night."[72]

The decision was announced by Young on July 4, Billings's thirty-seventh birthday: the Court recommended 6–1 against a pardon, on the grounds that Billings had had a fair and impartial trial. The Court acknowledged that the testimony of the Edeaus had been discredited, but held that the testimony of Estelle Smith and John McDonald had been upheld: McDonald's original testimony "bears the stamp of truth," but not his 1921 repudiation. The Court also exonerated Fickert of improper motives or methods:

> It is an almost irresistible conclusion that if Warren K. Billings did not himself prepare and plant the deadly time bomb of the Preparedness Day disaster, he and his intimate associates and co-defendant Mooney know and have always ... known who did ... and the deadly purpose for which it was prepared and planted.
>
> Yet there has never come from the lips of either of these defendants, or from the inner circle of their associates, the slightest tangible hint or aid to the public officials or to anyone else which might lead to a discovery of the real perpetrators ... if these two defendants were not the guilty ones.[73]

The lone dissenter was Justice William H. Langdon, who had been Fickert's predecessor as District Attorney of San Francisco and prosecutor of the Ruef machine.* Langdon stated that he was not free of doubt, and preferred a recommendation that would free Young to follow his own judgment.[74]

"I'm not licked yet," said Mooney. "It seems to me it takes a good deal to offset the word of perjured witnesses." His own petition was yet to be decided. Young, secluding himself in Los Angeles, awaited

---

* Langdon was the only member of the high bench who had lived in San Francisco through the Ruef era. He was elected to the Supreme Court in 1926 from the district court with the support of Northern California progressives. (*Chronicle*, August 20, 1926; *Who's Who in America*, *1930–1931*.) John W. Preston was the other San Franciscan on the Supreme Court. A native of Tennessee and a former State Assemblyman from Ukiah, he was appointed the United States District Attorney in San Francisco in 1913.

the Advisory Pardon Board's recommendation. It appeared promptly: the Board recommended against Mooney.[75] Although it did repudiate Oxman and the Edeaus as fully discredited witnesses, "the evidence remaining after such eliminations definitely establishes petitioner's guilt." The testimony of McDonald, "the most important witness for the State," stood unimpeached; his 1921 affidavit was *ex parte,* and he had refused to be questioned on it under oath by the San Francisco grand jury.[76]

Young then denied the pardon. The Court's recommendation against Billings, he said, "must apply with equal force to the case of Mooney," and he echoed his board: Oxman was thoroughly discredited, "a publicity-seeking romancer," but because of McDonald's testimony the case held up.[77] Mooney denounced the Governor to newspapermen so abusively that he was ordered back to his cell. That did not stop dissatisfied editors. "O Lord! give us a Governor with intestinal fortitude," petitioned one of them.[78]

The Court, Board, and Governor had all stressed McDonald. No one had examined him in person; no one had even looked for him; but Young, taking an idea from the Court, announced that if McDonald could prove that his repudiations were trustworthy, he should be given a hearing. The difficulty was that McDonald had not been heard from since 1923. The Scripps-Howard papers offered a $500 reward for his discovery, and a search spread at once. Three days after Young's remark, McDonald was found in Baltimore. He had been there all along, working as a night watchman. The Baltimore police took him into custody.[79]

McDonald was a broken old man. His hair was white, his face pale and haggard, his eyes bloodshot. He hobbled about the police station on a cane, nervously smoking cigarettes. He told the police that his part in the trials weighed heavily on his mind. When Walsh and Nockels arrived to see him, he made a new affidavit repudiating completely his original testimony against Mooney. He stated that he had perjured himself, and charged that his testimony against Mooney was procured through promises of money by Fickert's office and the police; that they coached his identifications and other testimony; and that they pointed out Mooney to him and urged him to swear falsely. "Every word in that [1921] affidavit is true and I wish to stand by it," he said.[80]

Accompanied by Walsh, Nockels, and two Baltimore attorneys, McDonald entrained for California to testify in a new hearing before the Supreme Court. Theoretically he was still liable for arrest in California for committing perjury in 1916 and 1917, but that risk was no longer real: he was the key eyewitness, now that Oxman was repudiated.

X

The justices examined a score of witnesses in the Billings rehearing. Among them McDonald was prime. The defense attorneys had billed McDonald as a man of sound mind. It was wishful thinking.[81]

Justice John W. Preston, the most effective cross-examiner on the bench, examined McDonald. Under relentless questioning, the witness contradicted himself, failed to recollect, broke down in tears, and took refuge in his handkerchief. But he stuck doggedly to his claim that his identifications of Mooney and Billings had been false—"a whole pack of lies, bumped into my head."

Q. A pack of lies that bumped into your head. When did you begin to pack those lies into your head?

A. I did not pack them in my head.

Q. Who was the first man that started putting them in your head?

A. Mr. Fickert.[82]

McDonald said that he had been at Steuart and Market at 1:50 P.M. on the day of the bombing, and had seen two men, one with a suitcase, but that he did not get a good look at them. He said that he had lied when he changed his testimony to 1:30–45 in Mooney's trial. "Q. Any other way you lied about it the second time? A. The whole thing." He said that Cunha had told him to make the time 1:30. He said that after the arrests, Fickert had promised him that he would get the biggest slice of the reward. He was "in the clutches of Mr. Fickert." He thought he was still in somebody's clutches, but he could not tell whose. A few minutes later, under Preston's questioning, he exonerated Fickert of coaching false testimony from him and said his identifications had been honest, though imperfect. But when Ed McKenzie questioned him, he returned to his contention that his trial testimony had been fraudulent and corrupt.

Q. [McKenzie] There was not any mistake about it, is that right?

A. No, sir.

Q. No mistake at all—it just depends on which one of us have him last.

MR. JUSTICE PRESTON: I pass.[83]

When Preston confronted him with his letter to Matheson of January 11, 1921, which contradicted his affidavit of the following month, McDonald could not explain the change. "Your Honor, all I could say is: The whole thing is a bunch of lies."

Q. You feel ashamed of yourself, do you?

A. I am, your Honor. (Witness breaks down.)

. . .

Q. Well, you have felt in coming out here that you are apt to be punished, haven't you, Mr. MacDonald?

A. Yes, sir.

Q. Are you willing to accept that punishment? (The witness breaks down.)[84]

McDonald presently went to Sacramento for a collateral hearing before the Governor, the Advisory Pardon Board, and four rows of newspapermen. He testified for about three hours and in certain respects contradicted what he had told the Supreme Court justices. He now said that he had been drinking on the day of the parade: two whiskies and a glass of beer. The Board cut the examination short, and McDonald returned to San Francisco to conclude his testimony before the Court. "Suppose MacDonald testified one thing in Sacramento and another thing here, what does it show?" asked Preston.[85] McDonald returned to Baltimore shortly thereafter. He found he had no job there and no place to go. He wrote Nockels that things were coming to an end. Nockels sent him $10 and tried to cheer him up.[86]

The other witnesses to appear before the Court included Cunha, Brennan, McNutt, Nockels, Estelle Smith, Older, and Billings. Estelle Smith had been an important witness at Billings's trial, and she was now heard at length with interest. Her testimony was rambling, incoherent, and sometimes self-contradictory, but from her own and Older's testimony, there emerged a bizarre tale:

Older in 1917 took it upon himself to cultivate Estelle Smith's acquaintance, in the belief that he might persuade her to admit her mistake in identifying Billings at 721 Market Street. He invited her to his office, and apologized for the defense committee's slanderous

attacks on her reputation. ("Estelle Smith was living a perfectly regular life" by that time, he said.) He explained his own views about
women who were "under [a] cloud and all that sort of thing": "we
were all just human beings, doing the best we could in life." She told
him her life story, and he pointed out the similarities between her
own impoverished childhood and Billings's. She said she was willing
to help him. Together they went to the city jail to see Billings, who
told her about himself. When he finished, according to Older, "she
arose weeping, and said, "Mr. Billings, I am awfully sorry for what
has happened, and I am going to help you in every way I can. Your
story is so much like mine. . . . But you were at 721 Market Street,
weren't you?" Billings said he was not. Later she told Older that she
had doubts about her identification of Billings, and intimated that she
had been "suggestionized" by Swanson. She gave Older the affidavit
which he published in the *Bulletin* during the initial Oxman exposé,
that Oxman had offered her a "sum in five figures" to perjure herself.[87] Older was encouraged. He took her to dinner regularly, and
gave her some presents; she gave him presents in return, and he became, she said, a "wonderful friend."[88]

Older in turn regarded Miss Smith highly; "she has compassion
and pity, which I consider are two of the highest virtues." Later she
moved to Sacramento, where she was running a whorehouse on K
Street at the time of the Supreme Court hearing.[89]

At Older's office in 1929 Estelle Smith made another affidavit, in
which she stated that her testimony against Billings had been false;
that "it was done through fear of District Attorney Fickert who told
me if I changed my testimony he would send me to San Quentin"; and
that she was a morphine addict at the time of Billings's trial and took
morphine during court recess.[90] However, at the 1930 rehearing she
denied parts of the affidavit, particularly those relating to morphine;
she said, rather, that she had been taking a prescription medicine that
had some morphine in it.[91] Nevertheless, the notary public who had
taken the statement in 1929 testified that she had sworn it after he
read it back to her.[92]

Justice Preston's questioning of Older was filled with innuendo.
Miss Smith, he said, was Older's "very dear friend":

MR. MCKENZIE: I resent the imputation.

MR. JUSTICE PRESTON: All right, "friend," cut out the "dear."

MR. MCKENZIE: I know.

MR. JUSTICE PRESTON: He knows I use these words for euphony.

MR. MCKENZIE: Then you ought to put your apology in because the Chronicle will have the head-lines tomorrow just like they had before. We don't want to damage any more reputations.

. . .

Q. [Preston] Do you think Estelle Smith committed perjury?—This bosom friend of yours with whom you associated daily and weekly?

MR. MCKENZIE: I want to again protest these expressions and insinuations.

THE WITNESS: Never mind.
MR. MCKENZIE: ... The word "bosom" I resent ... and I note the laughter of the Justice. ...

MR. JUSTICE PRESTON: You are trying to make a thing out of it I never thought of.

THE WITNESS: Never mind. ...

. . .

Q. [Preston] Did you think the female nature was more easily persuaded than the male nature? ...

MR. MCKENZIE: There we get again these insinuations. ...

MR. JUSTICE PRESTON: I just wanted to see if you were alive, Eddie.

MR. MCKENZIE: But I resent this. As a matter of fact, when I get to be 74 if you cast an insinuation like that on me I will welcome it, but I surely regret it when you do it with Mr. Older. ...

MR. JUSTICE PRESTON: What I really wanted to ask you was, if MacDonald had worn skirts, would you have thought him an important witness. ...

MR. MCKENZIE: Well, that is sort of up-country district attorney style, too.[93]

The style was adaptable:

Q. [Preston] What do you mean now about Christian religion ... ?

A. [Older] I mean that Christ's philosophy was "Resist not evil" ....

Q. "If my brother smite me on the one cheek, turn the other also," and "If he hit you twice, fight"? ...

MR. MCKENZIE: He don't even fight under this examination.

A. ... I think if the world is ever saved it will be saved by the doctrine of Christ, [by] Love, not by Hate.

Q. What are we going to do pending the arrival of the millenium, is the point?

A. Do the best we can, be as kind to each other as we can, and do as little judging as we can.

Q. What do you want done with this case? You have judged it ever since you took the witness stand?

A. [I] have not judged any human being since I have been on the witness stand.

Q. You . . . have been judging these people to be innocent. . . .

A. I have been convinced of their innocence for years. . . . I think you are, too.

Q. What?

A. Convinced of it.

Q. You want me to tell you what my opinion is, do you?

A. Not especially.

Q. I am afraid it would not go in the Call-Bulletin tomorrow.

MR. MCKENZIE: The Chronicle would give it a scoop.

A. I think we are all convinced.*

The justices decided during the course of the hearing to interrogate Billings. They did not subpoena him, but went to Folsom because they were technically sitting as the Governor's advisers rather than as the Court. Warden Court Smith converted the lobby of the prison's administration building into an investigating chamber; leased wires were installed by press services; and eighty people jammed into the stifling room one day after the 5 P.M. lock-up. Billings, dressed in a suit, was seated in a chair with his back to the solid steel door of the old cell block, where a major riot had been staged three years earlier.[94]

Preston on behalf of his colleagues questioned Billings about his belated alibi of spraying acid on cars, which the rehearing had just

---

* California Supreme Court, "In re Billings," III: 1707–9. Older's relations with Miss Smith may in fact have gone beyond the call of justice: according to one member of the Mooney Defense Committee, who made an investigation in Sacramento some time after January 1933, Estelle Smith had another house of prostitution on Seventh Street, and a boy about ten years old, whom she said was her nephew: and his name was Fremont. (Byrd Kelso, undated memorandum [1933?], Mooney Papers.)

revealed: Billings had told his story privately at Folsom to several persons, including James Brennan and Ed Gleeson in 1921 ("Can you imagine such a damned fool?" Brennan had said to Gleeson on their way back to San Francisco. "He stands trial for his life when he could have pleaded guilty to practically a battery"). Now for the first time it was public information.[95] But for the most part Preston's questioning was unrelated to the events of July 22, 1916. It was a tendentious inquest designed to show that Billings had been a scoundrel. Billings was inclined to agree, and Preston had a field day:

Q. I don't want to disgrace you below what the facts demand, but what I want to know is this: whom were you associated with besides anarchists? Just mention one legitimate associate that you had that was not an anarchist?

A. Well, I might mention several people, they would not be any credit to me, either, being saloon keepers, gamblers, and other obnoxious characters of that type. . . .

Q. And following this so-called slimy trail, if you will permit the word, you sit here and want us to recommend a pardon for you and are not even asking for commutation or parole, is that right?

A. Well, . . . I think that I ought to be given honest justice.

. . .

Q. . . . don't you have a real pity for your former self?

A. Not a pity, no, sir.

Q. What is it?

A. Well, distress, I imagine.

Q. Now you are 35 or 36 years of age?

A. 37.

Q. With a wasted ruined life lost. Does it not strike you as a sad commentary on human existence?

A. In a way I imagine it is, yes, sir.

Q. Have you any contrition or compunction about it now?

A. Yes, sir, I have, certainly.

Q. . . . Don't you think if you uncovered your soul here tonight you would be lots happier and have at least half of your life to live in better pursuits?

A. I have uncovered as far as I can. . . .

Q. You know [you] were down at 721 Market Street on the day of the Parade, don't you?

. . .

A. No, sir, I was not.

Q. [You were] against law and order or against business of most every kind, weren't you?

A. Against capitalism; my ideas were against capitalism.

Q. ... What is capitalism? You have got as good clothes as any man in the room haven't you?

A. They might appear so at a distance; they wouldn't appear so under closer inspection.

MR. MCKENZIE: They are borrowed for the night.

THE WITNESS: The shirt and necktie are borrowed property and the trousers ... are regular issue trousers.

MR. JUSTICE PRESTON: If you had the money you would enjoy the luxuries that any other human being would enjoy wouldn't you?

A. Probably so.

Q. You would like to eat and drink and smoke and swear like the rest of the world?

A. Yes, sir, I don't like to swear very much.

Q. That is only thrown in for euphony. ... How about capitalism now?

A. ... Capitalism can be good and bad, like everything else; it can be benevolent or it can be despotic.

Q. If you had it in your power tonight to reform the government, what would you do first?

A. What would I do first?

Q. Abolish the Supreme Court, I guess, would you?

A. No, sir. I think the first thing I would do would be to elect a [D]emocratic governor, a Democratic president, and a Democratic senator.

Q. ... Would you abolish property rights?

A. No, sir.

Q. Would you establish a Soviet like Russia has?

A. No, sir.

Q. You are not in sympathy with that any more, if you ever were?

A. I never was in sympathy with Communism.

Q. What were your theories of government prior to the time you were arrested upon this charge?

A. Well, my theories and sympathies and politics have always been with the Democratic party.

Q. They are not throwing any acid on automobiles, are they?

A. No sir; that is aside from my politics.[96]

"All men of education must laugh and cry," a Los Angeles attorney later exclaimed after reading the transcript. Felix Frankfurter characterized Preston's conduct as a scandal that "wouldn't be allowed in the Old Bailey in its worst days." And years afterward Walsh remarked that the hearing was a nightmare to him every time he thought of it.[97] None of Preston's colleagues had objected to his methods, as far as the record shows. To put it charitably, the Supreme Court of California was at its worst in the Billings rehearing.

Billings was locked up and the assembly departed. The hearing concluded August 20.[98] The justices took several months to prepare their new recommendation. Meanwhile, Young was defeated by a narrow margin for renomination in the primary. His indecision in the Mooney case contributed to his defeat; not only was he criticized by newspapers sympathetic to Mooney; he was also attacked in others such as the Los Angeles *Times,* which accused him of cowardice. Young himself asserted that he had lost political support because he had spurned political "prostitution" to the Mooney crowd.[99] The Republican voters chose Mayor James Rolph, Jr., of San Francisco.[100]

The Court made its recommendation in November. Once again it was against Billings, 6–1. Langdon dissented at length, vigorously: "Suspicions, conjectures, unwarranted inferences, irreconcilable inconsistencies, and admitted perjuries are treated as facts. [The decision] is indefensible because it appeals to passion and prejudice."[101]

Technically Young was still free to pardon Mooney, but he showed no interest in doing so. Walsh refused to press the matter. Leaving office, Young reasserted the correctness of his decision. Meanwhile Mooney had turned his hopes to the incoming Governor. As for the Supreme Court, its members overwhelmingly favored eliminating the constitutional provision that required its consent for the pardon of a two-time loser.[102]

CHAPTER TWENTY-FOUR

Through the Rolph Administration

In the dim studio by the fire and highballs, we got hot and feverish, you remember, about Mooney and Billings.
—Letter in ACLU Papers

Alice in Wonderland was on a rest cure compared with this case.
—Defense attorney George Davis

ROLPH CAME to Sacramento accompanied by the blare of trumpets and a theme song, "Happy Days Are Here Again." The capital was gaily decorated with flags, banners, and signs proclaiming "Smile with Sunny Jim." The inaugural festivities included three days of whoopee, brass bands, a pioneer parade, "stars and things from Hollywood," and the first inaugural ball since the days of the Southern Pacific machine. Franklin Hichborn recalled the inauguration of Henry T. Gage in 1899, "with his bespangled colonels and captains," and predicted sourly that Rolph's administration would come to an equally bad end.[1]

If personal radiance could have cured California of economic depression and social venom, Rolph would have done the job, for he was a cheerful, jovial man of great warmth and popularity. Born and raised in the Mission District, successful there as a banker, shipper, and coal merchant, he had served his native city as mayor for nineteen years, the longest tenure of any American mayor in his generation.[2] A compassionate and generous man rather than a moralist, he enjoyed people; he had scorned crusading against despised minorities, whether prostitutes, rumrunners, Klansmen, or Reds. While city police from New York to Los Angeles clubbed Communist demonstrators during the unemployment marches of 1930, Rolph characteristically received the marchers at the steps of the San Francisco City Hall.[3] His tolerance stemmed from natural goodwill rather than conscious political courage or broad learning. (He once admitted privately that he read only detective stories.)[4] But he was not without convictions on controversial issues. As mayor he had favored municipal ownership of streetcars, water, and power facilities before World War I. During the 1920's he retreated from reform—a reasonable shift for a popular politician, although some said that it happened because he lost his personal fortune when ship values plummeted at the end of the war and he became heavily and permanently indebted to Herbert Fleishhacker, a conservative Republican of San Francisco who controlled the Anglo-California National Bank. Fleishhacker was one of Rolph's principal gubernatorial advisers.[5]

Rolph never mortgaged his cheer. He loved the limelight. With his silver moustache, sparkling boots, and ever-fresh gardenia, he cut a dapper figure. During the 1930 primary campaign he had avoided divisive issues and rivals, including the Mooney case and Young; he had relied on his personality, toured every county, and promised an era of confidence and "unity that would fill the State with smiles." He also proposed to relieve unemployment from the treasury surplus piled up by Young. As Governor-elect he hailed the passing of the depression: "Let us have faith in California." But perhaps his own faith withered, for Rolph, long a connoisseur of good liquor, was an alcoholic Governor.[6]

Mooney's friends had little faith in either California or Rolph. Some of them harried the inauguration with reminders of the case. A fifty-foot Mooney banner was unfurled from the Capitol dome during the inaugural address; Mooney leaflets were dropped on the dancers at the inaugural ball; a 75-year-old hearse that had come around the Horn quietly joined the pioneer parade, and, as it passed the reviewing stand, signs were flipped over proclaiming "CALIFORNIA JUSTICE IS DEAD" and "FREE TOM MOONEY." ("Was Rolph's face red! That nearly cause[d] a riot, but it certainly was funny.")[7] After the inauguration Rolph received many letters claiming that Young had been defeated for refusing to pardon Mooney, but there was no reason to think the new Governor wanted the case reopened. "Rolph has never been friendly to Mooney so we do not expect anything from him unless we can bring pressure to bear," wrote Mary Gallagher before his election. As Roger Baldwin summed it up: "He is liberal only on prohibition so far as I know."[8]

Early feelers were unpromising. Fleishhacker was approached privately by an old friend, Charles Erskine Scott Wood, accompanied by Older; the banker received them cordially, and promised to look into the case. But he later declared that Mooney was an S.O.B. and that Rolph should keep him where he was.[9] Wood retorted that Fleishhacker should care more about civil rights because he was a Jew. Fleishhacker blanched and said nothing; subsequently he withdrew his opposition but refused to support a pardon.[10] When he was approached again in New York by Lincoln Steffens, he said the only move he would sanction was parole. Commented Traverse Clements, who was "a sort of local ambassador" for Roger Baldwin: "Rolph is not going to go farther than that unless Fleishhacker changes his mind —which is damn unlikely according to every one who knows him."[11]

Walsh heard that Rolph was willing to take up the case. Sources close to the Governor told him Rolph was disposed to provide a fair hearing and even looked favorably on the effort for a pardon.[12] But when Dorothy Murphy of the defense committee called on Rolph in May with Robert Whitaker, who in 1916 had been the first American pastor to protest the case, the Governor said that he was busy with matters of state. "Then of a sudden, with a dramatic throwing out of his hands, he exclaimed, . . . 'Who killed them? Who killed them? Somebody killed them. I was there; I saw the blood and the brains scattered about; I called the hospital; I led the parade; the people followed me, their leader. I led the parade. Who killed them?' "[13] The conclusion that Rolph would not act favorably was reinforced a few weeks later when he appointed Fickert, who was then living in Los Angeles, as attorney for the State Board of Medical Examiners.[14] Dorothy Murphy proposed that Rolph's gravestone read: " 'He appointed Fickert to a good state job.' Nothing more need ever be said about him."[15]

As Walsh and Baldwin were preparing a new pardon application, Rabbi Rudolph I. Coffee of Oakland, who had long supported the pardon efforts, suggested that they enlist the services of Aaron Sapiro. Sapiro, a prominent attorney, raised in San Francisco (he was once a pupil of C. C. Young), was nationally known for his work for the farm cooperative movement and the American Farm Bureau Federation in the 1920's. He was idealistic and influential. He had moved to New York, but knew Rolph and California politics intimately, and was anxious to help.[16] Baldwin took up Rabbi Coffee's proposal with elation. "If anybody can swing Rolph, Sapiro can, and he is astute enough to know how to do it with the least possible comeback."[17] The first step was to persuade Rolph to grant an open hearing.

Sapiro made four trips to California in 1931 to see Rolph and his advisers. He went as an attorney for the American Civil Liberties

Union, largely at his own expense and without publicity.[18] In conference he emphasized Oxman's perjury and pointed out the Supreme Court's inability to pass on it. He quoted a statement of Theodore J. Roche, one of Rolph's close advisers and for many years the president of the San Francisco police commission, that Oxman was " 'the damndest perjurer who ever took the stand in the State of California.' " Rolph replied that Roche had never said that to him; but Roche acknowledged the statement. He added that he had been asked to serve as a special prosecutor in the trial of Oxman, and had declined because he had not been guaranteed a free hand. Rolph said that he would rely on the recommendations of his advisers, including Roche; another would be Judge Matt I. Sullivan. Plans were made for a hearing.[19]

While Sapiro's negotiations were in process, Walsh fell into conversation about Mooney with the mayor of New York at luncheon one day. The mayor was Jimmy Walker, the dapper habitué of Broadway, former songwriter and trial lawyer, and dashing, popular son of Tammany. He told Walsh that he had read about the case and had been impressed by editorials defending Mooney's innocence. Some time later Walsh, learning from Sapiro that Walker stood high in Rolph's esteem, suggested to the mayor that a sympathetic letter to the Governor might help their efforts. Walker obliged.[20] After the hearing before Rolph had been arranged, Walsh proposed to Walker that he join them in person. The mayor replied he was not really needed. A movement then arose for his participation. The scheme reached the newspapers and he was flooded with requests—one of them from Mooney's mother, whose telegram was thrust into his hand during a press conference. "Dear Mayor Walker: I am eighty years old; afraid am breaking down at last. They want to take me to a hospital tomorrow. In the name of God and His blessed mother won't you come out to help my boy."[21] Walker began to read it aloud, but his eyes filled with tears and he handed it to a reporter to finish. The next day he announced his decision to go to California. He added, as congratulatory messages from labor leaders and clergymen arrived, that he had made only one other commitment for this trip: the Notre Dame–Southern California football game. The announcement of his coming surprised Californians, but Rolph said the latchstring would be out for his friend.[22]

The party included Walker, Walsh, Sapiro, and Nockels. Walker went over some Mooney documents en route. On arriving in San Francisco, Walsh and Nockels went to San Quentin; Walker went to tea at the Presidio, and was received presently by Rolph and Mayor

Angelo Rossi in frock coats and silk hats with the municipal band playing "The Sidewalks of New York" and "Happy Days Are Here Again," followed by a motor parade to the City Hall, whose dome, Rolph never tired of pointing out, was 27 feet higher than that of the national Capitol.[23] Walker visited Mooney's mother at her little white house in the Mission District, and encouraged her in the belief that her son would soon be free. He told her that his own father had come to America from Ireland with all his possessions in one suitcase. She asked him to stay for an Irish-style chicken luncheon, but he excused himself, after posing for the photographers.[24]

Privately Walker worried about popular hostility to his intervention. He remarked that "atmosphere" was almost as important as the evidence; and the atmosphere was chilly. The *Examiner* urged him to go home and attend to his own business. A Native Son addressed him as "Mr. New York Champion Jackass." Others wrote to Rolph: "A supreme exhibition of crust"; "What does the Pope know about the guilt or innocence of Mooney?" "It is to laugh. And he really believes he can get away with that bunk in Calif."[25] Declared the *Chronicle*: "New Yorkers propose that we deliver up Mooney—INNOCENT OR GUILTY—as blackmail to the emissaries of Moscow! Every red-blooded American must boil with resentment." (Editor The Chronicle—Sir: "Hurrah for The Chronicle and its courageous stand!")[26] Not all the responses were unfriendly. Walker was enthusiastically received by the San Francisco Downtown Association; he made other public appearances, and acquired a new popularity with men who had previously held him in low esteem. In spite of heavy social engagements and a severe "Eastern" cold, he visited San Quentin and went over the bomb scenes with Walsh.

The public hearing was held in the high-ceilinged, semi-circular chamber of the Supreme Court in the city on December 1. Rolph was present with his legal advisers, Matt I. Sullivan, former Chief Justice of the California Supreme Court; Daniel O'Brien, state director of penology; and Lewis F. Byington, a former District Attorney of San Francisco. Roche had excused himself. Walsh, Walker, and Sapiro spoke for Mooney. Ed Cunha had asked to speak, too, but that side was not invited.[27]

Walker, severely attired in black morning dress, made no apology for appearing: "even as Mr. Bourke Cockran . . . so has your humble servant come."[28] He was indifferently prepared, and turned to Walsh occasionally for prompting. His main arguments were that Oxman and McDonald had been discredited and that Griffin and the jurors favored Mooney's pardon. His plea was broadly emotional and was directed at Rolph. Stephens, Richardson, and Young had pardoned 126 men; Rolph had pardoned seven; was the innocence of any of them, he asked, as clear as Mooney's?[29] Walker had one surprise. He produced a message from Fickert, who was in San Francisco: it stated that, in view of Young's conclusion that Oxman was discredited, "You are probably right in maintaining that it would be to the best interest of the state that clemency should be granted to Mooney." Fickert at last had seemingly changed heart. But not for long. He had been invited to a party at Walker's hotel suite the evening he made this concession. When it was made public, he promptly qualified it beyond recognition: "I meant that this might be true if Governor Young were right. Oxman always stuck to his story. I believed it during the trial and after that. To the day of his death Oxman maintained that it was true. I still think so and I am not changing my position against clemency for Mooney."[30]

Outside the court building a Communist-organized demonstration was held as Walker made his plea. Police permission had been obtained and some three hundred policemen were there. Suddenly the demonstrators, chanting "We want Mooney," made a rush on the entrance. Several people were injured, demonstrators were chased all over the Civic Center—three of them into the plaza fountain—and up the side streets; a score or more were shoved into patrol wagons and bundled off to station houses as thousands of spectators looked on. (One possible cause of the disturbance was that admission to this public hearing had been by ticket only, and Rolph controlled the tickets.)[31]

At the close of the hearing, Rolph said that he would confer with his advisers and render a decision as soon as possible. He later added that it would take at least three months.[32]

The Walker caper remained controversial. One of the critics was Hearst, but Hearst was persuaded to modify his view after Sapiro arranged with Louis B. Mayer of Metro-Goldwyn-Mayer to win over the publisher's mistress, Marion Davies—a maneuver that was not available in 1916.[33] Mooney himself believed that Rolph would have avoided the hearing had Walker not come.[34] The most that could be said for the mayor was said by the New York *Times*: Walker, with a great burst of limelight, had "brought the Mooney question to the front of the American scene as probably no other man could have done it." But the net effect on California, as the *Times* said, could safely be put down as zero.[35] After the flashbulbs and the blarney died, the captain of the Tammany tribe departed for New York by way of

Albuquerque, where he attended an Indian ceremony at the University of New Mexico, was sprinkled with sacred corn, and received a Navajo title, "He Whose Heart Is Big." Sheer sentiment had undoubtedly spurred his trip west, but so, perhaps, had ulterior motives, for Walker at the time was under investigation by the Seabury commission of New York for dereliction in office. Ten months later, facing the prospect of imminent removal by Governor Franklin D. Roosevelt, he resigned.[36]

II

The defense surveyed the situation at the end of 1931 with mixed feelings. "The whole procedure smacks of another Sacco–Vanzetti decision," said Mooney, "and there is very little difference between the behavior of Governor Fuller of Massachusetts and Governor[s] Stephens, Richardson, Young, and Rolph of California."[37] Traverse Clements considered the local antagonism to Walker a bad sign. But others pointed out that Rolph would naturally delay a pardon so that Walker—whose trip had made front-page news in Europe—would not get the lion's share of the credit.[38] And Baldwin suspected that Rolph's solution would be to commute Mooney's sentence to time served, "without any reference whatever to his innocence or guilt. It is a cowardly escape, but it is the best, I think, we can expect."[39]

The advisers to whom Rolph referred the question were Sullivan, Roche, and Byington. Byington had been District Attorney of San Francisco during the palmy days of Abe Ruef. He was a brother-in-law of Tirey L. Ford, the Southern Pacific attorney who had been involved in the graft prosecutions, and served as Ford's assistant counsel during the trials.[40] He was not deeply involved in the Mooney issue; about a month after the Walker hearing, he met McKenzie on a streetcar, and reportedly asked him such questions as where the Eilers Building and 721 Market Street were, and attacked Walsh as a radical. Anyone who would defend Mooney, he said, was un-American.[41] Roche, on the other hand, was rumored to be solidly on Mooney's side and doing what he could to influence Sullivan, his law partner.[42]

At 75 Matt Sullivan, a progressive Democrat, was a lifelong friend of Rolph, whom he had persuaded to run for mayor in 1911. Sullivan had practiced law in San Francisco for half a century. He had been involved in two municipal reform movements—one in the 1880's against Chris Buckley, the blind boss, and the other against Ruef.

Hiram Johnson in 1914 had appointed him Chief Justice, in recognition of his public service; he served but a few months, completing his predecessor's term, and returned to private practice. Sullivan was widely respected, and carried weight in the city on a variety of municipal issues. His views on the Mooney case were not known, but Sapiro thought he might be sympathetic.[43] ("Sapiro thinks that while Sullivan is a stubborn old cuss and would be quite willing to find some real reason for denying a pardon, he is not as hopeless as appears," Mooney learned from his defense committee.)[44]

For several months in 1932 there were the usual rumors of an early decision; another rumor circulated that some radicals were going to kidnap Rolph's infant grandchild, to hold as a hostage until Mooney was pardoned.[45] In April, Sullivan and Byington called in McKenzie for a conference; McKenzie surmised that they had already made a decision, and felt that the conference was a pretense at fairness. Rolph held some secret meetings with his advisers. He let on that he had given many hours to a study of the record. The decision finally came on April 21: the pardon was formally denied. Rolph said that he was convinced of Mooney's guilt.[46]

Among the many satisfied was Congressman Thomas L. Blanton, the Texas Red Scare patriot, still on Capitol Hill; interrupting deliberations on an appropriation bill, Blanton praised Rolph's decision.[47] And another pleased citizen was Rolph's brother, William, of San Francisco, who blithely wrote the Governor's private secretary:

I wish you would tell him for me that we all feel very proud and happy over his decision in the Mooney case. I heard the news the last day I was in Honolulu, and I talked with many people . . . on the steamer, and one old friend of the Governor, Bill Llewellyn, (now of Los Angeles, but formerly of the Llewellyn Iron Works of San Francisco) asked me to be sure to tell the Governor that his decision in the Mooney case is the finest thing he has ever done. Mr. Llewellyn was on the "Mariposa" Tour, and he told me that lots of pools were made up among the passengers over the Mooney case, and when the decision came out, Mr. Llewellyn said he won over a hundred dollars, as he backed the Governor to a finish that he would decide the way he did. Mr. Llewellyn asked me to be sure to tell the Governor he had done the right thing.*

---

* Will Rolph to William A. Smith, May 3, 1932, in Mooney file, Governor's Office Record Group, California State Archives. Smith replied: "Your account of the incident on board the 'Mariposa' was indeed amusing and the Governor wishes you to thank Mr. Llewellyn for him at your first opportunity." (W. A. Smith to Will Rolph, May 9, 1932, same file.)

Along with his denial of the pardon, Rolph released the report prepared by Sullivan, which had been undertaken, according to Rolph, "in a spirit of absolute fairness, and without any bias or prejudice of any kind against Thomas J. Mooney."[48] It stated that Mooney should not have been convicted "if in fact he is innocent," but found that he was not innocent, because he was convicted: "the final judgment of conviction necessitates a conclusive presumption of guilt."[49] Oxman's testimony had not been crucial: "whether true or false, the other evidence in the case suffices to sustain the verdict of 'guilty.'" Among that evidence was McDonald's testimony. His 1921 affidavit was "a worthless scrap of paper," made for money.[50] Less than a quarter of Sullivan's report directly concerned the crime. Rather, he dwelt on associations, character, and opinions. He quoted Dunne extensively; Griffin's views were "fulminations." He was less interested in the bomb than the *Blast,* to which he turned again and again, to show that Mooney was capable of perpetrating the crime he had committed; for anarchists "sanction or condone every kind of crime, even murder, in the war of 'Reds' against the State," and Mooney was one of these revolutionists, "disloyal to our government, the best on earth." Sullivan also found that the defense had raised "an enormous sum of money in aid of vicious propaganda based upon slander, libel and attacks upon our State." In consequence, many well-meaning but uninformed persons had joined the protesting army, including Albert Einstein and Yehudi Menuhin.[51]

"No one who knows Matt I. Sullivan, his high character and his complete independence, can doubt that his finding represents solely his honest and complete conviction," editorialized the *Chronicle.* It expressed the desire to hear no more "din and clamor" about the case.[52] But the din and clamor about the Sullivan report had just begun.

Sapiro, among others, was outraged at such a performance by a member of the Bar. He drafted a letter of rebuttal ("The difficulty is restraint") and gave it to Baldwin for criticism.[53] The letter charged Sullivan with ignoring fundamental principles of law and logic, permitting his prejudices to rule his judgment, misleading Rolph, and keeping an innocent man in prison from hatred of his labor views and activities. "You ignored fundamental issues and obscured others. Your 88-page report,—an amazing document coming from a lawyer and former judge,—bristles with evasions, misrepresentations, insinuations, cheap emotionalism, and bitter prejudice."[54] Baldwin sought the signatures of a number of liberals before sending the letter. Rob-

ert L. Duffus, by then with the New York *Times,* considered it superfluous; the report spoke for itself, he said. Clarence Darrow said the
letter would do no good: "he would only come back with another!
... human beings are hopelessly cruel." But thirteen signed it in addition to Sapiro and Baldwin: Harry Elmer Barnes, John Dewey, Norman Hapgood, Arthur Garfield Hays, John Haynes Holmes, Ernest
Jerome Hopkins, Henry T. Hunt, Fannie Hurst, Fremont Older,
Lemuel F. Parton, Oswald Garrison Villard, Harry F. Ward, and Rabbi Stephen S. Wise: "The Famous Fifteen," Sullivan called them.[55]
Most of them were members of the ACLU-affiliated National Mooney-Billings Committee in New York.

San Francisco newspapers published the letter and Sullivan's reply:

a group made up of parlor Bolsheviks, accommodating publicity seekers,
intellectual irresponsibles and tricky special pleaders, fitly headed by a
female romancer, have sent me a letter ... denouncing my report, with
characteristic neurotic intemperateness and disregard of facts.

... Their letter is a reckless perversion of the report and abounds in
misstatements and libelous epithets and personal abuse. ...

The entire pro-Mooney propaganda, liberally financed by Reds, radicals and revolutionists throughout the world, is founded on falsehood and
venal imposture. It cannot prevail against the conclusively established fact
that Tom Mooney committed the dreadful crime of which he was convicted.[56]

Rolph said he agreed with Sullivan, which led Duffus to remark that
of the two, Rolph was the worse, "because I think his natural instincts
are kindly and he has had to go further to make the display of himself
he has."[57]

Sullivan also heard directly from Rabbi Wise, who called him a
"bitterly vindictive 'old man.' " He replied: "Perhaps you are merely
performing a Mooney goose step, like the rest of the wooden soldiers
on parade for Mooney whenever the journalistic master of the show
pulls them out of the box. In the last parade I missed from the ranks
those two deep students of the Mooney case, Yehudi Menuhin and
Professor Einstein." He added that Baldwin had been called before
a Congressional investigating committee for his defense of Communists. ("I am rather proud of his answer," Wise wrote Baldwin. "It
shows that there is no reason for keeping Mooney in prison except
that you testified before the Fish Committee and that Menuhin, Einstein, and I are Jews.")[58]

III

The defense had long wished for a new federal investigation. The Mediation Commission's report had been widely publicized in its day, and had contributed to the rescue of Mooney from the gallows. Although no federal inquiry could substitute for a pardon, it was natural to cast about for one when the prospects for clemency were so bleak. Shortly after the California Supreme Court's first recommendation against Billings, the National Mooney-Billings Committee decided that if nothing came of the McDonald hearing, the Committee should promote various investigations, including one by President Hoover's National Commission on Law Observance and Enforcement.[59]

The Wickersham Commission, as it was popularly called, had been set up in the early months of the Hoover administration as a temporary, fact-finding body of experts—mainly distinguished men of law— to investigate the rising problems of crime and law enforcement, under the chairmanship of George Wickersham, who had been the Attorney General in the cabinet of William Howard Taft. It was the most prominent of many temporary federal commissions created at Hoover's request. Originally conceived to deal with the problem of Prohibition, the Wickersham Commission came under strenuous political pressure in its first year, and compromised itself in handling that issue; but there was good reason to hope that its subsequent work might be enlightened and influential.[60] The proposed investigations were to cover eleven fields of study, one of which concerned lawless and unfair practices of police officers and prosecutors. This section was entitled "Lawlessness in Law Enforcement." It was headed by Judge William S. Kenyon of the United States Circuit Court, a former Progressive Republican Senator from Iowa and a man of liberal convictions.[61] Two other commissioners served in this section. One of them was Newton D. Baker, who had been Woodrow Wilson's Secretary of War and confidant.

Assisting the Kenyon section as special counsel, with staff and budgetary support from the Commission, were three unusually able, scholarly attorneys, all of them dedicated to civil liberties: Zechariah Chafee, Jr., of the Harvard law faculty, Walter H. Pollak of the New York Bar, and Carl S. Stern, a partner of Pollak. As Walsh remarked, they were men with "plenty of courage."[62] Chafee was a life-long defender of free speech. In 1919–20 he had investigated and criticized the illegal activities of the Department of Justice, which led to an extraordinary academic trial of Chafee by a committee of the Harvard Board of Overseers.* Pollak, who had worked with Benjamin Cardozo before World War I, had contributed to the constitutional expansion of civil rights in cases before the United States Supreme Court (including Anita Whitney's); he assisted Clarence Darrow in the defense of John Thomas Scopes in the Tennessee "monkey trial"; and in 1928 he helped Roger Baldwin found the National Mooney-Billings Committee.[63]

Baldwin turned to the Kenyon section. He learned from one of the Commissioners in July 1930 that they already had an inquiry in mind, but several months went by with no apparent progress. Walsh asked Roy Howard of the Scripps-Howard press for an appeal, and a syndicated Scripps-Howard editorial was published urging the investigation.[64] The matter was also taken up by Gardner Jackson, a freelance journalist and lobbyist-publicist for lost causes ("The damn S[acco]–V[anzetti] experience got into my blood and I can't get rid of it").[65] Jackson pointed out the editorial to Commissioner Baker: the public, he said, had a right to know whether public funds would be used to consider the case. Baker replied: "I do not know how far, if at all, it is being investigated, but ordinarily a Commission of the kind President Hoover has created cannot be expected to investigate and report upon individual cases, except as their investigation is a part of the material from which general conclusions can be drawn."[66] This did not satisfy Mooney's friends. "Of course," Jackson confided to Henry T. Hunt, "the only value we can expect from having the legal lawlessness report include material from the Mooney case is merely a louder sounding board for further action."[67] General conclusions were insufficient.

After discussing the question at a meeting in November, the Commissioners unanimously adopted a motion proposed by Baker, "that it was beyond the province of the Commission to investigate individual cases with a view to making recommendations as to their disposition, particularly in State courts, and one reason for that is that the commission has no power to examine witnesses or redetermine facts." Wickersham gave out this formula to the press.[68] Jackson protested

---

* The so-called "Harvard Club Trial," conducted by an appointed body of distinguished jurists, May 22, 1921. Accused of impropriety, willful error, and unfitness for "the training of youth," Chafee was narrowly exonerated. (Arthur E. Sutherland, *The Law at Harvard: A History of Ideas and Men, 1817–1967* [1967], pp. 251–58.)

that a recommendation as to the disposition of the case was not at issue, but only an investigation of its lawlessness. He kept after Baker, whose position grew sharper:

I am so clear that the Wickersham Commission has no jurisdiction to conduct a proper investigation of the Mooney case and so clear that any correction of that situation must be brought about in California, and probably by Californians, that I doubt whether there is anything that would justify a further discussion of the case with me. It seems to me that the administration of justice in California, so far as it involves a violation of the laws of that State, is essentially a domestic problem, and that any outside attempt to intervene is more likely to have the effect of delaying and discouraging than expediting the local application of remedies.*

On this view the Kenyon section had no right to investigate the lawlessness of any contemporary State officials that had resulted in convictions—a position which neither Kenyon nor his counsel approved. The day after this letter was written, Kenyon stated his preference for an investigation of the case.[69]

Kenyon was already deeply involved in the matter. He had asked Jackson to gather documents and Judge Griffin to send a report. (Griffin responded that all the major witnesses had testified falsely and sent Kenyon a number of documents.) Kenyon asked Walsh, an old friend, if it were true that the prosecution had knowingly introduced perjured testimony; Walsh replied that it was. He and Kenyon talked the case over with the section's counsel. The latter, at Kenyon's request, subsequently undertook the investigation, which took about four months.[70] Spadework was done by a young New York attorney, Thomas A. Halleran, who called on Walsh for material. Pollak, Chafee, and Stern each went over the work.[71] The report was hurried toward completion ("Pollak et al are splitting their guts," Jackson said privately to Baldwin), and it was submitted to Kenyon in June: a 240-page analysis accompanied by documents.[72] Kenyon presented the report to the Commission as it was winding up affairs and preparing to go out of business. Wickersham objected: he had not realized, he said, that any such study had been contemplated. He called it "unauthorized and uncalled for" and too late for consideration. Other Commissioners, including Baker, also disapproved.[73]

---

* Baker to Jackson, March 4, 1931, as quoted in Jackson to Baker, June 8, 1931, ACLU Papers, v. 482a. Felix Frankfurter commented a few months later, "I'm afraid Baker's liberalism has largely evaporated. 'The tired radical' was more than a happy phrase by Walter Weyl." (Frankfurter to Bruce Bliven, January 9, 1932, Frankfurter Papers.)

Kenyon wanted the report adopted, but did not insist. Ironically, the *coup de grace* came from Roger Baldwin, who urged Kenyon that it not be released just then, for fear of offending Governor Rolph, with whom Walsh and Sapiro were negotiating for a hearing. Might the release be delayed for at least a month? "It seems to me we all owe at least that much courtesy to the Governor."[74] The Commissioners, informed of Baldwin's request, decided not to accept the report. They drafted a letter to Pollak, Chafee, and Stern, invoking the Baker resolution, the tardy submission, and the action before Rolph. The report was not officially rejected, it was simply set aside.[75] As Chafee advised Baldwin, "the Commission will not publish before August 1—or before the U.S. joins the League of Nations." ("Ah, if we could only have worked for Al Smith!" he wrote Pollak.)[76]

When Mooney learned of Baldwin's intervention he was incensed, for he had no confidence in Rolph, courtesy or no courtesy. But given the attitude of Wickersham and Baker, the report probably would have been shelved anyway. There was one consolation: the Commission's section report on "Criminal Procedure," published in July, referred briefly to the case; it described the inadequacy of the laws of California as "shocking to one's sense of justice." This finding was played up in the press.[77]

That fall Baldwin tried to call forth the Pollack report and it would not come. No one seemed to know who had the authority to release it. He concluded that Congress was his only recourse. Jackson enlisted the help of several progressive Senators ("the newspaper gang down here are eager as hell to put their hands on the report"); a resolution was adopted requesting it from the administration. The Department of Justice had no copy, and had to ask Stern for one, which was delivered to the Senate. Publication was another matter: the estimated cost was $1,800 (reported as $1,800,000 in several California newspapers), and in the end the Judiciary Committee's recommendation died in the Senate. Eventually Baldwin was able to have the report published privately. It appeared in the fall of 1932 as *The Mooney-Billings Report Suppressed by the Wickersham Commission*.[78]

The *Mooney-Billings Report* was a systematic examination of unlawful aspects of the Mooney-Billings cases, drawn for the most part from the trial transcripts and related legal documents. Its findings were not new or sensational, but they comprised a sober indictment of the law enforcement practices to which the defendants had been subjected. It did not claim their innocence; it did not claim that they were class victims; it did not make recommendations on the disposition of their cases. Rather, it found plainly unfair conduct and grave violations of the American Bar Association's standard of professional ethics.[79] The report concluded that the preliminary investigation of the crime had been improperly turned over to Swanson; that the police investigation "was reduced to a hunt for evidence to convict the arrested defendants"; that there were flagrant violations of law in the arrests, detentions, and searches; that witnesses' identifications were accepted without tests; that the prosecuting officials deliberately sought to arouse public prejudice through interviews given to the press; that the prosecution deliberately concealed information impairing the credibility of witnesses; that in producing witnesses despite knowledge of their prior contradictory stories, the prosecution was "vouching for perjured testimony"; that the witnesses were coached to a degree approximating subornation of perjury; and that the prosecuting attorneys made intemperate and prejudicial opening and closing statements to the jury. "After the trials, the disclosures casting doubt on the justice of the convictions were minimized, and every attempt made to defeat the liberation of the defendants, by a campaign of misrepresentation and propaganda carried on by the officials who had prosecuted them."[80]

The report became popularly known as "the Wickersham Report," allegedly suppressed for reasons of political expediency.[81] It became a standard reference in the 1930's for advocates of Mooney's pardon.

IV

Executive clemency had no substitute. In its absence the struggle for freedom took many forms. The elusive goal was pursued through meetings and demonstrations, schemes, protests, and legal action. The defense committee circulated pamphlets and newsletters. People forswore vacationing in California and boycotted California oranges. Sinclair Lewis organized an authors' petition for Mooney's release; among the signers were Sherwood Anderson, Mary Austin, Stephen Vincent Benet, John Erskine, Edna Ferber, Dorothy Canfield Fisher, Will Irwin, Robinson Jeffers, Carl Sandburg, and William Allen White.[82] In a letter to Mooney from Hearst's castle, San Simeon, George Bernard Shaw satirized the whole situation:

If somebody would bomb the Mooney Defense Committee out of existence —if it were made a crime to mention your name in the papers—if only you could be allowed to take your true present position as an amiable elderly gentleman whose career as a Labor pioneer was cut short many years ago by a verdict vaguely remembered as having been much questioned at the time, and whose imprisonment has gone to a length which is now out-of-date and shocking, then perhaps the remonstrances I have made in response to Press inquiries might have some effect.[83]

At the closing ceremony of the 1932 Olympics in the Los Angeles Coliseum, six young radicals raced around the stadium track wearing "Free Tom Mooney" signs, as thousands booed and the band played "The Star Spangled Banner"; the demonstrators were held on suspicion of criminal syndicalism, and sentenced to nine months in the county jail for disturbing the peace.[84] Their attorney, Leo Gallagher, a left-wing member of the ACLU, was dismissed from his teaching post at a local law school: "There is a limit of what we can take for Gallagher's principles," said the law school dean. This local spleen prompted the *New Republic* to remark that California was "the most stupidly reactionary state in the country."[85]

The defense effort to renew legal action involved obtaining a trial on the old remaining indictment against Mooney. Since a new trial, whatever the verdict, could not in itself free him, its purpose was basically the same as that of the extra-legal stunts and measures, to create new arguments and pressures on the Governor and to keep the case alive.

The idea of retrying Mooney had rested since the year Governor Stephens refused to pardon him as the preliminary to a new trial. In August 1931 a motion for a new trial was filed in San Francisco Superior Court by an obscure Oakland attorney, Carl L. Shinn, acting independently of Walsh and Sapiro, and considerably embarrassing them in their efforts to obtain a pardon hearing before Rolph. Shinn's connection with Mooney is unclear: Mooney later repeatedly denied that he had hired him, but he must at least have given his approval, in hopes of seeing what could be accomplished. Judge Louis H. Ward, on whose calendar the indictment stood, stated that he was prepared to order Mooney brought for a trial; that testimony of deceased or absent witnesses from the first trial might be read by stipulation; and that the former prosecuting attorneys might be engaged to assist the present District Attorney, Matthew Brady.[86] However, because of the simultaneous efforts to obtain a pardon, Shinn withdrew his action.

Several months later, after Rolph denied the pardon, Sapiro and Walsh returned to the matter of a new trial. The outlook was poor. Oxman was dead and the purpose of the trial dubious. Brady declined to cooperate. He protested sympathy, but declared he would have no case; a trial would be a farce. He told Theodore Dreiser that he would ask for a dismissal of the indictment on the grounds that he believed Mooney innocent.[87] Walsh, however, felt that the effort to get a new trial for Mooney "would vastly aid his cause throughout the world."[88] Sapiro did not join him, for he had withdrawn from the case following a dispute with Mooney; in his place Walsh, at Mooney's request, chose Leo Gallagher, the dismissed law professor.

In the absence of Brady's cooperation Judge Ward requested Attorney General Webb to appoint a special prosecutor. Webb refused: Brady was qualified, he said, and could either try the case or insist on dismissal; if Ward refused dismissal, the District Attorney could ask the Appellate Court for a writ of *mandamus* ordering it.[89] Brady did not go to the latter extreme. His assistant was in court on April 26, 1933, the date Ward set for the trial. "California is very, very tired of Mr. Mooney and looks with distaste upon the spectacle about to be presented," said the New York *Times*; "there is little doubt that [legalized] beer comes first so far as public interest is concerned." But around the Hall of Justice the streets and Portsmouth Square were lined that morning with men shouting "Free Tom Mooney!" The police had learned that radicals were planning a demonstration, and were there in force to push them back. The shouts penetrated the courtroom through closed windows and caused the judge to postpone the case.[90]

Three weeks later Ward quietly ordered Mooney's return to court. Mooney was not informed in advance; when the sheriff's deputies arrived at San Quentin, he was peeling potatoes. There was a brief delay while he changed clothes and Warden Holohan consulted Webb about the legality of the order. Then the prisoner was called from his cell, handcuffed, loaded into the sheriff's sedan before two or three dozen news cameras, and taken to San Francisco in a private motorboat. He arrived at the Hall of Justice in good humor but not optimistic about the outcome of the proceedings. Walsh had come from New York; the state was represented by an Assistant District Attorney, William Murphy. This time there were no demonstrations.[91]

It was an odd spectacle—a murder trial in which the defense sought a rigorous prosecution and the prosecution sought an acquittal. Said the judge:

Before proceeding, I wish to state there can be no practical advantage in this trial in view of the District Attorney's determination not to present evidence. Without the people's evidence a verdict of not guilty would be worthless in the eyes of the world. . . .

I do not propose to permit this trial to become a means of refuting evidence given at any previous trial, and the defense here will be permitted to answer only such evidence as is produced at this trial. In view of the attitude of the District Attorney, I had hoped that the defense would decide to give up this trial. Do you still wish to go on trial?

"We do," said Mooney.[92]

Twelve jurors were found with no discernible fixed opinions, and the trial commenced. Gallagher read a list of out-of-town witnesses and asked for subpoenas; Ward replied, "the County is broke," and denied the request. Murphy then asked for a directed acquittal. "We believe there to be no question that the evidence is insufficient to warrant a conviction," he said, and proved it by refusing to offer any evidence.[93] Mooney argued his own defense for a real prosecution:

The District Attorney states here that as a result of seventeen years these witnesses are no longer available. That is not true. There is only one witness, to my knowledge, that is vital in this case that is not available now, and that is Frank C. Oxman. . . . The real object of this hearing is for the purposes of proving to this jury that I am not guilty of this charge, and if I am not guilty of this charge, inferentially the world will draw their deduction that I am not guilty on the other charge, and that cannot properly be done unless all of the evidence is presented to this jury.

Oxman's testimony might be entered from the record, he said, provided impeaching testimony were permitted also.

. . . the tragedy of the situation [is] this; that he [Murphy] says there's no case, and four Governors of this State have held that the very evidence he can not use in this case is sufficient to keep me in prison. It is available. The Supreme Court has held that evidence is sufficient to keep me in prison. It has held it is sufficient to keep Billings in prison. . . . And also the Advisory Pardon Board, under Governor Young, and Governor Rolph's personal legal advisors . . . have held that evidence is not only ample but sufficient. And if it is ample and sufficient to convict us . . . and keep us in prison for seventeen years, surely it must be worthy of consideration of this jury.[94]

The plea was poignant, but Murphy saw its weakness: "the only relief that can be granted must be granted by the Governor. It has passed out of our hands. . . . Nothing that we might do in this case could affect the prior judgment." He also acknowledged in effect the absurdity of it all:

There are only four witnesses that connected Mooney with the commission of this affair; one was McDonald, another was Oxman, and the two Edeau women. McDonald is out of the State. He has refused [refuted?] his testimony. Oxman is dead. There are many ways of impeaching Oxman. The Edeau women have been impeached. And when you eliminate those four witnesses and you call upon us some seventeen years after a thing has happened, . . . we can't do it.[95]

Ward directed the jury to bring in a verdict of not guilty, and they acquitted him without retiring to the jury room. Within a few hours Mooney was back in San Quentin peeling potatoes.[96]

"It's too late to correct it," said the Red Queen: "when you've once said a thing, that fixes it, and you must take the consequences."

V

The sterility of Mooney's trial left him nothing more than the bare acquittal on which to base a new pardon appeal. The appeal was not made. Not only was it considered futile, but it might have interfered with a new line of legal action then under way, the search for a federal writ of habeas corpus. The defense committee supported a recall movement against Rolph that had been initiated earlier, for unrelated reasons, by the State Grange; Mooney hoped that Langdon or Griffin might run for governor—or, barring them, he himself. "Rolph WILL NOT switch," said Older during the movement: "pardoning Mooney would finish him."[97] But the movement lacked the strength to force a recall election.

Rolph died in office seven months before his term's end. Government by radiance had failed to meet the crises of the depression. Fatigued by his duties and travels, weakened by illness, hounded by the state's financial problems and a State Senate investigation of his office, he went on a fence-mending tour and was stricken by a lung infection that brought on his death. "He was a man of heart more than head," said Matt Sullivan, "and whatever his faults were, the reason was that his heart was too big."* He had pardoned more criminals than his three predecessors combined.[98]

---

* Long afterward a *Chronicle* editor judged Rolph more severely as "an amiable Republican knucklehead." (Paul C. Smith, *Personal File* [1964], p. 174.)

As his body lay in state in the city hall he had loved, the responsibilities of governorship were taken over by the 68-year-old Lieutenant Governor, Frank F. Merriam of Long Beach, a colorless, pious, rightwing Republican who had been Friend W. Richardson's campaign manager in 1926.[99] In Hichborn's words, "By friend and foe alike he was regarded as a reactionary"; according to a Long Beach admirer who styled herself a "Lincoln greenback silver *Republican*," he was a "Perfected Gentleman of brotherly kindness."[100]

Mooney's attorneys at once prepared a new pardon petition. They considered the prospect hopeless, but Mooney was anxious to try. The application was *pro forma:* "It is being made for the purpose of keeping a record of applications to each successive Governor," one attorney confided.[101] Merriam had said that he was unprejudiced about the case and would give it fair consideration. But after the petition was filed, he declared that since Rolph had denied one pardon application in the present four-year term, there was no immediate need to consider another, and that he would not do so unless elected to a full term of office.[102] In this election the opponent he faced was Upton Sinclair.

Sinclair was a romantic Socialist reformer of many crusades. The nation's best known pamphleteer, he was the author of the muckraking *Jungle* and dozens of other books on American ills, including the Mooney-Billings affair: in 1920 Fremont Older had suggested to him that he write a "pure and simple" novel about the case, and the prompt result was a fictionalized tract entitled *100%: The Story of a Patriot.* (The *Nation* praised it, and Theodore Dreiser called it an important work of social criticism, but *100%* lacked both literary and historical merit.* Sinclair sold 35,000 copies and was left with a large warehouse surplus, which he sought unsuccessfully to dispose of, below cost, to the Mooney defense committee.)[103] Twice Sinclair had

---

* Sinclair wrote two autobiographies (*Candid Reminiscences: My first Thirty Years* [1932], and *The Autobiography of Upton Sinclair* [1962]), in neither of which he mentioned *100%*. In the second, he discussed nearly all of his first forty-seven books; but *100%* was better forgotten. In the following passage (p. 34) most of the allusions are transparent:

"Jim Goober [Mooney] was a prominent labor leader. He had organized the employees of the Traction Trust, and had called and led a tremendous strike. Also he had called building strikes, and some people said he had used dynamite upon uncompleted buildings, and made a joke of it. Anyhow, the businessmen of the city wanted to put him where he could no longer trouble them; and when some maniac unknown had flung a dynamite bomb into the path of the Preparedness parade, the big fellows of the city had decided that now was the opportunity they were seeking. Guffey [Swanson], the man who had taken charge of Peter [McDonald?], was head of the secret service of the Traction Trust, and the big fellows had put him in complete charge. They wanted action, and would take no chances with the graft-ridden and incompetent police of the city."

run for Governor of California on the Socialist ticket. But in 1933 he left his "small political sect" and announced his candidacy for the governorship as a Democrat. His platform was a program to "End Poverty in California" by putting the jobless to work at idle machines and on idle land, in State-run colonies producing goods for exchange through a system of scrip: production for use, helped along by an immense bond issue and heavy taxes on those who produced for profit. He also proposed substantial old-age pensions. The whole plan, felicitously called EPIC, was sanguine and economically naïve, but a dramatic response to despair, reaction, and emergency: "We have only a year or two in which to save ourselves," he said.[104]

Few people took Sinclair seriously at first. Nine candidates aspired to the Democratic nomination, including Woodrow Wilson's wartime propaganda head, George Creel, whose horizons were fixed by old-fashioned Progressivism; to Creel and other regular Democrats, Sinclair was a crackpot interloper, his candidacy a joke. But the electorate responded more warmly to Sinclair's visions, particularly in Southern California, where the depression had flattened a populace of shallow economic roots. In 1934 more than 1,250,000 Californians were dependent on relief, and 70 per cent of them were in Southern California.[105] Los Angeles, the bright lotus land of the 1920's, was exceptionally vulnerable to depression hardships; having boomed with tourists, orange groves, oil speculation, subdivision schemes, retirement income, and borrowed money, its defenses against national penury were weak. Elderly midwesterners, small-town Iowans who had settled in the sunshine, found that their modest structures of financial security had caved in. Small businessmen in the overcrowded service industries were bankrupt. Many of these desperate people had once supported Hoover, but their plight now drew them to Sinclair as they had earlier been drawn to evangelists, faith healers, and stock promoters.[106]

Sinclair had practically no newspaper support, but he published a weekly campaign paper, *EPIC News,* and by July he also had in print 200,000 copies of his campaign booklet, *I, Governor of California and How I Ended Poverty.* He addressed meetings endlessly; hundreds of local EPIC clubs held picnics and rallies; in Los Angeles transfigured throngs sang "Jerusalem the Golden" and waved American flags as they gathered to hear the new prophet. He preached a brand of radicalism they understood: not proletarian supremacy, but the speedy recapture of Elysium ("revolution by bankruptcy," the *Chronicle* called it), and he restored hope as he described the new covenant of prosperity. In the August primaries Southern Californians overwhelmed the Democratic preferences of San Francisco and the Central Valley and gave Sinclair the nomination of a badly divided party. Meanwhile that summer Governor Merriam had intensified his conservative image by calling out the National Guard in the San Francisco general strike and making Communism a campaign issue. He defeated C. C. Young and two other Republican rivals to win renomination—by 90,000 fewer votes than were cast for Sinclair. (Sinclair received 436,000, an absolute majority in the Democratic primary.)[107]

Mooney was jubilant over Sinclair's preliminary victory, for Sinclair had publicly promised to pardon him and apologize on behalf of California as his first gubernatorial act. Sinclair had said that he did not know whether Mooney was innocent or guilty, but that Mooney had been convicted on perjured testimony: "I have been told that by the judge who tried him." Before the primary he had asked President Roosevelt to intervene and seek a pardon; he himself called on Merriam with such a request. (He advised Merriam that Mooney's friends had been able to defeat every candidate for Governor who had opposed pardon. Merriam replied that he would not be influenced by political threats.)[108]

The EPIC fever swept on that fall. California's organized eccentrics were united with the dispossessed, for Sinclair had mobilized the supporters of other quivering crusades, including the briefly powerful Utopian Society. The movement was hampered, to be sure, by acute shortages of campaign funds; by the defection of moderates, including Creel; and by the fickleness of Roosevelt and his master of political ceremonies, Jim Farley, who progressed from curiosity and amiability to an endorsement of Sinclair that he later repudiated. But more important were the tactics of the opposition. The propertied voters saw in EPIC the threat of a social and economic upheaval. They argued that Sinclair's election would mean the ruin of private business, that workers would lose their jobs, public utilities would be taxed out of existence, capital would flee from the state; that credit would be destroyed, property confiscated, and the banking system laid prostrate.[109] They assailed Sinclair in a personal smear campaign that Arthur M. Schlesinger, Jr., has described as "the first all-out public relations *Blitzkrieg* in American politics." The public relations firm of Clem Whitaker and Leone Baxter directed this assault—its first venture into politics—despite Sinclair's longstanding friendship with the Whitaker family. Their strategy was to shift attention from EPIC to Sinclair's intellectual idiosyncrasies. Sinclair was vulnerable, since his books comprised a great treasury of social dissent from which alarming quotations could be extracted. Thousands were; many were affixed to cartoons and distributed to newspapers around the state. Sinclair was denounced as an atheist, anarchist, Communist, vegetarian, and advocate of free love. Highway billboards warned against his election. (On the beach at Santa Cruz two Italian clam diggers told Franklin Hichborn that they were going to vote for Merriam because Sinclair's election would "offend the Virgin.") *EPIC News* retorted with its own epithets, but the match was hardly even.[110]

Hollywood movie magnates, frightened by Sinclair's tax program, threatened to remove the movie industry to Florida (a ploy that was not taken seriously), and launched their own anti-Sinclair campaign. They made political speeches on studio lots, assessed their movie stars and other high-salaried employees a day's pay for Merriam's campaign, and faked a newsreel with bit actors depicting an influx into California of hoboes attracted by Sinclair's promises. (This and similar counterfeit newsreels were distributed to motion-picture theaters throughout the state.) The State Registrar of Motor Vehicles, a political appointee, warned that the unemployed were indeed entering the state at the rate of 100 a day—an alarming number if one overlooked the familiar pattern of winter migration to California of unemployed, homeless Americans. Probably more damaging to Sinclair was his own remark—which he claimed the press misrepresented—that if he were elected, half the unemployed in the United States would come to California.[111]

Sinclair's forces were kept busy trying to meet various strategems. Fabricated Communist endorsements of Sinclair circulated even though the Communist Party had its own candidate, Sam Darcy, and had denounced Sinclair as a social fascist. A *Literary Digest* poll released shortly before the election gave Merriam 62 per cent of the total vote—a wildly inaccurate prediction, since he actually received less than 49 per cent; Sinclair charged that Merriam workers were paid 25c for every *Digest* ballot they could turn in. Republican officials in Los Angeles attempted to disfranchise 25,000 or more county relief beneficiaries on the grounds of illegal registration, but before election day the State Supreme Court prohibited wholesale disqualification of these registrants. And another controversy involved the alleged coercion of voters in the motion-picture studios, which Sinclair's managers sought to have investigated by the Los Angeles grand jury. "After I am elected Governor," said Sinclair, "if you will bring me evidence of vote intimidation by employers, I will see they are sent to prison to take the place of Tom Mooney."[112]

During the campaign Sinclair received financial support from Mooney's friends, particularly Aline Barnsdall of Los Angeles, who pledged $10,000 for radio broadcasts. The Mooney defense committee publicized Sinclair's promise of a pardon and boosted his political rallies in San Francisco; at one of them Sinclair recognized Mooney's mother and sister by prearrangement and brought them to the platform before a wildly cheering crowd.[113] Mooney, apprehensive that Sinclair's support might be undermined by a contrived act of violence, reminded Sinclair of the bombing of the executive mansion on the eve of Fickert's recall. The *EPIC News* expressed parallel apprehensions: it warned that plots were afoot to connect Sinclair with the Preparedness Day bombing, and to circulate a rumor that Mooney had confessed.* These fears proved unfounded, but the Mooney case of course entered into the vilification heaped on the candidate. The Sacramento *Bee* declared that Mooney's liberation would encourage Bolshevism and that Sinclair's promise was enough to damn him in the eyes of the electorate. Merriam punsters printed "Sincliar" dollars, "good only in California or Russia," signed by "Utopian Sincliar," Governor, and "Tom Phoney," Secretary of Finance. Commented Sinclair, "the same men who employed perjurers against Mooney employ perjurers against me."[114]

The publicity barrage had its effect. "The amount of lying and dishonesty in this campaign exceeds belief," said the victim. Before the end it was apparent that Sinclair would lose. Moderates who could not bring themselves to vote for Merriam had the alternative of voting helplessly for Raymond Haight, the Progressive Party candidate, and many did. Haight, the grandson of a California governor, although supported by the McClatchy newspapers, had no chance of winning; he made lurid predictions of bloodshed if either Sinclair or Merriam won, and demanded federal intervention to prevent a civil war.[115] The final count was as follows: Merriam, 1,138,620; Sinclair, 879,557; Haight, 302,519; and Darcy, 5,826. Merriam claimed that his election demonstrated "the essential common sense of the people of Califor-

* There was a precedent for this in the confession of the Los Angeles *Times* bombing shortly before the defeat of Job Harriman, the Socialist candidate for mayor of Los Angeles, in 1911.

nia." Sinclair, in his concession statement, said the election had been stolen. In any event it had not been an expression of confidence in Merriam, but a rejection of Sinclair; and with his defeat went Mooney's hopes for a pardon. "It was the best possible chance for freedom we had," Mooney said.[116]

When Merriam's new term began, Sinclair asked him to pardon Mooney. "More than six months ago you promised me you would investigate the case." The Governor replied that he would consider the pardon application when the duties of office permitted.[117] ("The old political bunk—wait," a defense committee member said in 1921.) As Sinclair, surveying the political scene, had remarked, "we shall have to get most of our laughs in 1935 out of watching Merriam trying to look like a progressive. We shall not have much else to laugh at, for it is going to be a terrible year."[118]

CHAPTER TWENTY-FIVE

The Defense Committee and the Reds

Like the Sacco–Vanzetti *case, the* Mooney *case has
been used for world-wide ballyhoo.*
—Elizabeth Dilling, testifying
before the United States Senate

*The worst thing you could do for any movement
is to let it become inactive.*
—Mooney

COMMUNIST INTEREST in Mooney began early and lasted throughout
the years of his imprisonment. Robert Minor, the defense committee's
first secretary and later a Communist Party functionary, was for many
years a personal link between the CP and Mooney; so was William Z.
Foster, the veteran CP leader, who knew Mooney from the Socialist
activities they shared in 1913. The party understood Mooney's value
to the movement. As Minor wrote Foster in 1922, "We will need
every ounce of weight that can be attached to his name." Foster's
Trade Union Educational League, a CP-controlled organization of
the early 1920's, had the cooperation of Mooney's defense committee
"as far as possible," according to Rena Mooney.[1] However, Communist involvement in the case became significant only with the formation of the International Labor Defense, the most influential of the
CP's early fronts.

The ILD was an offshoot of the International Red Aid, a Comintern front set up in Moscow in 1922. It was created by the party in the
United States in 1925 for the legal defense and prison relief of "class-
war prisoners." In the late 1920's, under the control of James P. Cannon, its national secretary, the ILD waged fund-raising and propaganda campaigns on behalf of radical labor prisoners, including Sacco
and Vanzetti, J. B. McNamara, the Centralia IWW prisoners, the
Harlan miners in Kentucky, and Mooney and Billings.[2] Part of the
ILD's program was to send these prisoners small personal allowances.

In 1926, for instance, it sent each of 106 "class-war prisoners," mostly IWW's, $5 a month. Mooney received a total of $230 by June 1929, and his mother $130. Billings was treated similarly.[3]

The ILD stressed the Mooney case in its activities. ILD branches all over the country held meetings, dances, bazaars, and picnics to support demands for Mooney's freedom and raise money. The funds collected in his name did not, however, go to the Tom Mooney Molders Defense Committee. The TMMDC was not informed of the meetings or the amounts raised, or told how the money was spent.* Mary Gallagher did learn of one ILD Mooney meeting in Portland, Oregon, at which Elizabeth Gurley Flynn raised $56; following Mary's protest, the ILD sent the defense committee its first contribution—$5. "My dear," she wrote Tom, "I have something to . . . frame and save for your grandchildren."[4] Mooney complained to Alfred Wagenknecht, the ILD executive secretary in New York, that he was being exploited. In reply Wagenknecht explained the organization's position:

Although Mooney and Billings are the outstanding class war prisoners in America, we must assist in bringing about the release of all other class war prisoners, as well, and especially the Centralia prisoners. Our campaign must take the form of mobilizing all the workers in the cities in protest against the further incarceration of these class war prisoners. Toward this end we must route national organizers and speakers. We must rent halls. We must establish a press service. We must print hundreds of thousands of petitions to be circulated in America and other foreign countries [sic!], demanding the immediate release of Mooney, Billings and all class war prisoners. Funds for a campaign such as this must be collected as the campaign develops and proceeds.

. . . We feel that you are sufficiently interested in the fate of all class war prisoners, to agree with us that to make a campaign to free Mooney and Billings alone, would make it appear as if we had forsaken the rest.[5]

Wagenknecht claimed that Walsh and others had agreed in December 1928 to a division of responsibilities among the National Mooney-Billings Committee, the TMMDC, the Chicago Federation of Labor, and the ILD; the ILD alone was to organize a mass movement and collect funds. Mooney rejected this nonsensical claim and the ILD's strategy. Mary Gallagher told Wagenknecht, "if you can mobilize the well known working class to think, act or feel the same about any idea . . . , go ahead, I am for it. Don't wait for anybody's signed agreement." And to Benjamin Gitlow she added, "I want to see Tom Moo-

---

* The annual collections of the ILD from all sources amounted to $50–60,000, according to Roger Baldwin. (Baldwin to Mooney, January 14, 1929, in ACLU Papers, v. 371.)

ney and Warren Billings out of prison. I am not mingling the work for them with any propaganda of any sort whatever."[6]

Mooney refrained for years from public criticism of the ILD. He tolerated Communists, in keeping with his firm and long-standing faith in the unity and cooperation of all radicals. He himself never joined the party; as early as 1921 he told Nockels that the Communists were "a bunch of nuts."[7] To Mary he wrote, "I do hope that you and Lena [Morrow Lewis] will not blow up completely because of the new vermin that seems to be irritating you both. They never stopped or started anything. . . . They cannot do much harm. If they hold a big demonstration or Parade it will have a few hundred at the most." Communist revolutionary tactics, he pointed out, had not saved Sacco and Vanzetti.* In 1929—after the party had been Stalinized and its Trotskyist and Lovestone factions expelled—Mooney believed that the Communist movement was declining.[8]

Sometimes his tolerance was sorely tried. At an important mass meeting in the Los Angeles Trinity Auditorium, August 9, 1929, when Judge Griffin made his sole major public address on the case, the ILD distributed leaflets denouncing the occasion as a liberal maneuver to destroy the issue's working-class character. ILD members heckled the speakers and refused to leave (Mary scrupled to call in the police). Afterward Mooney wrote bitterly, "You know that they will attack any and all things that they do not have complete control of. They are the only saviours of the world. It is laughable in spite of its tragedy." He made public his complaint against the ILD; it was picked up editorially by the New York *Times*. At the same time Billings, after seeing the leaflet, wrote ILD headquarters and asked them to drop his case. They did not oblige. The Communists continued to raise funds in Mooney's name for their own purposes, over Mooney's continuing protests.[9]

II

Mooney's defense committee carried on its own fund-raising and publicity campaigns with the help of non-Communist radicals, particularly old-time Socialists and Wobblies who, like Mary Gallagher, were deeply committed to his cause. In one of their demonstrations on Mooney's behalf, the Socialists in Los Angeles paraded the ancient

* Mary Donovan Hapgood, formerly of the Sacco–Vanzetti Defense Committee, wrote Mooney: "You are having the same experience with the I.L.D. that we had with them in the Sacco–Vanzetti Defense Committee. I am glad you have found them out." (February 13, 1929, Mooney Papers.)

hearse used at Rolph's inauguration, outfitted with the giant placards, "California Justice Is Dead," and a rented skeleton. The incident received nationwide press publicity. Mooney was taken with the idea of sending the hearse on a national tour to symbolize his plight. "A skeleton can be rented very readily and cheaply," advised the owner, a Socialist newspaperman. Two days after Rolph's inauguration the macabre rig, which Mooney euphemistically—or superstitiously—called "the Symbol," set forth on a tour of the United States that covered 25,000 miles in fifteen months.[10]

The driver and custodian of the Symbol was Byrd Kelso, an old-time Wobbly and former member of the IWW General Executive Board, who had preached Mooney's cause on Sacramento soapboxes and hawked TMMDC literature in the state of Washington. Kelso took along a helper, David Emerick. They worked their way across the country, addressing unions, visiting local dignitaries, holding street rallies, and selling Mooney's pamphlets. Keeping themselves and the rig on the road cost about $30 a week. They had to make the tour self-supporting, but they were accustomed to rough, hand-to-mouth living, and made do with very little. ("For the past twenty-five years," said Kelso, "I never knew that a Turkey or Chicken was anything else outside of NECKS and WINGS.")[11]

The tour was a bizarre odyssey of depression America. The hearse jolted over poor roads, through dust storms, snow, and sleet. Tires blew out, valves stuck, gears broke: "it sure takes many kinds of hustling," Kelso reported. In Montana he found that Butte was "solid" for Mooney: "I never met so many Tom Mooney friends in all of my young life, even if they are poor." A hundred miles west of Fargo, North Dakota, the Symbol stuck in the mud. Kelso and Emerick hired a farmer and his team to pull them out for $1.50, which was half price: "He knows of the Mooney case." Things were tough. "Believe me, they are tough in North Dakota." However, Kelso was able to talk with the mayor of Fargo about the case.

In Wisconsin the Symbol was sideswiped by a truck and knocked over a fifty-foot embankment. Kelso was pulled out unconscious. A few days later he reported that he was as good as ever, "due to liberal applications of Sloans Linement." But the hearse was a wreck. He traded it for a 1927 Ford and went on to Milwaukee, where Socialists gave him an enthusiastic reception and held a mass meeting in the Court House Square, with the sheriff and other officials among the speakers. There Kelso swapped the car and $40 for a new hearse body, which he mounted on a 1925 Ford pickup chassis with three new tires and California license plates. (The plates were critical: without them he and Emerick would have been taken for imposters.) They put on new "California Justice Is Dead" signs and a coat of paint. Before leaving Wisconsin, Kelso visited Governor Philip La Follette and thanked him for the stand he had taken in favor of Mooney's pardon.[12]

In Chicago thousands saw his exhibit. Chased out of the Loop for blocking traffic, he sold pamphlets at factory gates. "I am attracting big crowds at various park and street meetings," he reported. "The most impossible ones are the Communists. At a meeting last night, one fanatic said that the I.L.D. . . . put up $5000 to start the hearses out, and that Tom Mooney has turned the future of his case over to them entirely. . . . these 'Comics' are sure trying at times." On they went through mining districts to Pittsburgh and across the Alleghenies. The Socialist Party had arranged meetings at small towns along the way. Kelso's audiences gave him a big hand when he asked them to boycott California goods. The Communists among his listeners were jealous of his hearse; they called it a ruse to get money for a bunch of fakers in San Francisco. He permitted them to sell their literature, although he thought it reduced his own sales, but they were still "IMPOSSIBLE." "I shall continue to contact them, to see if it is possible to meet any decent ones, and ones who are not so darn crazy." Arriving at Philadelphia—unemployed population, 200,000—Kelso found bigger crowds to address, but few people who could afford his ten-cent pamphlet. "I have many of them tell me this and they look at it. . . . And then I meet quite a few who have given up all hope in any kind of a struggle. They seem very tired."[13]

In New York Kelso looked up another old-time Wobbly, John W. Jenkins, who had worked for the Mooney defense as early in 1917. Although not currently accredited by the TMMDC, Jenkins was "a single purpose fellow whose only goal in life is to help Tom Mooney." He called himself a box-car bum. He had served three times in a Georgia chain-gang ("they can't fool a class war prisoner"), had been beaten and slugged, and had recently been in the New York "Tombs," charged with felonious assault on a policeman during a Mooney rally in Union Square. The arresting officer had been attempting to break up a fight between Jenkins's followers and a Communist group and was set upon by the crowd; he was rescued by taxi drivers armed with tire irons.[14] Jenkins despised practically everybody, from "Full Belly Hoover" and "Kerensky" Roosevelt to "four flushing" Roger Baldwin and "these Communist Lice." At the TMMDC office in San Francisco he was considered a nut.* Mooney had always resolved doubts in Jenkins's favor because Jenkins was trying to help the cause. When Kelso found him, he was talking up the Mooney case on street corners, but Kelso felt he could not depend on him.[15]

Kelso's major project in New York was to prepare a giant rally for Mooney in Union Square. More than three hundred delegates of New York labor organizations attended a preliminary conference at the Labor Temple on East 84th Street, at which Kelso, following Mooney's instructions, called for united-front action of all labor factions in his behalf. The chairman, Abraham Lefkowitz of the New York Teachers Union, objected to the inclusion of the Communists, who had been disruptive and were attacking the arrangements committee.[16] Although the CP was not officially represented, the ILD was. Kelso reported:

one of their women delegates immediately began to heckle and ... tried her very best to inform the delegates that this was not a proper Conference and the I.L.D. and they only were legally empowered to represent Tom Mooney, and most of those present were fakers, etc, their usual "canned" and copyrighted insults. ... This woman also kept shouting that the Communist Party Demonstration (which they called for October 17 at Union Square, to try and injure our demonstration) was the only legal one to be held. [While she was] demanding attention and shouting that everything was a "fake," the body passed a motion unanimously that "the ILD Delegates be bared from the Hall and this Conference. ..." As soon as this motion was carried this woman arose and screaming at the top of her voice "Long Live the Soviet," [she] started to leave the hall. And she screamed so loud that she fainted. ... Anyway she finaly reached the corridors and left.[17]

The rally was held at Union Square a week after the Communist rally. The meeting opened with "the 'Internationale' and other dear tunes and songs of the working class. ... NO JAZZ." Kelso estimated the attendance at 10,000. The speakers included Norman Thomas, Arthur Garfield Hays, and A. J. Muste, chairman of the Conference for Progressive Labor Action and long prominent in eastern left-wing

* When Governor Young was in his fourth year of postponing a pardon decision, Jenkins wrote Mooney suggesting that some of Young's family might "volunteer to give their blood to pay for the mistake of their father." Mary Gallagher was irked: "If that letter had gone to prison ... instead of to our office ... it would have been copied and sent to Governor Young and used as another excuse for showing the bad character of Mooney and his associates." (Jenkins to Mooney, June 19, 1930, and Mary Gallagher to Charles Blome, June 24, 1930, Mooney Papers.)

circles. Muste proposed a general strike for Mooney: "Let us do something to strike fear into the hearts of the masters of America." Kelso delivered another message from Mooney asking for labor unity: "The workers are divided into bickering groups on the question of what to do for class war prisoners, and while you bicker we rot in penitentiaries and jails." About a hundred Communists were present. They booed Norman Thomas and got into scuffles. Kelso was disgusted.[18]

As the fall progressed, the weather turned too cold for outdoor meetings. Kelso could not afford to rent halls. On the streets he often had trouble with police: "most of them despise our hearse." In December, when Congress convened, Kelso and Emerick went to Washington as they had planned and paraded the Symbol in front of the White House and the Capitol. On the second day the police shooed them off. Kelso looked for someone with influence to intercede, but without success. "These are all funny people here, very high class, of course. They do not want me to even mention or use the hearse. They all seem to be afraid of it." However, a public meeting was arranged at the Friends Meeting House where Hoover was a member, with speakers that included Senators Burton K. Wheeler and Gerald P. Nye. Kelso also went to the White House. By administrative error he was admitted to see the President, to whom he presented a petition. Hoover sent him out to his secretary.[19]

The journey home was dismal. Skirting the Deep South ("the Hearse is not a suitable thing for that part of the country"), Kelso and his companion crossed Tennessee, Arkansas, and Texas. In most of the larger towns, officials refused to let Kelso sell his pamphlets. In Texas he encountered "endless thrills, such as, Wind and violent sand storms, rain and high water, hostile police and unfriendly morons, slight motor trouble, water in our gasoline, etc. . . . ."

Our best thrill was in Dallas, Texas, when the Chief of Police threatened to give us some "Texas 45 Justice," whatever that means. There are many expressions down here that I do not understand. When I tried to reason with this moronic chief, all that I could get was this: "I attended the National Chief of Police's Convention last year, and the Tom Mooney case was thoroughly discussed, and most of them agreed that Calif. should have hung that dynamiting s— of a b———." Being unable to reason with him, I stayed in Dallas one day more and managed to "bootleg" some pamphlets. I have tried hard to hold some open air meetings in every suitable town, enroute, but they simply do not know what free speech is down this way.[20]

Kelso timed his visit to Tucson to coincide with a cowboy parade, whose guest of honor was James Rolph, Jr. "He looked very mad." In Phoenix, Kelso asked the mayor for permission to hold street meetings. The mayor flew into a rage, saying, " 'Tom Mooney is guilty as Hell, I know all about the case because Wm. Burns, the great detective told me all about it.' After producing voluminous proof, he quieted down and . . . admitted that he meant the McNamara case." Permission being denied anyway, Kelso rented a parking lot for $1 and exercised his constitutional right of free speech undisturbed on private property.[21]

Then back to California by way of the Imperial Valley: "We traveled most all of one night to outdistance a small mob at Brawley, Calif. who were determined to wreck the car. And then we were successful because we completely bluffed them by making them think that we had a machine gun in the car. I put my partner inside of the hearse, and this strategy worked. This perhaps sounds too ridiculous, but it is *true*."[22] At San Bernardino, Colton, and Riverside, they were chased out of town. They preferred that to arrest, for Kelso was ill. After visiting coastal towns on the final lap they arrived back in San Francisco in the spring of 1932. Two or three months later Kelso was ready for the road again, "but we are going to have nothing to do with any more hearses or exhibits." He intended to visit unions in an ordinary car.[23]

Kelso was one of the few friends for whom Mooney had only compliments. He frequently told visitors at San Quentin that he wished he had a hundred Kelsos on the road. Looking back in 1935, Mooney noted appreciatively, "for years you have worked on our case for your bare meager living expenses." The TMMDC did put another Symbol on tour, but it proved too costly and troublesome to keep going. The idea of the Symbol lingered on, however; a plan to use one turned up in Oklahoma City in 1937. The chairman of the Labor Day parade committee barred the vehicle from the parade, on the ground that it would be too grisly.[24]

III

The TMMDC underwent successive changes in the early 1930's. They began with the resignation of Mary Gallagher, Mooney's able secretary, whose loss Mooney's dictatorial habits made inevitable. The break finally came in the fall of 1930 over his determination to attack Governor Young publicly for shilly-shallying. Mary opposed the plan, since a slim hope of a pardon from Young still remained.[25] After her departure the committee was never the same again; other defense secretaries came and went, but none was her equal.

For a brief time the organization was rudderless. The records, mailbox, and funds were in quarreling hands. After a month or so an abortive attempt was made to reorganize under Walter W. Liggett, a free-lance, left-wing journalist who had worked for the Sacco–Vanzetti defense and had performed useful services for Mooney in Washington, D.C. Liggett, although a resourceful publicist, was unable to cope with his new job. Mooney was bossy; the office was in chaos; several of the women who worked there, particularly Mooney's sister, Anna, were suspicious of Liggett and his good salary, which had been underwritten by a wealthy friend of radical causes, Aline Barnsdall of Los Angeles. Liggett stood the gaff for two months and departed, leaving the committee temporarily in Anna's hands.[26]

Anna Mooney was a simple, conscientious woman of little schooling and no administrative talent. By trade she was a waitress. She had served briefly as the committee caretaker before Liggett, and was to be the regular secretary for several years after 1933. Having little interest in the social implications of the case, she served her brother out of personal loyalty. Tom, eight years older than she, had been like a father to her when she was a child. In the years since the Preparedness Day bombing, she had been repeatedly humiliated and occasionally fired from jobs because she defended him. "I do hope things will straighten out soon," she wrote after Liggett's departure, "as it has been a living death for me this last 13 years, of unjust punishment— wherever I went, worked, lived—people, like vicious animals ready to criticise attack, anything & everything to hurt me. . . . Well, we must make the best of it, kicking dont help." Her story was as simple as her character. "Life is sure a struggle work just to keep a roof over our heads, & cloth[e] ourselves and that keeps us busy." That and the committee: to set it running again she sold most of her possessions, including her furniture and radio, and moved into the committee office with the proceeds, $95. "I put the whole amount into your fight, as it meant nothing to me," she told Tom.[27] To please him she accepted all his instructions uncritically, and served him as an informer about everyone else on the defense committee. She was willing to work for her brother when others could no longer stand it. Mooney abused his sister as he did the others, but he never lost Anna's affection.[28]

In the spring of 1931 Mooney arranged for another secretary, Arthur Stuart Scott, who remained with the TMMDC for more than two years. Scott was a mysterious, conspiratorial figure, the most elusive person in the history of the Mooney case save the unknown bomber. A Communist, Scott's objective was to capture Mooney's cause for the Communist Party.

Scott came from a family of theatrical people. His father, Joseph Margolis, ran a restaurant, "Pierre's Chateau," on Baker Street near the Presidio. Arthur's childhood was evidently insecure and bitter; he hated his father for having remarried, and at the age of thirteen he was left on his own. He educated himself without help from his family. An intelligent and musically talented youth, he studied at the Brussels Conservatory, and was an outstanding student at the Yale School of Music from 1918 to 1920.[29] By that time he had changed his legal name to Arthur Kent. Later he joined the musicians' union and played in a Los Angeles orchestra. Information about him is too fragmentary to show why he jeopardized his career, but in 1928 he was convicted of burglarizing four homes in Beverly Hills and was sentenced to four years in San Quentin. There he met J. B. McNamara, Matt Schmidt, and Tom Mooney.[30] Presumably Kent was the "Arthur" who in 1928 helped Mooney secretly mimeograph his documents. In 1931 Kent joined the San Quentin cell of the Communist Party. He took the party name of Arthur Stuart Scott, and was known as Scott to the non-Communists connected with the Mooney defense although he initially concealed his party membership.[31] He went to work for the TMMDC following his parole.

Whatever Scott's personal interest in Mooney may have been, the Mooney cause was a prize objective for the CP. The party had tried to exploit other labor cases—Centralia, Sacco–Vanzetti, the Gastonia strike, the Harlan miners; the Communists also had their own Algernon Herndon case, and later gained control, for a time, of the Scottsboro defense. These cases were exploited among liberals and Negroes. After the execution of Sacco and Vanzetti in 1927, Mooney and Billings were the most attractive prospects for dramatic labor-prisoner, class-war propaganda.* All that kept the party from taking over Mooney's defense committee was Mooney; and Scott was Mooney's friend.

Scott's task was not simple. Mooney was just as critical, indepen-

---

* As another Communist in the TMMDC wrote: "There is no doubt in the minds of anyone of us who is sincerely devoted to the working class struggle that the Mooney case represents one of the pivotal points around which the working class must be rallied in the class struggle and that very effective blows can be given through the Mooney case to the disintegrating body of capitalism." (Louis B. Scott to TMMDC, January 3, 1933, Mooney Papers.)

dent, stubborn, and suspicious as ever. He gave Scott the TMMDC office because, just as Scott wanted to use him, he wanted to use Scott and the Communist Party. The contest of wills lasted for more than two years. Initially Scott was circumspect, keeping his purposes to himself. Other Communists and members of the ILD were brought into the defense committee, including Norma (Noni) Perrie, Sam Goodwin, Louis B. Scott, and Benjamin A. Ellisberg. Scott frequently used Ellisberg's initials to sign letters that would be seen by San Quentin censors: "We try to be careful and delete all matters the warden should not read." After several months on the committee he wrote Mooney disarmingly that their best worker was Byrd Kelso, and that "the persons at the head of the party here [in San Francisco] are so stupid that they have not got enough vision to try to 'capture' the office."[32] But Anna was suspicious of Scott. The two could not get along together. Scott appealed to Mooney:

She is *stupid*. For three months I have tried to make you understand this fact, but it is very plain you do not. We talk about her lack of training, etc. That is all nonesense [*sic*]. Her lack of training has nothing to do with the matter. It is her lack of intelligence. Certainly Anne [*sic*] is personally trustworthy, certainly she is devoted to you, certainly she does her utmost to help, certainly she worries herself sick trying to carry out your instructions, but all these qualities when of[f]set by gross stupidity spell disaster.[33]

Mooney urged him to be tolerant. Anna was "truly typical of all the working class," he said; "she will average up very well with them." He reminded Scott of their own "more or less mutual views on the greater problems of the day that cry out for solution. If there is no change on your part, surely there is none on my part."[34]

Scott hoped to bring about closer cooperation between the TMMDC and the ILD. He told Mooney that the ILD had a new interest in the case, and tried to persuade him to give up directing the work of the TMMDC. He promoted the circulation of a new pamphlet, "Labor Leaders Betray Tom Mooney," which assailed Paul Scharrenberg and other AFL leaders bitterly for not supporting the TMMDC. And over Mooney's name he sent out Communist propaganda, such as a May Day greeting to the Friends of the Soviet Union:

What an inspiring spectacle it must be to see millions of happy workers in the Soviet Union demonstrating before the workers of the world their glorious achievements in constructing a new land, abolishing unemployment, raising the standard of living and the cultural level of the toiling masses.[35]

Mooney learned what was going on from his friends. Kelso wrote from New York that he had heard rumors about Scott. Anna reported that "Darsey [Sam Darcy, San Francisco CP leader] calls up A. very often, and they seem to meet every day outside. Also the I.L.D.'s." Roger Baldwin warned: "the impression has gone abroad that you have sort of appointed the I.L.D. as your exclusive agents and others are moved not to cooperate unless they are pretty far to the left themselves." Nockels told Mooney bluntly that he should stop playing the martyr for the Communists.[36]

Mooney was determined to hold the reins, but he wanted the Communists to make a world-wide issue of his case. He believed they would succeed if only they stopped "playing politics" with it. He acknowledged to Kelso that there were ILD's in the office "and they may be CP's also for all I know—this I am not interested in, but am interested in the splendid work that they are and have been doing in my behalf that I am unable to get done by others."[37] He kept a close watch on Scott, warning him at one point that there were too many Communists on a local committee planning a mass meeting on his behalf. Another time he castigated Scott's faction for publicizing the history of the case without mention of Alexander Berkman, who had repudiated Communism after his deportation and experiences in Russia.[38] And he warned Scott not to assume more power than Rena, Mary, or Liggett had: "I'm wondering who you are working for? It seems to me at times that the work of my committee must be subordinated to the work of the Party and the ILD. I dont propose that this should be so. . . . I give you fair warning, that I have made changes before and I will again make them and damn soon if you dont fit into the scheem [sic] of this case as I see it."[39] But on other occasions he reassured Scott of his complete confidence.

IV

Early in 1932 the ILD approached Mooney with a proposal to take his mother on a national publicity tour to campaign for his freedom. Mary Mooney was not a radical. She had never cared much about the labor movement. But she did care about her son, and, like Anna and John, her younger son, had suffered ostracism because of Tom. Her solicitude was unwavering. Regularly every other week she went to San Quentin, often alone, to see him. She visited the defense committee office daily. Quietly she attended labor meetings and other gatherings where the case was discussed, and reported what she heard to

Tom. Public attention had been drawn to her by her appeal to Mayor Walker. She was present at his hearing; a few days afterward, suffering a nervous collapse, she was hospitalized. Her main desire thereafter was to live long enough to see her son free. Since she was 84 years old and her eyesight was failing, her physician considered the proposed national tour suicidal, but Mrs. Mooney said she would go anywhere to help her son. Tom, assured by his committee that his mother would be well cared for, encouraged her to make the tour. In February 1932, accompanied by Scott and Noni Perrie, Mary Mooney left for New York.[40]

The tour lasted a month. Sympathizers greeted Mother Mooney in New York with a tumultuous demonstration. She was too weak to attend an ILD-sponsored rally at the Bronx Coliseum, but a week later she called at the White House in an unsuccessful attempt to see President Hoover. The tour covered fourteen cities and received considerable publicity. Although she suffered a heart attack on the way home, she arrived in San Francisco safely and in good spirits. From the ILD's point of view, the tour had been a success.[41]

Scott now pressed Mooney to give Communism his full support. He urged a new campaign of class-conscious militancy without liberals or politicians: the Walkers, Baldwins, governors, lawyers, and federal commissions could not free him; gubernatorial contests were useless. "Why should we dissipate our energies trying to defeat one tool of the capitalists in order to put another one in office?" He argued that the international Communist movement would not fight for Mooney unless he placed his case wholeheartedly in the hands of the workers. Scott proposed another tour for Mother Mooney, this time with Louis Engdahl, the head of the ILD and a national party functionary. "I am sure you will agree that capitalism is definitely on the downward path, and if ever there was a time when you should adopt a radical and militant position it is now."[42]

Mooney, too canny to endorse the whole plan, did approve another tour for his mother. She was still obliging. This time Mother Mooney was accompanied by Richard B. Moore of the ILD executive committee and, as a personal traveling companion, Anne Rosenfield of the TMMDC. In three months they visited sixty towns and cities. The old woman was a continuing success. Her companions reported that their audiences "would rather hear a speech of twenty five words from Mother than an hour's talk from all the rest of the speakers— they hug and kiss her everywhere she goes."[43]

The ILD next wanted to extend the tour to Western Europe.

Once again Mooney approved. When the plan was scotched by the International Red Aid, on the grounds that the mother of one of the Scottsboro boys had just made such a tour, the ILD took Mother Mooney to Russia instead; she went as an honorary ILD representative to a world congress of the International Red Aid, held during the fifteenth anniversary of the Bolshevik Revolution.[44] Looking sprightly in a fur coat, she sailed with the delegation on the *Europa* on October 28, 1932, accompanied by a nurse. She had been promised that the trip would greatly help the fight for her son's release, and that he "would be hailed as a hero of labor in the land where the Red Flag flies, as are all honest, steadfast fighters of the class struggle." She also had hopes of stopping in Ireland and seeing her old home and her brothers for the first time in sixty years.[45]

After their arrival in Moscow the New York *Times* reported that Mrs. Mooney might present her son's greetings to Stalin in person. No personal presentation followed, but the letter of greetings, which had been written by the TMMDC, was published in the ILD's *Labor Defender*. In it Mooney thanked Stalin

for the magnificent spirit of international working-class solidarity by the militant workers of Russia in defense of my fight for freedom, and for the freedom of all class-war and political prisoners. Were it not for the revolutionary workers of Petrograd, led by our beloved Comrade Lenin, in militant demonstrations before the American Ambassador on April 25, 1917, I would not now be addressing these greetings to you. Thus my life was saved and my usefulness to the revolutionary working class prolonged.... All hail to the Russian revolution and the dictatorship of the proletariat. I'm for it hook, line, and sinker....

TOM MOONEY, 31921 [46]

Leaving the Soviet Union, the delegation (minus Engdahl, who died in Moscow) visited Berlin, Hamburg, Amsterdam, Rotterdam, Paris, and London—but not Mother Mooney's home, on the excuse that "holding a really great demonstration in Ireland during the winter" was too difficult.[47] The old woman had her revenge: on arriving in New York she told a *Times* reporter, to the embarrassment of the Communist welcoming party at the pier, that she was "completely wore out" and would not live in Russia if she were invited.[48]

Before returning to California, Mrs. Mooney went with an ILD delegation to Albany to ask Governor Franklin D. Roosevelt to intercede in the case. The President-elect saw her and agreed to send Rolph her appeal. Since it was his last day as Governor, he said he would write unofficially, as "an old friend" of Rolph's. The letter, a cautious appeal, constituted Roosevelt's only involvement in the case. Altogether, as the *Times* commented, the effort to make "Red capital" of the case through his mother had done Mooney little good.[49]

Mary Mooney lived to the autumn of 1934, long enough to enjoy the hope that her son would be freed by Upton Sinclair. She was stricken at home alone one day after returning from San Quentin. Neighbors called the hospital. One of them said she cried "My poor Tom," just before the ambulance took her away. A few minutes later she was dead.[50] Her funeral cortege stopped just outside the gates of San Quentin. It was a bitter gesture, for everyone knew that the Warden had refused to waive the prison rules so that Mooney could see his mother's coffin. Her last rites were held in the Civic Auditorium. They were working-class rites; she had left the Church, but Anna placed a crucifix on her casket. Mourners came in thousands. She was buried in a San Rafael cemetery three miles from her son. The estate she left was valued at $1,300.[51]

V

The Communist Party in the early 1930's created a number of united front organizations with liberals, Socialists, and other radicals, for propaganda purposes. Not surprisingly, the formation of a united front for Mooney figured in Arthur Scott's plans. He envisioned the creation of local United Front Pardon Mooney committees that would prepare for a national Free Tom Mooney Congress to dramatize Mooney's plight. The project recalled the 1919 Chicago Mooney Congress —or rather, what that congress would have been like had the Bolshevik faction controlled it. The new convention, like the old, was to be held in Chicago. Scott wrote his comrades in New York:

Will you carefully bear in mind at all times that what we are seeking to do is to attract the timid but more or less progressive elements within the working class. Therefore, great judgment must be exercised. We must also be very careful to make it plain that the entire project is under the control of the Tom Mooney Molders' Defense Committee and that we are not affiliated with any particular organization. We shall seek the cooperation of all organizations, but naturally we cannot help it if some do not respond.[52]

We would advise you not to concentrate very much on the Party and affiliated organizations which we are certain of. Already you have secured the endorsement of the ACLU. Now you should go after the Socialist Party, the Socialist-Labor Party, the C.P.L.A. [Conference for Progressive Labor Action] (Muste group), the I.W.W. the Anarchists and the other organizations. . . . As much as possible . . . the middle-class elements and the intellectuals should be kept in the background. It is workers that Tom wishes to attract to the Congress—especially members of organized labor.[53]

Especially in view of the E.C.C.I. [Executive Committee of the Communist International] should we strive to form such a united front organization. Surely the Mooney Case is an ideal basis on which to form a united front and we must not be satisfied until we have exhausted every possibility.

Our experiences in San Francisco prove that, correctly handled, the Mooney Case has tremendous appeal to the A.F. of L.[54]

The groundwork was laid in the ILD headquarters, which sent out Carl Hacker to arrange with branches in every large district city "to seek out some outstanding and sympathetic personality, not directly connected with any of the radical organizations, upon whom to fasten the responsibility for rallying the widest united front. This person is primarily to be sought among the AFL leaders."[55] Mooney liked the project and the publicity it promised; previously he had even embraced the idea of having United Front Pardon Mooney committees campaign for him as President in the 1932 election, for the sake of the publicity such a campaign would bring him.*

In New York, Louis B. Scott of the TMMDC discussed plans for the front with Earl Browder and Robert Minor. They told him that the project was important to the party and that "every issue of the entire range of the working class struggle must be linked up with the case and the Congress."[56] The difficulty lay in convincing other important organizations besides the ACLU to go along. The Socialists refused; as one of them said, they had been assailed by "Communist Jesuitism and gangsterism" too often to be deceived. The Chicago Federation of Labor also declined.[57] The CP showed its strong-arm tactics at the organizational meeting of a united front rally in San Francisco for Mooney. The meeting was packed with Communist paper organization representatives, and the outcome was so obvious that non-Communists left in disgust. However, 12,000–15,000 people attended the rally, held in the Civic Auditorium in March 1933. Ellis-

---

* Mooney thought it would be "the most effective weapon we could possibly have. Debs polled a Million votes while in Atlanta in 1920 on the S. P. Ticket." (Mooney to Arthur [Scott], September 6, 1932, Mooney Papers.)

berg, Minor, Darcy, and Lincoln Steffens led the meeting.[58] Mooney called it an overwhelming success, but one spectator described it as

the most insulting and un-American meeting that I ever witnessed.... Your ignorant audience hissed at our great President's name ..., the man that has showed great courage and leadership during these two weeks....

Lincoln Steffens should drop the name Lincoln as he is a disgrace to any good American.... How he did enjoy the hissing.

I am one of the un-employed and ... would give my last dollar to help ..., but for Lincoln Steffens, Sam Ornitz and the rest of your un-Americans that attended the meeting ... I would sooner give to a collection that would ship them all back to Russia with Emma Goldman and the rest of the instigators....

P.S. It is Sir in America and Comrade in Russia. so forget the Comrade stuff in a Union mans country.[59]

More than 1,000 delegates participated in the Free Tom Mooney Congress in Chicago on May 1–3. They described themselves, incorrectly, as the first national united front gathering in the history of the American labor movement. The sessions were largely of a "purely agitational character." Preoccupied with tactical hairsplitting, the delegates failed to settle on any plan to free Mooney.* The IWW delegates advocated a general strike, but the Communists voted it down. The congress proclaimed that Mooney's imprisonment was the keystone in the persecution of workers, farmers, and Negroes, and was "connected" with the rearmament appropriations of capitalist countries for war against the USSR. It also announced a "National Tom Mooney Council of Action—a United Front for Workers Rights and the Rights of the Negro People," and called for mass pressure.[60]

The congress climaxed with a parade and a mass meeting in the Chicago Coliseum. Just before the meeting began, the assemblage was deluged by a counterrevolutionary downpour; thousands departed before the collection was taken, and the sponsors who had rented the stadium were left with a deficit of $2,000, half of which was owed the CP and the ILD. Altogether it was not much of a congress. The *Daily Worker* called it "one of the greatest expressions of working-class unity," and then forgot about it.[61]

* Reported one of the Trotskyites: "The Left Opposition differed with both the Lovestoneite and Stalinist positions. We were opposed to the Stalinist attempt to turn the Mooney Committee into a Mooney-Scottsboro Committee, but we were equally opposed to the Lovestone right wing attempt to separate the Mooney case from the Scottsboro case." (Hugo Oehler, in New York *Militant*, May 13, 1933.)

The fiasco of the congress shook Mooney's own united front with the Communist Party. The alliance with Scott and his cohorts lasted but a month longer; it appears to have been dissolved by mutual consent. Mooney expressed regret to Scott at losing his services, but pointed out that he had not abided by the rules.[62] To those who remained Mooney wrote: "If the point should be rasied [*sic*] to you on the Communist[s] run[n]ing my defense committee—say this for me: They have not had any official connection with my Defense Committee since last June. They became impossible to work with and I move[d] them out. Anna is in complete charge . . . at a Salary of $12.00 weekly."[63]

Mooney's experiences did not destroy his faith in left-wing unity. In this respect he had learned nothing. The following winter he hoped once again to unite all groups and factions in a campaign on his behalf—the AFL, churches, Socialists, Socialist Labor Party, anarchists, Proletarian Party, and Communists. Nothing came of it. Furthermore, he had to repudiate the National Tom Mooney Council of Action, which had been raising money in his name without cooperating with the TMMDC. "The united front program worked out in Chicago has obviously flopped," concluded Baldwin.[64]

Mooney's relationship with the Communist Party was never so close again. No special front for Mooney was reestablished after 1933. Neither side repudiated the other, however, or relinquished the advantages that the other offered; to the end of the case, the one had money and machinery, the other a cause. The Communist Party gave at least $2,000 directly to the TMMDC in the mid-1930's, when contributions were exceptionally hard to come by. Throughout the decade virtually every issue of the ILD's monthly pictorial magazine, *Labor Defender*, contained a Mooney news item or photograph. Mooney became a member of the ILD national advisory board; Vito Marcantonio, the ILD president and later a Congressman from Harlem, worked on Mooney's behalf in 1937 and 1938.[65] These were propaganda steps; they stopped short of intimacy and allegiance. The relationship was based on convenience, not on mutual trust.

Mooney was on closer terms with the Lovestone faction of the Communist movement than with the CP after 1933. The Lovestone faction, or Communist Party of the U.S.A. (Opposition), had been expelled from the CP by the Comintern in its 1929 Stalinist purge. Mooney shared many confidences with Jay Lovestone. In 1936 the Lovestoneites talked grandly of running Mooney for President on a united labor ticket. The Lovestone faction, however, was minuscule, and, outside the CIO's United Automobile Workers Union, it exercised very little influence in radical labor circles.[66]

Few Communist-hunters in the 1930's accused Mooney of being a Communist. One witness for Martin Dies's House of Representatives Committee on Un-American Activities, Harper L. Knowles, who headed the Radical Research Department of the American Legion in California, asserted that Mooney was "of course" a Communist, and that the TMMDC was a Communist creation. But Knowles's remarks in that investigation did not represent the gist of the testimony about Mooney, which was, rather, that exploiting the Mooney case was the sort of thing Communists did. Arthur Scott was mentioned as a Communist in these hearings, but not in connection with the case.[67] In 1941 Eugene Lyons barely noticed Mooney in *The Red Decade,* a polemic survey of "Bolshevism in our country"; subsequently the California legislature's miniature Dies committee, headed by State Senator Jack B. Tenney, of Los Angeles, found nothing to add. Nor, later, did Mooney's name figure in the loyalty probes of the McCarthy era. Evidently most Red-hunters would have agreed with William Z. Foster's remark that Mooney was a "warm sympathizer of the Communist Party"—that, and nothing more.[68] In the last analysis Mooney's virtual immunity to Red witch-hunting stemmed from his own character: from his conviction that the Communist Party was incorrigibly sectarian, and from the indomitable vanity that kept all others from gaining control of his cause.

VI

Scott continued his devious career after leaving the committee. At the time of his departure he took with him some committee property worth about $200.[69] He remained in the CP for several years; in 1936 and 1937 he was the CP membership director in San Francisco. But in the latter year he was ousted from the party on suspicion of being a stool pigeon, for he was in the employ of a Colonel Henry R. Sanborn and an ex-Legionnaire, Stanley M. Doyle, who represented anti-radical and anti-labor interests, particularly the San Francisco shipowners.[70] For a short time in 1936 Scott was back on Mooney's payroll, "vitally interested in a big way in the cause" and "a Trojan for work," according to Mooney; but the friction with Anna was greater than ever. She and her brother John quit the committee in disgust. A month later Mooney dropped Scott and recovered his sister and brother.[71]

Scott, now calling himself Arthur Kent once again, was arrested in Ojai, California, in December 1937, on charges of burglarizing thirteen houses in Beverly Hills. He confessed, claiming that he was robbing the rich (of $15,000 or $20,000) to aid the poor and the Communist Party. Stanley Doyle took an interest in the case, since Kent was expected to testify in the deportation hearing against Harry Bridges, the West Coast maritime leader and alleged Communist.[72] In March 1938 Kent obtained the services of an American Legion attorney, Ray Nimmo, who figured prominently that year at the Dies committee hearings, as Harper R. Knowles's colleague. Subsequently most of the charges against Kent were dismissed. He pleaded guilty on two counts and was sentenced to Folsom: the sentences were to run concurrently, said the judge, in recognition of Kent's "patriotic" services in exposing Communist activities.[73] According to the records of the California Department of Corrections, Kent was never transferred to Folsom. A few days before California's general elections in 1938, he made an affidavit in the Los Angeles county jail that was inserted in the Dies committee hearings and given wide publicity. Kent alleged that several high-ranking Democratic candidates for state office, whom he named, were Communist Party members and had been meeting in secret sessions with Communist state leaders. As it turned out, these sensational charges, and others like them, failed to prevent the election of most of the Democratic ticket. Nevertheless, the defeated Governor, Frank Merriam, on his last day in office commuted Kent's sentence to time served.[74] Years afterward Kent boasted of these shabby events to a young woman in a Los Angeles bar.[75] Without knowing it, he was talking to Mary Gallagher's daughter.

CHAPTER TWENTY-SIX

Habeas Corpus, 1933-1938

*Dear Comrade: I got into an arguement with a
civics teacher who insisted Tom Mooney should
be shot. Please send me details to use in his defense.*
—Postcard to Roger Baldwin

*Rolph wouldn't give you a break. I only hope
that Chief Justice Hughes is a better sport.*
—Letter to Mooney, 1934

FOR MANY YEARS Billings had been convinced that he might gain his
freedom by a federal writ of habeas corpus. Shortly after his imprisonment he had begun to study the law, as prisoners are wont to do. To
him the matter was simple: judgment based on perjured testimony
could not be due process of law; therefore, he and Mooney were "entitled to release on habeas corpus" by virtue of the Fifth Amendment.
But practicing lawyers dismissed his claim; even Clarence Darrow
called his scheme impossible.[1] After the fruitless review of his case in
1930 Billings pressed his plan on Roger Baldwin. Baldwin consulted
Frank Walsh and Arthur Garfield Hays, the general counsel for the
ACLU. The attorneys replied that there was nothing in it. Said Billings: "All I have to say in rebuttal is that if there IS no legal remedy
for this judicial error then this is ONE HELL OF A COUNTRY TO LIVE IN."[2]

Billings was a layman; the "freedom writ" was recondite. In the
federal courts its availability was severely limited. Habeas corpus was
an independent civil proceeding—not an appeal—which asserted the
right to personal liberty by challenging either the legality of a detention, or the jurisdiction of the court or other detaining authorities.
It was not a substitute for a writ of error, not a method of testing
alleged errors of fact or law occurring at a criminal trial.[3] As Walsh
told Baldwin, "a habeas corpus proceeding will not lie to correct judgments founded on erroneous facts, to-wit, in this particular case, per-

jured testimony. . . . The question as to the fairness or unfairness of the trial given the defendant are objections that must be raised by a Writ of Error to the proper Appellate authority."[4] Hays added:

We tried this procedure in the Sacco–Vanzetti case, appealing to practically all the judges of the Supreme Court, including Holmes. The court took the position that nothing outside the record could be considered unless perhaps it was perfectly clear that there was a mere shadow and not the substance of a trial. Certainly the court could not regard perjured testimony as warranting the interference of the federal courts.[5]

Yet habeas corpus, in the venerable words of John Marshall, was for "the liberation of those who may be imprisoned without sufficient cause," and according to Holmes, it was "the usual remedy for unlawful imprisonment."[6] Were these generalities irrelevant to the circumstances of Mooney and Billings? According to the federal Judiciary Act of 1867, the writ was available to any person held in custody "in violation of the constitution";[7] and the Fourteenth Amendment prohibited imprisonment without due process of law. Did "due process" encompass the falsehoods of Oxman, McDonald, Crowley, the Edeaus, and Estelle Smith? or the prosecution's offering of these witnesses? The key questions were whether the convictions had been unlawful, as opposed to unjust or merely unwise; and, if so, whether federal jurisdiction might apply.[8]

Unquestionably the defense attorneys knew the law. But the law was changing. "Due process" was an organic and malleable concept. Habeas corpus was an expandable, adaptable writ. The Judiciary Act of 1867 went beyond common-law usage, and in at least one case by the 1920's the Supreme Court had granted an appeal for the writ against a state criminal conviction that offended the Court's basic ideas of just processes.* To be sure, the federal courts rarely interfered this way in state cases; but by 1931 federal application of the writ was about to undergo extraordinary expansion, as a means of voiding state convictions achieved under conditions that made a sham of justice. Prompted by its own growing sensitivity to civil liberties, and moving in an environment of expanding federal powers, the Supreme Court in the 1930's and 1940's greatly increased the scope of its review of state court practices, and broadened the application of the writ to cover many abuses that had not previously been reviewed by the federal courts. The Fourteenth Amendment, which until then

---

* *Moore v. Dempsey*, 261 U.S. 82 (1923). The threat of mob violence dominated the trial.

the courts had generously applied to protect property interests against state interference, came into its own as a bulwark of personal civil liberties. And one of the many steps in this transformation was taken in the Supreme Court's decision of 1935 relating to the Mooney case.[9]

The idea that a federal "due process" case might be made out of the Preparedness Day trials was explored independently in 1932 by two attorneys, neither of whom was then connected with the defense: John Beardsley, chairman of the ACLU organization in Los Angeles, and John F. Finerty, a prominent attorney of Washington, D.C., who had tried to convince Justice Holmes in 1927 to grant a writ of habeas corpus to Sacco and Vanzetti.[10] Beardsley proposed to seek a federal writ of habeas corpus for Mooney on the novel grounds that California's penal code was inadequate, since the state had "no law under which the wrongs we complain of can be righted." Baldwin referred the plan to his own ACLU legal advisers. They considered it desperate, and it was dropped.[11] Finerty's approach was different. He singled out Fickert:

The Wickersham report [he wrote Baldwin] makes it clear that the District Attorney knowingly suppressed material evidence, some of which, had it been before the court and jury, would, according to the statements of the presiding judge and of certain jurors, have prevented a verdict of guilty.... It, therefore, could be urged that the District Attorney as an agent of the state, perpetrated a fraud upon the court itself, and irrespective of the fact that the court acted in good faith, and that proper forms of procedure were adhered to, there was, nevertheless, lack of due process of law.

To make a federal case, Finerty drew on the United States Supreme Court's decision in the Leo Frank case: if the Fourteenth Amendment be violated, the Court had said, "it makes no difference in a court of the United States by what agency of the state this is done." Fickert had been the agent of California.[12]

Baldwin and Walsh were receptive to Finerty's argument, and Finerty joined the defense. Hopes for successful action were considerably buoyed that fall by the Supreme Court's decision in the Scottsboro case, *Powell v. Alabama,* in which the Court set aside the Alabama convictions and death sentences of seven Negro youths charged with rape, and accepted the argument presented by Walter Pollak and Carl Stern that the failure of the trial court to accord the right of counsel constituted a denial of due process. The Fourteenth Amendment was now admittedly violated by a state's denial of the right of counsel; perhaps it was also violated if a state knowingly offered perjured evidence. In the Scottsboro case, however, the Supreme Court had found its evidence in the trial record; in the Mooney case that would not be possible. This increased the uncertainties for Mooney's attorneys.[13]

Finerty decided that the federal District Court for Northern California was the place to begin, since the United States Supreme Court rarely issued an original writ of habeas corpus. Needing an associate in San Francisco, he and Walsh arranged for the assistance of George T. Davis, a young graduate of the University of California law school in Berkeley. All three worked without pay; Finerty's initial expenses were financed by the ACLU with funds from the estate of a Wellesley College professor. Finerty flew to San Francisco, conferred with persons who knew the case, including Maxwell McNutt and Ed McKenzie, and hired stenographers to transcribe documents. "He has the true crusading spirit," Walsh wrote Mooney, "plus deep sympathy for you, and a head full of brains."[14] Mooney, though torn between his attorneys' optimism and his own disbelief in American courts, gave all the help he could with TMMDC funds and his own detailed knowledge of the case.

In May 1934 the District Court denied the attorneys' petition; that summer the federal circuit court also denied a hearing. An appeal was then taken to the United States Supreme Court, in the form of a motion for leave to file a petition for an original writ of habeas corpus. The chief clerk of the court confided to Finerty that he thought the chances of success were good—in Finerty's words, "that we had an excellent chance of convincing the Court that the deliberate use of perjured testimony by the State was as much a domination of the Court as if the State had used military force or permitted the Court to be dominated by mob violence." Finerty submitted an enormous, twelve-volume record in support of the motion. Chief Justice Charles Evans Hughes undertook an analysis for presentation to his colleagues in conference. In November the Court ordered Warden James Holohan of San Quentin to show cause why Mooney's attorneys should not be permitted to file their petition. ("Good news!" said Mooney, peeling potatoes.)[15]

The motion was opposed by California's Attorney General, U. S. Webb, and his assistant, William F. Cleary. Webb contended that the only remedy lay with the Governor, that the courts had no power to reopen the case, that the acts of a prosecuting attorney could not in themselves amount to a denial of due process, and that the petitioner had raised no federal question. He pointed out that the petitioner was trying to change the accepted meaning of the Constitution, and warned that if his contention were sustained, the Supreme Court would become "the Court not only of last but of ever continuing resort."[16]

The decision was handed down in January 1935. Hughes, speaking for the Court, stated that a federal question was involved, and lectured the State of California on the character of justice:

we are unable to approve this narrow view of the requirement of due process. That requirement, in safeguarding the liberty of the citizen against deprivation through the action of the State, embodies the fundamental conceptions of justice which lie at the base of our civil and political institutions. . . . It is a requirement that cannot be deemed to be satisfied by mere notice and hearing if a State has contrived a conviction through the pretense of a trial which in truth is but used as a means of depriving a defendant of liberty through a deliberate deception of court and jury by the presentation of testimony known to be perjured. Such a contrivance by a State to procure the conviction and imprisonment of a defendant is as inconsistent with the rudimentary demands of justice as is the obtaining of a like result by intimidation. And the action of prosecuting officers on behalf of the State, like that of administrative officers in the execution of its laws, may constitute state action within the purview of the Fourteenth Amendment. . . .

Reasoning from the premise that the petitioner has failed to show a denial of due process . . . , the Attorney General urges that the State was not required to afford any corrective judicial process to remedy the alleged wrong. The argument falls with the premise.[17]

For the rest Hughes was cautious; the comity of state and federal courts made this type of review—in the phrase of an earlier Supreme Court decision—"an exceedingly delicate jurisdiction."[18] He stated that Mooney should first seek a writ of habeas corpus in the California courts, because the Supreme Court was not satisfied that California had failed to provide a corrective judicial process.[19]

Thus *Mooney v. Holohan* was a victory, but less for Mooney than for civil rights under the Fourteenth Amendment. The decision became the leading case for the federal principle that due process in criminal proceedings is denied if a state obtains a conviction by means of testimony known to the prosecution to be perjured.[20]

Mooney knew he was a long way from freedom. He expected the State Supreme Court to deny the writ, and predicted that it would take fifteen months and $10,000 to bring the case back through the United States Supreme Court. He said he was less worried about the time than the money.[21] Walsh was worried, too. If the California Supreme Court were to refuse a hearing, the United States Supreme Court would grant one, he was confident; but supposing the California Supreme Court were to issue a preliminary writ of habeas corpus, "and give us a hearing, or an alleged hearing," and then refuse liberty? What then? Hughes had not said. "Maybe a long time experience with courts has curbed my enthusiasm for 'apparent victories.'" If California denied the writ on the merits of the case, the effect might be to reduce Mooney's chances for ultimate federal relief.[22]

And so the process began again in California. The Superior Court in San Rafael and the State District Court of Appeals in San Francisco both refused to grant the writ. The defense hoped the State Supreme Court would do likewise. When the appeal was taken there in May 1935, Finerty sought to persuade the justices that they lacked jurisdiction.[23] The court was caught in a dilemma: it had previously held that Mooney's only remedy lay with the Governor, but now it was faced with the prospect that the United States Supreme Court would do in its place what it had said it could not do itself. *Mooney v. Holohan* was a mandate it could not disregard. The court ordered a hearing on the writ.[24] No one close to Mooney supposed, "in view of past performances," that the judges' finding would be favorable; as Finerty said, "apparently they think that under the decision of the Supreme Court of the United States, they cannot get out of granting it, but hope to beat us on the facts."[25] There was nothing for it but to go along. The attorneys supposed the hearings would take about four weeks. Instead, they lasted for thirteen months.

II

The habeas corpus hearings constituted an exceptionally comprehensive review of the case. Formally, there were three issues: whether any witness against Mooney had committed perjury in his trial; whether the District Attorney or any of his assistants had knowingly caused or permitted perjured testimony to be introduced at the trial; and whether he or his assistants had suppressed evidence favorable to the defense. Virtually no restrictions were made on the scope of testimony. In the interests of a full hearing, everything went into the record that Mooney or the attorneys for either side considered material, although much of it was technically subject to later exclusion.[26]

41. Mooney in San Quentin, 1930

42. Arthur Kent, alias Arthur Stuart Scott

43. Mary Gallagher

44. Mayor Jimmy Walker with Mooney at San Quentin, 1931

46. Mary Mooney

45. Mooney working in his cell at San Quentin

47. Mother Mooney's funeral cortege at the gates of San Quentin, 1934

48. "The Symbol." Byrd Kelso (right) and David Emerick on their national tour, 1931.

49. A Communist demonstration in San Francisco, 1932

50. Demonstrators at the courthouse during Mooney's retrial, 1933

51. Mooney at the San Francisco County Jail for the Habeas Corpus hearings, 1935

52. John F. Finerty

53. Frank P. Walsh

54-55. Fickert and Mooney at the time of the Habeas Corpus hearings

56. Governor Culbert L. Olson

58. Celebrating the pardon, with Harry Bridges

57. Leaving San Quentin for the last time,
January 7, 1939

59. Billings leaving Folsom Prison, October 17, 1939, accompanied by the warden (left) and
defense attorney George T. Davis

60. The victory procession up Market Street, January 8, 1939. Marching in the front line behind Mooney are Harry Bridges, Belle Hammerberg, Rena Mooney, George Davis, Anna Mooney, John Mooney, and John Shelley, later Mayor of San Francisco.

Among the witnesses were many principals: Tom and Rena Mooney, Billings, Nolan, Weinberg, McDonald, Hatcher, Hand, Peterson, William Smith, Matheson, Goff, Bunner, McNutt, McKenzie, Lawlor, Fickert, Cunha, Brennan, and Griffin. Others had died in the intervening years, including Crowley, Swanson, Oxman, O'Connor, Cockran, and Older. Many testified who had not done so previously. The total record covered 13,400 pages of typescript in twenty volumes, plus hundreds of exhibits—a nightmare to brief, but a storehouse of documents and recollections.

Before testimony commenced, the justices decided not to participate personally. Instead they appointed a referee, an elderly, obscure attorney named Addison E. Shaw, who had been a classmate of the Chief Justice, William H. Waste. Shaw was inexperienced in criminal law.[27] The arrangement was objectionable to Mooney's attorneys. Finerty flew to Washington to renew his application for habeas corpus from the United States Supreme Court; he argued that the California justices' refusal to see and hear the witnesses firsthand was a procedural denial of due process. But the Court refused to interfere. Shaw took the testimony. Deputy Attorney General Cleary, a hulking figure with a high-pitched voice, represented the state.[28]

The proceedings were extraordinary and in some ways bizarre. The testimony began in August 1935 in the surgical theater of the Baltimore City Hospital, for the twelfth solemn encounter of truth and John McDonald, whose physical condition had worsened. His affliction was the same: syphilis of the central nervous system.[29] But the attorneys on both sides proceeded on the supposition that he was still competent. McDonald had stated that he was eager to "expose Mr. Fickert and his bunch of crooked lawyers." Partly paralyzed and sitting in a wheelchair, he testified at length; he asserted once again that he had never seen Mooney before viewing him in jail. Said Cleary after cross-examining him, "I do believe that, after the ten years in which he has been worked on by Mooney sympathizers, he really does not know what happened." This was McDonald's final appearance in the case. Before the habeas corpus proceedings had ended, he was dead.[30]

When the proceedings shifted to San Francisco in September, Mooney was brought to the city in a police boat, the "D. A. White," under the escort of ten men. He was lodged once more in the County Jail on Dunbar Alley, off Washington Street, just behind the Hall of Justice. More than fifty police officers patroled the courthouse and nearby streets to prevent any demonstration. Mooney had gained twenty pounds and looked healthy, but was grayer than he had been when last in the city two years previously. In his jail cell he wept with excitement.[31]

Through his attorneys' efforts and the consent of officials, Mooney remained in San Francisco throughout the hearings and ensuing reviews—all told, nearly two years. Apart from his own testimony, his presence at the hearings was valuable because he knew so much about the case. He sat with his attorneys at the sessions and assisted (or, on one occasion, interfered) with their presentation.* Between sessions he worked at the jail, assembling materials, receiving visitors, and answering letters, often until the early hours of the morning. The routine at the jail was more relaxed than at the prison. Lock-up was later, letter-writing was unrestricted, local newspapers were permitted, and Mooney could have radical literature that was banned at San Quentin. The regular jail fare he considered terrible, but from the commissary the inmates were permitted to purchase meat and eggs, fresh dairy products, fruit, and vegetables.

Mooney was also quietly accorded a number of special privileges. He carried on his business in the jail office, enjoyed unlimited use of the telephone, and received callers privately after visiting hours. A secretary came regularly from the defense committee. He even acquired a dictaphone. One evening he arranged to produce a sound-track film of himself reviewing his plight in the basement of the jail. Arrangements were also made for eye treatment and dental work outside the premises.[32] As he said, "it is almost tantamount to freedom to be able to sit down without restraint or restriction and work on my case, to make my fight for freedom more effective without being questioned or censured."[33] To protect his privileges he was circumspect, guarding against careless boasts or public criticism of the law's delays. Indeed, the longer the hearings lasted, the longer he was able to stay in San Francisco.† Billings was in town for eleven months of the proceedings, and he, too, was accorded privileges.

One of their privileges was priceless. Early in the hearings Mooney

* He demanded the inclusion of the jury-tampering issue (pp. 192–93 above), which Walsh and Davis considered irrelevant. (California Supreme Court, "Habeas Corpus," X: 6142–51.)

† "If I were to begin making public statements too hostile to the Court and the Referee," he confided after sixteen months, "they would soon discipline me by returning me to San Quentin. I am here at their sufferance. I am long overdue at the penitentiary. There is no legitimate excuse for my remaining here." (Mooney to William Z. Foster, Robert Minor, and Earl Browder, January 30, 1937, Mooney Papers.)

had routinely been returned to jail for the noon recess. This impeded consultations with his attorneys. Davis obtained permission from Shaw for Mooney and Billings to take lunch at any restaurant in the neighborhood of the courthouse. The two prisoners were always accompanied by a deputy sheriff, Archie McAllister, whose superior, Daniel C. Murphy, a former president of the State Federation of Labor, had long believed in Mooney's innocence. Murphy was an understanding sheriff, and under McAllister's indulgent eye—he never handcuffed his charges, and sometimes neglected to take his gun—the "neighborhood" included a great part of San Francisco. Luncheons were held with attorneys, friends, a Hollywood star or two, and a number of labor leaders, including Scharrenberg and Harry Bridges. The gatherings were known to certain newsmen, but they kept quiet, and the arrangements went unspoiled; "the boys . . . had a very good time on the quiet."[34] Billings did have a bad moment when he was separated from McAllister at a crowded intersection, but he found his guardian without mishap.[35]

The luncheon arrangements improved as the hearings tapered off to short morning sessions and the lunch hours expanded. McAllister would accompany Mooney and Billings to an unobtrusive rented cottage at the end of Polk Street, near the waterfront, for afternoons with labor and radical friends, and women. One of the women, a tall, lanky left-winger named Myrtle Childs, was a professional cook, a caterer for Peninsula society weddings. She prepared roasts and spreads at the Polk Street retreat, and occasionally brought back left-over bottles of Peninsula champagne.[36] The tales of cottage life do not all tally, but as Davis said, Mooney and Billings were "having a good vacation at the county jail" and were most anxious that the hearings continue.* Every evening they returned to jail for the night: lock-up was at 8 P.M., and special privileges could not be stretched indefinitely.[37] "They have been very good to me here," Mooney once remarked, "and I do not like to impose on them." He deeply appreciated the referee's "splendid order" for the lunches out. "That was a great treat

---

* Davis to Finerty, May 9, 1936, Walsh Papers. According to one participant in the cottage gatherings, McAllister once had too much to drink and the prisoners went back to jail unaccompanied on the streetcar. Another participant questions this story: he points out that private automobiles were available in such circumstances. He recalls, however, that Billings once overindulged and had to be plied with strong coffee and walked up and down on the waterfront to sober up for the return to jail. But a third participant says that neither Mooney nor Billings drank on these occasions. (Author's interviews and correspondence [names withheld].)

that can be little understood or appreciated by one who has not known what we have endured."[38]

Following the conclusion of testimony, Davis importuned Chief Justice Waste to allow Mooney to remain in the city so he might be be accessible to counsel pending oral argument. After the interview Davis reported that Waste "was very friendly and volunteered the statement that Tom need not worry about being returned to San Quentin until his case is concluded. The Chief [Justice] further stated there was no need to return Tom to San Quentin because he has been a model prisoner in San Francisco and has proven that it is not at all unsafe to keep him in the County Jail."[39] Mooney was relieved. Walsh was pleased, too: Mooney would be helpful in marshaling the voluminous details, and the longer he was away from San Quentin, Walsh felt, the more apparent it would be to the public that he was not a dangerous dynamiter. On the other hand, little excuse could be found for Billings's further dalliance, and he was returned to Folsom.[40]

III

Fickert was another for whom the habeas corpus hearings were quietly beneficent. He was a pathetic figure, for he had become an alcoholic and had recently been divorced by his wife, after a separation of many years, for intemperance and habitual gambling. Unable to continue paying installments on the $4,000 awarded her, he lived in poverty and obscurity on his Kern County ranch. At 63 he was a shell of the man that had prosecuted Mooney: partially deaf, his hair thin and gray, his face lined and blotchy, his eyes dull, his clothes hanging loosely on his large frame. For months during the hearings he received $10 a week from the Attorney General's office as a consultant and witness. His reappearance in San Francisco elicited a response that was not without sympathy. The press refrained from publicizing his condition, and the football chronicler of the University of California recalled that Fickert had been unjustly denied a place on the honor roll of All American players.[41]

As a witness Fickert adhered to his former views. He admitted no irregularities, no fraud; he denied that there had been any perjury by any witness or any subornation of witnesses by the prosecution. His testimony added few facts or insights. His memory was faulty, his perspective unchanged.

Shortly before the writ was denied the following year, Fickert attended a Stanford football game in the rain and came down with pneumonia. A week later he was dead. Hopes proved vain that documents disclosing "the truth of the notorious frameup" might be found among his effects. Some onlookers saw in his decline and death the righteousness and judgment of God. More charitably, the San Francisco *News* saw his life as an "American Tragedy," a subject worthy of a Dreiser novel: "visualizing the fine, big lad of 38 years ago, just up from Stanford, we say that only the bitter and the myopic will withhold their pity." Billings said he bore him no malice, but Mooney remained unforgiving.[42]

IV

The habeas corpus hearings produced no revelations comparable to the Oxman letters or the Kansas City affidavit. In the basement of the Hall of Justice were found boxes of old police reports and records of the District Attorney's office on the Preparedness Day crime that had not been examined since the trials. Mooney and Davis asked permission to examine them for evidence of official fraud, and Cleary agreed to the project. For more than a month his office in the State Building was the scene of diligent sifting by half a dozen people, including Davis, Mooney, and Belle Hammerberg, Mooney's sister-in-law. The old papers harbored unexpected entertainment as well as information, as Belle wrote Walsh. The file of the *Revolt* showed Mooney running for sheriff: "George read his platform into the record . . . we found many amusing things." Everyone relaxed. Shaw lit his pipe. "It looks as if we are in for several days (or weeks) of enjoyment."[43] Several thousand documents later the search was concluded. Not more than a dozen items were of any importance. One valuable find was the police transcript of Mooney's "third degree." Another was a photograph of Steuart and Market from across Market about one minute before the explosion, showing a man on the roof of the saloon: it revived the old defense theory that the bomb had been dropped from that roof. But nothing was conclusive. Mooney thought that some of the records had been removed, but there was no way to prove it.[44]

By the time the hearings ended, the last evidence that either side ever uncovered on the Mooney case was in. Months were spent in briefing. Cleary's findings on behalf of the state were uniformly negative. He even found no perjury. Shaw prepared his own findings of fact, on a tardy directive from the State Supreme Court, and in January 1937 submitted his report. In it the material issues were resolved against Mooney without exception. Shaw found that Mooney had had a fair and impartial trial, that he had been prosecuted in good faith, that no state officials had abetted the presentation of perjured testimony or willfully concealed favorable evidence; and he concluded that Mooney had not been denied any right guaranteed to him by the state or federal constitution.[45] "Simply awful," said Walsh after reading the report, and added in an unguarded moment of bitterness, "had the decision been otherwise, I feel sure that the petitioner and all of his counsel would have fallen dead in every direction."[46]

Argument was held in April before the justices of the State Supreme Court and a sizable audience of lawyers and law students. The atmosphere was relaxed, in contrast to the rancor that had developed during the 1930 hearings. (Preston was no longer on the bench; he had resigned and returned to private practice.) Davis, who had noticeably lost weight, argued the case for five days, while Mooney sat at the counsel table and maintained a discreet silence. The argument concluded in a friendly atmosphere. The court clerk, a dignified gentleman, shook Mooney's hand and wished him good luck. Although many spectators thought the justices' friendliness a good omen, experience kept Mooney skeptical. "However," he added, "with all the agitation that is going on all over the country in favor of President Roosevelt's court reform program and the general upsurge of the labor movement on all fronts, it is just impossible to predict what can and cannot happen in these matters."[47]

V

For a while Mooney was permitted to remain at the jail, but things had changed: there were no hearings and no lunch hours. Mooney missed the sunshine and exercise that had been part of his life at San Quentin. He hoped for a speedy decision, which was neither realistic nor fair: the case was labyrinthine, the judges were not to be rushed. Days turned to weeks. Once again Mooney's health gave way and he was removed in a serious condition to the city hospital. There, with competent care, his ulcer stopped bleeding and he began to mend. After two weeks the hospital authorities wished to discharge him, but since the jail was a poor place for convalescence, Mooney pulled wires all over town, and was permitted to remain at the hospital a third week.[48] Davis remarked that Mooney had many visitors: "you know that as soon as the first flush or two of illness would pass,

Tom would resume his station in life as general of the free Mooney movement, and would be interviewing all and sundry the important persons visiting San Francisco. Consequently, our sick general interviewed Brophy, Zaritsky, Father O'Flanagan, and God know[s] who else, from his hospital bed."* At the end of his hospital stay the Supreme Court ordered Mooney's return to San Quentin. "The honeymoon is over," he said. He looked like a tired old man.[49]

San Quentin had no nursing quarters. After a few days in the prison hospital, Mooney was assigned to stoop labor in the vegetable garden. There he fainted. Subsequently he was reassigned to the mess room at the prison hog ranch, where he could have fresh milk and eggs, though not the rest of the special diet prescribed for him by the city hospital.[50] He was deeply depressed. He was being treated like a "fish," a new prisoner without privileges, and deprived of his books, papers, typewriter, and other belongings. The preceding occupant of his new cell had been syphilitic. The prison ranch assignment meant long walks to receive visitors or return to the cell. Mooney felt that the new warden was harassing him, perhaps looking for an excuse to transfer him to Folsom, or even dispose of him by the "backdoor parole." He complained to the defense committee, which notified friendly newspapers and labor unions. Warden Court Smith and the Prison Board were deluged with protests. A party of eighteen, including four State Assemblymen, called on Smith to demand that Mooney be placed on the diet prescribed by the city hospital. Complaints were made to Governor Merriam. The authorities also heard from Roger Baldwin, the Communist Party, and members of the Hollywood Actors Guild—James Cagney, Boris Karloff, Edward G. Robinson, and others.[51] Ultimately, orders were given for the special diet, and Mooney was returned to his old cell "with all of its bookshelves and domestic appurtenances," including his typewriter.[52] However, the rich, creamy diet proved a mistake, for he had not only ulcers, but also a gallbladder infection. Soon he was back in the hospital, in great pain, but properly diagnosed. Although too weak for an operation, Mooney improved in time, and was assigned odd jobs around the hospital while he awaited the outcome of the habeas corpus proceedings.[53]

---

* Davis to Walsh, June 10, 1937, Walsh Papers. John Brophy was a leader of the CIO; Max Zaritsky was one of its founders. Michael O'Flanagan, former vice-president of the Irish Republic, was touring the United States in behalf of the Spanish Loyalists. (Irving Howe and Lewis Coser, *American Communist Party*, pp. 264–65, 371; New York *Times*, October 8, 1936, April 25, 1937, and May 19, 1938.)

VI

In October 1937 the State Supreme Court denied the writ of habeas corpus. The vote was 5–1, Langdon dissenting. The members of the Court had not relied alone on the findings of Shaw or the final arguments of the attorneys; they had studied the record. The decision filled 85 pages. It was the most comprehensive opinion on the Mooney case ever issued by a court. The judges rejected the petition not on procedural grounds—they conceded the availability of the writ—but on the grounds that neither fraud nor perjury nor suppression of evidence had been established.[54] The Court made only one concession to the petitioner: it found that the Oxman letters were "suspicious and questionable in character." However, no injury was done Mooney by "such assumed corruption" on Oxman's part, since Rigall did not testify in Mooney's trial. "At the most, the letters indicate an attempted subornation of perjury."[55]

Otherwise the petitioner had established nothing. The Court found that John McDonald told the truth at the 1916 grand jury hearing, at the trials, and in his letter to Duncan Matheson in January 1921; thereafter he perjured himself, in his affidavit of February 1921, his 1930 testimony, and his habeas corpus testimony. The change occurred when Nockels gave him the $500 to come to California. Thereafter his testimony and statements "were a sequence of inconsistencies, contradictions and obvious falsehood, indicating patent perjury and a corrupt attempt to destroy his trial testimony."[56] But prior to this corruption, such variations as had occurred in McDonald's testimony were inconsequential, particularly those relating to the time at which Mooney and Billings arrived at Steuart and Market on the day of the explosion: "it is apparent that the witness was not attempting definitely to fix the exact time of the occurrence of the events. MacDonald [sic] was merely estimating and approximating the time of the occurrences described by him. His testimony upon the Billings and Mooney trials is susceptible of no other construction."* Nor was there "irreconcilable conflict" between the eyewitness accounts of McDonald and Oxman, since they were standing on opposite sides of the crowded street.[57] And as for the fact that McDonald's original identifications in the police reports were not descriptive of Mooney and Billings, "we do not attach the significance or materiality to said reports

---

* McDonald's inconsistency is discussed above, pp. 184–85. See also pp. 347–48 and 393.

that petitioner does. The description therein merely inaccurately stated the heights, weights and ages of the persons involved. No glaring discrepancy appears."[58]

Oxman's Kansas City affidavit the Court similarly found of no great importance:

In the main, there is no great deviation between the substance of the averments of the affidavit and the material portions of Oxman's subsequent testimony upon petitioner's trial. As to the persons he had observed, their manner of approach to the scene and their conduct while there, the two are substantially the same. . . .

. . . Oxman averred in his affidavit that he "noticed them talking in a foreign language", which was not mentioned by him upon the trial. . . . it might be argued that the "foreign language" may have been uttered by the unidentified man whom Oxman designated as being with the others at the scene of the explosion and, according to Fickert's testimony herein [*i.e.*, the habeas corpus hearings], whom Oxman designated on one occasion in the district attorney's office as "a foreigner."

The Court also suggested that the foreigner might have been the Spaniard or Mexican whom John Crowley described in Billings's trial as being with Billings at Steuart and Mission streets. The Court did not suggest who might have been listening to the foreigner. Moreover, the Court quoted from Oxman's trial testimony relating the words between Mooney and Billings (" 'Give it to him and let him go; we must get away from here; the bulls will be after us' "), but it did not mention that Oxman's Kansas City affidavit stated, in connection with the foreign language, "I could not understand what was said."[59]

The Court found the testimony of Earl Hatcher and his wife "a tissue of falsehoods" because of Hatcher's signed statement during Oxman's trial, and other statements of Hatcher's before 1921, that Oxman was in San Francisco before the bomb exploded; and because the Hatchers gave unsatisfactory reasons for their long silence. "It was not until after Oxman refused to loan him $10,000 that he made any claim that he did not leave Woodland until afternoon." The Court found that Hatcher's incorrect timing of the afternoon train from Woodland impeached his own testimony, since the timetables disclosed no passenger train leaving Woodland at 2:15, or enabling passengers to reach San Francisco by 6:00 P.M., but revealed, rather, a train leaving Woodland at 2:55 P.M., enabling passengers to arrive by boat in San Francisco at 6:30: "It must be remembered in this connection, that Hatcher testified herein that Oxman phoned him from San Francisco about 6:00 P.M. Had Oxman taken the 2:55 P.M. train he could not have phoned from San Francisco at 6:00 P.M."[60] But the Court did not acknowledge that the same hearings also showed that in 1921 Hatcher testified to the San Francisco grand jury that Oxman telephoned "I think it was about six or seven o'clock."[61]

Further concerning Oxman, the Court found no adequate reason to believe that he had not seen Weinberg's jitney at Steuart and Market as he testified. "It is not for us to speculate as to the course taken by the automobile prior to Oxman's observation of it. We do not think the testimony of the officers [i.e., the eighteen policemen stationed on Market Street] is capable of all that the petitioner claims for it." In sum, "we find and conclude that petitioner has not established by any substantial, credible evidence his charge that Oxman perjured himself."[62]

The Court went to the rescue of Mellie and Sadie Edeau, in contrast to its 1930 dismissal of them. Plunging into the thick of the evidence, it emerged thirteen pages later bearing the scalps of Police Chief Walter J. Peterson ("most evasive, uncertain and forgetful," "equivocal and indefinite," and of "questionable moral standard") and Officer William H. Smith ("he is subject to the same criticism"). It retrieved the ladies' virtue: Mrs. Edeau had denied the "assertion" of Peterson and McKenzie that she told them she was at 721 Market Street in her astral body. "We are satisfied . . . that petitioner has not here established . . . that either Mellie or Sadie Edeau committed perjury upon his trial."[63]

Other findings of the Court included these: the clock alibi from the Eilers Building photographs was unconvincing, because Mooney "might have participated in the bombing and still have been present at the time and place indicated by the pictures." Mooney's possessions in Nolan's basement included "explosives and articles similar to those found at the scene of the explosion," and Mooney had possessed other "incriminating articles at his residence."[64] Although Mooney had been acquitted at Martinez, "there was testimony that . . . some of the articles were subsequently reclaimed on his affidavit."*

Finally, the opinion dealt briefly with the petitioner's background,

---

* 10 *California Reports* (2d ser.) 8 (1937). T. D. Johnson, associate counsel with Mc-Nutt in the Martinez case, had testified in the habeas corpus hearings that he received two of the weapons from the Martinez arsenal after the trial. "I think I filed an affidavit. . . . My impression is that Mooney made the affidavit, but . . . I would not want to be

"his revolutionary activities which clearly establish his aim and purpose to weaken and undermine, with the view of ultimate destruction, both by violent and insidious means, the entire social and political structure of the nation. Such was the character of his associates and his own professed writings. In other words, he was outspokenly hostile to our system of government."[65]

Many things were not mentioned. The Court virtually ignored the manner in which the case was prepared by the police and District Attorney. No note was taken of the arrests without warrants, the grilling of Mooney, detentions incommunicado, identifications without line-ups, the newspaper releases, the Kidwell affair. The Court did not mention McDonald's cerebral spinal lues, diagnosed in 1914, or explain why, under the circumstances, he was trustworthy thereafter. It did not mention any unfavorable character evidence against Oxman; the Spain case it dismissed as immaterial. It did not criticize Oxman for failing to offer his testimony in Billings's trial, yet it criticized Peterson and Smith for failing to offer theirs in Mooney's. It mentioned Judge Griffin's denial of the motions for a new trial and for the writ of *coram nobis*, but not his request that Attorney General Webb consent to a reversal, his protests to Governor Stephens, or anything else respecting the trial judge's views after the exposure of Oxman. Upon all these and other omissions the Court closed the door: "Points not discussed herein are lacking in merit and do not require further notice."[66]

Langdon's dissent was brief. He said that no useful purpose would be served by reviewing the evidence. "The preponderance of the material, credible evidence in the record leads me to conclude that on his trial petitioner was not accorded due process of law."[67] Chief Justice Waste announced that the proceedings had cost the state $17,664.24. "It was the most expensive luxury in the history of the court," he said.[68] Thus concluded the habeas corpus proceedings for Mooney in the state of California.*

---

bound by that. ... now as to what the property [was] that he made the affidavit as to ownership of I would not be prepared to state.... I wanted to hold this property [the two guns] until I got some pay." A search of the Contra Costa records failed to turn up the affidavit. (California Supreme Court, "Habeas Corpus," XVII: 11,251–60.)

 * The California Supreme Court has been studied too little and too superficially to warrant an explanation of its bias on the grounds of class or reactionary sentiment as an unqualified assertion. Suffice it to note here that mediocre governors appointed most of the judges of 1937. For uncritical biographical sketches of the judges, see J. Edward Johnson, *History of the Supreme Court Justices of California, 1900–1950* (1966).

VII

The defense returned to the United States Supreme Court, its goal for so many years. The attorneys decided to seek a review of the California decision rather than an original writ of habeas corpus. Davis did most of the work. He moved to New York, set up a temporary office near Walsh, and was admitted to practice before the United States Supreme Court. After four years on the case he still found its legal problems and possibilities stimulating—"a fortunate miracle for both of us," as he wrote Mooney.[69] The task of briefing anew was staggering. The work extended through long days and many hours of night. Three stenographers were constantly employed—one of them out of Walsh's pocket. Mooney was anxious for a decision before the end of the Court's session in June 1938, "lest there be no necessity for a decision at all in this case."[70] If the Court made no decision by then, he threatened to withdraw the appeal altogether, in order to clear the deck for renewed political action. Governor Merriam was up for re-election. "I am determined that Merriam shall not be able to avail himself of the argument that our case is still in the courts," Mooney wrote his attorneys. This precipitated a crisis, but it passed and the work continued.[71]

In March 1938 the attorneys filed a condensed, 187-page brief in support of their petition for a writ of certiorari. The brief charged that the California Supreme Court had "become a party to the frame-up," and "by its deliberate misrepresentations, distortions, suppressions and evasions of material evidence . . . has itself been guilty of what is the moral equivalent of the prosecutor's knowing use of perjury and deliberate suppression of evidence."[72] This charge was denounced by the opposition: Attorney General Webb called it insulting; the Sacramento *Bee* said it was "an hysterical and flamboyant attack on the good name, the impartiality, the honesty, and the integrity of the justices of the California Supreme Court"—qualities that were indeed at question. The prospects for the defense were not good; as one sympathetic attorney remarked to Walsh, "you sure have put the U.S. Supreme Court in a peculiar spot where they will have to hold that the Supreme Court of California was corrupt and . . . are part of a conspiracy against Tom Mooney."[73]

The Supreme Court needed the summer months to inspect the record and exhibits, and postponed decision until October. "What a travesty upon justice, the idea of spending five calendar years in obtaining a writ of habeas corpus!" exclaimed Mooney. He turned meanwhile to the political scene, and threw all he had into the campaign to nominate Democratic State Senator Culbert L. Olson for the governorship in the August primaries.[74]

The petition for certiorari was denied in October. Justices Hugo Black and Stanley Reed, both Roosevelt appointees, dissented. No opinion accompanied the decision. The high court seldom went behind findings of fact by a state court; in effect, it found the state court's findings of fact conclusive.[75] Finerty applied once again for an original writ of habeas corpus, but by that time attention was almost entirely on California politics. It was little noticed when the United States Supreme Court denied the petition, in December 1938.[76] The Mooney case in state and federal courts had come to an end.

CHAPTER TWENTY-SEVEN

The Politics of Freedom, 1935-1938

Boost for your California! ... Boost for its beauty, its comfort and its opportunities. Boost for its inheritance of the spirit of the pioneers and for its achievement in the spirit of today.... Boost for its learning, its teaching, its literature, its art and its social structure. Be proud of your share in this final foreground of one civilization and opening gateway toward another. Boost for your California!
—*Chronicle*, July 22, 1936

You have reached the dazzling heights of State Senator—I don't say that sarcastically; it is a position of honor, although some of us would rather learn to play the harmonica as an achievement.
—Ed McKenzie

THE LATE DEPRESSION times of 1935–38 were years of anguished searching for social justice. New Dealers and exploited minorities were seeking security, social equality, and a renewed sense of purpose. One of the symbols that dramatized the quest, as many a banner and placard proclaimed, was Tom Mooney behind bars. To be sure, Mooney and Billings did not inspire the radical 1930's as profoundly as the memory of Sacco and Vanzetti, for the California case had inherent dramatic weaknesses: it had dragged on for a generation, its principals less than heroic, its details lost in the haze of years. (Children born in the year of Mooney's trial voted in 1938.) Yet Mooney remained a powerful image for the times, his freedom a goal of radicals, labor, and reformers. Nowhere was this image more powerful than in California—and nowhere was the opposition more formidable.

Upton Sinclair's defeat for the governorship in 1934 did not leave the progressive elements in California politically powerless. The new legislature that convened the following January, when Merriam began his first full term of office, included a number of dissident voices. The Depression and the much-maligned EPIC movement had thrust up some thirty Democratic Assemblymen committed in varying degrees to the EPIC program. Most of them came from Southern California. Comprising more than a third of the lower house, they worked as a bloc—an uncommon phenomenon in Sacramento—to pass reform legislation. They conferred daily on measures and means, and introduced jointly a number of progressive bills, ranging in subject from the 30-hour week and higher inheritance taxes to repeal of the Criminal Syndicalism law. One of their measures was a concurrent resolution calling on Governor Merriam for an immediate and unconditional pardon of Mooney.[1]

The idea of legislative intervention for a pardon was not new. As early as 1931 a pardon resolution for Mooney had been introduced in the Assembly. At that time the move, having virtually no support, served only to embarrass the cause.[2] But the climate had changed by 1935. In addition to the concurrent resolution for a pardon, the EPIC bloc introduced several bills to change the legal codes for Mooney's benefit. One measure provided for the writ of *coram nobis*; another permitted a new trial if new evidence were found within 60 days; a third enabled appellate courts to make findings of fact outside the record; and a fourth proposed that "A writ of habeas corpus may be procured by every person who has been convicted through a pretense of a trial which in truth is but used as a means of depriving a defendant through a deliberate deception of court and jury by the presentation of testimony known to be perjured."[3] Unexpectedly, in the midst of these there appeared a resolution requesting Merriam to commute Mooney's sentence to time served. It came not from the EPIC bloc, but from Billings's prosecutor, James F. Brennan, now a San Francisco Assemblyman.

Brennan's plan won sudden popularity. Among groups hostile to Mooney and Billings, the commutation scheme looked attractive in the aftermath of the *Mooney v. Holohan* decision, which seemed to offer the prospect of long, costly proceedings that would humiliate the state and probably end in Mooney's vindication by the United States Supreme Court. Editors asked on behalf of a long-suffering public to be spared further agitation for Mooney: might he not be freed and forgotten?[4] With a minimum of inconvenience and no loss of honor, the state, through Merriam, could deprive Mooney of his martyrdom by turning him out. Mooney could not refuse a commutation, as he could a parole; commutation would not exonerate him, as a pardon might; it would simply end a vexed and contentious problem. That the proposal should have been introduced by Brennan seems particularly fitting: it was a crude compromise born of exasperation.

Some of Mooney's supporters, including Baldwin and Walsh, had long since privately concluded that a commutation would be acceptable. As Baldwin said in 1931, "to overcome that hard-boiled gang by making them confess error is to ask, I think, the impossible." This was a common view in 1935. Although Brennan's resolution was criticized both by Mooney, who wanted vindication, and by some of his enemies, who wanted to keep him behind bars, the EPIC bloc joined in supporting it, and it was adopted, 51–28.[5]

Mooney believed the worst of Merriam—that he would comply, and kill the hopes raised by *Mooney v. Holohan*. But the Governor, who had, after all, been free right along to commute the sentence without legislative prodding, remained impervious to the Assembly's importuning, and did nothing. The "master propagandist," Brennan said, was left in San Quentin to "sit there and agitate till he finally gets out with a clean bill of health." As for the progressive-bloc measures of uncompromising relief for Mooney, all were buried in committee. Merriam was not required to act on them.[6]

II

California in the mid-1930's was harvesting the fruits of economic disorder, unimaginative leadership, and irresponsible public life. Unemployment and inadequate remedies left widespread physical suffering and a corrosive social malaise that spread across the state from the Sacramento Valley to the Mexican border. Anxiety, hatred, and fear of radicalism frequently erupted into violence and repression. The tone was set in 1934, by the gubernatorial panic of that year; by Communist efforts to organize agricultural labor; and by the San Francisco general strike that summer, which resulted in dead and wounded strikers, anti-Communist hysteria, and Governor Merriam's calling of the National Guard. (San Francisco businessmen formed a Citizens' Committee, headed by Thornwell Mullally—the grand marshal of the 1916 Preparedness Day parade—"to cope with the Red menace.")[7] The tensions grew with the influx of tens of thousands of poverty-stricken "Oakies" and "Arkies" from the midcontinental Dust Bowl to the fertile valleys of California, where they moved as pickers from crop to crop in misery and squalor, exploited by the farmers (who themselves lived in fear of bankruptcy), and terrorized by armed guards in the pay of large landholding companies.

Throughout the state, personal freedoms were abused, as in the prewar years of IWW persecution. The record of repression included rural violence: the intimidation, flogging, and killing of migratory farm laborers by vigilantes and deputized residents. It included police lawlessness: the unlawful arrests of radicals, of indigents, of picketing strikers in the cities. It included the tarring and feathering of radicals in Santa Rosa, the shooting of strikers on the San Pedro waterfront, the beating of gold miners on strike in the Mother Lode country, the beating of workingmen in San Jose vigilante raids, the deputizing of "Citizens Armies" to suppress strikers in Salinas and Stockton. The Los Angeles police operated a Red Squad and an elaborate spy system against radical groups and AFL unions; the police chief stationed officers on the distant borders of the state, without authorization, to turn back impoverished and unemployed migrants, lest they become a burden to Los Angeles County. Rural county ordinances restricted the right of assembly: in Tulare County, for instance, no more than 25 persons might lawfully gather without a permit. Private paramilitary bodies such as the "Berkeley Nationals" and the "California Cavaliers" were formed. Rioters attacked radical meeting places in the Bay Area. The Criminal Syndicalism Law was used in Sacramento by the District Attorney and the so-called Associated Farmers of California—an organization of powerful corporations with important financial interests in agriculture—against a group of Communist organizers; the Associated Farmers maintained their own espionage system and worked alongside state and local law enforcement agencies. In the Imperial Valley a federal commission found the law trampled underfoot by citizens and local officials alike; "outside agitators" there were met with tear gas, indiscriminate arrests, and unreasonable bail. Governors seemed to share the local attitudes: Rolph on one occasion publicly approved the lynching of two kidnap-murder suspects in San Jose,* and Merriam condoned vigilante action. And in one session of the State Assembly, more than a score of bills were introduced to limit civil liberties; one bill would have established a state espionage system; another would have made it a felony to advocate pacifism.[8] Of the California scene, Lillian Symes wrote in *Harper's*: "It was like this, I imagine, in Rome in 1922, in Berlin in 1932."[9]

Mooney, in one of his own mildly aphoristic moments, once re-

---

* "I believe that it was a fine lesson to the whole Nation," he said. "If anyone is arrested for the good job, I'll pardon them all." (As quoted, *Chronicle*, November 28, 1933.) George West later wrote in the New York *Times* (May 20, 1934), "He said what perhaps nine out of ten persons said when they first heard of the lynching. . . . Californians agreed with the sentiment while deploring the fact that it had been uttered by a man in Mr. Rolph's position."

marked: "It does not take much to stir up a red scare in California."[10] He knew it from personal experience in San Quentin, for the "dubious battle" reached even there; the prison had its own red scare in 1935, touched off by efforts of two con-politicians to discredit a prison lieutenant who had removed them from privileged positions. They told Warden Holohan that Communist agitators were active among the inmates and that radical publications were getting through the lieutenant's office to them. Alarmed, Holohan reprimanded the officer and ordered the prison guards to confiscate all such literature. Three guards were assigned to raid the cells of known radicals, of whom there were 28 by one count, including McNamara and Mooney. The radicals had a common library of some seven hundred books contributed from friends outside. The guards began with Mooney's cell.[11] It was "knocked over," in prison parlance, and for the first time in his prison term, his books, papers, magazines, and pamphlets were seized. "When this search of my cell was finished, it looked a wreck—it was a wreck . . . and in my terribly upset condition for the next several days, I forgot about everything else but my loss." Holohan found from the records of the group's circulating librarian that about three hundred convicts were using the radical library, and concluded that Communist influence in the prison was indeed a menace.[12]

San Quentin's red scare passed, but not conservative Californians' hatred of Mooney. Though he was said to be one of four Americans whose names were best known in Europe (the others were Franklin D. Roosevelt, Charles A. Lindbergh, and Henry Ford),[13] in his own state it remained anathema. "There has not been a commuters' train or a street car . . . in which somewhat acrimonious discussion of the Mooney case did not sooner or later arise amidst the passengers," commented the *Examiner*. When Aline Barnsdall of Los Angeles put up "Free Mooney" billboards along her estate on Wilshire Boulevard, she was accused of being a Communist; when a Los Angeles sculptress, Martha Oathout Ayres, made a bust of Mooney, a local paper accused her of lacking patriotism. As the *Nation* said, "Mooney is California's bogey man extraordinary; the hysteria with which he is hated and feared is not amenable to reasoned argument."[14]

III

The Democrats took control of the State Assembly in 1937 for the first time in many years, with 47 of the 80 seats.[15] Their number included the EPIC progressives. Though less conspicuous as a bloc, they led a renewed campaign in the Assembly to free Mooney. They pinned their hopes on an extraordinary resolution proposing that the legislature itself pardon Mooney, without reference to the Governor. Mooney himself appears to have originated the idea: in 1934 he had asked Upton Sinclair and his party campaign manager, Culbert L. Olson, to draft a bill for the legislature to pardon him; nothing then came of it. Following the 1936 elections Mooney pressed the idea upon Paul Richie, an EPIC Democratic Assemblyman and former Socialist, from San Diego, who had been disturbed about the Mooney case since his childhood.[16] Richie responded: "I am amazed, if it is really true that the Legislature has the power to pardon or free any prisoner by a Legislative act. I never knew that."[17] He thought such a resolution more promising than any addressed to Merriam. He conferred with the leader of the bloc, William Moseley Jones of Montebello (Los Angeles County), who thought offhand that it would work. Since Jones was the new Speaker, Richie was encouraged: "Jones will stack every important committee with Democrats, and believes beyond a doubt the Committee on Judiciary would report favorably," he informed Mooney.[18] Richie also consulted Olson, the one State Senator to whom he could turn for advice. Olson recommended that instead of introducing a bill, which could be vetoed by the Governor, they work for a concurrent resolution, which he thought would have the same legal force in this situation as a statute.[19]

No one knew whether the legislature had the constitutional authority to pardon a convict. The Legislative Counsel thought not. The constitution was not explicit: it empowered the Governor to grant pardons, except in cases of treason or impeachment, in which only the legislature could grant them, and provided that neither the Governor nor the legislature could pardon a recidivist without the approval of the Supreme Court.[20] Did this mean the legislature might pardon a first-term convict? It had never been tried, so far as the record showed, and no court had ruled on the question. "I can see a mile off that our opponents will attack us on constitutional grounds," said Richie. He wondered if it might not be wisest to argue that the constitutional point could be settled after the resolution had passed. It was ticklish business: "Of course what we want them to do is to vote their convictions on the Mooney case, not vote on a point of law; but at the same time we want to create and preserve confidence in the validity of our measure, as having the force and effect of law if we pass it, and we want the Governor, the courts, or the Warden to regard it as dangerous business to attempt to defy the will of the legislature."[21]

The resolution was jointly introduced by 27 Assemblymen. Richie worked assiduously on doubtful members.* After a lengthy debate in March before a packed gallery, the measure passed, 45 to 28. "A pure political gesture," said the *Chronicle*; "What is the constitution among friends?"[22] The measure then went to the Senate. There was the rub: the upper chamber was overwhelmingly controlled by rural county votes. The people of Los Angeles, San Francisco, Alameda, and San Diego counties, comprising more than two-thirds of the population, elected only four of the 40 Senators; 21 members—a majority—represented only about 13 per cent of the population.[23] Most of the small-county Senators were not even farmers or ranchers, but businessmen and attorneys.† There was no possibility that the overwhelmingly conservative Senate might adopt the pardon resolution.

However, the resolution was not abandoned without a fight. The TMMDC, with a dozen clerical workers on the job from morning to midnight, mailed 15,000 letters to labor, liberal, and radical Californians, urging them to put pressure on the Senate. The response was heavy.[24] "Some of the members are howling that an effort is being made to intimidate them," said Richie. It was no use. "The trouble with the Senators is that few of them *know* anything about the case, and they will not read."[25] Olson, leading the Senate debate, said he became convinced of Mooney's innocence after reading the Wickersham report and briefs of the case. He pleaded for broad construction of the powers of the legislature. Several Senators, including the assistant publisher of the Oakland *Tribune,* William F. Knowland, spoke against the resolution. It lost, 34–5; the five came from heavily populated counties, and, for what consolation it was worth, represented more Californians than did the other 34.[26] Richie said he would at

---

* The constitutional scruples of some Assemblymen were overcome by other considerations. Kennett B. Dawson, who represented a silk-stocking district in San Francisco, was "a stickler for forms," but on the roll call he voted for the resolution because he found it preposterous that Mooney's application for the writ of *habeas corpus* had gone unresolved for more than two years. (Mooney to Richie, March 8, 1937, Mooney Papers; California Legislature, 52d Sess., 1937, *Assembly Journal,* p. 773.)

† The Senate "has become the reactionary house of the Legislature, where the dirt farmers have found small comfort," observed Franklin Hichborn. "When the dirt farmers have wanted help they have depended upon the city-elected Assembly, not the rural-elected Senate." (Hichborn, "Answers to Arguments against the One-House Legislature," n.d., p. 4, Olson Papers.) According to Olson, "a majority of the [Senate's] members are there to represent the interests of the Standard Oil Company, the banking interests, the cement trust, the insurance companies' interests, the power companies' interests, the railroads and the privately owned public utilities and other special interests. They are there to oppose any legislation objected by the interests they represent, and to secure the passage of legislation for their special benefit." (Culbert L. Olson, script of speech in Trinity Auditorium, Los Angeles, July 19, 1935, pp. 6–7, Olson Papers.)

once introduce a concurrent resolution asking Merriam to pardon Mooney. He expected the Senate to kill it, "but this resolution will show if any member was honest in talking about the constitution instead of talking about the fake conviction of Mooney."[27]

The new resolution was no more palatable than the old. It passed the Assembly with a net loss of three votes, and lost in the Senate with a net gain of three votes.[28] So much for the constitution. In a philosophical mood Richie remarked:

It is difficult for an outsider who has not served, or closely observed, to really understand the legislature. One would think we must be careless and callous and rather illogical. I think we are—but I will say the boys are literally overwhelmed with a deluge of stuff their minds can't digest. They can't read half the total material that is sent them on 57 subjects. They are under pressure and receive a grist of letters pro and con on everything from court procedure to cosmetics. They haven't much chance here during the one hundred or so days to learn anything new. They are lucky if they can keep in their heads what little they do know without going nuts, many of the Senate have been there a long time, and I sometimes wonder if that is what makes half of them bald headed, *and all dumb.*

. . . the situation is something like . . . kindling a dead fire that time or the rain has put out. It wouldn't be so if members were really intellectual and logical or if they had the *fire* in them they ought to have. A lot of them are weak bundles of capricious emotion—and that is the way God or somebody made them.[29]

Mooney's next request of Richie was a nonconcurrent resolution of the Assembly memorializing Merriam for a pardon. Richie thought such a resolution superfluous, but he went along with it, probably to gratify Mooney's supporters. The resolution passed; nothing came of it except additional publicity, which was all that Mooney expected.[30] Then he wanted Richie to prepare a pardon measure for a statewide referendum. Such a move would have raised the same constitutional question as a legislative pardon, and so Richie's team proposed instead a constitutional amendment; for, as even the Legislative Counsel had to admit, the voters could free Mooney, if they chose, by inserting his pardon in the state constitution! However, putting the measure before the people required a two-thirds vote of both houses. Richie failed to get the proposal through the Assembly Committee on Constitutional Amendments.[31] "It does not matter, Tom," he wrote;

this assembly will get a rebuke later on. My only comment is to quote Chic Hanson, correspondent for the L. A. Times. Several days ago in the midst of a hubbub characteristic of the closing days of a session Hanson said to me: "My last story about this session of the legislature . . . will have a lead that will read as follows,—'The monkeys have come down out of the trees and headed for home.' The editor, of course, might cut it."[32]

That summer, after the legislature had adjourned, a proposed constitutional amendment that was to be adopted by popular initiative did circulate among voters for signatures. This amendment would have provided for pardons by popular vote, through the initiative process. Sponsored by someone in Los Angeles with the bona fide name of Irving Fig Newton, who had no connections with the TMMDC, the measure came to naught.[33]

Early in 1938 Governor Merriam called a special session of the legislature to deal with a number of pressing problems. The Mooney case was not one of them. However, once the session convened, Richie and his associates introduced a new legislative pardon resolution. Then, to dramatize it, they introduced and passed another resolution directing Mooney and Warden Court Smith of San Quentin to appear before the Assembly two days later, so that Mooney might address the legislators, sitting as a committee of the whole, and be questioned in connection with the proposed pardon.[34]

What some legislators thought of this gambit was unprintable. The Assembly's subpoena was denounced as "hippodroming," which it doubtless was, for there was nothing Mooney could say that had not been said already; as the *Chronicle* remarked, Mooney telling his story in a morning to the legislature "is like asking Balzac to boil down La Comédie Humaine to a short story."[35] The plan was, indeed, a publicity stunt at the expense of the legislature; it was part of the mold that grew in the darkness of California's prolonged disgrace. For a time it was uncertain whether Smith would honor the subpoena. He consulted the Attorney General, who advised him that the Assembly was within its rights. Early the next morning Mooney and Smith stepped into a chauffered limousine and set off for the state Capitol.[36]

The Assembly chamber was crowded to overflowing. Mooney was in good spirits. Dressed in a neat, dark suit with matching necktie and pocket handkerchief, he looked more like a middle-aged businessman than a convict. He shook hands with friends in the chamber, and, mounting the speaker's rostrum, beamed and bowed as a thunder of applause rolled down from the gallery. About half the Senate sat with the Assembly; Merriam had also been invited, but did not attend. Mooney's address was a long, somewhat rambling discourse without histrionics, a review of his life and the case. At the end he thanked the Assembly and burst into tears.[37]

A few minutes later the Assembly voted on the pardon resolution. It did not pass. The prisoner was taken back to prison, while Richie tried to round up absent legislators for another vote. The Assembly remained in session until one o'clock the following morning, but the resolution's supporters could not muster a majority of the house.[38] Perhaps the matter would have ended there but for the determination of Captain Goff in San Francisco to be heard in the Assembly, too. (Mooney described Goff as the "generalissimo of the frame-up forces," which had been roughly true since Fickert's death.) Goff wired the Assembly and requested an appearance. His request was granted. For three hours he berated Mooney and the defense's evidence. The Assembly reacted by passing the pardon resolution, 41-29. The Senate tabled it without a roll call, and the affair was over. As Mooney said a few days later, it was hard to realize that the thing had actually happened.[39]

IV

The failure of California authorities in 1937 and 1938 to release Mooney intensified national political interest in his plight. His supporters attempted to involve Congress in the movement to free him, and after long effort they obtained a Congressional investigation of the case. Publicly this phase of the case began with a House speech on the Wickersham Report in late March 1937 by Congresswoman Caroline O'Day of Rye, New York. A liberal Democrat, Mrs. O'Day had been concerned about the case as far back as the 1920 Democratic National Convention in San Francisco, and had more recently asked President Roosevelt to intercede.[40] Other New Deal Congressmen joined her, among them Congresswoman Nan Wood Honeyman of Portland, Oregon (daughter of C. E. S. Wood, who had long been involved in the case), and Jerry J. O'Connell of Butte, Montana; so did Usher L. Burdick of North Dakota, a maverick Republican. On March 29, O'Connell introduced a joint resolution in the House, calling on Merriam to pardon Mooney; a few days later Senator James E. Murray—like O'Connell, an ardent New Dealer from Butte—introduced the resolution in the Senate.[41]

Support for the Murray-O'Connell resolution was fostered by the TMMDC, AFL, CIO, and Chicago Federation of Labor. For months it was urged upon the legislators and the public by two offbeat lobbyists: Gardner Jackson and—incredible as it may seem—John Jenkins, Mooney's salty, zealous old Wobbly friend, who was now chairman of the TMMDC-affiliated Washington Mooney Defense Committee. Jenkins carried on his campaign from the offices of several sympathetic Congressmen. He lobbied around the Capitol in a frayed old suit (and, he said, no underwear), mimeographing news releases, franking pro-Mooney Congressional speeches by the sack, and surviving on handouts from friends or at breadlines.[42] He and Jackson succeeded by July in gathering the signatures of two hundred members of Congress, among them 27 Senators, in support of the resolution. ("I think we can get all of New York except Ham[ilton] Fish who states that Tom Mooney is guilty and he knows it and told me to get the Hell out of his office," Jenkins reported.)* Much of the support no doubt was politically motivated; as one Senator remarked, "some who pretend to be so interested in Tom Mooney are interested to get the support of his followers rather than get his freedom."†

Mooney had no illusions about the effect of a Congressional hearing. Even if the resolution were passed, Merriam would not pardon him. For Mooney, the value of the resolution lay in its propaganda possibilities. Moreover, he was most anxious to be subpoenaed to testify in Washington—and then, hopefully, to be kept around for a long hearing there, as he had been in San Francisco. It did not work out that way, even briefly, but not for want of trying. The House and Senate Judiciary subcommittees to which the resolution was referred both decided that they lacked the power to issue the subpoena. The chairman of the House subcommittee, Emanuel Celler of New York, asked Merriam to let Mooney come to Washington, but Merriam replied that he had no authority to do so.[43]

* New York *Times*, August 7, 1937; Sara Eliaser to Herbert Resner, July 30, 1937 (Mooney Papers). Fish was the reactionary Republican who chaired the 1930 House committee investigation of Communism. See above, p. 411. (Telford Taylor, *Grand Inquest: The Story of Congressional Investigations* [1955], pp. 71–72.)

† Rush D. Holt (Democrat, West Virginia) to C. W. Kirkendall, January 28, 1938, Mooney Papers. In Jenkins's own opinion, Congressmen were a contemptible lot. He wrote Mooney: "Some of those who claim to represent labor dont even know you have been arrested. Senator James Davis of Pa. told me that while he was Sec'y of Labor [1921–30] no one ever told him about it." Later he added, "I have been here over twenty-five years off and on and all I know is that [Congress] is the biggest pile of junk that I ever saw piled up in one pile." (Jenkins to Mooney, April 4 and May 4, 1938, Mooney Papers.)

The Senate subcommittee acted first. Chaired by Joseph O'Mahoney of Wyoming (an old friend of Frank Walsh) and dominated by sympathetic New Dealers, it held a one-day session in December 1937. Walsh, Davis, Jenkins, and numerous reporters were present. The subcommittee decided to recommend the resolution's passage solely on the basis of the record, without hearing witnesses. The resolution was subsequently buried in the Senate Judiciary Committee, allegedly on Senator Hiram Johnson's request of the committee chairman.[44] The House subcommittee, in contrast, called witnesses and held a public hearing. For two days in May 1938, the subcommittee heard half a dozen important witnesses—all pro-Mooney—including Walsh, Davis, Weinberg, Claude Ellis, Captain Peterson, and the Hatchers. Afterward, Celler went on the radio to report that Mooney should be pardoned immediately: "I shall never rest until this foul wrong is righted."[45] Though his subcommittee did its part, there the matter rested. All that Mooney had gained was the publicity.

V

State Senator Culbert L. Olson declared himself a candidate for the governorship of California in the late summer of 1937. The Democratic primary was a full year off, but Olson wanted an early lead, and as it turned out, he dominated a crowded field all the way to the polls. It was Olson who ultimately was to free Mooney.

Olson had a wealth of experience to draw on. He was born and raised on a farm in Utah Territory, of a Scandinavian immigrant and a devout Mormon mother. His mother was very active in the women's suffrage movement and in causes for the underprivileged, and she profoundly influenced her son's social outlook. As a youth he worked on his father's farm. In high school and college he worked as a railroad telegraph operator and brakeman, and witnessed the effects of the economic depression of the 1890's—the unemployed riding the rails, and Coxey's army. In 1896, although still too young to vote, he campaigned for William Jennings Bryan. After graduation from Brigham Young University he was city editor of the Ogden *Standard* for a time, and then went to Washington as secretary for his cousin William H. King, a Congressman. There he also served as a newspaper correspondent, and earned a law degree at George Washington University.

Back in Salt Lake City after the turn of the century, Olson practiced law, engaged in mining and other businesses, and went into politics. In the Utah State Senate from 1916 to 1920 he headed the judiciary committee and sponsored a variety of progressive reforms, including initiative and referendum, child labor legislation, and a workmen's compensation act. In 1920, as a delegate to the Democratic National Convention at San Francisco, he urged the platform committee to adopt a program hopelessly advanced for the day: expanded government ownership and control of public utilities, government regulation of agriculture and industry, labor legislation—a foreshadowing of the New Deal. That year Olson moved his family to Los Angeles. Those were boom times for Southern California, and in his law practice he fought against business frauds and worthless stock promotion. He also pursued his convictions by supporting the Presidential candidacy of Robert La Follette and the Progressive movement in 1924, but in general Olson played no part in California politics until the depths of the Depression.[46]

In 1933 members of the Los Angeles County Democratic club urged Olson to enter the coming gubernatorial race. He liked the idea, but hesitated because although he was well-known in Southern California, he was relatively unknown in the state as a whole. Upton Sinclair decided for him: when Sinclair announced his Democratic candidacy that fall, Olson realized that apart from the problem of his own limited reputation, his candidacy in the primary would split the progressive vote. He chose to support Sinclair, and ran instead for State Senator from Los Angeles County, with Sinclair's endorsement, and won the primary easily against seven other candidates.[47] Had Sinclair not run, it is possible that Olson would have entered and won the primary (as Southern California's progressive candidate, over Northern California's New Deal regular, George Creel) and gone on to defeat Merriam; for Olson was less extreme and less offensive to regular Democrats than Sinclair was. California would in that case have had a timely rather than tardy state New Deal administration, and Mooney would presumably have been freed in 1935 by the man who freed him in 1939.

The 1934 Democratic state convention, which followed the primary, was dominated by EPIC delegates, who chose Olson as their state chairman.[48] He managed the Democratic campaign that fall. He was the only EPIC-progressive candidate to win a seat in the Senate; with Sinclair's defeat and withdrawal from active politics and the rapid decline of the EPIC clubs, Olson was left as head of the progressive Democratic forces. They were at loggerheads with the regulars, led by United States Senator William Gibbs McAdoo,[49] but in spite of the factionalism, the party rose from strength to strength because of the times, the New Deal, and the vacuity of Republican leadership.

During his four years in the State Senate, Olson pressed his progressive creed. He fought for higher taxes on corporations and inheritances, for an EPIC-inspired "production for use" bill, and above all for public control of the tidelands oil deposits.[50] He believed in an advanced New Deal for California—in "economic security from the cradle to the grave, under a government that recognizes the right to an education, to employment on a basis of just reward, and to retirement at old age in comfort and decency, as inalienable as the right to life itself."[51] To his Senate colleagues he was an extremist, who even wanted to abolish their chamber; but in Hichborn's judgment, his consistency, ability, fearlessness, and independence brought him "the golden opinion of all sorts of people." Tall, strong, silver-haired, articulate, Olson looked good for 1938.[52]

Seven other candidates besides Olson sought the Democratic nomination for Governor. They included Sheriff Daniel Murphy of San Francisco, who had the endorsement of the California State Federation of Labor; Congressman John F. Dockweiler of Los Angeles, a native son New Dealer with substantial old-line Democratic support; and the ubiquitous Raymond L. Haight, a former Republican, who had run for Governor in 1934 as the candidate of the Progressive Party.[53] (Haight was seeking the gubernatorial nominations of three parties in 1938—an arrangement permitted by California's peculiar "cross-filing" law, which enabled voters in the primaries to pick candidates who were not of their party.)[54] These were Olson's three serious challengers.

Olson was also up against Southern California's latest economic craze, the "Ham and Eggs" pension plan, or Thirty Dollars Every Thursday for all idle Californians over 50: an impossible scheme of brief but breathtaking popularity, masterminded from Hollywood by a pair of scoundrels. Olson did not quite endorse it in the primary, but Dockweiler did, and it brought grief to them both, for "Ham and Eggs" was the epic issue of 1938.[55]

Olson's campaign machinery was professional. According to his primary opponents, it was also richly financed. Olson did not share that view; although by his own report he received more than $90,000 in contributions, he spent $13,000 more than that,[56] and considered himself a needy candidate. He therefore sought funds from his supporters, including Mooney and his friends.

Olson clearly felt that he and Mooney needed each other. He intended to pardon Mooney if he became Governor; in the meantime he valued Mooney's support, which might have gone to Murphy. The connection was a natural one. Mooney described it to Aline Barnsdall, his benefactress, that June:

Olson visited me last week and told about the desperate plight in which he finds himself with regard to the necessary finances in order to conduct a vigorous campaign. . . . It is not a push-over for him by any means. This is our one sure shot for freedom if he is elected and in the event that the United States Supreme Court fails to liberate me in the Fall.

Inasmuch as I am the one to be personally benefited by his act, he naturally and logically expects me to bend every effort in support of his fight for nomination and election. He definitely asked me to try to raise $10 000 for his campaign. I told him I doubted if this could be done. I pointed out the many obstacles we have had to hurdle in the past, and the fact which is always ever present with us: that we must spend over half of our money in getting it.[57]

Mooney promised to do his best. He particularly had Miss Barnsdall in mind; she had done so well for Sinclair in 1934. She had already given Olson $500 and much more was to come. The TMMDC also contributed heavily, though for the most part indirectly: it spent $9,000 or more for Olson's primary candidacy. It printed and circulated 300,000 copies of an illustrated pamphlet boosting Olson, at a cost of more than $6,000; it paid George Davis $1,360 in expenses to campaign for Olson; it contributed $500 directly to the Olson campaign chest.[58] Aline Barnsdall paid for five statewide broadcasts for Olson, and spent an additional $3,000 for radio time in the general election.[59]

Olson in turn made secret, written pledges to Davis and Miss Barnsdall that he would pardon Mooney if elected.[60] He thereby compromised the office he sought, but not his convictions; his belief that Mooney deserved a pardon was no secret. He did not make a campaign issue of the case, for he was anxious not to antagonize the McClatchy press—a powerful political force in the Central Valley. The McClatchy papers were progressive, as in days of old, and friendly to Olson, who badly needed newspaper support; but for Mooney they harbored perpetual hatred. According to Mooney, Olson had received assurance of McClatchy support if he did not make an issue of the case.[61] As matters developed, the McClatchy papers endorsed no one but remained sympathetic to Olson, and Olson ran especially well in the Central Valley.[62]

Mooney aided Olson with a will. He believed that the Senator's prospects were good: "he will not have all the odium attached to him that Sinclair had. . . . They hung everything on Sinclair that he had written for the past thirty years."[63] Mooney appealed privately for funds from the Chicago Federation of Labor, the ACLU, the garment trades unions, and the Communist Party in New York. He appealed to sympathetic Hollywood celebrities.* From some of these came help; the ILGWU and the Communist Party each contributed $500. (The Communists, who claimed six thousand members in California and had considerable influence for their numbers, did not back Olson openly, but were supporting his nomination.)[64]

Davis, too, was hard at work. He was a member of the Democratic State Central Committee. In 1936 he had been chairman of the Progressive State Committee for Roosevelt, and he used his connections to urge Progressive Party members not to split the liberal opposition to Merriam by nominating Haight. Haight won the Progressive nomination anyway.[65] Otherwise, however, the primary results in August were gratifying. Olson won the Democratic nomination by a plurality of 42 per cent, with more votes than were cast for Dockweiler, Haight, and Murphy combined.[66]

At the same time both the Republican and the Democratic nominations for Attorney General were won by Earl Warren, Alameda County's conservative Republican District Attorney. "Earl Warren is the 1936–37 edition of Charles M. Fickert," said Mooney.[67] Davis and the Olson crowd had hoped to see that nomination go to a Southern Californian, Pat Cooney, who was running on the platform "Free Mooney by Voting for Cooney," but he lost.[68]

The Mooney defense played no active part, even behind the scenes, in Olson's fight that fall against Merriam. The TMMDC had exhausted its resources in the primary—it owed $5,000 to the printer alone—and Olson told Davis more than once that he wanted Mooney, Davis, and the defense committee to lay low. Davis agreed: "no press

* Among them were James Cagney, Douglas Fairbanks, Jr., George Gershwin, Humphrey Cobb, Fredric March, and Dorothy Parker.

releases, no statements, and no public gestures of any kind."[69] When the United States Supreme Court refused in October to reopen the case, Mooney did make a statement, which was carried in the press and on the radio, saying that he pinned his hopes on Olson. He also claimed that Olson had made no promises.[70]

Merriam had the advantage of the active support of nearly all the newspapers in the state, heavy financing for billboards and ballyhoo, Olson's continued embarrassment by "Ham and Eggs"—which Merriam had the sense to oppose—and a right-wing smear campaign against Olson. The Dies Committee in Washington provided testimony, including Arthur Kent's affidavit, that Olson's running mate and state chairman were Communists, and that Olson accepted Communist Party strategy; newspapers splattered him with the charges. But the accusers made themselves ridiculous by labeling Shirley Temple, the child movie star, a Communist front. "I am sorry Comrade Shirley Temple is not here," Olson told one of his audiences. "She should be here to aid us in plotting the overthrow of the government of the United States of America."[71]

Merriam's advantages were not enough to offset Olson's. A New Dealer late in New Deal times, Olson had the endorsement of the national administration, the nearly unanimous support of California's organized labor, a skillful organization, the support of most of his Democratic primary rivals, the backing of two major newspapers, and the withdrawal of Haight from the contest in October. His strongest support came from Los Angeles County and the Central Valley. After a vigorous campaign against an uninspired opponent, Olson won by the substantial margin of 220,000 votes.[72] California had at last chosen a liberal Governor.

CHAPTER TWENTY-EIGHT

Freedom and Death

I have a song in my heart.
                    —Mooney, November 9, 1938

Nerts to you.
                    —Anonymous to Governor Olson,
                    January 8, 1939

OLSON MADE a public statement on the case the day after his election. He did not say explicitly that he would pardon Mooney, but the inference was clear. He said that he would consider a pardon application in the belief that Mooney had been convicted on perjured testimony and was innocent. Lest his action appear arbitrary, he promised a hearing for "any and all entitled" to show why he should not grant the pardon.[1]

Olson's administration began January 2, 1939. His inaugural address upheld the collective welfare and the policies of the New Deal, in terms broad enough to be widely taken as conciliatory. Less than an hour after taking the oath of office, he received a group headed by Davis, Richie, and Harry Bridges, who presented a formal application for Mooney's pardon.[2] Olson promptly set the hearing for the following Saturday, January 7, in the chamber of the State Assembly, and notified Warden Court Smith to have Mooney there at 10 A.M. He stated that he was willing to hear from anyone who had new evidence, but that the hearing would not be permitted to drag out interminably or become a free-for-all. "If I pardon him," he said, "I will make the announcement then and there, and the pardon will become effective forthwith."[3]

Mooney spent his last day at San Quentin in high spirits and nervous excitement. He gathered his personal things together—he had previously sent out fifteen cases of letters and papers—and said farewell to convict friends, including Matt Schmidt, with whom he ate breakfast. The prison tailor put the final touches on a neat gray pinstripe suit. Early the following morning Mooney emerged for the last time through San Quentin's gate. He greeted his wife and Davis and a crowd of well-wishers. Rena was crying for joy. "These twenty-two long years have been moth-eaten," she said. "Life to me has been something like a cloak. There is little left but the tatters. However, even they amount to something."[4] A motorcade of thirty cars set out for Sacramento, escorted by the state highway patrol.

Several thousand people jammed the Capitol corridors before the doors of the Assembly chamber. About a thousand, including many of the legislators, were able to witness the proceedings from within. The Governor took the rostrum before a bank of microphones and klieg lights. He reviewed the case briefly, and asked if anyone with information not in the record desired to be heard. There was a long pause. No one came forward. Following an address from Davis, who spoke in praise of Judge Griffin and Justice Langdon, Olson laid the shame of the Mooney case at the feet of his five predecessors and the State Supreme Court. Turning to Mooney, he reiterated his belief in Mooney's innocence, and admonished him to prove in his future deeds that he was incapable of having committed the Preparedness Day crime.[5]

Mooney stood up. The Governor gave him a handsomely printed document. It declared that his conviction had been based wholly on perjured testimony, and bore a full and unconditional pardon, restoring Mooney's full privileges as a citizen. The Governor's last words were drowned out as the spectators, standing in their seats, clapped and cheered. Mooney, invited by the Governor to address the public by radio, pledged himself to work for Billings's freedom, the labor movement, and the common good of democracy.[6]

After twenty-two and a half years, Mooney was free. Surrounded by friends and well-wishers, he made his way out of the chamber and headed for Folsom to visit Billings. The next day, January 8, he made a triumphant return to San Francisco. Marching at the head of a giant parade, he led thousands of union men and women up Market Street —pausing at Steuart Street—to the Civic Center, where Mooney, Davis, and others addressed a crowd of 25,000 that had turned out for his homecoming celebration.[7]

The public response to Olson's act was mixed. Some of his critics were abusive or threatening. One of the many hostile letters he received was from Judge Dunne; and the McClatchy papers vented their animus to the last.[8] But the average Californian, according to earlier Gallup polls, approved the pardon of Mooney, and public opinion in the nation as a whole supported it overwhelmingly.* The reception of Mooney himself continued to be enthusiastic. At the Los Angeles Coliseum a week after the pardon, a crowd of 50,000 turned out to see him under CIO and AFL sponsorship; other mass rallies followed in Oakland and Stockton.[9]

II

Mooney had no intention of fading quietly into history. He was a good showman, he loved the limelight, and he was $20,000 in debt.[10] He planned an extended lecture tour of the labor circuit, to champion the elusive goal of labor unity that had been so central to his beliefs for over thirty years. Although his sympathies were strongly with the left-wing elements of the CIO and their commitment to industrial unionism and mass labor organization, Mooney wanted to do all he could to end the animosities between the CIO and the AFL.[11] But two things interfered with his hopes and relegated him to obscurity: his marital plans and his health.

For sixteen years Mooney had treated his wife coldly. Rena loved and wanted him, and had made occasional public appearances on his behalf. But she had left his defense committee in the 1920's. She did not share his beliefs, and in her loneliness had become an alcoholic. (Once Mooney sent her a bottle of whiskey for a birthday present. An incensed friend exclaimed that she should have "broken it over his head the son-of-a-bitch. . . . Oh, people, people, how they can hurt each other.")[12] Having lost her pupils, she was reduced to the $52 a month she earned as a copyist on a WPA music project: a blighted, shabby life. For him the old ties had long been dead. Once out of prison, he foolishly asked her for a divorce. She refused. "We've been through too much to be separated now," she said. The matter got into

* Nationally, 64 per cent of those giving opinions in January 1938 favored a pardon —although only 53 per cent thought Mooney innocent—and 36 per cent opposed it. By regions, the Middle Atlantic respondents were the most favorable to a pardon (77 per cent), Southerners the least favorable (52 per cent); in California, where only 48 per cent believed Mooney innocent, 55 per cent favored a pardon. The survey also found the younger generation much more sympathetic than the older to Mooney. Of all those interviewed, however, 56 per cent said they were unfamiliar with the case or declined to give an opinion. In December 1938 another Gallup poll showed undiminished national support for Mooney: 66 per cent of those giving opinions thought Olson should free him. This time only 15 per cent had "never heard of the case." (Washington Post, January 30, 1938; George Gallup and Claude Robinson, "American Institute of Public Opinion— Surveys, 1935–38," Public Opinion Quarterly, July 1938, p. 391; New York Times, December 4, 1938; San Francisco News, December 5, 1938.)

the papers, which brought a cry of outrage from those whose goodwill Mooney needed.[13] Ingratitude was part of his makeup, but his friends had shielded that embarrassing fact from the public gaze. His request for a divorce made it painfully obvious. Unbelieving, people wrote asking if it was not a plot of his enemies; they called him a cad, canceled contributions, told him to go back to prison, urged that he be dumped off a bridge. Said a postcard "from 2 nut Splitters" in Texas: "wee sure think you are a pure ole Bum. if you ever want to quit that good woman that done every thing a person could Have done to get you out of your Trouble."[14] Although Mooney did not take legal steps toward a divorce, there was no reconciliation, and the damage had been done.[15]

Barely a month after his pardon he fell ill in Los Angeles and had to cancel his tour. He returned to San Francisco, where surgeons removed his gallbladder.[16] Recovery was slow, but he was well enough by June to resume his tour. Arriving at Grand Central Station in New York, he was received in a tumultuous demonstration of 15,000 admirers; cheering and singing "Solidarity," they marched him to his hotel. He held a press conference; Mayor Fiorello LaGuardia received him; the crowds turned out again to hear him at Madison Square Garden.[17] The tour continued to other major cities and back to California. Addressing labor conventions and local meetings, Mooney urged unity, supported the New Deal, and condemned the international menace of fascism.[18] The strenuous pace resulted in rehospitalization in July and again in October. He was in Pittsburgh when the remainder of a second eastern tour had to be canceled.[19] The old ulcers, bleeding again, undermined his strength and required another operation for the removal of part of his stomach. ("You know that French cooking that I had in San Quentin for twenty-three years didn't do my stomach any good.")[20] From this illness he never recovered. Most of the last two years of his life were spent in the hospital.[21] His role as labor's martyr may have been weakened by his pardon and his personal failings, but it was his illness, brought on in the years of imprisonment, that caused his complete obscurity before death.

III

Billings remained in Folsom Prison for ten months after Mooney's pardon. Olson could not pardon him without the approval of the Supreme Court, whose members remained unsympathetic. The Governor might have seen to a parole, but Billings, who had applied for a parole six years earlier and been turned down, was no longer willing to accept one. He wanted full exoneration.[22] Olson sought the support of the State Advisory Pardon Board early in the year, but it voted 3–2 against recommending a pardon. The new Attorney General, Earl Warren, voted with the majority against Lieutenant Governor Ellis E. Patterson and Warden Court Smith. Warren cited Dunne and said that there was no justification for a pardon.[23]

There the matter rested until after Olson had appointed two new members to the Supreme Court. Then he requested a pardon recommendation. The majority was still unwilling to reverse itself and approve a pardon, but in tacit recognition that the continuing imprisonment of Billings was an absurdity, the justices recommended commutation of his sentence to time served. Immediately, on October 16, Olson commuted Billings's sentence, and in a brief ceremony the next day apologized for not being able to making it a full pardon.[24] "I believe you have served a prison sentence for a crime you did not commit," he said.[25]

Billings's life in prison had been very different from Mooney's. Folsom was the harsher penitentiary of the two—a maximum security prison in the foothills of the Sierra, remote from most visitors and regulated strictly.[26] For many years Billings had worked in the stone quarry. He saw virtually no one from the outside for the first six years or more. Seeking publicity had never been his preoccupation; he found no calling in labor martyrdom. He spent his free time in recreation, study, and teaching himself the skills of a watch repairman; he was the official prison watchmaker in his later years there. The wardens considered him a model prisoner. Some of his letters were understandably bitter, but on the whole he had adjusted well to prison life.[27] As he wrote a Berkeley Quaker in 1930:

In "doing time" the true philosopher takes the wholly reasonable view of the matter that instead of "doing time" he is merely living here,—just as a settler on his frontier ranch lived for years in one little community among the same friends and relatives, making the best of conditions as he found them,—doing whatever work became necessary and getting what enjoyment he could out of his meagre existence. In fact in the final analysis my prison is no different than your own,—a little more restricted perhaps. . . . Mentally there are no restrictions,—we set our own horizons.[28]

When he finally emerged from Folsom he was in good health, with plans to marry and settle down in a mantle of obscurity. He set up a small jeweler's shop on Market Street and moved to a San Mateo cottage with his wife.[29]

Olson never had the opportunity to pardon Billings, which meant that Billings was denied the full rights of citizenship as well as formal exoneration. In 1945 James F. Brennan drew up a "certificate of rehabilitation" and presented it to Maxwell McNutt, who was then a Superior Judge of San Mateo County. McNutt, signing it, remarked that it was incorrectly titled: it ought to have read, "In the Matter of an Application for Atonement by the State of California."[30] Many years later Governor Edmund G. Brown obtained the State Supreme Court's consent, and in December 1961 extended to Billings a complete pardon.[31] Thus, forty-five years after the Preparedness Day crime, the State of California made its final peace with the defendants.

IV

Everything considered, Mooney's last months were cheerful. He followed the Second World War and international events from his hospital bed in San Francisco, with an unflagging interest in public affairs, and enjoyed visits from old supporters. In March 1942 he underwent another major operation, his fourth since freedom. "I guess I'm just too tough to die," he told his surgeon afterward. "I pulled through again." But death came on March 6, a little more than three years after his pardon. He was 58 years old and still $6,000 in debt.[32] As his friends said, it was a pity that he had not enjoyed a few years of peace. Rena, still separated at the end, and living on her WPA earnings, had never lost her feelings for him: "We spent five happy years together before the arrest. They were the only happy years of our life. His courage in life has been an inspiration to me through many years of loneliness and travail. . . . I have only one grief deeper than my sorrow at his passing, and that is that I could not have given my life, so that Tom might have lived to enjoy his freedom."[33]

Last rites were held in the Civic Auditorium. McNutt and Minor were among those who spoke. Thousands filed past Mooney's bier— elderly working people, for the most part.[34] Mooney was buried in a cemetery south of the city, rather than beside his mother. As Billings said, "we felt Tom would have wanted to be laid to rest far from San Quentin."[35]

The Mooney case never inspired novelists or poets. The verses of his admirers are best left to oblivion, along with Upton Sinclair's

100% and a play called "Precedent," by Isadore J. Golden, a St. Louis lawyer.[36] The able writers who cared about the case, like Sinclair Lewis and Dreiser, did not lend it their talents. Mooney often called for a Zola, but no Zola ever came.[37] The case was too complex, the human qualities too mottled, to stir the artist's spirit. Unlike Bartolomeo Vanzetti, a radical humanist of deep sensitivity, Mooney was vain and repelled many of his own friends. Except for a few, including Finerty and Baldwin, those who knew him personally did not admire him. He was a small man of mixed clay. Moreover, there was no execution to heighten the tragedy. The injustice simply dragged to its tardy, untidy end, which came in political acts of justice, slightly soiled by the circumstances of politics.

The Preparedness Day bomber was never found. Over the course of many years, countless tips, some new accounts of the crime by alleged eyewitnesses, and a few confessions—including one from an inmate of a California state mental hospital—were given to the defense. Many leads were followed up, occasionally with a flurry of excitement and publicity, but none ever led to the solution of the crime. Various hypotheses were advanced to explain the bombing. One view, that the bomb had been planted by Mexicans in the heat of the United States–Mexican border fighting, was supported by eyewitness reports that one or two Mexicans had set down a suitcase at the spot where the bomb exploded. The most attractive hypothesis, however, was one put forward in 1920 by Baron Wilhelm von Brincken, who had been an attaché of the German Consul General in San Francisco in 1916, that the bomb had probably been a time bomb intended for one of the munitions vessels on the waterfront; in 1916 active German agents on the West Coast were sabotaging American munitions shipments to the Allies. Von Brincken speculated that an agent, making his way to the waterfront on foot, had been held up by the marchers, police barricades, and crowds, and had simply abandoned the bomb.[38]

The Mooney case festered unresolved for more than twenty years, its causes widespread, its consequences pernicious. The trials and imprisonment of Mooney and Billings revealed dramatically the intolerance and injustice accorded radical dissenters before, during, and long after the First World War. The case, developing out of class social tensions and public anxieties accompanying the Preparedness Day crime, was forged through the repeated abuse of fair procedures by local law enforcement officials. It came ultimately to involve the inadequacies of the law itself (including the state constitution), the bias of the State Supreme Court, and the timidity of California's governors. The attitudes of Governor Olson's predecessors reflected public indifference and hostility to the defendants rather than the merits of the case. By and large, the public—particularly in California—preferred not to consider legal abuses and the law's inadequacies, but insisted that respect for law and order took precedence over the fate of two radicals.

A generation and more has passed since the freeing of Mooney and Billings. The law has changed since their days in court. In recent years the United States Supreme Court, preceptor to a reluctant nation, has handed down constitutional interpretations designed to compel scrupulously fair procedures in the prosecution of state criminal cases. Although these decisions have provoked widespread resentment ("There is no substitute for law and order," writes former Congressman Hamilton Fish, calling to mind the San Francisco *Examiner* of 1916), the Supreme Court has significantly advanced the centuries-old libertarian aim of English and American constitutional law—to protect the individual from zealous and unscrupulous exercise of authority.[39] Under the leadership of Earl Warren, California's once intractable Attorney General who succeeded Olson as Governor before being appointed Chief Justice, the Supreme Court has made binding on state courts the provisions of the Bill of Rights essential to a fair trial. The Warren Court has required the prompt arraignment of criminal suspects; it has condemned incommunicado interrogation, and upheld the right of a suspect to counsel during police questioning; it has ruled that evidence illegally gathered in unreasonable searches and seizures is inadmissible in state criminal courts as in federal courts; and it has found that "massive, pervasive, and prejudicial publicity" attending a state trial may constitute a violation of due process.[40] In all these respects, Mooney and Billings had been denied fair proceedings; and it is not too much to infer that had the United States Supreme Court established these same safeguards half a century ago, there would have been no Mooney case. Certainly there would have been no Mooney case after the appellate courts had finished with it.

Moreover, if the California Supreme Court had subscribed to the principles of criminal procedure that it has recently upheld, there would have been no need to seek redress in the federal courts; for the California Supreme Court is one of the most libertarian state supreme courts in the nation, and in some respects has anticipated the Warren Court. For instance, it anteceded the Warren Court by several years in barring state use of evidence secured through illegal search and seizure. Since 1956 it has progressively established the principle of "criminal discovery"—the sharing of information by both sides before the trial—in order to minimize the sporting element in criminal trials and increase the likelihood that cases will proceed on their merits. A defendant in California now generally has the right to know in advance the names and addresses of prosecution witnesses, and to examine documents that may be used against him.[41] Had such rules existed in 1916, they would have enabled Mooney's attorneys to obtain the Eilers Building photographs before Billings's trial, and to make a careful advance check on Frank Oxman's assorted surprises.

For many years Mooney lacked access to the United States Supreme Court—access that has been available since the 1930's to many petitioners seeking protection of their rights in state criminal cases. The Mooney case itself contributed to the protection of these rights, by providing the occasion for expanding the writ of habeas corpus. Over the years since Chief Justice Hughes announced the Court's opinion, the Supreme Court has made *Mooney v. Holohan* bedrock constitutional law. The Court has cited the decision in more than fifty cases since 1935. In 1967, explaining a unanimous reversal of an Illinois rape-murder conviction (and death sentence), Associate Justice Potter Stewart said bluntly: "More than 30 years ago this Court held that the Fourteenth Amendment cannot tolerate a state criminal conviction obtained by the knowing use of false evidence. There has been no deviation from that established principle. There can be no retreat from that principle here."[42] That principle, guaranteeing the constitutional rights of the accused, is a living monument to Tom Mooney and Warren Billings, and to those who defended them.

Oxman's Kansas City Affidavit

October 26, 1916

I ARRIVED at San Francisco on Saturday, July 22nd, about noon. I have forgotten the number of the train I rode on. This train arrived at San Francisco Bay just before noon, or about noon. I had gotten on at the Willows that morning, and I know we had a light breakfast, and I was about hungry. As I stopped at the terminal [Terminal Hotel] while on Washington Street within San Francisco, I proceeded to go from the Ferry Boat to the hotel. When going out of the Ferry building I was fronted with a multitude of people, and being practically a stranger and didn't know exactly what it meant, I went on to the hotel and the clerk told me he couldn't give me a good room right then, but before night he would have plenty of them. I left my grip, and remained around the lobby for a few minutes, and I proceeded to go out to get something to eat, and I found difficulty in getting a seat in the restaurants in the vicinity. I proceeded to go down Market Street toward the Ferry, passing a restaurant on the left hand side as I went down. I went to a restaurant—I don't remember the name. I frequently eat there,—a kind of dairy lunch. It was on the left side of the street as you proceed to go from Washington Street, near the Bay Hotel. That place being full, I proceeded to go across through the crowd to the left hand side of Washington Street where I know of about two or three small restaurants in there. They were also crowded. I proceeded to go up Washington Street from the Ferry building on the left hand side of the street when I became a little bit disgusted, and thought my chances to get something to eat were not very good. I remained on the corner of a side street leading out from Washington Street to the left, being, I think, the first street leading out from the west after leaving Front Street [the Embarcadero?]. I remained there on the corner a few moments, and my attention was called to a jitney—I think a Ford, stopped near me. My attention was drawn because it worked its way through the mass of people. It was driven by a driver, three people in the back seat, two in the front seat, one of which was the driver. One of the five people was a lady. Very soon after the car stopped, two gentlemen from the rear seat got out. The second gentleman to get out handed to the first gentleman to get out, a common looking suitcase, being of brown paper or cheap leather. While I was standing on the corner one of the gentlemen carrying the suitcase pushed me to one side. The second gentleman also rubbed up against me. They proceeded on a few feet when the gentleman carrying the suitcase handed it back to the gentleman which had given it to him after they left the automobile. This gentleman proceeded about ten feet and set it down by the side of a brick building, just a little beyond where a boot black was very busy shining shoes. They proceeded back and also seemed to be a little frustrated, and pushed me aside for the second time. I was good natured and fat, and didn't pay much attention to it. I noticed them talking in a foreign language, and I could not understand what was said. But the gentleman that had the suitcase [who] got out of the car first and taken [sic] the suitcase from the gentleman that got out second, did not return in the car. The other party spoke some words to the driver, and they proceeded to move off. While the gentleman that didn't get in proceeded to turn towards the Ferry. I then went across to the hotel and waited a few moments and went down on the street, being the first street on the left-hand side as you go towards the restaurant from the Ferry, where I proceeded to get something to eat, and while settling my bill I heard the explosion. I proceeded to go back to the hotel, and being a stranger, I was probably a little slow in catching on that there had been an accident. However, I heard there had been a bomb exploded; also seen the crowd of people at this certain place. I did not go near the crowd until the next morning. In going by I heard some person say something about a bomb exploded there. I proceeded up a little closer. It had a rope stretched around it by that time. The ruins were still there, so far as the mortar and broken and blown up bricks were concerned. My attention was called to some small pieces of grip lying around which I identified as being a part of the grip I had seen the two gentlemen with. This [is] the first I had any knowledge that I had seen or knew anything of it. Then I realized that the grip that had been sat down by the wall of the building was the same identical grip as the bomb had been stored in. A lady was in the hind seat with the two gentlemen that left the car. She wore a broad brimmed cheap hat, and had a very prominent and bold face.

The picture of Warren K. Billings looks to me as being that of the man who handed the grip to the other party that got out. The other fellow carried it to the sidewalk and proceeded a piece, and this man took it and sat [sic] it down.

The picture of Israel Weinberg is the picture of the man that drove the car, as near as I can recognize the picture.

The picture of Thomas J. Mooney is the man that remained in the car, sitting by the driver.

This man looked to be 25 or 27 years old, medium build, I should say about five feet six inches. He was pretty much the height of the other gentlemen, maybe a little larger. He looked like he would weigh one hundred and fifty-five or sixty. His complexion, I wouldn't class him as sandy, but as light, blue eyes.

—California Supreme Court, "Habeas Corpus," V: 2551–54

Notes

Notes

Abbreviations and Short Forms

All letters (except to the author) cited without collection are in the Mooney papers in the Bancroft Library at the University of California, Berkeley, as are all trial transcripts, hearings, petitions, and briefs on the Mooney case, excluding published appellate court decisions. All San Francisco newspapers and labor journals are cited without the city. The following abbreviations and short forms are used in the text and the Notes:

ACLU. American Civil Liberties Union

ACLU P. American Civil Liberties Union Papers, New York Public Library (microfilm)

AFL. American Federation of Labor

Bul. San Francisco *Bulletin*

Cal Dept of Corrections. California State Department of Corrections, Sacramento

Cal S Ct, "In re Billings." California Supreme Court, "Before the Members of the Supreme Court ... Sitting as a Nonjudicial Fact-finding Commission for the Purpose of Hearing Testimony in Re the Petition of Warren K. Billings for a Pardon." 1930. Typescript, 3 vols.

Cal State Archives, Atty Gen Records. California State Archives, Attorney General's Records, San Francisco

Cal State Archives, Gov's Off. California State Archives, Governor's Office Record Group, Sacramento: Transcripts and Prison Records, Mooney file

Cal State F of L. California State Federation of Labor

Chr. San Francisco *Chronicle*

Cockran P. Bourke Cockran Papers, New York Public Library

CP. Communist Party

DAB Supl. *Dictionary of American Biography,* Supplement

Densmore Report. U.S. House of Representatives, 66th Congress, 1st Session, Document No. 157, *Connection of Certain Department of Labor Employees with the Case of Thomas J. Mooney.* 1919

EPIC. End Poverty in California

Exmr. San Francisco *Examiner*

Francis P.   David R. Francis Papers, Hoover Institution, Stanford, California (microfilm)

Frankfurter P.   Felix Frankfurter Papers, Harvard Law School (microfilm)

Gompers Corres.   Samuel Gompers letterbooks, AFL-CIO Library

"Habeas Corpus."   California Supreme Court, "In the Matter of the Application of Thomas J. Mooney for a Writ of Habeas Corpus." 1935–36. Typescript, 20 vols.

Hichborn, "California Politics."   Franklin Hichborn, "California Politics, 1891–1939," typescript photocopy, University of California Law School Library, Berkeley. 5 vols.

House P.   Edward M. House Papers, Yale University Library

HR.   House of Representatives

IAM.   International Association of Machinists

IBEW.   International Brotherhood of Electrical Workers

ILD.   International Labor Defense

ILGWU.   International Ladies' Garment Workers Union

IMU.   International Molders Union

Inglis P.   Agnes Inglis Papers, Labadie Library, University of Michigan

IWDL.   International Workers Defense League

IWW.   Industrial Workers of the World

Johnson P.   Hiram Johnson Papers, Bancroft Library

Lang P.   Lucy Robins Lang Papers, Institute of Industrial Relations, University of California at Los Angeles (microfilm)

Lewis P.   Austin Lewis Papers, Bancroft Library

M.   Mooney

M & M.   Merchants and Manufacturers Association

M-B Report.   Walter H. Pollak, Zechariah Chafee, Jr., and Carl Stern [for the U.S. National Commission on Law Observance and Enforcement], *The Mooney-Billings* Report. 1932.

McNutt, *Before the Commission.*   Maxwell McNutt, *Before the Special Commission Appointed by the President of the United States: People v. Warren K. Billings, Israel Weinberg, Thomas J. Mooney, Rena Mooney and Edward D. Nolan: Significant Facts Concerning the Cases.* 1917.

Merriam P.   Frank F. Merriam Papers, Bancroft Library

MP.   Thomas J. Mooney Papers, Bancroft Library

Nat Archives.   National Archives

Older P.   Fremont Older Papers, Bancroft Library

Olson P.   Culbert L. Olson Papers, Bancroft Library

Oral Hist. Proj.   University of California, Berkeley, Oral History Project

PG&E.   Pacific Gas and Electric Company

Rolph, *In re Mooney Pardon.*   James Rolph, Jr., *In the Matter of the Application Made on Behalf of Thomas J. Mooney for a Pardon: Decision of Hon. James Rolph, Jr., Governor of the State of California, Together with the Report of Hon. Matt I. Sullivan. . . .* 1932.

Rowell P.   Chester Rowell Papers, Bancroft Library

SF C of C.   San Francisco Chamber of Commerce

TMMDC.   Tom Mooney Molders Defense Committee

UHT.   United Hebrew Trades

UMW. United Mine Workers
URR. United Railroads
U.S. Commn. on I. R., *Final Report.* United States Commission on Industrial Re-
lations, *Final Report and Testimony Submitted to Congress by the Commis-
sion on Industrial Relations.* 1916. 11 vols.
Walsh P. Frank P. Walsh Papers, New York Public Library
Wm B. Wilson P. William B. Wilson Papers, Historical Society of Pennsylvania
Woodrow Wilson P. Woodrow Wilson Papers, Library of Congress

1 The Early Careers of Mooney and Fickert

EPIGRAPH: M to Kate Jackson, 14 Je '35.

1. [Anna] Marcet Haldeman-Julius, "Amazing Frameup of Mooney and Billings" (1931), 28–29; Belle Hammerberg testimony, Cal S Ct, "In re Billings," III: 1965; M to H. A. Thompson, 13 N '32; M to Joe Doyle, 19 S '33; TMMDC circular, 18 Mr '32; "Habeas Corpus," XX: 12,836–38.

2. Haldeman-Julius, "Frameup," 29; M. J. Keough to M, 3 My '27 (MP); "Habeas Corpus," I: 362–63, II: 728; Agnes Inglis to Mary Gallagher, 29 Je '39, Inglis P.

3. Haldeman-Julius, 31–33.

4. *Ibid.*, 33–34; Harold U. Faulkner, *Decline of Laissez Faire, 1897–1917* (1951), 30; M to Waldo Cook, 3 N '27.

5. H. Wayne Morgan, "Eugene V. Debs and the Campaign of 1908," *Indiana Magazine of History*, Sept. 1958, 224–25; Haldeman-Julius, 34–35; Miriam Allen DeFord, *Up-Hill All the Way: The Life of Maynard Shipley* (1956), 135.

6. Debs to M, 28 Je '09, as quoted, SF *Revolt,* 23 N '11.

7. Haldeman-Julius, 35; M to May Wood Simmons, 16 Mr '36.

8. Oakland *World,* 22 D '16.

9. Walton Bean, *Boss Ruef's San Francisco* (1952), chs. 7–9, 19, 20; Franklin Hichborn, *"The System," as Uncovered by the San Francisco Graft Prosecution* (1915), ch. 18.

10. Bean, 264–67, 297; Hichborn, chs. 21, 25, 27.

11. Stanford *Alumni Directory,* II (1910), 106; author's interview, Ruth Fickert Pitt, 13 Jl '65.

12. Fickert interview by Pauline Jacobson in *Bul,* 22 Je '18.

13. Ernest Allen Lane in "Habeas Corpus," XIX: 12,410–11. Lane, Fickert's Assistant District Attorney in 1910, was several

classes behind Fickert at Stanford. *News,* 3 Au '10; Stanford University, *Register for 1900–01,* 189.

14. Pitt interview. See *Chr,* 25 Oc 1897.

15. *Bul,* 22 Je '18; *Stanford Quad '99* (1898), 29.

16. *Chr,* 27 N 1896, 25 Oc, 13 N 1897.

17. *Stanford Quad '99,* 77; *Chr,* 27 N 1896, 25 Oc 1897.

18. *Stanford Quad '99,* 29.

19. *Call,* 16, 28 S '09.

20. SF *News Letter,* 25 S '09; *Call,* 23 Jl '09; *Crocker-Langley San Francisco Directory,* 1891–1900 eds., *passim; Daily Alta California,* 21 Ap 1870; George T. Clark, *Leland Stanford* (1931), 8.

21. *Exmr,* 21 Oc '37.

22. *Chr,* 24 N '00; Pete Grothe, ed., *Great Moments in Stanford Sports* (1952), 116; Brick Morse, *California Football History* (1924), 77, 79, 84.

23. *Bul,* 16 Je '05.

24. *Call,* 8 Mr '04, 17 Je '05.

25. *Exmr, Call,* 17 Je '05.

26. NY *Tribune,* 3 Je '17.

27. Bailey Millard, *History of the San Francisco Bay Region* (1924), III: 152; *San Francisco Blue Book, 1906,* 93; *Call,* 23 Jl '09.

28. *Call,* 26 F '07; Brennan testimony, "Habeas Corpus," XI: 6368–70; Fickert testimony, *ibid.,* XIV: 9229, 9231; Ira Cross, *Collective Bargaining and Metal Trade Agreements in the Brewery, Metal, Teaming and Building Trades of San Francisco, California* (1918), 240–42.

29. *Exmr,* 23 Je '09.

30. *Chr,* 7 Jl '09; *Call,* 8 Jl '09; Hichborn, *System,* 257–58n, 410n; *Stanford Quad '99,* 31; George E. Mowry, *California Progressives* (1951), 36, 254ff.

31. *Call,* 10 Jl '09; Bean, 91–95, 298; Chester Rowell to Hichborn, 19 Jl '16, Rowell P.

32. Bean, 297; Hichborn, 409–14, 418–20.

33. *Call*, 25 Oc '09; SF *News Letter*, 25 S '09.

34. *Call*, 7, 12, 17, 18, 28–30 Oc '09.

35. As quoted, *Bul*, 27 Oc '09.

36. *Who's Who in America, 1910–1911*, 894; *Bul*, 24 Je '14.

37. *Call*, 30 Oc '09.

38. *Bul*, 6 Oc '09.

39. *Bul*, 12, 13 Oc '09, 4 Mr '15; William Martin Camp, *San Francisco: Port of Gold* (1947), 211, 327, and *passim*; *Coast Seamen's Journal*, 20 Oc '09, 8 N '11.

40. As quoted, *Call*, 1 N '09.

41. Bean, *Ruef*, 299; *Call*, 3 N '09.

42. *Call*, 12, 8 F '10.

43. Univ. of Calif., Berkeley, Oral Hist. Proj., "Warren K. Billings" (1957), 156.

44. Hyman Weintraub, "The I.W.W. in California, 1905–1931," M.A. thesis, UCLA (1947), 32–34; Emma Goldman, *Living My Life* (1934), II: 510–14; *Labor Clarion*, 12 My '11; *Chr*, 27 D '13.

45. "Habeas Corpus," I: 451; M to Thomas Corbet, 12 My '13, in *People v. Rena Mooney*, III: 1313–16; Elizabeth Gurley Flynn, *I Speak My Own Piece* (1955), 101, 183; M to Alexander Berkman, 13 Je '15, in *People v. Rena Mooney*, IV: 1707–10; Bill Haywood to M, 29 Jan '16, in *ibid.*, IV: 1827.

46. Joseph Noel, *Footloose in Arcadia* (1940), 24; Lucy Robins Lang, *Tomorrow Is Beautiful* (1948), 85.

47. W. Jett Lauck and Edgar Sydenstricker, *Conditions of Labor in American Industries* (1917), 173; Carlton H. Parker testimony, in *Final Report and Testimony Submitted to Congress by the Commission on Industrial Relations* (1916), V: 4934; Carlton H. Parker, *The Casual Laborer and Other Essays* (1920), chs. 2, 3; *Chr*, 2 S '16.

48. Louise D. Harding, in Oakland *Tri-City Labor Review*, 29 D '16: "Mooney is not, and never has been, affiliated with the I.W.W." Haldeman-Julius, "Frameup," ignores the IWW altogether. On the other hand, Matt I. Sullivan's report in James Rolph, Jr., *In the Matter of the Application . . . of Thomas J. Mooney for a Pardon . . .* (1932), 23, distorted Mooney's IWW role. The Sacramento *Bee* exploited it persistently, to his detriment.

49. Haldeman-Julius, 36; Ralph E. Shaffer, "A History of the Socialist Party of California," M.A. thesis, Univ. of Calif., Berkeley (1955), 1, 84–86, 115–17; Grace Heilman Stimson, *Rise of the Labor Movement in Los Angeles* (1955), chs. 19–21.

50. See, e.g., Austin Lewis, *Militant Proletariat* (1911); *Revolt, passim*.

51. Shaffer, "Socialist Party," 58, 74; Oakland *World*, 25 Au '16; *Revolt*, 30 My '11, 13 Jan '12. See also *Chr*, 26 Mr '42.

52. Shaffer, 47, 68; Gertrude Atherton, *My San Francisco* (1946), 190; Lewis, *Militant Proletariat*, 11–179 *passim*; *Revolt*, 11 N '11, 30 Mr '12; Lewis testimony in U.S. Commn. on I. R., *Final Report*, V: 5007. See also Paul Scharrenberg testimony, *ibid.*, 5050; Debs to Lewis, 24 N '11, in *Revolt*, 2 D '11.

53. *Revolt*, 20 My '11; *People v. Rena Mooney*, III: 1361; *San Francisco Directory* (1911), 1156.

54. *Revolt*, 20 My, 1–29 Jl '11; San Francisco Young Socialists' "Initial Grand Ball" (1911), misc. pamphlets, Socialist Party in California, v. 3, Bancroft Library.

55. Ernest J. Hopkins, *What Happened in the Mooney Case* (1932), 83.

56. *Revolt*, 1 My '11.

57. *Ibid.*, 15 Jl '11; M testimony, "Habeas Corpus," XVIII: 11,758.

58. *Revolt*, 8 Jl, 9 S, 21 Oc, 18 N '11; 6 Jan, 3 F '12.

59. *Ibid.*, 1–16 Mr '11; 20, 27 Ap, 11 My '12.

60. *Ibid.*, 9 S '11.

61. *Ibid.*, 10 Je '11.

62. *California Blue Book, 1911*, 347; *Bul*, 28 S '11.

63. M to Leonard Shober, 19 Ap '13, in "Habeas Corpus," XIII: 8272–74.

64. M to M. J. Knudsen, 18 My '13, in "Habeas Corpus," XIII: 8375.

65. *Labor Clarion*, 12 Jan, 15 Mr, 12 Jl '12, and *passim*.

66. Edgar T. Gleeson to Evelyn Wells, 18 Mr '59, Older P.

67. William Z. Foster, "The Molders' Convention," *International Socialist Review*, Dec. 1912, 486.

68. *International Molders Journal, Proceedings . . . 1912*, 173.

69. *Ibid.*, 220.

70. *Ibid.*, 220–21.

71. M to Fred Marchant, 22 Je '13, in "Habeas Corpus," XIII: 8336–38. See also Haldeman-Julius, 36–37; "Habeas Corpus," XIX: 12,762–63; *International Molders Journal, Proceedings . . . 1912*, 1, 123, 124, 163, 173, 181, 193, 195, 226, 228, 272–76; *International Molders Journal*, Dec. 1912, 963.

72. William Z. Foster, *From Bryan to Stalin* (1937), 65; M to "Fellow Officers," 1 D '12, M to Fred Marchant, 9 Ap '13, M to

Frank Cerney, 11 My '13, M to Thomas Corbet, 12 My '13, M to Jack Laurensen, 11 My '13, all in "Habeas Corpus," XIII: 8248–51, 8270–71, 8253–62, 8282–86, 8368–70.

II Labor Strife, 1913–1914

EPIGRAPH: H. H. Bancroft, *Retrospection* (1915 ed.), 386.

1. It has erroneously been said that Billings was sentenced to six months' imprisonment: See, e.g., Rolph, *In re Mooney Pardon*, 8.

2. Oral Hist. Proj., "Billings," ch. 1; Haldeman-Julius, "Frameup," 44–45.

3. Oral Hist. Proj., "Billings," 22–25, 51–55, 144; F. Monaco, "San Francisco's Shoe Workers' Strike," *International Socialist Review*, May 1913, 819; Haldeman-Julius, 40, 45; *Labor Clarion*, 16 My '13.

4. *News*, 12 F '13, M to E. A. Carlson, 6 F '16, in "Habeas Corpus," XIII: 8314–26; *ibid.*, XX: 12,870–71; Oral Hist. Proj., "Billings," 56.

5. *Labor Clarion*, 25 Ap '13.

6. Oral Hist. Proj., "Billings," 60–81.

7. Sacramento *Bee*, 5 Ap, 7, 12 My '13; Charles Franklin Marsh, *Trade Unionism in the Light and Power Industry* (1928), 55–56; *Labor Clarion*, 7 Mr '13.

8. PG&E, "History of Strike of Pacific Gas and Electric Company Called by Light and Power Council of California May 7, 1913," a confidential company report summarized in "Habeas Corpus," XX: 13,277–87; *ibid.*, 13,008–9; *Labor Clarion*, 14 F, 4, 18 Ap, 9, 23, 30 My, 27 Je, 23 S '13; *ibid.*, 26 Je '14; Sacramento *Bee*, 8 My, 27 S, 1 Oc '13; *Bul*, 26 Jl, 16 Au, 13, 19 S, 24 N '13; Charles M. Coleman, *P. G. and E. of California* (1952), 253; Marsh, *Trade Unionism*, 61. See also Robert Edward Lee Knight, *Industrial Relations in the San Francisco Bay Area, 1900–1918* (1960), 280–84.

9. *Labor Clarion*, 23 My '13.

10. Sacramento *Bee*, 12, 13, 15, 19 My, 2 Je, 25 Au '13; *News*, 1 S '13; Martinez *Standard*, 18 D '13; U.S. Commn. on I. R., *Final Report*, VI: 5423–25; "Habeas Corpus," XX: 13,081, 13,086–87, 13,277–87; Swanson testimony, *People v. Rena Mooney*, IV: 1480, 1485; Ed Delaney and M. T. Rice, *Bloodstained Trail* (1927), 87.

11. "Habeas Corpus," XX: 13,008–9, XIX: 12,646, III: 1603–8, XIII: 8314–26; Oral Hist. Proj., "Billings," 82–83, 96.

12. *Bul*, 4 Oc '11.

13. Sacramento *Bee*, 15, 20 S '13; Oral Hist. Proj., "Billings," 83–103; Haldeman-Julius, "Frameup," 64.

14. Sacramento *Bee*, 15 S '13.

15. *Ibid.*, 19 N '13; M testimony, "Habeas Corpus," XX: 12,826–27.

16. Sacramento *Bee*, 19, 20, 28 N '13; Oral Hist. Proj., "Billings," 103–7.

17. Fickert testimony, "Habeas Corpus," VIII: 4651, XIV: 9257; *People v. Rena Mooney*, IV: 1480–87.

18. [Alexander Berkman], "The Billings Trial," *Blast*, 15 S '16.

19. Bruce Smith, *State Police* (1925), 54–57.

20. U.S. Commn. on I. R., *Final Report*, V: 5011.

21. Cal Legislature, 41st Sess., 1915, *Senate Bills*: S.B. 20, and *Final Calendar*, 77.

22. Martinez *Standard*, 16 Jan '14; SF C of C *Activities*, 4, 18 F, 18 Mr '15; Franklin Hichborn, *Story of the California Legislature, 1915 Session* (1916), 18; Sacramento *Bee*, 28 N '13; *Labor Clarion*, 13 F, 21 Au '14, 15 Jan '15.

23. Martinez *Standard*, 16 Jan '14; U.S. Commn. on I. R., *Final Report*, V: 4979–80 (testimony of George L. Bell, attorney for the state Commission on Immigration and Housing); *Labor Clarion*, 27 Mr, 10 Ap '14; Sacramento *Bee*, 21 N '13. See also *Bul*, 7 S '12; Oakland *World*, 4 Mr '11; *Chr*, 19 Jan '11.

24. Robert Glass Cleland, *California in Our Time, 1900–1940* (1947), 90–93; Carey McWilliams, *Factories in the Field: The Story of Migratory Farm Labor in California* (1939), 158–61; *Survey*, 21 Mr '14; Woodrow C. Whitten, "The Wheatland Episode," *Pacific Historical Review*, Feb. 1948, 37–42. See also Graham Adams, Jr., *Age of Industrial Violence, 1910–1915* (1966), 195–97.

25. McWilliams, 161–62; U.S. Commn. on I. R., *Final Report*, V: 5011; Sacramento *Bee*, 27 S '13.

26. U.S. Commn. on I. R., *Final Report*, V: 5001; Joseph A. McGowan, *History of the Sacramento Valley* (1961), II: 111; Sacramento *Bee*, 24 D '13.

27. Martinez *Standard*, 16 Jan '14.

28. Sacramento *Bee*, 17, 24 N '13, 14 Jan–12 Mr '14; Martinez *Standard*, 16, 17, 21 Jan '14; Inez Haynes Gilmore, "The Marysville Strike," *Harper's Weekly*, 4 Ap '14.

29. Sacramento *Bee*, 15, 20 N, 1 D '13; Martinez *Standard*, 16, 22 Jan, 16 My '14;

U.S. Commn. on I. R., *Final Report*, V: 4996–98.

30. Haldeman-Julius, 65; M to E. A. Carlson, 6 F '16, in "Habeas Corpus," XIII: 8314–26; *ibid.*, XX: 12,820, 13,009–38, 13,049; R. N. Ruiz testimony, Richmond Police Court, *People v. Thomas J. Mooney, Joe Brown, and H. G. Hanlon, Preliminary Inquiry*, 5 Jan '14, p. 22 (in MP).

31. "Habeas Corpus," XX: 12,821; *Chr*, 28, 29 D '13; Richmond *Independent*, 28 D '13; Martinez *Contra Costa Gazette*, 3 Jan '14; Martinez *Standard*, 5 Jan '14.

32. *People v. Rena Mooney*, IV: 1482–84; "Habeas Corpus," II: 818–22, 844, XX: 13,054; Martinez *Standard*, 30 D '13, 6 Ap '14; Martinez *Contra Costa Gazette*, 24 Jan '14; Sacramento *Bee*, 7 Ap '14.

33. Haldeman-Julius, 66–67; Rolph, *In re Mooney Pardon*, 18–20.

34. "Habeas Corpus," XX: 13,048; Martinez *Standard*, 7 F, 30 Mr '14, 6 N '18; *Bul*, 1 N '13; *Bench and Bar of California, 1937–38*, 129.

35. Martinez *Contra Costa Gazette*, 28 F, 18 Ap, 27 Je '14; *Bul*, 7 Ap '14. The quotation is from the Martinez *Standard*, 24 Mr '14.

36. Franklin Hichborn, *Story of the California Legislature of 1911* (1911), 136, 136n; Martinez *Standard*, 24 Mr, 2, 9, 24 Ap '14; *Bul*, 2 Ap '14; *Chr*, 1 Ap '14; McNutt statement in *People v. Weinberg*, quoted in "Habeas Corpus," II: 846–47; *ibid.*, XX: 12,827. The quotation from the *Standard* is 2 Ap '14.

37. *Labor Clarion*, 27 F, 6, 20 Mr '14; Richmond *Terminal*, 6 Mr '14; *Bul*, 21 F, 6 Mr '14; Martinez *Contra Costa Gazette*, 28 F '14.

38. Martinez *Standard*, 22 Ap '14.

39. McKenzie testimony, U.S. Commn. on I. R., *Final Report*, V: 4995, 4997; Martinez *Contra Costa Gazette*, 25 Ap '14; Martinez *Standard*, 27, 28, 30 Ap '14.

40. *Bul*, 17 F, 20 Je '14.

41. Haldeman-Julius, 66; Martinez *Standard*, 4–6, 16 My, 13 Je '14; *Bul*, 7 My, 12 Je '14.

42. Haldeman-Julius, 66; Swanson testimony, *People v. Rena Mooney*, IV: 1480; Martinez *Standard*, 26 My, 27 Je '14; Martinez *Contra Costa Gazette*, 16 My, 27 Je '14; *Bul*, 20 Je '14.

43. Martinez *Standard*, 1, 27 Ap '14; M testimony, "Habeas Corpus," XX: 12,824; McKenzie testimony, U.S. Commn. on I. R., *Final Report*, V: 4994.

44. Martinez *Standard*, 6 F '14.

45. The *Standard* is the best available source of information on the Martinez trials; the trial record was not transcribed and preserved, since Mooney was acquitted. The only surviving legal document on the case was the preliminary hearing. "Habeas Corpus," XX: 12,890, 13,037–40. Mooney's later denunciation of the *Standard* was reckless.

46. Martinez *Standard*, 30 D '13, 28 Mr, 6, 8 Ap, 13, 16 Je '14; Richmond *Daily News*, 17, 20 Je '14.

47. Martinez *Contra Costa Gazette*, 11 Ap, 20 Je '14; Martinez *Standard*, 24 Ap '14.

48. "Habeas Corpus," XX: 13,068–69, 13,105; PG&E, "History of Strike," in *ibid.*, 13,277–87; Britton testimony, U.S. Commn. on I. R., *Final Report*, VI: 5423–25; Rolph, *In re Mooney Pardon*, 18; Sacramento *Bee*, 27 Oc '13; *Bul*, 6 D '13.

49. Oral Hist. Proj., "Billings," 108; *Chr*, 29 D '13; Martinez *Standard*, 21 Jan, 23 Mr '14. Edward Cunha, Fickert's Assistant District Attorney, declared later that if Mooney had dynamited the Carquinez tower it might have fallen on a passing ship or railroad train and killed hundreds of people. "Habeas Corpus," XII: 7661.

50. See *Chr*, 1 Ap '14; Finerty statement, "Habeas Corpus," XIII: 8528.

51. Schulberg to M, 2 Jan '14, in "Habeas Corpus," XIII: 8406–7.

52. McNutt testimony, *ibid.*, III: 1759. See also McNutt testimony, Cal S Ct, "In re Billings," II: 1261.

III The Radicals

EPIGRAPH: M to Noble Burton, 26 My '36.

1. Oral Hist. Proj., "Billings," 109; E. B. Morton to Ed Nolan and M, 27 Oc '15, in *People v. Rena Mooney*, IV: 1717–19; M to Mother Jones, 15 D '15, in "Habeas Corpus," XI: 6387–93; *Mother Earth*, Apr. 1916, 492.

2. Cross, *Collective Bargaining*, 240–42, 287; Oral Hist. Proj., "Billings," 104–6, 156; *Labor Clarion*, 29 Oc '15 and *passim*, 1911–16; M to Mother Jones, 28 Oc '14 and 15 D '15, in "Habeas Corpus," XVI: 10,373–76 and XI: 6387–93.

3. The most damaging of these letters were entered into the trial records of *People v. Rena Mooney* and *People v. Israel Weinberg* in 1917.

4. *Bul*, 24 Mr, 15, 22, 29 D '13, 30 Mr, 4

My '14, 16 F, 27 Jl '15, 4 Ap '16; David Milder to C. F. Grow, 7 My '15, and M to Dan Regan, 19 Ap '16, in "Habeas Corpus," XIII: 8403–4 and XVIII: 12,029.

5. *Bul*, 11 N '13, 2, 17 Mr, 17 Jl '14, 10 Je '15; Milder testimony, *People v. Rena Mooney* III: 1336–38; "Habeas Corpus," XX: 13,078–79; Hutchins Hapgood, *The Spirit of Labor* (1905), and *Victorian in the Modern World* (1939), 189, 196; Grace Heilman Stimson, *Rise of the Labor Movement in Los Angeles*, 334.

6. Milder testimony, *People v. Rena Mooney*, III: 1340; William J. Burns, *Masked War* (1913), 287–89; Louis Adamic, *Dynamite* (1931), 201–9; Lucy Robins Lang, *Tomorrow Is Beautiful*, 40–46; Harold U. Faulkner, *Politics, Reform and Expansion, 1890–1900* (1959), 132; Alexander Berkman, *Prison Memoirs of an Anarchist* (1912), chs. 33, 36; *Bul*, 13 Oc '13, 3 Jan '14, 5 Jan, 6 My '15; *Labor Clarion*, 27 Oc '11, 7 Je '12, 12 Jan, 4 Jl '13; Billings, McKenzie testimony, Cal S Ct, "In re Billings," II: 1476, 1550.

7. *Blast*, 15 Au '16.

8. *Bul*, 5 Jan, 4 My, 8 D '14, 22 Oc '15; *Labor Clarion*, 27 N '14; M to E. A. Carlson, 6 F '16, in "Habeas Corpus," XIII: 8314–26; M testimony, *ibid.*, XX: 12,832.

9. M to Mother Jones, 15 D '15, in "Habeas Corpus," XI: 6387–93. Misspellings are in source.

10. *People v. Rena Mooney*, III: 1287; Rolph, *In re Mooney Pardon*, 21.

11. *Solidarity* (Chicago), 2 Oc '15, in "Habeas Corpus," XX: 13,146–49. See also Rolph, 28.

12. Sacramento *Bee*, 11 S '15.

13. *Bul*, 5 F, 24 Jl '14, 11 S '15; *Labor Clarion*, 31 Jl '14; M to E. A. Carlson, 6 F '16, in "Habeas Corpus," XIII: 8314–26; *ibid.*, XX: 12,873.

14. M to Alexander Berkman, 26 Jan '16, in "Habeas Corpus," XIII: 8035–37.

15. *Bul*, 4 Oc '15.

16. *Bul*, 4, 5, 8 Oc '15; M to Berkman, 26 Jan '16, in "Habeas Corpus," XIII: 8035–37.

17. M to William Spry, 27 S '15, in Cal State Archives, Atty Gen Records, Box 222.

18. *Bul*, 15, 16, 19 N '15; Sacramento *Bee*, 18 N '15.

19. Berkman, circular letter, n.d. [Nov. 1915?], in "Habeas Corpus," XIII: 8017–18.

20. *Ibid.*; Berkman to Mrs. J. Sergeant Cram, 16 Oc '15, and E. B. Morton to Ed Nolan and M, n.d. [Nov.? 1915], both in

"Habeas Corpus," XIII: 8010–14; Berkman to J. Cohen, 26 N '30, and Berkman to Philip Grosser, 11 Ap '32, in Berkman P, II, III, International Institute of Social History, Amsterdam (notes courtesy of Richard Drinnon).

21. "Habeas Corpus," XVIII: 11,761.

22. *Ibid.*, XX: 12,834–35, 13,208; M to C. L. Lambert, 13 F '16, in *ibid.*, XIII: 8064–66.

23. *Blast*, 1 Jan '16–1 D '17; Joseph North, *Robert Minor: Artist and Crusader* (1956), 152 and *passim*; Walter Woehlke, "The Mooney Case," *Sunset*, Jan. 1919; Lang, *Tomorrow*, 87–88.

24. Nolan to Morton, 22 Jan '16, in *People v. Weinberg*, II: 1026.

25. *Blast*, 4 Mr '16.

26. *Blast*, 4 Mr, 15 Ap, 1 My '16; *Mother Earth*, May 1916, 512.

27. *Blast*, 1 My '16.

28. *Blast*, 5 F, 15 Ap, 1 My '16; "Habeas Corpus," XIX: 12,777.

29. *Blast*, 1 Ap '16.

30. M testimony, "Habeas Corpus," XVIII: 11,760–71.

31. *Call*, 24 F, 2–6, 29 Mr, 10 Ap '08; *Independent*, 5, 12 Mr, 2 Ap '08; *Nation*, 2 Ap '08; *Outlook*, 11 Ap '08. See also Sidney Fine, "Anarchism and the Assassination of McKinley," *American Historical Review*, July 1955, 777–79.

32. NY *Times*, 6, 7 Jl, 12–15 N '14, 3, 30 Mr '15; *Bul*, 2, 4 Mr '15. See also Emma Goldman, *Living My Life*, 533–34.

33. Erwin G. Gudde, "Vita Nostra Brevis Est" (1959), 6, reprinted from *Names*, Mar. 1959.

34. Sacramento *Bee*, 26 Mr '14; *Bul*, 24 S '12, 2, 4 Mr, 17 Ap '15; *Exmr*, 13 Je '16; *Labor Clarion*, 3 Mr, 1, 29 D '16; Berkeley *Courier*, 23 S '16; Oakland *World*, 1 My '09; Lang, *Tomorrow*, 42; Weintraub, "I.W.W. in California, 1905–31," M.A. thesis, UCLA, 298–99; *Blast*, 1 Ap '16.

35. *Mother Earth*, Aug. 1916; *Call*, 15–20 Jan, 1, 27 F '09.

36. *Exmr*, 13, 15, 18 F '16; Robert Hunter, *Violence and the Labor Movement* (1919), 87; *Chr*, 21 F '16; NY *Times*, 13, 17–19 F '16.

37. *Exmr*, 15 F '16.

38. *Chr*, 18 F '16.

39. *Chr*, 19 F '16.

40. *Chr*, 25 F '16. Cf. NY *Times*, 28 F, 22 Mr '16, which indicates that the identity of the suicide was probably not Crones.

41. *Exmr*, 9 Ap '16.

42. *Exmr*, 10 Ap '16.
43. *Exmr*, 13, 16, 17, 27 Ap, 10 My '16.
44. *Exmr*, 29 My '16.
45. *Exmr*, 27 My, 6 Je, 23 Jl '16; *Chr*, 7, 8 Je '16.

IV   San Francisco Tensions,
1914–1916

EPIGRAPHS: Octavius Thorndike Howe, *Argonauts of '49* (1923), 115; Steffens's *Autobiography*, 847.

1. Benjamin Rastall, "Industrial Survey Report," serialized in *Bul*, 18 Jan–13 F '17; *SF C of C Journal*, July 1911–Mar. 1913, *passim*; SF C of C *Activities*, 4 My '16 and *passim*.

2. See testimony of five San Francisco building-trades employers (Grant Fee, Sam J. Eva, G. H. Wendling, L. H. Sly, and James Tyson) in U.S. Commn. on I. R., *Final Report*, VI: 5171–258; Cross, *Collective Bargaining*, 235–42; Rastall, "Report." See also Knight, *Industrial Relations in the San Francisco Bay Area, 1900–1918*, 370–93.

3. *SF C of C* Journal, Dec. 1912, Feb. 1913; SF C of C *Activities*, 2 Ap, 28 Jl '14, 5, 26 Au '15.

4. SF C of C *Activities*, 17 D '14.

5. *Ibid.*

6. Frederick W. Kellogg testimony, in U.S. Commn. on I. R., *Final Report*, VI: 5482–83.

7. *Bul*, 2 Mr '15; SF C of C *Activities*, 1915, *passim*.

8. U.S. Commn. on I. R., *Final Report*, V: 4776, 4797, 4822–23, 4893, 4899; Mowry, *California Progressives*, 199.

9. Irving Martin testimony, in U.S. Commn. on I. R., *Final Report*, V: 4878; *ibid.*, 4857; *Bul*, 25 Jl '14.

10. His name is sometimes given as J. P. Emerson or Emmerson.

11. Sacramento *Bee*, 26, 28 S '14; *Labor Clarion*, 9, 23 Oc '14; M testimony, "Habeas Corpus," XX: 12,908–12.

12. *Chr*, 27 S '14; M testimony, "Habeas Corpus," XX: 12,906–11; Haldeman-Julius, "Frameup," 69.

13. See Robert Minor, "The Frame-up System" (1916), 3–4; *Labor Clarion*, 30 Oc '14, 9 Ap '15; Stockton *Record*, 31 Mr '15; Oakland *Tri-City Labor Review*, 8 D '16.

14. *Labor Clarion*, 27 N, 4 D '14; Oakland *Tri-City Labor Review*, 16 My '19.

15. SF C of C *Activities*, 4, 25 My, 8 Je, 27 Jl '16; *Bul*, 17 Jan '17. Rastall's doctoral dissertation, *Labor History of the Cripple Creek District* (Univ. of Wisconsin, 1908), dispassionately criticized both the Western Federation of Miners and the mine owners.

16. SF C of C *Activities*, 1 Je '16.

17. Cal State F of L, *Proceedings of the Seventeenth Annual Convention* (1916), 58; *Argonaut*, 30 D '16; *Walker's Manual of California Securities . . . 1920*, 121, 564; Frank Morton Todd, *Story of the Exposition* (1921), I: 229, II: 227; *Town Talk*, 15, 22 Jl '16; SF C of C *Activities*, 4 My '16; *Exmr*, 25 N '17.

18. *Labor Clarion*, 9, 16 Je '16; Carey McWilliams, *California: The Great Exception* (1949), 143–44; Knight, *Industrial Relations in the San Francisco Bay Area*, 302–3.

19. SF C of C, "Law and Order in San Francisco: A Beginning" (1916), 8–9.

20. *Ibid.*, 5, 9–10; Knight, 303–4.

21. SF C of C, "Law and Order," 12–14; NY *Weekly People*, 19 Au '16; *Coast Review*, July 1916; *Exmr*, 2 Je, 6 Jl '16; *Labor Clarion*, 7 Jl '16; *Town Talk*, 15 Jl '16.

22. SF C of C *Activities*, 13 Jl '16; SF C of C, "Law and Order," 15.

23. SF C of C, "Law and Order," 17–19.

24. *Bul*, 2 S '15; *Town Talk*, 16 D '16; *Labor Clarion*, 7 Jl '16; SF C of C, *Sixty-First Annual Report* (1910), 256; Hopkins, *What Happened in the Mooney Case*, 11.

25. SF *News Letter*, 15 Jl '16. See also *Argonaut*, 15 Jl '16, and *Town Talk*, 15, 22 Jl '16.

26. *Memoirs of Robert Dollar* (1928), III–IV, 67. See also *Labor Clarion*, 9 Je '16; George T. Davis remarks in "Habeas Corpus," XV: 9612–13, 9652.

27. Sacramento *Bee*, 10 D '16.

28. *Exmr*, 10 Jan, 4 F, 6 Mr, 17, 24 Ap '16. See also *Chr*, 9 Jan '16.

29. *Chr*, 18 N '01, 9 Jan '16; *Exmr*, 10 Jan, 4 F, 6, 9, 16 Mr, 17, 24 Ap '16; *Bul*, 17 My '16.

30. *Exmr*, 9, 17 F '16.

31. SF C of C *Journal*, Dec. 1912, Feb. 1913; SF C of C unpublished minutes, 5 Jan '15, III: 31, in the SF C of C's archives.

32. SF C of C *Activities*, 29 Jl, 23 S '15.

33. *Exmr*, 12 Ap '16.

34. *Exmr*, 28 Jan, 6, 27 F, 18 My, 23 Jl, and *passim*, Mar.–May 1916; *Who's Who Among California Women* (1922), 601.

35. *Bul*, 5 Mr '13, 23 My, 20 Jl '14; John Eshleman, "Does the Regulation of Public Utilities Hurt Business?", SF C of C *Activities*, 6 Au '16; *Who's Who in California, 1928–29*, 381; Bean, *Ruef*, 115, 131, 218,

240, 303; *Exmr*, 9 F, 18 My '16; author's interview, Edgar T. Gleeson, 6 F '60.

36. *Exmr*, 18, 25, 27–29, 31 My '16; Will Irwin, *City That Was* (1906), 42.

37. *Town Talk*, 9 Jan '15; *Coast Seamen's Journal*, 28 Je '16; *Bul*, 5 Mr '13; Oakland *Observer*, 24 F '17.

38. Sacramento *Bee*, 21 Mr '14; *Exmr*, 23 F '16; NY *Weekly People*, 5 Au '16; *Grizzly Bear*, Feb. 1916, 5.

39. Robert L. Duffus, *The Tower of Jewels: Memories of San Francisco* (1960), 93ff; *Bul*, 14 Au '15, 10, 26 My '16; memorandum, Older to Johnson, 7 Jl '16, in Johnson P. On the national anti-preparedness response, see Arthur S. Link, *Wilson: Confusions and Crises, 1915–1916* (1965), 23–33.

40. *Bul*, 23 Ap '14, 16 My '16; Lewis Lorwin, *American Federation of Labor* (1933), 140–45; *Labor Clarion*, 26 My '16.

41. *Bul*, 15, 16, 26 F '16; *Labor Clarion*, 26 My, 2, 9 Je '16; *Blast*, 15 My '16; *Exmr*, 26 F '16.

42. Bul, 14 Au '15; *Exmr*, 30 Ap, 3, 24, 28 My, 4 Je, 10, 16 Jl '16.

43. See *Coast Seamen's Journal*, Jan.–Feb. issues, 1917.

44. Evelyn Wells, *Fremont Older* (1936), 221, 310.

45. *Bul*, 24 Jl, 17 Au '15, 5 F '16, and *passim*, 1913–16; Bean, *Ruef*, 230. Cf. Fremont Older, *My Own Story* (1919), and Cora Miranda Older, *William Randolph Hearst* (1936).

46. Cora Older, *Hearst*, 346.

47. *Bul*, 21, 25 My, 2, 3 Je '15, 31 Oc, 1 N '16; Gleeson interview.

48. Duffus recalled in later years, "I loved that newspaper as a young man loves a young woman and a sailor loves the sea, purely and with all my heart." *Tower of Jewels*, 49.

49. Jerome A. Hart, *In Our Second Century, from an Editor's Notebook* (1931), 114, 118; *Organized Labor*, 16 My '14; *Bul*, 18 S '13, and *passim*, 1913–16; Gleeson interview; *Who's Who in America, 1960–61*; Duffus, ch. 6.

50. Rowell to Caspar Whitney, 28 S '17, Rowell P.

51. Older, *My Own Story* (1925 ed.), 103.

52. *Ibid.*, chs. 1–8, 32–37; Fremont Older, *Growing Up* (1931), chs. 1–6, 13, 14; Wells, *Older*, 124–26, 240–55; Delany and Rice, *Bloodstained Trail*, 86; Gleeson interview.

53. Max Eastman, *Enjoyment of Living* (1948), 424–25.

54. *Bul*, 24 D '13; Gleeson interview.

55. See Older–Charles Aked exchanges, *Bul*, 29 Ap and *passim*, Apr.–May 1914.

56. *Bul*, 1 My '14.

57. R. C. Miller to editor, *Bul*, 4 My '14.

58. Martinez *Contra Costa Gazette*, 27 D '13.

59. SF *News Letter*, 24 My '13. See also *ibid.*, 3 Au '12, 28 Je '13.

60. *Exmr*, *Chr*, 24 D '13; Sacramento *Bee*, 17 Mr '14.

61. Walter Woehlke, "The Mooney Case," *Sunset*, Jan. 1919, contains a thoughtful, though unappreciative, characterization of Older.

v Mooney's Car Strike

1. Franck R. Havenner, "Progressives Get the Scalp of Calhoun," Sacramento *Bee*, 6 S '13. Calhoun's misuse of URR funds was not known when this article was written, but was presumably the reason for his refusal to show the State Railroad Commission the URR books. Bean, *Ruef*, 304.

2. Havenner, "Calhoun's Scalp"; A. W. Voorsanger, ed., *Western Jewry* (1916), 205–6; Gertrude Atherton, *My San Francisco*, 158–63; *Bul*, 22 Oc '13, 15 Jan '14; "Habeas Corpus," XI: 6652–66. For an analysis of the URR's overcapitalization, see *Exmr*, 22 Je '16.

3. Minor, "Frame-up System," 4; Oakland *World*, 22 D '16; *Bul*, 14, 15 Jan '14.

4. William D. Mahon, quoted in NY *World*, 5 Au '16; M to A. L. Wilde, 18 My '16, in *People v. Rena Mooney*, IV: 1712–15; "Habeas Corpus," I: 464–66.

5. M to E. A. Carlson, 6 F '16, and M to R. C. Greenley, 29 Ap '16, in "Habeas Corpus," XIII: 8314–23 and I: 510–24.

6. Belle Hammerberg testimony, Cal S Ct, "In re Billings," III: 1969.

7. "Habeas Corpus," XX: 12,865–66, 13,-136–38; M to R. C. Greenley, 29 Ap '16, in *ibid.*, I: 510–24.

8. M testimony, "Habeas Corpus," I: 470–72, II: 770–72; four letters to and from W. D. Mahon, May–July 1916, in *ibid.*, II: 764–69, XIII: 8419–21, XVIII: 12,051–55; M circular letter, 12 Jl '16, in *ibid.*, XVIII: 12,042–44; *Exmr*, 15 Jl '16; *Labor Clarion*, 21 Jl '16.

9. "Habeas Corpus," XIII: 8454–62.

10. Quoted in Henry T. Hunt, *The Case of Thomas J. Mooney and Warren K. Billings* (1929), 25.

11. "Habeas Corpus," XX: 12,875–76; XIX: 12,749–50; I: 630, 633.

12. The notice is reprinted in Hunt, *Case of Mooney*, 29.

13. SF *News Letter*, 17 Je '16.

14. Hunt, *Case of Mooney*, 26–27; *Town Talk*, 22 Jl '16; Rena Mooney and M testimonies, "Habeas Corpus," I: 570 and XX: 12,931–32, 13,125; Oral Hist. Proj., "Billings," 204–5; *Exmr*, 15, 19 Jl '16; *Bul*, 18 Jl '16; SF *News Letter*, 20 Jl '16; *Labor Clarion*, 21 Jl '16.

15. Hunt, 24; Swanson testimony, *People v. Rena Mooney*, IV: 1476, 1487, 1519; Swanson testimony, *People v. Weinberg*, in "Habeas Corpus," II: 849.

16. Minor, "Frame-up System," 3; L. D. Harding to Bourke Cockran, 23 F '17, in Cockran P; *Labor Clarion*, 7 Jl '16; *People v. Mooney*, III: 1453–55; *People v. Rena Mooney*, V: 2241, 2256–59, 2270–71; *People v. Weinberg*, II: 1127–28, III: 1463; "Habeas Corpus," III, 1318.

17. Weinberg testimony, in *People v. Rena Mooney*, V: 2272–77, and in *People v. Mooney*, III: 1610.

18. Weinberg testimony, *People v. Mooney*, III: 1612–13.

19. *Ibid.*, 1614–15.

20. Swanson testimony, *People v. Rena Mooney*, IV: 1508–22, 1544.

21. Oral Hist. Proj., "Billings," 122–46, 160–220.

22. Swanson testimony, *People v. Rena Mooney*, IV: 1498–1505.

23. George P. West, "The Mooney Case Today," *Nation*, 27 Ap '21; Hopkins, *What Happened in the Mooney Case*, 8–9; Edgar T. Gleeson to Evelyn Wells, 18 Mr '59, in Older P; Duffus, *Tower of Jewels*, 137–40; Lang, *Tomorrow*, 88.

24. M to Fred Hagmann, 11 My '13, in "Habeas Corpus," XIII: 8339–41.

25. M to Thomas Corbet, 12 My '13, in *ibid.*, 8282–86.

26. *Ibid.*; M to Henry Murray, 18 Ap '13, and M to L. L. Ketterfield, 16 Jan '13, both in "Habeas Corpus," XIII: 8342–44 and 8288–91; M testimony, *ibid.*, I: 450, XIX: 12,781–82, and XX: 13,233–39.

VI The Parade Is Bombed

EPIGRAPH: Cal S Ct, "In re Billings," II: 1304.

1. NY *Times*, 13 My '16; *Exmr*, 14 My, 17 Je '16.

2. *Exmr*, 16 My '16.

3. *Exmr*, 3 Je '16.

4. *Exmr*, 4, 7, 10 Je '16; *San Francisco Directory, 1916*, 613, 1314; *Densmore Report*, 10.

5. *Exmr*, 16 My, 7 Je '16.

6. *Exmr*, 16 My '16.

7. *Labor Clarion*, 9 Je '16.

8. *Organized Labor*, 22 Jl '16.

9. *Exmr*, 24 My, 2, 13, 20 Je '16.

10. As quoted in *Exmr*, 9 Je '16.

11. *Exmr*, 10 Je, 19 Jl '16; U.S. Dept. of Commerce, *Statistical Abstract of the United States: 1916* (1917), 54.

12. *Exmr*, *Call*, Jl '16, *passim*; SF C of C *Activities*, 29 Jl '16; *Chr*, 20 Jl '16; *Bul*, *News*, *Labor Clarion*, June–July 1916, *passim*; Emma Goldman, *Living My Life*, II: 577.

13. As quoted in *Exmr*, 30 Je '16. See Hunt, *Case of Mooney*, 9, for another like it.

14. *Exmr*, 30 Je '16.

15. *Labor Clarion*, 14 Jl '16; *Bul*, 18–21 Jl '16; Wells, *Older*, 291–92; author's interview, Sara Bard Field, 18 S '59.

16. As quoted in *Bul*, 21 Jl '16.

17. *Ibid.*

18. As quoted in *Coast Seamen's Journal*, 26 Jl '16.

19. As quoted in *Chr*, 25 Jl '16.

20. *Chr*, 21, 25 Jl '16; *Exmr*, *Bul*, *Call*, *News*, 21 Jl '16; Older, *My Own Story* (1925 ed.), 181.

21. *Exmr*, *Chr*, 23 Jl '16; *Bul*, 24 Jl '16. *Bulletin* counters tallied 22,428; the *Examiner* claimed an adding-machine tally of 51,329.

22. *Exmr*, 23 Jl '16.

23. *Chr*, 23 Jl '16; *Bul*, 24 Jl '16.

24. *Chr*, 23 Jl '16; Hopkins, *What Happened in the Mooney Case*, 14–20.

25. *Chr*, 23 Jl '16.

26. *Chr*, *Exmr*, 23 Jl '16, and *Call*, 24 Jl '16, offer eyewitness accounts. See also Matheson testimony, "Habeas Corpus," X: 5887–88; and medical testimony, *People v. Billings*, I: 21 ff, esp. 48.

27. *Exmr*, 23 Jl '16; *Chr*, 20, 23, 24 Jl '16; Cal S Ct, "In re Billings," III: 1891.

28. *Chr*, 23 Jl '16; *Exmr*, 24, 25 Jl '16; Hopkins, 32; [U.S. National Commission on Law Observance and Enforcement,] *Mooney-Billings Report*, 2.

29. *People v. Mooney*, II: 881; Matheson, Bunner testimonies, *ibid.*, II: 639–43, 658–59, 706–36.

30. *Ibid.*, II: 639–43, 658–59, 706–36; Hopkins, 40.

31. Colburn testimony, *People v. Mooney*, II: 600–624, 562, 729; author's interview, Edgar T. Gleeson, 6 F '60. (Gleeson, a *Bulletin* reporter who was on the scene of the explosion, overheard Brennan's comment.)

32. Matheson testimony, *People v. Mooney*, II: 668–69.

33. Hopkins, 34.

34. *Ibid.*

35. *Exmr, Chr,* 23 Jl, 3–5 Je '16. Each newspaper had a reporter covering the parade at Steuart Street when the explosion occurred. One was hit. *People v. Billings,* I: 160–71.

36. *Bul,* 24 Jl '16; Older testimony, Cal S Ct, "In re Billings," III: 1650; Mullally as quoted in *Exmr,* 23 Jl '16; *Chr,* 25 Jl '16; *Call,* 24 Jl '16.

37. *Bul,* 25 Jl '16.

38. Fresno *Republican,* 25 Jl '16.

39. As quoted in *Bul,* 24 Jl '16. For Lathrop's civic career in San Francisco, see *Call,* 27 Ap, 27 Oc '08, 13 Ap, 4 My '13. Author's interview, the Rev. Harold S. Kelly (archivist, Episcopal Diocese of California), 21 Jan '60.

40. Sacramento *Bee,* 24 Jl '16.

41. Stockton *Record,* 27 Jl '16.

42. Fresno *Republican,* 25 Jl '16.

43. See Rowell to Caspar Whitney, 28 S '17, in Rowell P.

44. Fresno *Republican,* 25 Jl '16.

45. *Bul,* 21 Mr '18, 17 Au '16; *Coast Seamen's Journal,* 9 Au '16; *Chr,* 26 Jl '16.

46. *Exmr,* 23 Jl '16.

47. See *Exmr, Call,* and *Chr,* 23–26 Jl '16.

48. Goldman, *Living My Life,* II: 577; *Mother Earth,* Aug., Sept. 1916; NY *Weekly People,* Sept. 1916 issues.

49. As quoted, 23 Jl '16.

50. As quoted in *Call,* 25 Jl '16; *Bul,* 24 Jl '16.

51. *Chr,* 23, 25 Jl '16; L. P. Russell, as quoted in *Chr,* 26 Jl '16; White and Rolph, as quoted in *Exmr,* 24 Jl '16.

52. *Exmr,* 23–25 Jl '16; *Chr,* 23, 25, 26 Jl '16.

53. White, as quoted in *Chr,* 24 Jl '16.

54. *Chr,* 26 Jl, 11 Au '16.

55. *Bul, Chr, Exmr,* NY *Times,* 25 Jl '16.

56. NY *Times,* 26 Jl '16.

57. As quoted in *Exmr,* 23 Jl '16.

58. *Coast Review,* July 1916.

59. *Grizzly Bear,* Aug. 1916; SF *News Letter,* 5 Au '16.

60. Koster, as quoted in *Bul,* 24, 25 Jl '16.

61. *Bul, Chr,* 25 Jl '16.

62. *Exmr,* 27 Jl '16.

63. *Exmr,* 25 Jl '16.

64. As quoted in *Exmr,* 27 Jl '16.

65. *Ibid.*

66. Edward H. Hurlbut in *Call,* 27 Jl '16. See also Edward H. Hamilton in *Exmr,* 27 Jl '16.

67. *Call,* 24 Jl '16; Matheson testimony, "Habeas Corpus," IX: 5574.

68. *Bul,* 24 Jl '16; Matheson and Goff testimony, "Habeas Corpus," X: 5888–89, XI: 7072–76; Peterson testimony, *ibid.,* VIII: 4519–20.

69. *People v. Mooney,* I: 382–88.

70. *Exmr,* 24 Jl '16; *Bul,* 25 Jl '16; *Chr,* 24, 26 Jl '16.

71. M testimony, "Habeas Corpus," XI: 6362.

72. Older, quoted in Wells, *Older,* 295. See also Duffus, *Tower of Jewels,* 160.

73. Matheson testimony, "Habeas Corpus," X: 5889 and IX: 5699–700.

74. Kytka to Matheson, 6 Au '16, in "Habeas Corpus," XVI: 10,308–09. This is the same letter which was discredited in another regard; see note, p. 74 above. But this part of it McNutt apparently did not deny.

75. Brennan testimony, "Habeas Corpus," XVI: 10,380–89. Brennan denied that Swanson was the "main source," but in the light of his own testimony he was equivocating. See also Maxwell McNutt, *Before the Special Commission Appointed by the President of the United States . . .* (1917), 19–20.

76. E.g., Hunt, *Case of Mooney,* vi; *M-B Report,* 41–42, 46–47, 57–58.

77. "Habeas Corpus," XIV: 9244, XV: 9518.

78. *Ibid.,* IX: 5706–7.

79. Swanson testimony, SF Police Commission, "In re Police Officer Draper Hand," 13 Ap '21, in *ibid.,* X: 5797–98, 5808; McNutt, *Before the Special Commission,* 7.

80. Minor, "Frame-up System," 5, 7. See also Federal Mediation Commission Report, in U.S. Commission on Public Information, *Official Bulletin,* 28 Jan '18, 14–15.

81. *M-B Report,* 46–47; author's interview, Edgar T. Gleeson, 6 F '60.

82. McNutt to Bourke Cockran, 24 N '16, in Cockran P.

83. Until Feb. 1, 1917. *People v. Rena Mooney,* IV: 1478.

84. Fickert testimony, "Habeas Corpus," XIV: 9244–45, 9249.

85. *Ibid.,* 9296.

86. Brennan testimony, *ibid.*, XVI: 10,600.
87. *People v. Rena Mooney*, II: 675–77.
88. Brennan testimony, "Habeas Corpus," XVI: 10,295, 10,522.
89. *Ibid.*, XVI: 10,623.
90. SF Police Commission, "In re Draper Hand," 13 Ap '21, in *ibid.*, X: 5781–831.
91. Swanson testimony, *People v. Rena Mooney*, IV: 1490–98, 1535–36.
92. Brennan testimony, "Habeas Corpus," XVI: 10,628.
93. Memorandum, Swanson to Fickert, 15 Au '16, in *ibid.*, IX: 5611–20; testimony of John Dowd (URR investigator, 1916), in *ibid.*, XVI: 10,739; SF Police Commission, "In re Draper Hand," 13 Ap '21, in *ibid.*, X: 5805.
94. Swanson testimony, SF Police Commission, "In re Draper Hand," in *ibid.*, X: 5800–5805.

VII   The Arrests

EPIGRAPHS: Cal S Ct, "In re Billings," II: 1049; M to H. C. Carrasco, 20 Je '36.

1. Author's interview, Warren K. Billings, 29 Au '61; *M-B Report*, 50–51; Bunner testimony, *People v. Billings*, I: 201–2; Bunner testimony, *People v. Mooney*, II: 1087–91, 1096; C. M. Fickert, *Before the Governor of the State of California in the Matter of the Application of Thomas J. Mooney for a Pardon* (n.d. [1918], 20; *Exmr*, 27 Jl '16; *Chr*, 27 Jl, 3 Au '16; Billings testimony, "Habeas Corpus," XIX: 12,546.
2. Hunt, *Case of Mooney*, vii; *M-B Report*, 66–67; Hand testimony, *People v. Mooney*, II: 1102; Weinberg testimony, *ibid.*, III: 1477–79, 1485–86; Sergeant W. R. Proll testimony, *ibid.*, II: 1123–31; McNutt, *Before the Special Commission*, 19.
3. Officer Ernest E. Gable testimony, *People v. Mooney*, III: 1635–36.
4. Rena Mooney testimony, *ibid.*, III: 1369–72; M and Rena Mooney testimonies, "Habeas Corpus," I: 398–401, 550–53; *Exmr*, 27 Jl '16.
5. *People v. Mooney*, III: 1380.
6. "Habeas Corpus," I: 555.
7. *Ibid.*, I: 554; *People v. Mooney*, III: 1372–74.
8. *Exmr*, 27, 28 Jl '16; *People v. Mooney*, II: 699, III: 1375, 1405, 1406; "Habeas Corpus," I: 403–9, 460, II: 661; police report of William C. O'Brien, *ibid.*, XVIII: 12,059–60; McKenzie statement, Cal S Ct, "In re Billings," II: 1571.

9. Police stenographer's transcript of M interrogation, 28 Jl '16, in "Habeas Corpus," II: 661–731.
10. *Ibid.*, 661.
11. Rena Mooney testimony, *ibid.*, I: 558, 561.
12. *Chr*, 30 Jl '16.
13. *People v. Mooney*, III: 1406–7.
14. See *Encounter*, Mar. 1967, 91.
15. See *M-B Report*, 94–108; Older, *My Own Story* (1925 ed.), 182.
16. *Chr*, 27 Jl '16.
17. *Chr*, 1 Au '16.
18. *Chr*, 27–31 Jl, 1, 4, 15 Au '16.
19. *Exmr*, 2 Au '16.
20. *Bul*, 26 Jl '16.
21. *Bul*, 27 Jl '16.
22. Older, *My Own Story*, 182; Wells, *Older*, 296–97.
23. *M-B Report*, 94n.
24. *Chr*, 28, 30 Jl, 4 Au '16.
25. As quoted, *Chr*, 30 Jl '16.
26. *Chr*, 7 Au '16.
27. *Exmr*, 1 Jl '16; *Chr*, 26 Jl, 7 Au '16.
28. *Chr*, 28 Jl '16.
29. McKenzie testimony, "Habeas Corpus," III: 1738; William J. Burns, *Masked War*, 45.
30. *Exmr*, 24 Je '16; *Chr*, 28 Jl, 1 Au '16; McIntosh testimony, "Habeas Corpus," VIII: 4565ff; SF Grand Jury, "Testimony . . . on Indictment of Warren K. Billings [*et al.*]" (1916), 2–4 and *passim*.
31. McIntosh testimony, "Habeas Corpus," VIII: 4565–628.
32. Fresno *Republican*, 28 Jl '16; *Chr*, 28 Jl, 2 Au '16; Oakland *World*, 4 My '11 *et seq.*
33. *Chr*, 30 Jl '16.
34. *Ibid.*; Louise D. Harding (Mrs. Alexander Horr) to Bourke Cockran, 27 F '17, Cockran P.
35. Hichborn, *Story of the California Legislature, 1915 Session*, 107–8, 226; Hichborn testimony, "Habeas Corpus," XIX: 12,150.
36. Fickert as quoted, *Chr*, 10 Au '16.
37. *Chr*, 29 Jl, 13 Au '16; *M-B Report*, 23–24, 32–35.
38. *M-B Report*, 55–57.
39. Hopkins, *What Happened in the Mooney Case*, 126–27.
40. Rena Mooney testimony, "Habeas Corpus," I: 563–64.
41. Burke testimony, SF Grand Jury, "Indictment of Billings *et al.*," 70.
42. Hughes testimony, *ibid.*, 62–63.
43. Burke testimony, *ibid.*, 68, 70.
44. *M-B Report*, 2; *Chr*, 4 Au '16.

45. *M-B Report*, 62–63.

46. West, letter to the ed., *Nation*, 5 Oc '21.

47. *Exmr*, 1 N '13. See also *Bench and Bar of California, 1937–1938*, 129.

48. *Exmr*, 1 N '13; *Nation*, 5 Oc '21.

49. *Call*, 3 D '08, 25 Oc '21; *Chr*, 15 Jan, 23 Oc '19, 8 Je '48.

VIII The Prosecution Commences

EPIGRAPH: *Call*, 13 N '20.

1. *M-B Report*, 2–6.

2. *Ibid.*, 125; Hunt, *Case of Mooney*, 220–26; Fickert, *Before the Governor in re Application of Mooney for a Pardon*, i–vi, 1–13, 21–23, 29–31, 73–103.

3. *People v. Billings, Appellant's Brief* (1917), 132–35; Maxwell McNutt, *Before the Governor of the State of California: Petition for Pardon of Thomas J. Mooney* (1918), 6, 93–94, and *passim*, and 117–20 of the appendix.

4. *M-B Report*, 27–28, 124, 125, 128–33; SF Grand Jury, "Indictment of Billings *et al.*," 12–17; *People v. Billings*, I: 381, 384; *People v. Mooney*, II: 744, 751; *People v. Billings, Appellant's Brief*, 8–13.

5. Goff testimony, "Habeas Corpus," XII: 7110.

6. *M-B Report*, 67–93.

7. Statement of John McDonald, 24 Jl '16: photostat in MP. Cf. report, Officer Peter Hughes to Duncan Matheson, 24 Jl '16, quoted in *M-B Report*, 70–71.

8. *People v. Mooney*, II: 797.

9. As quoted, *Bul*, 28 Jl '16.

10. *Chr*, 29 Jl '16.

11. Hopkins, *What Happened in the Mooney Case*, 137; *Chr, Exmr*, 29 Jl '16.

12. SF Grand Jury, "Indictment of Billings *et al.*," 17–20.

13. *M-B Report*, 180–81. A slightly different version appears in *Bul*, 25 S '16.

14. Sara Eliaser (for M) to Humphrey Cobb, 20 S '37.

15. *Ibid.*

16. See Fickert testimony, "Habeas Corpus," XV: 9356, 9784, 9956; Fickert, *Before the Governor in re Application of Mooney for a Pardon*, 52 and *passim*.

17. *Exmr*, 1 Au '16.

18. *Call*, 2 Ap, 12 Jl '13.

19. *M-B Report*, 125, 182; Hopkins, 145.

20. Theodore Bonnet in *Town Talk*, 21 Oc '16.

21. Hand testimony, "Habeas Corpus," XI: 6764–65.

22. Brennan testimony, *ibid.*, XVI: 10,547.

23. *Ibid.*, 10,397–409, 10,417–18, 10,546–48.

24. *Nation*, 14 Je '33; Hopkins, 31–32; *Chr*, 12 S '16; *Bul*, 11 S '16 *et seq.*

25. *Chr, Bul*, 12, 13 S '16.

26. *Bul*, 12, 13 S '16; *Chr*, 13 S '16; *People v. Billings*, I: 97.

27. Brennan testimony, "Habeas Corpus," XI: 6397–99.

28. *Bul*, 12, 13 S '16.

29. As quoted, *Chr*, 15 S '16.

30. Judge Dunne, as quoted, *Bul*, 14 S '16. The argument on the admissibility of the conspiracy evidence, having been made in the absence of the jury, is not in the trial transcript; the *Bulletin* and *Chronicle* accounts are in substantial agreement, however.

31. *Chr*, 15 S '16; *People v. Billings*, I: 246–48.

32. *Chr*, 15, 16 S '16.

33. *People v. Billings*, I: 269–77.

34. *Ibid.*, 105, 145.

35. *Ibid.*, 204–6.

36. *Ibid.*, 209–10; *People v. Billings, Appellant's Brief*, 138–46.

37. *People v. Billings*, I: 280, 289–96.

38. *Ibid.*, 305–16.

39. *Ibid.*, 316–21.

40. *Ibid.*, 291, 295, 307, 309, 318–19.

41. *Ibid.*, 322–34.

42. As quoted, *Chr*, 16 S '16.

43. *People v. Billings*, I: 362–63. This quotation came from Estelle Smith's grand jury testimony, and was entered in the trial record by stipulation.

44. *Ibid.*, 371–77.

45. *Chr*, 20 S '16; *People v. Billings*, *passim*.

46. McDonald testimony, *People v. Billings*, I: 381–86.

47. Crowley testimony, *ibid.*, 395–98.

48. *Ibid.*, 399–402.

49. De Caccia *et al.* testimonies, *ibid.*, II: 439–67; *M-B Report*, 30.

50. Billings testimony, *People v. Billings*, II: 491–514; testimonies of Patek *et al.*, *ibid.*, 514–25; *M-B Report*, 32.

51. *People v. Billings*, II: Brennan rebuttal, 33–36. See also Goff, White, Riehl testimonies, *ibid.*, I: 251–63, 267–68.

52. Billings testimony, Cal S Ct, "In re Billings," II: 1495–1500.

53. McNutt testimony, *ibid.*, 1245–48; Billings testimony, *ibid.*, 1547.

54. Billings testimony, *ibid.*, 1497.

55. *People v. Billings,* II: Fickert argument, 15–16.

56. Brennan, Billings, Older testimonies, Cal S Ct, "In re Billings," II: 1004–5, 1546, 1574, III: 1603.

57. Belle Lavin, Frank Lee testimonies, *People v. Billings,* II: 467–76, 526–32. See also *People v. Billings, Appellant's Brief,* 147.

58. Tom Mooney, Rena Mooney, Belle Hammerberg, Mrs. R. C. Timberlake testimonies, *People v. Billings,* II: 569–94, 639–46; Lawlor, Mendell, Crisafulli, and De Lorenzo testimonies, *ibid.,* 594–600, 609–14.

59. Bodechtel testimony, *People v. Billings,* I: 218–23.

60. *Ibid.,* II: McNutt's argument, 13, 28; *People v. Billings, Appellant's Brief,* 21–26, 60, 67–69.

61. Watson, Moss, Pendergast testimonies, *People v. Billings,* II: 533ff, 550–62; *M-B Report,* 34.

62. Logan, Requa, Sumney testimonies, *People v. Billings,* II: 598–604, 606–9, 614–29; McNutt, Fickert statements, *ibid.,* 633–34.

63. *Ibid.,* 652–63, 665–66.

64. *Ibid.,* II: Fickert argument, 4, 10, 16, 18, 22, 26.

65. *Ibid.,* 3, 5.

66. *People v. Billings,* II: McNutt argument, 1.

67. *Ibid.,* 2–3.

68. *Ibid.,* 3.

69. *Ibid.,* 9.

70. *Ibid.,* Brennan rebuttal, 17, 24, 30, 44.

71. *Bul,* 21 S '16.

72. *People v. Billings,* II: Brennan rebuttal, 62.

73. *Bul,* 23 S '16.

74. Gleeson testimony, Cal S Ct, "In re Billings," III: 1901.

75. *Chr,* 24 S '16.

76. *Ibid.*

77. *Ibid.*

78. As quoted, *Bul,* 25 S '16.

79. *Ibid.*

80. As quoted, *Chr,* 25 S '16.

IX   The Early Defense Movement

EPIGRAPHS: "Habeas Corpus," IX: 5429; Oakland *World,* 8 S '16.

1. See Emma Goldman, *Living My Life,* II: 580; Richard Drinnon, *Rebel in Paradise: A Biography of Emma Goldman* (1961), ch. 19; Joseph North, *Robert Minor,*

78–97; James McGurrin, *Bourke Cockran* (1948), 293ff; Wells, *Older,* 301ff; Lang, *Tomorrow Is Beautiful,* 127; and Philip Taft, *A. F. of L. in the Time of Gompers* (1957), 374–77.

2. *Exmr,* 28 Jl '16.

3. North, *Minor,* 77; Emma Goldman, *Living My Life,* II: 580. According to Miss Goldman, it was Berkman who wired Minor; according to North, Lydia Gibson: anarchist credits anarchist, and Communist credits a latter-day Communist. Miss Goldman does give Minor credit in *Living My Life* for assisting Berkman in Mooney's rescue, but as far as North is concerned, Minor ran the defense himself. Nowhere in North's book is Berkman mentioned. See comment of Theodore Draper, *Roots of American Communism* (1957), 418n.

4. Draper, *Roots,* 122.

5. *Exmr,* 9 Au '16; *Masses,* Aug.-Nov. 1915; North, 44–77.

6. Oakland *World,* 25 Au '16; *Exmr,* 9 Au '16; North, 79–81.

7. Emma Goldman, *Living My Life,* II: 598–625; NY *Worker,* 13 S '33; Draper, 123.

8. As quoted, Oakland *World,* 8 S '16.

9. Minor, "Frame-up System," 4.

10. *Ibid.,* 10–16.

11. Robert Minor, "Fickert Has Ravished Justice" (n.d. [1917]), 1.

12. Alexander Berkman, "Planning Judicial Murder," *Mother Earth,* Sept. 1916; Emma Goldman, *Living My Life,* II: 579; Oakland *World,* 28 Jl, 4 Au, 1 S '16; Oakland *Tri-City Labor Review,* 18 Au '16 *et seq.*

13. Margaret C. Anderson, *My Thirty Years' War* (1930), 69, 74, 112–19; Frederick J. Hoffman *et al., The Little Magazine: A History and Bibliography* (1946), 57; *Little Review,* Sept. 1916.

14. *Mother Earth,* Sept. 1916.

15. Oakland *Tri-City Labor Review,* 25 Au, 8 S '16; Oakland *World,* 8 S '16; Minor, "Frame-up System," 2.

16. *Bul,* 22 S '16; see Frederick Ely's labor columns, *Bul,* Aug.–Oct. 1916.

17. SF *Blue Book and Club Directory, 1928,* 507; Oakland *Tri-City Labor Review,* 30 Je, 15 S '16; *Bul,* 11 S '16.

18. See NY *Public,* 12 Jl '19; *Labor Clarion,* 5 Je '15; Graham Adams, Jr., *Age of Industrial Violence: 1910–1915,* 56–57, 173–75.

19. John R. Commons, *Myself* (1934), 140.

20. *Bul,* 13 S '11, 11 S '16; Marguerite Green, *National Civic Federation and the*

American Labor Movement, 1900–1925 (1956), 234; Oakland *World*, 6 Oc '16; Minor to Walsh, 19 Au '16, and Walsh to Minor, 30 Au '16, in Walsh P.

21. As quoted, *Blast*, 15 S '16.

22. *Bul*, 9 S '16.

23. Author's interview, Sara Bard Field, Aug. 1959.

24. (Cleveland-Chicago) *Solidarity*, 1 Jl–23 D '16; Lowell S. Hawley and Ralph B. Potts, *Counsel for the Damned: A Biography of George Francis Vanderveer* (1953), 171–93.

25. *Solidarity*, 14 Oc '16; Elizabeth Gurley Flynn, *I Speak My Own Piece* (1955), 188, 212; Ralph Chaplin, *Wobbly* (1948), 178.

26. Herbert R. Collie to ed., *Solidarity*, 2 D '16.

27. NY *Weekly People*, 22 Jl '16–5 My '17; Mary Eleanor Fitzgerald to ed., *ibid.*, 9 Je '17.

28. Brennan testimony, "Habeas Corpus," XVI: 10,279–84, 10,302.

29. Cal State F of L, *Proceedings of the Seventeenth Annual Convention, 1916*, 77–89. See also Scharrenberg's Commonwealth Club address of 2 S '16, in *ibid.*, 53–59; *Bul*, 2 Oc '16.

30. Cal State F of L, *Proceedings, 1916*, 33–34.

31. *Labor Clarion*, 13 Oc '16.

32. *Ibid.*

33. *Ibid.*

34. *Bul*, 6 Oc '16.

35. Cal State F of L, *Proceedings, 1916*, 34, 88, and *passim*.

36. Frederick Ely in *Bul*, 4 Oc '16.

37. *Labor Clarion*, 20 Oc '16.

38. *Town Talk*, 16 D '16.

39. Oakland *Tri-City Labor Review*, 22 D '16; *Town Talk*, 16 D '16; *Bul*, 13 Oc '16.

40. Berkman to Johannsen, 13 Ap '15, in Rolph, *In re Mooney Pardon*, 69.

41. *Blast*, 1 N '16.

42. Morris Hillquit, *Loose Leaves from a Busy Life* (1934), 17–18, 206–7; Harry Rogoff, *East Side Epic: The Life and Work of Meyer London* (1930), 31, 60, 114–15; Benjamin Stolberg, *Tailor's Progress* (1944), 37; Taft, *A. F. of L. in the Time of Gompers*, 180–82; Matthew Josephson, *Sidney Hillman* (1952), 115–37; John Herman Randall, *Problem of Group Responsibility in Society: An Interpretation of the History of American Labor* (1922), 206, 229–30; Joel Seidman, *Needle Trades* (1942), 138–40. See also Moses Rischin,

The Promised City: New York's Jews, 1870–1914 (1962), 175ff. For a novelist's portrayal of the anarchist and Socialist spirit of the New York Jewish garment workers' community, see Abraham Cahan, *Rise of David Levinsky* (1917).

43. *Mother Earth*, Dec. 1916; United Hebrew Trades, form letter, n. d. [Nov. 1916], in Cockran P.

44. *Mother Earth*, Dec. 1916.

45. Berkman to Agnes Inglis, 30 Jan '17, in Inglis Papers, Labadie Library; Max Eastman, *Enjoyment of Living* (1948), 553n and *passim*; NY *Call*, 18 N '16.

46. NY *Call*, 4 D '16. Emma Goldman states that Walsh addressed this meeting, but she is in error. *Living My Life*, II: 588.

47. *Mother Earth*, Dec. 1916; NY *Call*, 26 N, 1, 4 D '16.

48. Robert Ford to Cockran, 22 S '16, [IWDL] to Cockran, 23 Oc '16, Cockran to M and Billings, 9 N '16, and Cockran to Maxwell McNutt, 17 N '16, all in Cockran P; Emma Goldman, *Living My Life*, II: 586; NY *Call*, 14, 30 N '16; *Mother Earth*, Dec. 1916; *Bul*, 30 D '16, 4 Jan '17.

49. Ambrose Kennedy, *American Orator: Bourke Cockran, His Life and Politics* (1948), *passim*; *Nation*, 27 S '17.

50. *Call*, 12 F '17.

51. *Town Talk*, 18 N '16, 27 Jan '17; McNutt to Cockran, 13 N '16, and Cockran to McNutt, 14 N '16, in Cockran P.

52. Cockran to Anna M. Sloan, 24 N '16, Cockran P (Letterbook).

53. Ed Nolan to Cockran, 2 Jan '17, Cockran P.

54. Mrs. Clare Cram to M and Billings, 8 N '16, Cockran to M, 11 N '16, and McNutt to Cockran, 17 N '16, all in Cockran P; *Chr*, 14 N '16; *Bul*, 17 N, 30 D '16.

x Jury Duty in San Francisco

EPIGRAPH: *In These Latter Days*, p. 239.

1. *Fairall's Code of Civil Procedure* (1916), section 198, p. 104; *West's Annotated California Codes: Code of Civil Procedure* (1954), section 198.

2. *People v. Thompson*, 34 Cal 672 (1868); *Fairall's Code of Civil Procedure*, sec. 198, p. 105.

3. *Fairall's Code of Civil Proc.*, sec. 190, p. 103; *Statutes of California Passed at the Extra Session of the Forty-First Legislature* (1917), ch. 692.

4. *West's Annotated Cal Codes: Civil*

Proc., sec. 199 and historical note, pp. 272–73.

5. *Ibid.*, sec. 200 and historical note, pp. 274–77.

6. *Smith v. Texas*, 311 U.S. 128 (1940), 130; U.S. Sen., 88th Congr., 1st Sess., Doc. 39, Norman J. Small, ed., *Constitution of the United States of America: Analysis and Interpretation* (1964), 1318–20.

7. See Rita M. James, "Status and Competence of Jurors," *American Journal of Sociology*, May 1959, 563–70; W. S. Robinson, "Bias, Probability, and Trial by Jury," *American Sociological Review*, February 1950, 73–78; "Jury Selection in California," *Stanford Law Review*, V (1952–53): 247-73.

8. *Stanford Law Review*, V: 247–73; *West's Annotated Cal Codes: Civil Proc.*, sec. 204, historical note, p. 283; *Livesey v. Stock*, 208 Cal 315 (1929), 321.

9. Minor, "Frame-up System," 13.

10. For the modern practice of investigating jurors through agencies, see *Baugh v. Beatty*, 91 Cal App 2d 786 (1949).

11. *Chr*, 17 Jan '16. I have found no references to judicial patronage in San Francisco. I am indebted for the hypothesis to Professor Geoffrey C. Hazard, Jr., Univ. of Chicago, formerly of the Univ. of Calif. Law School, Berkeley.

12. Minor, "Frame-up System," 13.

13. Robert Minor, "Shall Mooney Hang" (12th ed., "Frame-up System," n. d. [1918]), 39.

14. *People v. Quijada*, 154 Cal 243 (1908), 245.

15. In 1926 the Ninth Circuit Court of Appeals ruled that prior service within a year was ground for exemption only, and in 1935 the California court of appeal followed suit. *White v. U. S.* 16 F. (2d) 870; *Silman v. Reghetti*, 82 Cal App 21. See *California Law Review* XXIV: 346–49. The author of this concludes: "If the legislature intended to eliminate professional jurors, its purpose has been frustrated, unless the *Silman* case should be overruled."

16. *Bul*, 6 Mr '14.

17. *News*, 23 Jan '17.

18. Minor, "Shall Mooney Hang?", 39. His place was taken by the alternate.

19. *Bul*, 31 My '17.

20. Cockran to Edward A. Michael, 17 My '17, Cockran P (Letterbook).

21. Alan Valentine, *Vigilante Justice* (1956), 86.

22. Harold R. Medina, *Anatomy of Freedom* (1959), 119.

23. *Stanford Law Review*, V: 264.

24. Cockran to Edward A. Michael, 17 My '17, Cockran P (Letterbook).

25. Max Eastman, "The Trial of Eugene Debs," *Liberator*, Nov. 1918; Zechariah Chafee, Jr., *Free Speech in the United States* (1942), 73, 249.

26. *Chr*, 11 Jan '17.

27. *Bul*, 15, 18 Jan '17.

28. Minor to Walsh, 17 S '16, Walsh P.

29. *Exmr*, 2 Oc '16; *Labor Clarion*, 29 S, 6 Oc '16; Oakland *World*, 6 Oc '16.

30. *Chr*, 9 N '16.

31. *Bul*, 10 N '16; Al Richmond, *Native Daughter: The Story of Anita Whitney* (1942), 98–99.

32. *Exmr*, 14 N '16; *Town Talk*, 18 N '16.

33. *Labor Clarion*, 17 N '16.

34. *Ibid.*, 8 D '16.

35. *Ibid.*, 19 Jan '17; Cal Legislature, 42d Sess., 1917, *Assembly Bills*, No. 17, and *Final Calendar of Legislative Business*, 66.

36. Cal Legislature, 42d Sess., 1917, *Senate Bills*, Nos. 387–390, 756, and *Journal of the Senate*, 1053, and *Final Calendar*, 5, 203; *West's Annotated Cal Codes: Civil Proc.*, sec. 199, pp. 272–73.

XI The Prosecution Shifts Witnesses

EPIGRAPH: *Call*, 13 N '20.

1. Hunt, *Case of Mooney*, 70–71; "Habeas Corpus," XIX: 12,681–705, XV: 9838–43; Hopkins, *What Happened in the Mooney Case*, 163–65.

2. Estelle Smith testimony, Cal S Ct, "In re Billings," I: 470.

3. *Ibid.*, 477ff; Hopkins, 137–38.

4. Hopkins, 167–68; hospital reports for McDonald, in Cal S Ct, "In re Billings," III: appendix.

5. *Chr*, 7 Oc '16.

6. Hopkins, 203–4; Hunt, *Case of Mooney*, 286–88; testimonies of Lt. Bunner, Earl Hatcher, and residents of Durkee, in "Habeas Corpus," IV: 2529, VI: 3673–74, VII: 4146–56.

7. Hunt, 284–85; Hopkins, 205; *John Spain v. Oregon and Washington Railroad and Navigation Company* (1914), 5, 100–107, and *passim* (in MP); B. C. Wilson to A. C. Spencer, 19 Jl '18, and B. C. Wilson to Governor Stephens, 27 Jl '18, both in Walsh P; testimonies of Frank H. Mytenger (the railroad conductor) and B. C.

Wilson, in "Habeas Corpus," IV: 2346–49, VII: 4176–98, 4292–332.

8. Affidavits of Earl K. Hatcher and his wife, 1926, in Cal S Ct, "Exhibits Referred to in the Petition of Thomas J. Mooney for a Writ of Habeas Corpus," nos. 25, 26; Hatcher testimonies, SF Grand Jury, "In re Thomas J. Mooney," 28, 31 My '21 (in MP); Earl Hatcher testimony, "Habeas Corpus," VI: 3586–618, 3673–74; Hunt, 257–58; Hopkins, 207.

9. Frank Woods testimony, "Habeas Corpus," VII: 4200–211.

10. James A. Tate testimony, *ibid.*, 4161–65.

11. Oliver Oscar Baisley testimony, *ibid.*, 4342.

12. *People v. Oxman* (1917), II: 469.

13. Fickert to Woods, 23 S '16 and 9 Oc '16, in *ibid.*, 470–73. See also *ibid.*, 546, and Hunt, *Case of Mooney*, 238.

14. *Densmore Report*, 90.

15. Fickert testimony, SF Grand Jury, "Testimony . . . In re F. C. Oxman" (1917), 162; Fickert testimony, "Habeas Corpus," XV: 9314–16, 9865–66; Hatcher testimony, SF Grand Jury, "In re Mooney," 28 My '21, pp. 11, 13.

16. Tate, Baisley testimonies, "Habeas Corpus," VII: 4173–74, 4334–43.

17. Hunt, *Case of Mooney*, 239.

18. Frank H. Tharp (Burns Agency manager) to Kansas City office, 19 Oc '16, in "Habeas Corpus," IV: 2432–36.

19. Kansas City Investigator #61 reports, 26 Oc '16, in "Habeas Corpus," IV: 2440–47.

20. Cunha testimony, "Habeas Corpus," XII: 7,623–24.

21. *People v. Oxman*, II: 381; "Habeas Corpus," IV: 2510–19, XIV: 9065–74, XVIII: 11,700, XIX: 12,767a.

22. Brennan testimony, "Habeas Corpus," XVI: 10,347, 10,584–627; *Bul*, 6 D '16.

23. Bunner testimony, SF Grand Jury, "Testimoney in re Oxman," 75–79.

24. Oxman testimony, *People v. Oxman*, II: 349.

25. Bunner testimony, SF Grand Jury, "Testimony in re Oxman," 78.

26. Oxman, Fickert, Cunha testimonies, *People v. Oxman*, II: 387–89, 515–18, 572.

27. *People v. Oxman*, I: [30–31].

28. *Ibid.*, I: 34.

29. From facsimile in Minor, "Frame-up System," 3d ed. (n.d. [1917]), 24.

30. *People v. Oxman*, I: 273–74, 35–36.

XII Mooney's Trial

EPIGRAPHS: *Stanford Quad '06*, 354; and Fickert to Mrs. F. C. Oxman, 29 Jan '17, in Cal State Archives, Atty Gen Records, Box 222.

1. *Bul*, 12 Au '13, 29, 31 Oc '14; *Chr*, 12 Jan '16. Most of the newspaper citations in this and the following nine chapters are from scrapbook clippings, 1917–23, assembled by the Mooney defense and now in the Bancroft Library. These clippings are largely from the five San Francisco dailies and from labor weeklies around the country.

2. *Chr*, 30 Jl '16.

3. *People v. Mooney*, I: 14.

4. *Bul*, 30 D '16, 1, 8 Jan '17; *Exmr*, 8 Jan '17.

5. Fickert as quoted, *Bul*, 1, 3 Jan '17.

6. *Bul*, 3 Jan '17.

7. *Exmr*, 4 Jan '17.

8. *News, Call*, 4, 18 Jan '17; *Bul*, 3, 5 Jan '17.

9. *Chr, Exmr*, 8 Jan '17.

10. *Bul*, 8 Jan '17; *People v. Mooney*, I: 8.

11. *People v. Mooney*, I: 9.

12. *Ibid.*, 10.

13. *Ibid.*, 24.

14. *Bul, Exmr*, 10 Jan '17; *Chr*, 11 Jan '17.

15. *Chr, Exmr*, 12 Jan '17.

16. *People v. Mooney*, I: 32.

17. *Ibid.*, 33–34.

18. *Ibid.*, 35–39, 49–51.

19. *Chr*, NY *Times*, 13 Jan '17.

20. *People v. Mooney*, I: 60–61.

21. *Ibid.*, 78–91.

22. *Ibid.*, 69–78.

23. Rigall testimony, SF Grand Jury, "Testimony in re Oxman," 16, 53–55; SF Police Court, *People v. Oxman* (Preliminary Hearing), 135.

24. Rigall testimony, *People v. Oxman* (Preliminary Hearing), 217, 221; "Habeas Corpus," VIII: 5098–5103.

25. Rigall testimony, SF Grand Jury, "Testimony in re Oxman," 15, 18, 35–36, 39; Rigall testimony, *People v. Oxman* (Preliminary Hearing), 65–66, 136, 174; Rigall testimony, SF Superior Court, *People v. Oxman*, I: [29].

26. Rigall testimony, *People v. Oxman* (Preliminary Hearing), 72, 73, 78, 85, 103–7, 116, 157, 164; Rigall testimony, *People v. Oxman*, I: 45, 100; Oxman testimony, SF Grand Jury, "Testimony in re Oxman," in "Habeas Corpus," VI: 3312.

27. Rigall testimony, *People v. Oxman* (Preliminary Hearing), 72, 95, 161, 178; Fickert and Oxman testimonies, "Habeas Corpus," V: 2932–33, VI: 3312.

28. Rigall testimony, *People v. Oxman* (Preliminary Hearing), 103–4, 129, 160; *Bul,* 12 Ap '17.

29. Hand testimony, "Habeas Corpus," XI: 6931–32.

30. Hand testimony, *ibid.,* 6780–81.

31. *Ibid.,* 6891–92.

32. Hand testimony, *ibid.,* 6930.

33. Rigall testimony, SF Grand Jury, "Testimony in re Oxman," 27.

34. Rigall testimony, *People v. Oxman* (Preliminary Hearing), 183–85.

35. Oxman testimony, *People v. Mooney,* II: 823.

36. *Ibid.,* 822.

37. Oxman testimony, *ibid.,* 795–803.

38. *Ibid.,* 814–17.

39. *Ibid.,* 828.

40. *Ibid.,* 831.

41. *Ibid.,* 833.

42. *Ibid.,* 852, 853, 862.

43. *People v. Mooney,* II: 804–36, 845–62; C. E. S. Wood to Cockran, 1 F '17, in Cockran P.

44. *Bul,* 27 Jan '17.

45. Matheson, Goff testimonies, *People v. Mooney,* II: 1164–72; Spangler testimony, *ibid.,* 1545–54.

46. "Habeas Corpus," III: 1768–70, IX: 5214–23.

47. Rigall testimony, SF Police Court, *People v. Oxman* (Preliminary Hearing), 203, 210, 227.

48. *News,* 27 Jan '17. See also *Call,* 27 Jan '17.

49. *Chr,* 28 Jan '17.

50. Sadie Edeau testimony, *People v. Mooney,* II: 891–903. Cf. Sadie Edeau testimony, *People v. Billings,* I: 330–34.

51. Sadie Edeau testimony, *People v. Mooney,* II: 913.

52. Mellie Edeau testimony, *ibid.,* II: 978.

53. Edeau affidavits, 8 D '19, in "Habeas Corpus," VIII: 5039–43.

54. Hammerberg, Timberlake *et al.* testimonies, *People v. Mooney,* briefed in Hunt, *Case of Mooney,* 172–79, 192–95.

55. Hamilton, Cunha, Kytka testimonies, *People v. Mooney,* II: 1262–84.

56. McDonald testimony, *People v. Billings,* I: 381–86.

57. *People v. Mooney,* II: 744, 751, 761–74.

58. *Ibid.,* 1270–76.

59. "Habeas Corpus," XIV: 8732.

60. *People v. Lee Chuck,* 78 Cal 317 (1884).

61. See *M-B Report,* 189, and Minor, "Frame-up System," 2.

62. Dahl, Hollfelder, Eris testimonies, *People v. Mooney,* III: 1207–23.

63. Compton testimony, *ibid.,* III: 1224–28.

64. Nancy Jane Parrott (Mrs. Jane Compton) testimony, "Habeas Corpus," VIII: 4648–50.

65. As quoted, *Bul,* 7 F '17.

66. As quoted, *Call,* 7 F '17.

67. As quoted, *News,* 7 F '17.

68. As quoted, *Bul,* 7 F '17.

69. *Ibid.*

70. Author's interview, Edgar T. Gleeson, 6 F '60; *Bul,* 7 F '17.

71. *Bul,* 7 F '17.

72. *Exmr,* 8 F '17.

73. *Call,* 8 F '17.

74. As quoted, *Bul,* 8 F '17.

75. *Ibid.*

76. As quoted, *Bul,* 9 F '17. Capitalization of "Blasters" in this and next quotation is mine.

77. *Ibid.*

78. *Chr,* 10 F '17.

79. As quoted, *Bul,* 9 F '17.

80. *Ibid.*

81. *Chr,* 10 F '17.

82. *News, Bul,* 9 F '17.

83. *Chr,* 10 F '17; Edwin V. McKenzie testimony, "Habeas Corpus," IX: 5262, 5287–88.

84. *Chr, Bul,* 10 F '17.

85. As quoted, *Bul,* 10 F '17.

86. Fickert, as quoted, *ibid.*

87. *Chr,* 11 F '17.

88. *Exmr,* 11 F '17.

89. *Call,* 10 F '17; *Bul,* 12 F '17.

90. As quoted, *Chr,* 10 F '17.

91. *Bul,* 12 F '17.

92. McKenzie testimony, "Habeas Corpus," IX: 5262, 5289, 5295; Bean, *Boss Ruef's San Francisco,* 198–212.

93. *Bul,* 5 Jan '17.

94. Carrie MacNevin affidavit, 28 Jl '22, in "Habeas Corpus," X: 6111–22; McKenzie testimony, *ibid.,* IX: 5262–64, 5400; Zimdars testimony, *ibid.,* 5452–505.

95. MacNevin affidavit, 19 N '30, in "Habeas Corpus," IX: 5506–17; MacNevin to James Walker, 30 N '31, in Rolph, *In re Mooney Pardon,* 71–73.

XIII Rigall Has an Idea

EPIGRAPHS: Cunha testimony, "Habeas Corpus," XIV: 8915; *People v. Oxman* (Preliminary Hearing), 138.

1. Minor to Cockran, 29 Mr '17, in Cockran P; *News*, 13 F '17; *Exmr*, 14, 18 F '17; *Bul*, 20 F '17; *Chr*, 25 F '17.
2. Charlotte W. LaPosee affidavit, 13 F '17, in "Habeas Corpus," XII: 7784–88; *Bul, Call*, 13 F '17.
3. *Chr*, 15 F '17.
4. *Exmr*, 20 F '17.
5. *Bul*, 24 F '17.
6. *Ibid.*
7. Rigall testimony, SF Grand Jury, "Testimony in re Oxman," 29–30; Rigall testimony, SF Police Court, *People v. Oxman* (Preliminary Hearing), 185.
8. Rigall testimony, SF Grand Jury, "Testimony in re Oxman," 42.
9. *Ibid.*, 22.
10. Rigall testimony, *People v. Oxman* (Preliminary Hearing), 79–81, 159–73.
11. *Ibid.*, 189.
12. *People v. Oxman*, 600.
13. *Ibid.*, 601–2.
14. Cunha testimony, "Habeas Corpus," XIII: 8985.
15. See *ibid.*, XII: 7794.
16. See *ibid.*, 7797; *Chr*, 15, 16 Ap '17.
17. Cunha testimony, "Habeas Corpus," XII: 7796–97.
18. *Ibid.*, 7798; *Chr, Exmr*, 20 F '17.
19. Matheson testimony, SF Grand Jury, "Testimony in re Oxman," 12.
20. Fickert testimony, "Habeas Corpus," V: 2935. See also Cunha testimony, *ibid.*, XIII: 7942–43.
21. "Habeas Corpus," XIII: 7621.
22. M testimony, *ibid.*, XX: 12,923–24.
23. Nockels testimony, Cal S Ct, "In re Billings," II: 786, 819.
24. Rigall testimony, *People v. Oxman* (Preliminary Hearing), 299–300; Ellis affidavit, 8 N '17, paraphrased in Hunt, *Case of Mooney*, 264–65.
25. Ellis testimony, *People v. Oxman* (Preliminary Hearing), 330; Nockels testimony, "In re Billings," II: 787.
26. McKenzie testimony, "Habeas Corpus," IX: 5330–31.
27. Ellis to Mulholland, quoted in Mulholland to Cockran, 12 Mr '17, Cockran P.
28. Transcript from the Princeton, Indiana, *Daily Democrat*, 2 Jan '01, in Cockran P.

29. Mulholland to Cockran, 12 Mr '17, Cockran P.
30. Mulholland to Cockran, 4 Ap '17, Cockran P.
31. Cockran to Mulholland, 19 Ap '17, Cockran P (Letterbook).
32. Ellis interview, *Bul*, 23 Ap '17.
33. Mulholland to Cockran, 4 Ap '17, Cockran P.
34. *Ibid.*; Cockran to Mulholland, 5 Ap '17, in Cockran P (Letterbook); McKenzie testimony, *People v. Oxman* (Preliminary Hearing), 252–53; Taft, *A. F. of L. in the Time of Gompers*, 300; McKenzie testimony, "Habeas Corpus," IX: 5334.
35. Re McKenzie's career: *Labor Clarion*, 12 N '15; *Town Talk*, 23 D '16; McKenzie testimony, Cal S Ct, "In re Billings," II: 881–82; Robert E. L. Knight interview of McKenzie, 24 My '56 (author's transcript, courtesy of interviewer). For a sketch of O'Connor, see *Call*, 10 F '20.
36. McKenzie testimony, "Habeas Corpus," IX: 5380–82, 5259, 5334–35; McKenzie testimony, *People v. Oxman* (Preliminary Hearing), 250.
37. McKenzie testimony, "Habeas Corpus," IX: 5291.
38. *Ibid.*, 5337–38.
39. *Ibid.*, 5290–91, 5332.
40. Nockels to Walsh, 9 Jl '35, Walsh P.
41. Cunha testimony, SF Grand Jury, "Testimony in re Oxman," 200.
42. *People v. Oxman* (Preliminary Hearing), 280–81.
43. Rigall testimony, *ibid.*, 188.
44. *Ibid.*, 347.
45. McKenzie testimony, "Habeas Corpus," IX: 5314.
46. *Ibid.*, 5315.
47. Older, *My Own Story* (1925 ed.), 182.
48. *Ibid.* See also Wells, *Older*, 303.
49. McKenzie testimony, "Habeas Corpus," IX: 5257–58; *Bul*, 11 Ap '17.
50. *Bul*, 12 Ap '17. Misspellings of Rigall's name in quotations from this issue have been corrected.
51. As quoted, *ibid.*
52. *Exmr, Chr*, 14 Ap '17.
53. *Call*, 12 Ap '17; *Chr, Bul*, 13 Ap '17.
54. *Chr*, 14, 15 Ap '17; *Exmr*, 15 Ap '17. See also Matheson testimony, "Habeas Corpus," X: 5917–19.
55. As quoted, *Bul*, 17 Ap '17.
56. *Ibid.*
57. *Bul*, 13 Ap '17; *News, Call, Bul*, 20 F '17.

58. Peterson testimony, "Habeas Corpus," VIII: 4548. See also Smith report to Peterson, 28 Jl '16, in Cal State Archives, Atty Gen Records, Box 222.

59. Smith report to Peterson, 30 Jan '17, "Habeas Corpus," VIII: 5024; Smith testimony, *People v. Rena Mooney*, IV: 1904; Smith affidavit, 18 Ap '18, in "Habeas Corpus," VII: 4396–400. (In 1935 Smith said that he did not recall Fickert's remarks of 30 Jan '17, or the affidavit of 18 Ap '18, but acknowledged his signature on the latter. Smith testimony, "Habeas Corpus," VII: 4391–403, 4469.)
For corroborating evidence, see *Bul*, 13 Ap '17; Peterson testimony, *People v. Weinberg*, II: 1008–12; and Peterson testimony, "Habeas Corpus," VII: 4477, VIII: 4483–84. See also *M-B Report*, 145.

60. Smith, as quoted, *Bul*, 13 Ap '17.

61. Peterson testimony, "Habeas Corpus," VIII: 4529–38. See also affidavit of Thomas Stout (the Oakland tailor), 19 F '17, in "Habeas Corpus," VII: 3896–99; Stout, Burgess testimonies, "Habeas Corpus," VII: 3863–76, 3903.

62. *Bul*, 13 Ap '17.

63. As quoted, *Exmr*, 13 Ap '17.

64. McKenzie testimony, "Habeas Corpus," IX: 5423.

65. *Bul*, 16 Ap '17.

66. See Hopkins, *What Happened in the Mooney Case*, 215. Hopkins thought that Estelle Smith was jealous of Oxman.

67. As quoted, *Call*, 16 Ap '17.

68. Cunha testimony, "Habeas Corpus," IX: 7815–16.

69. Older, O'Connor statements, *Bul*, 20 Ap '17; McKenzie testimony, "Habeas Corpus," IX: 5260.

70. McKenzie statement, *Bul*, 20 Ap '17.

71. McKenzie testimony, "Habeas Corpus," IX: 5262–63.

72. *Ibid.*, 5261, 5311.

73. McKenzie statement, *Bul*, 20 Ap '17; McKenzie testimony, "Habeas Corpus," IX: 5304–35.

74. McKenzie testimony, "Habeas Corpus," IX: 5386–87, 5314.

75. McKenzie statement, *Bul*, 20 Ap '17; McKenzie testimony, "Habeas Corpus," IX: 5267–68.

76. McKenzie testimony, "Habeas Corpus," IX: 5268.

77. *Bul*, 17, 18, 20 Ap '17; *Call*, 18 Ap '17.

78. As quoted, *Bul*, 18 Ap '17.

79. *Bul*, 18 Ap '17; *Chr, Exmr, Call*, 19 Ap '17.

80. *Bul*, 18, 20 Ap '17.

81. McKenzie testimony, "Habeas Corpus," IX: 5426. See also pp. 5268–71.

82. Older, McKenzie, O'Connor statements, *Bul*, 20 Ap '17.

83. *Chr*, 19 Ap '17; *Bul*, 20 Ap '17; McKenzie testimony, "Habeas Corpus," IX: 5426–31.

84. Lately Thomas, *Debonair Scoundrel: An Episode in the Moral History of San Francisco* (1962), 160; Bean, *Ruef*, 160; Franklin Hichborn, "California Politics, 1891–1939" (typescript photocopy, Univ. of Calif., Berkeley, Law School Library), III: 1775–76, IV: 2338, 2352n.

85. *Exmr*, 20 Ap '17.

86. *Bul*, 19 Ap '17.

87. As quoted, *Exmr*, 20 Ap '17.

88. *Bul*, 20 Ap '17.

89. *Bul*, 19 Ap '17; *Chr*, 20, 21 Ap '17.

90. *Exmr*, 21 Ap '17.

91. *Bul, Exmr*, 26 Ap '17.

92. *Exmr, Call, News, Chr, Bul*, 13–21 Ap '17.

93. *Chr*, 21 Ap '17.

94. *Chr*, 24 Ap '17.

95. Hunt, *Case of Mooney*, 15–16.

96. *Bul*, 21 Ap '17; *Chr*, 22 Ap '17.

97. *Chr, Exmr, Bul*, 23 Ap '17.

98. Sacramento *Bee*, 22 Ap '17. Among other out-of-town papers, see San Jose *Mercury-Herald*, 24 Ap '17, and Sacramento *Union*, 24 Ap '17.

99. *Town Talk*, 21 Ap '17. See also *Argonaut*, 28 Ap '17.

100. SF Labor Council minutes, in *Labor Clarion*, 27 Ap '17; *Chr, Exmr*, 24 Ap '17.

101. *Exmr*, 24 Ap '17.

102. Minor to Cockran, 26 Ap '17, Cockran P.

103. *Exmr*, 28 Ap '17.

104. Law and Order Committee, "Law and Order in San Francisco," 20; SF C of C *Activities*, 26 Jl '17.

105. *Exmr*, 28 Ap '17.

106. *Ibid.* (capitals omitted).

107. *Bul*, 30 Ap '17.

108. *News*, 28 Ap '17.

109. *Call*, 22 S '07, 7 Jan '08; *Bul*, 3 F '15.

110. *Call, Bul*, 23 Ap '17.

111. *Chr*, 25 Ap '17.

112. *People v. Oxman* (Preliminary Hearing), 144–48.

113. *Exmr*, 25 Ap '17.

114. As quoted, *Chr*, 25 Ap '17.

115. *SF News Letter*, 28 Ap '17.

116. *People v. Oxman* (Preliminary Hearing), 217, 220.

117. Complaints and warrants concerning the abduction of Nora Biford, stamped by Burns Agency in Chicago, 29 Ap '17, in "Habeas Corpus," VIII: 5098–5103.

118. *Chr,* 28 Ap '17.

119. *Bul,* 28, 30 Ap '17.

120. *Call,* 29 My '12; *Chr, Bul,* 28 Ap '17.

121. *Chr,* 1 My '17; *Bul,* 1–3 My '17.

122. Oxman testimony, SF Grand Jury, "Testimony in re Oxman," 117, 118.

123. *Ibid.,* 119–20.

124. *Ibid.,* 121–24.

125. *Ibid.,* 127–29.

126. *Ibid.,* 131, 135–36.

127. Fickert testimony, SF Grand Jury, "Testimony in re Oxman," 159–66.

128. *Ibid.,* 168–78.

129. *Ibid.,* 183, 184.

130. *Ibid.,* 179.

131. *Exmr,* 4 My '17; *Bul,* 4, 5 My '17.

132. *Exmr,* 4 My '17.

133. *Chr,* 4, 6 My '17; *Bul,* 4, 5 My '17.

134. *Chr,* 7, 15–18 My '17; *Bul,* 15, 24 My '17; *Exmr,* 25 My '17.

xiv The Trial of Rena Mooney

FIRST EPIGRAPH: The *Blast,* June 1, 1916.

1. As quoted, *Bul,* 30 Ap '17.

2. See esp. *Bul,* 1 My '17.

3. *Call,* 7, 12 My '17.

4. *Call,* 2 My '17.

5. *Bul,* 3 My '17.

6. *Call,* 14 My '17.

7. *Bul,* 14, 21 My '17.

8. *Exmr,* 31 My '17.

9. *Chr,* 11 Je '17.

10. *Ibid.; Exmr,* 11, 12 Je '17; *Bul,* 12 Je '17.

11. *Bul,* 11 Je '17.

12. *News,* 11 Je '17.

13. *Ibid.;* author's interview, Sara Bard Field, 18 S '59; *Chr,* 29 Jan '16; *Blast,* 15 Jan '16; *Bul,* 12 D '17, 4 Mr '18; *Town Talk,* 9 Mr '18.

14. *Argonaut,* 5 My '17.

15. *Ibid.,* 16 Je '17.

16. John W. Preston to Asst Atty Gen William C. Fitts, 6 Je '17, in Nat Archives, RG 60, file 185354.

17. Preston to Atty Gen T. W. Gregory, 15 Oc '17, in *ibid.*

18. Rowell to Theodore Roosevelt, 1 D '17, Rowell P. For other circumstances exacerbating this conflict, including another URR streetcar strike, see *Coast Seamen's*

Journal, 29 Au '17, and Knight, *Industrial Relations in the San Francisco Bay Area,* 344–47.

19. *Chr,* 24 My '17; *Bul,* 31 My '17.

20. *Exmr,* 1 Je '17; *Bul,* 2 Je '17.

21. *Chr,* 12 Jan '16.

22. *Call,* 11 Je '17.

23. *People v. Rena Mooney,* I: 7–31.

24. *Bul,* 12 Je '17.

25. *People v. Rena Mooney,* I: 33–34; *Chr,* 16, 17, 21, 27 Je '17.

26. *People v. Rena Mooney,* II: 620–39; *Call,* 19 Je '17.

27. *People v. Rena Mooney,* II: 813, 823–24, 833–34; *Bul, Call,* 21 Je '17; *Chr,* 22 Je '17.

28. McDonald testimony, *People v. Rena Mooney,* III: 943, 951, 960; *News,* 22 Je '17.

29. *Who's Who in America, 1918–1919* and *1924–1925.*

30. Fitch memorandum, 14 Je '17, in "Habeas Corpus," IV: 2360–62.

31. *Ibid.,* 2362–64.

32. Fitch testimony and memorandum, in *ibid.,* 2359–73.

33. *Survey,* 7 Jl '17.

34. Franklin Hichborn in *Bul,* 17 D '17; Fitch to William D. Stephens, 15 Mr '18, in Cal State Archives, Gov's Off.

35. Cunha testimony, "Habeas Corpus," XII: 7619–7704.

36. *Call,* 27 Je '17; *Chr, News, Exmr,* 28 Je '17.

37. *People v. Rena Mooney,* III: 1454–71, IV: 1472–1548; *Bul, Call,* 29 Je '17; *Exmr,* 30 Je '17.

38. *People v. Rena Mooney,* V: 2063–64; *Bul, News,* 9 Jl '17; *Chr,* 10 Jl '17.

39. Juror Beal, in *People v. Rena Mooney,* IV: 1747.

40. *Ibid.,* IV: 1750–51.

41. *Call,* 6 Jl '17; *Bul,* 6, 11, 12 Jl '17.

42. Charles Buschweit testimony, *People v. Rena Mooney,* V: 2404–14.

43. *Bul,* 13 Jl '17.

44. Eisert testimony, *People v. Rena Mooney,* VI: 2798–2858. See also *Bul,* 16 Jl '17, and *Chr,* 17 Jl '17.

45. Rena Mooney testimony, *People v. Rena Mooney,* VI: 2859–70 *et seq.,* 2937.

46. *Ibid.,* VI: 2951–52.

47. *Chr,* 18 Jl '17.

48. *Bul,* 18 Jl '17.

49. *Bul,* 20 Jl '17.

50. *Exmr,* 24 Jl '17.

51. *News, Chr,* 24 Jl '17; *Chr, Bul, Call,* 25 Jl '17.

52. Madeline Wieland to Lucy Lang, 7 Au '17, in Lang P.

53. *Ibid.; Bul, Call,* 25 Jl '17; *Chr,* 26 Jl '17.

54. As quoted, *Chr, Call,* 26 Jl '17.

55. *Call, Bul,* 26 Jl '17.

56. *Exmr,* 29 Jl '17.

57. *Bul,* 4 Au '17.

58. *California Outlook,* Sept. 1917.

59. *Chr,* 27, 28, 31 Jl '17; Oakland *Tribune,* 6 Au '17.

60. *Bul,* 14, 24, 25 Au '17; *Exmr,* 17 Au '17; *News, Call,* 17, 18 Au '17.

61. *E.g.,* Seattle *Union Record,* 1 S '17; Joliet *Illinois Tribune,* 30 Au '17; Richmond, Va., *Square Deal,* 7 S '17.

xv   The Trials of Oxman and Weinberg

EPIGRAPHS: Beatty, quoted in *News,* 19 Mr '38; Matheson, quoted in Hopkins, *What Happened in the Mooney Case,* 308.

1. *Call,* 26 Jl '17; Daniel Murphy and Paul Scharrenberg, circular letter to the Cal State F of L unions, 9 Jl '17, in MP (Scrapbook); *News,* 18 Jl '17; *Labor Clarion,* 3 Au '17; *Bul,* 30 Jl '17.

2. *Bul,* 30 Jl '17; *M–B Report,* 4.

3. Minor, "Justice Raped in California" ("Frame-up System," 5th ed., n.d. [1917]), 46.

4. Fickert statement, *Exmr,* 1 Au '17.

5. The Supreme Court's statement is in *Call,* 6 Au '17.

6. *Bul, Call,* 4 S '17.

7. *Bul,* 4 S '17.

8. Excerpts from the Supreme Court's ruling are in *Exmr,* 12 S '17.

9. Gleeson to author, 23 Je '67; Southern Pacific RR, "Shasta Route" schedule, June 1916; *Call,* 16 Je '17.

10. As quoted, *Chr,* 15 Je '17.

11. Hatcher testimony, SF Grand Jury, "In re Thomas J. Mooney" (1921), in "Habeas Corpus," VI: 3728–32, 3746.

12. Woodland *Democrat,* 14 Je '17, cited in Paul Leake testimony, "Habeas Corpus," XVI: 10,433ff.

13. Hatcher testimony, SF Grand Jury, "In re Thomas J. Mooney," in "Habeas Corpus," VI: 3662, 3714, 3750.

14. *Ibid.,* 3725–26.

15. *Call,* 26 Jl '17; *Chr,* 27 Jl '17.

16. As quoted, *Exmr,* 9 Au '17.

17. *Chr, Call, Exmr, News,* 9 Au '17; *Labor Clarion,* 17 Au '17; *Bul,* 1 S '17.

18. *Bul,* 25 Au '17; Oakland *Enquirer,* 18 Au '17; *Exmr,* 19 Au '17; *Call,* 31 Au '17;

Al Richmond, *Native Daughter: The Story of Anita Whitney,* 101, 105–9.

19. *Bul,* 3 S '17; *Call,* 1 S '17.

20. Hatcher testimony, and Hatcher statement of Sept. 1917, in "Habeas Corpus," VI: 3652, 3656–60, 3686–703. See also Hatcher testimony, SF Grand Jury, "In re Thomas J. Mooney," in "Habeas Corpus," VI: 3732–34, 3737.

21. *Bul,* 4 S '17.

22. *Bul,* 11 S '17.

23. *People v. Oxman,* I: 383, 239–40.

24. *Chr,* 26 S '17.

25. *People v. Oxman,* I: 240–49, II: 515–51, 612–58, and *passim; Bul,* 15, 28, 29 S '17; *Chr, Exmr,* 26 S '17.

26. *People v. Oxman,* II: 535–36.

27. *Chr, Exmr, Bul,* 28 S '17; Fickert as quoted in Oakland *Enquirer* and *Exmr,* 28 S '17; *Bul,* 28 S '17.

28. *People v. Oxman,* I: 127.

29. See *ibid.,* 30, 123–49.

30. *Ibid.,* I: 352, 362, II: 447, 505–9; *Exmr,* 27 S '17.

31. *People v. Oxman,* II: 407.

32. *Ibid.*

33. *News,* 25 S '17. The trial transcript does not mention Dunne's interruption, but other newspapers confirm its occurrence, without mentioning its point in the testimony. (See *Chr, Exmr,* 26 S '17.) There is evidence that the court reporter was partisan: when the case was concluded, he appended his own comments to the transcript, praising Dunne and the jury. (*People v. Oxman,* II: [670–72].)

34. *Bul,* 29 S '17.

35. *Ibid.*

36. *Call,* 1 Oc '17.

37. *Bul,* 1, 3 Oc '17; Hatcher testimony, "Habeas Corpus," VI: 3650, 3693–94, 3705–13; *Exmr,* 4 Oc '17.

38. Shortridge testimony, "Habeas Corpus," VIII: 5076; *Chr,* Oakland *Enquirer,* 6 Oc '17.

39. M to Oxman, 17 Je '29.

40. Mary Gallagher to M, 22 D '28.

41. Mrs. Charles Anderson to M, 1 Jan '33.

42. *Chr,* 23 Jl '31.

43. Rena Mooney to Ed Nockels, 28 F '22.

44. Emma Goldman, *Living My Life,* II: 591–622, 627–29.

45. *Exmr,* 28 Je, 14 Jl '17; *Chr,* 6, 12, 19, 20 Jl '17; M to Walsh, 21 Mr '36, Walsh P.

46. *Call,* 20 Jl '17; NY *Call,* 9 S '17.

47. *Call,* 8 Au, 11, 12 S '17; [NY] Trade-Union Conference for the Defense of the California Labor Cases, "A Call for Immediate Action in the Mooney Appeal," cir-

cular letter, 17 S '17, in MP (Scrapbook); Lang, *Tomorrow Is Beautiful*, 114–15, 118–19; Goldman, *Living My Life*, II: 630–39; NY *Call*, 2 Oc '17.

48. NY *Call*, 25 S '17, 2 Oc '17; Charles M. Travis to Walter Lippmann, 2 Oc '17, in Nat Archives, RG 174, file 16/510. See also Drinnon, *Rebel in Paradise*, 181.

49. *Chr*, 3 Oc '17; *Chicago Labor News*, 25 Jan '18.

50. *Bul*, 1, 9 Oc '17; *News*, 8 Oc '17; *Call*, 9, 15, 16 Oc '17; *Chr*, 17, 18, 20, 23 Oc '17.

51. *People v. Weinberg*, I: 7–22; *Call*, 23 Oc '17; *Chr*, 24 Oc '17.

52. *Exmr*, 25, 30 Oc '17; *Bul, Call*, 29 Oc '17; *Chr*, 30 Oc '17.

53. *Call*, 31 Oc '17; *Exmr*, 24 Oc '17; Older testimony, Cal S Ct, "In re Billings," III: 1591ff.

54. *Bul*, 7 N '17; *Chr*, 8 N '17.

55. *People v. Weinberg*, I: 560–63.

56. *Ibid.*, II: 946–50, 1036.

57. *Ibid.*, 1019–20, 1029–30.

58. *Call*, 27 N '17.

59. Langdon E. Boyle, as quoted in *Chr*, 28 N '17.

60. As quoted, *Chr, Exmr*, 28 N '17.

61. *Bul*, 28 N, 1 D '17.

62. *News*, 5 D '17.

63. *Call*, 29 N '17.

64. *Bul*, 5 D '17.

65. As quoted, *Call*, 5 D '17. This is a newspaper reporter's version; Dunne prohibited the court stenographer from writing up his notes for the press. There are slight variations in *Bul*, 5 D '17, and *Exmr* and *Chr*, 6 D '17.

66. *Bul*, 8 D '17; *Chr*, 6, 9 D '17, 10 Jan '18.

67. *Bul*, 2, 6, 13, 26 F '18; *Call*, 11, 25 F '18; *Exmr*, 14 F '18.

68. *Chr*, 2 Mr '18; *Bul, News*, 18 Mr '18.

69. *Call*, 21 Mr '18.

70. *Call*, 22 Mr '18. Since the *Call* was the only paper that picked up the quip, there may be some doubt of its authenticity.

71. E.g., Weinberg testimony, House of Representatives, Committee on the Judiciary, 75th Congr., 3d Sess. (1938), *Tom Mooney: Hearings Before Subcommittee No. 1 . . .*, 52–62.

72. *Bul*, 16 Mr '18; *Chr*, 25, 26, 28, 31 Mr '18; *Call*, 26, 30 Mr '18.

XVI   Fickert Faces Recall

1. *Chr*, 24 Ap '17; *Exmr*, 24, 28 Ap '17; *Call*, 24, 25 Ap '17; *Crocker-Langley San Francisco Directory, 1917*, 232; *California Outlook*, Dec. 1917; *Bul*, 26 Ap '17.

2. *News*, 28 Ap, 10 My, 6 Je '17; *Exmr*, 29 Ap, 8 My '17; *Call*, 5 My '17.

3. *Call*, 21 Jl '17.

4. *Bul, News*, 28 Ap '17; all SF dailies and *Labor Clarion*, My–Je '17, *passim*; J. G. Lawlor to Bourke Cockran, 25 My '17, in Cockran P.

5. *News, Bul*, 21 Jl '17.

6. As quoted, *Call*, 21 Jl '17.

7. *Bul*, 25 Jl, 8, 21 Au, 18 S '17; *Chr*, 29 Jl, 3, 10, 31 Au, 5 S '17, 8 Jan '18; *News*, 1, 2 Au, 22 S, 11 D '17; *Exmr*, 2, 7, 8, 16, 17, 26 Au, 1, 29 S '17, 20 Jan '18; *Call*, 29 S, 13 D '17.

8. *Exmr*, 31 Au, 3 Oc '17; *News*, 22 S '17.

9. *Who's Who in America, 1916–1917*; *News*, 8 Oc '17; Haynes, as quoted in Los Angeles *Tribune*, 14 Oc, *Bul*, 10 Oc, and *News*, 11 Oc '17.

10. *Bul*, 29 S '17; *News*, 11 Oc '17; Los Angeles *Tribune*, 14 Oc '17.

11. *Bul*, 20, 26 Oc '17; *Chr*, 21, 25 Oc '17; Oakland *Tribune*, 24 Oc '17; *Exmr*, 25 Oc '17.

12. As quoted, *Call*, 26 Oc '17. See also *Labor Clarion*, 2 N '17.

13. *Labor Clarion*, 2 N '17; *Call*, 6 N '17; *Exmr*, 9 N '17; *News*, 8 N '17.

14. *Call*, 13, 16 Au, 13 N '17.

15. Franklin Hichborn, in *Bul*, 10 D '17; Hichborn, "California Politics," III: 1576–77, 1588. See also Paul Smith statement, *Call*, 16 Au '17.

16. *Exmr*, 13 N '17.

17. Rowell to Julia George, 6 Oc '17, Rowell P.

18. *Bul*, 17 D '17.

19. *Town Talk*, 8 Jan '16, 14 Jl '17; *Webster's Biographical Dictionary* (1943), 1294; *Bul*, 23 N '17; Hanlon to Moore, 15 N '17, in *Call*, 23 N '17.

20. Quoted in Howard Lawrence Hurwitz, *Theodore Roosevelt and Labor in New York State, 1880–1900* (1943), 283.

21. Theodore Roosevelt, *Autobiography* (1913), 532. See also Henry F. Pringle, *Theodore Roosevelt, A Biography* (1931), 111, 153.

22. Roosevelt to Fickert, 17 N '17, in possession of Ruth Fickert Pitt.

23. *Call*, 20 N '17.

24. *Call*, 19 N '17.

25. As quoted, *ibid.*

26. Moore to Paul Smith, 20 N '17, in *Call*, 21 N '17.

27. As quoted, *Call*, 22 N '17.

28. As quoted, *Bul*, 22 N '17.

29. *Exmr*, 4 D '17.

30. Joseph R. Tobin to Roosevelt, 22 N '17, Rowell P.

31. Roosevelt to Rowell, 23 N '17, Rowell P.

32. Roosevelt to Rowell, 12 D '17, in Elting E. Morison, ed., *Letters of Theodore Roosevelt* (1951), VIII: 1260.

33. *California Outlook*, Jan. 1918; *Bul*, 17 D '17; *News*, 13 D '17; SF *News Letter*, 8 D '17.

34. *Exmr*, 8 D '17; M to Walsh, 23 Mr '18, Walsh P.

35. As quoted, *Bul*, 7, 8 D '17.

36. *Exmr*, 5 D '17.

37. *Call*, 13, 17 D '17.

38. *Chr, Exmr*, 19 D '17.

39. *Call*, 21 D '17.

40. *Chr*, 19 D '17; *Town Talk*, 22 D '17; *Retail Grocers' Advocate*, 21 D '17.

41. *Chr*, 5, 10, 11 D '17; *California Outlook*, Jan. 1918; *Labor Clarion*, 14 D '17; *Call*, 19 D '17; *Coast Seamen's Journal*, 16 Jan '18; Hichborn, "California Politics," III: 1595; Robert Knight, *Industrial Relations in the San Francisco Bay Area*, 349.

42. *Bul*, 19 D '17.

43. Sacramento *Bee*, 19 D '17; *Chr*, 21 D '17.

44. Sacramento *Bee*, 19 D '17 and 1913–17, *passim*; Sacramento *Union* and *Star*, 1916–17, *passim*; *Chr*, 18–30 D '17, 3 Jan '18; *Call*, 18, 24 D '17.

45. *Chr*, 19 D '17.

46. *Chr*, 23, 25 D '17, 6 Jan '18; Sacramento *Bee*, 8, 16 F '18.

47. IWW report to E. S. Doree, IWW national secretary, in *Chr*, 30 D '17.

48. *Call*, 24 D '17; *Chr*, 25, 28–30 D '17; Sacramento *Bee*, 5, 8, F '18; H. C. Peterson and Gilbert C. Fite, *Opponents of War, 1917–1918* (1957), 177–78, 244, 245. See also Harvey Duff, *Silent Defenders: Courts and Capitalism in California* (1919); and Philip Taft, "The Federal Trials of the IWW," *Labor History*, Winter 1962, 76–79.

XVII   The Labor Defense Movement, 1917

EPIGRAPH: A. J. Rogers to U. S. Webb, 26 Jl '17, in Cal State Archives, Atty Gen Records, Box 222.

1. Taft, *A. F. of L. in the Time of Gompers*, 385, 453. See also Eugene Staley, *History of the Illinois State Federation of Labor* (1930), 362–63. On Fitzpatrick see Stolberg, *Tailor's Progress*, 143.

2. *Chicago Labor News*, 5 Jan '17.

3. *Ibid.*; Lang, *Tomorrow Is Beautiful*, 100–106.

4. Cockran to M, 11 F '17, in M P; *Chicago Labor News*, 23 F '17; Nockels to Cockran, 19 F '17 and 8 Mr '17, in Cockran P.

5. NY *Call*, 12 Mr '17; NY *Irish World*, 24 Mr '17; Cockran to Nockels, 27 F '17, and Cockran to M, 30 Mr '17, in Cockran P.

6. Cockran to M, 30 Mr '17, and Mooney form letters to IMU and streetcar locals, 17 Ap '17, in Cockran P; Oakland *Tri-City Labor Review*, 30 Mr '17; Chicago *Tribune*, 26 Mr '17.

7. Cockran to M, 30 Mr '17, M to Nockels, Cockran, *et al.*, 3 Ap '17, and Louise D. Harding to Cockran, 9 Ap '17, all in Cockran P.

8. Gompers to Cockran, 21 Mr '17, Cockran to M, 30 Ap '17, and Cockran to McNutt, 4 Ap '17, all in Cockran P; Frederic L. Paxson, *American Democracy and the World War: America at War, 1917–1918* (1939), 20, 25, 28.

9. Cockran to McNutt, 4 Ap '17, Cockran P.

10. Cockran to M, 20 My '17, Cockran P (Letterbook). See also Cockran to Mulholland, 13 Ap '17, Cockran P.

11. Cockran to Nockels, 28 Mr '17, in Cockran P (Letterbook); Felix Frankfurter, *Felix Frankfurter Reminisces* (1960), 122, 127.

12. Gompers to John O'Connell, in *Labor Clarion*, 18 My '17; William C. Fitts to Rep. Carl Hayden, 22 My '17, in Nat Archives, RG 60, file 185354.

13. Draft of a resolution for the House of Representatives, 1917, Walsh P.

14. John W. Preston to Gregory, 6 Je '17, Nat Archives, RG 60, file 185354.

15. Gompers to Cockran, 10 My '17, Cockran P.

16. Cockran to M, 20 My '17, Cockran P (Letterbook).

17. Draft of a bill, 1917, Walsh P.

18. Walsh to M, 23 Je '17, Walsh P.

19. Draft of res. for H. R., 1917, Walsh P.

20. Walsh to M, 23 Je '17, Nockels to Older, 1 Je '17, Walsh to M, 30 My '17, Nockels and Furuseth to Older, 30 My '17, and Nockels to Walsh, 11 Je '17, all in Walsh P; Louise D. Harding to Cockran,

9 Ap '17, in Cockran P; *Congressional Record,* 65th Congr., 1st Sess., v. 55:3, p. 3253, and v. 55:8, "History of Bills and Resolutions," p. 112.

21. Walsh to M, 23 Je '17, Walsh P.

22. Walsh to Nockels, 16 Je '17, and Walsh to M, 23 Je '17, in Walsh P; *Congressional Record,* 65th Congr., 1st Sess., v. 55: index and *passim.*

23. *Coast Seamen's Journal,* Aug. 1916–Apr. 1917.

24. *Ibid.,* 17 Jan '17; *Bul,* 18 Jan '17; SF C of C, "Law and Order in San Francisco," 20–40.

25. *Coast Seamen's Journal,* 21 F, 25 Ap '17, and *passim,* Apr.–Jl. '17.

26. Labor Council minutes, meetings of 17, 24 N '16, in *Labor Clarion,* 24 N, 1 D '16.

27. *Bul,* 29 Mr '16; Knight, *Industrial Relations in the San Francisco Bay Area,* 348; Louise D. Harding to Cockran, 23 F '17, Cockran P.

28. *Labor Clarion,* 23 F, 6, 27 Ap, 3 Au, 5 Oc '17.

29. *Labor Clarion,* 11 My '17; *Bul,* 7 Ap '17; IWDL, "Financial Statement . . . August 1916 to January 1918," in MP (Scrapbook).

30. Older to Nockels, 9 Je '17, Walsh P.

31. A. W. Brouillet to Older, 20 Au '17, in *Labor Clarion,* 24 Au '17. See also *Bul,* 9, 21 Au '17.

32. As quoted, Sacramento *Bee,* 5 Oc '17.

33. *Bul,* 5 Oc '17. See also Sacramento *Union,* 5 Oc '17.

34. As quoted, Sacramento *Bee,* 5 Oc '17.

35. As quoted, *Bul,* 5 Oc '17.

36. *Ibid.*

37. Labor Council minutes for meetings of 12 Oc–7 D '17, in *Labor Clarion,* 19 Oc–14 D '17; Louise D. Harding to Cockran, 23 F '17, in Cockran P. Haggerty was a member of Nolan's union. See also SF *News Letter,* 27 Oc '17, 3 N '17; Knight, *Industrial Relations in the San Francisco Bay Area,* 348.

38. Nat Archives, RG 60, file 185354.

39. NY *Call,* 8 Mr '17.

40. Nat Archives, RG 60, file 185354. See also *Bul,* 2 Mr '17, and *Exmr,* 10 Mr '17.

41. Resolution as quoted, *International Socialist Review,* July 1917.

42. H. B. Brawn [*sic*] (secretary, Maine State F of L), to Cockran, 19 Je '17, in Cockran P.

43. *Railway Federationist,* 8 D '17.

44. Newark *Union Labor Bulletin,* Feb. 1917.

45. IWDL, "Financial Statement, 1916–18," 25.

46. *Union Labor Bulletin,* May 1917.

47. Michael Gannon, "A Personal View," in *ibid.*

48. *Union Labor Bulletin,* June, July 1917; Newark *News,* undated clipping [June? 1917], in MP (Scrapbook).

49. *Union Labor Bulletin,* Mar., Aug., Sept., Dec., 1918.

50. *Exmr,* 22 Au '16.

51. Minor to Cockran, 26 Ap '17, Cockran P.

52. IWDL, "Financial Statement, 1916–18," *passim.*

53. *Ibid.*

54. *Ibid.,* 57–62.

55. M to Cockran, 3 Ap '17, and Cockran to Minor, 21 Ap '17, both in Cockran P.

56. Minor to Cockran, 7 Ap '17, Cockran P.

57. Minor to Cockran, 26 Ap '17, Cockran P.

58. *Labor Clarion,* 16 Mr '17.

59. *Appeal to Reason,* 20 Oc '17.

60. M to Walsh, 18 Au '18, Walsh P.

61. Nolan to Cockran, 20 Mr '17, in Cockran P; IWDL, "Financial Statement, 1916–18," 60; Joliet, Illinois, *Herald-News,* 14 Oc '17.

62. IWDL, "Financial Statement, 1916–18," 60–61; Stockton *Record,* 23 Ap '17; Sacramento *Union,* 26 Ap '17; Martinez *Standard,* 28 Ap '14; Oakland *Tri-City Labor Review,* 18 Au, 3 N '16, 11 My '17; Oakland *World,* 24 N '16; Los Angeles *Citizen,* 15, 22 Je '17; San Jose *Mercury-Herald,* 12 Ap '17; Modesto *Herald,* 2 My '17.

63. Chicago *American,* 24 N '17; Chicago *Examiner,* 24 N '17; White House memorandum, 23 N '17, in Woodrow Wilson P, Series VI, file 4261.

64. *Chr.* 20, 21 Ap '18; *Bul,* 25 Ap '18. The NY *Call,* 22 Je '18, indicates that another IWDL representative, William D. Patterson, was threatened or assaulted in Iowa.

65. Marc Karson, *American Labor Unions and Politics, 1900–1918* (1958), 141–43; American Federation of Labor, *Report of the Proceedings of the . . . Annual Convention* (1916–18), v. 36: 192, 231, 348; v. 37: 459–61; v. 38: 325–26; Taft, *A. F. of L. in the Time of Gompers,* 278–85, 374–76.

XVIII   Petrograd and Washington

EPIGRAPHS: Both letters are in Cal State Archives, Gov's Off. Morison's letter is misdated as April 5, 1917.

1. Isaac Deutscher, *The Prophet Armed: Trotsky, 1879–1921* (1956), 246; Thomas J. Tunney, *Throttled! The Detection of the German and Anarchist Bomb Plotters* (1919), 269.

2. Emma Goldman, *Living My Life*, II: 562, 595–96; Frederick R. Wedge, *Inside the I.W.W.* (1924), 35; NY *Call*, 3, 26 D '16; Edgar Sisson, *One Hundred Red Days* (1931), 342; William Hard, *Raymond Robins' Own Story* (1920) 188–89. See also Albert Rhys Williams, *Through the Russian Revolution* (1921), 117.

3. Los Angeles *Times*, 18 Au '18; *Call*, 22 Mr '22.

4. Francis gave four accounts of the affair, each one varying slightly from the others. In chronological order they are: Francis to Lansing, 24 Ap '17, in Nat Archives, RG 59, 124.61/11; Francis, "Private News Letter," 24 Ap '17, paraphrasing "R.V." [Petrograd *Russkaya Volya*?], in Francis P; U. S. Sen. Judiciary Subcommittee, 65th Congr., 3d Sess., *Bolshevik Propaganda . . .* (1919), 961–62; and David R. Francis, *Russia from the American Embassy* (1921), 101–2.

5. Francis to Lansing, 24 Ap '17, in Nat Archives, RG 59, 124.61/11.

6. Lansing to Francis, 30 Ap '17, *ibid.*

7. Francis, *Russia from the American Embassy*, 105.

8. NY *Times*, 15, 25 Ap '17. See also Sacramento *Union*, 25 Ap '17.

9. NY *World*, 26 Ap '17.

10. Upton Sinclair, *The Brass Check: A Study of American Journalism* (1931 ed.), 352.

11. NY *Tribune*, 3 Je '17. The demonstration was also reported in the NY *Sun*, NY *World*, and NY *Globe*, all 25 Ap '17. See also Philadelphia *Public Ledger*, 24 S '17.

12. NY *Times*, 27 Ap '17.

13. Gompers to Cockran, 10 My '17, Cockran P.

14. Ray Stannard Baker, *Woodrow Wilson, Life and Letters* (1927–39), VII: 65–66.

15. Stephens to Wilson, 11 My '17, in Woodrow Wilson P, Series VI, file 4261.

16. Baker, *Wilson*, VII: 66n.

17. Lawlor to Cockran, 1 S '17, in Cockran P. See also M. E. Fitzgerald to Cockran, 26 S '17, in Cockran P.

18. U. S. Dept. of State, *Foreign Relations: 1918: Russia*, I: 146; Philadelphia *Public Ledger*, 24 S '17; Sacramento *Star*, 4 Oc '17.

19. F. L. Paxson, *America at War: 1917–1918*, 169; Preston William Slosson, *Great Crusade and After, 1914–1928* (1930), 68; Frankfurter, *Felix Frankfurter Reminisces*, 118–19; *New Republic*, 21 Jl '17, 320–22, 22 S '17, 215–17, 29 S '17, 242–44, and 8 D '17, 140; *Survey*, 8 D '17, 291–92; Council of Nat Defense minutes, 25 Au '17, in Wm B. Wilson P. On the importance of Sitka spruce in airplane construction, see Harold Hyman, *Soldiers and Spruce* (1963), 43–44.

20. *Nation*, 28 F '18, 235; Gompers to Woodrow Wilson, 2, 10 Au '17, in Gompers Corres. (Letterbook, v. 236); nine other letters from Gompers to C. L. Myers, Wm B. Wilson, Thomas A. French, David C. Coates, C. O. Edwards, Claude O. Taylor, William H. Johnston, and John G. Riege, 17–31 Au '17, in Gompers Corres. (Letterbook, v. 237, 238); Council of Nat Defense minutes, 12, 18 Jl, 1, 25, 29 Au '17, in Wm B. Wilson P; Wm B. Wilson to Woodrow Wilson, 31 Au '17, in Woodrow Wilson P.

21. Frankfurter to E. M. House, 1 S '17, House P.

22. Frankfurter to House, 4 S '17, House P.

23. Wm B. Wilson to Woodrow Wilson, 31 Au '17, in Woodrow Wilson P, Series II; Council of Nat Defense minutes, 1 Au '17, in Wm B. Wilson P; Gompers to Wm B. Wilson, 27 Au '17, in Gompers Corres. (Letterbook, v. 237); J. L. Spangler to Wm B. Wilson, 12 My '17, in Wm B. Wilson P, Series V, file 142.

24. Presidential order, 19 S '17, in Nat Archives, RG 174, file 20/473.

25. E. M. House diary, 20 S '17 (XI: 285), in House P; Berkman later believed that House went to Albany at the President's request to see Governor Whitman, but there is no note of that in House's diary or letters. Berkman to J. Cohen, 26 N '30, in Berkman Papers, Bundle II (International Institute for Social History, Amsterdam), courtesy of Richard Drinnon.

26. Morgan to House, 20 S '17, House P.

27. As spelled, House to Woodrow Wilson, 21 S '17, House P.

28. Philadelphia *Public Ledger*, 24, 25 S '17.

29. Woodrow Wilson to Gregory, 24 S '17, in Baker, *Wilson*, VII: 282. See also House diary, 26 S '17 (XII: 293), in House Papers: "The President is . . . having an investigation made of the Thos. J. Mooney case in San Francisco as I advised."

30. Among them the NY *Globe, Post, World*, and *Evening Mail*, the Springfield *Republican*, and the Philadelphia *Public Ledger*.

31. *Chr*, 4 Oc '17.

32. *Argonaut*, 6 Oc '17.

33. Philadelphia *Public Ledger*, 26 S '17.

34. Preston to Gregory, 15 Oc, 9 N '17, and Gregory to Woodrow Wilson, 17 N '17, all in Nat Archives, RG 174, 16/510.

35. Sacramento *Bee*, 31 Au '17.

36. Memorandum, Wm B. Wilson to Woodrow Wilson, 31 Au '17, in Woodrow Wilson P, Series II.

37. *Ibid.*; *Chr*, 10 N '17; Frankfurter, *Felix Frankfurter Reminisces*, 117; J. L. Spangler to Wm B. Wilson, 18 F '16 and 12 My '17, in Wm B. Wilson P, Series V, file 142; broadside for Spangler genealogical reunion, same file.

38. Frankfurter to Stanley King, 25 Oc '17, in Nat Archives, RG 174, box 193; Denver *Labor Bulletin*, 9 Je '17; Sacramento *Union*, 28 S '17.

39. Frankfurter, *Felix Frankfurter Reminisces*, 96–97, 123, 124, 146; Archibald MacLeish and E. F. Prichard, Jr., eds., *Law and Politics: Occasional Papers of Felix Frankfurter, 1913–1938* (1939), introd.; *Chr*, 10 N '17; Frankfurter testimony, U. S. Sen., 76th Congr., 1st Sess. (1939), *Hearings on the Nomination of Felix Frankfurter*, 114.

40. See Louis B. Wehle, *Hidden Threads of History: Wilson through Roosevelt* (1953), 54.

41. *Chr, Exmr*, 10 N '17.

42. As quoted, Sacramento *Union*, 11 N '17.

43. Preston to Gregory, 9 N '17, in Nat Archives, RG 174, file 16/510.

44. G. S. Arnold to Frankfurter, 31 D '17, in Nat Archives, RG 174, file 20/473. An excerpt from this letter, p. 248n above, indicates Arnold's impartiality. See also McNutt, *Before the Special Commission*, and Bourke Cockran, *To the Commissioners Appointed by the President to Investigate the Conditions Under Which Thomas J. Mooney Was Convicted of Murder . . .* [Nov. 1917].

45. *Call*, 10 N '17.

46. G. S. Arnold to Gov. Stephens, 15 Ap '18, in *Bul*, 30 Ap '18.

47. *New Republic*, 18 Jan '22, 220, 221.

48. Wm B. Wilson to Agnes Hart Wilson, 24 N '17, in Wm B. Wilson P, Series V, folder 4-C; Frankfurter, *Felix Frankfurter Reminisces*, 127, 131; U. S. Committee on Public Information, *Official Bulletin*, 28 Jan '18, 15; Wm B. Wilson to Woodrow Wilson, 22 Jan '18, in Nat Archives, RG 174, file 16/510A.

49. "Report on the Mooney Dynamite Cases in San Francisco Submitted by President Wilson's Mediation Commission," in U. S. Committee on Public Information, *Official Bulletin*, 28 Jan '18, 14–15.

50. Woodrow Wilson to Stephens, 22 Jan '18, in Baker, *Wilson*, VII: 488–89.

51. Baker, VII: 489n; Stephens to Wilson, 30 Jan '18, in Woodrow Wilson P, Series VI, file 4261.

52. White House memorandum, 23 Jan '18, *ibid.*

53. Memorandum, Tumulty to Woodrow Wilson, 23 Jan '18, *ibid.*

54. Attached note on *ibid.*

55. Albert Rhys Williams, "The Spirit of Internationalism," in Socialist Publication Society, *One Year* (n.d. [1918]), 19–20; Francis to Lansing, 29 S '17 and 1 Oc '17, in Nat Archives, RG 59, 861.00/564 and /567; Francis, *Russia from the American Embassy*, 136, 165–67; Granville Hicks, *John Reed* (1936), 256–60. These sources mention only Berkman, but Louise Bryant, who was there, stated that the meeting was in Mooney's behalf. Seattle *Union Record*, 30 Jan '19. See also Goldman, *Living My Life*, II: 638.

56. Hicks, *Reed*, 280; *News*, 8 Ap '19; Francis testimony, U. S. Sen. Judiciary Subcommittee, 65th Congr., 3d Sess., *Bolshevik Propaganda*, 961–62.

57. George F. Kennan, *Soviet-American Relations, 1917–1920: Russia Leaves the War* (1956), 356.

58. As quoted in Francis to Lansing, 19 Jan '18, in U.S. Dept. of State, *Foreign Relations: 1918: Russia*, I: 353–54.

59. *Ibid.*

60. Kennan, *Russia Leaves the War*, 357–58; Francis, *Russia from the American Embassy*, 209–10.

61. Kennan, 403.

62. Sisson, *One Hundred Red Days*, 283. On Sisson, see Kennan, 50–52 and *passim*.

63. Stockton *Record*, 30 Jan '18.

64. Kennan, 430–37, 509–16.

65. Wm B. Wilson to Gompers, 3 Ap '18, in Nat Archives, RG 174, file 16/510. In February the Secretary of Labor wrote the President: "The failure to dispose of the cases . . . is having an unwholesome effect upon Labor of the Pacific Coast." Wm B. Wilson to Woodrow Wilson, 23 F '18, *ibid.*

66. Lane to Woodrow Wilson, 26 Mar '18; Wilson to Stephens, 27 Mr '18; Stephens to Wilson, 30 Mr '18, all in Woodrow Wilson P, Series VI, file 4261.

67. Oakland *World,* 29 Je '17; Morgan to House, 20 S '17, in House P.

68. NY *Times,* 27 Au '31; Shaw as quoted, IWDL Newsletter #26 [Dec.(?) 1917].

69. Lansing to Woodrow Wilson, 23 My '18, and memorandum, Wilson to Lansing, 24 My '18, in Woodrow Wilson P, Series VI, file 4261.

70. Page to Lansing, 16 My '18, in Nat Archives, RG 174, box 57, file 16/510D. He reported that the British requests were inspired by AFL action on the case.

71. Nat Archives: RG 174, box 57, file 16/510E; RG 60, file 185354; and RG 59, 311.1121/51. See also *Call,* 6 Au '18.

72. *News,* 3 Jl '18; Oakland *Tri-City Labor Review,* 28 Je '18.

73. Nat Archives, RG 174, box 57, file 16/510E.

74. *Christian Science Monitor,* 28 Je '18; Oakland *Tri-City Labor Review,* 28 Je '18; *News,* 8 Je, 12 Oc '18; *Call,* 15 Oc '18.

75. *Bul, Call,* 27 Au '18.

76. *Call,* 5 Oc '18.

77. Memorandum, Lansing to Woodrow Wilson, 13 S '18, in Woodrow Wilson P, Series VI, file 4261.

78. Frankfurter to Arnold, 1 Ap '18, and Arnold to Frankfurter, 4 Ap '18, in Nat Archives, RG 174, files 20/473 and 16/510; *New Republic,* 18 Jan '22, 222; Arnold to Gov. Stephens, 15 Ap '18, in Nat Archives, RG 174, file 20/473.

79. *Wasp,* 2 F '18; Los Angeles *Times,* 31 Jan '18.

80. As quoted, *Exmr,* 27 Jan '18 and *Bul,* 29 Jan '18.

81. Sacramento *Bee,* 28 Jan '18.

82. Fickert to Woodrow Wilson, 16 F '18, in Woodrow Wilson P, Series VI, file 4261; *Exmr,* 17 Mr '18; *Labor Clarion,* 12 Ap '18; *Chr,* 13 Ap '18.

83. Cf. issues of the *Blast* and original parade threat note in Older P.

84. C. M. Fickert, "In the Matter of the Investigation of the Case of The People vs. Thomas J. Mooney et al., by the United States Commission on Mediation: Brief of The People of the State of California" (n.d. [1918]), 3–4, 5–6, 8, 24, 61, 62.

85. *Ibid.,* 109–16.

86. Frankfurter to Arnold, 3 Ap '18; Arnold to Frankfurter, 4 Ap '18; Frankfurter to Wm B. Wilson, 5 Ap '18, and Wilson's endorsement of same, all in Nat Archives, RG 174, file 16/510.

87. *Bul,* 30 Ap '18; *Exmr, Call,* 1 My '18.

88. Fickert to Stephens, 30 Ap '18, **in Nat** Archives, RG 174, file 16/510.

89. Maxwell McNutt, *Before the Governor of the State of California: Reply of Thomas J. Mooney to Brief Filed by District Attorney of . . . San Francisco Against Petition for Pardon* (1918), 1; Fickert, *Before the Governor in re Application of Mooney for a Pardon,* 109–10; *Chr,* 26 Jl '18.

90. M. C. Sloss to Frankfurter, 26 Jl '18, in Nat Archives, RG 174, file 20/473; *Bul,* 30 Jl '18.

91. As quoted, *News,* 26 Jl '18.

92. *Bul,* 27 Jl '18.

93. *New Republic,* 3 Au '18.

XIX From Intervention to Commutation

EPIGRAPH: In the records of the Cal Dept of Corrections.

1. *People v. Mooney, Appellant's Opening Brief* (1917), 42, 69–72.

2. Shaw to John R. Haynes, 23 Au '29, in Cal State Archives, Gov's Off.

3. Author's interview, Justice Raymond E. Peters, 25 My '65.

4. *Call,* 2 Mr '18; *Exmr,* 4 Mr '18; *Chr,* 2, 4 Mr '18; Fickert, *Before the Governor in re Application of Mooney for a Pardon,* 11–21; *Call,* 10 Je '18.

5. Oakland *Enquirer,* 2 Mr '18; *Bul,* 1, 5, 19 Mr, 2 Ap '18; Sacramento *Bee,* 4 Ap '18.

6. Woodrow Wilson to J. H. Beckmeyer, 18 Ap '18, in *Exmr,* 25 Ap '18.

7. As quoted, *News,* 25 Ap '18.

8. As quoted, *News,* 3 Ap '18.

9. Abraham L. Freedman, "The Writ of Coram Nobis," *Temple Law Quarterly,* III (1928–29); 370–71 [citations omitted].

10. *Sanders v. State* (85 Ind. 318). This was the leading criminal case in which the writ had been applied in a state court. See Freedman, 373ff.

11. *People v. Mooney: Arguments of Counsel on Motion for a Writ of Coram Nobis* (1918), 1–86, typescript, MP.

12. Griffin's decision is in SF Superior Court, "People v. Mooney, Opinion of the Court on the Demurrer of the People to the Amended Petition for a Writ of Audita Querela" (1921), flyleaf, in MP, Legal Documents, v. 40.

13. As quoted, *Bul*, 21 My '18.

14. *Bul*, 22 Jl '18; *People v. Mooney*, 178 Cal 525–28 (1918).

15. George H. Tinkham, *History of Stanislaus County, California* (1921), 465; Modesto *Evening News*, 13 Jl '18, 3 F '19; William J. Brown (Hindman's law partner) to the author, 14 Ap '58.

16. Jay A. Hindman, "The Mooney Case," *American Law Review* LII (1918): 743–76.

17. H. Brett Melendy and Benjamin F. Gilbert, *The Governors of California: Peter H. Burnett to Edmund G. Brown* (1965), 322–33; Mowry, *California Progressives*, 117, 279–83; Hiram Johnson to Joseph Scott, 23 Mr '17, in Johnson P; Kent, quoted in Russell M. Posner, "State Politics and the Bank of America, 1920–1934," Ph.D. diss., Univ. of Calif., Berkeley (1956), 147; Rowell to Hiram Johnson, 24 Mr '17, in Johnson P; Hichborn, "California Politics," III: 1519, 1927.

18. *Bul*, 28 My, 17 Jl '18.

19. *Chr*, 6, 13 Je '18.

20. *Bul*, 6 Je '18.

21. *Bul*, 27 Jl '18; Richard H. Frost, "The Mooney Case in California Politics," M.A. thesis, Univ. of Calif., Berkeley (1954), ch. 3.

22. NY *American*, 14 Mr '18.

23. *Bul*, 21 Mr '18.

24. *Call*, 17 Au '18; Older, *Growing Up*, 156–58; Wells, *Older*, 306; Ed Nolan to Bourke Cockran, 2 My '17, in Cockran P; Duffus, *Tower of Jewels*, 240.

25. Author's interview, Edgar T. Gleeson, 6 F '60; Oakland *Enquirer*, 31 Jl '18.

26. Author's interview, Robert L. Duffus, 14 Je '62.

27. Wells, *Older*, 308.

28. Author's interview, Sara Bard Field, 18 S '59.

29. Wells, *Older*, 307, 315.

30. Author's interview, Edgar T. Gleeson, 6 F '60; Oakland *Enquirer*, 31 Jl '18.

31. Author's interview, Sara Bard Field, 18 S '59.

32. See *Public*, 10 Au '18; Sacramento *Bee*, 19 Au '18.

33. See Hearst to Older, 2 Jan, 30 Ap '19, Older P.

34. *Bul*, 23, 25 Jl '18; Chicago *American*, 29 Jl '18.

35. *Bul*, 29 Jl '18.

36. Sacramento *Bee*, 5, 12 Au '18.

37. Cockran to M, 5 Jl '18, N. A. James to Cockran, 18 Jl '18, John D. Barry to Cockran, 24 Jl '18, and Cockran memorial to Woodrow Wilson, 8 Au '18, all in Cockran P; Woodrow Wilson–Tumulty memoranda, 17, 22, 23 Jl '18, in Woodrow Wilson P, Series VI, file 4261; Lang, *Tomorrow Is Beautiful*, 131–34.

38. See Sacramento *Union*, 28 Jl '18, and Stockton *Record*, 1, 13, 17 Au '18.

39. *News*, 20 Au '18.

40. Sacramento *Bee*, 18 Oc '18.

41. Los Angeles *Times*, 28 Jl '18.

42. *Exmr*, 28 Jl '18.

43. M to Woodrow Wilson, 29 Ap '18, in Woodrow Wilson P, Series VI, file 4261.

44. *Bul*, 18 N '18; 248 U.S. 579.

45. *Call, News*, 19 N '18.

46. *Bul*, 19, 21 N '18.

47. *Bul*, 19, 21, 23, 26 N '18; *News*, 19, 20 N '18; Oakland *World*, 22, 29 N '18; San Jose *Mercury*, 20, 21, 27 N '18; *Exmr*, 28 N '18; Oakland *Tri-City Labor Review*, 29 N '18. See also Robert L. Friedheim, *Seattle General Strike* (1964), 81–82.

48. Griffin to Stephens, 19 N '18, in *Bul*, 21 N '18.

49. *Bul*, 27 N '18; *Call*, 28 N '18.

50. *Densmore Report*, 2, 6, 7, 19; Parson to Older, 17 F '21, and McCarthy to C. C. Young, 10 S '29, in Mooney Collection, NY Pub. Libr.

51. Parson, as quoted by Older in *Growing Up*, 160.

52. *Densmore Report*, 26, 27.

53. *Ibid.*, 33.

54. *Ibid.*, 19.

55. *Ibid.*

56. Edgar T. Gleeson interview of Mrs. Judd, 31 Oc '18, in *Densmore Report*, 88–90.

57. Older, *My Own Story* (1925 ed.), 111–14; *Densmore Report*, 33, 50, 55, 76–88; *Call*, 23 N '18.

58. *Call, Exmr, Bul*, 23 N '18; *Town Talk*, 30 N '18.

59. *Bul*, 23 N '18.

60. *Chr*, 25 N '18.

61. *Densmore Report*, 75.

62. *Ibid.*, 4.

63. *Ibid.*, 6.

64. Sacramento *Bee*, 25 N '18. See also SF *News Letter*, 30 N '18.

65. As quoted, *Exmr*, 29 N '18.

66. *Ibid.*

67. *Call*, 4 D '18.

68. Stockton *Record*, 29 N '18.

69. *Call*, 4 D '18.

70. Judge George A. Sturtevant to Stephens, 16 D '18, in Cal State Archives, Gov's Off; *Exmr*, 29 N '18; Stockton *Record*, 13 Au, 29 N '18; Sacramento *Union*, 30 N '18.

71. Stephens to George A. Sturtevant, 20 D '18, in Cal State Archives, Gov's Off.

72. 2 D '18, Cockran P.

73. *Survey*, 7 D '18.

74. Walsh as quoted, *Call*, 2 D '18; M as quoted, *News*, 29 N '18.

xx Mooney and the Red Scare, 1919

EPIGRAPHS: R. W. Anderson to Wm B. Wilson, in Nat Archives, RG 174, 16/510 F; Robert Hunter, "The General Strike," reprinted from *National Socialist* in *Labor Clarion*, 14 F '13.

1. *Liberator*, Mar. 1919, 20.

2. *Exmr*, 3 D '18; NY *Call*, 20 D '18; Seattle *Union Record*, 28 N '18; *Bul*, 26 N, 9 D '18; Seattle *International Weekly*, 6 D '18.

3. *Bul*, 8 Jan '19; *Christian Science Monitor*, 4 D '18; *Exmr*, 3 D '18; *Call*, 6 D '18, 14 Jan '19; Oakland *Tri-City Labor Review*, 14 F '19; Chicago *American*, 15 Jan '19.

4. Taft, *A. F. of L. in the Time of Gompers*, 376–77.

5. "Proceedings of National Labor Congress on the Mooney Case, . . . 1919," 64, in MP (Scrapbook).

6. *Ibid.*, *passim*; Crystal Eastman, "The Mooney Congress," *Liberator*, Mar. 1919, 19–24; Anton Johannsen to Walsh, 22 Jan '19, in Walsh P; Lang, *Tomorrow Is Beautiful*, 139. See also newspaper citations below.

7. Richmond *Square Deal*, 10 Jan '19.

8. *Labor Clarion*, 14 F '19 and *passim*; Newark, N.J., *Union Labor Bulletin*, Jan. 1919; "Habeas Corpus," XX: 13,407–8.

9. Mooney Congress, "Proceedings," 4–19; Anton Johannsen, "Report to the Officers and Delegates of the Carpenters District Council of Chicago," 18 Jan '19, in Walsh P; *Thirty-ninth Annual Convention of the American Federation of Labor, 1919, Report of Proceedings*, xiv–xix; *Bul*, 20, 28 D '18.

10. Oakland *Tri-City Labor Review*, 17 Jan '19; *Exmr*, 15, 16 Jan '19; Johannsen, "Report"; Johannsen to Walsh, 22 Jan '19, in Walsh P; Chicago *American*, 15 Jan '19; *Liberator*, Mar. 1919; *News*, 15 Jan '19.

11. Cockran addressed the congress, although Walsh was unable to attend. *News*, 1 Jan '19; Walsh to Fitzpatrick, 15 Jan '19, in Walsh P; *Exmr*, 15 Jan '19; Mooney Congress, "Proceedings," 34; *Call*, 17 Jan '19.

12. Mooney Congress, "Proceedings," 3, 4, 15–19, 28–29; *Liberator*, Mar. 1919; *Chr*, 16 Jan '19; *Bul*, 15 Jan '19.

13. *Exmr*, 16 Jan '19; Mooney Congress, "Proceedings," 15–19; Johannsen to Walsh, 22 Jan '19, in Walsh P; Johannsen, "Report."

14. As quoted, *Liberator*, Mar. 1919. See also Mooney Congress, "Proceedings," 65–67. On Kate (Sadler) Greenhalgh's career, see Harvey O'Connor, *Revolution in Seattle* (1964), 97–99, 122–24, 206.

15. Mooney Congress, "Proceedings," 68.

16. *Ibid.*, 69–70; Johannsen to Walsh, 22 Jan '19, Walsh P; Johannsen, "Report."

17. *Liberator*, Mar. 1919; NY *Weekly People*, 1 F '19; Chicago *Herald-Examiner*, 18 Jan '19; Seattle *Union Record*, 22 F '19; Seattle General Strike Committee, *Seattle General Strike* (1919), 12; Robert K. Murray, *Red Scare: A Study in National Hysteria, 1919–1920* (1955), 59–61; Friedheim, *Seattle General Strike*, 81–93, 110–11; comment of Harvey O'Connor in *Pacific Northwest Quarterly*, Jan. 1965, 42; O'Connor, *Revolution in Seattle*, *passim*. Seattle's general strike was not the first in the U.S. See Wilfrid H. Crook, *Communism and the General Strike* (1960), ch. 3.

18. *National Civic Federation Review*, 5 Mr '19; *Labor Clarion*, 14 F '19; Rock Island *Tri-City Labor Review*, 28 F '19; UMW *Journal*, Jan.–Feb. 1919.

19. San Diego *Labor Leader*, 28 Mr '19; *News*, 17 Ap '19.

20. Seattle *Union Record*, 14 Ap '19.

21. *Ibid.*, 19 Ap '19; *News*, *Call*, 19 Ap '19.

22. Philadelphia *Trades Union News*, 10 Ap '19; *Chr*, 20 Ap '19; *American Federationist*, Apr. 1919.

23. *Liberator*, Mar. 1919.

24. *News*, 21 F '19; *Call*, 22, 28 F, 10 Ap '19; *Chr*, 13 Ap '19.

25. *Labor Clarion,* 14 Mr '19.

26. *Chr,* 27 Ap '19; *Call,* 28 Ap '19; *Labor Clarion,* 25 Ap '19.

27. *Chr,* 27 F '19; *Bul,* 4 Mr '19; *Call,* 3 Mr, 11 Ap '19; NY *Call,* 5 Mr '19; Oakland *Tri-City Labor Review,* 21 Mr, 18 Ap '19; Chicago *New Majority,* 19 Ap '19.

28. Seattle *Union Record,* 22 F '19; NY *Call,* 7 Mr '19.

29. Oakland *Tribune,* 14 N '18; *Chr, Exmr,* 13 N '18; Dixon Wecter, *When Johnny Comes Marching Home* (1944), 262–63, 431.

30. Amalgamated Clothing Workers Association, *General Executive Board Report, 1920,* 177–79; NY *World,* 1, 2 My '19; NY *Times, Herald, Sun,* 2 My '19; NY *Call,* 2, 3 My '19; *New Republic,* 10 My '19. The newspaper accounts are all similar; where details vary, the *Times* is followed.

31. NY *Herald, World, Times, Call,* 2–4 My '19; *Christian Science Monitor,* 2 My '19; Wecter, *When Johnny Comes Marching Home,* 431–32; James R. Mock and Evangeline Thurber, *Report on Demobilization* (1944), 76; Murray, *Red Scare,* 73–76.

32. Murray, 69–71; *Bul,* 30 Ap '19; Oakland *Tribune,* 26 Ap, 1 My '19; *News,* 28, 30 Ap, 1, 3 My '19.

33. As quoted, *Exmr,* 1 My '19.

34. As quoted, *Call,* 1 My '19.

35. *Chr,* 8 Ap '19.

36. Woodrow C. Whitten, "Criminal Syndicalism and the Law in California, 1919–1927," Ph.D. diss., Univ. of Calif., Berkeley (1946), 97–98.

37. *Chr,* 3 My '19.

38. Oakland *World,* 12 S '19; *Call,* 19 My '19; Oakland *Tri-City Labor Review,* 30 My '19; IWDL circular letter, 17 Je '19, MP.

39. *Grizzly Bear,* June 1919, 26; *Coast Review,* May 1919, 325, June 1919, 431; *Signs of the Times,* 20 My '19; NY *World,* 18 My '19.

40. The question of numerical strength of trade-union radicals in 1919 has not been adequately explored. Their convention voting strength was indicated by a roll-call vote on a contested election between the organization's candidate, from the United Garment Workers, and the radicals' candidate, from the Journeymen Tailors; the former won, 28,229 to 2,661. *Thirty-ninth Annual Convention of the American Federation of Labor, 1919, Report of Proceedings,* 425–26. See also *ibid.,*

v–xxiii; Chicago *New Majority,* 28 Je '19; NY *World,* 18 Je '19; Taft, *A. F. of L. in the Time of Gompers,* 376–77, 448ff; James O. Morris, *Conflict Within the AFL: A Study of Craft Versus Industrial Unionism, 1901–1938* (1958), 44, 46; John Reed, "Convention of the Dead," *Liberator,* Aug. 1919; Staley, *History of the Illinois State Federation of Labor,* 350ff.

41. AFL, *1919 Proceedings,* 267–68.

42. *Ibid.,* 298.

43. NY *World,* 18 Je '19; *Chr,* 18 Je '19.

44. AFL, *1919 Proceedings,* 336–37; *Exmr, Chr, Call,* 18 Je '19; Seattle *Union Record,* 18, 25 Je '19.

45. AFL, *1919 Proceedings,* 328, 333, 345; Chicago *New Majority,* 28 Je '19; *Call,* 18 Je '19; NY *Times,* 10, 20, 21 Je '19.

46. Oakland *Tri-City Labor Review,* 27 Je '19; *News,* 18 Je '19; NY *Call,* 11 Je '19; Altoona *Mirror,* 13 Je '19; Pittsburgh *Post,* 16 Je '19; Youngstown *Vindicator,* 19 Je '19; Chicago *New Majority,* 21 Je '19; Seattle *Union Record,* 23 Je '19; *Christian Science Monitor,* 2 Jl '19.

47. *News,* 27, 28 Je '19; NY *Times,* 3 Jl '19; *Bul,* 26 Je '19; Oakland *Tri-City Labor Review,* 13 Je '19; *Christian Science Monitor,* 2 Jl '19.

48. *Who's Who in America, 1914–1915* and *1920–1921;* Rheta Childe Dorr, *Woman of Fifty* (1924), 117, 218, 219, 322, and *passim,* and *Inside the Russian Revolution* (1917), 233.

49. NY *Evening Mail,* 14 My '19.

50. NY *Call,* 8 Je '19; *Chr,* 3 Je '19.

51. Frederic L. Paxson, *American Democracy and the World War: Postwar Years: Normalcy, 1918–1923* (1948), 88; Murray, *Red Scare,* 78.

52. *Exmr,* 3 Je '19.

53. Boston *Evening Transcript,* 3 Je '19.

54. NY *Call,* 8 Je '19; *Exmr,* Boston *Evening Transcript,* 4 Je '19.

55. NY *Times,* 3, 20–22 Je, 30 Au '19.

56. Max Lowenthal, *The Federal Bureau of Investigation* (1950), 77–79; Stanley Coben, *A. Mitchell Palmer: Politician* (1963), chs. 10–13; NY *Times,* 13 Je '19; NY *World,* 19 Je '19.

57. NY *Times,* 13, 14 Je '19.

58. *Exmr, Chr,* NY *Times,* NY *World,* Boston *Evening Transcript,* 19 Je '19.

59. *Exmr,* NY *Times,* NY *World,* 19 Je '19.

60. NY *Times,* 27 Je '19.

61. *Ibid.,* 13, 19 Je '19.

62. *Ibid.,* 1 Jl '19.

63. *Who's Who in America, 1918–1919*; NY *Call*, 7 Je '19.

64. Seattle *Union Record*, 24 Je '19.

65. Chicago *Tribune*, 3, 4 Jl '19; Murray, *Red Scare*, 116; NY *Times*, 1, 3–5 Jl '19; *Nation*, 12 Jl '19; Oakland *Tribune*, 2 Jl '19.

66. *Chr*, 1–4 Jl '19; *Exmr*, *Bul*, 1–5 Jl '19; Sacramento *Bee*, 4 Jl '19; Oakland *Tribune*, 1–8 Jl '19.

67. Chicago *Tribune*, 5 Jl '19; NY *Times*, 7 Jl '19; 30 Ap '20; Seattle *Union Record*, 12 Jl '19; *Bul*, 7 Jl '19; *Chr*, 8 Jl '19; *Nation*, 12 Jl '19.

68. *Call*, 3, 7 Jl '19; NY *Call*, 7–10 Jl '19; *Chr*, 8 Jl '19; Butte *Daily Bulletin*, 9 Jl '19; Sacramento *Bee*, 9 Jl '19; Minneapolis *Labor Review*, 4 Jl '19.

69. 41 *U.S. Statutes* 207; Murray, *Red Scare*, 195–209; Drinnon, *Rebel in Paradise*, 210–11, 221–22.

70. Duluth *News Tribune*, 14 Jl '19; *News*, 24 Jl '19; *Call*, 28 Jl '19; UMW, *Proceedings of the ... Convention ... 1919*, 598–606; Seattle *Union Record*, 1 Au '19; *Bul*, 15 N '19.

71. *News*, 7 Oc '19; *Call*, 7, 8 Oc '19; NY *Call*, 20 Oc '19.

72. *Call*, 11 Jl '19.

73. NY *Times*, 7 Ap '22.

74. *Ibid.*, 18, 19 F, 28 Oc '21, 16 F '27, 30 Au '36.

75. Mock and Thurber, *Report on Demobilization*, 141, 200, 208–9; *Survey*, 5 F, 5 Jl '19, 30 Jan '20; NY *Times*, 30 My, 15, 27, 28 Je, 24, 25 Jl, 2, 15, 30 Au '19; *Bul*, 24, 28 Jl '19; *Exmr*, 25 Jl '19; Washington *Post*, NY *Tribune*, 24 Jl '19; *News*, 29, 31 Jl '19; *Congressional Record*, 66th Congr., 1st Sess. (1919), v. 58: 422, 652, 655, 1489, 1511, 1927–29, 2521, 3868–69, 5528–32, 8939–62.

76. Norman Hapgood, ed., *Professional Patriots* (1928), 192; Philadelphia *City Directory* (1919–20), 1221; NY *Times*, 6 Ap '38; Welsh, "America's Greatest Peril," *passim*; *Call*, 3 Mr '19.

77. *Congressional Record*, v. 58:2, 1513; Francis R. Welsh to C. C. Young, 31 My '29, in Cal State Archives, Gov's Off.

78. Deutscher, *Prophet Armed*, 241–46; SF *Star*, Feb. 1918, 20; *Densmore Report*, 16, 25, 33.

79. *Call*, 6 D '19.

80. *Nation*, 12 N '19.

81. *Bul*, 4 Au, 10, 17 Oc '19; *Call*, 5 Au, 13 S '19; *News*, 5, 7 Au, 23 Oc '19; *Chr*, 27 Oc '19.

82. *Chr*, 24 Oc '19; *Exmr*, 27 Oc '19.

83. *Exmr*, 6 N '19; *Call*, 1 My '20.

84. *Chr*, 6 N '19; *Bul*, 13 N '19, 17 F '21; *Nation*, 27 Ap '21.

85. *Call*, 19 Oc, 7 N '23.

XXI   New Discoveries and Eclipse

EPIGRAPHS: Cal S Ct, "In re Billings," I: 118; A. Plotkin to Mary Gallagher, 19 Jl '30.

1. As quoted, *Bul*, 8 D '19 and *Call*, 7 Jan '20.

2. *News*, 8 D '19; *Bul*, 1, 8 D '19, 6 Jan '20; *Call*, 6 Jan '20; *Chr*, 8 Jan '20.

3. *News*, 8 Jan '20.

4. *Ibid.*; *Call*, 5, 30 D '19.

5. As quoted, *Bul*, 2 Jan '20.

6. *Call*, 2, 30 Jan, 13 F, 27 Ap, 14 My '20; *Bul*, 14 My '20.

7. Minor to Rena Mooney, 17 F '21; M circular letter, 28 F '21; George Stewart to M, 7 Jan '24; Stockton *Labor Review*, 15 Oc '20.

8. *Tom Mooney's Monthly*, Aug. 1920–Apr. 1923; [George T. Sayles] to George Stewart, 27 My '21; Sayles to Richard Rohman, 17 Oc '22; Sayles to Leonard Craig, 4 Ap '23; Rena Mooney to R. L. Apple, 20 Au '23; Rena Mooney [?] to National Labor Forum, 18 Jl '23; Nockels to Rena Mooney, 27 Jan '22; Rena Mooney to George Stewart, 20 F '22; George Stewart to Rena Mooney, n.d.; Sayles to Billings, 19 Je '22; Rena Mooney to Leonard Craig, 6 Au '21 (all MP).

Sayles was a parolee from San Quentin, where he had made friends with Mooney. He was able to meet the parole requirements by working for the Defense Committee. (Author's interview, Warren Billings, 29 Au '61.)

9. *Call*, 12 N '20.

10. *Chr*, 13 N '20.

11. Rigall testimony, SF Grand Jury, "Testimony in re Oxman," 57–58.

12. Bunner testimony, *ibid.*, 74, 75.

13. As quoted, *News*, 13 N '20.

14. *Exmr*, 14 N '20; *Call*, 15 N '20.

15. *Exmr*, 21 D '20; Matheson testimony, "Habeas Corpus," X: 5829; SF Police Commissioners, "In re Police Officer Draper Hand," *ibid.*, 5780–832.

16. M to Mary Gallagher, in Gallagher to Roger N. Baldwin, 18 F '29, ACLU P, v. 371.

17. Mary Gallagher to Traverse Clement, 11 F '29, ACLU P, v. 371.

18. "Habeas Corpus," X: 6132–33; M to

Arthur [Scott], 6 S '31; [Scott] to M, 9 F '32; M to Cora Older, 26 Oc '35. Hand did testify for the defense in 1936.

19. As quoted, *Call*, 17 N '20.

20. As quoted, *Call*, 18 N '20.

21. *Call*, 23 N '20.

22. *Call, News*, 23, 30 N '20.

23. *News*, 27 Jan '21.

24. *Call*, 7 F '21; Preston interrogation, Cal S Ct, "In re Billings," I: 119–20; Nockels testimony, *ibid.*, II: 792.

25. Nockels testimony, Cal S Ct, "In re Billings," II: 766–70, 793–98, 819–23.

26. McDonald to Matheson, 11 Jan '21, in Cal State Archives, Atty Gen Records, Box 222. See also McDonald testimony, Cal S Ct, "In re Billings," I: 50.

27. Matheson testimony, Cal S Ct, "In re Billings," I: 227.

28. Nockels testimony, *ibid.*, II: 804–8.

29. Matheson testimony, *ibid.*, I: 226.

30. McDonald testimony, *ibid.*, 49, 57–58, 189–90, 194–95.

31. Max Kesselman affidavit, 16 Jl '30, Cal State Archives, Atty Gen Records, Box 224.

32. McDonald testimony, Cal S Ct, "In re Billings," I: 53.

33. Kesselman affidavit, 16 Jl '30, in Cal State Archives, Atty Gen Records, Box 224.

34. McDonald testimony, Cal S Ct, "In re Billings," I: 54–62.

35. As published in *Call*, 7 F '21.

36. Walsh to Older, 9 F '21, MP.

37. *Call*, 8 F '21; *Bul*, 8, 9, 14 F '21.

38. McDonald testimony, Cal S Ct, "In re Billings," I: 64, II: 826–27; Nockels testimony, *ibid.*, II: 773, 881.

39. Nockels testimony, *ibid.*, II: 811–12; McDonald testimony, *ibid.*, 827.

40. *Call*, 9 F '21; McDonald testimony, Cal S Ct, "In re Billings," I: 64–70; *News*, 14 F '21; *Exmr*, 15 F '21.

41. *News*, 21, 22 F '21; *Bul*, 25 F '21; *Call*, 25, 28 F, 1 Mr '21.

42. Foreman Curtis Clifford, as quoted, *Call*, 1 Mr '21.

43. *Call*, 3 Mr '21; *Labor Clarion*, 4 Mr '21.

44. *Call*, 1–3 Mr '21; Matheson, as quoted, *Call*, 8 Mr '21.

45. Cockran to Rena Mooney, 12 Jan '21. See *Frank v. Mangum*, 237 U.S. 309 (1915), 326: "it is perfectly well settled that a criminal prosecution in the courts of a State, based upon a law not in itself repugnant to the Federal Constitution, and conducted according to the settled course of judicial proceedings as established by

the law of the State . . . , is 'due process' in the constitutional sense." Holmes and Hughes dissented.

46. Laurence Todd to Rena Mooney, 6 Ap '22.

47. *News*, 19 Mr '21; *Exmr*, 20 Mr '21; *Bul*, 15 Ap '21.

48. 3 *Blackstone's Commentaries* 406 (1825 ed.).

49. Charles E. Bennett, "Form of Action —Audita Querela . . . ," *Boston University Law Review*, XXXVI: 304–8; "Argument on Audita Querela," 6, 19, 119, and *passim*.

50. *Bul*, 15 Ap '21; *News*, 20 Ap '21.

51. *Call, Bul, News*, 2 My '21.

52. U'Ren, in "Argument on Audita Querela," 19.

53. Wickes, in *ibid.*, 47, 73.

54. *Ibid.*, 153–55.

55. U'Ren, in *ibid.*, 138, 149.

56. SF Superior Court, "People v. Mooney, Opinion of the Court on the Demurrer of the People to the Amended Petition for a Writ of Audita Querela," 6–7, and appended remarks, 1; *Call*, 27 My '21.

57. Sayles to Billings, 9 Mr '22 (MP); *Call*, 8 My '22.

58. Oxman to Hatcher, 12 Jl '18, in "Habeas Corpus," XVIII: 12,066–67.

59. Hatcher to Nichols, 3 Oc '18, in Cal State Archives, Atty Gen Records, Box 222.

60. Cunha testimony, "Habeas Corpus," XIV: 8614–15.

61. Hatcher testimony, SF Grand Jury, "In re Thomas J. Mooney," 12, 32–34.

62. *Call*, 23 My '21.

63. Hatcher testimony, SF Grand Jury, "In re Thomas J. Mooney," 11–34.

64. Mrs. E. K. Hatcher testimony, *ibid.*, pt. 2, 12.

65. Leake testimony, *ibid.*, pt. 2, 2.

66. *Call*, 23 My, 7 Oc '21, 19 Ap '22; M to Nockels, 27 N '21; Rena Mooney to Minor, 4 My '22.

67. As quoted, *Call*, 18 Ap '22.

68. Sacramento *Bee*, 19 Ap '22.

69. *Call*, 27 My '21; Arnold to Frankfurter, 18 D '20, in Frankfurter P (microfilm reel 12, Harvard Law School).

70. Rena Mooney to R. L. Apple, 20 Au '23; Rena Mooney to H. Weinberger, 27 Oc '24; George Stewart to M, 7 Jan '24 (all in MP); Philip Taft, *A. F. of L. from the Death of Gompers to the Merger* (1959), chs. 1, 2.

71. As quoted, *Call*, 8 F '23.

72. NY *Times*, 23 My '23.

73. *E.g., Call*, 1–28 Jan '24.

74. *Call,* Jan. 1920–Dec. 1929; Older, *My Own Story* and *Growing Up, passim.* See also Lillian Symes's review of Wells's *Older* in *Nation,* 28 N '36.

75. Craig to Rena Mooney, 6 S '23.

76. Rena Mooney to Nockels, 17 My '22.

77. As quoted, *Rank and File,* 15 My '22.

78. *Exmr,* 16 My '22; [Rena Mooney] to Craig, 2, 15 My '22.

79. Melendy and Gilbert, *Governors of California,* 337; Posner, "State Politics and the Bank of America," 159–62; Edward Hamilton in *Exmr,* 12 Je '23.

80. *Exmr,* 12 Je '23.

81. Sayles to Craig, 14 Oc '22; M to Nockels, 27 N '21.

82. Rena Mooney to Nockels, 6 Je '22; *Exmr,* 16 My '22.

83. TMMDC to Craig, 31 Oc '22. Mooney's editorial assistant found his instructions for this issue "so repugnant to me that I simply slammed it together." [Sayles] to Richard Rohman, 17 Oc '22.

84. John Mooney as quoted, *Exmr,* 16 My '22; *Call,* 16 Au '22; M to Nockels, 18 S '22 (MP); Oakland *World,* 3 N '22 (typescript copy, Cal Dept of Corrections, Inmate file 31921).

85. Posner, 163; Rena Mooney to Craig, 5 S '22; *Call,* 10 Au '22.

86. As quoted, *News,* 15 S '22.

87. Sayles to Craig, 14 Oc '22; Older to Stephens, 20 Oc '22; Stephens to Older, 23 Oc '22 (all in MP).

88. Posner, 165–73; Melendy and Gilbert, *Governors of California,* 339ff; *Call,* 2 Jl '23, 30 Au '26.

89. *Call,* 27 Au '23, 28 F, 3 N '25.

90. Friend W. Richardson, "Rules Governing Applications for Executive Clemency," in "Petition for Pardon of Thomas J. Mooney" (1926), I: 1; Rena Mooney to Craig, 24 Oc '23.

91. Ellis to Rena Mooney, 28 Oc '20, Rena Mooney to Ellis, 6 Je '23, Belle Hammerberg to James Rolph, Jr., 19 Je '24, and Sayles to M, 26 F '24 (all in MP); B. C. Wilson to Stephens, 27 Jl '18, Walsh P.

92. M to Fickert, 17 F, 6 Ap '24; Fickert to M, 19 F '24; M–Cunha and M–F. H. Tharp letters, 13 F–5 Mr '24; M to Walsh, 24 S '26; M to Belle Hammerberg, 24 S '26 (all in MP); "Habeas Corpus," IV: 2512–16.

93. Fickert to M, 26 Oc '26, in "Petition for Pardon of Thomas J. Mooney" (1926), I: 10–11.

94. McNutt to M, 3 N '26.

95. Letters and statements of Brady, Griffin, jurors, Belle Hammerberg, Matheson, Goff, and Brennan, in "Petition for Pardon of Thomas J. Mooney" (1926), I: 3ff.

96. As quoted, NY *Times,* 30 D '26.

XXII   San Quentin

SECOND EPIGRAPH: Arthur Heeb to Mary Gallagher, 29 Ap '30 (MP).

1. *Call,* 18 My '27; Kenneth Lamott, *Chronicles of San Quentin* (1961), 18–19.

2. Leo L. Stanley, *Men at Their Worst* (1940), 7; J. L. Clifton, "The Truth about San Quentin," *Pacific Weekly,* 23 Mr '36; *News,* 21 Au '22; Gerald Breckenridge, "Biggest Big House," *Saturday Evening Post,* 8 N '41, 20.

3. Inez Haynes Irwin, *The Native Son* (1919), 3–4.

4. David A. Lamson, *We Who Are About to Die* (1936), 43–44.

5. M to Lucy Lang, 16 Jl '18, Lang P.

6. Stanley, *Men at Their Worst,* 250; Herbert Resner to Humphrey Cobb, 27 Oc '37 (MP); M, as quoted, *News,* 25 Au '22.

7. M circular letter, 22 D '32; *Atlantic Monthly,* July 1922, 38; Tom Mooney, "Sixteen Years," *American Spectator,* Feb. 1933. The *American Spectator* was a folio periodical published in New York and edited by a literary group that included Theodore Dreiser, James Branch Cabell, and Eugene O'Neill. According to one of Dreiser's biographers, Robert H. Elias, Mooney smuggled this article out of prison. But more likely it was ghostwritten. (Mooney did smuggle letters out of prison, but not for publication. Ordinarily he observed prison regulations scrupulously, in order to keep out of trouble and retain his privileges. Moreover, the article is not in his style.) It was probably the work of someone who had visited him, such as Dreiser, and had learned about his prison routine. (Robert H. Elias, *Theodore Dreiser: Apostle of Nature* [1948], 266, 347. Cf. the statement of Warden Holohan, quoted in NY *Times,* 25 Jan '33: "Although Mooney does not write the material, the public is given the impression that he does. Persons from the Mooney Defense League and others interview him and write later what he says, signing his name.")

8. *Nation,* 1 Au '23, 114; Cal Dept of Corrections, Inmate file 31921; *News,* 25 Au

'22; Lamott, *Chronicles of San Quentin,* 142–43, 195; NY *Times,* 21 Ap '32. See also Oral Hist. Proj., "Mary Gallagher," 95.

9. *American Spectator,* Feb. 1933.

10. Herbert Resner to Amelia Richie, 6 D '37; M to Joe Doyal, 19 F '35; M to Minor, 9 Jl '35 (all in MP).

11. *American Spectator,* Feb. 1933; Warden J. A. Johnston to Sayles, 5 D '22; M to Theodore Dreiser, 11 Oc '28; M to Joe Perroni, 5 Jan '33.

12. M to Older, 12 D '28; M to Mary Gallagher, 12 D '28.

13. M to Older, 7 D '28.

14. Oral Hist. Proj., "Mary Gallagher," 95; Smith, as quoted, *Call-Bul,* 14 S '29. See also Anna Mooney to M, 23 D '28.

15. M to Mary Gallagher, 26 Oc '29.

16. M to Mary Mooney, 11 Mr '32.

17. *Outlook and Independent,* 2 S '31.

18. C. B. King to Walsh, 15 S '30, Walsh P; Baldwin to Older, 10 My '29, in ACLU P, v. 371; Walsh to M, 19 Mr '35 (MP); Walsh to Baldwin, 6 Ap '31, in ACLU P, v. 481; Older to Baldwin, 14 My '29, in ACLU P, v. 371.

19. Stanley, *Men at Their Worst,* 258; M to "Sidney," 13 N '31 (MP); J. L. Clifton, "Truth About San Quentin," *Pacific Weekly,* 6 Ap '36; J. B. McNamara to Baldwin, 20 Ap '32, in ACLU P, v. 561; J. B. McNamara to Older, 19 Jan '26, Older P; unnamed convicts, quoted in Ben Reitman to M, 20 Jan '39 (MP), and in Stanley, 251.

20. M to Nockels, 4 Jl '27; M to IMU Local 164, 7 Oc '28; M to Baldwin, 2 Ap '29; Anne Vantz to Mary Gallagher, 8 S '30; M to Mary Gallagher, 8, 9 Je '29 (all in MP); Lena Morrow Lewis to Baldwin, 26 Jan '31, in ACLU P, v. 481; ed'l, *Nation,* 25 Jl '36.

21. Stanley, 251.

22. M to Abby Scott Baker, 5 Au '25; Cal Dept of Corrections, Inmate file 31921, record card; M to Harry Weinberger, 5 Au '25; M to — Miller, 29 Jan '26; M to John R. Haynes, 3 Mr '28; M to Mary K. Jensen, 5 Jl '32.

23. M to William McNevin, 2 S '26; M to Mary Jensen, 5 Jl '32; [Mary Gallagher] to Don Evans, 26 My '29 (all in MP); *Call,* 15 N '28; Austin Lewis to Baldwin, 29 [?] May '29, in ACLU P, v. 371; Mary Gallagher to Aline Barnsdall, 2 My '29 (MP); Baldwin to Austin Lewis, 31 My '29, in ACLU P, v. 371; M to Mary Gallagher, 4 Je '29.

24. M to Ruth Kennell, 21 S '28 (MP); *New Republic,* 9 Oc '29; Paul U. Kellogg memorandum, n.d., in Kellogg to C. C. Young, 23 Jl '29, in Cal State Archives, Gov's Off.

25. Traverse Clements to Baldwin, 14 Jl '31, in ACLU P, v. 480; M to Baldwin, 15 S '28; M to Rena Mooney, 24 Jl '22; M to Walter W. Liggett, 24 Mr '29 (all in MP); Orrick Johns, *Time of Our Lives: The Story of My Father and Myself* (1937), 327; Mark Schorer, *Sinclair Lewis: An American Life* (1961), 532; Lincoln Steffens, *Autobiography of Lincoln Steffens* (1931), 847; Ella Winter, *And Not to Yield* (1963), 123; Theodore Dreiser to M, 10 N '28 (MP).

26. *Bul,* 20 Jan '22.

27. Rena Mooney to John Mooney, 26 Jl, 6 Au '21.

28. Ed Nolan to Rena Mooney, 24 Jan '21.

29. *Exmr,* 12 Je '23.

30. Rena Mooney, "One Small Chapter of an 'Agitator's?' Life" (MP); Haldeman-Julius, "Frameup," 53–59; Rena Mooney testimony, "Habeas Corpus," I: 526–27; adv. in *Call,* 27 D '24.

31. Author's interviews, Warren Billings, 29 Au '61, and John F. Finerty, 7 Je '62.

32. M to Rena Mooney, 20 Au '29.

33. M to Rena Mooney, 29 Mr '27; Mary Gallagher to Leonard Craig, 26 Au '30; Rena Mooney to M, 6 Au '25, 27 Jan '26, 8 D '28 (all in MP).

34. M to Mary Gallagher, 1 Au, 24 N '28.

35. Oral Hist. Proj., "Mary Gallagher," intro., 1–5, 11, 19ff; Mary Gallagher to Billings, 3 Jan '29 (MP); Mary Gallagher to Lucy Lang, 4 Mr '18, in Lang P; Clinton J. Taft to Baldwin, 14 My '29, in ACLU P, v. 371.

36. M to Older, 30 N '28; M to Mary Gallagher, 24 N '28.

37. Oral Hist. Proj., "Mary Gallagher," 48–51; Mary Gallagher to M, 23 N '28.

38. M to Mary Gallagher, 12 D and 24 N '28.

39. M to Mary Gallagher, 20 Mr, 23 Je, 14 Au '29, 28 D '28.

40. M to Mary Gallagher, 24 N '28, 6 Je, 18 F, 16 Ap, 20 F, 7 Oc '29.

41. Mary Gallagher to M, 7 Oc, 21, 22 N, 14 D '28, 12 Jan '29.

42. Mary Gallagher to M, 29 D '28, [? F '29], 2, 3 F '29.

43. Mary Gallagher to M [June 1929?].

44. M to Mary Gallagher, 6 Je, 7 Oc, 2 My, 14 Ap, 10 F, 4 Ap, 20 S '29.

45. M to Mary Gallagher, 16 N '29; M. M. Travassos to M, 6 D '31; Charlie Mooney to M, 25 D '28.

46. Theodore Dreiser to M, 10 N '28 and [? Au '30], in Robert H. Elias, ed., *Letters of Theodore Dreiser: A Selection* (1959), II: 481, 505–6.

47. As quoted, *Chr*, 13 Oc '31.

48. "Mooney" [Arthur Stuart Scott?] to Noel Sullivan, 24 D '32.

49. Sherwood Anderson to Lucia Trent, 11 Jl '31 (MP).

XXIII The Pale Cast of C. C. Young

EPIGRAPHS: C. C. Young, quoted in Franklin Hichborn, "California Politics, 1891–1939," V: 2701; Univ. of Calif., Berkeley, *Daily Californian*, 20 Au '30.

1. M to Older, 6 Jan '27.

2. M to Felix Frankfurter, 3 F '27.

3. Univ. of Calif., Berkeley, Oral Hist. Proj., "Max Thelan," 9; Hichborn, "California Politics," II: 902, 919–21, III: 1632–33, 1675, IV: 2306–20, 2398n, 2539–51, 2570; Posner, "State Politics and the Bank of America," 194–96, 227; *Call*, 7 Jan '27.

4. *Call*, 5 Jan '27; M to C. C. Young, 5 Jan '27; M to Walsh, 6 F, 16 Mr '27; M to Mary Gallagher, 3 S '29.

5. Older to M, 14 Ap '27 (MP); Older to Young, 19 Ap '27, and C. S[pence] to Older, 25 Ap '27, in Cal State Archives, Gov's Off. See also State Constitution, Art IV, Sect. 16.

6. Older to the Rt. Rev. James P. Cantwell, 18 My '27 (MP).

7. *Call*, 27 Oc '25, 16 My, 7, 9, 20 Je '27.

8. *Call*, 21 Je '27; Older to M, 21 D '27.

9. M to Older and Rowell, 19 D '27.

10. Older to M, 21 D '27.

11. Rowell to Older, 30 Au '27 (MP).

12. Older to Rowell, 16 S '27, Rowell P.

13. Older to M, 22 Je '27; McNutt to M, 7 Jl '27.

14. Young to Rowell, 24 S '27 (MP).

15. Older to Young, 28 S '27, in Cal State Archives, Gov's Off.

16. Young to Older, 30 S '27, in Cal State Archives, Gov's Off.

17. M to Older, 24 Je '27.

18. Older to M, 22 Je, 12 Oc '27.

19. Mencken to M, 25 Oc '28.

20. M to Mencken, – N '28; M to Frank Brown, 1 Je '28; M to Baldwin, 16 F '28;

M to Older and Rowell, 19 D '27; *Call*, 8 Je '28.

21. Older to Rowell, 8 D '27 (MP); *Call*, 8 Je '28.

22. Griffin to Young, 20 Jan '28 (MP).

23. Worth M. Tippy to Mary Gallagher, 21 Je '28.

24. Older to M, 23 Jan '28.

25. M to Martin Eagan, 10 My '28.

26. Older to M, 23 Jan '28.

27. Older to Walsh, 27 Mr '28; Older to M, 10, 16 Ap '28; M to Walter Lippmann, 29 Je '28 (all in MP).

28. Walsh to M, 25 F '28.

29. M to Older, 19 Jl '28.

30. Young to Older, 13 D '28, and Older to Young, 17 D '28, in Cal State Archives, Gov's Off.

31. M to Older, 29 Au '28; M to Dan Regan, 29 Au '28; M to Michael J. Keough, 27 S '28; M to Walsh, 25 S '28; M to Baldwin, 31 Au '28; Nockels to Keough, 7 S '28 (MP).

32. Young to Scharrenberg, 19 S '28, in Cal State Archives, Gov's Off.

33. M to Young, 7 D '28.

34. Young to Scharrenberg, 9 Jl '28, as quoted in M to Robert Whitaker, 20 Oc '28; M to Keough, 23 Oc '28.

35. M to Edward Keating, 12 Jl '28. See also M to Keough, 27 Jl '28.

36. M to John F. McNamee, 25 Je '28.

37. Mary Gallagher to Rose Paul, 24 Ap '29; Darrow to M, 4, 24 Jl, 27 S, 10 N '28; M to Walsh, 1 S '28 (all in MP).

38. M to Walsh, 16 N '28.

39. M to Frank Brown, 25 Oc '28; M to Mary Gallagher, 5 Oc '28; M to Walsh and Nockels, 6 Oc '28.

40. Mary Gallagher to M, 8 D '28; Mary Gallagher to Mrs. Parker Maddux, 23 My '30; M to Older, 18 D '28.

41. *Call*, 10 Jan '29.

42. Max Stern to Baldwin, 11 Mr '29, in ACLU P, v. 371.

43. Older to Baldwin, 15 Mr '29, in ACLU P, v. 371.

44. Excerpts from about 25 letters to C. C. Young, 1927–30, in Cal State Archives, Gov's Off. (Misspellings are in sources.)

45. *Call*, 2 Au '29; M to Mary Gallagher, 3 S '29.

46. M to Older, 1 S '29.

47. *Call-Bul*, 4 S '29, 25 N '31. (The San Francisco *Bulletin* was purchased by Hearst and merged with the *Call* under Older's editorship in August 1929.)

48. *Call-Bul*, 17 S '29.

49. *Call-Bul*, 7 N '29; Mary Gallagher to Joe Schlossberg, 3 Jl '29.

50. M to Older, 23 S '29.

51. M to Billings, 23 S '29.

52. M to Older, 23 S '29.

53. Mary Gallagher to Aline Barnsdall, 5 Oc '29; Dorothy Murphy to M, 26 S '29; Lena Morrow Lewis to M, 27 S '29; Lena Morrow Lewis to Billings, 27 S '29 (all in MP).

54. Mary Gallagher to Aline Barnsdall, 5 Oc '29; Mary Gallagher to Baldwin, 5 Oc '29 (both in MP); *Call-Bul*, 6, 7, 20, 21 N '29.

55. *Call-Bul*, 21 N '29.

56. Lewis to Baldwin, 6 D '29, in Lewis P.

57. Older to M, 16 D '29.

58. *Call-Bul*, 18 D '29.

59. *Ibid.*, 19 D '29.

60. Mary Gallagher to Aline Barnsdall, 30 D '29.

61. M to Mary Gallagher, 19 D '29.

62. Billings to Mary Gallagher, 15 D '29, 5 Jan '30; Mary Gallagher to Arthur Heeb, 14 My '30 (all in MP).

63. *Chr*, 12 Mr '30; Heeb to Young, 30 D '28, to Mary Gallagher, 14 My '29, 11 F '30, and to M, 12 Jan '30 (all in MP).

64. *Chr*, 12 Mr '30; Mary Gallagher to Dorothy Verplank, 7 Mr '30; Peter Guldbrandsen to M, 3 F '30.

65. Mary Gallagher to Baldwin, 11 Mr '30.

66. J. Murray Luck memorandum, n.d. [March 1930?]; Heeb to Mary Gallagher, 14 Mr '30; Luck to Mary Gallagher, 22 Mr '30 (all in MP).

67. Heeb to Mary Gallagher, 19 Mr '30; *Chr*, 12 Mr '30.

68. Luck memorandum; Mary Gallagher to Oswald Garrison Villard, 12 Mr '30.

69. "O. A. W.", undated memorandum [1929?], in Cal State Archives, Gov's Off.

70. Traverse Clements to Baldwin, 14 F '31, in ACLU P, v. 480.

71. Older to M, 18 Jan '30; Mary Gallagher to Baldwin, 29 Mr, 10 My '30; *Exmr*, *News*, 24 Ap '30; Older to M, 26 My '30.

72. *Chr*, 29 My '30; *Call-Bul*, 5 Je '30; Haldeman-Julius to M, 27 My '30; Frost, "Mooney Case in California Politics," 144; Lena Morrow Lewis to M, 22 Je '30.

73. Supreme Court as quoted, *Exmr*, 5 Jl '30.

74. *Exmr*, 5 Jl '30.

75. M as quoted, *ibid.*; *Exmr*, 6–8 Jl '30.

76. *Exmr*, 8 Jl '30.

77. As quoted, *Exmr*, 9 Jl '30.

78. *Exmr*, 9 Jl '30; San Rafael *Independent*, 7 Au '30.

79. *Exmr*, 9, 11 Jl '30; *News*, 9, 10 Jl '30; Cal S Ct, "In re Billings," I: 75; NY *Times*, 12 Jl '30.

80. NY *Times*, 13–15 Jl '30; *Exmr*, 13, 14, 18 Jl '30.

81. *Exmr*, 21 Jl '30.

82. Cal S Ct, "In re Billings," I: 24.

83. *Ibid.*, I: 12, 24–27, 271–72, 283–85, 289.

84. *Ibid.*, 53, 106–7, 124.

85. *Exmr*, 31 Jl, 3 Au '30; Cal S Ct, "In re Billings," II: 862–65.

86. McDonald to Nockels, 7 S '30, and Nockels to McDonald, 9 S '30, Walsh P.

87. Older testimony, Cal S Ct, "In re Billings," III: 1591, 1609, 1611, 1594–95.

88. Estelle Smith testimony, *ibid.*, I: 411.

89. Older testimony, *ibid.*, III: 1614; Dorothy Murphy to A. J. Harder, 5 S '30 (MP).

90. *Call*, 21 Mr '29; Cal S Ct, "In re Billings," II: 684–96.

91. Estelle Smith testimony, *ibid.*, I: 477–93.

92. Alpheus Duffee testimony, *ibid.*, II: 742–48.

93. Older testimony, *ibid.*, III: 1618–19, 1665, 1839–40.

94. *Exmr*, 15 Au '30.

95. Brennan testimony, Cal S Ct, "In re Billings," II: 1004–5; Gleeson testimony, *ibid.*, III: 1895; Walsh statement, *ibid.*, I: 441; *Exmr*, 16 Au '30.

96. Cal S Ct, "In re Billings," II: 1477–78, 1492–93, 1511–14.

97. Thomas R. Lynch to Edward C. Krauss, 17 Ap '37 (MP); Frankfurter to Baldwin, 19 Au '30, in ACLU P, v. 416; M to John F. Finerty, 9 Au '35, Walsh P.

98. *Exmr*, 21 Au '30.

99. Young to C. K. McClatchy, in Fresno *Bee*, 15 My '31.

100. See Frost, "Mooney Case in California Politics," 147–60.

101. "Mr. Justice Langdon Dissents" (1930), 6.

102. Walsh to C. B. King, 8 D '30, Walsh P; *Chr*, 6 Jan '31, 15 Jl '32.

XXIV Through the Rolph Administration

EPIGRAPHS: Roger William Riis to Harwood A. White, 20 F '31, in ACLU P, v. 481; George Davis to Frank Walsh and John F. Finerty, 26 S '36, Walsh P.

1. Luther Whiteman and Samuel L. Lew-

is, *Glory Roads* (1936), 1; *Chr*, 3–5 Jan '31; Hichborn, "California Politics," V: 2603–4.

2. Ernest J. Hopkins, *Our Lawless Police: A Study of the Unlawful Enforcement of the Law* (1931), 159; *Who's Who in America, 1932–1933.*

3. *Chr*, 7 Mr '30, 21 Je '34; *Nation*, 14 Jan '31.

4. Rolph to W. A. Pinkerton, 12 N '14, cited in Liston Sabraw, "Mayor James Rolph, Jr., and the End of the Barbary Coast," M.A. thesis, SF State College (1960), 85.

5. Posner, "State Politics and the Bank of America," 50, 171; Dorothy Murphy to Baldwin, 21 My '31, in ACLU P, v. 481; Traverse Clements to Baldwin, 26 F '31, in ACLU P, v. 480. See also Ernest J. Hopkins, in *New Republic*, 11 My '32.

6. On Rolph's alcoholism—which is said to have been a matter of common knowledge—see Upton Sinclair, *I, Candidate for Governor: And How I Got Licked* (1934), 4, 14. Other traits of Rolph's are described in *Chr*, 11 S '31, 26 Jan '34; *Nation*, 14 Jan '31; *Labor Clarion*, 8 Je '34; Herman G. Goldbeck, "The Political Career of James Rolph, Jr.: A Preliminary Study," M.A. thesis, Univ. of Calif., Berkeley (1936), 13. The two quotations are from *Chr*, 28 Je '34 and 2 Jan '31.

7. Dorothy Murphy to William Busick, 24 S '31; *Open Forum*, 16 Ap '32; Anna Mooney to M, 27 Je '35.

8. W. A. Smith memorandum to Rolph, 29 Jan '31, in Cal State Archives, Gov's Off; *Nation*, 14 Jan '31; Mary Gallagher to Baldwin, 23 Oc '30, in ACLU P, v. 416; Baldwin to Sinclair Lewis, 6 Ap '31, ACLU P, v. 482a.

9. Traverse Clements to Baldwin, 16 Jan '31, ACLU P, v. 480.

10. Author's interview, Sara Bard Field (Mrs. C. E. S. Wood), Aug. '59; Clements to Baldwin, 16 Mr '31, ACLU P, v. 480.

11. C. B. King to Walsh, 17 F '31, Walsh P; Clements to Baldwin, 26 F '31, ACLU P, v. 480. See also Baldwin to Clements, 18 Mr '31, same file.

12. Walsh to C. B. King, 11 F '31, Walsh P.

13. Robert Whitaker to Walsh, 6 My '31 (MP). See also Dorothy Murphy to Baldwin, 21 My '31, ACLU P, v. 481.

14. M to John A. Gahan, 2 S '31.

15. Dorothy Murphy to George Wagner, 19 S '31.

16. Sapiro to C. C. Young, 15 Jl '30, in Cal State Archives, Gov's Off; Traverse Clements to Baldwin, 31 Jan '31, Baldwin to Clements, 10 F '31, and Clements to Baldwin, 5 Mr '31, all in ACLU P, v. 480; *Who's Who in America, 1932–1933*; John D. Hicks, *Republican Ascendancy, 1921–1933* (1960), 194–95.

17. Baldwin to Clements, 1 Je '31, ACLU P, v. 480.

18. Baldwin, circular letter to the National Mooney-Billings Committee, 1 Mr '32, Sapiro to Baldwin, 7 My '31, and Baldwin to Billings, 22 N '32, in ACLU P, vs. 559, 482a, and 561, respectively.

19. Sapiro to Rolph, 3 Au '31, in ACLU P, v. 482a; Roche to Zechariah Chafee, Jr., 5 S '31, in Nat Archives, RG 10, #78, NCLOE 4-D1; Sapiro to Walsh, 20 Oc '31, ACLU P, v. 481.

20. Louis J. Gribetz and Joseph Kaye, *Jimmie Walker: The Story of a Personality* (1932), 91, 106–8. See also Baldwin to Gardner Jackson, 20 Jl '31, in ACLU P, v. 482a.

21. NY *Times*, 19 N '31.

22. *Ibid.*, 19, 20 N '31; *Chr*, 24 N '31.

23. *Chr*, 23–25 N '31; *New Republic*, 11 My '32.

24. NY *Times*, 26 N '31.

25. *Ibid.*, 27 N '31; *Exmr*, 27 N '31; "A Native Son" to Walker, 21 N '31, C. D. Kimball to Rolph, 23 N '31, Alexander Sifford to Rolph, 24 N '31, and M. S. Curtis to Rolph, 20 N '31, all in Cal State Archives, Gov's Off.

26. *Chr*, 26 N, 1 D '31.

27. NY *Times*, 27, 29, 30 N, 1, 2, 4 D '31.

28. As quoted, *ibid.*, 2 D '31.

29. *Ibid.*; Rolph, *In re Mooney Pardon*, 82–85.

30. Fickert to Walker, 30 N '31, in *ibid.*, 89; NY *Times*, 3 D '31.

31. NY *Times*, 1, 2 D '31; *Exmr*, 2 D '31; *Labor Clarion*, 4 D '31; M to Byrd Kelso, 3 Au '32.

32. NY *Times*, 2, 4 D '31.

33. Norma Perrie to M, 7 Jan '32. See also W. A. Swanberg, *Citizen Hearst* (1961), 305, 341.

34. M to Arthur [Scott], 25 Jl '32.

35. NY *Times*, 4, 6 D '31.

36. *Ibid.*, 9 D '31; Albuquerque *Journal*, 9 D '31; Frank Freidel, *Franklin D. Roosevelt: The Triumph* (1956), 333–36.

37. TMMDC circular letter, 26 D '31 (MP).

38. Clements to Baldwin, 7 D '31, in ACLU P, v. 480; *Nation*, 16 D '31; Peter Gulbrandsen to Rolph, 14 Ap '32, in Cal State Archives, Gov's Off.

39. Baldwin to Clements, 11 D '31, ACLU P, v. 480.

40. Thomas, *Debonair Scoundrel*, 287.

41. Norma Perrie to M, 6 Ap '32; Sam Goodwin to Aline Barnsdall, 8 Ap '32.

42. Norma Perrie to M, 7 Jan '32; *Chr*, 4 N '33.

43. *Chr*, 5 My, 4 N '33, 3 Je, 1 S '34; Mowry, *California Progressives*, 36; Lewis F. Byington and Oscar Lewis, eds., *History of San Francisco* (1931), III: 5–10; J. Edward Johnson, *History of the Supreme Court Justices of California, 1900–1950* (1966), 7, 34; Hichborn, "California Politics," IV: 2354; *New Republic*, 11 My '32; *Labor Clarion*, 13 Au '37.

44. Norma Perrie to M, 7 Jan '32.

45. NY *Times*, 7 Jan, 14, 22 Mr '32; *Exmr*, 15 Mr '32; Sam Goodwin to Aline Barnsdall, 17 Mr '32.

46. Sam Goodwin to Norma Perrie, 16 Ap '32; *Chr*, 12, 19, 22 Ap '32.

47. *Chr*, 23 Ap '32.

48. Rolph, *In re Mooney Pardon*, 2.

49. *Ibid.*, 23, 22.

50. *Ibid.*, 68, 61.

51. *Ibid.*, 17, 78, 72, and *passim*.

52. *Chr*, 22 Ap '32.

53. Baldwin to E. L. Parsons, 17 N '32, and Sapiro to Baldwin, 20 [?] Ap '32, both in ACLU P, v. 560.

54. "Open Letter to Judge Matt I. Sullivan," [22] N '32, ACLU P, v. 560.

55. Duffus to Baldwin, 11 N '32, Barrow to Baldwin, 15 N '32, Barnes *et al.* to Sullivan, 22 N '32, and Sullivan to Stephen S. Wise, 15 D '32, all in ACLU P, v. 560.

56. As quoted, *Exmr*, 30 N '32.

57. Baldwin to the signers of the open letter, 5 D '32, and Duffus to Baldwin, 5 D '32, both in ACLU P, v. 560.

58. Wise to Sullivan, 7 D '32, in Nat Archives, RG 10, NCLOE #78, 4-D1; Sullivan to Wise, 15 D '32, and Wise to Baldwin, 20 D '32, both in ACLU P, v. 560.

59. National Mooney-Billings Committee minutes, 16 Jl '30, in Baldwin circular letter, 31 Jl '30 (MP).

60. Charles Merz, *The Dry Decade* (1931), 237–39; NY *Times*, 17 Jan, 5, 6 Mr, 23 Ap, 21, 23, 29 My, 8 Au '29, 9 Oc '30, 16 Je '31; *Outlook*, 5 Je '29; *Nation*, 21 Jan, 15 Jl '31; *New Republic*, 4 F '31.

61. Earle A. Ross, "Kenyon," *DAB Supl* I.

62. Walsh to C. B. King, 11 F '31, Walsh P.

63. NY *Times*, 9, 23 F '57; "Chafee," *Who's Who in America, 1930–1931*; Zechariah Chafee, Jr., *Blessings of Liberty* (1956), 72–73, and *Inquiring Mind* (1928), 117n; Chafee, "Pollak," *DAB Supl* II; *Gitlow v. New York*, 268 U.S. 652 (1925); Carl S. Stern, "Memorial of Walter Heilprin Pollak," in NY Bar Assn, *Year Book, 1941*, 507–13; L. Sprague de Camp, *The Great Monkey Trial* (1968), 462; Nat. M-B Comm. minutes, 16 N '28, in Baldwin to M, 19 N '28 (MP).

64. Nat. M-B Comm. minutes, 16 Jl '30, in Baldwin circular letter, 31 Jl '30, MP; Walsh to C. B. King, 18 Oc '30, Walsh P; Anne Vantz to Mrs. Haldeman-Julius, 14 N '30 (MP).

65. Drew Pearson and Robert S. Allen, "Washington Daily Merry-Go-Round" (syndicated column), 1 Mr '37 (MP); Gardner Jackson to Henry T. Hunt, 10 Jan '31, ACLU P, v. 481.

66. Jackson to Newton D. Baker, 10 N '30, and Baker to Jackson, 14 N '30, as quoted in Jackson to Baker, 8 Je '31, ACLU P, v. 482a. See also *Chr*, 1 Mr '37, 18 Ap '65.

67. Jackson to Henry T. Hunt, 10 Jan '31, ACLU P, v. 481.

68. Extracts of the minutes of the Commission, 24 N '30, in U.S. Senate, 72d Congr., 1st Sess., Report 256; NY *Times*, 23 D '30.

69. Wickersham to Kenyon, 17 Je '31, in Senate Report 256, "Minority Report," 4.

70. NY *Times*, 9 Jan '32; Cyrus B. King to Walsh, 8 Jan '31, Kenyon to Walsh, 30 Jan '31, Walsh to Kenyon, 3 F '31, all in Walsh P; Stern to Wickersham, 1 Jl '31, and Pollack to Chafee, 29 Je '31, both in Nat Archives, RG 10, #78, NCLOE 4-D1.

71. Walsh memorandum, 18 F '31, and Thomas A. Halleran to Walsh, 4 My '31, both in Walsh P; Walsh to Anna Mooney, 18 My '31 (MP); Baldwin to Sapiro, 29 F '32, in ACLU P, v. 560.

72. Jackson to Baldwin, 10 Je '31, in ACLU P, v. 482a; Baldwin to Sapiro, 29 F '32, in ACLU P, v. 560.

73. Wickersham to Kenyon, 17 Je '30, in Senate Report 256, 4; Jackson to Kenyon, 25 Je '31, in ACLU P, v. 482a; NY *Times*, 27 Je '31; Baker to M, 5 Au '31.

74. Baldwin to Kenyon, 20 Je '31, in Nat Archives, RG 10, #78, NCLOE 4-D1.

75. Wickersham to Chafee, Pollak, and Stern, 24 Je '31, in Nat Archives, same file; Kenyon to Baldwin, 24 S '31, in ACLU P, v. 482a; Kenyon to Baldwin, 4 Mr '32, in ACLU P, v. 560.

76. Chafee to Baldwin, 23 Je '31, in ACLU P, v. 482a; Chafee to Pollak, 30 Je '31, in Nat Archives, RG 10, #78, NCLOE 4-D1.

77. M to TMMDC, 1 Jl '31; NY *Times*, 16 Jl '31; *Chr*, 16, 17 Jl '31; Baldwin to Jackson, 20 Jl '31, in ACLU P, v. 481. The criticism recalls the 1918 law review article by Jay Hindman.

78. Jackson to Pollak, 1 Jl '31, in Nat Archives, RG 10, #78, NCLOE 4-D1; Baldwin to Kenyon, 2 Oc '31, Kenyon to Baldwin, 12 Oc '31, and Baldwin to Pollak, 15 Oc '31, all in ACLU P, v. 482a; Lawrence Todd to TMMDC, 9 Jan '32 (MP); *Congressional Record*, 72d Congr., 1st Sess., v. 75:2, 913; Baldwin to Helen Tufts Bailie, 9 Jan '32, in ACLU P, v. 560; NY *Times*, 7, 8 Jan, 26 Oc '32; Senate Report 256, 1–3; *Chr*, 17 F '32; G. W. Alexander to TMMDC, 29 F '32 (MP).

79. *M-B Report*, 13, 46, 193, and *passim*.

80. *Ibid.*, 242–43. The list of conclusions was not originally part of the report, but was added at the time of its release. (Baldwin to Sapiro, 29 F '32, in ACLU P, v. 560.)

81. See, e.g., *New Republic*, 4 F, 19 Au '31.

82. *Argonaut*, 30 Oc '31; Sinclair Lewis *et al.* to Rolph, 11 My '31, ACLU P, v. 482a.

83. Shaw to M, 27 Mr '33.

84. Los Angeles *Times*, 15 Au '32; *Open Forum*, 10 S '32; *Daily Worker*, 16 S '32.

85. Upton Sinclair memorandum, 1 S '32 (MP); *New Republic*, 21 S '32.

86. Traverse Clements to Baldwin, 3 S '31, in ACLU P, v. 480; Cyrus B. King to Walsh, 8, 14 S '31, Walsh P; *Chr*, 1 S '31, 23 Jan '32; M to TMMDC, 16 Jan '32; NY *Times*, 1 S '31; TMMDC to Norma Perrie, 26 Jan '32.

87. Traverse Clements to Baldwin, 2 My '32, in ACLU P, v. 561; Arthur Stuart Scott [?] to Max Stern, 18 N '32 (MP).

88. Walsh to Anna Mooney, 23 N '32 (MP).

89. NY *Times*, 27, 29 Mr '33.

90. *Ibid.*, 2 Ap '33; Chr, 27 Ap '33.

91. NY *Times*, 19 My '33; *Chr*, 19, 24 My '33.

92. NY *Times*, 24 My '33.

93. *People v. Mooney* (1933), 4, 6, in Cal Dept of Corrections, Inmate file 31921.

94. *Ibid.*, 9–10, 21.

95. *Ibid.*, 25–26.

96. *Exmr*, NY *Times*, 25 My '33.

97. *Chr*, 21, 22 Oc '32; M to TMMDC, 20 Jan '33 (MP); Older to Baldwin, 2 F '33, in ACLU P, v. 650.

98. Melendy and Gilbert, *Governors of California*, 333, 345, 359, 374–77; *Chr*, 1, 2, 24 Mr '34; Sullivan, as quoted, *Chr*, 3 Je '34.

99. Melendy and Gilbert, 381, 382; Posner, "State Politics and the Bank of America," 306; Whiteman and Lewis, *Glory Roads*, 1–2.

100. Hichborn, "California Politics," V: 2746; Hattie Belle Gandy to Merriam, n.d., Merriam P.

101. *Chr*, 9 Je '34; John F. Finerty to John Walsh, 12 Je '34, Walsh P; Finerty to A. L. Wirin, 17 Au '34, in ACLU P, v. 733.

102. *Labor Clarion*, 8, 15 Je, 31 Au '34; Thomas R. Lynch to Frank P. Walsh, 8 S '34, Walsh P; M to Charles Blome, 22 Au '34 (MP).

103. Arthur M. Schlesinger, Jr., *The Age of Roosevelt: The Politics of Upheaval* (1960), 111; Older to Sinclair, 15 Je '20, in Upton Sinclair, *My Lifetime in Letters* (1960), 223–25; *ibid.*, 258–59; Sinclair leaflet, "Opinions of 'Co-op,'" n.d., in Sinclair to M, 25 N '36 (MP); Arnold Peter Biella, "Upton Sinclair: Crusader," Ph.D. diss., Stanford Univ. (1954), 10; Sinclair to TMMDC, 12 Jan '23.

104. Upton Sinclair, *I, Governor of California and How I Ended Poverty* (1933), 20 and *passim*.

105. NY *Times*, 30 Au '34; *Harper's*, Feb. 1935, 366; Joseph A. McGowan, *History of the Sacramento Valley*, II: 278; Otis L. Graham, Jr., *An Encore for Reform: The Old Progressives and the New Deal* (1967), 89–91; George Creel, *Rebel at Large: Recollections of Fifty Crowded Years* (1947), 281ff; Robert Glass Cleland, *California in Our Time*, 211.

106. NY *Times*, 9 S, 4 N '34; Dixon Wecter, *Age of the Great Depression* (1948), 202; *Collier's*, 27 Oc '34, 13; *Harper's*, Feb. 1935, 367. See also Oliver Carlson, *Mirror for Californians* (1941), 281–84; and Carey McWilliams, *Southern California Country* (1946), 291–93.

107. Upton Sinclair, *I, Candidate for Governor: And How I Got Licked*, 21, 33–34; Schlesinger, *Politics of Upheaval*, 114; *Collier's*, 27 Oc '34, 12; NY *Times*, 5, 31 Au

'34; McGowan, II: 280; *Statement of the Vote of the State of California*, Aug. 28, 1934, 4, 5.

108. NY *Times*, 30 Au '34; Sinclair, *I, Candidate*, 39; Sinclair to Franklin D. Roosevelt, 12 My '34 (MP); *Chr*, 8 Je, 31 Au '34.

109. *Ibid.*, 21, 27 Oc '34; Sinclair, *I, Candidate*, 24; Rexford G. Tugwell, *The Democratic Roosevelt* (1957), 298; Schlesinger, 116–17, 120.

110. Schlesinger, 118; Irwin Ross, *The Image Makers* (1959), 65–70; Hichborn, "California Politics," V: 2739–41; [J. F. Carter], *American Messiahs* (1935), 67.

111. Clarence F. McIntosh, "Upton Sinclair and the EPIC Movement, 1933–1936," Ph.D. diss., Stanford Univ. (1955), 235; Leo Rosten, *Hollywood: The Movie Colony and Movie Makers* (1941), 134–37; NY *Times*, 6, 14, 19, 23, 28 Oc, 4 N '34; Sinclair, *I, Candidate*, 125–27.

112. McGowan, II: 279–80; Sinclair, *I, Candidate*, 45–46, 54; Mary Craig Sinclair, *Southern Belle*, 350; *Statement of the Vote*, November 6, 1934, 6; NY *Times*, 21, 25, 28 Oc, 1, 2 N '34, and (for the Sinclair quotation) 5 N '34.

113. Mary Sinclair, *Southern Belle*, 356–57; M to Aline Barnsdall, 25 S '34.

114. TMMDC to Sinclair, 24 Au '34; *EPIC News*, 24 Oc '34; McIntosh, "Upton Sinclair," 245; Sinclair, *I, Candidate*, 148, 149 illus., and 39.

115. *Nation*, 28 N '34; Schlesinger, 121; NY *Times*, 3, 4, N '34.

116. *Statement of the Vote*, Nov. 6, 1934, 6; NY *Times*, 8 N '34; M to James Oscar Yatesy, 1 F '36.

117. Sinclair to Merriam, 10 Jan '35 (MP); *Chr*, 15 Jan '35.

118. William J. Sheehan to Rena Mooney, 18 D '21; *EPIC News*, 7 Jan '35.

xxv   The Defense Committee and the Reds

EPIGRAPHS: U. S. Senate, 76th Congr., 1st Sess., Judiciary Committee, *Hearings on the Nomination of Felix Frankfurter to the Supreme Court* (1939), 38; M to Albert A. Shanks, 22 Ap '37.

1. Minor to Foster, 22 My '22; Rena Mooney to Minor, 4 My '22 (both in MP).

2. Theodore Draper, *American Communism and Soviet Russia* (1960), 180–81.

3. Carl Hacker to Mary Gallagher, 25 Je '29; Billings to M, 27 Jan '30.

4. ILD leaflet, "An Important Xmas Appeal Addressed Personally to You," n.d. [1928]; Mary Gallagher to Wanda Greenberg, 21 Mr '29, Mary Gallagher to Arthur Moulton, 1 Ap '29, Alma Reinis to TMMDC, 22 Ap '29, and Mary Gallagher to M, 25 Ap '29 (all in MP).

5. M to Wagenknecht, 13 Jan '29; Wagenknecht to M, Billings, and Mary Gallagher, 11 F '29.

6. Wagenknecht to Ella Reeve Bloor, 1 D '28; Wagenknecht to Mary Gallagher, 8 Jan '29; Mary Gallagher to Wagenknecht, 18 F '29, and to Gitlow, 7 My '29 (all in MP).

7. M to Nockels, 27 N '21.

8. M to Mary Gallagher, 5, 14 Mr, 14 D '29. See also Irving Howe and Lewis Coser, *The American Communist Party* (1957), chs. 4, 5.

9. Leaflet, "The International Labor Defense Calls upon the Working Class to Fight for . . . Mooney and Billings . . . ," n.d. [1929], MP; M to Dorothy Murphy, 5 Au '31; NY *Times*, 15 Au '29; Mary Gallagher to Harry Hodgman, 23 Au '29; Charles Harmon to Mary Gallagher, 19 Jl '30; M to Minor, 14 S '31.

10. Mary Gallagher to William Busick, Jr., 5 Oc '30, and Busick to Mary Gallagher, 8 Oc '30; *Open Forum*, 16 Ap '32.

11. Kelso to Mary Gallagher, 23 Je, 5 Au '30; Kelso to Anna Mooney, 27 My '31; M to TMMDC, 3 Au '31 (all in MP); Kelso to Forrest Bailey, 1 D '31, in ACLU P, v. 482a.

12. Kelso to Anna Mooney, 4, 11, 15, 24, 27, 28 My, 11 Je '31; Kelso to TMMDC, 19, 27 Je '31; *Open Forum*, 16 Ap '32.

13. Kelso to TMMDC, 22, 27 Je, 24 Jl, 3, 4, 15, 18 Au '31.

14. Jenkins to TMMDC, 30 Jl '31, 7 N '34; George T. Davis to M, 18 N '37; Jenkins, mimeographed leaflet, "The 'Justice' Racket in the United States," n.d., MP; Jenkins to M, 22 N '34, 4 My '38; Jenkins to Mary Mooney, n.d. [1931]; NY *Times*, 19, 20 Jl '31.

15. Jenkins to "Daisy," 23 Mr '38; Jenkins to Mother Mooney, 8 Mr '34; Jenkins to M, 10 D '37; Jenkins to TMMDC, 10 Oc '32; Mary Gallagher to M, 16 Jl '30; M to Gardner Jackson and John Jenkins, 24 Oc '35; Kelso to TMMDC, 1 S '31.

16. NY *Times*, 25 S '31.

17. Kelso to TMMDC, 25 S '31. (Some

caps omitted.) See Howe and Coser, *American Communist Party*, ch. 5, for background of the CP "Third Period."

18. Kelso to M, 7, 10 Oc '31; NY *Times*, 11 Oc '31.

19. Kelso to M, 21 D '31; Kelso to TMMDC, 10 D '31; Norma Perrie to TMMDC, memorandum, 31 Jan '32; Kelso to Norma Perrie, 7 Jan '32; *Open Forum*, 7 Jan, 16 Ap '32.

20. Kelso to M, 21 D '31; Kelso memorandum, 27 Jan '32; Kelso to TMMDC, 5, 13 F '32.

21. Kelso to TMMDC, 20, 25 F '32.

22. Kelso to TMMDC, 3 Mr '32.

23. *Ibid.*; Kelso to Joseph Gwatkin, 20 Je '32.

24. M to Kelso, 13 N '31, 24 Oc '35; Benjamin A. Ellisberg to Kelso, 22 Jl '31; Clarence Senior to TMMDC, 7 S '31; Oklahoma City *Oklahoma News*, 31 Au '37.

25. Mary Gallagher to Aline Barnsdall, 28 My '30; Anne Vantz to Billings, 22 N, 1 D '30.

26. Mary Gallagher to Baldwin, 14 N, 4 D '30; Raymond Burns to M, 4, 8 D '30; Liggett to M, 15 Jan '29 (all in MP); Mary Gallagher to Baldwin, 23 Mr '29, in ACLU P, v. 371; Liggett to Walsh, 27 Mr '31, in ACLU P, v. 482a.

27. Anna Mooney to M, 2 D '28, 30 N '29, 13 My '30, 16 My '31; Anna Mooney memorandum, n.d.; Mary Gallagher to M, 30 Mr '29; M to M. A. Thompson, 13 N '32; M to Waitresses' Union #48, 17 Jl '35; M to Aline Barnsdall, 24 S '36.

28. A. S. Scott to M, 20 My '31; M to Anna Mooney, 13 Jan '35; Anna Mooney to M, 17 S '38.

29. Joseph William Marcus testimony, U.S. Immigration and Naturalization Service, "In re Harry Bridges: Deportation Hearing," typescript (1939), IX: 1331–33, 1352, in Univ. of Calif., Berkeley, Law School library; Louis B. Scott to M, 17 D '37 (MP); Marjory L. Jones, Yale Alumni Records Office, to author, 26 Ap '65.

30. M to A. S. Scott, 6 Jan '32; author's interview, Mary Gallagher, 22 Au '64; *People v. Arthur James Kent* (Los Angeles Superior Court, No. 70596, 9 Mr '38, transcript from the Records Office of that court), 7–8; Los Angeles *Herald-Express*, 22 D '37.

31. Arthur Kent affidavit, 2 N '38, in U.S. House of Representatives, 75th–77th Congr., *Hearings Before a Special Committee on Un-American Activities* (1938–

42), II: 2083–85; Forest Bailey to Traverse Clements, 15 Oc '31, ACLU P, v. 480.

32. A. S. Scott to Louis B. Scott, 11 F '33; "B.A.E." to M, 25 Jl, 21 Au '31.

33. "B.A.E." to M, 25 Jl '31.

34. M to TMMDC, 31 Jl '31; M to "Dear Member of the Committee," 22 Au '31.

35. "B.A.E." to M, 3, 13 Oc '31; TMMDC to G. Akerman, 10 Je '31; NY *Times*, 21 Ap '31.

36. Kelso to M, 12 Oc '31; Anna Mooney to M, 17 S '31; Nockels to M, 1 S '31 (all in MP); Baldwin to M, 27 S '32, in ACLU P, v. 561.

37. M to "Sidney," 16 N '31; M to Kelso, 13 N '31, 3 Au '32.

38. M to TMMDC, 10, 27 Oc '32; Emma Goldman, *Living My Life*, ch. 52.

39. M to TMMDC, 26 N '32.

40. M to Scott and Noni Perrie, 12 F '32; Anne Rosenfield to Mary Mooney, 15 Mr '32; NY *Times*, 6 D '31, 25 F '32, 3 S '34; Sam Goodwin to Mary Mooney, 10 Mr '32.

41. NY *Times*, 22, 25 F, 6 Mr '32; M to Aline Barnsdall, 8 Au '32; Anne Rosenfield to Mary Mooney, 17 Mr ['32]; Anna Mooney to M, 31 Mr '32; S[am] G[oodwin] to F. E. Starkins, 7 Ap '32.

42. [A. S. Scott] to M, 6 Ap '32.

43. M to TMMDC, 13 My, 11 Je '32; M to Anne Rosenfield, 4 Jl '32; M to Kelso, 3 Au '32; NY *Times*, 15 Je '32.

44. TMMDC to NY ILD, 23 Au '32; M to Aline Barnsdall, 8 Au '32; NY *Times*, 23 Oc '32; Anne Raynor to Scott and Noni Perrie, 28 Oc '32.

45. NY *Times*, 28 Oc '32; "F. S." to TMMDC, 31 Oc '32; Harriet Silverman to M, 27 Oc '32; M to TMMDC, 14 S '32.

46. NY *Times*, 24 N '32; M to Mary Mooney, 22 Oc '32; M's greetings, in U.S. Sen. Jud. Comm., *Hearings on the Nomination of Frankfurter*, 38.

47. William Taylor to M, 13 D '32; [Louis B. Scott] to TMMDC, 2 D '32.

48. NY *Times*, 23 D '32. Cf. the ILD's explanation, *ibid.*, 29 D '32.

49. *Ibid.*, 30, 31 D, and ed'l, 25 N, '32; *Chr*, 10 Jan '33.

50. M to Aline Barnsdall, 25 S '34.

51. *Ibid.*; *Chr*, 8 S '34; Belle Hammerberg to Walsh, 23 N '36, Walsh P; NY *Times*, 9 S '34; M memorandum, 30 My '35, in Anna Mooney folder, MP; M to Anna Mooney, 10 Mr '35.

52. A. S. Scott to Louis B. Scott, 7 D '32.

53. *Ibid.*, 14 D '32.

54. A. S. Scott to "John Brown," 9 Ap '33.

55. [Louis B. Scott] to M, 20 D '32.

56. Louis B. Scott to A. S. Scott, 26 Jan '33.

57. Clarence Senior to Louis B. Scott, 9 F '33; *Labor Clarion*, 31 Mr '33.

58. *Labor Clarion*, 17 Mr '33; unidentified clipping, Scrapbook 27, MP. See also Orrick Johns, *Time of Our Lives*, 326.

59. M to Baldwin, 1 Ap '33; Jack McGrath to M, n.d. [Mr '33].

60. NY *Militant*, 13, 27 My '33; Chicago *Industrial Worker*, 11 My '33.

61. Baldwin to A. S. Scott, 2 Je '33 (MP); Baldwin to M, 6 Oc '33, in ACLU P, v. 650; National Tom Mooney Congress, "Secretariat" minutes, 20 Oc '33, in ACLU P, v. 651; *Daily Worker*, 3 My '33 et seq.

62. M to A. S. Scott, 2 Jl '33.

63. M to TMMDC, 27 Jl '33.

64. M to Frank Palmer, 31 D '33 (MP); Baldwin to Lillian Symes, 12 Jan '34, in ACLU P, v. 734; M to Baldwin, 20 Ap '34 (MP); Baldwin memorandum, n.d. [S? '33], in ACLU P, v. 650.

65. M to Paul S. McCormick, 9 Je '37; *Labor Defender*, 1930–39, *passim*; Vito Marcantonio, "We Accuse! The Story of Tom Mooney" (1938); Harvey Goldberg, ed., *American Radicals* (1957), 146, 148.

66. Howe and Coser, *American Communist Party*, 173; Draper, *American Communism and Soviet Russia*, ch. 18; "Lovestone" folder, MP; "B.A.E." to Kelso, 4 S '31; NY *Workers Age*, 1 F '36; Walter Galenson, *The CIO Challenge to the AFL: A History of the American Labor Movement, 1935–1941* (1960), 151.

67. Knowles testimony, U.S. House of Representatives, 75th Congr., *Hearings on Un-American Activities*, 2038, 2044; *ibid.*, 535, 600, 645, 2276, 4794.

68. Eugene Lyons, *The Red Decade* (1941), 14, 15, 242, 331; California Senate, 55th Sess., Joint Fact-Finding Committee on Un-American Activities in California, *Report* (1943), 63; William Z. Foster, *History of the Communist Party of the United States* (1952), 380. See also Martin Dies, *The Trojan Horse in America* (1940), 129, 183, 295.

69. Anna Mooney to Walsh, 19 S '36, Walsh P; M to A. S. Scott, 2 Jl '33.

70. Arthur Kent affidavit, 2 N '38, in U.S. House of Representatives, 75th Congr., *Hearings on Un-American Activities*, II:

2083–85; author's interview, Mitchell Slobodek, 15 N '63; *Industrial Unionist*, 18 D '37; King-Ramsay-Connor Defense Committee, Maritime Federation of the Pacific, "Punishment Without Crime: An Unfinished Story," n.d. [1940?], 7–8; Harper Knowles testimony, "In re Harry Bridges: Deportation Hearing" XX: 3410.

71. M to John Mooney, 12 S '36; M to Jay Lovestone, 27 My, 22 Je '36; M to Anna Mooney, 21 Je '36 (all in MP); M to Baldwin, 11 Jan '37, in ACLU P, v. 1030.

72. Aaron Sapiro testimony, "In re Harry Bridges: Deportation Hearing," VIII: 1208.

73. *Ibid.*, 1268–70; John J. Keegan testimony, *ibid.*, XXI: 3710ff; *People v. Arthur James Kent* (Los Angeles Superior Court, No. 70596, 9 Mr '38), 9–10.

74. Philip D. Guthrie, Cal State Dept of Corrections, to author, 28 Jl '67; Kent affidavit, 2 N '38, in *Hearings on Un-American Activities*, II: 2083–85; Robert E. Burke, *Olson's New Deal for California* (1953), 29–30, 33; M to Baldwin, 29 Jl '39; Sapiro testimony, "In re Harry Bridges," IX: 1269–70.

75. Author's interview, Jean Douglas Robson, 26 Au '64.

XXVI   Habeas Corpus, 1933–1938

EPIGRAPHS: Aillie Carlson to ACLU, 6 N '35, in ACLU P, v. 829; Michael E. Astroh to M, 26 Oc '34, MP.

1. Billings to Baldwin, 8 F '31, in ACLU P, v. 480; remarks of Older in *Labor Clarion*, 16 N '34.

2. Billings to Baldwin, 22 F '31; Baldwin to Hays, Hunt, and Walsh, 2 Mr '31; Baldwin to Billings, 18 Mr '31; Billings to Madeline Wieland, 26 Ap '31, all in ACLU P, v. 480.

3. Ronald P. Sokol, *A Handbook of Federal Habeas Corpus* (1965), 2–5.

4. Walsh memorandum in Baldwin to Billings, 18 Mr '31, ACLU P, v. 480.

5. Hays to Baldwin, 19 Mr '31, ACLU P, v. 480.

6. *Ex parte Watkins*, 28 U.S. (3 Peters) 201 (1830), and *Chin Yow v. United States*, 208 U.S. 13 (1908), quoted in Sokol, 2.

7. C. Herman Pritchett, *American Constitution* (1959), 101.

8. See Zechariah Chafee, Jr., "The Most Important Human Right in the Constitution," *Boston University Law Review*, XXII (1952), 159.

9. Pritchett, ch. 30; David Fellman, *The Defendant's Rights* (1958), ch. 5; Charles Warren, "The New 'Liberty' Under the Fourteenth Amendment," *Harvard Law Review*, XXXIX (1926), 431; Frank A. Peters, "Collateral Attack by Habeas Corpus upon Federal Judgments in Criminal Cases," *Washington Law Review and State Bar Journal*, XXIII (1948), 94–98 and *passim*; "The Freedom Writ—The Expanding Use of Federal Habeas Corpus," *Harvard Law Review*, LXI (1948), 657; U.S. Sen., 88th Congr., 1st Sess., Doc. 39, Norman J. Small, ed., *The Constitution of the United States of America: Analysis and Interpretation*, 1257 and *passim*.

10. Baldwin to Morris Ernst, 25 My '32, in ACLU P, v. 561; Francis Russell, *Tragedy in Dedham: The Story of the Sacco-Vanzetti Case* (1962), 422, 446; *Who's Who in America, 1966–1967*.

11. Beardsley to Baldwin, 4 My '32, and Baldwin correspondence with Morris Ernst, Arthur Garfield Hays, George W. Anderson, and Felix Frankfurter, 10–31 May '32, all in ACLU P, v. 561.

12. Finerty to Baldwin, 23 Je '32, ACLU P, v. 561.

13. *Ozzie Powell et al. v. Alabama*, 287 U.S. 45 (Nov. 1932); Aaron Sapiro to Baldwin, 22 N '32, ACLU P, v. 561.

14. Finerty to Walsh, 21 N '33, ACLU P, v. 650; Finerty to Walsh, 28 Mr, 3 Ap '34, Walsh P; author's interviews, John F. Finerty, 7 Je '62, and George T. Davis, 19 Jl '65; M to Baldwin, 5 My '34, and Baldwin to M, 10 My '34 (MP); Walsh to M, 24 Jan '35, Walsh P.

15. "Thomas J. Mooney v. James B. Holohan," U.S. District Court, Northern District of California, Habeas Corpus No. 21766–S, Walsh P; Finerty to M, 19 S '34, Walsh P; Merlo J. Pusey, *Charles Evans Hughes* (1951), II: 722; NY *Times*, 21 Au 13 N '34.

16. *Mooney v. Holohan*, 294 U.S. 103 (1935), 106, 109–12.

17. *Ibid.*, 112–13.

18. *Baker v. Grice*, 169 U.S. 284 (1898), quoted in *Darr v. Buford*, 339 US 200 (1950), 206.

19. *Mooney v. Holohan*, 294 U.S. 103, 113–15.

20. Paul G. Kauper, *Constitutional Law: Cases and Materials*, 2d ed. (1960), 935; Small, *Constitution of the United States*, 1257.

21. M to Mrs. John D. Casserly, 11 F '35; M to Fannia M. Cohn, 9 F '35; *New Republic*, 17 Ap '35.

22. Walsh to Anton Johannsen, 24 Jan '35, Walsh P. See also *Columbia Law Review*, XXXV (1935), 415–16.

23. NY *Times*, 13, 20, 30 Ap '35; Walsh to Baldwin, 14 My '35, Walsh P.

24. M to Miriam Allen de Ford, 6 Je '35; NY *Times*, 23 Je '35.

25. M to John Mooney, 24 My '35 (MP); Finerty to M, 20 My '35, Walsh P.

26. "In re the Application of Thomas J. Mooney for a Writ of Habeas Corpus," 10 *California Reports* (2d ser.) 1 (1937), 16.

27. Cleary statement, "Habeas Corpus," VI: 3327; NY *Times*, 30 Jl '35; *Nation*, 29 Au '36; *News*, 30 Au, 3 Oc '35; M to Nockels, 3 Au '35; Davis interview, 19 Jl '65.

28. NY *Times*, 3, 15, 21, 29 Oc '35; Finerty interview, 6 Je '62.

29. Finerty interview, 7 Je '62; Dr. Robert A. Reiter to Davis, 26 Jl '35, Walsh P; NY *Times*, 14–16 Au '35.

30. McDonald to Baldwin, 28 Je '35, in ACLU P, v. 829; Cleary, as quoted, NY *Times*, 16 Au '35; John Jenkins to TMMDC, 30 S '37.

31. *News*, 17 S '35; NY *Times*, 18, 19 S '35.

32. M to Jay Lovestone, 29 F '36, 23 Mr '36, 29 Ap '37; M to Draper Hand, 1 Mr '36; M to Martha D. Mohai, 29 Jan '36; M to Baldwin, 14 Ap '36; M to Walsh, 17 D '36. The film included brief newsreel clips of early scenes in the case. It is in the Mooney Papers, Bancroft Library; rental or purchase copies, entitled "The Mooney Case," are available from the University of California Extension Media Center, Berkeley, Calif.

33. M to Lovestone, 29 F '36.

34. M to Paul Pierce, 6 My '37; M to Lovestone, 23 Mr '36; Davis and Finerty interviews; Belle Hammerberg to Walsh, 1 My '36, Walsh P.

35. Finerty interview.

36. Author's interviews [name withheld on request], Davis, and Finerty.

37. M to Draper Hand, 1 Mr '36; Finerty interview.

38. M to Anga M. Bjornson, 3 D '36; M to Walsh, 17 D '36.

39 Davis to Walsh, 12 Jan '37, Walsh P.

40. *Ibid.*; Walsh to Davis, 28 Jl '36, Walsh P; M to Aline Barnsdall, 27 Au '36.

41. Author's interviews, Edgar T. Gleeson, 6 F '60, and Ruth Fickert Pitt, 13 Jl

'65; *Call-Bul,* 20 Oc '37; *Labor Clarion,* 24 Ap '36; *News,* 20 Oc '37; *Chr,* 4 Ap '36, 24 Oc '37; Belle Hammerberg to Walsh, 15 Ap '36, Walsh P; Brick Morse in "Sporting Green," *Chr,* 10 D '35.

42. *Exmr,* 21 Oc '37; *Voice of the Federation,* 21 Oc '37; *Irish World,* 6 N '37; *News,* 21 Oc '37; *Chr,* 21 Oc '37.

43. Belle Hammerberg to Walsh, 9 Je '36, Walsh P.

44. *News,* 22 Je '36; Davis to Walsh, 17 Je '36; M to Walsh, 30 Je '36, Walsh P.

45. NY *Times,* 8 Jan '37; Finerty to Davis, 8 My '36, Davis to Walsh, 6 Au '36, and Davis to Finerty, 12 D '36, all in Walsh P; *In re Mooney,* 10 Cal (2d) 1, 16–17; *Call-Bul,* 18 Jan '37.

46. Walsh to Belle Hammerberg and Walsh to Davis, both 4 F '37, Walsh P.

47. Davis to Walsh, 19 Ap, 7 My '37, Walsh P; M to Walsh, 19 Ap '37; M to Albert A. Shanks, 19 Ap '37; M to Charles Zimmerman, 23 Ap '37.

48. Davis to Finerty, 2 Je '37, Walsh P; M to Sarah I. Metcalf, 17 Je '37.

49. M to Jay Lovestone, 17 Je '37 (MP); Davis to Walsh, 10, 16 Je '37, Walsh P.

50. *Exmr,* 10 Mr '38; J. C. Geiger, M.D., to "City Editor," 15 Je '37 (MP); Cal Dept of Corrections, Prison record card, Inmate file 31921; Davis to Walsh, 1 Jl '37, Walsh P.

51. Davis to Walsh, 1 Jl '37, Walsh P; Herbert Resner to Humphrey Cobb, 23 Je '37; Resner to Anna Damon, 21 Jl '37; Court Smith to Merriam, 12 Jl '37; *Labor Clarion,* 9 Jl '37; Humphrey Cobb *et al.* to Merriam, 8 Jl '37.

52. Davis to Walsh, 13 Jl '37, Walsh P.

53. Davis to Walsh, 6 Au '37, Walsh P; Cal Dept of Corrections, Prison record card, Inmate file 31921; Resner to Cobb, 12 N '37.

54. *In re Mooney,* 10 Cal (2d) 1, 1 and 85.

55. *Ibid.,* 45.

56. *Ibid.,* 21–22, 2.

57. *Ibid.,* 2–3, 18, 33–34.

58. *Ibid.,* 31.

59. *Ibid.,* 32–39 and *passim.*

60. *Ibid.,* 4, 53–56.

61. "Habeas Corpus," VI: 3753.

62. 10 Cal. (2d) 1, 57, 59–60.

63. *Ibid.,* 60–73.

64. *Ibid.,* 5, 7.

65. *Ibid.,* 84.

66. *Ibid.,* 85.

67. *Ibid.,* 85–86.

68. As quoted, *Chr,* 31 Oc '37.

69. Davis to M, 9 N '37, Walsh P; Baldwin to M, 24 F '38; NY *Times,* 18 N '37; Davis to M, 14 Jan '38.

70. Walsh to M, 20 Jan '38, and M to Davis, 17 F '38, both in Walsh P.

71. M to Finerty and Walsh, 21 F '38; Davis to M, 24 F '38.

72. Davis to M, 15 Mr '38; NY *Times,* 17 Mr '38.

73. Sacramento *Bee,* as quoted, *News,* 19 Mr '38; Weinberger to Walsh, 23 Ap '38, Walsh P.

74. M to Walsh, 20 S '38, Walsh P; NY *Times,* 1, 5 Je '38.

75. *News,* 10 Oc '38. See also Small, *Constitution of the United States,* 1277.

76. Finerty to TMMDC, 12 D '38; *Chron,* NY *Times,* 13 D '38.

XXVII The Politics of Freedom, 1935–1938

SECOND EPIGRAPH: McKenzie statement to Ed Hurley, Cal S Ct, "In re Billings," III: 1813–14.

1. Whiteman and Lewis, *Glory Roads,* 238; *EPIC News,* 4 F, 22 Ap, 13 My '35; Dewey Anderson, *California State Government* (1942), 86; Robert E. Burke, *Olson's New Deal for California,* 5; *California Assembly Journal,* 1935, I: 155.

2. Frost, "Mooney Case in California Politics," 183; Dorothy Murphy to Anna Mooney, 27 Ap '31; Traverse Clements to Baldwin, 6, 8, 12 My '31, ACLU P, v. 480.

3. Northern California Committee, ACLU, circular letter, Mr '35; Cal Legislature, 51st Sess., 1935, *Assembly Bills,* II: Nos. 319–21; X: No. 1821.

4. See, e.g., *Chr,* 23, 27 Jan '35.

5. Baldwin to Walter W. Liggett, 3 F '31 (MP); M to Gross W. Alexander, 17 My '35; *EPIC News,* 6 My '35 (cf. 12 N '34); *Cal Assembly Journal,* 1935, I: 2408.

6. Brennan, as quoted, *Chr,* 17 My '35; Cal Legislature, 51st Sess., 1935, *Final Calendar: Assembly,* 200–201, 547, 711.

7. *Chr,* 13 Au '34.

8. George P. West, "California Sees Red," *Current History,* Sept. 1934; *Chr,* 6 Jl '34; David W. Mabon, "West Coast Waterfront and Sympathy Strikes of 1934," Ph.D. diss., Univ. of Calif., Berkeley (1966), 118, 149–54; John Steinbeck, *Their Blood Is Strong* (1938), *passim;* Carey McWilliams, *Facto-*

ries in the Field, chs. 13, 14; Clarke A. Chambers, *California Farm Organizations* (1952?), 39–52, 108; Louis B. Perry and Richard S. Perry, *History of the Los Angeles Labor Movement, 1911–1941* (1963), 267–70; *Labor Clarion*, 23 F '34; *Nation*, 29 Ap '31, 8, 15, 29 Au '34, 12 S '34, 5 Je, 24 Jl, 25 S '35, 26 Oc '36; *New Republic*, 22 My, 26 Je '35. See also Jerold S. Auerbach, *Labor and Liberty: The La Follette Committee and the New Deal* (1966), ch. 8.

9. *Harper's*, Feb. 1935, 366.
10. M to William Z. Foster, Robert Minor, and Earl Browder, 30 Jan '37.
11. J. L. Clifton articles in *Pacific Weekly*, 6, 13, 20 Ap '36.
12. M to Thomas A. Bailey, 10 Je '35; *Pacific Weekly*, 20 Ap '36.
13. John D. Barry in *News*, 22 Jan '35.
14. *Exmr*, 27 N '31; Aline Barnsdall to M, 9 Jl '29; Martha Oathout Ayres to M, 20 My '37; *Nation*, 2 Oc '35.
15. Royce D. Delmatier, "The Rebirth of the Democratic Party in California, 1928–1938," Ph.D. diss., Univ. of Calif., Berkeley (1955), 51.
16. M to Richie, 22, 29 D '36; M to Baldwin, 11 Jan '37; memorandum on Richie's remarks at a Mooney rally in Sacramento, n.d. (MP).
17. Richie to M, n.d. [Dec. 1936?].
18. Richie memorandum, n.d. [Dec. 1936?].
19. Richie to M, 12 Jan '37.
20. Olson to Richie, 8 Jan '37 (MP).
21. Richie to Herbert Resner, 5 F '37 (MP).
22. Cal Legislature, 52d Sess., 1937, *Final Calendar: Assembly*, 742; Richie to M, 5 Mr '37; *Chr*, 11, 12 Mr '37.
23. Culbert L. Olson, radiobroadcast script, 27 My '35, Olson P.
24. M to Olson, 13 Mr '37 (MP).
25. Richie to M, 1 Ap '37.
26. Cal Legislature, 52d Sess., 1937, *Senate Journal*, 5, 6, 825–41; NY *Times*, 17 Mr '37.
27. *Chr*, 17 Mr '37; Richie to M, 16 Mr '37.
28. Cal Legislature, 52d Sess., 1937, *Assembly Journal*, 1421; ibid., *Senate Journal*, 1507.
29. Richie to M, 31 Mr '37.
30. M to Leigh Athearn, 7 Ap '37; Richie to M, 1, 10 Ap '37; M to Walsh, 19 Ap '37, Walsh P; M to Richie, 24 Ap '37.
31. Richie to M, 11, 13, 17 My '37.
32. Richie to M, 23 [?] My '37.

33. NY *Times*, 17 Jl '37; M to Albert A. Shanks, 14 D '37.
34. Cal Legislature, 52d (Extra) Sess., 1938, *Assembly Journal*, 38, 45, 46.
35. Sacramento *Bee*, 9 Mr '38; *Chr*, 10 Mr '38.
36. *Chr*, 8, 10 Mr '38; Oakland *Post-Enquirer*, 10 Mr '38.
37. *News*, *Call-Bul*, 10 Mr '38.
38. Sacramento *Union*, 11 Mr '38; *Assembly Journal*, *1938*, 105.
39. *Chr*, 12, 13 Mr '38; *News*, 12 Mr '38; M to Baldwin, 16 Mr '38.
40. *Congressional Record*, 75th Congr., 1st Sess., v. 81:3, p. 2841; John Jenkins to M, 10 Ap '37; *Who's Who in America*, *1934–35*; Caroline O'Day to Baldwin, 13 Oc '31, in ACLU P, v. 480; Caroline O'Day to Franklin D. Roosevelt, 2 Ap '35, in Walsh P.
41. *Who's Who in America, 1938–39*; Jenkins to M, 14 My '38; *Congressional Record*, v. 81:3, pp. 2858, 3215; William E. Leuchtenburg, *Franklin D. Roosevelt and the New Deal, 1932–1940* (1963), 272.
42. William Green to Hatton W. Sumners, 16 My '38; John Brophy to Emanuel Celler, 11 Ap '38; Lee Pressman to Celler, 12 My '38; John Fitzpatrick to TMMDC, 21 Jan '37; Gardner Jackson to Herbert Resner, 2 D '37; Jenkins to M, 5 Jan, 15, 17 Ap '37 (all in MP); NY *Times*, 26 Au '37; Jenkins to Walsh, 30 N '37, Walsh P; Jenkins to M, 4, 14 My '38, to Resner, 23 My '38, and to Sara Eliaser, 27 My '38; Gardner Jackson to John F. Finerty, 17 Je '37 (all in MP).
43. M to Harry Bridges, 2 Ap '38; M to Joseph O'Mahoney, 21 N '37; M to George Davis, 22 N '37; M to Baldwin, 8 D '37; Emanuel Celler to M, 23 Ap '38; Davis to M, 16 D '37; *Call-Bul*, 5 My '38. See also U. S. Webb to Hiram Johnson, 4 My '38, Cal State Archives, Atty Gen Records, Box 222.
44. NY *Times*, 16 D '37, 1 Mr '38; Davis to M, 16 D '37 (MP); Walsh to M, 22 S, 16 D '37, and M to Walsh, 27 Ap '38, all in Walsh P.
45. NY *Times*, 18 My '38; "Report of the Sub-committee of the House Judiciary Committee on H.R. Motion Memorializing Governor of California to Pardon Thomas J. Mooney" [n.d.]; script of radio address of Emanuel Celler, 28 My '38 (both in MP).
46. *Exmr*, 4 S '37; Burke, *Olson's New*

Deal for California, 6–8; *Who's Who in America,* 1940–41; T. William Goodman, "Culbert L. Olson and California Politics, 1933–1943," M.A. thesis, UCLA (1948), 2–3, 8; Culbert L. Olson, speeches, 17 Au '37 and 15 My '59, Olson P; Frank Scully, *The Next Governor of California* (n.d.), 31–32; Sacramento *Bee,* 9 N '38; Melendy and Gilbert, *Governors of California,* 395–96; Olson campaign leaflet, 1934, Olson P.

47. Goodman, 9, 13; Burke, 8.
48. Burke, 4.
49. *Ibid.,* 6, 8.
50. *Ibid.,* 8–10.
51. Olson, speech, 25 Ap '36, Olson P.
52. Hichborn, "California Politics," V: 2798; Whiteman and Lewis, *Glory Roads,* 239; Burke, *Olson's New Deal for California,* 6, 9.
53. *Labor Clarion,* 25 Mr, 15 Jl '38; Burke, 13, 14; Russell M. Posner, "A. P. Giannini and the 1934 Campaign in California," *Historical Society of Southern California Quarterly,* June 1957, 194–95.
54. See Dean E. McHenry, "Invitation to Masquerade," in David Farrelly and Ivan Hinderaker, eds., *Politics of California* (1951), 75–81. The "cross-filing" law was repealed in 1959.
55. Carey McWilliams, *Southern California Country,* 303–7; Cleland, *California in Our Time,* 231–41; Winston and Marian Moore, *Out of the Frying Pan* (1939), 15–46, 66, 83–84; Burke, *Olson's New Deal for California,* 15–16.
56. Burke, 18.
57. M to Aline Barnsdall, 13 Je '38.
58. *Ibid.;* "Tom Mooney's Message to Organized Labor . . . on the 1938 California Elections" (n.d.); M to Olson, 22 S '38.
59. M to Aline Barnsdall, 31 Au '38; Aline Barnsdall to M, 29 S '38.
60. Aline Barnsdall to M, 29 S '38; Davis to author, 12 S '66.
61. M to Aline Barnsdall, 13 Je '38.
62. Burke, *Olson's New Deal for California,* 21.
63. M to Aline Barnsdall, 13 Je '38.
64. M to John Fitzpatrick, 14 Je '38; M to Baldwin, 18 Je '38; M to Sidney Hillman, 29 Je '38; M to Charles S. Zimmerman, 30 Je '38; M to James Cagney, 15 Jl '38; M to Douglas Fairbanks, Jr., 16 Jl '38; M to Mrs. Alan Campbell, 16 Jl '38; M to David Dubinsky, 9 Au '38; M to Earl Browder, 3 S '38; *American Mercury,* April 1940, 413; Burke, 18–19.

65. Davis to Walsh, 30 Au '37, and Davis, circular letter, 26 Au '38 (both MP); Burke, 15.
66. Burke, 20.
67. M to Walsh, 20 S '38, Walsh P.
68. Davis to Robert Allen, 25 Au '38, Walsh P.
69. Davis to M, 3, 15 Oc '38.
70. M to Walsh, 12 Oc '38, Walsh P.
71. Burke, *Olson's New Deal for California,* 30–31.
72. *Ibid.,* 23–25.

XXVIII   Freedom and Death

EPIGRAPHS: *Call-Bul,* 9 N '38; Olson P.
1. Los Angeles *Examiner,* 10 N' 38.
2. Burke, *Olson's New Deal for California,* 40–44; *Exmr,* 3 Jan '39.
3. Sacramento *Bee,* 3 Jan '39; International News Service clipping, 3 Jan '39 (MP); *Chr,* 5 Jan '39.
4. NY *Times,* 7 Jan '39.
5. *News,* 7 Jan '39; *Chr,* 8 Jan '39.
6. *Exmr,* NY *Times,* 8 Jan '39. The pardon document, printed in black and green ink on heavy folio paper by the California State Printing Office, is preserved in the Governor's Pardon File, Secretary of State's file room, in the State Capitol.
7. NY *Times,* 8 Jan '39; *Chr,* 9 Jan '39.
8. Letters to Olson, Jan.–Feb. 1939 (MP); Burke, 57.
9. *People's World,* 17, 21 Jan '39; Stockton *Record,* 23 Jan '39.
10. M to Robert D. Cramer, 17 Jl '39.
11. See e.g., NY *Post,* 2 Je '39.
12. Madeline [Wieland] to Lucy Lang, 10 Jan '41, Lang P.
13. NY *Times,* 4, 5 F '39; Madeline [Wieland] to Lucy Lang, 10 Mr '42, Lang P.
14. Letters to M, Feb.–Mr. '39, among them the postcard, from P. Daily and T. A. Newlon, 13 F '39.
15. NY *Times,* 7 Mr '42. See also San Diego *Sun,* 14 Jan '39.
16. NY *Times,* 13, 26 F '39.
17. NY *Post, Tribune,* 2 Je '39; NY *Times,* 2, 6 Je '39.
18. M to Jerry O'Connell, 18 Jl '39; assorted newspaper clippings, June–Oct. 1939 (MP); M circular letter, 1 Ap '40.
19. M to Newton Short, 16 Jl '39; M to J. J. McNamara, 16 Oc '39; M to Joseph Baron, 11 Oc '39.
20. NY *Times,* 2 Ap '40; M to Charles Burr, 31 Oc '39.

21. NY *Times,* 7 Mr '42.

22. *Ibid.,* 12 Oc '33, 7 Jan '34; *News,* 6 F '39.

23. *Chr,* 24 F '39.

24. *Chr,* 14, 18 Oc '39; *Exmr,* 17 Oc '39.

25. NY *Times,* 22 D '61.

26. *Call,* 10 N '23.

27. Oral Hist. Proj., "Billings," 262–78; M to E. J. Costello, 4 Au '22; Billings to Lucy Lang, 22 Jan '33, Lang P; *Chr,* 18 Oc '39; Lena Morrow Lewis to Baldwin, 26 Jan '31, ACLU P, v. 481.

28. Billings to Arthur Heeb, 15 Je '30, quoted in Heeb to C. C. Young, 6 Jl '30 (MP).

29. Oral Hist. Proj., "Billings," 340–42; author's interview, Warren Billings, 30 Au '61.

30. NY *Times,* 22 D '61.

31. *Ibid.*

32. *Chr,* 7 Mr '42; Baldwin to Sara H. Eliaser, 6 Mr '42 (MP); *Exmr,* 7 Mr '42.

33. As quoted, *Exmr,* 7 Mr '42.

34. *Chr, Exmr,* 9 Mr '42.

35. As quoted, *Exmr,* 8 Mr '42.

36. *Nation,* 29 Ap '31. Mary Gallagher wrote a play based on the case; it was never published and evidently never produced. The manuscript is in the Labadie Library, Univ. of Michigan. See also Mary Gallagher to Agnes Inglis, 2 Je '39, in Inglis P.

37. E.g., M to John Haynes Holmes, 5 F '32.

38. *Bul,* 26 Oc '20. One of the agents working for the German consulate was a saboteur named Louis J. Smith, who supposedly made a death-bed confession of the Preparedness Day crime to his family in 1922. That was not revealed for another seven years, however, by which time there was nothing more than the word of his relatives to go on. Moreover, Smith had had the reputation of a liar and n'er-do-well. *Call-Bul,* 9, 11, 12 N '29; NY *Times,* 10, 12 N '29; Older to M, 8 N '27, and Baldwin to Mary Gallagher, 29 Jan '30 (in MP). For further speculation on these and other possible causes, see Hopkins, *What Happened in the Mooney Case,* 49–71, or Curt Gentry, *Frame-up: The Incredible Case of*

Tom Mooney and Warren Billings (1967), 441–77.

39. On the historic teaching role of the federal judiciary, see Ralph Lerner, "The Supreme Court as Republican Schoolmaster," in Philip B. Kurland, ed., *The Supreme Court Review: 1967* (1967), 129–80. As Lerner states, "teaching is inseparable from judging in a democratic regime" (180). Recent public response to such tutelage, respecting criminal procedure, has been decidedly hostile: according to a national poll in 1966, 65 per cent of those interviewed disapproved of the Court's disallowing confessions without counsel. G. Theodore Mitau, *Decade of Decision: The Supreme Court and the Constitutional Revolution, 1954–1964* (1967), 7. See also Arthur E. Sutherland, "Crime and Confession," in *Harvard Law Review,* v. 79 (1965), 21–41. Hamilton Fish's statement appears in his letter to the NY *Times,* 19 Je '66.

40. *Mallory v. U.S.,* 354 U.S. 449 (1957); *Miranda v. Arizona,* 384 U.S. 436 (1966); *Mapp v. Ohio,* 367 U.S. 643 (1961); *Sheppard v. Maxwell,* 384 U.S. 333 (1966).

41. On the scope, merits, and problems of criminal discovery in California, see Roger J. Traynor (now Chief Justice of the California Supreme Court), "Ground Lost and Found in Criminal Discovery," *NYU Law Review,* v. 39 (1964), 228–50; David W. Louisell, "Criminal Discovery: Dilemma Real or Apparent?" in *California Law Review,* v. 49 (1961), 56–103, or his *Modern California Discovery* (1963), ch. 13; and Kendall R. Bishop, "The Self-Incrimination Privilege: Barrier to Criminal Discovery," in *California Law Review,* v. 51 (1963), 135.

42. *Miller v. Pate,* 386 U.S. 1 (1967), 7 [citations omitted]. Other references to *Mooney v. Holohan* are in *U.S. Reports,* vols. 296–388; it is discussed, e.g., in *Johnson v. Zerbst,* 304 U.S. 458 (1938), 467; *Hawk v. Olson,* 326 U.S. 271 (1945), 275; *Brady v. Maryland,* 373 U.S. 83 (1963), 87. The last of these states: "The principle of *Mooney v. Holohan* is not punishment of society for the misdeeds of a prosecutor but avoidance of an unfair trial to the accused."

Index